高水平专业群教材建设专项项目
新时代新理念职业教育教材
“互联网+”新形态立体化教学资源特色教材

铁道车辆技术

Technology for Railway Vehicles

中英双语

主　编　李文久　孙志才
副主编　王伟楠　曹立达　柳重阳　才　宇
主　审　王学明

扫码获取相关配套资源

U0913435

北京交通大学出版社
·北京·

内容简介

本书共包含 9 个项目，主要介绍铁道车辆技术。项目 1 为铁道车辆概述，简要介绍铁道车辆的作用和发展；项目 2 为铁路车辆基本知识，主要介绍铁道车辆的组成、分类、代码、标记及主要技术参数等；项目 3 为轮对，重点介绍车轴、车轮的结构及作用；项目 4 为滚动轴承（轴箱）装置，重点介绍铁路客、货车滚动轴承（轴箱）装置的结构；项目 5 为客、货车转向架，重点介绍铁路客、货车转向架的结构、主要技术参数等；项目 6 为车钩缓冲装置，重点介绍铁路客、货车车钩结构及缓冲器；项目 7 为客车车体，重点介绍铁路客车的车体结构；项目 8 为货车车体，重点介绍铁路货车的车体结构；项目 9 为动力集中电动车组，重点介绍 160 km/h 动力集中电动车组。

本书可供职业教育铁道车辆技术相关专业的学生作为教材使用，也可供相关从业人员学习参考。

版权所有，侵权必究。

图书在版编目（CIP）数据

铁道车辆技术 / 李文久，孙志才主编. — 北京 ：北京交通大学出版社，2025.1
新时代新理念职业教育教材　高水平专业群教材建设专项项目
ISBN 978-7-5121-4902-1

Ⅰ. ① 铁…　Ⅱ. ① 李…　② 孙…　Ⅲ. ① 铁路车辆－高等职业教育－教材　Ⅳ. ① U27

中国国家版本馆 CIP 数据核字（2023）第 040446 号

铁道车辆技术
TIEDAO CHELIANG JISHU

项目总策划：陈　颖
责 任 编 辑：张利军
出 版 发 行：北京交通大学出版社　　电话：010-51686414　　http://www.bjtup.com.cn
地　　　址：北京市海淀区高梁桥斜街 44 号　　邮编：100044
印　刷　者：北京虎彩文化传播有限公司
经　　　销：全国新华书店
开　　　本：185 mm×260 mm　　印张：22.5　　字数：660 千字
版　印　次：2025 年 1 月第 1 版　　2025 年 1 月第 1 次印刷
定　　　价：79.00 元

本书如有质量问题，请向北京交通大学出版社质监组反映。对您的意见和批评，我们表示欢迎和感谢。
投诉电话：010-51686043，51686008；传真：010-62225406；E-mail：press@bjtu.edu.cn。

前　言

本书是根据铁道车辆技术专业基于工作过程和认知规律开发制定的“铁道车辆技术”课程教学大纲编写的。

“学生工作页”是根据行动导向教学法、按照项目教学和任务导向式教学思路设计的“工作－学习”（简称为“工学”）任务，包括信息、策划、计划、实施、检查、评价等项目过程，以及项目名称、目标、类型、分解任务、自我评价等具体内容。“学生工作页”作为一种新型的教学、学习工具和载体，能够在课堂教学、现场实训、作业、答疑、考核等多个教学环节使用，例如在课堂环境下模拟现场的岗位情境、具体工作过程，参照行业标准模拟岗位任务等。通过模拟任务的完成过程，使学生学习和掌握专业知识和技能，并培养学生团结协作、自主学习、自我评价、归纳总结等多种能力及素质。

“学生工作页”主要面向职业教育学生的教学实践及企业职工的岗前培训，其内容既针对某一岗位的专有知识和技能，又兼顾相关岗位群的通用知识，并为适应现场技术装备的快速更新奠定基础。因此，本书既可供职业教育院校铁道车辆技术专业的学生在校学习使用，也可供车辆系统各相关岗位的新职工岗前培训使用。

本书综合介绍了我国铁道车辆的发展历程、铁道车辆的基本知识、轮对、滚动轴承（轴箱）装置、主型客货车转向架、车钩缓冲装置、车体、CR200J动力集中电动车组，重点介绍铁道车辆的基本原理、类型、总体结构、布局，以及车辆必备的、最基本的、共同具有的设备，具体包括设备的名称、作用、基本原理，同时也简单地介绍了国外一些车型、转向架等的相关知识点。

本书紧密结合现场实际，力求由浅入深、通俗易懂，以期大幅提高教与学的效率，节约教与学的成本。本书注重实际应用能力的训练和自主适应新技术装备能力的培养，同时尽量将形状结构、技术参数等内容与理论推导、技术分类、发展历史等内容一并给出，以便于学生理解所学知识。

本书由吉林铁道职业技术学院李文久、孙志才担任主编，吉林铁道职业技术学院王伟楠、曹立达、柳重阳、才宇担任副主编，吉林铁道职业技术学院王学明担任主审。

特别需要说明的是，本书涉及的技术数据、结构参数，均属于一般的通识性知识，与现场真实情况难免有所出入，因此不可作为技术文件使用。

受编者水平所限，书中难免存在不足和疏漏之处，诚恳请有关专家、教师、学生提出宝贵意见。

编　者

2024年12月

目　录

项目 1

Project 1

铁道车辆概述

Overview of Railway Vehicles

本项目以了解铁道车辆的作用及铁道车辆的发展过程为工学任务，通过课堂任务的完成过程，着重介绍车辆的总体作用，并以此为引导，简单介绍铁路提速的新成果；通过课后任务的完成，了解铁道车辆的作用及今后的发展。

The main task of this project is to understand the functions of railway vehicles and their development process. In the classroom, the main focus is on introducing the overall function of railway vehicles, and the recent advancements in railway speed improvements. Through after-class tasks, students will gain an understanding of the role of railway vehicles and its future development.

学生工作页 Student Worksheet

工学任务描述 Task description	预期目标 Expected goals
任务名称：认识铁道车辆的作用 Task name: Understanding of the functions of railway vehicles 任务编号：CJ-01 Task number: CJ-01 知识类型：认知型+理论 Knowledge type: Cognitive + theory 适用范围：车辆系统各岗位群 Applicable scope: All post groups of the system of railway vehicles 完成时间：　　　学时 Completion time:　　　class hours	初级：掌握铁道车辆的作用 Elementary level: Master the functions of railway vehicles 中级：掌握铁路提速的内容 Intermediate level: Master the content of railway speed-up campaigns 高级：理解铁路第六次提速的成果；理解关键知识点 Advanced level: Understand the results of the sixth railway speed-up campaign; Understand the key knowledge points

知识回顾+小组讨论

Knowledge review + group discussion

1. 小组讨论：在铁路的六次提速中，你认为哪一次影响力最大？

Group discussion: Among the six railway speed-up campaign, which one do you think has the greatest impact?

2. 小组讨论+学习记录：你所知的铁路对车辆的要求都有哪些？

Group discussion + learning record: What do you know about the requirements of the railway vehicles?

序号 S/N	车辆类型 Type	作　用 Function	铁路对车辆的要求 Requirements
1			
2			
3			
4			
5			
6			
7			
8			
9			

3. 归纳总结：铁道车辆的基本作用及对铁道车辆的基本要求。

Summary: basic functions of the railway vehicles and basic requirements for the railway vehicles.

4. 总结并记录：铁路第六次提速所采用的新成果。

Summary and record: the new achievements adopted in the sixth railway speed-up campaign.

新成果名称 New achievement	内　容 Description

课后任务

After-class tasks

1. 查阅资料：随着铁道车辆的发展，今后对铁路客车及货车还可能提出哪些新要求？

Look up data and information: What new requirements may be put forward for the railway passenger cars and freight cars with the development of railway vehicles in the future?

种　类 Category	车　型 Model	速　度 Speed	发　展 Development	新要求 New requirements

2. 按兴趣建立工学小组，并明确目标、确定分工。

Establish work-and-study teams according to the interests, and clearly define the objectives and responsibilities of each group member.

小组成员 Group member	分　工 Responsibility	小组成员 Group member	分　工 Responsibility

学习效果评价 Learning effect evaluation

年 Year　　月 Month　　日 Day

专业班级： Major & class:	姓名： Name:		学号： Student number:
工学小组及分工： Work-and-study team and responsibility division:			
专业（知识/技能）收获 Professional gains (knowledge/skills)	（非专业）能力素质收获 (Non-professional) ability and quality gains		

评价考核项目 Evaluation item	自我评价 Self-evaluation	小组评价 Group evaluation	教师评价 Teacher's evaluation
已掌握铁路对车辆的基本要求 Have mastered the basic requirements for railway vehicles			
已掌握第六次大提速的内容 Have mastered the contents of the sixth railway speed-up campaign			
已掌握相关客、货车的发展趋势 Have mastered the development trend of passenger cars and freight cars			
已掌握相关知识点的数量 Number of knowledge points mastered			
课外学习时间（学时） After-school learning time (hours)			
兴趣内容自主学习（收集相关知识点的数量） Autonomous learning of interested content (the number of knowledge points collected)			
工作态度（课堂、课后任务完成情况） Work attitude (completion condition of classroom tasks and after-class tasks)	☆☆☆☆ ☆☆☆☆	☆☆☆☆ ☆☆☆☆	☆☆☆☆ ☆☆☆☆
合作意识及协调能力 Cooperation consciousness and coordination ability	☆☆☆☆ ☆☆☆☆	☆☆☆☆ ☆☆☆☆	☆☆☆☆ ☆☆☆☆
正确表达和沟通能力 Correct expression and communication skills	☆☆☆☆ ☆☆☆☆	☆☆☆☆ ☆☆☆☆	☆☆☆☆ ☆☆☆☆
自律能力（缺勤/旷课/迟到/违纪次数） Self-discipline (absences/absenteeism/lateness/disciplinary violations)			

任务 1.1　铁路运输业对车辆的要求

Task 1.1　Requirements of the railway transportation industry for vehicles

我国铁路具有高度集中、大动脉、半军事化的特点，在国民经济建设中起着重要的作用，尤其在抗震救灾、抗击冰雪灾害中发挥着重要的作用。在现有公路、水路、航空、管道等运输方式中，铁路担负着我国大部分的运输任务，是国民经济发展的先导。铁路的客、货运量占我国总运量的 60%左右。近年来，随着人民生活水平的不断提高及旅游事业的发展，乘坐铁路客车出行的人越来越多。激烈的运输业竞争对铁路提出了新的要求——铁路部门应提供运行平稳、安全可靠、乘坐舒适、方便快捷的旅客列车。为达到这一目的，客车上应配备运行品质良好的走行装置，客室内应有舒适的座席和卧铺、明亮开阔的窗户、性能良好的通风装置，具备加温、降温、去湿功能的空调设施，以及为缓解旅客的旅途疲劳而设置的广播、电视、通信、信息设备，为保证安全可靠而设置的必要的轴温报警装置。随着国民经济的不断发展及货运量的增加，要求铁路提供载重量大、防雨、防晒、保鲜及承担特大特重货物运输任务的车辆。由于运输要求的不同，所以客运车辆有硬座车、硬卧车、软卧车、餐车、行李车、邮政车、发电车、公务车等，货运车辆有平车、敞车、棚车、罐车、自翻车、漏斗车、冷藏车、家畜车等。

Railway transportation in China, which is characterized by high artery concentration and semi-militarization management, plays an important role in national economic construction, especially in the relief against earthquakes as well as ice and snow disasters. Among all transportation means, including road, waterway, airline, and pipelines, the railway undertakes most transport tasks in China, and is the forerunner of national economic development. Passenger and freight traffic volume of railway accounts for about 60% of total traffic volume in China. Recent years, with improvement in living standards and development in the tourism industry, more and more people choose to take passenger cars for travel. However, the fierce competition in the transportation industry proposes new requirements for the railway - the railway department should provide smooth, safe, and reliable passenger cars that are comfortable, convenient, and fast. In view of this, high-quality running gear shall be adopted, and in the passenger cars, comfortable seats and sleepers, bright and wide windows as well as high-performance heating, ventilation, and dehumidifying air conditioning units, entertainment facilities to relieve the passengers' fatigue such as radio, television, communication, and information equipment, and axle temperature alarms required for safe and reliable operation shall be installed. With the continuous development of the national economy, the increase in freight traffic volume entails railway vehicles with heavy loading capacity as well as rain-proof, sun-proof, and fresh-keeping functions to transport extra-large and extra-heavy cargoes. To meet different transportation requirements, passenger cars available include semi-cushioned seat coaches, semi-cushioned berth sleepers, cushioned-berth sleepers, dining cars, luggage cars, mail cars, generator cars, official business cars, etc.; and freight cars available include flat cars, gondola cars, box cars, tank cars, dump cars, hopper cars, refrigerator cars, livestock cars, and others.

铁道车辆是编组成列运行的，所以在机车车辆间及两车辆间装有车钩缓冲装置，以便于列车编组分解和调车作业；在每辆车上均装有制动装置，以便于车辆减速或停车，缓解的操纵是在列车端部的机车上，因此要求车辆上的制动装置应能使整列车辆互相配合、动作一致。为达到对客、货车的要求，在车辆上加装的各种设备越来越多，结构也越来越复杂，如车辆速度提高以后为保证在规定距离内停车，车辆上采用了盘型制动装置、单元制动缸，以及双层客车空重车的调整装置、抗侧滚扭杆、25T 型客车的集便装置、电子防滑器、客车行车安全检测诊断系统、高原客车制氧系统。这些设备的安装使车辆的自重越来越大，在相同的列车重量下，所运送的旅客和货物量就会越来越少。尤其是在提速的情况下，这是不允许的。为解决这一矛盾，车辆在设计和制造上采用新材料、新工艺、新结构、新技术来降低车辆自重，以提高运输效益。

The railway vehicles operate in formation, so a coupler and draft gear are installed between two cars for the convenience of decoupling and switching service. All cars are equipped with braking devices for slowing down or stopping, and the release control of braking devices is installed in the locomotive(s) at the end(s) of the train. Therefore, it is required that the braking devices on the whole train should cooperate with each other and act in a consistent manner. To ensure the realization of the required purposes, the passenger and freight cars are installed with more complex equipment, such as the disc braking device and the unit brake cylinder to ensure that the train is stopped within a certain distance after speed-up, unloaded/loaded car adjustment device for double-deck cars, anti-rolling torsion bar, dejecta collecting device for 25T type coach, electronic anti-skid device, passenger car operation safety detection & diagnosis system, and passenger car plateau oxygen generation system. As the installation of those devices, the tare weight of the railway vehicles increases, but accordingly, the number of passengers and cargoes transported will reduce under the same train weight. This is undesirable, especially under the background of speed-up. To solve it, new materials, new processes, new structures, and new technologies are adopted in the design and manufacture of railway vehicles to reduce the tare weight of railway vehicles and improve transportation efficiency.

任务 1.2　我国的新型铁路货车

Task 1.2　New freight cars in China

我国的新型铁路货车满足了时速 120 km 的需要，实现了铁路货车单车载重由 60 t 提高到 70 t 的跨越。2006 年铁道部招标采购的 2.5 万辆货车，全部是在许多方面具有国际先进水平的车辆，标志着我国货车开始由单车载重 60 t 向 70 t 跨越，也标志着铁路在自主创新、实施内涵、扩大再生产方面又迈出了坚实的一步。目前，我国铁路货物运输在用的 60 多万辆货车基本为载重 60 t、时速 80 km 的车辆，与国民经济发展对铁路运输的要求相距甚远。70 t 货车从整车设计到每个零件全部实现了技术创新和技术升级，每列运量由 3 500～5 000 t 提高到

5 000～10 000 t，轴重由 21 t 提到 23 t，运输能力提高了 16.7%，在 5 年的使用寿命期内，可减少辅修 50 次、段修 4 次，厂修周期也由过去运行约 90 万 km 提高到 120 万～160 万 km，节约了维修费用，减少了行车事故。首批 70 t 货车在大秦铁路投入使用。

New railway freight cars of China meet the operation speed requirement of 120 km/h and realize the leap of load capacity from 60 t to 70 t. All the 25,000 freight cars purchased by the Ministry of Railways through bidding in 2006 reached an internationally advanced level in many aspects, which marks not only the leap in one-car load capacity of freight cars from 60 t to 70 t but also the progress of railway in independent innovation as well as implementation and expansion of reproduction. At present, the 600,000+ in-service freight cars in China generally have a load capacity of 60 t and an operation speed of 80 km/h, which are far from the requirements of national economic development for railway transportation. The 70 t freight cars have realized technological innovation and upgrading from the design of the complete car to each part. Specifically, the transportation volume of each train increased from 3,500–5,000 t to 5,000–10,000 t, the axle weight increased from 21 t to 23 t, the transportation capacity increased by 16.7%, and throughout the service life of 5 years, the number of minor repairs is reduced by 50 times, the number of repairs at the depot is reduced by 4 times, while the interval of repair in works is increased from about 900,000 km to 1,200,000–1,600,000 km, ensuring low maintenance cost, high safety and reliability, and less operation accident. The first batch of 70 t freight cars has been put into operation Dalian-Qinhuangdao Railway.

任务 1.3　我国铁路提速的进程

Task 1.3　China's railway speed-up process

（1）1994 年 1 月，在沈大线上首创了时速 120 km 客车，开创了国内铁路既有线上的提速。

In January 1994, the passenger cars on the Shenyang-Dalian Railway first operated at a speed of 120 km/h, marking the start of China's railway speed-up.

（2）1996 年 4 月，在京沪线上，南京—上海的客车实现了时速 160 km。

In April 1996, the passenger cars on the Nanjing-Shanghai Railway operated at a speed of 160 km/h.

（3）1996 年 7 月，北京—北戴河实现了时速 130 km。

In July 1996, the passenger cars on the Beijing-Beidaihe Railway operated at 130 km/h.

有了这几次提速的基础和经验，我国于 1997 年在全路开始了第一次大规模提速，列车运行速度大幅度提高。

Based on the experience of these speed-ups, China initiated the first railway speed-up campaign in 1997, with greatly increased train speed.

（4）1998 年 10 月，实现了第二次大提速，在京广、京沪、京哈三大干线上最高运行速度达到 160 km/h。

In October 1998, the second railway speed-up campaign was launched, with the maximum operation speed on Beijing-Guangzhou Railway, Beijing-Shanghai Railway, and Beijing-Harbin railway increasing to 160 km/h.

（5）2000 年 10 月，实现了第三次大提速，这次提速的重点是陇海、兰新等连接西部地区的铁路干线。

In October 2000, the third railway speed-up campaign was launched, which is mainly implemented on main railway lines connecting the western region, such as Lianyungang-Lanzhou Railway and Lanzhou-Xinjiang Railway.

（6）2001 年 10 月，中国铁路实施第四次大提速。四次大面积提速基本形成了四纵四横的提速网络。经过四次大提速，客车平均速度提高了 25%，列车最高时速从 120 km 提高到 140 km、160 km。广州—深圳的最高时速达到 200 km。中国铁路现代化标志性工程秦沈客运专线试验速度创造了 321.5 km 的时速。

In October 2001, China implemented the fourth railway speed-up campaign. And after that, a railway speed-up network covering four east-west railway lines and four north-south railway lines was formed. The average operation speed of passenger cars increased by 25%, with the maximum operation speed rising from 120 km/h to 140 km/h and 160km/h. The maximum operation speed on Guangzhou–Shenzhen Railway reached 200 km/h. The experimental operation speed on the Qinhuangdao–Shenzhen Passenger-dedicated Railway, a landmark project of China's railway modernization, realized a maximum test speed of 321.5 km/h.

（7）2004 年 4 月，中国铁路实施了第五次大提速，客车运行最高速度达到了 200 km/h。为使提速线路的货车速度与客车速度相匹配（在客货混跑的条件下），同时实施货车提速，由提速前时速不足 80 km，提高到时速 120 km。第五次大提速后，中国铁路初步建成以上海、北京、广州为中心的三大提速圈。以这三个城市为圆心，半径在 500 km 左右的城市实现了朝发夕至，半径在 1 200～1 500 km 左右的城市实现了夕发朝至，半径在 2 000～2 500 km 左右的城市实现了一日到达。

In April 2004, China Railway implemented the fifth railway speed-up campaign, with the maximum operation speed of passenger cars increasing to 200 km/h. In order to match the speed of the freight car with the speed of the passenger car (under the condition of mixed passenger and freight cars running), the speed of the freight car is increased from less than 80 km/h before the speed-up to 120 km/h. After the fifth railway speed-up campaign, three speed-up railway circles centered on Shanghai, Beijing, and Guangzhou were formed. With these three cities as the center of the circle, cities within a radius of about 500 km achieved morning departure and evening return, cities within a radius of about 1,200–1,500 km achieved evening departure and morning arrival, and cities within a radius of 2,000–2,500 km have achieved arrival within one day.

（8）2007 年 4 月 18 日，对中国来说，是个不平凡的日子。这一天，中国铁路第六次大面积提速调图正式实施，140 对最高运行时速达 200～250 km 的国产化动车组列车开始正式运行在中国的铁路线上。中国铁路将以此大提速为起点，进入一个全新的高速时代，并且以具有中国特色的方式开始谱写高速铁路发展的新篇章。第六次大提速共涉及京哈、京广、京沪、京九、陇海、沪昆、胶济、广深、兰新等 18 条线路。第六次大提速以动车组、直达快车、朝发夕至列车为重点，打造铁路快速客运新品牌，不仅优化了旅客列车的运行方案，还推广了以开行跨局大型货物直达列车、“五定”班列、行包专列为重点的三大货运产品板块。经过第六次大提速，三亚站开通了至北京、上海、广州的过海列车。海南西环铁路翻开了三亚铁路史上新的一页，天涯海角从此不再遥远，天涯海角成咫尺的梦想终于实现。

April 18, 2007, was an extraordinary day for China. On this day, the sixth large-scale speed-up adjustment map of China Railway was officially implemented. The 140 pairs of domestically-made EMU trains with a maximum operating speed of 200–250 km/h began to be officially operated on China's railway lines. China's railway will take this as a starting point, enter a new high-speed era, and begin to write a new chapter in the development of high-speed railways in a way with Chinese characteristics. The sixth railway speed-up campaign involved 18 railway lines, including Beijing-Harbin Railway, Beijing-Guangzhou Railway, Beijing-Shanghai Railway, Beijing-Kowloon Railway, Lanzhou-Lianyungang Railway, Shanghai-Kunming Railway, Qingdao-Jinan Railway, Guangzhou-Shenzhen Railway, and Lanzhou-Xinjiang Railway. This speed-up campaign is focused on multiple units, direct express trains, and morning departure & evening arrival trains to create a new railway brand of rapid passenger transport. In addition to the optimization of the passenger car operation plan, this speed-up campaign also promoted the operation of three freight transportation product modules, including cross-bureau large direct freight cars, unscheduled trains, and special trains. In the sixth railway speed-up campaign, the cross-sea trains from Haikou to Beijing, Shanghai, and Guangzhou were opened. Hainan West Ring Railway turned a new page in the history of Sanya Railway, making arrival to Tianya Haijiao possible.

第六次大面积提速调图在技术创新上取得了以下 7 个方面的新成果。

The sixth railway speed-up campaign has reaped new achievements in the following 7 aspects of technological innovation.

（1）成本系统集成技术，掌握了既有线时速 200 km 及以上提速成本系统集成技术，实现了旅客列车 5 min 追踪间隔。

The cost system integration technology for the speed-up of existing railway lines of 200 km/h or above is developed, and a 5-minute tracking interval for passenger cars is achieved.

（2）车组全面系统地引进国外先进成熟的动车组设计制造技术，形成了中国铁路高速动车组的技术体系和知识产权，实现了国产化，打造了最高运行速度达 250 km/h 的中国 CRH 品牌。

The technical embodiment and intellectual property rights of the high-speed EMU with special Chinese characteristics are formed based on the introduction and localization of foreign advanced and mature EMU design and manufacturing technologies, creating the Chinese CRH brand with an operation speed as high as 250 km.

（3）列车运行控制系统采用具有中国特色、自主知识产权的 CTCS-2 级列控系统，完成了列控车载设备地面应答器和 LEU 电子单元的技术引进、消化吸收和系统集成。

The Chinese Train Control System (CTCS) - a Class 2 train control system and column control center equipment, with Chinese characteristics and independent intellectual property rights, is adopted, realizing the introduction, digestion, absorption, and system integration of the ground transponder and LEU of the onboard train control equipment.

（4）通信上首次采用 GSM-R 通信系统和新型的机车综合无线通信设备。

GSM-R communication system and cab-integrated radio communication equipment (CIR) are adopted for the first time.

（5）在繁忙干线上采用分散自律调度集中系统，在主要干线上实现列车调度指挥系统（TDCS）的覆盖。

The discrete self-discipline centralized train control system is adopted for the busy trunk line, and the train operation dispatching command system (TDCS) is deployed on the main trunk lines.

（6）工务工程、路基工程首次研制了 18 号有砟轨道并验证了其平顺性和适用性，轨道技术水平已达到国际先进水平。

For public works engineering and roadbed engineering, the No.18 ballasted track is developed firstly with its smoothness and applicability verified, marking that the technical level of the track has reached an international advanced level.

（7）牵引供电这次采用接触导线最低高度 6 330 mm 条件，验证了弓网适用性，在时速 200 km 的条件下，应用自动过分相装置，验证交流传动技术对谐波等电能质量的影响及适用性。

The contact line with a minimum height of 6,330 mm is adopted for the traction power supply, the applicability of the traction electric network is verified, the automatic splitting phase device is applied when the operation speed is 200 km/h, and the influence of AC drive technology on the power quality such as harmonics as well as its applicability is verified.

项目 2

Project 2

铁道车辆基本知识

Basic Knowledge of Railway Vehicles

本项目以分析、分解铁道车辆的功能单元为工学任务，通过课堂任务的完成过程，着重以车辆的标记和用途区分不同种类的车辆，并以此为引导，简单介绍各种类型的车辆；通过课后任务的完成，了解车辆的组成、分类、代码、标记、主要技术参数等。

The main task of this project is the analysis and disassembly of railway vehicles. In the classroom, the main focus is on identifying different types of railway vehicles based on their markings and uses, and providing a brief introduction to each type. Through after-class tasks, students will learn about the composition, classification, codes, markings, and key technical parameters of railway vehicles.

学生工作页 Student Worksheet

工学任务描述 Task description	预期目标 Expected goals
任务名称：认识、分解铁道车辆（火车） Task name: Understanding and disassembly of railway vehicles 任务编号：CJ-02 Task number: CJ-02 任务类型：认知型+原理型 Task type: Cognitive + structural principle 适用范围：车辆系统各岗位群 Applicable scope: All post groups of the system of railway vehicles 完成时间：　　　　学时 Completion time: 　　　class hours	初级：掌握铁道车辆的特点、组成 Elementary level: Master the characteristics and composition of railway vehicles 中级：掌握铁道车辆的用途、分类 Intermediate level: Master the classification of railway vehicles by purpose 高级：掌握铁道车辆的代码、标记和方位的确定，以及主要技术参数 Advanced level: Master the code, marking, location as well as the main technical parameters of cars

知识回顾+小组讨论

Knowledge review + group discussion

1. 小组讨论：

   Group discussion:

（1）列举你所见过的 5 种以上的铁道车辆，并在小组讨论之后，简单解释各种车辆的作用。

List more than 5 kinds of railway vehicles you have seen. After group discussion, briefly explain the functions of each kind of railway vehicles.

（2）尝试对所列举的铁道车辆进行分类，你所在小组的分类依据是什么？

Try to classify the listed railway vehicles. What is the basis of the classification in your group?

2. 小组讨论+学习记录：你所知的车辆有哪些基本功能单元（比如汽车），或者你认为应该具备哪些基本功能单元？

Group discussion + learning record: What basic functional units do you know about the railway vehicles (such as cars), or what basic functional units do you think a railway vehicle should have?

	基本功能单元 Basic functional unit	功能/作用 Function
1		
2		
3		
4		
5		

3. 归纳总结：针对铁道车辆的种类和组成，归纳一下铁道车辆的特点。

Summary: summarize the characteristics of railway vehicles according to the types and composition of railway vehicles.

4. 识别车辆代码：

Identification of car code:

（1）通过查阅资料，注明以下车辆代码的含义。

Refer to relevant documents and describe the meaning of the following codes for railway vehicles.

RW_{25Z} 31688：______

YZ_{25G} 46188：______

P_{64} 3408290：______

G_{70T} 999999：______

K_{18AT} 0338718：______

L_{18} 0236543：______

（2）归纳总结：每组代码由哪几部分组成？如果你是设计师，你会把代码涂在车辆的哪个部位？

Summary: What's the composition of each code for railway vehicle? Where would you put the code on the car, if you are a designer?

5. 小组讨论：如何评价车辆的性能？通过查阅资料，列举车辆的技术参数。

Group discussion: How to evaluate car performance? Refer to relevant documents and list the technical parameters of railway vehicles.

6. 识别车辆标记：

Identification of car marking:

（1）回忆一下你见过的车辆，除了车辆代码以外还有哪些图案、数字？

Recall the railway vehicles you have seen. What are the patterns and numbers you have found on the car in addition to the car code?

（2）如果你是车辆检修人员，接到一辆车时，你觉得应该了解什么；检修完一辆车后，你觉得应该记载什么？

If you are a maintenance person, what do you think you should know about the car after you receive it? And what do you think should be recorded after it is serviced?

（3）学习并记录、总结车辆的标记及作用。

Learn, record, and summarize the marking and function of cars.

标记类型 Type of marking	作　用 Function

课后任务

After-class tasks

学习并理解车辆的主要技术参数，填写 P_{64}、G_{70T}、YZ_{25K} 的主要技术参数，对照找出其中的共同点与不同点；学会自己查阅资料，选择所喜欢的车型，填写主要技术参数。

Learn and understand the main technical parameters of the car, fill in the main technical parameters of P_{64}, G_{70T}, and YZ_{25K}, and identify the common points and differences by comparison; learn to look up information, choose your favorite model, and fill in the main technical parameters.

主要技术参数 Main technical parameters	车型 Model			
	P_{64}	G_{70T}	YZ_{25K}	所喜欢的车型 Favorite model
自重系数/每个定员所占自重 Ratio of tare weight to loading capacity/Tare weight per passenger capacity				
比容系数/车辆每米长所占自重 Specific volume/Tare weight per meter				
最高运行速度 Max. operating speed				
最高试验速度 Max. test speed				
轴重 Axle load				
每延米轨道载重 Load per meter of track				
通过最小曲线半径 Min. radius of curvature negotiated				
传动方式 Transmission mode				

学习效果评价
Learning effect evaluation

年 Year　　月 Month　　日 Day

专业班级： Major & class:	姓名： Name:	学号： Student number:
工学小组及分工： Work-and-study team and responsibility division:		

专业（知识/技能）收获 Professional gains (knowledge/skills)	（非专业）能力素质收获 (Non-professional) ability and quality gains

评价考核项目 Evaluation item	自我评价 Self-evaluation	小组评价 Group evaluation	教师评价 Teacher's evaluation
已掌握构成车辆的基本功能单元 Have mastered the basic functional units of the car			
已掌握车辆主要技术参数 Have mastered the main technical parameters of the car			
已理解各型铁道车辆的用途 Have understood the function of each type of the railway vehicles			
已掌握相关知识点的数量 Number of knowledge points mastered			
主动提出问题的数量 Number of questions proposed			
课外学习时间（学时） After-school learning time (hours)			
兴趣车型自主学习（收集相关知识点的数量） Autonomous learning of interested model (the number of knowledge points collected)			
工作态度（课堂、课后任务完成情况） Work attitude (completion condition of classroom tasks and after-class tasks)	☆☆☆☆ ☆☆☆☆	☆☆☆☆ ☆☆☆☆	☆☆☆☆ ☆☆☆☆
合作意识及协调能力 Cooperation consciousness and coordination ability	☆☆☆☆ ☆☆☆☆	☆☆☆☆ ☆☆☆☆	☆☆☆☆ ☆☆☆☆
正确表达和沟通能力 Correct expression and communication skills	☆☆☆☆ ☆☆☆☆	☆☆☆☆ ☆☆☆☆	☆☆☆☆ ☆☆☆☆
自律能力（缺勤/旷课/迟到/违纪次数） Self-discipline (absences/absenteeism/lateness/disciplinary violations)			

任务 2.1　铁道车辆的组成

Task 2.1　Compositions of railway vehicles

为适应和满足旅客和货物运输的不同要求，铁道车辆虽有很多类型，构造也各有不同，但从基本结构来看，一般均由五大部分组成，如图 2–1 所示。

The railway vehicle is divided into many kinds to adapt to and meet different requirements of passenger and cargo transportation. Though different in construction, railway vehicles of different kinds generally consist of five modules, as shown in Figure 2-1.

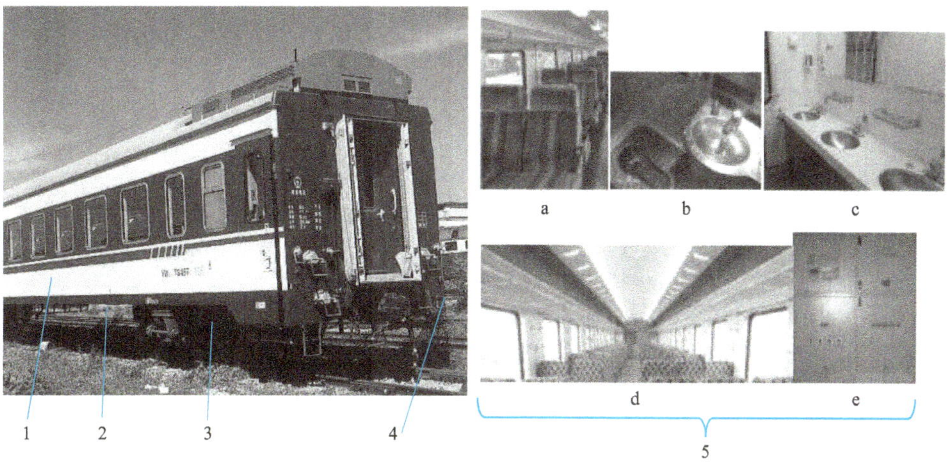

1—车体；2—制动装置；3—转向架；4—车钩缓冲装置；
5—车内设备（a—座椅及行李架；b—卫生设备；c—洗脸间；d—空调装置；e—电气装置）。
1—Car body; 2—Braking device; 3—Bogie; 4—Coupler and draft gear;
5—In-car equipment (a—Seat and luggage rack; b—Sanitary equipment; c—Face washing room; d—Air conditioning; e—Electrical apparatus).

图 2–1　铁道车辆的组成
Figure 2-1　Compositions of Railway Vehicle

1. 车体

Car body

车体是容纳旅客、装载货物及整备品等的部分。车体主要由底架、侧墙、端墙、车顶等部分组成，其结构如图 2–2 所示。其中，底架是车体的基础，底架上有许多纵向梁和横向梁，和车体一起承受着作用于车辆上的各种载荷。因此，它应具有足够的强度和刚度。

The car body is the part that accommodates passengers, cargo, and accessories. It is mainly composed of the underframe, side wall, end wall, roof, and other parts, as shown in Figure 2-2. The underframe is the foundation of the car body, and on the underframe, longitudinal beams and cross beams are installed to bear various loads acting on the car together with the car body. Therefore, it should have sufficient strength and rigidity.

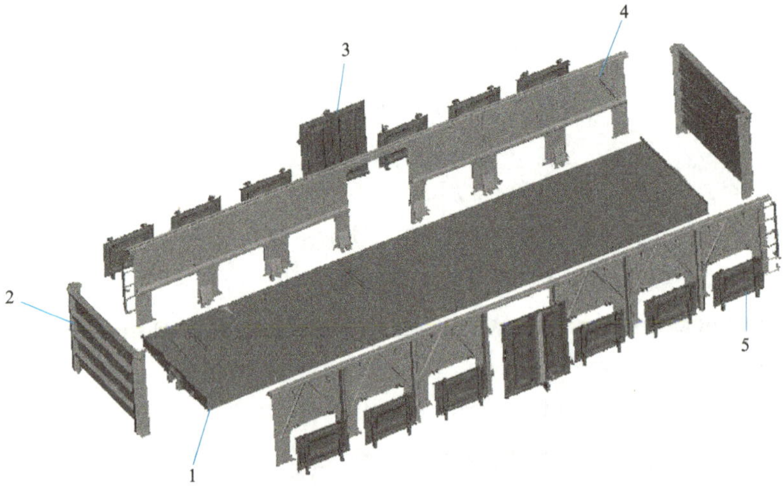

1—底架；2—端墙；3—侧开门；4—侧墙；5—下开门。

1—Underframe; 2—End wall; 3—Side swinging door; 4—Side wall; 5—Downward swinging door.

图 2–2　车体的结构

Figure 2-2　Structure of Car Body

2. 制动装置

Braking device

制动装置是车辆上起制动作用的零部件所组成的整套机构。它的主要作用是保证运行中的列车减速及在规定的距离内停车或防止静止的车辆溜走，以保证行车安全。制动装置一般由空气制动机、手制动机和基础制动装置三部分组成，其结构如图 2–3 所示。制动装置是通过压缩空气或人力推动基础制动装置来实现制动作用的。

The braking device is a complete mechanism composed of parts and components for braking the car. It is mainly intended for decelerating the train during operation, stopping the train within the specified distance, and preventing the stationary car from sliding, thus ensuring safe operation. The braking device is generally composed of an air brake, hand brake, and foundation braking device, as shown in Figure 2-3. The braking device works by driving the foundation braking device with compressed air or human power.

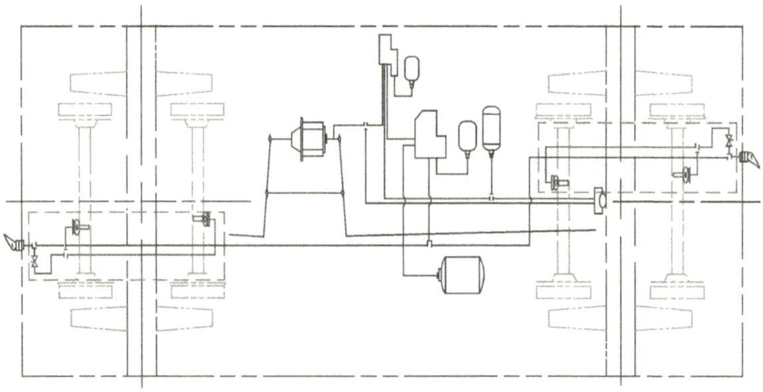

图 2–3　车辆制动装置的结构

Figure 2-3　Structure of Braking Device

3. 转向架（走行部）

Bogie (running gear)

走行部承受着车体的自重和载重，并由机车牵引行驶在钢轨上，是保证车辆运行品质的关键部件。对于四轴及多轴车，一般将两轴或多轴组成一个能相对车体回转的整体，称为转向架，俗称台车。转向架一般由构架（侧架）、轮对、滚动轴承（轴箱）装置、弹簧减振装置、基础制动装置等部分组成，如图 2–4 所示。

The running gear, as the key part to ensure the running quality of the car, bears the tare weight and load of the car body, and is towed by the locomotive on the rail. For four-axle cars and multi-axle cars, generally two axles or multiple axles constitute an assembly that can rotate relative to the car body, which is called a bogie. The bogie is generally composed of a frame (side frame), a wheelset, a roller bearing (axle box) assembly, a spring & vibration damper assembly, and a foundation braking device, as shown in Figure 2-4.

图 2–4 转向架（走行部）
Figure 2-4 Bogie (Running Gear)

4. 车钩缓冲装置

Coupler and draft gear

车钩缓冲装置是将机车与车辆或车辆与车辆进行互相连挂的装置，它具有传递纵向力并缓和各车辆之间冲击力的作用。车钩缓冲装置主要由车钩、缓冲器、解钩装置及附属配件等组成，如图 2–5 所示。车钩缓冲装置安装在车体底架的两端。

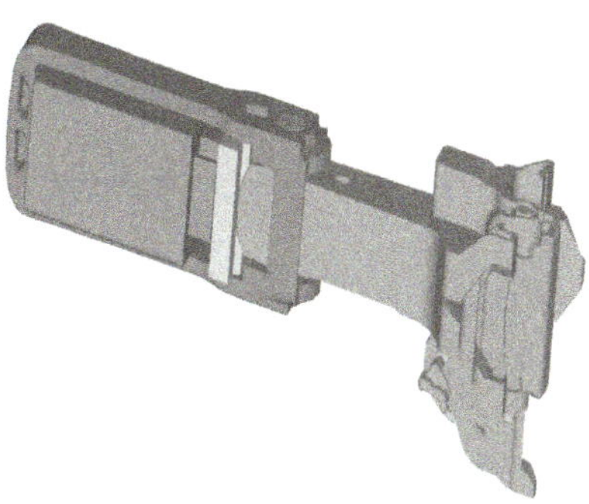

图 2–5 车钩缓冲装置
Figure 2-5 Coupler and Draft Gear

The coupler and draft gear is a device that connects the locomotive and the car or connects the cars for transmitting longitudinal force and mitigating the dynamic effect between cars. The coupler and draft gear is mainly composed of a coupler, draft gear, uncoupling device, and accessories, as shown in Figure 2-5. The coupler and draft gear is installed at both ends of the car body underframe.

5. 车内设备

In-car equipment

车内设备是指能良好地为运输对象服务而设于车体内的一些固定附属装置，如图 2-6 所示。例如，客车车内设备主要包括给水装置、空调装置、电气装置、座席、卧铺、行李架、卫生设施等，有的客车上还设有媒体和通信装置等。货车由于类型不同，车内设备也各不相同，一般来说比客车简单，如保温车中装设的制冷设备和乘务员的生活设备。

In-car equipment refers to some fixed attachments installed in the car body to well serve the transportation object, as shown in Figure 2-6. For example, the equipment in passenger cars mainly includes water supply equipment, air conditioning, electrical apparatus, seats, sleepers, luggage racks, sanitary facilities, etc., and some passenger cars are also equipped with media and communication devices. The in-car equipment in freight cars depends on the type of freight cars and generally the configuration of the in-car equipment of freight cars is simpler than that of the passenger cars, for example, the refrigerator car is equipped with refrigerator and living equipment for the crew.

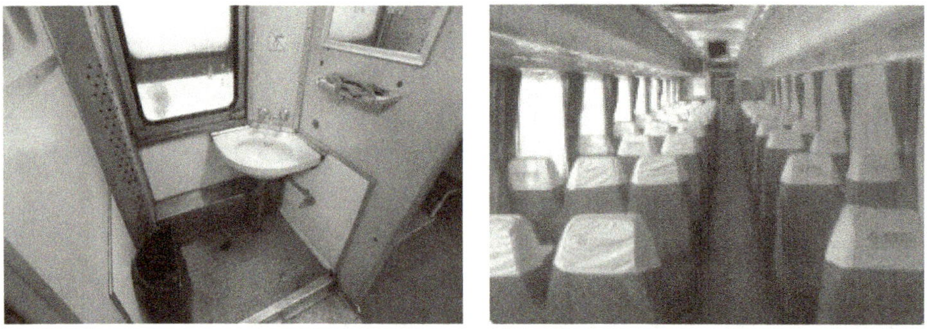

图 2-6　车内设备
Figure 2-6　In-car equipment

任务 2.2　铁道车辆的分类

Task 2.2　Classification of railway vehicles

铁道车辆按用途分为客车、货车。

Railway vehicles are classified into passenger cars and freight cars according to their use.

1. 客车

Passenger car

客车是指供运送旅客和为旅客服务的或原则上编组在旅客列车中具有特殊用途的铁道车辆。

A passenger car refers to a kind of railway vehicle used for transporting and serving passengers, and it is in principle grouped in passenger cars for special purposes.

客车的一般外形特点是：两侧墙上有车窗；两车厢连接处有供旅客通行的车端装置与渡板；有运行品质较好的转向架；车身一般比较长等。客车的主要用途是运送旅客或提供某种为旅客服务的功能。还有一些客车，既不运送旅客，又不为旅客服务，但因某种特殊的用途编在旅客列车中或单独几辆编组按旅客列车在线路上运行，如邮政车、试验车、检轨车、公务车等。

The general appearance characteristics of passenger cars are as follows: there are doors and windows on both side walls; there are end devices and walkways at the connection of two cars for passengers to pass; the bogies have good operating quality; the car body is generally long, etc. The main purpose of the passenger car is for transporting passengers or providing a certain kind of service for passengers. Some passenger cars may be used neither for transporting passengers nor providing service for passengers, but they are grouped in passenger cars or grouped together to operate on the line as a passenger train for some special purpose, such as mail cars, test cars, rail inspection cars, official business cars, etc.

2. 货车

Freight car

货车是用以运输货物和为此服务的或原则上编组在货物列车中使用的车辆。按其用途的不同，货车分为通用货车、专用货车和特种货车 3 类。

A freight car is a railway vehicle used for transporting cargo and providing cargo transportation service, or which is grouped in the freight train for operation. The freight car is classed according to use into general-purpose freight cars, special-purpose freight cars, and particular-class cars.

任务 2.3　铁道车辆代码、标记及车辆方位的确定

Task 2.3　Code, marking, and orientation determination of railway vehicles

为了车辆运用和管理上的需要，将车辆的性能、配属及使用注意事项等在车体明显处用符号标示出来，这些符号称为车辆标记，如图 2-7 所示的客车车种称号和车号。

To facilitate the operation and management of cars, the performance, attributes, and operation precautions are marked by symbols in the obvious places of the car body. These symbols are called markings, as shown in Figure 2-7.

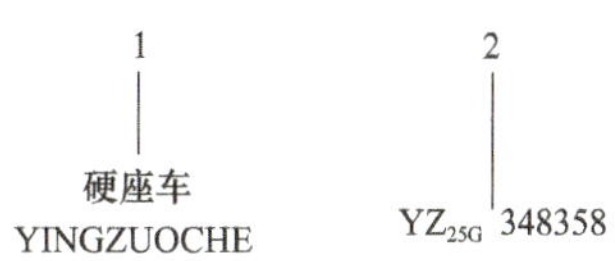

1—车种；2—车号。

1—Type of the car; 2—Serial number of the car.

图 2-7　客车车种称号和车号

Figure 2-7　Type and Serial Number of Passenger Car

1. 铁道车辆代码
Railway vehicle code

为了对车辆进行识别与管理，特别因全国铁路用微机联网管理的需要，必须对运用中的每一辆车都进行编码，且每一辆车的代码唯一。代码分车种、车型、车号三段。车种代码原则上在该车种汉语拼音名称中选取一个或两个大写字母构成，具体可见表 2-1。其中，客车用两个字母，而货车仅用一个字母。车型代码必须与车种代码连用，它是为区分同一车种中因结构、装载量等不同而设的，一般由 1～2 个数字构成，必要时其后还可再加大写字母。车型代码是车种代码的后缀，原则上两种代码合在一起不得超过 5 个字符。举例如下：

C_{62B}　　C（车种）　　62（顺序系列）　　B（结构区别）
N_{17A}　　N（车种）　　17（顺序系列）　　A（结构区别）
YW_{25G}　　YW（车种）　　25（车长系列）　　G（结构区别）

For the purpose of car identification and management, and especially for the national railway microcomputer network management, each car in service shall be uniquely coded. The code consists of three parts, namely car type, car model, car number. In principle, the code of the car type is generally composed of one or two capital letters in the pinyin of the car, as shown in Table 2-1,with the passenger car represented by two letters while the freight car by one. The code of the car model must be used in conjunction with the type code for the car to distinguish the difference between cars of the same type in structure and load capacity. It is generally composed of 1–2 numbers, which may be suffixed with capitalized letters when necessary. The model code for the car is the suffix of the type code for the car, and, in principle, the length of these two codes shall not exceed five characters. Example:

C_{62B}　　C (type of car)　　62 (sequence series)　　B (structural difference)
N_{17A}　　N (type of car)　　17 (sequence series)　　A (structural difference)
YW_{25G}　　YW (type of car)　　25 (car length series)　　G (structural difference)

表 2-1　铁道车辆代码
Table 2-1　Railway vehicle code

客　车 Passenger car			货　车 Freight car		
序　号 S/N	车　种 Type	代　码 Code	序　号 S/N	车　种 Type	代　码 Code
1	软座车 Cushioned seat coach	RZ	1	棚车 Box car	P
2	硬座车 Semi-cushioned seat coach	YZ	2	敞车 Gondola car	C
3	硬卧车 Semi-cushioned berth sleeper	YW	3	平车 Flat car	N
4	软卧车 Cushioned berth sleeper	RW	4	集装箱平车 Flat car for containers	X

续表
Continued

客　车 Passenger car			货　车 Freight car		
序　号 S/N	车　种 Type	代　码 Code	序　号 S/N	车　种 Type	代　码 Code
5	餐车 Dining car	CA	5	矿石车（自翻车） Ore car (dump car)	F（KF）
6	行李车 Luggage car	XL	6	长大货物车 High-capacity freight car	D
7	邮政车 Mail car	UZ	7	罐车 Tank car	G
8	厨房车 Kitchen car	CF	8	保温车 Refrigerator car	B
9	公务车 Official business car	GW	9	毒品车 Poison car	W
10	医务车 Medical car	YI	10	家畜车 Livestock car	J
11	卫生车 Ambulance car	WS	11	水泥车 Cement car	U
12	试验车 Test car	SY	12	粮食车 Grain car	L
13	维修车 Maintenance car	EX	13	特种车 Special car	T
14	文教车 Culture and education car	WJ	14	守车 Guards van	S
15	特种车 Special car	TZ			
16	代用座车 Substitute coach	ZP			
17	代用行李车 Substitute luggage car	XP			
18	简易座车 Simple car	DP			

车号代码均为数字，因车种、车型不同，区分了使用数字的范围。

The car number is only composed of figures, and the range of applicable numbers depends on the type and model of the car.

一辆车的代码是该车的重要标识，必须涂刷在车辆明显的位置（如侧墙）上。

The code of a car is an important identification and must be painted on a conspicuous position of the car (such as the side wall).

2. 铁道车辆标记

Railway vehicle markings

习惯上把车辆标记分为运用、产权、检修、制造 4 种类型。但实质上这些标记主要是为了在运用及检修等情况下便于管理和识别所设置的。

The operation marking is generally divided into operation marking, ownership marking, inspection & repair marking, and manufacturing marking. However, these markings are essentially set for easy management and identification in the case of operation and maintenance.

1）运用标记

Operation marking

（1）自重：空车时，车辆自身的全部质量称为车辆自重。自重以 t 为计量单位，保留 1 位小数。检修及改造中若发生 100 kg 及以上的质量差异时，检衡后应更改自重标记。

Tare weight: Tare weight refers to the total mass of cars when it is empty, which is expressed in t and rounded off to the first place after the decimal point. If a mass difference of 100 kg or more occurs during maintenance and renovation, the tare weight marking shall be changed after weighing.

（2）载重：车辆允许的正常最大装载质量称为车辆的载重。载重以 t 为计量单位。

Load capacity: Load capacity refers to the normal maximum loading mass allowed by the car, which is expressed in t.

（3）容积：车辆内部可容纳货物的体积称为车辆的容积。以车体内部长、宽、高的乘积表示，以 m^3 为计量单位，保留 1 位小数。容积下面附括号，在括号内列出长、宽、高标记，以 m 为计量单位，保留 1 位小数。敞车、煤车在括号内仅涂打长、宽标记；棚车、冷藏车、通风车、家畜车等在括号内涂打长、宽、高标记；平车、砂石车、长大货物车不涂打容积标记，仅涂打长、宽标记；罐车在容积标记下方应涂打“容量计表”标记，除规定的淘汰型罐车和路用水槽车外，罐车还应在罐体两侧端板中部涂打“容量计表”标记。

Volume: Volume refers to the volume of cargo that can be accommodated inside the car, which is expressed as the product of the length, width, and height of the car body in m^3, and rounded off to the first place after the decimal point. A bracket is provided below the volume, in which the length, width, and height of the car body are listed, expressed in m, and rounded off to the first place after the decimal point. For gondola cars and coal cars, only markings for length and width are made in the bracket; for box cars, refrigerator cars, ventilated box cars, and livestock cars, markings for length, width, and height are made in the bracket; for flat cars, ore cars and high-capacity cars, no volume marking is made, and only markings for length and width are painted; for tank cars, markings for number and volume calculation table shall be painted under the volume marking, and except for specified obsolete tank cars and on-road water tank cars, the marking for “volume calculation table” shall also be painted on the end plate of two sides of the tank body.

（4）车辆全长及换长：车辆全长为该车两端车钩处于闭锁位时两钩舌内侧面间的距离，以 m 为单位。换长等于全长除以 11，保留 1 位小数，尾数四舍五入。换长也可以称为计算长度，说明该车折合 11 m 长的车辆（以解放初期 30 t 敞车平均长度为计算标准）时，相当于它的多少倍，以便在运营中估算列车的总长度。

Full length and converted length of car: Full length refers to the length over the inner side faces of coupler knuckles in a locking position, which is expressed in m. The converted length is equal to the total length divided by 11 and is rounded off to the first place after the decimal point. Converted length, which is also called calculated length, indicates the multiple of the original car length to an 11 m-long car (taking the average length of a 30 t gondola car in the early liberation period as the calculation standard) to estimate the total length of the train in operation.

（5）车辆定位标记：以阿拉伯数字 1 或 2 标记之，货车涂在车体两侧的端下角，客车涂在脚蹬的外侧面及车内两端墙上部。

Orientation marking: It is represented by the Arabic numeral 1 or 2, and is painted in the bottom corner on both sides of the car body for freight cars, and at the outer side face of the footsteps and the upper part of the end walls for passenger cars.

（6）表示车辆（主要指货车）设备、用途及结构特点的各种标记：

Markings for identifying the equipment, use, and structural characteristics of cars (mainly freight cars):

(MC)——表示可以参加国际联运的客货车。

representing passenger cars or freight cars allowed for international operation.

——表示禁止通过机械化驼峰调车场的货车，如长大货物车、自翻车、液化气体罐车等。

representing freight cars not allowed to pass through the mechanized hump yard, such as high-capacity freight cars, dump cars, liquefied gas tank cars, etc.

(人)——表示具有车窗、车顶烟筒、床托架等的棚车，必要时供运送人员使用。

representing box cars with door windows, roof chimneys, berth brackets, etc. for transportation personnel when necessary.

——表示具有拴马环或其他拴马装置的货车。

representing freight cars with horse-tying rings or other horse-tying devices.

(特)——表示可以装运坦克及特殊货物的车辆。

representing cars for transporting tanks and special cargo.

(卷)——表示车辆侧梁端部装有卷扬机的挂钩，可以卷扬倒车。

representing the end of the side beam of the railway vehicle is equipped with the hook of the hoist, which can be lifted and reversed.

——表示顶车作业的指定部位。

representing the location designated for jacking.

——表示吊装作业的指定部位。

representing the location designated for hoisting.

水平环形色带——运送危险货物的罐车标识，在罐体纵向中部，涂打一条宽 200 mm 的表示所运货物主要特征的水平环形色带，红色表示易燃，黄色表示有毒，黑色表示腐蚀；液化气体罐车的色带宽 300 mm，上层 200 mm 涂蓝色，下层 100 mm 涂其他颜色，红色表示易燃液体，黄色表示剧毒液体，白色表示不燃无毒液体；色带留一空处，涂打专用货物名称及其危险性，并用分子分母形式表示，如为遇水会发生剧烈化学反应的货物，还须在分母内，涂打“禁水”二字。

Horizontal circular color strip—the tank car markings for transporting dangerous goods, in the longitudinal middle of the tank, a horizontal circular color strip painted of 200 mm wide indicating the main characteristics of the goods transported, red indicates flammable, yellow indicates toxic, black indicates corrosion; The color bandwidth of the liquefied gas tank car is 300 mm, the upper 200 mm is painted blue, the lower 100 mm is painted with other colors, red indicates flammable liquid, yellow indicates highly toxic liquid, and white indicates non-combustible non-toxic liquid. The color bandwidth is left empty, and the name of the special goods and its danger are painted, and expressed in the form of numerator and denominator. If the goods will have a violent chemical reaction in the water, the word “forbidden water” must be painted in the denominator.

——表示救援列车，在车辆的两侧墙中央涂打宽为 200 mm 的白色横线。

representing rescue cars, with a 200 mm-wide white horizontal line painted to the center of both side walls of the car.

——毒品车标志，涂刷在车门左侧，并在车门的车号标记下面涂打“毒品专用车”标记。

representing poison car, which is painted on the left side of the door, and accompanied by a marking reading “DEDICATED FOR POISON” under the car number on the door.

此外，车辆上还有客车运行区间牌、色票插、货票插及特种票插等，供运输部门及车辆部门放置色票、货票等使用。

In addition, there are passenger car operating section cards, color ticket jacks, cargo ticket jacks, and special ticket jacks on the car for the transportation department and the vehicle department to place color tickets, cargo tickets, etc.

有时根据一定时期内检修、实验、统计等工作的需要，也可以涂打某些临时性标记。例如，客车滚动轴承结构改进后，涂刷一定的标记以区分该轴承是否改进；对以 120 km/h 或 160 km/h 等速度运行的客车涂打速度标记，以确定该车能编挂在何种运行速度的列车上。

Sometimes, temporary markings may be made when required by maintenance, experiment, statistics, and other work within a certain period of time, such as a marking for distinguishing the improvement of the roller bearing of a passenger car after its structural improvement, as well as speed marking made on a passenger car operating at a speed of 120 km/h, 160 km/h or others to determine the operating speed of trains applicable for the coupling of the car.

客车车种汉字标记及定员标记：为了便于旅客识别，在客车侧墙上的车号前必须用汉字涂刷车种名称，如“硬座车 YZ_{25G} 46188”。有车门灯的客车还可以在车门灯玻璃上涂刷车种汉字名称，以便旅客夜间识别。在客车客室内端墙上方的特制标牌上，标明车号及按座席或铺位可容纳的人数，例如：

Chinese character marking the type of passenger car and marking for passenger capacity: to facilitate identification by passengers, the name of the type of passenger car must be painted with Chinese characters before the serial number on the side wall of the passenger car, such as “semi-cushioned seat coach YZ_{25G} 46188”. Passenger cars with door lights can also be painted with the car in Chinese characters on the door light glass for passengers to identify at night. The serial number of the car and the passenger capacity by seat or berth are indicated on a special sign on the end wall of the passenger compartment of the passenger car, for example:

RW_{25Z} 31688
定员：36 人 Passenger capacity: 36 people

YZ_{25G} 46188
定员：128 人 Passenger capacity: 128 people

2）产权标记
Ownership marking

（1）国徽：凡参加国际联运的客车须在侧墙中部悬挂特制的国徽。

National emblem: a special national emblem shall be attached in the middle of the side wall of all passenger cars in international operations.

（2）路徽：凡产权归中国国家铁路集团有限公司的车辆，均应在侧墙或端墙适当部位涂刷路徽，对于货车还应在侧梁适当部位安装中国国家铁路集团有限公司的产权牌（用金属制作的、椭圆形的路徽标志牌）。我国的路徽为 ，含有“人民铁道”之意。其他国家或公司所属的铁道车辆也各有其自己的标志。参加国际联运的货车虽无国徽，一旦离开产权所有国，可凭路徽标志回送至产权国而不会混淆使用。

Railway logo: for cars with ownership under China Railway, a railway logo shall be painted on the appropriate part of the side wall or end wall, and for freight cars, the ownership signboard (an oval-shaped railway logo signboard made of metal) shall be installed on the appropriate part of the side rail. The railway logo of China is , meaning the “people’s railway”. The railway vehicle owned by other countries or companies also has its own logo. Once the freight cars involving in international operations leave the country of ownership, they can be returned to the country of ownership with the railway logo without confusion though they have no national emblem.

（3）路外厂矿企业自备车辆的产权标志：我国各路外厂矿企业的自备车因运送货物或委托路内厂、段检修而需在正线上行驶，为避免铁路运输部门混淆使用，必须有明显的产权标志。

Ownership marking of cars owned by factories and mines out of the jurisdiction of Railway Bureau: the cars owned by factories and mines out of the jurisdiction of Railway Bureau, when they are operating on the railway for transportation of goods or are entrusted for repair in works or repair in depot shall be provided obvious ownership marking to avoid confusion with cars of railway transportation departments.

一般在侧墙上或其他相应的部位用汉字涂刷上“×××企业自备车”字样，并注明该企业所在地的特殊到站，如图 2-8 所示。

Generally, the words “Self-owned Cars of ××× (enterprise name)” are painted on the side wall or other corresponding parts with Chinese characters, and the special arrival station where the enterprise is located shall be indicated, as shown in Figure 2-8.

图 2-8　自备车
Figure 2-8　Self-owned Cars

（4）配属标记：所有客车及某些有固定配属的货车，必须涂刷上所属局、段的简称（各车辆修、造厂及车辆段的简称及代号见厂修、段修规程）。例如，标有“广铁广段（牌）”的车表示广州铁路局广州车辆段的配属车，如图 2-9 所示；部属车以带边框的部字表示。客车配属标记均涂刷在端墙左下角处。

Allocation entity marking: all passenger cars and some freight cars with fixed allocation entity must be painted with the abbreviations of the bureaus and sections to which they belong (see Regulations for repairs in works and at the depot for abbreviations and codes of each repair, workshop, and depot). For example, the car marked with “Guangzhou Bureau Guangzhou Section” represents the cars allocated by Guangzhou Depot of Guangzhou Railway Bureau, as shown in Figure 2-9; Cars belonging to departments are marked by the word with borders. The allocation entity marking of passenger cars is painted at the lower left corner of the end wall.

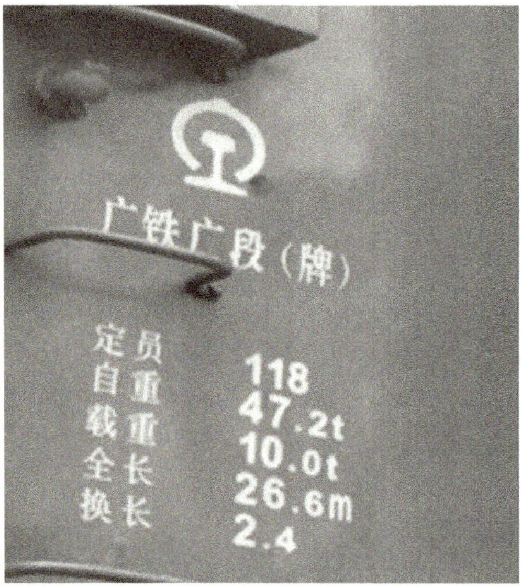

图 2-9　配属标记
Figure 2-9　Allocation Entity Marking

3）检修标记

Maintenance marking

检修标记是便于车辆计划预防修理制度执行与管理的标记，共有两种。它记下本次修程、类型及检修责任单位并提醒下一次同类修程应在何时进行等，且车辆一旦发生重大行车事故，可借此追查与车辆检修有关的责任单位及责任者。

The maintenance marking has two kinds and is intended for facilitating the implementation and management of the scheduled preventive repair system of cars. It records the maintenance process, type of maintenance, and the responsible unit and reminds the time when the next similar repair is due. It can be used as a basis for tracing the responsible unit and personnel for car inspection and maintenance when a serious operation accident occurs.

定期修理标记：段修、厂修两栏。例如：

Scheduled repair marking: including repair at depot and repair in works. For example:

07.9	06.3	成成
14.3	06.9	柳厂

07.11	06.5	成成东
14.11	06.11	眉厂

上述标记中，横线上部为段修标记，横线下部为厂修标记，左侧为下次检修年月，右侧为本次检修年月及检修单位的简称。若为新造车，也须在横线下部右侧填写制造年月及单位简称。此种标记的涂刷规定为：货车涂刷在两侧墙左下角；客车涂刷在两外侧端墙右下角。

As shown above, the marking above the horizontal line is for repair at the depot, and the marking below the horizontal line is for repair in works. The left part is the date of the next maintenance, and the right part is the date and responsible unit of current maintenance. In the case of a newly-built car, the manufacture date and unit are to be marked on the right lower part of the horizontal line. As specified, this marking shall be painted at the lower left corner of the two side walls for freight cars, and at the lower right corner of the two outer end walls for passenger cars.

4）制造标记

Manufacturing marking

在每一车辆上有一块生产厂家的金属标志牌，形式由各厂家自定。此外，车辆的主要零部件，如车轮、车轴、转向架、车钩及制动分配阀等，在其上一般均有该零部件生产厂家的某种代号，锻件常打出数码代号，铸件常铸出铸造代号。这些标记的基本作用是在发生事故后可据此追查责任。

A metal nameplate of the manufacturer is installed on each car, with the form determined by the manufacturer. In addition, the main parts and components of cars including wheels, axles, bogies, couplers, brake distribution valves and others are generally marked with the code of their manufacturer. Forgings are usually marked with digital code while castings are usually cast with casting code. This marking is generally used for tracing the responsible unit of an accident.

3. 铁道车辆方位的确定

Determination of railway vehicle's orientation

铁道车辆在前后、左右方向是一个基本对称的结构，但不完全对称，如轮对、轴箱装置是对称的，制动系统就是不对称的，在横向、纵向对称轴或对称部位上有许多结构相同或相近的零部件。为了在检修、运用中对车辆不良处所的修复及事故的调查处理准确无误，需要给车辆的每个零部件确定一个像数字坐标一样准确的方位。那么，如何确定呢？

The railway vehicle is basically but not completely symmetrical in the front, rear, left, and right directions. For example, the wheelset and axle box devices are symmetrical while the braking system is asymmetrical. On the horizontal, longitudinal symmetrical axles, or symmetrical parts, many parts have the same or similar structure. To ensure proper repair of defects and accurate investigation of accidents during maintenance and operation, each part on the car should be given an accurate position like digital coordinates. So, how to determine it?

1）车辆方位的确定

Determination of car's orientation

车辆方位一般以制动缸活塞杆推出的方向为一位，相反的方向为二位，并在车上规定的部位涂刷方位标志，如图 2-10 所示。对于有多个制动缸的情况，则以手制动装置安装的位置为一位。若按上述方法确定方位仍有困难，则以出厂时涂打的标记为准。若客车转向架使用盘型制动装置时制动缸数量较多，则以手制动端为一位。一些长大货车使用转向架群，手制动装置也可能有数个，则可以出厂时涂打的标记为准。

For the orientation of the car, generally, the pushing direction of the brake cylinder piston rod is taken as “B” end, and the direction opposite to it is taken as “A” end. The orientation markings shall be painted on the specified position of the car, as shown in Figure 2-10. If there are multiple brake cylinders, the position where the hand brake is installed will be taken as “B” end. When the orientation is hard to be determined by the methods described above, the marking made before delivery shall be referenced. If multiple brake cylinders are present when the disc braking device is used for the passenger car bogie, the end of the hand brake end will be taken as “B” end. Some high-capacity freight cars are equipped with bogie clusters and possibly several hand brakes, and in this case, marking is recommended to be made before delivery.

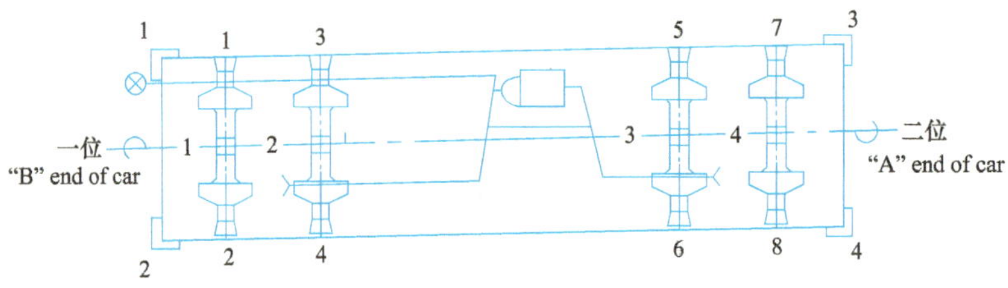

图 2-10　车辆方位

Figure 2-10　Car's Orientation

2）零部件位置的确定

Determination of parts' position

对于车辆的车轴、车轮、轴箱、车钩、转向架、车底架各梁和其他部件的位置确定，如果是纵向排列的，是由一位端起至二位端止以自然数顺次标注。如果位置是左右对称的，则站在一位端，面向二位端，从一位端起，从左向右以自然数顺次标注到二位端止，如图 2-11 所示。

For the determination of positions of axles, wheels, axle boxes, couplers, bogies, underframe beams, and other parts of the car, if arranged longitudinally, they will be marked in sequence with natural numbers from "B" end of car to "A" end of car. And if arranged symmetrically from left to right, they will be marked in sequence, with natural numbers from left to right (viewed from "B" end of car towards "A" end of car) with "B" end of car as starting point and "A" end of car as the endpoint, as shown in Figure 2-11.

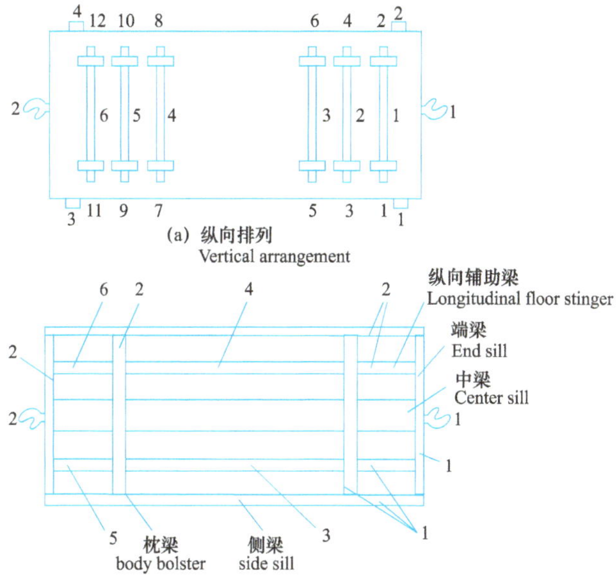

图 2-11　车辆零件位置的确定

Figure 2-11　Determination of Parts' Position

任务 2.4　铁道车辆的技术参数

Task 2.4　Technical parameters of railway vehicles

车辆技术参数是从总体上表征车辆性能及结构的一些数字，一般分为性能参数与尺寸参数两大类。

Technical parameters of a car are some figures that characterize the performance and structure of the car and generally include performance parameters and dimension parameters.

1. 车辆性能参数

Performance parameters

性能参数中的自重、载重、容积等在前面已做了说明，此外还有以下几项。

The performance parameters, including tare weight, load, volume, etc., have been described before, and the following are some other performance parameters to be explained.

（1）自重系数：指运送每单位标记载重所需的自重，其数值为车辆自重与标记载重的比值。对于一般货车而言，这是一个重要的技术参数。例如，C_{70} 型敞车的标记载重为 70 t，自重为 23.8 t，则自重系数为 0.34。

Ratio of tare weight to loading capacity: it refers to the tare weight required to transport each unit of marked load, expressed as the ratio of tare weight to marked loading capacity. It is an important technical parameter for general freight cars. For example, if the marked loading capacity of a C_{70} gondola car is 70 t and its tare weight is 23.8 t, the ratio of tare weight to loading capacity is 0.34.

（2）比容系数：该参数是针对一般货车而言的，它是设计容积与标记载重的比值。不同类型的货车因装载货物种类不同，要求不同的比容系数。例如，P_{70} 型棚车的标记载重为 70 t，设计容积为 145 m^3，故比容系数为 2.07 m^3/t；C_{70} 型敞车的标记载重为 70 t，设计容积为 77 m^3，则比容系数为 1.1 m^3/t。某些类型的货车没有这项参数或改用别的参数代替，例如平车就没有比容系数，而罐车则一般采用比容系数的倒数，称为“容重系数”。

Specific volume: it is applicable for general freight cars, and expressed as the ratio of design volume to marked loading capacity. The required specific volume of a freight car depends on the type of cargo to be loaded. For example, if the marked loading capacity of P_{70} box car is 70 t, and the design volume is 145 m^3, the specific volume is 2.07 m^3/t; if the marked loading capacity of C_{70} gondola car is 70 t and the design volume is 77 m^3, the specific volume is 1.1 m^3/t. For some types of freight cars, this parameter is not available or is substituted by another parameter. For example, the flat car is not defined with the specific volume, and the tank car is applied with the reciprocal of specific volume, i.e. “Capacity coefficient”.

（3）最高运行速度：除满足安全及结构强度条件外，还必须满足连续以该速度运行时车辆有足够良好的运行性能。以往常用“构造速度”作为参数，因其概念不够明确，现多以“最高试验速度”和“最高运行速度”来替代它。

Max. operating speed: this parameter shall meet the requirements in safety and structural strength, and shall ensure that a good operation performance is possible. Historically, “construction speed” was commonly used. But this concept is not clear enough and is now replaced by “max. test speed” and “max. operating speed”.

（4）最高试验速度：指设计车辆时安全及结构强度等条件所允许的车辆最高行驶速度。

Max. test speed: it refers to the maximum speed allowed by the safety and structural strength of the car in the process of car design.

（5）轴重：指按车轴型式及在某个运行速度范围内该轴允许负担的包括轮对自身在内的最大总质量。轴重的选择与线路、桥梁及车辆走行部的设计标准有关。

Axle load: it refers to the maximum total mass, including the mass of the wheelset, that the axle is allowed to bear within a certain operating speed range based on the type of axle. The selection of axle load depends on the design standard of the track, bridge, and running gear of the railway vehicle.

（6）每延米轨道载重：是车辆设计中与桥梁、线路强度密切相关的一个指标，同时又是能否充分利用站线长度、提高运输能力的一个指标，其数值是车辆总重与车辆全长的比值，其单位为 t/m。按目前的桥梁设计规范，允许车辆每延米轨道载重可取到 8 t。在车辆设计中，希望尽量接近这个数值。例如，C_{70} 型敞车的总质量为 93.8 t，全长 13.976 m，每延米轨道载重约为 6.71 t。

Load per meter of track: it is an indicator closely related to the strength of the bridge and track in car design, and also an indicator to measure whether the length of station track is fully utilized and to improve the transportation capacity, and expressed by the ratio of total mass of car to the total length in t/m. According to the current design specification of the bridge, a load per meter of track up to 8 t is allowed, and in the process of car design, a load per meter of track as close as possible to this value is preferred. For example, if the C_{70} gondola car has a total mass of 93.8 t and a total length of 13.976 m, the load per meter of track is 6.71 t.

（7）通过最小曲线半径：指配用某种型式转向架的车辆在站场或厂、段内调车时所能安全通过的最小曲线半径。当车辆在此曲线区段上行驶时不得出现脱轨、倾覆等危及行车安全的事故，也不允许转向架与车体底架或与车下其他悬挂物相碰。

Min. radius of curvature negotiated: It refers to the minimum curve radius that a car with a certain type of bogie can pass safely during shunting in the station yard, workshop, or depot. When the car runs on this curve section, there shall be no derailment, overturning, or other accidents endangering driving safety, and the bogie shall not collide with the underframe of the car body or other suspended objects under the car.

对于客车，一般没有自重系数与比容系数。直接载客的客车车种，如硬座车、软座车、硬卧车、软卧车等，均给出了 3 个参数，即“每定员所占自重”“车辆每米长所能容纳的定员”“车辆每米长所占自重”。

For passenger cars, the ratio of tare weight to loading capacity and specific volume are generally not defined. Passenger cars for direct passenger carrying, such as semi-cushioned seat coach, cushioned seat coach, semi-cushioned berth sleeper, and cushioned berth sleeper are defined with three parameters, namely, “tare weight per passenger”, “passenger capacity per meter of car”, and “tare weight per meter of car”.

2. 车辆尺寸参数

Dimension parameters

车辆运行在曲线路段时，车体或转向架的中心线与线路不一致，这种不一致的程度越大，轮缘与钢轨之间的磨损就越大。为了克服这种缺点，除在线路铺设上应限制曲线半径不得过小，外轨应适当加高且轨距加宽外，在车辆的制造上，对轮轴距离也加以规定和限制。

When the car is running in a curved section, the center line of the car body or bogie is inconsistent with the track. The greater this inconsistency, the greater the wear between the rim and the rail. To overcome this shortcoming, we can control the curve radius not too small in the track laying. In addition, the outer rail can be properly increased in height and track gauge and the wheelbase can be limited as specified in the manufacture of cars.

车辆的尺寸参数除前述的车辆全长、换长以外，还有以下几项。

Dimension parameters of cars include total length, converted length, and the following:

（1）全轴距：车辆两端最外侧的车轴中心线间的水平距离称为全轴距，即图 2–12 上的 B。全轴距过小时，会引起车体激烈的点头振动，容易引起脱轨或脱钩事故，并易使货物损坏或倒塌。

Total wheelbase: it refers to the horizontal distance between the outermost axle center lines at both ends of the car, as shown by *B* in Figure 2-12,as a small total wheelbase will cause intense car body nodding, possibly leading to derailment or decoupling accidents, as well as damage or collapse of cargoes.

（2）车辆定距：指车体两端支承处之间的距离。有转向架的车辆为两心盘中心线之间的水平距离，车辆定距又称为转向架中心间距，即图 2-12 中的 *C*。

Fixed distance: it refers to the distance between the supports at both ends of the car body. For cars with bogies, it refers to the horizontal distance between the center lines of the two center plates, and thus it is also called the distance between bogie centers, as shown by *C* in Figure 2-12.

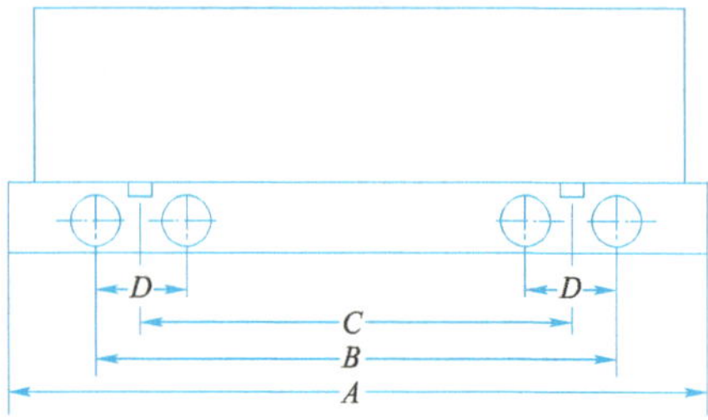

图 2-12　全轴距、车辆定距、转向架固定轴距

Figure 2-12　Total Wheelbase, Fixed Distance, and Bogie Fixed Wheelbase

（3）转向架固定轴距：不论是二轴转向架，还是多轴转向架，同一转向架最前位轮轴中心线与最后位轮轴中心线之间的距离称为转向架固定轴距，即图 2-12 中的 *D*。转向架固定轴距的大小对车辆的运行有很大的影响。若固定轴距过大，车辆在曲线半径小的线路上运行时，外侧车轮轮缘压迫钢轨内侧面，不但易加剧轮缘与钢轨间的磨耗，而且容易因扩大轨距而造成脱轨事故。若固定轴距过小，会增大车辆的振动，使车辆上的螺栓等紧固件容易松弛，各零件及货物易损坏。常规货车的固定轴距一般小于 2 000 mm，如我国新造货车二轴转向架的固定轴距为 1 830 mm（转 K6 型转向架）和 1 800 mm（转 K5 型、转 K7 型转向架）；新造客车二轴转向架的固定轴距多为 2 500 mm。三轴转向架的固定轴距为 2 400～2 600 mm。

Bogie fixed wheelbase: it refers to the distance between the center of the front axle and the center line of the rear axle of the same bogie, regardless of two-axle bogie or multi-axle bogie, as shown by *D* in Figure 2-12. The dimension of bogie fixed wheelbase has a great influence on the operation of the car. If the fixed wheelbase is too large, when the car is running on a track with a small curve radius, the outer wheel flange will press the inner side of the rail, which is likely to not only aggravate the wear between the flange and the rail but also expand the gauge, leading to derailment accident. If the fixed wheelbase is too small, the vibration of the car will be aggravated, making the bolts and other fasteners on the car easy to loosen, and the parts and cargo easy to be damaged. The fixed wheelbase of conventional freight cars is generally less than 2,000 mm. For example, the fixed wheelbase of the two-axle bogie of newly-built freight cars in China is 1,830 mm (for bogie type ZK-6) and 1,800 mm (for bogie type ZK-5 and ZK-7); and the fixed wheelbase of the two-axle bogie of newly-built passenger cars is mostly 2,500 mm, and that of a three-axle bogie is 2,400–2,600 mm.

（4）车辆最大宽度、最大高度：车辆最大宽度指车体最宽部分的尺寸；车辆最大高度指车辆顶部最高点离钢轨水平面之间的距离。这两个尺寸均需符合机车车辆限界的要求。

Max. width and height of cars: the maximum width of the car refers to the size of the widest part of the car body; the maximum height of the car refers to the distance between the highest point of the top of the car and the horizontal plane of the rail. Both max. width and max. height shall meet the requirements for the railway rolling stock clearance limit.

（5）车体长、宽、高：有车体外部与内部之分，但车体内部的长、宽、高必须满足货物装载或旅客乘坐等要求。

Length, width, and height of the car body: The length/width/height of the car body includes inner length/width/height and outer length/width/height, and the inner length/width/height shall meet the requirements of cargo loading, passenger riding and others.

（6）车钩中心线距轨面高度：简称钩高，指车钩钩舌外侧面的中心线至轨面的高度。列车中车辆与车辆及车辆与机车的钩高基本一致，是保证正常传递牵引力及列车运行时不会发生脱钩事故所必需的。我国规定新造或修竣后的空车标准钩高为 870～890 mm。其他国家由各自的历史条件决定了其所使用的车钩高度。如俄罗斯及东欧各国的钩高（或盘形缓冲器的中心线高）定为 1 060 mm。

Height from the center line of the coupler to the rail surface (or coupler height for short): it refers to the height from the center line of the outer side of the coupler knuckle to the rail surface. The coupler heights between cars and the coupler height between car and locomotive in a train should be basically the same, which is necessary to ensure the normal transmission of traction and the elimination of decoupling when the train is running. The national standard stipulates that the unloaded coupler height of the standard coupler of newly-built or repaired cars should be 870–890 mm; the coupler height specification of other countries depends on their respective historical conditions. For example, the coupler height (or the height of the center line of the disc buffer) in Russia and Eastern European countries is set at 1,060 mm.

（7）地板面高度：地板面距轨面的高度。与钩高一样，均指新造或修竣后空车的数值。它将受到两方面的制约，一是车辆本身某些结构高度的限制，如钩高及转向架下心盘面的高度。

Height of floor from rail top (or floor height for short): the height of floor from rail top. Similar to coupler height, the height of floor from rail top is based on the unloading condition of a newly-built car or repaired car. It is subject to two constraints, and one is the height of some structures, such as the coupler height and the bogie’s lower center plate height.

项目 3

Project 3

轮　　对

Wheelset

本项目以了解轮对的结构组成为工学任务，通过课堂任务的完成过程，着重介绍轮对的结构组成，并以此为引导，介绍轮对的作用、组装技术要求；通过课后任务，了解各类型车辆的轮对在技术参数上和标记上的差别。

The main task of this project is to learn about the structural composition of wheelsets. In the classroom, the main focus is on introducing the structure and components of wheelsets, along with explaining their function and assembly requirements. Through after-class tasks, students will learn about the technical parameter differences and markings of wheelsets across different types of railway vehicles.

学生工作页 Student Worksheet

工学任务描述 Task description	预期目标 Expected goals
任务名称：认识轮对 Task name: Understanding of the wheelset 任务编号：CJ-03 Task number: CJ-03 任务类型：结构型+识记型 Task type: Structure + memory applicable 适用范围：车辆系统各岗位群 Applicable scope: All post groups of the system of railway vehicle 完成时间：　　　学时 Completion time:　　　class hours	初级：了解轮对的基本组成及作用 Elementary level: Understand the basic composition and function of wheelsets 中级：掌握轮对组装技术要求 Intermediate level: Master the assembling requirements of wheelsets 高级：掌握车轴及车轮标记的具体内容，为今后检修打下基础 Advanced level: Master the markings of axles and wheels to lay the foundation for maintenance in future

知识回顾+小组讨论

Knowledge review + group discussion

1. 以自行车车轮为例，尝试填写自行车车轮的结构部件、各部件的功能。你认为哪些是车辆轮对必须具备的部件。

Taking bicycle wheels as an example, try to fill in the name and functions of each component of bicycle wheels. Which components do you think are necessary for wheelsets.

	自行车车轮结构部件 Bicycle wheel structural components	功能/作用 Function	轮对对应的名称及作用 Name and function of wheelset
1			
2			
3			
4			
5			
6			
7			
8			

2. 识记车轴各部位的名称及作用。

Remember the name and function of each component of the axle.

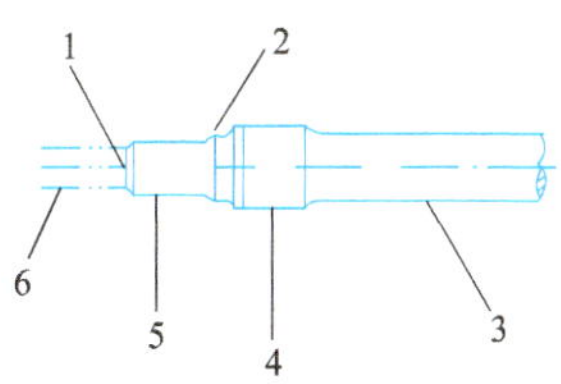

序 号 S/N	名 称 Name	作 用 Function
1		
2		
3		
4		
5		
6		

3. 识记车轮。

Remember the following knowledge of the wheel.

（1）识记车轮各部分的名称。

Remember the name of each component of the wheel.

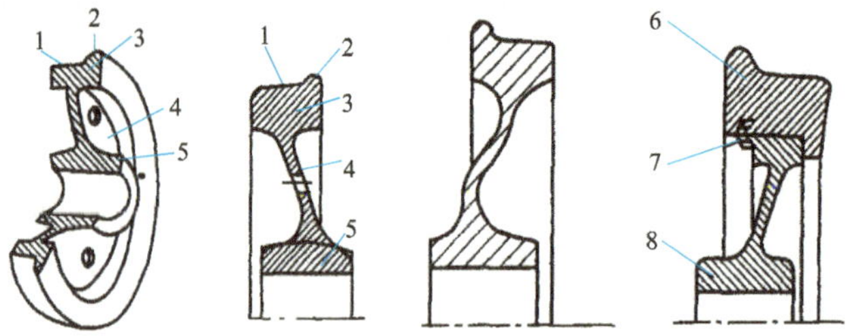

(a) (b) (c) (d)

序号 S/N	名　称 Name	序号 S/N	名　称 Name	序号 S/N	名　称 Name
1		4		7	
2		5		8	
3		6			

（2）小组讨论：

Group discussion:

① 观察车轮轮缘，总结车轮轮缘的特点。

Observe the wheel flange and summarize the characteristics of the wheel flange.

② 轮缘具有什么作用？

What are the functions of wheel flange?

③ 学习并记录轮缘的作用。

Learn and record the functions of wheel flange.

4. 查阅资料，识别轮对标记。

Refer to relevant documents and identify the wheelset markings.

（1）右图中的车轮标记表示什么？

What's the meaning of the wheel marking shown in the right figure?

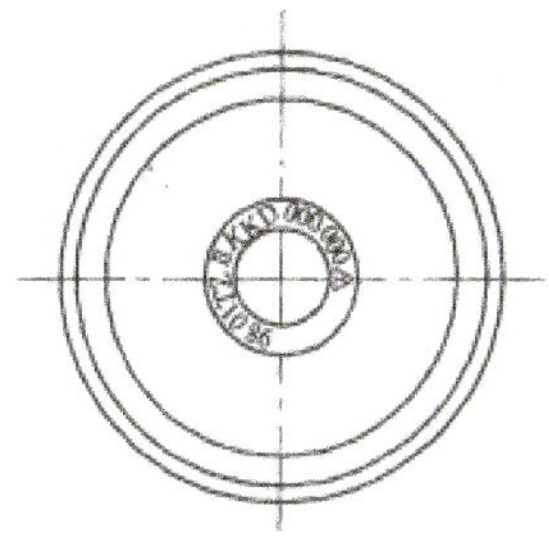

（2）右图中的标记表示什么？

What's the meaning of marking shown in the right figure?

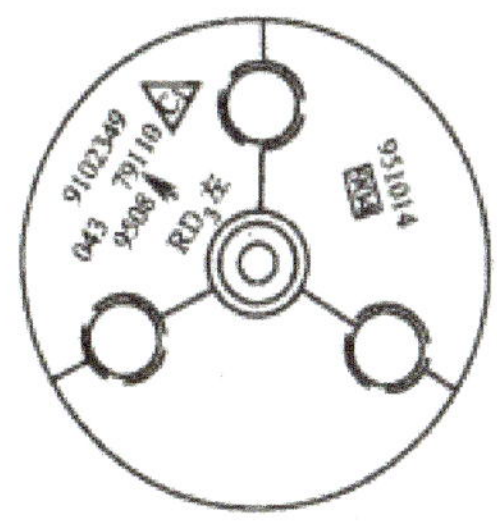

（3）查阅资料，总结车轮标记、车轴标记及标记位置。

Refer to relevant documents, and summarize the information and position of wheel markings and axle markings.

5. 查阅资料，写出轮轴组装的技术要求。

Refer to relevant documents, and mark the assembling requirements of the wheel and axle.

课后任务

After-class tasks

1. 查阅资料，比较不同轴型客车车轴的技术参数。

Refer to relevant documents, and compare the technical parameters of passenger car axles of different types.

轴型 Axle type	车轴主要尺寸/mm Main dimensions of axle/mm	使用轴承类型 Type of bearing used	轴重/t Axle load/t
RC_3			
RD_3			
RD_{3A}			
RD_{4A}			
RD_{3A1}			
RD_{1X}			
AM96			

2. 根据轮对分类的要求，比较不同类型的客车轮对的主要技术参数。

Compare the main technical parameters of different types of passenger car wheelsets according to the requirements for the classification of wheelsets.

分类 Classification	轮对型号 Wheelset model	车轴型号 Axle model	车轮型号 Wheel model	车轮材质 Wheel material	车轮原型公称直径/mm Nominal diameter of wheel prototype/mm	配套轴承型号 Matching bearing model	适用转向架型号 Applicable bogie model
标准型轮对 Standard wheel set	RC_3 RC_4						
	RD_3 RD_4						
	RD_{3A} RD_{4A}						
	RD_{3A1}						
非标准型轮对 Non-standard wheel set	RD_{1X}						
	AM96						

3. 针对轮对，提出你的问题。

Put forward your questions about the wheelset.

学习效果评价
Learning effect evaluation

年 Year 月 Month 日 Day

专业班级： Major & class:	姓名： Name:	学号： Student number:
工学小组及分工： Work-and-study team and responsibility division:		

专业（知识/技能）收获 Professional gains (knowledge/skills)	（非专业）能力素质收获 (Non-professional) ability and quality gains

评价考核项目 Evaluation item	自我评价 Self-evaluation	小组评价 Group evaluation	教师评价 Teacher’s evaluation
已掌握轮对的基本组成 Have mastered the basic composition of wheelsets			
已掌握相关知识点的数量 Number of knowledge points mastered			
主动提出问题的数量 Number of questions proposed			
课外学习时间（学时） After-school learning time (hours)			
工作态度（课堂、课后任务完成情况） Work attitude (completion condition of classroom tasks and after-class tasks)	☆☆☆☆ ☆☆☆☆	☆☆☆☆ ☆☆☆☆	☆☆☆☆ ☆☆☆☆
合作意识及协调能力 Cooperation consciousness and coordination ability	☆☆☆☆ ☆☆☆☆	☆☆☆☆ ☆☆☆☆	☆☆☆☆ ☆☆☆☆
正确表达和沟通能力 Correct expression and communication skills	☆☆☆☆ ☆☆☆☆	☆☆☆☆ ☆☆☆☆	☆☆☆☆ ☆☆☆☆
自律能力（缺勤/旷课/迟到/违纪次数） Self-discipline (absences/absenteeism/lateness/disciplinary violations)			

轮对是由一根车轴和两个相同的车轮按规定压力和规定尺寸通过过盈配合组装成一体，如图 3-1 所示。为了运行安全，绝不允许发生任何松动，因此对轮对有以下要求。

The wheelset is an assembly consisting of one axle and two similar wheels which are assembled together through interference fit according to the specified pressure and size, as shown in Figure 3-1. For the sake of operation safety, looseness is not allowed on wheelsets. Therefore, the wheelset shall meet the following requirements.

（1）具有足够的强度和刚度。

The wheelset shall have sufficient strength and rigidity.

（2）在保证安全的条件下，轮对质量小并具有一定弹性。

The wheelset shall have a small mass but certain elasticity, provided that safety is ensured.

（3）阻力小，耐磨性好。

The wheelset shall be subject to small resistance and have good wear resistance.

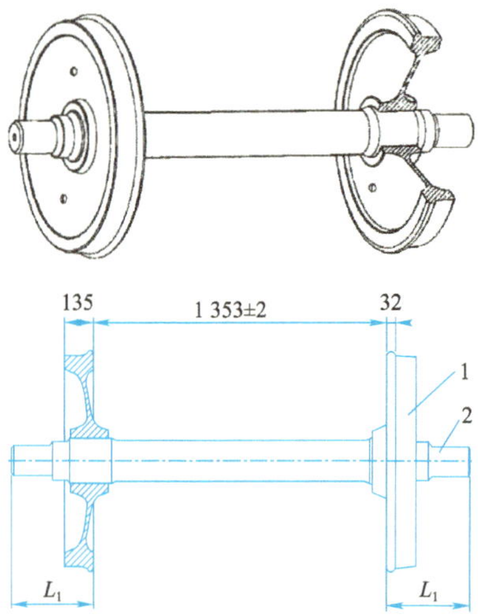

1—车轮；2—车轴。

1—Wheel; 2—Axle.

图 3-1　轮对

Figure 3-1　Wheelset

任务 3.1　车　　轴

Task 3.1　Axle

1. 车轴各部位的名称及作用

Name and function of each component of the axle

我国铁路车辆使用的车轴，绝大多数为圆截面实心车轴。由于各部位受力状态不同，其直径也不一样。车轴是用优质碳素钢（40 钢或 50 钢）锻造制成的。车轴表面需锻造光滑平整，不得有起层、裂纹、溶渣或其他危害性缺陷。

Most axles used on railway vehicles in China are solid axles with a circular cross-section.

Considering that the components are stressed differently, their diameters also vary. The axle is forged from high-quality carbon steel (40# steel or 50# steel). The surface of the axle shall be forged to be smooth without scaling, crack, slag, or other harmful defects.

车轴的构成如图 3-2 所示。

The composition of the axle is shown in Figure 3-2.

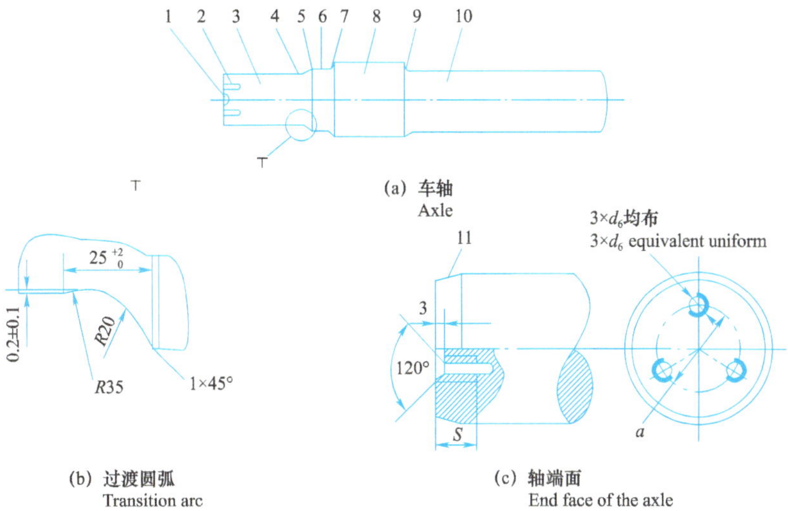

1—中心孔；2—轴端螺栓孔；3—轴颈；4—卸荷槽；5—轴颈后肩；6—防尘板座；7—轮座前肩；8—轮座；9—轮座后肩；10—轴身；11—轴端倒角。

1—Center hole; 2—Journal end bolt hole; 3—Journal; 4—Pressure relief groove; 5—Journal rear fillet; 6—Dust guard seat; 7—Wheel seat front fillet; 8—Wheel seat; 9—Wheel seat rear fillet; 10—Axle body; 11—Axle end chamfer.

图 3-2　车轴的构成

Figure 3-2　Composition of Axle

车轴各部位的名称和作用如下。

The names and functions of the various parts of the axle are as follows.

（1）中心孔：加工车轴和组装、加工轮对时机床顶针孔支点，并可以作为校对轴颈、车轮圆度的中心。

Center hole: It is the fulcrum of the top pinhole of the machine tool during the machining of axles as well as assembling and machining of wheelsets, and can be used as the center for checking the roundness of the journal and wheel.

（2）轴端螺栓孔：安装轴承前盖或压板，防止滚动轴承外移窜出。

Journal end bolt hole: It is for installing the bearing front cover or pressing plate to prevent the roller bearing from moving out.

（3）轴颈：用以安装滚动轴承，承担车辆重量，并传递各方向的静、动荷载。

Journal: It is for installing the roller bearing, bearing the weight of the car, and transmitting the static and dynamic loads in all directions.

（4）卸荷槽：为了磨削轴颈时便于砂轮退刀，起到退刀槽的作用，可以减少轴承内圈组装后与此处相互间的接触应力，有利于提高此处的疲劳强度。

Pressure relief groove: It can be used as a tool access groove during the grinding of a journal with an abrasive wheel, and can reduce the mutual contact stress between the assembled bearing inner ring and this position, thus helping improve the fatigue strength at this position.

（5）轴颈后肩：轴颈与防尘板座间的过渡圆弧，可以防止应力集中。

Journal rear fillet: It is the transition arc between the journal and the dust guard seat to prevent stress concentration.

（6）防尘板座：车轴与防尘板配合部位，其直径比轴颈直径大，比轮座直径小，介于两者之间，是轴颈和轮座的中间过渡部分，可以减少应力集中。

Dust guard seat: It is the part where the axle fits the dust guard, and it is the transition part between the journal and wheel seat to reduce stress concentration, with a diameter greater than the journal but smaller than the wheel seat.

（7）轮座前肩：防尘板座与轮座之间的过渡圆弧，可以防止应力集中。

Wheel seat front filler: It is a transition arc between the dust guard seat and the wheel seat to prevent stress concentration.

（8）轮座：车轴与车轮配合的部位。

Wheel seat: It is the part where the axle fits the wheel.

为了保证轮轴之间有足够的压紧力，轮座直径比车轮孔径要大 0.10～0.35 mm；同时，为了便于轮轴压装，减少应力集中，轮座外侧（靠防尘板座侧）直径向外逐渐减小，成为锥体，其小端直径比大端直径要小 1 mm，锥体长 12～16 mm。轮座是车轮受力最大的部位。

To ensure a sufficient pressing force between the wheel and the axle, the diameter of the wheel seat is 0.10–0.35 mm larger than the wheel bore, and to make the press-fitting of the wheel and axle easier and reduce stress concentration, the diameter of the outer side of the wheel seat (on the side of the dust guard seat) decreases gradually outward to form a cone of 12–16 mm long, with the diameter of the small end 1mm smaller than the diameter of the big end. The wheel seat is the most stressed part of the wheel.

（9）轮座后肩：轮座与轴身之间的过渡圆弧，可以防止应力集中。

Wheel seat rear filler: It is a transition arc between the wheel seat and the axle body to prevent stress concentration.

（10）轴身：车轴中央部分，该部位受力较小。

Axle body: It is the central part of the axle, and is less stressed.

（11）轴端倒角：轴端部设有 1:10 的倒角，其作用是在压装滚动轴承时起引导作用。

Axle end chamfer: A 1:10 chamfer is processed at the axle end to guide the roller bearing during press-fitting.

2. 车轴的材质及要求

Material and requirements of axle

车轴采用优质碳素钢，如平炉钢、电炉钢钢锭或专门的车轴钢坯加热锻压成型，经过热处理（正火或正火后再回火）和机械加工制成。

The axle is made of high-quality carbon steel, such as open-hearth steel, electric furnace steel ingots, or special axle billets through heating, forging, thermal treatment (normalizing or tempering after normalizing), and mechanical processing.

任务3.2 车 轮

Task 3.2 Wheel

1. 车轮各部分的名称及作用

Name and function of each part of the wheel

目前，我国铁路车辆上使用的车轮绝大多数是整体辗钢轮，它包括踏面、轮缘、轮辋、辐板和轮毂等部分，其构成如图3–3所示。车轮与钢轨的接触面称为踏面。一个突出的圆弧部分称为轮缘，是保持车辆沿钢轨运行、防止脱轨的重要部分。轮辋是踏面下部的实体部分。轮毂是车轮与车轴互相配合的部分，辐板是连接轮辋与轮毂的部分。辐板上有两个圆孔，便于轮对在切削加工时与机床固定及搬运轮对之用（现已取消）。

At present, railway vehicles in China are generally applied with the monobloc rolled steel wheel, which consists of wheel tread, wheel flange, wheel rim, plate, wheel hub and others, as shown in Figure 3-3. The wheel tread is the contact surface between the wheel and the rail. The wheel rim is a protruding arc part on the wheel, which is important in keeping the car running along the rail and preventing derailment. The wheel rim is a solid part below the wheel tread. The wheel hub is the part where the wheel fits the axle, and the plate is the part that connects the wheel rim and the wheel hub. There are two round holes on the plate for fixing the wheelset on the machine tool in the case of grinding and the handling of wheelsets (now canceled).

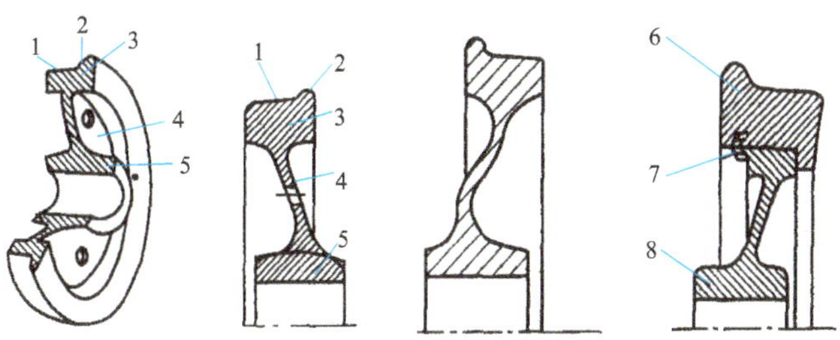

（a）整体轮 Integral wheel （b）直辐板形轮 Straight plate wheel （c）S形辐板轮 S-shaped plate wheel （d）轮箍轮 Tire wheel

1—踏面；2—轮缘；3—轮辋；4—辐板；5—轮毂；6—轮箍；7—扣球；8—轮心。

1—Wheel tread; 2—Wheel flange; 3—Wheel rim; 4—Plate; 5—Wheel hub; 6—Tire; 7—Spike; 8—Wheel center.

图3–3 车轮的构成

Figure 3-3 Composition of Wheel

车轮踏面需要做成一定的斜度（见图3–4），其作用如下。

The wheel tread is required to be made to a certain slope (see Figure 3-4), and its functions are as follows.

（1）便于通过曲线。车辆在曲线上运行，由于离心力的作用，轮对偏向外轨，于是在外轨上滚动的车轮与钢轨接触的部分直径较大，而沿内轨滚动的车轮与钢轨接触的部分直径较小，使滚动中的轮对中大直径的车轮沿外轨行走的路程长，小直径的车轮沿内轨行走的路程短，这正好和曲线区间线路外轨长、内轨短的情况相适应，这样可使轮对较顺利地通过曲线，减少车轮在钢轨上的滑行。

Easier curving. When the car runs on a curve, the wheelset deviates towards the outer rail under the action of centrifugal force, so the diameter of the part of the wheel rolling on the outer rail in contact with the rail is larger, while the diameter of the part of the wheel rolling along the inner rail is smaller. Therefore, in the wheelset, the distance of the wheel of larger diameter rolling along the outer rail is long, while that of the wheel of smaller diameter rolling along the inner rail is short, which fits well the situation that the outer rail of the curve track is long while the inner rail is short and ensures that the wheelset can pass the curve smoothly and reduce the sliding of the wheel on the rail.

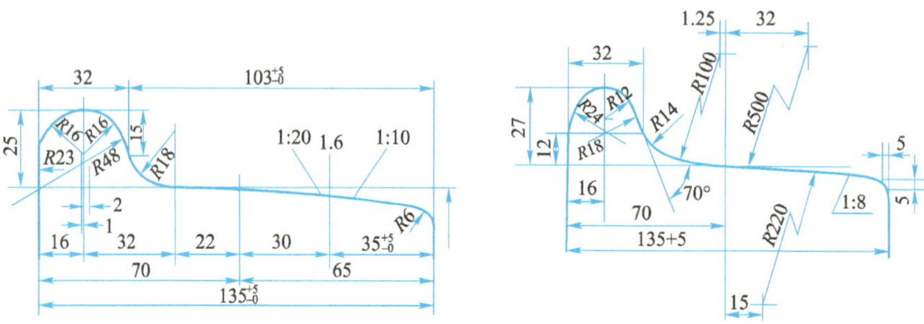

（a）TB 踏面
TB tread

（b）LM 型踏面
LM tread

图 3-4　车轮轮缘和踏面的外形
Figure 3-4　Profile of Wheel Flange and Wheel Tread

（2）可自动调中。在直线线路上运行时，如果车辆中心线与轨道中心线不一致，则轮对在滚动过程中能自动纠正偏离位置。

Automatic alignment. When the car runs on a straight track, if the center line of the car is inconsistent with the center line of the track, the wheelset can automatically correct the deviation during rolling.

（3）踏面磨耗沿宽度方向比较均匀。

Uniform tread wear along the width direction.

从上述分析可知，车轮踏面必须有斜度。而车轮踏面斜度的存在，也是轮对以至整个车辆发生自激蛇行运动的原因。

As analyzed above, the wheel tread must have a slope, which is also the reason for the self-excited hunting of wheelsets and even the whole railway rehicle.

2. 轮缘和踏面的形状

Profile of wheel rim and tread

为使轮对在钢轨上平稳运行，能顺利地通过曲线和道岔，且使踏面磨耗比较均匀，轮缘和踏面必须有相应的外形。我国铁路车辆所使用的车轮轮缘和踏面有锥型（TB 型）、磨耗型（LM 型）和高速磨耗型（HLM 型）3 种。磨耗型踏面是在锥型踏面的基础上发展起来的，其踏面外形较复杂，接近车轮磨耗后形成的曲面状态。

To make the wheelset run smoothly on the rail and pass the curve and turnout smoothly, and to make the tread wear more uniform, the wheel flange and tread shall have a certain profile. There are three types of wheel rims and treads used on railway vehicles in China: conical profile (TB), hollow type (LM), and high-speed worn profile (HLM). The hollow profile tread is developed on the basis of the original conical profile tread. This tread profile is complex, and similar to the curved state of the wheel after wear.

由于车轮踏面有斜度，各处直径不相同，所以按规定，在离轮缘内侧 70 mm 处测量所得的直径为名义直径。以名义直径为直径的圆称为滚动圆，即以滚动圆的直径作为车轮的名义直径。车轮直径的大小，对车辆本身各有利弊。轮径小，可以降低车辆重心，增大车体容积，减小车辆簧下质量，缩小转向架固定轴距，但阻力增加，轮轨接触应力增大，踏面磨耗较快；同时，小直径车轮通过轨道凹陷和接缝处对车辆振动的影响也将加大。轮径大的优缺点则与之相反。所以，车轮直径尺寸的选择，应视具体情况而定。我国货车的标准轮径为 840 mm，客车的标准轮径为 915 mm。

Considering that the wheel tread has a slope and the diameter varies from place to place, it is specified that the diameter of the steel wheel measured 70 mm from the inner side of the wheel flange is the nominal diameter. A circle with a nominal diameter is the tape circle. That is to say, the diameter of the tape circle is defined as the nominal diameter of the wheel. The wheel diameters of different magnitudes have positive and negative influences on the wheel. A small wheel diameter can lower the center of gravity of the car, increase the volume of the car body, and reduce the unsprung mass and the bogie fixed wheelbase, but will increase resistance and wheel-rail contact stress, and speed up the tread wear. Besides, it will increase the impact on the car vibration when the wheel passes through the sunken parts and joints of the track. The advantages and disadvantages of large wheel diameters are opposite to the small diameter wheel. Therefore, the wheel diameter should be selected depending on the specific situation. According to the national standard of China, the standard wheel diameter is 840 mm for freight cars and 915 mm for passenger cars.

任务 3.3 轮　对
Task 3.3 Wheelset

1. 轮对的分类
Classification of wheelsets

轮对的类型和名称，应根据车轴的类型和车轮的类型确定。

The type and name of the wheelset depend on the type of axles and wheels.

客车滚动轴承轮对与车轴型号一致，车轮为相应吨位客车车轮。例如，客车滚动轴承轮对 RD_3 型，分别配装 RD_3 型车轴和 KD 或 KDS 型车轮。

For passenger cars, the model of roller bearing wheelset shall be consistent with the model of the axle, and the wheels shall be suitable for the tonnage of the passenger car. For example, the model roller bearing wheelset of a passenger car is RD_3, and thus the RD_3 axle and KD/KDS wheels shall be used.

轮对的类型和名称须符合表 3–1 的规定。

The type and name of the wheelset shall be determined according to the type of axles and wheels and shall meet the requirements in Table 3-1.

表 3–1 轮对的类型和名称

Table 3-1 Type and Name of Wheelset

<table>
<tr><th>分类
Classification</th><th>轮对型号
Wheelset model</th><th>车轴型号
Axle model</th><th>车轮型号
Wheel model</th><th>车轮材质
Wheel material</th><th>车轮原型公称直径/mm
Nominal diameter of wheel prototype/mm</th><th>配套轴承型号
Matching bearing model</th><th>适用转向架型号
Applicable bogie model</th><th>备注
Remarks</th></tr>
<tr><td rowspan="4">标准型轮对
Standard wheel set</td><td>RC_3
RC_4</td><td>RC_3
RC_4</td><td>KC
KKD</td><td>辗钢
Rolled steel</td><td rowspan="4">915^{+10}_{0}</td><td>4(15)2724</td><td>202</td><td></td></tr>
<tr><td>RD_3
RD_4</td><td>RD_3
RD_4</td><td>KD
KDS
KKD</td><td>辗钢
Rolled steel</td><td rowspan="3">4(15)2726 P
NJ(P)3226X1
进口轴承
Imported bearing</td><td>206，209</td><td></td></tr>
<tr><td>RD_{3A}
RD_{4A}</td><td>RD_{3A}
RD_{4A}</td><td rowspan="2">KKD</td><td rowspan="2">辗钢
Rolled steel</td><td>209HS，206PK，SW–160，CW–1，CW–2，209P，206P，209PK</td><td></td></tr>
<tr><td>RD_{3A1}</td><td>RD_{3A1}</td><td>CW–2，CW–200，CW–220K，SW–220K</td><td></td></tr>
<tr><td rowspan="2">非标准型轮对
Non-standard wheel set</td><td>RD_{1X}</td><td>RD_{1X}</td><td>KD
KDS</td><td>辗钢
Rolled steel</td><td>915</td><td>4(15)2726
NJ(P)3226X1</td><td>211，212</td><td></td></tr>
<tr><td>AM96</td><td>AM96</td><td>R9T</td><td>辗钢
Rolled steel</td><td>915</td><td>BT2–8690 D
1639605E</td><td>AM96</td><td></td></tr>
</table>

2. 轮对标记

Wheelset marking

为了便于检查和发现轮对故障，确认轮对生产或检修质量的责任，在轮对的适当部位刻打或铸有不同的标记，用以辨认。轮对标记包括车轮标记、车轴标记。

To facilitate the inspection and identification of wheelset faults, and to confirm the responsible unit/individual of wheelset production or maintenance quality, different markings are engraved or cast on the appropriate parts of the wheelset for identification. The wheelset markings include wheel markings and axle markings.

1）车轮标记

Wheel markings

车轮上应有以下基本标记：制造年月、车轮型号、制造厂代号（标记）、车轮钢种标记、熔炼炉罐号。

The wheels shall be made with the following basic markings: manufacturing date, wheel model, manufacturer code (marking), wheel steel grade marking, and heat number.

车轮上的标记可采用热压、冷打等方式生成。

The marking on the wheels is recommended to be made by hot pressing, cold beating, etc.

车轮标记应出现在轮辋外侧面、轮毂内侧端面或辐板内侧面上。中国马鞍山钢铁股份有限公司车轮厂制造的整体辗钢车轮上的标记在轮辋外侧面或轮毂内侧端面上。

The wheel markings shall be made on the outer side of the wheel rim, the inner end face of the wheel hub, or the inner side of the plate. For the monobloc rolled steel wheels manufactured by the Wheel Factory of Maanshan Iron & Steel Company Limited (China), the marking is made on the outer side of the wheel rim or the inner end face of the wheel hub.

（1）在轮辋外侧面上标记。

Marked on the outer side of the wheel rim.

1993 年及以前的标记涂打如下：

As of 1993, the markings made are as follows:

① 制造年月（各 2 位数字）、冶炼年份、制造工厂标记、车轮钢种代号、车轮型号、熔炼炉罐号、班次。例如：

930892 ⊕ ⅡD21002 甲［见图 3–5（a）］

Manufacturing date (2 digits for year and month respectively), smelting year, manufacturer marking, wheel steel grade code, wheel model, heat number, and shift. For example:

930892 ⊕ ⅡD21002 A [See Figure 3-5 (a)]

② 制造年月（各 2 位数字）、冶炼年份、制造工厂代号、车轮钢种代号、车轮型号、熔炼炉罐号、班次。例如：

941094MGⅡD1072B［见图 3–5（b）］

Manufacturing date (2 digits for year and month respectively), smelting year, manufacturer code, wheel steel grade code, wheel model, heat number, and shift. For example:

941094MGⅡD1072B [See Figure 3-5 (b)]

2003 年及以后的标记涂打如下：制造年月（各 2 位数字）、制造工厂代号、车轮钢种代号、车轮型号、熔炼炉罐号（冶炼年份末 2 位数字+冶炼炉编号+本年度冶炼流水号）、车轮顺序号、检验人员标记。例如：

0511MGⅡKKD05-2-2541123M［见图 3–5（c）和图 3–5（d）］

As of 2003, the markings made are as follows: Manufacturing date (2 digits for year and month respectively), manufacturer code, wheel steel grade code, wheel model, heat number (the last two digits of smelting year-heat number-annual smelting serial number), wheel sequence number, and inspector marking. For example:

0511MGⅡKKD05-2-2541123M [See Figure 3-5 (c) and Figure 3-5 (d)]

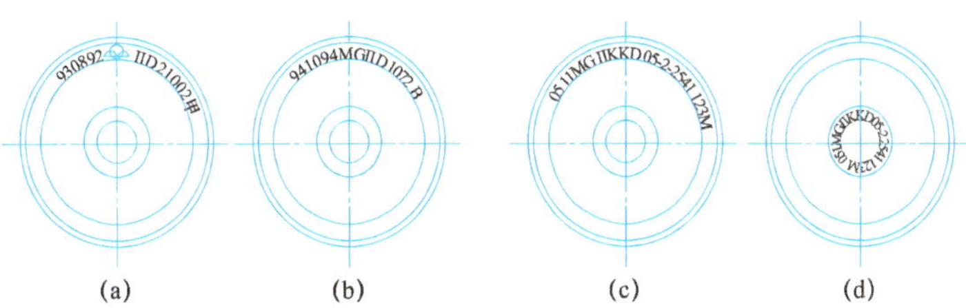

图 3–5　车轮标记示意图（一）

Figure 3-5　Schematic Diagram of Wheel Markings (I)

（2）在轮毂内侧端面上标记。

Marked on the inner end face of the wheel hub.

① 制造年月（各 2 位数字）、制造工厂代号、车轮钢种代号、车轮型号、熔炼炉罐号（冶炼年份末 2 位数字+冶炼炉编号+本年度冶炼流水号）、车轮顺序号、检验人员标记。例如：

0511MGⅡKKD05-2-2541123M

Manufacturing date (2 digits for year and month respectively), manufacturer code, wheel steel grade code, wheel model, heat number (the last two digits of smelting year-heat number-annual smelting serial number), wheel sequence number, and inspector marking. For example:

0511MGⅡKKD05-2-2541123M

中国太原重型机械（集团）有限公司制造的整体辗钢车轮标记在轮毂内侧端面上，如图 3−6 所示。

For the monobloc rolled steel wheel manufactured by Taiyuan Heavy Machinery Group Co., Ltd., the marking is made on the inner end face of the wheel hub, as shown in Figure 3-6.

② 制造年月（各 2 位数字）、制造工厂代号、钢种代号、车轮型号、车轮顺序号、检验人员标记。例如：

01TZⅡKKD000000Q

Manufacturing date (2 digits for year and month respectively), manufacturer code, steel grade code, wheel model, wheel sequence number, and inspector marking. For example:

01TZⅡKKD000000Q

乌克兰车轮制造厂制造的整体辗钢车轮标记在轮毂内端面上，如图 3−7 所示。

For the monobloc rolled steel wheel manufactured by Ukraine Wheel Factory, the marking is made on the inner end face of wheel hub, as shown in Figure 3-7.

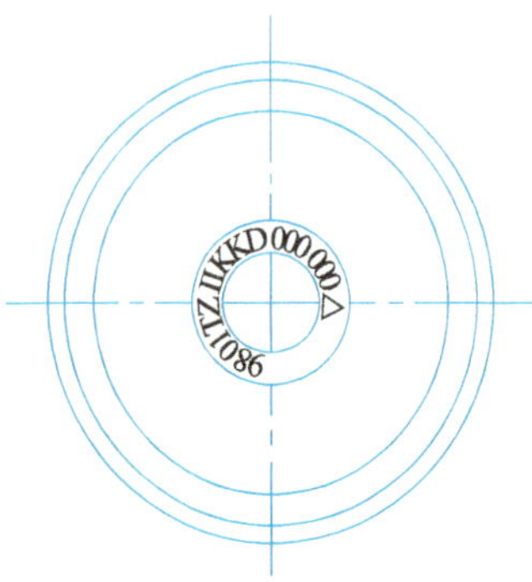

图 3−6 车轮标记示意图（二）
Figure 3-6 Schematic Diagram of Wheel Markings (II)

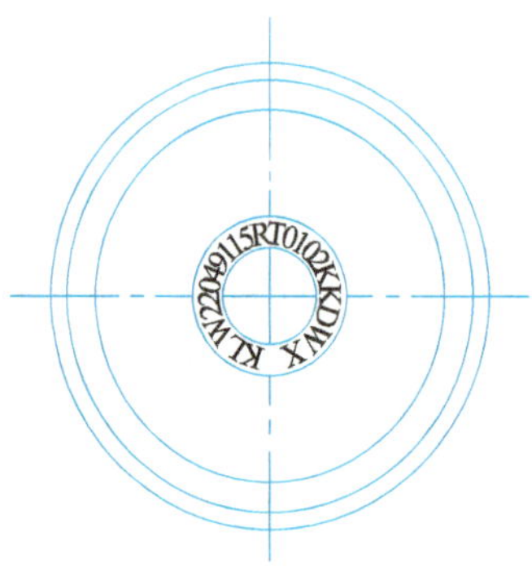

图 3−7 车轮标记示意图（三）
Figure 3-7 Schematic Diagram of Wheel Markings (III)

③ 制造工厂代号、熔炼炉罐号、车轮顺序号、车轮钢牌号、制造年月（各 2 位数字）、车轮型号、检验员代号。例如：

KLW22049115R7T0102KKDWX

Manufacturer code, heat number, wheel sequence number, wheel steel grace number, manufacturing date (2 digits for year and month respectively), wheel model, and inspector code.

For example:

KLW22049115R7T0102KKDWX

法国 TRI Source 公司进口客车车轮标记在轮毂内端面上（冷打方式），如图 3−8 所示。

For passenger car wheels imported from TRI Source, the marking is made on the inner end face of wheel hub (by cold beating), as shown in Figure 3-8.

④ 制造工厂代号、熔炼炉罐号、车轮顺序号、车轮钢牌号、制造年月（各 2 位数字）、车轮型号、检验员代号。例如：

UV000000000ER8T0707KKDX

Manufacturer code, heat number, wheel sequence number, wheel steel grace number, manufacturing date (2 digits for year and month respectively), wheel model, and inspector code. For example:

UV000000000ER8T0707KKDX

德国 BVV 公司制造的整体辗钢车轮标记在轮毂内端面上，如图 3−9 所示。

For the monobloc rolled steel wheel manufactured by BVV, the marking is made on the inner end face of wheel hub, as shown in Figure 3-9.

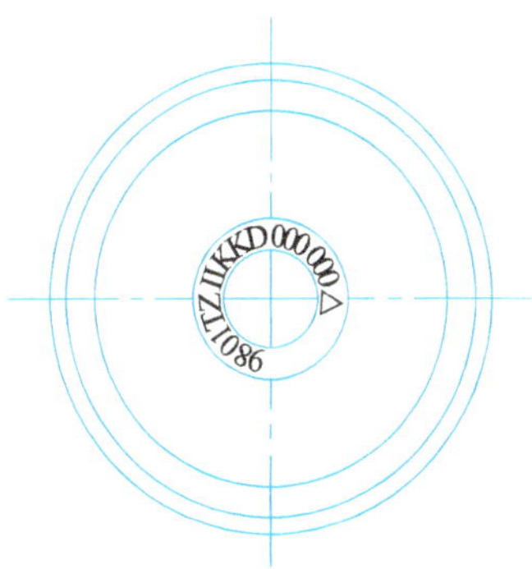

图 3−8　车轮标记示意图（四）
Figure 3-8　Schematic Diagram of Wheel Markings (IV)

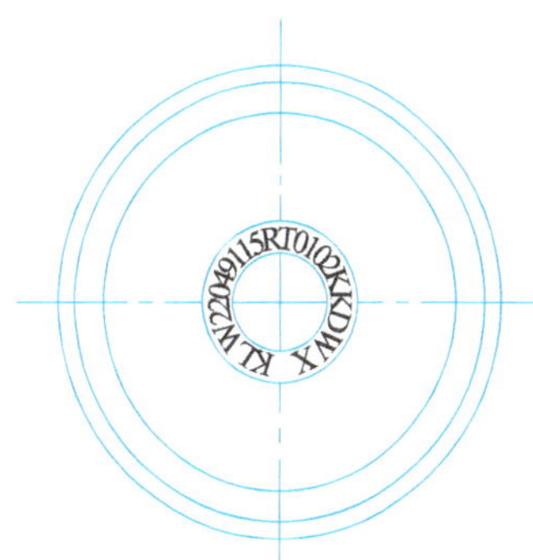

图 3−9　车轮标记示意图（五）
Figure 3-9　Schematic Diagram of Wheel Markings (V)

⑤ 制造厂标记、熔炼炉罐号及顺序号、车轮钢种代号、制造年月（各 2 位数字）、车轮型号。例如：

055737/00218 Ⅱ 0805KKD

Manufacturer marking, heat number, and sequence number, wheel steel grade code, manufacturing date (2 digits for year and month respectively), wheel model. For example:

055737/00218 Ⅱ 0805KKD

2）车轴标记

Axle markings

车轴标记包括车轴制造标记、轮对组装标记和特殊标记。在车轴两端面上，以轴端中心孔中心与轴端三个螺栓孔中心的假想连线及其延长线将轴端分成 3 等份，构成 3 个扇区，如图 3−10 所示。车轴标记须按规定刻打在某一扇区内。

Axle markings include axle manufacturing markings, wheelset assembly markings, and special markings. For the engraving position of axle markings, it is specified that, on the end faces of newly-manufactured or modified end-flush bearing axles, 3 sectors are uniformly divided by the imaginary lines passing through the center hole of the axle end, the center of the three bolt holes on the axle end, and their extension lines, as shown in Figure 3-10,and axle markings shall be made in any of the three sectors.

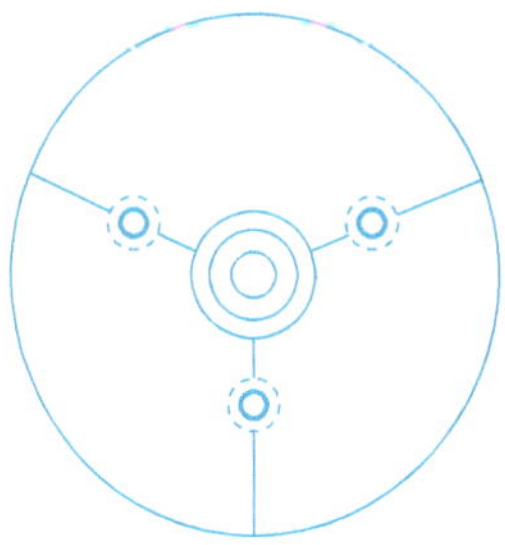

图 3-10 车轴扇区示意图
Figure 3-10 Schematic Diagram of Axle Sectors

（1）车轴制造标记。

Axle manufacturing markings.

① 车轴钢冶炼熔炼号：阿拉伯数字，如“9311288”，字体高 5 mm。

Axle steel smelting number: Arabic numerals such as “9311288”, with a font height of 5 mm.

② 车轴钢种标记：一个汉语拼音字母，字体高 7 mm，打在熔炼号后面（50 钢车轴钢钢种标记为“W”，40 钢车轴钢钢种标记省略）。

Axle steel grade marking: a Chinese pinyin with a font height of 7 mm, which is marked after the smelting number (axle made of 50# steel axle is marked with “W”, and marking for 40# steel is omitted).

③ 车轴制造（锻造）工厂代号：中国国家铁路集团有限公司公布的工厂代号，3 位阿拉伯数字，如“183”，字体高 7 mm。

Axle manufacturer (forging factory) code: factory code published by the China Railway, 3 Arabic numerals such as “183”, with a font height of 7 mm.

④ 车轴制造年月：年、月分别用 2 位阿拉伯数字表示，如“9508”，字体高 7 mm。

Axle manufacturing date: year and month respectively represented by 2 Arabic numerals such as “9508”, with a font height of 7 mm.

⑤ 车轴锻造顺序号（轴号）：5 位阿拉伯数字，从 00001～99999 循环刻打，如“79310”，字体高 7 mm。

Axle forging sequence number (axle number): 5 Arabic numerals in the cycle of 00001–99999, such as “79310”, with a font height of 7 mm.

⑥ 车轴方位标记：“左”字标记，字体高 7 mm。

Axle orientation marking: “LH”, with a font height of 7 mm.

⑦ 车轴轴型标记：RC_3、RD_3、RD_{3A} 等，字体高 7 mm，下角标高 5 mm。

Axle type marking: RC_3, RD_3, RD_{3A}, etc., with a font height of 7 mm and an angular elevation of 5 mm.

⑧ 车轴制造超声波穿透探伤检查钢印标记："↑" 标记，高 10 mm。

Stamped marking for ultrasonic penetration inspection of axle: "↑", with a height of 10 mm.

⑨ 超声波穿透探伤工作者的责任钢印标记："$\triangle$C1" 标记，字母 "C" 字体高 5 mm，超声波穿透探伤工作者编号 "1" 字体高 3 mm，三角形边框高 8 mm、下底宽 10 mm。

Stamped marking for ultrasonic penetration detection operator: "$\triangle$C1" mark, with font height of C of 5 mm, font height of ultrasonic penetration detection operator number "1" of 3 mm, height of triangle frame of 8 mm, and bottom width of 10 mm.

车轴制造标记须集中刻打在轴端的某一扇区之内，并永久保留，排列位置如图 3–11 所示。

The axle manufacturing marking shall be permanently made in a certain sector of the axle end as per a layout shown in Figure 3-11.

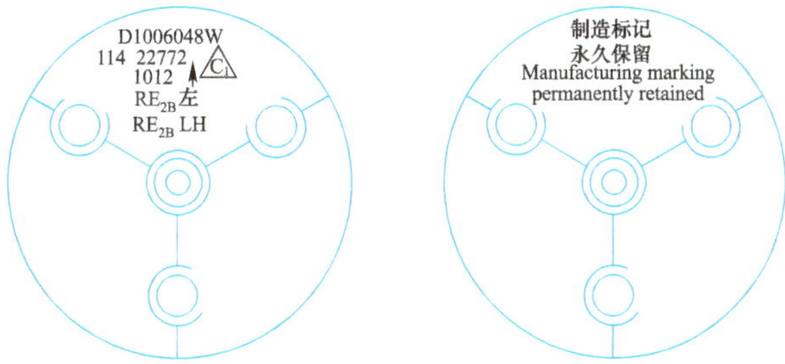

图 3–11　车轴制造标记示意图

Figure 3-11　Schematic Diagram of Axle Manufacturing Marking

（2）轮对组装标记。

Wheelset assembly markings.

① 轮对组装及组装单位标记：[×××] 标记，矩形框长 12 mm、高 7 mm，框内刻打轮对组装责任单位代号，字体高 5 mm，如 "904"。

Wheelset assembling marking and assembler marking: [×××] with a rectangular frame of 12 mm long and 7 mm high, and the code of the responsible unit for wheelset assembly engraved in the rectangular frame with a front height of 5 mm, such as "904".

② 轮对组装年月日标记：年、月、日分别用 2 位阿拉伯数字表示，字体高 7 mm，如 "951014"。

Wheelset assembly date marking: year, month, and day respectively represented by 2 Arabic numerals, such as "951014", with a font height of 7 mm.

轮对的第一次组装标记须在车轴制造标记所处扇区按顺时针方向排列的下一个扇区内刻打，排列位置如图 3–12 所示。轮对的第一次组装标记须永久保留。

The first assembly marking of wheelsets shall be permanently made in the sector next to the sector where the axle manufacturing marking is located (counted in the clockwise direction) as per a layout shown in Figure 3-12.

图 3–12　轮对组装标记示意图

Figure 3-12　Schematic Diagram of Wheelset Assembly Marking

轮对再次组装时，组装标记在轮对第一次组装标记所处扇区按顺时针方向排列的下一个扇区内刻打，左端打满后在右端刻打，依次类推。各扇区均打满后，依次选择第二次及以后各次组装标记中允许不保留者，将该扇区的所有标记全部磨除，重新刻打组装标记。

When the wheelset is assembled again, the assembly marking shall be made in the sector next to the sector where the first assembly marking is located (counted in the clockwise direction). When the leftmost sector is full, the marking is to be made in the rightmost sector. When all sectors are full, it is recommended to select a second assembly marking and markings for subsequent assemblies that are allowed to be removed and ground off for engraving assembly marking.

（3）特殊标记。

Special markings.

车轴经改轴后再组装使用时，必须在刻打本次轮对组装标记的扇区内增加改轴标记，刻打“改”字标记（字体高 7 mm）和改轴后的轴型标记（字体高 7 mm），如“改 RC_3”。车轴型号以改轴后的轴型为准，带有“改”字标记的扇区内的所有标记须永久保留，如图 3–13 所示。

When the axle is assembled after a change, a “CHANGE” word marking (with a font height of 7 mm) and the axle model marking (with a font height of 7 mm) after the axle is changed must be added in the sector where the wheelset assembly marking is engraved, such as “CHANGE RC_3”. The axle model after a change shall be applied, and all markings in the sector with “CHANGE” marking shall be all permanently retained, as shown in Figure 3-13.

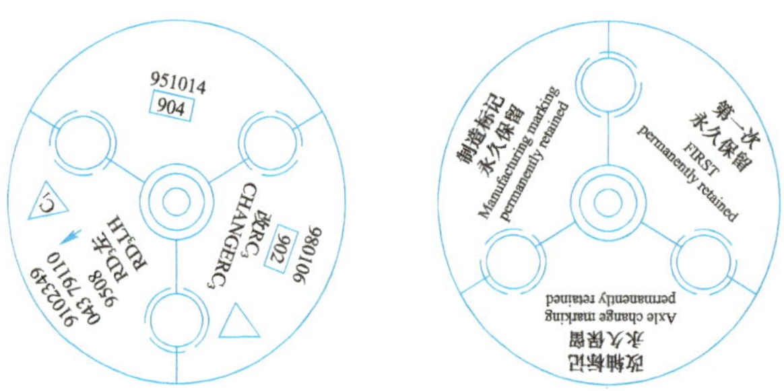

图 3–13　车轴改轴标记示意图

Figure 3-13　Schematic Diagram of Axle Change Marking

进口轮对轴端原有制造及组装等标记必须永久保留。改轴和改制轴端螺栓孔时，必须将需要永久保留的轴端标记依次转打在新刻制的各扇区内（按新的标记刻打规范）。车轴轴端标记必须刻打清晰、准确，除规定刻打的标记外，不允许刻打其他任何标记。

The original manufacturing and assembly marking and other markings at the journal end of imported wheelsets must be permanently retained. In the case of axle change and journal end bolt-hole modification, all axle end markings that need to be permanently retained must be transferred to the newly-engraved sectors in turn (according to the new marking engraving specification). The axle end markings must be engraved clearly and accurately, and no other markings than those specified are allowed.

项目 4

Project 4

滚动轴承（轴箱）装置

Roller Bearing (Axle Box) Assembly

本项目以了解滚动轴承（轴箱）装置的结构组成为工学任务，通过课堂任务的完成过程，着重介绍各种类型车辆滚动轴承（轴箱）装置的结构组成，并以此为引导，介绍滚动轴承（轴箱）装置的型号、作用；通过课后任务，了解各种类型车辆滚动轴承在结构上的主要差别。

The main task of this project is to understand the structure and composition of roller bearing (axle box) assembly. In the classroom, the main focus is on introducing the structure and composition of various types of roller bearing (axle box) assemblies for railway vehicles, and introducing their models and functions. Through after-class tasks, students will learn about the main structural differences of rolling bearings across different types of railway vehicles.

学生工作页 Student Worksheet

工学任务描述 Task description	预期目标 Expected goals
任务名称：认识车辆滚动轴承（轴箱）装置 Task name: Understanding of the roller bearing (axle box) assembly 任务编号：CJ-04 Task number: CJ-04 任务类型：结构型+工作过程型 Task type: Structure + work process 适用范围：车辆系统各岗位群 Applicable scope: All post groups of the car system 完成时间：　　　学时 Completion time:　　　class hours	初级：了解滚动轴承（轴箱）装置的基本结构组成 Elementary level: Understand the basic structure and composition of roller bearing (axle box) assembly 中级：掌握滚动轴承的型号及作用 Intermediate level: Master the model and function of roller bearings 高级：客、货车使用不同类型轴承的原因及轴承游隙的作用 Advanced level: Under the reasons for using different types of bearings for passenger cars and the function of bearing clearance

知识回顾+小组讨论

Knowledge review + group discussion

1. 滚动轴承装置的基本组成及要求。
Basic composition and requirements of roller bearing devices.

	基 本 组 成 Basic composition		相关知识点 Relevant knowledge points
1	轴承 Bearing		（1）原件具体结构 Specific structure of part （2）客、货车密封的不同之处 Differences in the seal between passenger cars and freight cars （3）轴箱的种类 Types of axle box
2	密封装置 Seal		
3	附属配件 Accessory		

2. 识记 SKF197726 型轴承装置的具体组成。
Remember the specific composition of the SKF197726 bearing device.

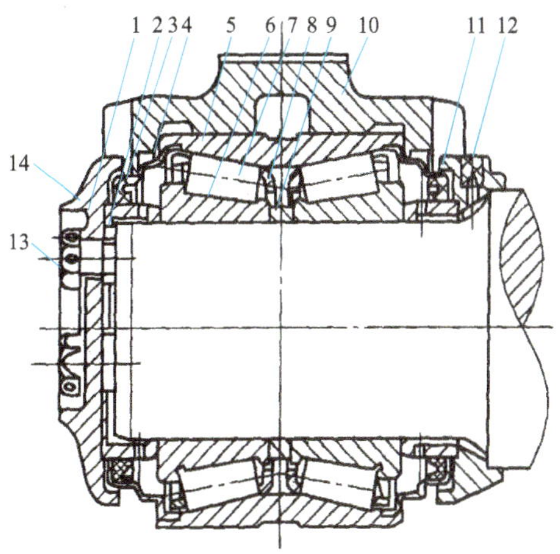

序号 S/N	名　称 Name	序号 S/N	名　称 Name	序号 S/N	名　称 Name
1		6		11	
2		7		12	
3		8		13	
4		9			
5		10			

3. 下图是 353130B 型滚动轴承的部分组成，写出图中各部分的名称。
The following figure is the part composition of the 353130B roller bearing, write the name of each part in the figure.

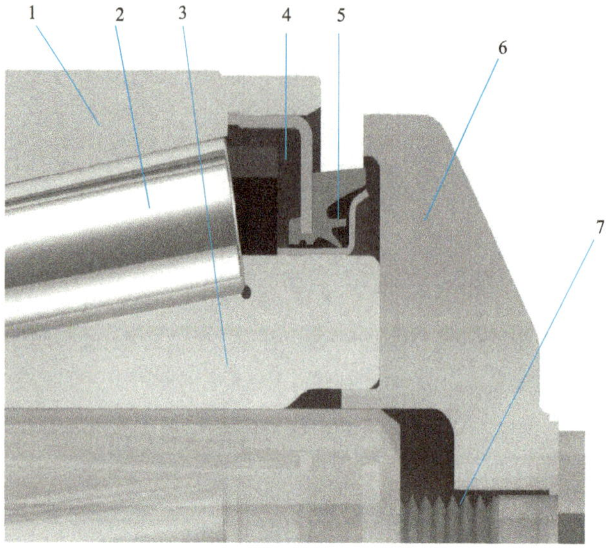

序号 S/N	名　称 Name	序号 S/N	名　称 Name	序号 S/N	名　称 Name
1		4		7	
2		5			
3		6			

4. 识记普通客车滚动轴承（轴箱）装置。

   Remember the roller bearing (axle box) assembly for ordinary passenger cars.

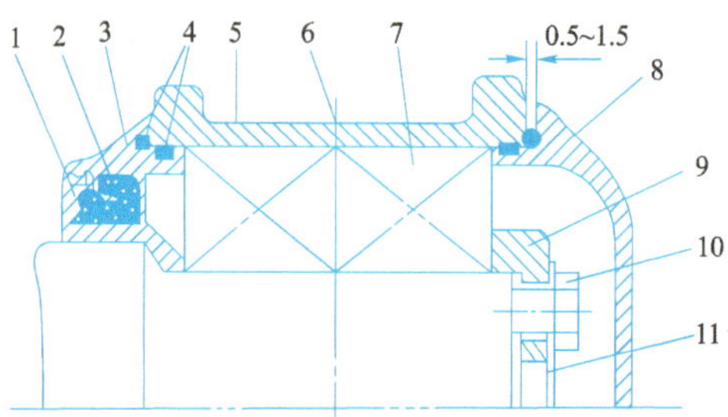

序号 S/N	名　称 Name	序号 S/N	名　称 Name	序号 S/N	名　称 Name
1		5		9	
2		6		10	
3		7		11	
4		8			

课后任务

After-class tasks

1. 查阅资料，写出各型号轴承游隙的大小。

   Refer to relevant documents and write down the clearance of each type of bearing.

轴承型号 Bearing model	SKF197726	352226X2–2RZ	42726T 152726T	353130B
径向游隙 Radial clearance				
轴向游隙 Axial clearance				

2. 分析各种客车滚动轴承（轴箱）装置的不同点。

Analyze the differences between various types of passenger car roller bearing (axle box) assemblies.

3. 试写出 RD_3 型滚动轴承（轴箱）装置的分解顺序。

Try to write the disassembly sequence of the RD_3 roller bearing (axle box) assembly.

4. 提出你的问题。

Put forward your questions.

5. 按兴趣建立工学小组，并明确目标、确定分工。

Establish work-and-study teams according to the interests, and clearly define the objectives and responsibilities of each group member.

小组成员 Group member	分　工 Responsibility	小组成员 Group member	分　工 Responsibility

学习效果评价
Learning effect evaluation

年 月 日
Year Month Day

专业班级： Major & class:	姓名： Name:	学号： Student number:
工学小组及分工： Work-and-study team and responsibility division:		

专业（知识/技能）收获 Professional gains (knowledge/skills)	（非专业）能力素质收获 (Non-professional) ability and quality gains

评价考核项目 Evaluation item	自我评价 Self-evaluation	小组评价 Group evaluation	教师评价 Teacher's evaluation
已掌握滚动轴承（轴箱）装置的基本结构组成 Have mastered the basic compositions of roller bearing (axle box) assembly			
已掌握相关知识点的数量 Number of knowledge points mastered			
主动提出问题的数量 Number of questions proposed			
课外学习时间（学时） After-school learning time (hours)			
工作态度（课堂、课后任务完成情况） Work attitude (completion condition of classroom tasks and after-class tasks)	☆☆☆☆☆ ☆☆☆☆☆	☆☆☆☆☆ ☆☆☆☆☆	☆☆☆☆☆ ☆☆☆☆☆
合作意识及协调能力 Cooperation consciousness and coordination ability	☆☆☆☆☆ ☆☆☆☆☆	☆☆☆☆☆ ☆☆☆☆☆	☆☆☆☆☆ ☆☆☆☆☆
正确表达和沟通能力 Correct expression and communication skills	☆☆☆☆☆ ☆☆☆☆☆	☆☆☆☆☆ ☆☆☆☆☆	☆☆☆☆☆ ☆☆☆☆☆
自律能力（缺勤/旷课/迟到/违纪次数） Self-discipline (absences/absenteeism/lateness/disciplinary violations)			

任务 4.1 货车滚动轴承装置

Task 4.1 Roller bearing device for freight cars

4.1.1 货车滚动轴承装置的结构特点和种类

Structural features and types of roller bearing devices for freight cars

我国铁路货车上（机械保温车除外）使用的滚动轴承均为无轴箱密封式双列圆锥滚子轴承（简称圆锥轴承），主要有以下几种型号：用于 D 型车轴的 197726 型、SKF197726 型、352226X2−2RZ 型、TBU130 型、AP130 型；用于 E 型车轴的 353130A 型、353130B 型、353130C 型、AP150 型、TBU 150 型等。D 型车轴与 E 型车轴所使用的轴承除内径及外形尺寸有所不同外，其他基本相同。

The roller bearings used on freight cars (except reefers) in China are all sealed double-row tapered roller bearings without axle box (hereinafter referred to as tapered bearings), which mainly include the following types: 197726, SKF197726, 352226X2-2RZ, TBU130 and AP130 for D-type axles; and 353130A, 353130B, 353130C, AP150, TBU 150, etc. for E-type axles. Bearings used for D-type axles and E-type axles are basically the same except for inner diameter and dimensions.

货车各种新型轴承的结构特点如表 4−1 所示。

The structural characteristics of various new bearings for freight cars are shown in Table 4-1.

表 4−1 货车各种新型轴承的结构特点

Table 4-1 Structural Features of Various New Types of Bearings for Freight Cars

	197726 型 Model 197726	SKFI97726 型 Model SKFI97726	352226X2−2RZ 型 Model 352226X2-2RZ	AP130 型 Model AP130
外形尺寸（内径×外径×宽度） Overall dimension (inner diameter/ outer diameter × width)(2, 2 × 2)	130 mm×230 mm×150 mm	130 mm×230 mm×150 mm	130 mm×230 mm×150 mm	130 mm×230 mm×150 mm
精度等级 Accuracy class	G 级（普通级） Class G (normal)	D 级 Class D	D 级 Class D	
保持架 Cage	钢板冲压保持架 Steel plate stamping cage	注射成型塑钢保持架 Injection molded plastic steel cage	钢板冲压保持架 Steel plate stamping cage	钢板冲压保持架 Steel plate stamping cage
滚子及挡边状态 Status of roller and rib	内圈大挡边为斜直挡边，滚子大端面为球基面，滚子为半凸度（滚动面素线为直线，两端修正线接触） The large rib of the inner ring is an inclined straight rib, the large end face of the roller is a spherical base surface, and the roller is semi-convex (the plain line of the rolling surface is a straight line, and the two ends are in contact with the correction line)	滚子全凸度（滚动面素线为对数曲线，内圈滚道带凸度） Full-convex roller (the rolling surface line is a logarithmic curve, and the inner raceway is convex)	内圈大挡边为斜直挡边，滚子大端面为球基面，滚子为全凸度，内圈滚道带凸度 The large rib of the inner ring is an inclined straight rib, the large end face of the roller is a spherical base surface, the roller is fully convex, and the inner raceway is convex.	

续表

Continued

	197726 型 Model 197726	SKFI97726 型 Model SKFI97726	352226X2-2RZ 型 Model 352226X2-2RZ	AP130 型 Model AP130
轴承密封 Bearing seal	直接接触式橡胶油封，后改进为非接触式橡胶迷宫油封 Direct contact rubber oil seal is changed to contactless rubber labyrinth oil seal for improvement	改进型的接触式橡胶油封 Improved contact rubber oil seal	非接触式橡胶迷宫油封 Contactless rubber labyrinth oil seal	HDL 型专用油封 HDL special oil seal
润滑脂 Grease	n 型锉基脂 n-type file-based grease	改进的 B 型锉基脂 Improved B-type file-based grease	改进的 B 型理基脂 Modified B-type lithium-based grease	B 型锉基脂 B-type file-based grease
设计单位和时间 Design unit and time	1978 年引进日本 KOYO 公司技术生产，1994 年由南口厂改进设计 In 1978, the production technology was imported from KOYO in Japan, and in 1994, the design was improved by the Nankou factory	1999 年由北京南口斯凯孚铁路轴承有限公司设计改进 In 1999, the design was improved by Beijing Nankou SKF Railway Bearing Co., Ltd.	1999 年由四方车辆研究所设计 In 1999, the design was conducted by Sifang Rolling Stock Research Institute	2000 年由美国引进 In 2000, technology was imported from the United States
使用类别 Type of bearing used	转 8A、转 8AG、转 8G Z8A, Z8AG, Z8G	转 SG、转 K1、转 K2、转 K3、转 K4 ZSG, ZK-1, ZK-2, ZK-3, ZK-4	转 8G、转 K1、转 K2、转 K3、转 K4 Z8G, ZK-1, ZK-2, ZK-3, ZK-4	转 Ka ZKa

轴承（轴箱）油润装置是铁道车辆的重要组成部分，将轮对和转向架构架连接在一起，把车辆的垂直、水平载荷传给轮对，不断地保持轴承的正常润滑，减小摩擦、降低运行阻力；防止热轴，限制轮对过大的横向移动；防止雨水、灰尘等异物侵入，保证车辆安全可靠运行。

The bearing (axle box) oil lubrication unit is an important part of railway vehicles. It connects the wheelset and the bogie frame together to transmit the vertical and horizontal loads of the car to the wheelset, continuously maintaining the normal lubrication of the bearing to reduce friction and running resistance; prevent hot box, limit the excessive lateral movement of the wheelset; and prevent the intrusion of rain, dust, and other foreign matters, thus ensuring the safe and reliable operation of the car.

其工作原理是：借助于内、外圈之间的滚动体滚动实现传力和滚动；内圈采用过盈配合装配在轴颈上，当车轮转动时随轴颈一起转动，外圈允许有少量转动，起支承作用。由于存在径向游隙和轴向游隙，可以保证滚动体自由转动。

Working principle: the force transmission and rolling are realized by means of the rolling elements between the inner and outer rings; the inner ring is assembled on the journal by interference fit so that it will rotate with the journal when the wheel rotates; and outer ring is allowed to rotate for supporting, thus ensuring that the rolling element can rotate freely in face of axial play and radial play.

其优点有：减小列车起动和运行的阻力，增大列车牵引重量；延长检修周期，减少材料消耗；承载均匀，减少燃轴事故，安全可靠；提高运行速度，适应现代化运输的需要。

Its advantages are as follows: reduce the starting and running resistance of the train, increase the traction weight of the train; extend the maintenance cycle, reduce material consumption; ensure uniform bearing, reduce axle burning accidents to ensure safe and reliable operation; and improve the operating speed to meet the needs of modern transportation.

下面将着重介绍 352226X2−2RZ 型、353130A 型、353130B 型、SKF197726 型轴承的结构特点。

The structural characteristics of bearings 352226X2-2RZ, 353130A, 353130B, and SKF197726 will be introduced later.

1. 352226X2−2RZ 型轴承
352226X2-2RZ bearing

352226X2−2RZ 型轴承是为了满足铁路货车提速的要求而设计制造的一种新型快速轴承，主要使用在转 K1、转 K2、转 K3、转 K4 等快速转向架上。该型轴承由四方车辆研究所于 1999 年开始设计研制，现已由成都天马轴承厂等多家轴承厂家进行批量生产并投入使用。

The 352226X2-2RZ bearing is a new type of high-speed bearing designed and manufactured by China Railway to meet the speed-up requirements of freight cars. It is mainly used on high-speed bogies such as ZK-1, ZK-2, ZK-3, and ZK-4. This type of bearing was designed and developed by the Sifang Rolling Stock Research Institute in 1999, and has been mass-produced by many bearing manufacturers such as Chengdu Tianma Railway Bearing Co., Ltd., and put into use.

352226X2−2RZ 型轴承装置由外圈、内圈、滚子、保持架、中隔圈及密封装置和附属配件组成，其结构如图 4−1 所示。

The 352226X2-2RZ bearing assembly consists of an outer ring, an inner ring, rollers, a cage, a middle spacer ring, a sealing assembly, and accessories, as shown in Figure 4-1.

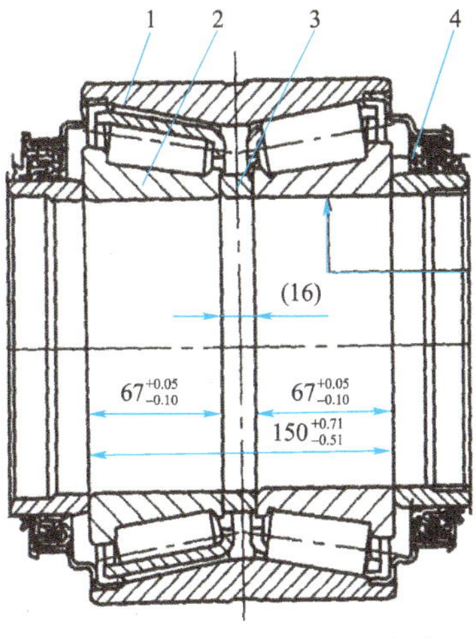

1—外圈；2—内圈；3—中隔圈；4—密封装置。

1—Outer ring; 2—Inner ring; 3—Middle spacer ring; 4—Sealing assembly.

图 4−1　352226X2−2RZ 型轴承的结构

Figure 4-1　Structure of 352226X2-2RZ Bearing

1）外圈

Outer ring

外圈带有两个倾斜的滚道，滚道的倾角为 10°0′。两端薄壁为牙口，在牙口根部设有油沟，以嵌入密封罩凸边，防止密封罩脱落或漏油脂。外圈的结构如图 4–2 所示。外圈采用 G20CrMoA 电渣重熔轴承钢制造，滚道表面进行渗碳处理，其有效渗碳层深度为 1.5～2.3 mm，表面含碳量为 0.8%～1.05%，表面硬度为 59～63 HRC，心部硬度不小于 32 HRC。这样轴承外圈表面耐磨性提高，内部却保持较高的韧性，从而提高了其抗压强度和冲击韧性。为了防止锈蚀和提高润滑效果，内、外圈的全部表面均施行磷化处理，磷化膜厚度为 0.003～0.005 mm。

The outer ring has two inclined raceways with an inclination of 10°0′. The thin walls at both ends are grippers, and an oil groove is designed at the root of the gripper to embed the flange of the sealing cover to prevent the sealing cover from falling off or leaking. The structure of the outer ring is shown in Figure 4-2. The outer ring is made of G20CrMoA electroslag remelting bearing steel, and the raceway surface is carburized with an effective carburized layer depth of 1.5–2.3 mm, a surface carbon content of 0.8%–1.05%, a surface hardness of 59–63 HRC, and a core hardness not less than 32 HRC, to improve the wear resistance of the outer face without prejudice to the toughness of the inside, and therefore improve its compressive strength and impact toughness. To prevent corrosion and improve the lubrication effect, the surface of the inner and outer rings is phosphated with a phosphating thickness of 0.003–0.005 mm.

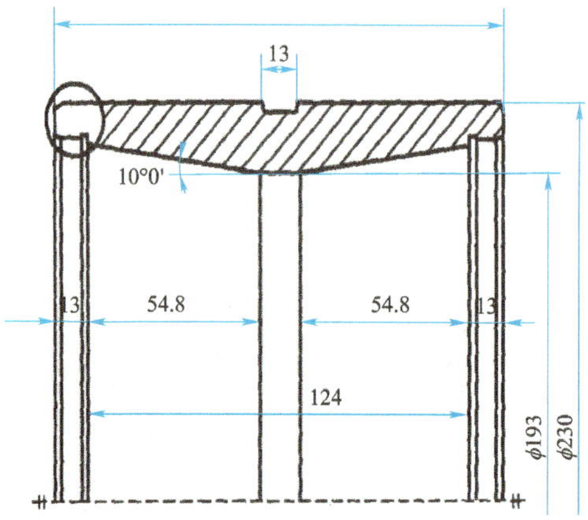

图 4–2　352226X2-2R2 型轴承的外圈

Figure 4-2　Outer Ring of 352226X2-2R2 Bearing

2）内圈

Inner ring

内圈为双挡边结构，外圆周面为倾斜角 7°40′的滚道，如图 4–3 所示。内圈与轴颈采用过盈配合，内圈大挡边的外端面刻有制造厂代号、制造年月及轴承型号。为了使大挡边与滚子球基面接触带控制在大挡边中部，便于润滑和减少摩擦，内圈大挡边内端面设计成 7°59′的锥面。内圈的材质、热处理及磷化处理等与外圈相同。

The inner ring takes a double rib structure, with the outer peripheral surface being a raceway with an inclination angle of 7°40′, as shown in Figure 4-3. The inner ring is assembled with the journal by interference fit, and the outer end face of the large rib of the inner ring is engraved with markings including manufacturer code, manufacturing date (year and month), and bearing model. In order to control the contact zone between the large rib and the roller spherical reference surface in the middle of the large rib for lubrication and friction reduction, the inner end face of the large rib of the inner ring is designed as a 7°59′ conical surface. The material, heat treatment, and phosphating requirements of the inner ring are the same as those of the outer ring.

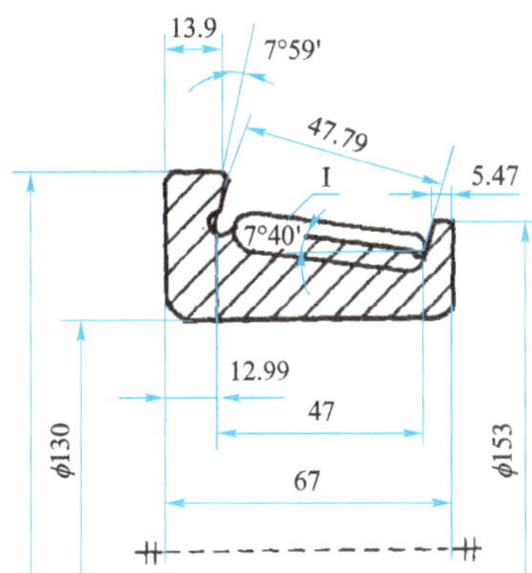

图 4-3　352226X2-2RZ 型轴承的内圈
Figure 4-3　Inner Ring of 352226X2-2RZ Bearing

3）滚子
Roller

滚子为圆锥体结构，其锥度角为 2°20′，如图 4-4 所示。为使滚子表面接触应力分布均匀，避免两端应力集中，滚子滚动面素线为一曲线。

The roller is a cone with a conical angle of 2°20′, as shown in Figure 4-4. To make the contact stress distribution on the roller surface uniform and avoid stress concentration at both ends, the plain line on the rolling surface of the roller is a curve.

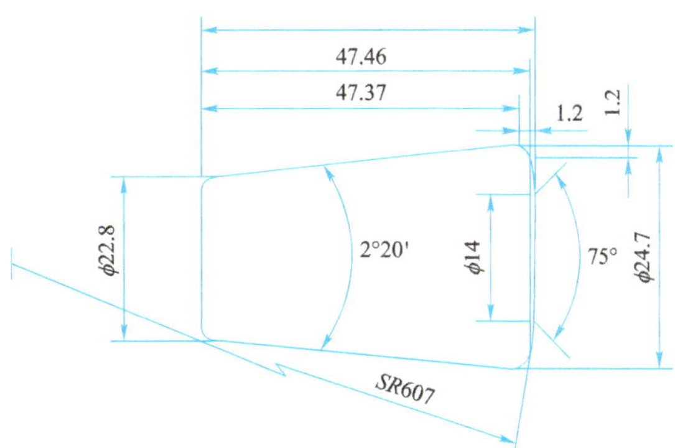

图 4-4　352226X2-2RZ 型轴承的滚子
Figure 4-4　Roller of 352226X2-2RZ Bearing

滚子采用 GCr15 电渣重熔钢冷拉制造，经表面热处理后硬度为 60～64 HRC。每套 352226X2–2RZ 型轴承共有 40 个滚子（比 SKF197726 型少 2 个），分两列排列。

The roller is made of GCr15 electroslag remelting steel by cold drawing, and the hardness is 60–64 HRC after surface heat treatment. Each set of 352226X2-2RZ bearings has 40 rollers (2 less than SKF197726 bearings) arranged in two rows.

4）保持架

Cage

保持架整体呈圆锥形，它将滚子与内圈组合在一起，圆周面上开有 20 个等分的窗孔，使滚子能沿滚道均匀分布，如图 4–5 所示。保持架采用 5 mm 厚的 08AIT 钢板冲压而成，并采用振动光饰或其他有效方法消除残余应力。其表面进行磷化处理，磷化膜厚度为 0.003～0.015 mm。保持架与滚子组合后，滚子径向游动量为 0.15～0.40 mm，窗孔侧隙不大于 1.5 mm。2004 年 9 月 1 日以后新造、大修的 352226X2–2RZ 型滚动轴承均需全部装用类似 SKF197726 型轴承的工程塑料保持架。

The cage is conical as a whole for combining the rollers with the inner ring. There are 20 orifices uniformly distributed on the circumference to enable the rollers to be evenly distributed along the raceway, as shown in Figure 4-5. The cage is stamped from a 5 mm thick 08AIT steel sheet, and is adopted with vibration finishing or other effective means to eliminate residual stress. Its surface is phosphated, with a phosphating film thickness of 0.003–0.015 mm. After the cage is combined with the roller, the radial play of the roller is 0.15–0.40 mm, and the side clearance of the orifice is not more than 1.5 mm. The 352226X2-2RZ roller bearings newly built and overhauled after September 1, 2004 shall all be equipped with an engineering plastic cage similar to that of SKF197726 bearings.

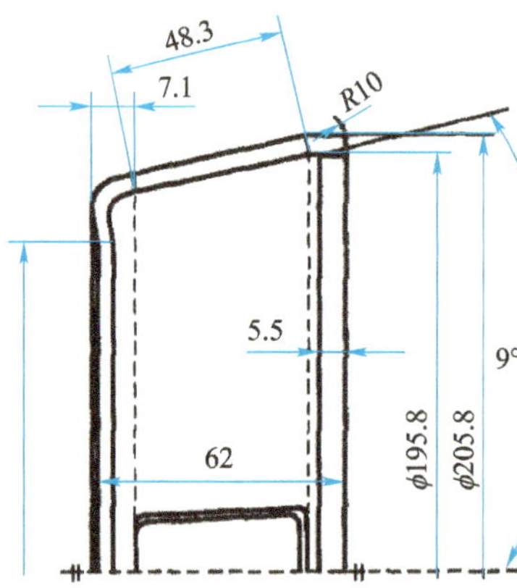

图 4–5 352226X2–2RZ 型轴承的保持架
Figure 4-5 Cage of 352226X2-2RZ Bearing

5）中隔圈

Middle spacer ring

352226X2–2R2 型轴承的中隔圈如图 4–6 所示。中隔圈由 45 号钢制造，其表面经磷化处理。中隔圈安装于两内圈之间，除隔离内圈外，还可用来调整轴承轴向间隙。在新装配或检修轴承时，选择适当厚度的中隔圈，即可获得所需要的轴向游隙值。

The middle spacer ring of 352226X2-2R2 bearing, as shown in Figure 4-6,is made of 45# steel with the surface phosphated. The middle spacer ring is installed between the two inner rings for isolating inner rings as well as adjusting the axial clearance of the bearing. When a new bearing is assembled or a bearing is repaired, a middle spacer ring of appropriate thickness should be selected to ensure the axial clearance meets your requirement.

6）密封装置

Sealing assembly

密封装置由密封罩、油封、密封座组成，轴承前后端各装一套。352226X2−2R2 型轴承的密封装置如图 4−7 所示。其作用是防止油脂外泄及外部沙尘、雨雪的侵入。

The sealing assembly consists of a sealing cover, oil seals, and sealing seat, which is installed at both the front end and the rear end of the bearing. The sealing assembly of 352226X2-2R2 bearing is as shown in Figure 4-7. The sealing assembly is intended for preventing the leakage of grease and the invasion of sand, rain, and snow.

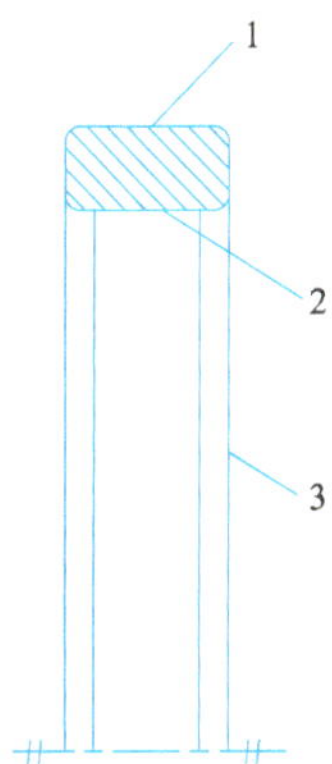

1—外径面；2—内径面；3—端面。

1—Outer diameter surface; 2—Inner diameter surface; 3—End face.

图 4−6 352226X2−2RZ 型轴承的中隔圈

Figure 4-6 Middle Spacer Ring of 352226X2-2RZ Bearing

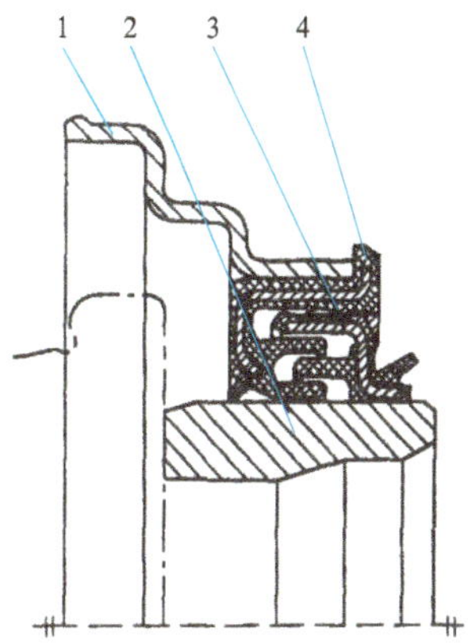

1—密封罩；2—密封座；3—内油封；4—外油封。

1—Sealing cover; 2—Sealing seat; 3—Inner oil seal; 4—Outer oil seal.

图 4−7 352226X2−2RZ 型轴承的密封装置

Figure 4-7 Sealing Assembly of 352226X2-2RZ Bearing

（1）密封罩。密封罩由 2.5 mm 厚的 T10 钢板（允许用 08AlT 钢代替）压型而成，表面进行磷化处理，磷化膜厚度为 0.003～0.015 mm。密封罩大端外圆周面有凸边，以嵌入外圈油沟，大端外圆与外圈牙口为过盈配合。密封罩小端为直通式，不再设油封挡边，以适应安装新型油封的需要。352226X2−2R2 型轴承密封罩的结构如图 4−8 所示。

Sealing cover. The sealing cover is pressed from a 2.5 mm thick T10 steel sheet (08AlT steel is allowed to be used for substitution), and the surface is phosphated with a 0.003−0.015 mm thick phosphating film. The outer circumferential surface of the large end of the sealing cover has a convex edge to be embedded in the outer ring oil groove, and the large end outer circle is assembled with the outer ring gripper by interference fit. The small end of the sealing cover is of straight-through type with no oil seal rib provided to meet the needs of installing new oil seals. The structure of the sealing cover of 352226X2-2R2 bearing is shown in Figure 4-8.

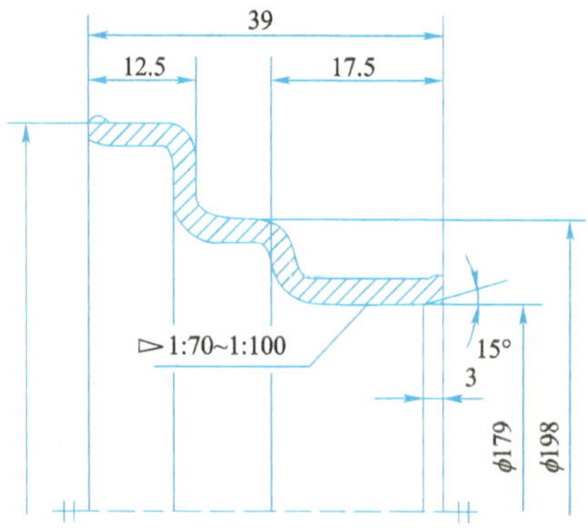

图 4-8　352226X2-2RZ 型轴承的密封罩
Figure 4-8　Sealing Cover of 352226X2-2RZ Bearing

（2）油封。油封为非接触式橡胶迷宫油封，由内油封和外油封组合而成，如图 4-9 所示。外油封安装在密封罩最小直径的圆周内，内油封则与密封座紧密配合。轴承压装后，内外油封之间并不接触，但它们之间的凹凸槽则相互配合形成密封迷宫。

Oil seal. The oil seal is a contactless rubber labyrinth oil seal that includes an inner oil seal and an outer oil seal, as shown in Figure 4-9. The outer oil seal is installed in the circumference of the smallest diameter of the sealing cover, and the inner oil seal is closely fitted with the sealing seat. After the bearing is press-fitted, the inner oil seal does not come in contact with the outer oil seal, but the concave and convex grooves between them will work with each other to form a sealing labyrinth.

内、外油封均为橡胶制品，内置钢骨架。钢骨架由厚度为 1.5 mm 的钢板压型而成，与橡胶油封硫化在一起。其作用是提高油封的刚度，减少变形。

Inner and outer oil seals are rubber products with a built-in steel frame. The steel frame is pressed from a steel sheet with a thickness of 1.5 mm and vulcanized with the rubber oil seal for increasing the rigidity of the oil seal and reducing deformation.

（3）密封座。密封座由 GCr15 钢制成，经热处理后硬度为 58～62 HRC，其断面为“门”状，如图 4-10 所示。内圈直径较小的圆周与轴颈过盈配合，直径较大的圆周上不再开有小孔，从而不再有加油或排气功能。前、后密封座与前盖及后挡配合后，还起到轴承内圈的定位作用。

Sealing seat. The sealing seat is made of GCr15 and heat-treated to a hardness of 58–62 HRC, with the cross-section in the shape of a “door”, as shown in Figure 4-10. The circumference of the inner ring with a smaller diameter is assembled with the journal by interference fit, and the circumference with a larger diameter is no longer drilled with holes, thus making oiling or venting unavailable. After fitting with the front cover and the rear rib, the front, and rear sealing seats can also play a role in positioning the inner ring of the bearing.

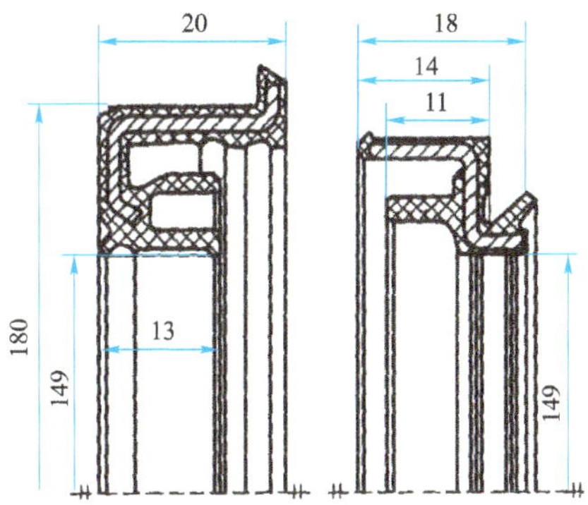

图 4-9 352226X2-2RZ 型轴承的油封
Figure 4-9 Oil Seal of 352226X2-2RZ Bearing

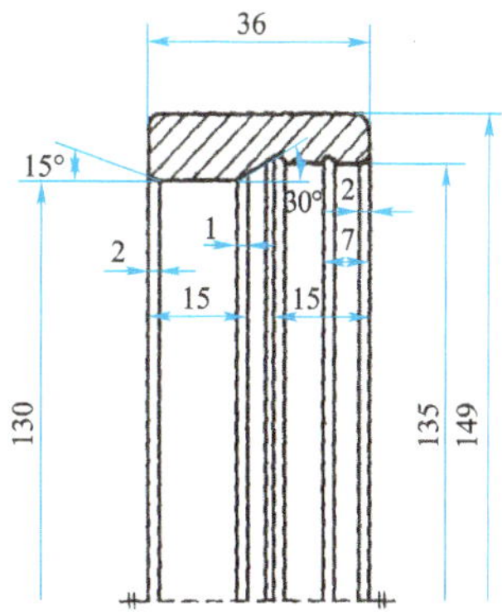

图 4-10 352226X2-2RZ 型轴承的密封座
Figure 4-10 Sealing Seat of 352226X2-2RZ Bearing

2. 353130A 型轴承

353130A bearing

为进一步满足铁路货车提速、重载的需要，提高轴承使用可靠性，开发了 353130A 紧凑型轴承。紧凑型轴承的主要特点是减少了轴承的零件，缩短了轴承总的轴向宽度，改善了微动磨损对轴承性能的影响，适应与之压装的 RE_{2B} 型车轴轴颈长度。

To further meet the needs of the speed-up and heavy load of freight cars, and to improve the operation reliability of bearing, the 353130A compact bearing is developed, and its main features are as follows: reduce the parts used in the bearing, shorten the total axial width of the bearing, improve the influence of fretting wear on the performance of the bearing, and adapt to the length of the RE_{2B} axle journal.

353130A 紧凑型轴承于 2005 年 7 月在青岛通过了当时铁道部组织的图样技术技术审查。

The 353130A compact bearing passed the technical review of the drawing organized by the Ministry of Railways at that time in Qingdao in July 2005.

353130A 紧凑型轴承的结构如图 4-11 所示。

The structure of the 353130A compact bearing is shown in Figure 4-11.

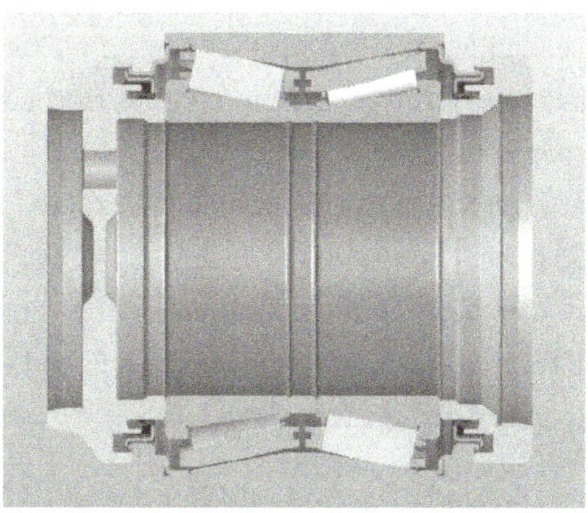

图 4-11 353130A 紧凑型轴承的结构
Figure 4-11 Structure of 353130A Compact Bearing

353130A 紧凑型轴承的特点如下。

The features of the 353130A compact bearing are as follows.

（1）取消内油封及密封座。

No inner oil seal and sealing seat available.

（2）缩短轴承的轴向宽度。

Reduced axial width of the bearing.

（3）采用塑料保持架。

Plastic cage used.

（4）密封效果稳定。

Stable sealing effect.

（5）适应既有的检修设备。

Compatible with existing maintenance equipment.

2005 年 9 月，当时铁道部安排 353130A 型轴承装车运用试验。2005 年装车 2 500 辆，2006 年装车 12 000 多辆。2006 年 4 月 30 日起停止 353130A 型轴承生产。2006 年 5 月，对试验的轴承进行了退卸分解检查，状态均良好。目前未接到 353130A 型轴承的不良反映。

In September 2005, the Ministry of Railways organized the in-car operation test for the 353130A bearing, and it was then installed on 2,500 cars in 2005 and more than 12,000 cars in 2006. The production of 353130A bearings was stopped on April 30, 2006. In May 2006, the test bearing was unloaded and disassembled and was inspected in good condition. Till now, no complaints about the 353130A bearing have been received.

3. 353130B 型轴承

353130A bearing

为了在较高的技术平台上制定我国统一的轴承标准，便于今后轴承的制造、检修、运用和管理，经过与国外轴承公司多次技术交流，当时铁道部最终确定引进 SKF 公司的 CTBU150。

To formulate a unified national bearing standard on a higher technology platform to facilitate the manufacture, maintenance, application, and management of bearings in the future, Ministry of Railway, after multiple technical exchanges with foreign bearing companies, finally decided to introduce the CTBU150 bearing from SKF.

2006 年 1 月，铁道部组织技术人员对 SKF 公司提供的 CTBU150 型轴承图样进行了技术审查，确定的轴承型号为 353130B（C353130），并在国内制造。

In January 2006, Ministry of Railway organized technical personnel to carry out a technical review of the drawing of CTBU150 bearings provided by SKF, and after this, the bearing model 353130B (C353130) was determined and manufactured locally.

353130B 紧凑型轴承的结构如图 4-12 所示。

The structure of the 353130B compact bearing is shown in Figure 4-12.

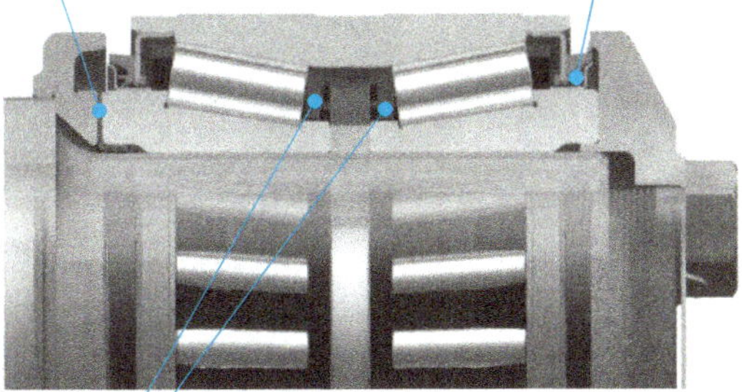

图 4-12　353130B 紧凑型轴承的结构

Figure 4-12　Structure of 353130B Compact Bearing

353130B 紧凑型轴承的主要结构及特点如下。

The main structure and characteristics of the 353130B compact bearing are as follows.

（1）取消了密封座，密封座的功能由内圈大挡边实现，如图 4-13 所示。

The sealing seat is not used, and the function of the sealing seat is realized by the large rib of the inner ring, as shown in Figure 4-13.

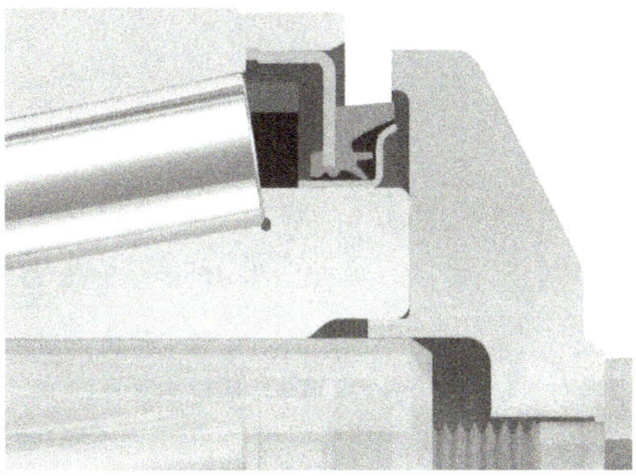

图 4-13　353130B 紧凑型轴承的密封部分

Figure 4-13　Sealing Part of 353130B Compact Bearing

（2）采用工程塑料保持架，增加一个特殊兜孔的设计，方便轴承的一般检修，如图 4-14 所示。

Engineering plastic cage is provided, and a special pocket is designed to facilitate the general maintenance of the bearing, as shown in Figure 4-14.

（3）后挡和内圈间的塑钢隔圈保证了接触面间无微振磨蚀颗粒，提供了更长的油脂寿命和维护周期，如图 4-15 所示。

The plastic steel spacer ring is installed between the rear rib and the inner ring to ensure that there are no micro-vibration abrasive particles between the contact surfaces, providing a longer grease life and maintenance interval, as shown in Figure 4-15.

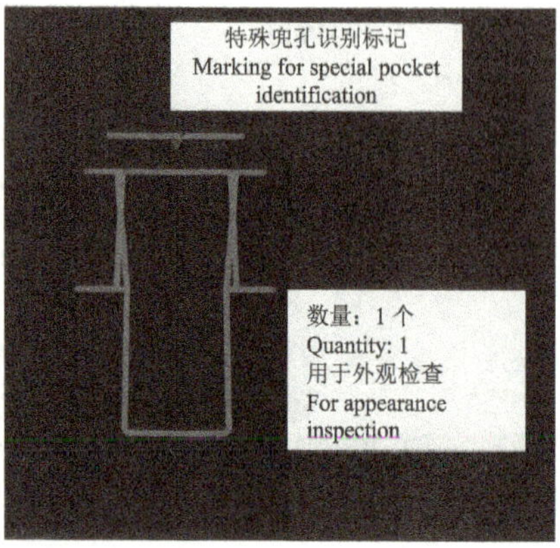

图 4-14　353130B 紧凑型轴承的保持架
Figure 4-14　Cage for 353130B Compact Bearing

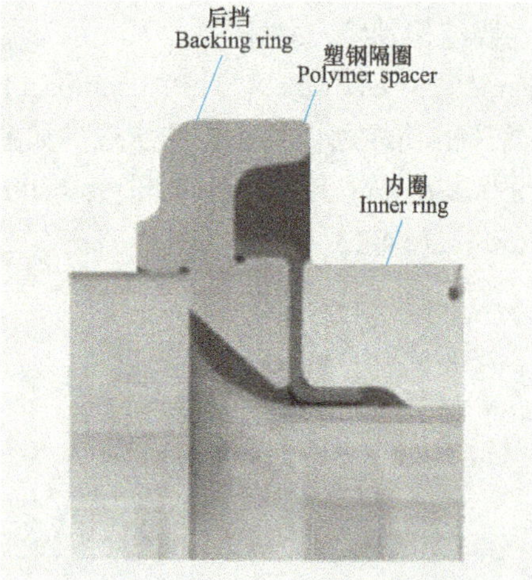

图 4-15　353130B 紧凑型轴承的塑钢隔圈
Figure 4-15　Plastic Steel Spacer Ring of 353130B Compact Bearing

353130B 紧凑型轴承的基本运用条件如下。

The basic operating conditions of the 353130B compact bearing are as follows.

（1）运用速度：120 km/h。

Operation speed: 120 km/h.

（2）轴重：25 t；轴载荷：23.83 t。

Axle load: 25 t; axle loading force: 23.83 t.

（3）最大轴向载荷：9.53 t。

Max. axial load: 9.53 t.

（4）环境条件：−45℃～+50℃；最大相对湿度：100%。

-45℃ – +50℃; maximum relative humidity: 100%.

（5）轴承最高允许温升：55℃。

Max. allowable temperature rise of the bearing: 55℃.

（6）定期检修：正常使用和维护条件下，80 万 km 或 8 年（以先到者为准）。

Regular maintenance: 800,000 km or 8 years under normal operation and maintenance conditions (whichever comes first).

353130B 紧凑型轴承在澳大利亚、瑞典、美国已得到广泛使用。

353130B compact bearings have been widely applied in Australia, Sweden, and the United States.

4. SKF197726 型轴承

SKF197726 bearing

SKF197726 型轴承是由北京南口斯凯孚铁路轴承有限公司（由瑞典 SKF 公司和中国机车车辆工业总公司南口工厂合资组建，厂家代号：SKF）为适应铁路“高速、重载”的需要而生产的新型快速轴承。该轴承能满足在静态轴重 21 t 时正常运行速度为 120 km/h 的运行要求。SKF197726 型轴承主要使用在转 8G、转 K1、转 K2、转 K3、转 K4 等型号的提速、快速转向架上。

SKF197726 bearing is a new type of high-speed bearing produced by Beijing Nankou SKF Railway Bearing Co., Ltd. (a joint venture established by AB SKF and Nankou Factory of China National Railway Locomotive & Rolling Stock Industry Corporation with a factory code of SKF) to meet the “high speed and heavy load” operation requirements of railway, and is suitable for the normal operating speed of 120 km/h under a static axle load of 21 t. The SKF197726 bearing is mainly applied to speed-up and high-speed bogies including Z8G, ZK-1, ZK-2, ZK-3, ZK-4, etc.

SKF197726 型滚动轴承是在我国现有的主型货车滚动轴承 197726 型的基础上进行了二大步五小点的创新改造而新设计生产的。

The SKF197726 roller bearing is newly designed on the basis of the mainstream freight car roller bearing, i.e. 197726 roller bearing through two steps of modifications and innovation in five aspects.

第一步创新改造（1998 年 1 月 1 日—1999 年 3 月 30 日期间制造的轴承）的目的是延长轴承使用寿命，进行了以下 3 点改造。

The first step of the innovation and modification (covering bearings manufactured from January 1, 1998 to March 30, 1999) is to extend the service life of the bearing, and a 3 transformation points are involved, as described below.

（1）保持架改造。新保持架的设计考虑了保持架的全体功能：保持架必须要把各滚动体平均分离，避免滚子搅动；避免滚子相互影响，即要使用轻质材料；摩擦性质，即材料要有特别低的摩擦系数；材料性质，即材料要软而富有韧性和弹性；制造性能，即材料能塑膜注射成型。

Cage modification. The design of the new cage takes into account all the functions of the cage, that is, the cage must be able to evenly separate the rolling elements to avoid roller agitation. To avoid roller interaction, lightweight material must be used, and besides, the material shall have extremely low friction efficiency in terms of friction performance, shall be soft and resilient in terms of material nature, and shall be able to be formed by plastic film injection molding in terms of manufacturing performance.

为了满足上述要求，新保持架采用了可以注射塑造的塑胶材料，它由滚子引导转动，同时将原每列 21 个滚子改成每列 20 个滚子，以提高保持架的强度和单个滚子的抗压强度。

To meet the above requirements, the new cage is made of plastic material that supports injection molding. The cage rotates under the guidance of rollers. Besides, the number of rollers per row is changed from 21 to 20 to improve the strength of the cage and the compressive strength of individual rollers.

（2）滚子与滚道表面微观几何形状改造。通过滚子与滚道表面微观几何尺寸的改造，使得滚子与滚道之间有更长的接触线，能够使滚动体保持平衡（无歪斜），滚动体不轻易滑行，有效防止擦伤。尤其是当滚子进入负荷地带时，优越性更为明显。

Surface micro geometry modification of roller and raceway surface. Through the modification of the surface micro-geometry of the roller and the raceway surface, the contact line between the roller and the raceway is longer, which can keep the rolling elements in balance (without skewness), make the rolling element slide easily, and effectively prevent scratches, especially when the roller is in the load zone.

（3）滚子球基面和挡边改造。滚子球基面和挡边都在磨削加工时磨成不同直径的球面形。当两体接触时，摩擦将会减少至最低限度，尤其是在轴承运转的磨合期不会产生磨损现象。

Modification of roller spherical reference surface and rib transformation. The roller spherical reference surface and the rib are ground into spheres of different diameters. When they are in contact, the friction will be reduced to the lowest limit, especially in the running-in period of bearing, when no wear will occur.

当轴承在高速运行时，摩擦系数小，故此轴承温度较低，更加保证了轴承寿命的延长。

When the bearing is running at high speed, the friction coefficient is small, so the bearing temperature is lower, which helps extend the service of the bearing.

第二步创新改造（1999 年 3 月 30 日以后制造的轴承）主要集中于油封和油脂上，主要目的是延长轴承使用期，提高速度，增加负荷量。

The second step of innovation and modification (covering bearings manufactured after March 30, 1999) mainly focuses on oil seals and grease. The main purpose of this modification is to extend the service life of bearings and increase the speed and the load.

（1）润滑脂的改造。为了改善滚子与内、外圈滚道之间，滚子与保持架之间，滚子端面与内圈挡边之间的工作状况，更为有效地延长滚动轴承的使用寿命，SKF197726 型轴承使用的润滑脂是改进型铁道滚动轴承 n 型锂基润滑脂，该润滑脂是在铁道滚动轴承 11 型锂基润滑脂的基础上改进而来的，并通过了 SKF 公司工程研究中心（荷兰）的测试、检验。

Modification of grease. To improve the working conditions between the roller and the inner/outer raceways, between the roller and the cage, and between the roller end face and the inner ring rib, and further effectively extend the service life of the roller bearing, the improved railway roller bearing n-type lithium-based grease is applied for SKF197726 bearing. This grease is improved on the basis of the railway roller bearing 11-type lithium-based grease, and passed the test and inspection of SKF Engineering Research Center (in the Netherlands).

（2）密封装置的改造。由于 197726 型轴承容易产生密封罩脱出、油封密封不严等不利于轴承正常使用的状况，为了消除这些不利状况，197726 型轴承曾做过一些改进，将接触式橡胶油封改成非接触式橡胶迷宫油封，但改进后的效果还不是很理想。因此，SKF197726 型轴承的密封装置又进行了较大的改进：①将密封罩的制造材料由 2.2 mm 钢板改成 2.5 mm 钢板以提高强度，防止密封罩变形脱出；②将橡胶油封由非接触式橡胶迷宫式改回接触式。该接触式油封与原 197726 型轴承的接触式油封不同，原 197726 型轴承的油封与密封罩为分体式，而 SKF197726 型轴承的油封与密封罩为一体式。经过改造后的密封装置基本杜绝了上述不良现象的产生，降低了轴承的故障率，满足了轴承提速的要求。

Modification of sealing assembly. Considering that the 197726 bearing is prone to have problems such as dislodgement of sealing covers, improper sealing of oil seals, and others, which are harmful to the normal operation of the bearing, some improvements are made on the 197726 bearing, for example, the contact rubber oil seal is changed to the contactless rubber labyrinth oil seal, but the effect fails to meet the expectation. Therefore, further improvements are then carried out on the SKF197726 bearing, as described below: ① The material of sealing cover is changed from 2.2 mm-thick steel sheet to 2.5 mm-thick steel sheet to improve the strength and prevent the sealing cover from deforming and coming out; ② The oil seal is changed from the contactless rubber labyrinth oil seal back to the contact rubber oil seal, but this contact oil seal is different from the original one on the 197726 bearings. Specifically speaking, the original oil seal on the 197726 bearings is separated from the sealing cover, but the oil seal on the SKF197726 bearing is integrated with the sealing cover. After the sealing assembly is modified, the bearing defects described above are basically eliminated, thus reducing the failure rate of the bearing and meeting the speed-up requirements of the bearing.

与 197726 型轴承相比，该轴承具有下列优越性：① 轴承寿命延长，由原来的 10 年增至 20 年；② 提高了货车质量，增加了负荷量；③ 操作顺畅，经济实惠；④ 轴承温度降低，可提高速度；⑤ 保持架耐磨损、耐振动。

Compared with the 197726 bearings, the SKF197726 bearing has the following advantages: ① The service life is prolonged from 10 years to 15 years; ② The quality of the freight car is improved, and the loading capacity is increased; ③ The operation becomes smooth and economical; ④ The bearing temperature is reduced, making speed-up possible; ⑤ The cage is resistant to wear and vibration.

SKF197726 型轴承由内圈、外圈、塑钢保持架、滚子、中隔圈、密封座和密封罩组件组成。SKF197726 型轴承的结构组成与 352226X2–2RZ 型轴承基本相似。因此，为了避免内容重复，在此不再做介绍。

The SKF197726 bearing is composed of an inner ring, outer ring, plastic steel cage, roller, middle spacer ring, sealing seat, and sealing cover assembly. The structure and composition of the SKF197726 bearing are basically similar to that of the 352226X2-2RZ bearing, and thus no introduction is given for this type of bearing to avoid repeated introduction.

4.1.2 352226X2-2RZ 型、353130A 型、353130B 型货车滚动轴承的附件 Accessories for 352226X2-2RZ, 353130A, and 353130B roller bearings of freight cars

197726 型、SKF197726 型、352226X2-2RZ 型滚动轴承都不使用轴箱（用在转 K3 型转向架上除外），除双列双内圈圆锥滚子轴承外，还有后挡、前盖、防松片、标志板、承载鞍、施封锁、轴端螺栓等附属配件。

For 197726, SKF197726, and 352226X2-2RZ roller bearings, the axle box (except for bogie type ZK-3) is not used, and the accessories for them, in addition to the double-row double inner ring tapered roller bearings, include rear retainer ring, front cover, lock washer, signboard, adapter, lead seal, journal end bolts, etc.

1. 后挡 Rear retainer ring

后挡如图 4-16 所示。后挡的凸起檐遮住密封罩后端，起保护作用。后挡的密封座槽为内侧密封座支撑，在老式后挡上有一个通气栓孔，内装通气栓。新式后挡现已取消通气栓。后挡的防尘座槽过盈配合于防尘板座上。后挡的组装图如图 4-17 所示。

The rear retainer ring is shown in Figure 4-16. The raised eave covers the rear end of the sealing cover for protection; the sealing seat groove is for supporting the inner sealing seat; for the old-version rear retainer ring, a vent plug hole is provided and a ventilation bolt is installed in it. The new-version rear retainer ring is not provided with the vent plug. The dust guard seat groove of the rear retainer ring is installed on the dust guard seat via an interference fit. The assembling diagram of the rear retainer ring is shown in Figure 4-17.

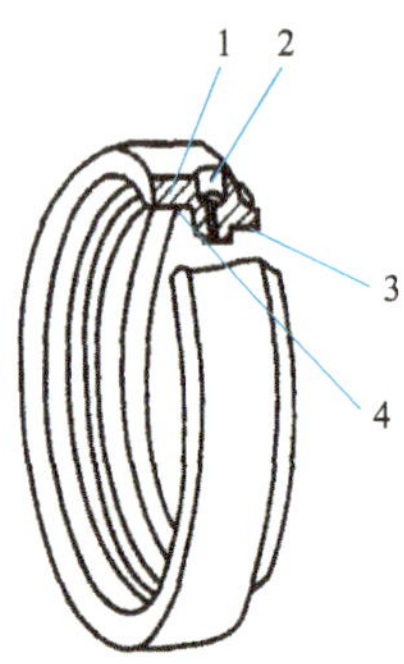

1—凸起檐；2—通气栓孔；3—防尘板座槽；4—密封座槽。
1—Raised eave; 2—Vent plug hole; 3—Dust guard seat groove; 4—Sealing seat groove.

图 4-16 后挡
Figure 4-16 Rear Retainer Ring

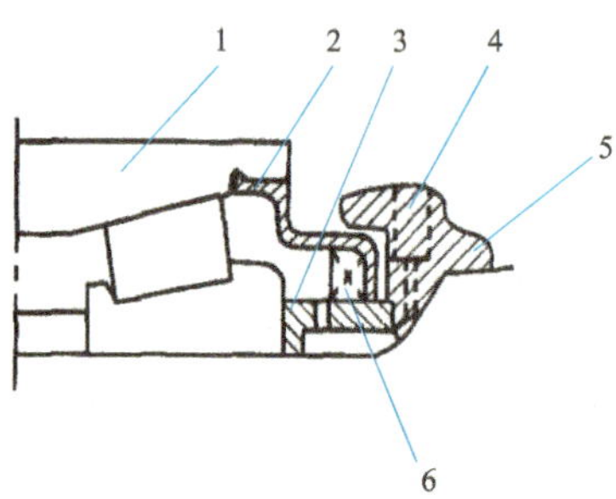

1—外圈；2—密封罩；3—密封座；4—通气栓孔；5—后挡；6—密封圈。
1—Outer ring; 2—Sealing cover; 3—Sealing seat; 4—Vent plug hole; 5—Rear retainer ring; 6—Sealing ring.

图 4-17 后挡的组装图
Figure 4-17 Assembling Diagram of Rear Retainer Ring

2. 前盖 Front cover

前盖如图 4-18 所示，其上有 3 个 M22 螺栓孔，用螺栓固定在车轴端面，作为轴承前端主要支承，压紧外侧密封座。凸起檐起保护密封罩作用。因前盖随车轴转动，前盖又称旋转前盖。

The front cover, as shown in Figure 4-18, has three M22 bolt holes, and is bolted to the end face of the axle for working as the main support for the front end of the bearing and pressing the outer sealing seat. The raised eave is for protecting the sealing cover. The front cover rotates with the axle, thus it is also called a rotating front cover.

3. 防松片

Lock washer

防松片由厚 1.5 mm 的钢板压制而成，如图 4–19 所示。轴端螺栓穿过防松片和轴承前盖后，把螺栓拧紧，将止耳翘起，挡住螺栓头部，防止其松动。每个防松片只可以使用一次，以免止耳裂损失去止转作用。

The lock washer is pressed from a 1.5 mm-thick steel sheet as shown in Figure 4-19. After the shaft end bolt passes through the lock washer and the bearing front cover, tighten the bolt, it is required to raise the stop lug to block the bolt head from loosening. Each lock washer can only be used once, so as to prevent the failure of the rotation locking function in case of stop lug cracking.

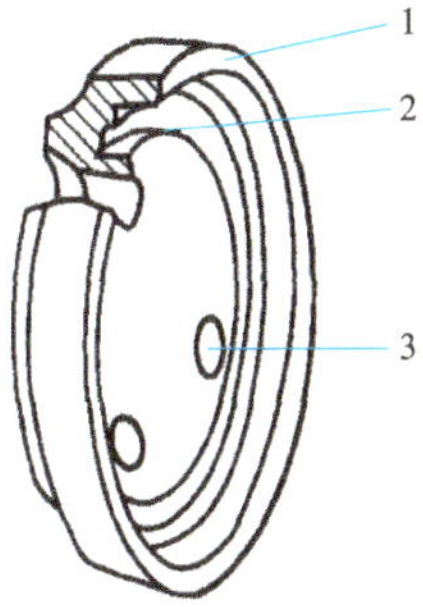

1—凸起檐；2—密封座槽；3—螺栓孔。

1—Raised eave; 2—Sealing seat groove; 3—Bolt hole.

图 4–18　前盖

Figure 4-18　Front Cover

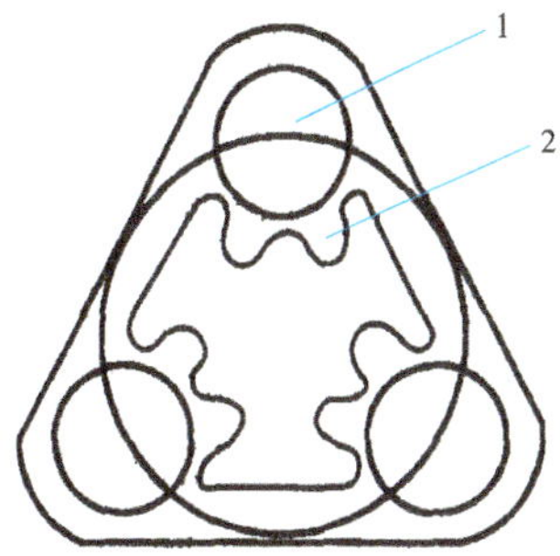

1—螺栓孔；2—止耳。

1—Bolt hole; 2—Stop lug.

图 4–19　防松片

Figure 4-19　Lock Washer

任务 4.2　客车滚动轴承装置

Task 4.2　Roller bearing for passenger cars

4.2.1　客车滚动轴承的结构和种类

Structure and types of roller bearings for passenger cars

铁路车辆用滚动轴承均配置在簧下，除承受车辆载荷外，还直接承受着轮轨间发生的振动、冲击，其可靠性直接关系行车安全，因此要求轴承耐振、耐冲击、寿命高、维护检修方便且要有较小的尺寸和重量。所以，铁路车辆轴承均设计为非标准系列的形式，并多采用滚动体为向心滚子的轴承。我国铁路车辆主要采用圆柱滚子轴承和圆锥滚子轴承。

Roller bearings for railway vehicles are placed under the spring for bearing car load as well as directly bearing the vibration and impact between the wheels and rails, and their reliability is directly related to driving safety. Therefore, features including vibration resistance, impact resistance, long service life, convenient maintenance, small size, and low weight are required for the bearings. In view of this, bearings for railway vehicles are designed as non-standard series and applied with radial rollers as rolling elements. Roller bearings used on railway vehicles in China mainly include cylindrical roller bearings and tapered roller bearings.

我国铁路客车上应用的滚动轴承均为单列向心短圆柱滚子轴承（简称圆柱轴承），主要有以下几种型式：42724QT 型、152724QT 型、42726QT 型、152726QT 型、NJ3226X1 型、NJP3226X1 型。42726QT 型和 152726QT 型曾是我国铁路客车主型轴承，大量装用于各型客车车辆转向架上。但随着铁路运输的不断发展，列车运行速度不断提高，该型轴承已不能满足运用要求。因此，当时铁道部规定：自 2001 年 1 月 1 日起停止生产 42726QT 型、152726QT 型轴承（现有库存产品允许继续使用，用完为止），改为生产 NJ3226X1 型、NJP3226Xl 型轴承，其外形尺寸与 42726QT 型、152726QT 型相同。25K 等客车采用 SKFBC1B322880AB、SKFBC1B322881AB 及日本 NSK 公司生产的 NSK42，结构与国产轴承相似，但精度较高。

The roller bearings used in passenger cars of China are single-row radial short cylindrical roller bearings (hereinafter referred to as cylindrical bearings) of the following types: 42724QT, 152724QT, 42726QT, 152726QT, NJ3226X1, and NJP3226X1. The 42726QT bearing and 152726QT bearing used to be mainstream bearings used in passenger cars, and were widely installed on bogies of passenger cars of various types. However, with the continuous development of railway transportation and the continuous increase of train operation speed, they became unable to meet the application requirements anymore. Therefore, Ministry of Railway specified to stop the production of 42726QT and 152726QT bearings (existing stock products are allowed to be used until they are used up) since January 1, 2001 and start the production of NJ3226X1 and NJP3226Xl bearings which have the same overall dimensions as the original 42726QT and 152726QT bearings. Passenger cars such as 25K are applied with the SKFBC1B322880AB bearing, SKFBC1B322881AB bearing as well as NSK42 bearing manufactured by NSK in Japan, which are similar to domestically-produced bearings in structure, but have a higher precision.

下面将着重以 NJ3226X1 型、NJP3226X1 型轴承为例来介绍圆柱滚子轴承。

The cylindrical roller bearings will be introduced with NJ3226X1 bearings and NJP3226X1 bearings as examples.

圆柱滚子轴承的结构、基本尺寸如图 4–20、图 4–21 所示。圆柱滚孔子轴承由内圈、外圈、滚动体（滚子）、保持架组成。外圈两侧带有挡边，内圈只有一侧有固定单挡边（或活动平挡圈），保持架、滚动体和外圈组合成一个组件，与内圈可以互相分离。圆柱滚子轴承的形式及基本尺寸如表 4–2 和图 4–21 所示。

The structure, form, and basic dimensions of cylindrical roller bearings are shown in Figure 4-20 and Figure 4-21. The cylindrical roller bearing is composed of an inner ring, outer ring, rolling elements (rollers), and cage. The outer ring is provided with ribs on both sides, but the inner ring is only provided with a fixed single rib (or a movable flat retainer ring) on one side. The cage, rolling element, and outer ring are combined into an assembly, which can be separated from the inner ring. The type and basic dimensions of cylindrical roller bearings are shown in Table 4-2 and Figure 4-21.

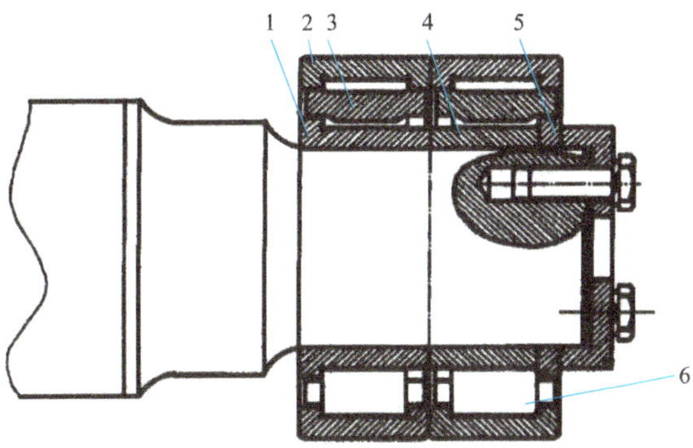

1—内圈（有固定挡边）；2—外圈；3—保持架；
4—内圈（无固定挡边）；5—平挡圈；6—滚子。
1—Inner ring (with fixed rib); 2—Outer ring; 3—Cage;
4—Inner ring (without fixed rib); 5—Flat retainer ring; 6—Roller.

图 4-20　圆柱滚子轴承的结构
Figure 4-20　Structure of Cylindrical Roller Bearing

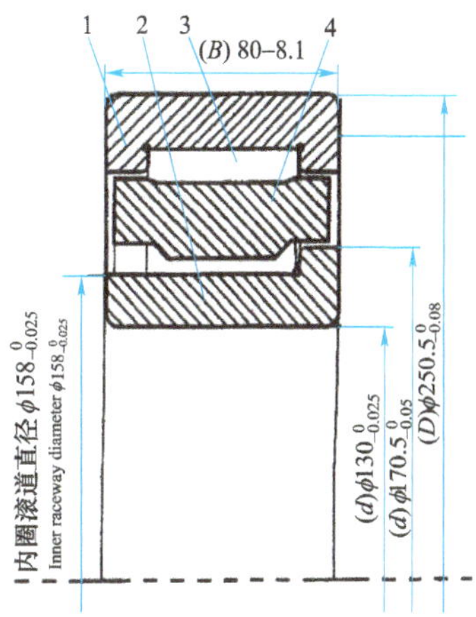

1—外圈；2—内圈；3—滚子；4—保持架。
1—Outer ring; 2—Inner ring; 3—Roller; 4—Cage.

图 4-21　圆柱滚子轴承的形式及基本尺寸
Figure 4-21　Types and Basic Dimensions of Cylindrical Roller Bearing

表 4-2　圆柱滚子轴承的基本尺寸　　**单位：mm**
Table 4-2 Basic Dimensions of Cylindrical Roller Bearing　　**Unit: mm**

型　号 Model	外形尺寸 Overall dimension			滚　子 Roller			内圈外径 Inner ring
	d	*D*	*B*	数量 Quantity	直径 Diameter	高度 Height	
NJ(P)3226X1	130	250	80	14	32	52	158
进口轴承 Imported bearing	130	250	80	14	32	52	158

1. 内圈
Inner ring

内圈与轴颈为过盈配合。圆柱滚子轴承的内圈、平挡圈示意图如图 4-22 所示。NJ3226X1 型轴承的内圈有固定单挡边，NJP3226X1 型轴承的内圈没有固定挡边，而设有活动平挡圈。

The inner ring is assembled with the journal via an interference fit. The inner ring and flat retainer ring of the cylindrical roller bearing are shown in Figure 4-22. The inner ring of the NJ3226X1 rearing has a fixed single rib, while the inner ring of the NJP3226X1 bearing is provided with a movable flat retainer ring instead of a fixed rib.

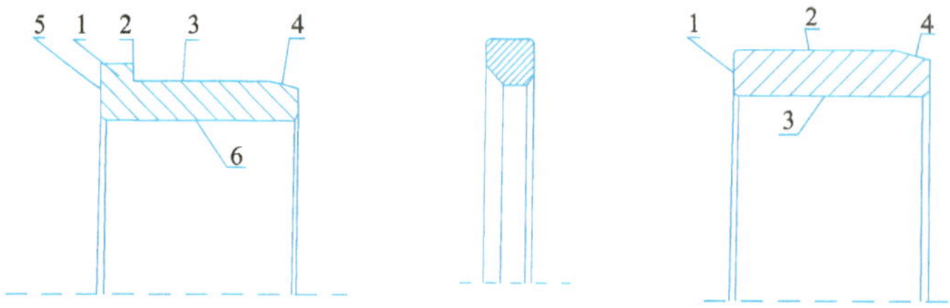

1—挡边；2—沟槽；3—滚道面；
4—斜坡；5—端面；6—内径面。
1—Rib; 2—Groove; 3—Raceway surface;
4—Slope; 5—End face; 6—Inner diameter surface.
(a) 内圈（有固定挡边）
Inner ring (with fixed rib)

(b) 平挡圈
Flat retainer ring

1—端面；2—滚动面；
3—内径面；4—斜坡。
1—Inner diameter surface; 2—Rolling surface;
3—Inner diameter surface; 4—Slope.
(c) 内圈（无固定挡边）
Inner ring (without fixed rib)

图 4-22 圆柱滚子轴承的内圈、平挡圈示意图

Figure 4-22 Schematic Diagram of Inner Ring and Flat Retainer Ring of Cylindrical Roller Bearing

内圈、平挡圈按内径大小不同分为三个级别，其标志与内径尺寸如图 4-23 和表 4-3 所示。

The inner ring and flat retainer ring are classified into three grades according to the inner diameter, and their markings and inner diameters are shown in Figure 4-23 and Table 4-3.

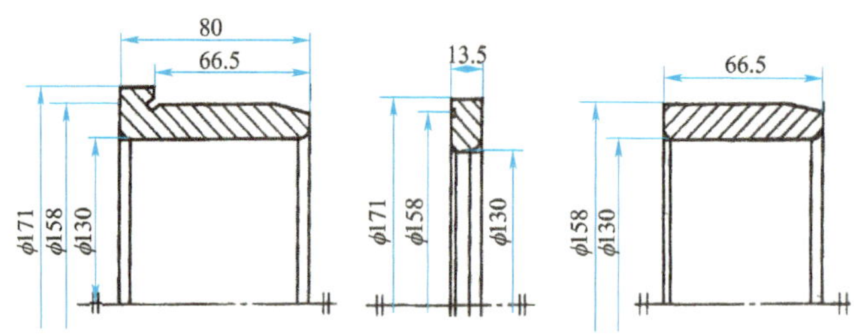

(a) NJ3226X1 型轴承的内圈
Inner ring of NJ3226X1 bearing

(b) 平挡圈
Flat retainer ring

(c) NJP3226X1 型轴承的内圈
Inner ring of NJP3226X1 bearing

图 4-23 圆柱滚子轴承内圈、平挡圈的基本尺寸

Figure 4-23 Basic Dimensions of Inner Ring and Flat Retainer Ring of Cylindrical Roller Bearing

表 4-3 圆柱滚子轴承内圈、平挡圈分类等级表

Table 4-3 Table of Classified Grade of Inner Ring and Flat Retainer Ring of Cylindrical Roller Bearing

等 级 Grade	内圈标志 Inner ring marking	内径尺寸/mm Inner diameter/mm	内圈标志 Inner ring marking	内径尺寸/mm Inner diameter/mm	平挡圈标志 Flat retainer ring marking	内径尺寸/mm Inner diameter/mm
原型 Prototype	NJ3226X1	130	NJP3226X1	130	NJP3226X1	130
第一等级 First grade	NJ3226XlK1	129.5	NJP3226XlK1	129.5	NJP3226XIK1	129.5
第二等级 Second grade	NJ3226XlK2	129	NJP3226XIK2	129	NJP3226XIK2	129

2. 外圈

Outer ring

外圈与轴箱筒体为间隙配合。外圈内滚道面为滚子滚道，且两边都有固定挡边。圆柱滚

子轴承的外圈示意图及基本尺寸如图 4–24 所示。

The outer ring is assembled with the axle box tube via clearance fit, and the inner rolling surface of the outer ring is roller raceway, and provides fixed rib on both sides. The schematic diagram and basic dimensions of outer ring of cylindrical roller bearing are as shown in Figure 4-24.

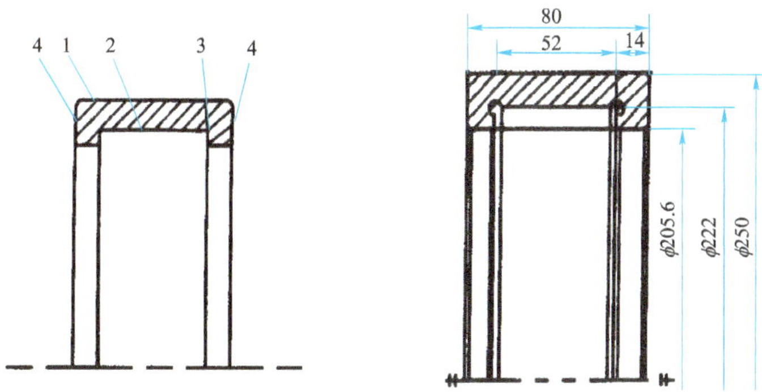

1—外径面；2—滚道；3—挡边；4—端面。

1—Outer diameter surface; 2—Raceway; 3—Rib; 4—End face.

图 4–24　圆柱滚子轴承的外圈示意图及基本尺寸

Figure 4-24　Schematic Diagram and Basic Dimensions of Outer Ring of Cylindrical Roller Bearing

3. 滚子

Roller

滚子为圆柱形。为了使滚子受力后应力均匀分布，滚子两端允许按双点线（ϕ18.5 mm）制作平端面，平端面的表面粗糙度为 *Ra*0.2 μm，并可制作 ϕ14 mm、深 1 mm 的凹穴。滚子承受载荷并产生滚动作用，滚子处于轴径水平中心线上侧时受力，处于下侧时不受力。圆柱滚子轴承滚子的示意图及基本尺寸如图 4–25 所示。

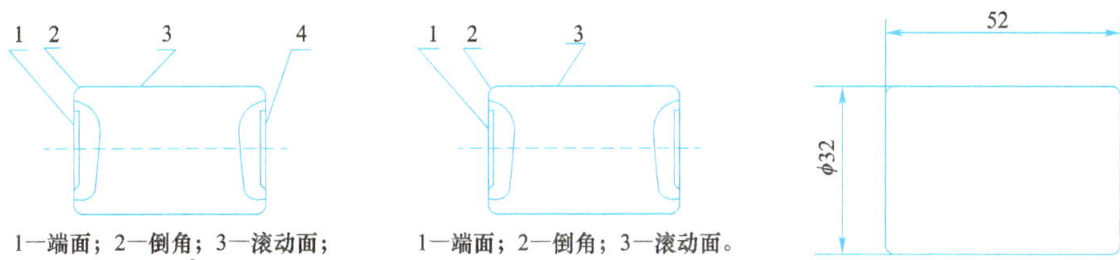

1—端面；2—倒角；3—滚动面；4—凹窝。
1—End face; 2—Chamfer; 3—Rolling surface; 4—Dimple.
(a) 普通轴承滚子
Ordinary bearing roller

1—端面；2—倒角；3—滚动面。
1—End face; 2—Chamfer; 3—Rolling surface.
(b) 国产提速、进口轴承滚子
Domestic speed-up/imported bearing rollers

(c) 基本尺寸
Basic dimensions

图 4–25　圆柱滚子轴承滚子的示意图及基本尺寸

Figure 4-25　Schematic Diagram and Basic Dimensions of Rollers of Cylindrical Roller Bearing

The roller is cylindrical. To ensure a uniform stress distribution on the roller, it is allowed to machine the ends of the roller to be flat end faces according to double dotted lines (ϕ 18.5 mm) with a surface roughness of Ra0.2 μm, and process dimples with a diameter of ϕ 14 mm and depth of 1 mm on them. The roller bears the load and rolls. The roller is stressed on the upper side of the horizontal center line of the axle diameter, and not stressed on the lower side of the horizontal center line of the axle diameter. The schematic diagram and basic dimensions of rollers of cylindrical roller bearing are as shown in Figure 4-25.

4. 保持架

Cage

保持架的作用是保持滚子沿滚道均匀分布，不发生偏斜，从而合理分布载荷。滚子从保持架兜孔外侧放入保持架正常位置后再向内移动一段距离，但不能从兜孔内侧脱出，使滚子装入后整体外圆直径小于外圈挡边内径。然后套上外圈，再装进内圈，使轴承成为一个整体。圆柱滚子轴承保持架的示意图及基本尺寸如图 4–26 所示。

The cage is intended for keeping the rollers evenly distributed along the raceway without deflection, to ensure that the load is reasonably distributed. After the roller is placed in the normal position from the outside of the cage pocket, it is required to move it inward for some distance so that it will not come out from the inside of the pocket, so that the overall outer circle diameter after the roller is installed is smaller than the inner diameter of the outer ring rib. Then the outer ring and inner ring should be installed to end the assembling of the bearing. The schematic diagram and basic dimensions of cage of cylindrical roller bearing are as shown in Figure 4-26.

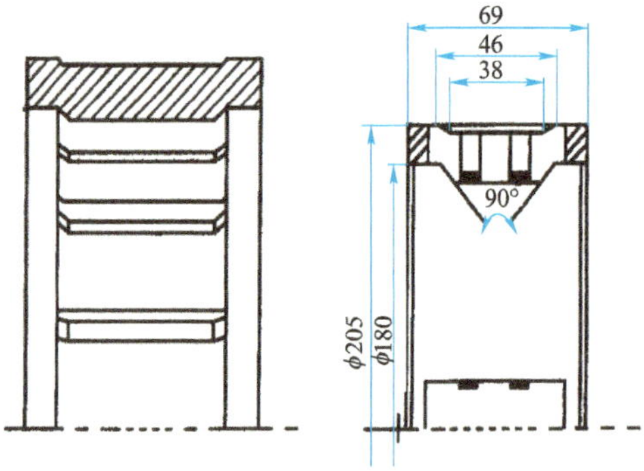

图 4–26　圆柱滚子轴承保持架的示意图及基本尺寸

Figure 4-26　Schematic Diagram and Basic Dimensions of Cage of Cylindrical Roller Bearing

客车轴承主要零件的材质如表 4–4 所示。

The material of the main parts of bearings for passenger cars is shown in Table 4-4.

表 4–4　客车轴承主要零件的材质

Table 4-4　Material of Main Parts of Bearings for Passenger Cars

型　号 Model	零件名称 Part name	材　料 Material
NJ(P)3226X1	外圈 Outer ring	GCr18Mo 钢（GB/T 18254—2016） Steel GCr18Mo (GB/T 18254—2016)
	内圈 Inner ring	GCr18Mo 钢（GB/T 18254—2016） Steel GCr18Mo (GB/T 18254—2016)
	滚子 Roller	GCr15 钢（GB/T 18254—2016） Steel GCr15 (GB/T 18254—2016)

续表
Continued

型　号 Model	零件名称 Part name	材　料 Material
NJ(P)3226X1	保持架 Cage	ZCuAL10Fe3Mn2 铝青铜（GB/T 1176—2013） Aluminium bronze ZCuAL10Fe3Mn2 (GB/T 1176—2013)
	平挡圈 Flat retainer ring	GCr18Mo 钢（GB/T 18254—2016） Steel GCr18Mo (GB/T 18254—2016)

4.2.2　客车滚动轴承的制造标记 Manufacturing markings of roller bearings for passenger cars

轴承制造标记有轴承型号、轴承制造厂代号和轴承制造年月。轴承制造标记分别刻写在内圈大端面和外圈端面上，轴承型号、轴承制造厂代号和轴承制造年月按顺序在圆周上均布。

The manufacturing markings of bearings include bearing model, bearing manufacturer code, and bearing manufacture date (including year and month). The manufacturing markings are respectively engraved on the large end face of the inner ring and the end face of the outer ring, with the bearing model, bearing manufacturer code, and bearing manufacturing date (including year and month) evenly distributed on the circumference in sequence.

轴承制造标记为永久性标记，须刻写清晰、易识别，可采用机械滚（挤）压、激光刻字或其他经过批准的方式刻写，标记字体高 5 mm。NJ(P)3226X1 型滚动轴承的制造标记示意图如图 4–27 所示。

The bearing manufacturing marking shall be permanent and legible and can be made by mechanical rolling (squeezing), laser engraving, or other approved methods, with a font height of 5 mm. The manufacturing marking of the NJ(P)3226X1 roller bearing is shown in Figure 4-27.

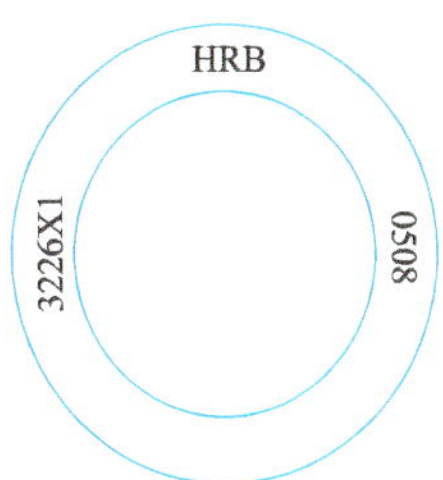

（a）外圈端面上刻写标记
Marking engraved on the end face of the outer ring

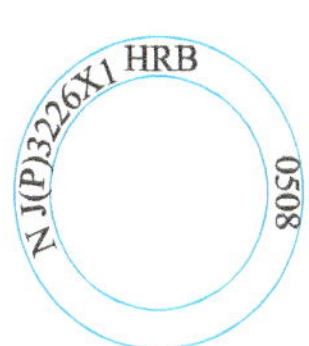

（b）内圈大端面上刻写标记
Marking engraved on the large end face of the inner ring

图 4–27　NJ(P)3226X1 型滚动轴承的制造标记示意图
Figure 4-27　Schematic Diagram Manufacturing Marking of NJ(P)3226X1 Roller Bearing

4.2.3 圆柱滚子轴承的轴箱装置

Axle box assembly of cylindrical roller bearing

我国客车上采用的滚动轴承轴箱装置按密封形式不同可分为橡胶油封密封式轴箱装置和金属迷宫密封式轴箱装置。

The roller bearing axle box assemblies used in passenger cars in China are classified according to sealing method into rubber oil seal type axle box assembly and metal labyrinth seal type axle box assembly.

1. 橡胶油封密封式轴箱装置

Rubber oil seal type axle box assembly

这种装置由轴箱体、轴箱后盖、防尘挡圈、橡胶油封、轴箱前盖、压板等组成，其结构如图 4–28 所示。

This type of axle box assembly is composed of an axle box body, axle box rear cover, dust retaining ring, rubber oil seal, axle box front cover, pressing plate, etc., as shown in Figure 4-28.

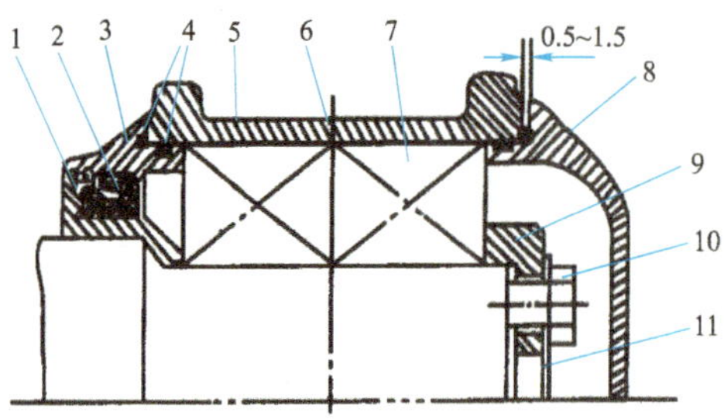

1—防尘挡圈；2—橡胶油封；3—轴箱后盖；4—密封圈；5—轴箱体；6—轴温报警器安装孔；7—圆柱滚子轴承；8—轴箱前盖；9—压板；10—压板螺栓；11—防松片。

1—Dust retaining ring; 2—Rubber oil seal; 3—Axle box rear cover; 4—Sealing ring; 5—Axle box body; 6—Axle temperature alarm mounting hole; 7—Cylindrical roller bearing; 8—Axle box front cover; 9—Pressing plate; 10—Pressing plate bolt; 11—Lock washer.

图 4–28　橡胶油封密封式轴箱装置的结构

Figure 4-28　Rubber Oil Seal Type Axle Box Assembly

（1）轴箱体。轴箱体为铸钢筒形结构，两侧铸有弹簧托盘，用来安装轴箱弹簧等配件，如图 4–29 所示。筒两端各有 4 个轴箱耳，分别与轴箱前、后盖用螺栓连接。轴箱筒内安装滚动轴承，与轴承外圈为间隙配合。其主要作用是组装、支承各零件，连接构架，传递载荷。

Axle box body. The axle box body takes a cast steel tube structure, with spring trays cast on both sides for installing axle box springs and other accessories, as shown in Figure 4-29. There are 4 axle box lugs at each end of the tube, which are respectively connected with the front and rear covers of the axle box by bolts. The axle box tube is housed with a roller bearing and is assembled with the bearing outer ring via an interference fit. Its main functions include assembling and supporting the parts, connecting the frames, and transmitting loads.

（2）轴箱后盖。如图 4–30 所示，轴箱后盖的内侧凸起缘嵌入轴箱体筒内，支承内侧轴承外圈。在凸起缘外圆周面上和根部设有密封圈槽，用以安装密封圈。在内圆周面安装橡胶油封。

Axle box rear cover. The axle box rear cover supports the outer bearing outer ring with the inner flange embedded in the axle box body tube, as shown in Figure 4-30. A sealing ring groove is provided on the outer circumferential surface and the root of the flange for installing the sealing ring. A rubber oil seal is installed on the inner circumferential surface.

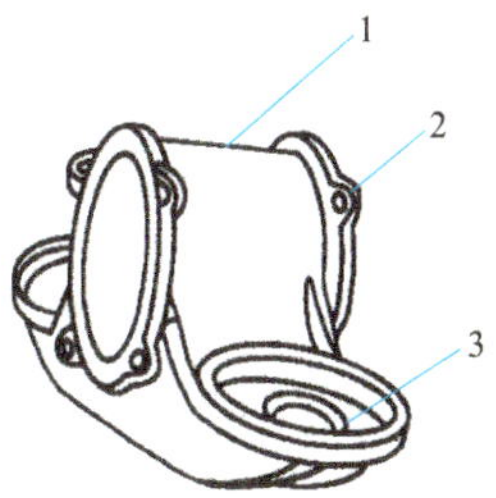

1—轴箱筒；2—轴箱耳；3—弹簧托盘。
1—Axle box tube; 2—Axle box lug; 3—Spring tray.

图 4-29　橡胶油封密封式轴箱装置的轴箱体
Figure 4-29　Axle Box Body of Rubber Oil Seal Type Axle Box Assembly

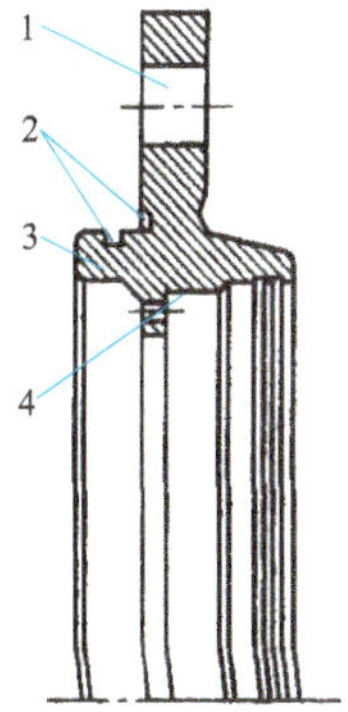

1—螺栓孔；2—密封圈槽；3—凸起缘；4—橡胶油封座。
1—Bolt hole, 2—Sealing ring groove; 3—Flange, 4—Rubber oil seal seat.

图 4-30　橡胶油封密封式轴箱装置的轴箱后盖
Figure 4-30　Axle Box Rear Cover of Rubber Oil Seal Type Axle Box Assembly

（3）防尘挡圈。防尘挡圈如图 4-31 所示，过盈配合于车轴防尘板座上，与橡胶油封配合起密封作用，其内圆周端面支承内侧轴承内圈端面。

Dust retaining ring. As shown in Figure 4-31, the dust retaining ring is mounted on the axle dust guard seat via an interference fit, and works with the rubber oil seal for sealing, with its inner circumferential end face supporting the end face of the inner bearing inner ring.

（4）橡胶油封。橡胶油封如图 4-32 所示，内有钢骨架，以增加其刚度。橡胶油封安装在轴箱后盖内圆周面上，与防尘挡圈配合。

Rubber oil seal. The rubber oil seal, as shown in Figure 4-32, is provided with a steel frame inside to increase its rigidity. The rubber oil seal is installed on the inner circumferential surface of the axle box rear cover and works in cooperation with the dust retaining ring.

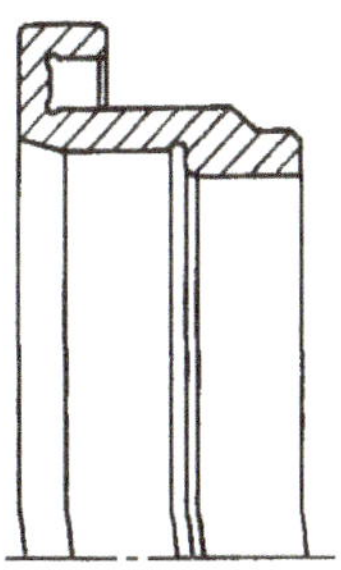

图 4-31　橡胶油封密封式轴箱装置的防尘挡圈
Figure 4-31　Dust Retaining Ring of Rubber Oil Seal Type Axle Box Assembly

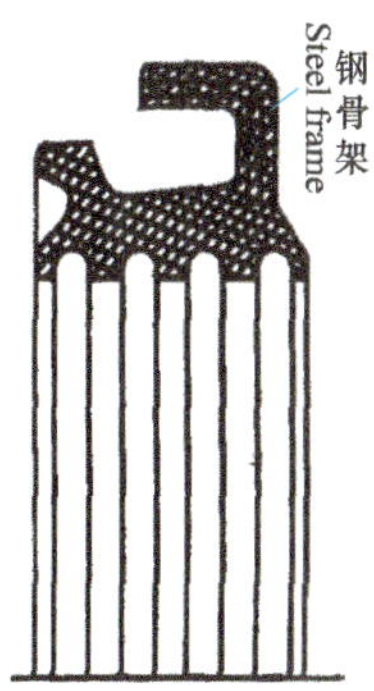

图 4-32　橡胶油封密封式轴箱装置的橡胶油封
Figure 4-32　Rubber Oil Seal of Rubber Oil Seal Type Axle Box Assembly

（5）轴箱前盖。轴箱前盖如图 4–33 所示，内侧凸起缘嵌入轴箱体筒内，支承外侧轴承外圈。在凸起缘外圆周上和根部设有密封圈槽，以安装密封圈。其作用是密封轴箱前部。橡胶油封密封式和金属迷宫密封式轴箱密封装置的前盖构造相同。

Axle box front cover. The axle box front cover supports the outer bearing outer ring with the inner flange embedded in the axle box body tube, as shown in Figure 4-33. A sealing ring groove is provided on the outer circumferential surface and the root of the flange for installing the sealing ring. It is intended for sealing the front part of the axle box. The front covers for rubber oil seal type axle box sealing assembly and metal labyrinth seal type axle box sealing assembly are similar in structure.

轴箱前盖组装时，其凸起缘必须压紧外侧轴承外圈端面。为此，前盖外缘与轴箱体前端面必须留有 0.5～1.5 mm 的间隙。

When assembling the axle box front cover, its flange must be pressed against the end face of the outer bearing outer ring. For this reason, a clearance of 0.5–1.5 mm must be reserved between the front cover flange and the axle box body front end face.

（6）压板。压板用 3 个螺栓固定在车轴端面上，在螺栓和压板之间安装防松片，以防止螺栓松动。压板内侧凸起缘顶在外侧轴承内圈端面，起支承作用。橡胶油封密封式和金属迷宫密封式轴箱密封装置的压板结构相同，如图 4–34 所示。

Pressing plate. The pressing plate is fixed on the end face of the axle with 3 bolts, and a lock washer is installed between the bolts and the pressing plate to prevent the bolts from loosening. The inner flange of the pressing plate is pressed against the end face of the outer bearing inner ring for support. The pressing plates for rubber oil seal type axle box sealing assembly and metal labyrinth seal type axle box sealing assembly are similar in structure, as shown in Figure 4-34.

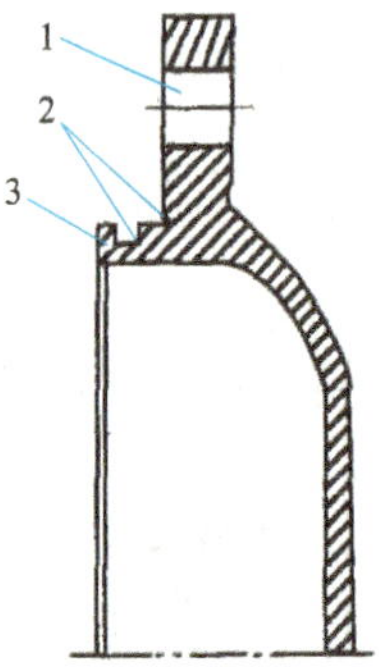

1—螺栓孔；2—密封圈槽；3—凸起缘。

1—Bolt hole; 2—Sealing ring groove; 3—Flange.

图 4–33 橡胶油封密封式轴箱装置的轴箱前盖

Figure 4-33 Axle Box Front Cover of Rubber Oil Seal Type Axle Box Assembly

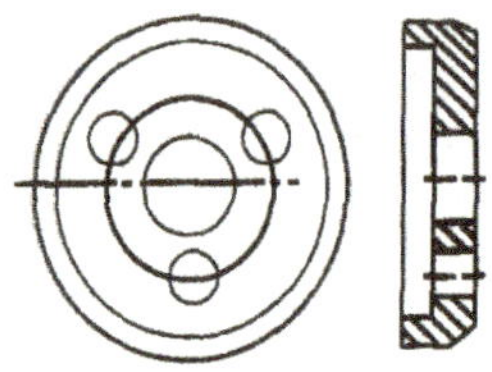

图 4–34 橡胶油封密封式轴箱装置的压板

Figure 4-34 Pressing Plate of Rubber Oil Seal Type Axle Box Assembly

采用 RD_4（RC_4）型车轴的轴箱装置，车轴一端安装有发电机皮带轮，如图 4–35 所示，除轴箱前盖和前端密封与 RD_3（RC_4）轴箱不同外，其余部分均相同。

The RD_4 (RC_4) axle box assembly is adopted, with a generator pulley installed at one end of the axle, as shown in Figure 4-35. This type of axle box assembly is basically the same as the RD_3 (RC_4) axle box, except for the front cover and front seal.

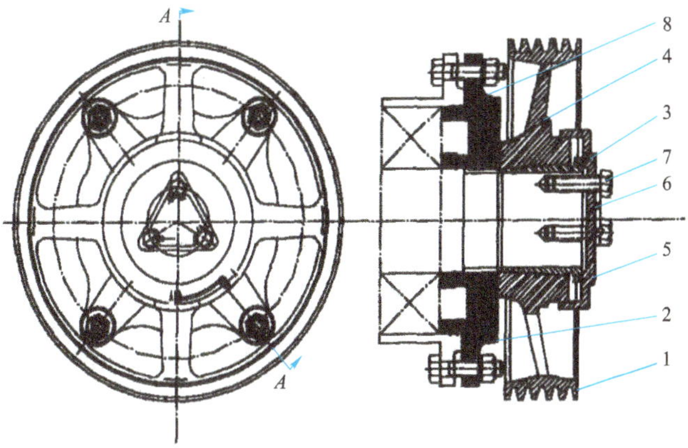

1—轴端三角皮带轮；2—轴箱前盖；3—退卸套；5—轴端压盖；6—防松片；7—螺栓；8—O 形密封圈。
1—Axle end V-belt pulley; 2—Axle box front cover; 3—Withdrawal sleeve; 5—Axle end gland; 6—Lock washer; 7—Bolt; 8—O-ring.

图 4-35　带轴端皮带轮传动装置的轴箱
Figure 4-35　Axle Box with Axle End Pulley Drive

2. 金属迷宫密封式轴箱装置
Metal labyrinth seal type axle box assembly

这种结构的轴箱，不带轴箱后盖，在轴箱体后端设有迷宫槽，迷宫槽的底部设有排水孔。在轴箱筒内后端设有凸台，以支承内侧轴承的外圈，其结构如图 4-36 所示。

The axle box of this structure does not have a rear cover, a labyrinth groove is provided at the rear end, and a water drain is provided at the bottom of the labyrinth groove. A boss is provided at the inner rear end of the axle box tube to support the outer ring of the inner bearing. The structure of this type of axle box assembly is shown in Figure 4-36.

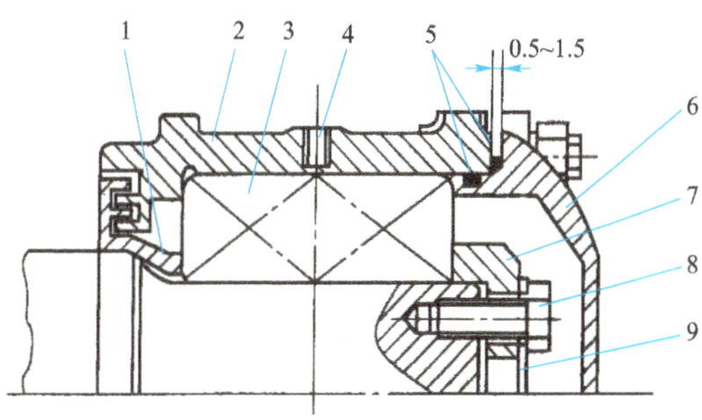

1—防尘挡圈；2—轴箱体；3—圆柱滚子轴承；4—轴温报警器安装孔；
5—密封图；6—轴箱前盖；7—压板；8—压板螺栓；9—防松片。
1—Dust retaining ring; 2—Axle box body; 3—Cylindrical roller bearing; 4—Axle temperature alarm mounting hole;
5—Seal; 6—Axle box front cover; 7—Pressing plate; 8—Pressing plate bolt; 9—Lock washer.

图 4-36　金属迷宫密封式轴箱装置的结构
Figure 4-36　Metal Labyrinth Seal Type Axle Box Assembly

（1）轴箱体。轴箱体与橡胶油封密封式轴箱装置的轴箱体基本相同，所不同的是轴箱体后端不设轴箱耳（没有轴箱后盖），而设有迷宫槽，与防尘挡圈迷宫槽配合，起密封作用，并在轴箱筒内的后端设有凸台，以支承内侧轴承的外圈，如图 4–37 所示。

Axle box body. The axle box body of this type of axle box assembly is basically the same as the rubber oil seal type axle box assembly, except that the rear end of the axle box body is not provided with an axle box lug (as there is no axle box rear cover) but with a labyrinth seal groove, which works with the dust retaining ring labyrinth groove for sealing, and a boss is designed in the rear end of axle box tube to support the inner bearing outer ring, as shown in Figure 4-37.

CW–2 型准高速客车转向架采用了转臂式轴箱定位装置，其轴箱装置采用金属迷宫密封式，轴承为短圆柱滚子轴承。轴箱体只有一侧铸有弹簧托盘，弹簧托盘外侧铸有垂直液压减振器安装孔和轴箱控制杆定位销孔；轴箱体的另一侧铸有弹性定位套孔。轴箱体通过弹性定位套与构架上的定位座相连。轴箱结构的设计可使垂直载荷在轴箱弹簧和弹性定位套之间的分配比例为 2:1，这样可改善轴箱弹簧受力状态。转臂式轴箱的外形结构如图 4–38 所示。

For bogie type CW-2 on the quasi-high-speed passenger car, a rotary arm axle box guidance device is applied, and the axle box assembly is equipped with the metal labyrinth seal and the short cylindrical roller bearing. Only one side of the axle box is cast with a spring tray, and the outer side of the spring tray is cast with a vertical hydraulic damper mounting hole and an axle box control lever positioning pin hole; the other side of the axle box is cast with an elastic positioning bushing hole. It is connected with the positioning seat on the frame through the elastic positioning bushing. The axle box is so structurally designed that the distribution ratio of the vertical load between the axle box spring and the elastic positioning bushing is 2:1, thus improving the stressing state of the axle box spring. The outer structure of the rotary arm axle box is shown in Figure 4-38.

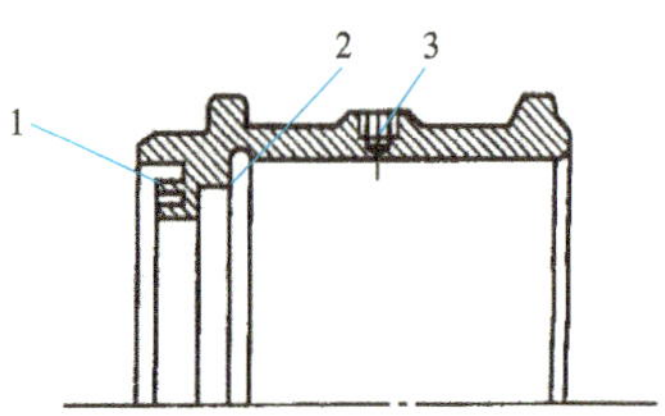

1—迷宫；2—台阶；3—轴温报警器安装孔。
1—Labyrinth; 2—Step; 3—Axle temperature alarm mounting hole.

图 4–37 金属迷宫密封式轴箱装置的轴箱体
Figure 4-37 Axle Box Body of Metal Labyrinth Seal Type Axle Box Assembly

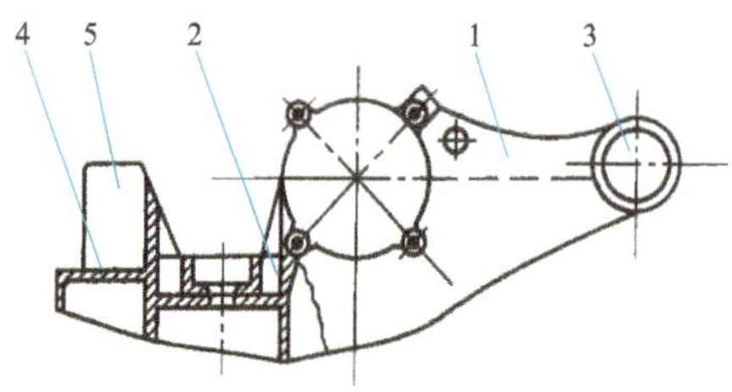

1—轴箱体；2—弹簧托盘；3—弹性定位套孔；
4—液压减振器安装孔；5—轴箱控制杆座。
1—Axle box body; 2—Spring tray; 3—Elastic positioning bushing hole; 4—Hydraulic damper mounting hole; 5—Axle box control lever seat.

图 4–38 转臂式轴箱的外形结构
Figure 4-38 Rotary Arm Axle Box of Metal Labyrinth Seal Type Axle Box Assembly

（2）防尘挡圈。防尘挡圈与防尘板座过盈配合，其外圆设有迷宫槽，与轴箱体上的迷宫槽配合。内圆端面支承内侧轴承内圈大端面，如图 4–39 所示。

Dust retaining ring. The dust retaining ring is assembled with the dust guard seat via an interference fit, and its outer circle is provided with a labyrinth seal groove, which works in cooperation with the labyrinth seal groove on the axle box body. The inner circle end face supports the end face of the inner bearing inner ring, as shown in Figure 4-39.

（3）安装发电机皮带轮车轴轴箱前盖装置。这种装置由前盖和顶套等组成，如图 4-40 所示。

Axle box front cover assembly for installing generator pulley. This assembly consists of a front cover and a top bushing, as shown in Figure 4-40.

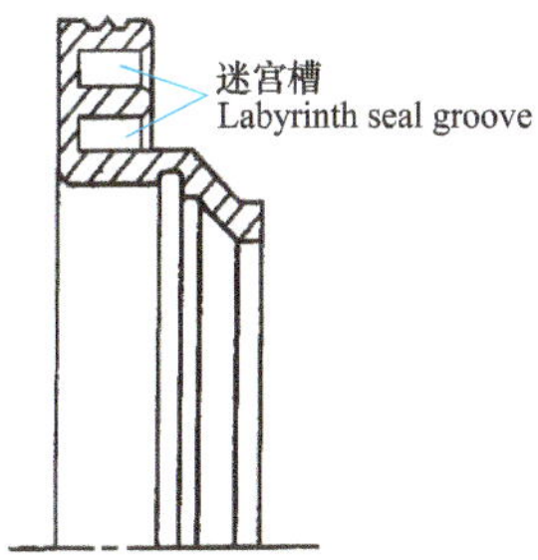

图 4-39　金属迷宫密封式轴箱装置的防尘挡圈
Figure 4-39　Dust Retaining Ring of Metal Labyrinth Seal Type Axle Box Assembly

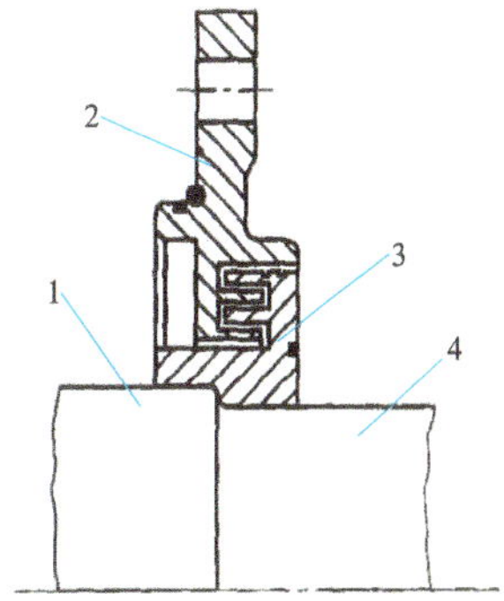

1—轴颈；2—前盖；3—顶套；4—皮带轮座。
1—Journal; 2—Front cover; 3—Top bushing; 4—Pulley seat.

图 4-40　安装发电机皮带轮车轴轴箱前盖装置
Figure 4-40　Axle Box Front Cover Assembly for Installing Generator Pulley

① 前盖。与一般前盖基本相同，中间为一透孔，设有迷宫槽，与顶套迷宫槽配合，起密封作用，如图 4-41 所示。

Front cover. Basically the same as the general front cover, it is provided with a through hole in the middle, and a labyrinth seal groove, which works in cooperation with the labyrinth seal groove on the top bushing for sealing, as shown in Figure 4-41.

② 顶套。顶套外圆设有迷宫槽，与前盖迷宫槽配合。内圆端面支承外侧轴承的内圈。外端面上设有密封圈槽，以安装密封圈，与皮带轮配合起密封作用，如图 4-42 所示。

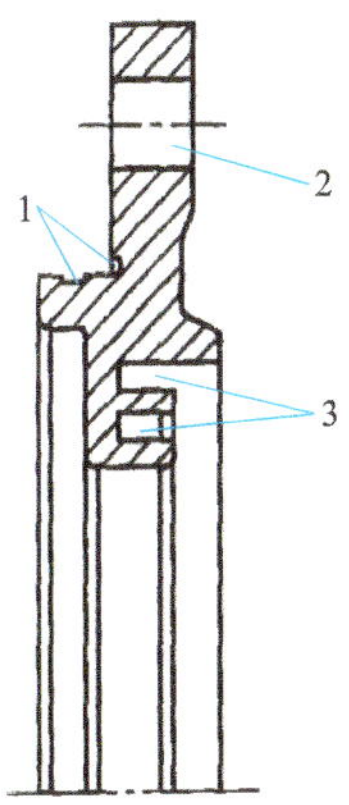

1—密封圈槽；2—螺栓孔；3—迷宫槽。
1—Sealing ring groove; 2—Bolt hole; 3—Labyrinth seal groove.

图 4-41　前盖
Figure 4-41　Front Cover

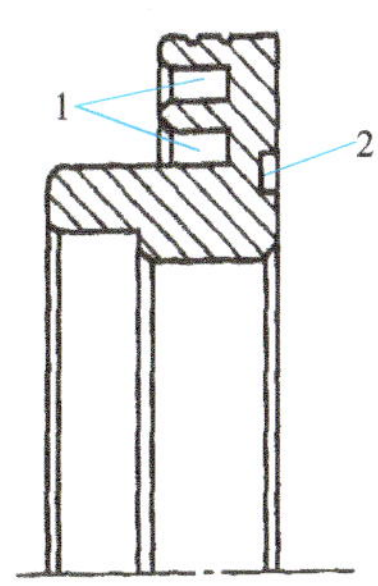

1—迷宫槽；2—密封圈槽。
1—Labyrinth seal groove; 2—Sealing ring groove.

图 4-42　顶套
Figure 4-42　Top Bushing

Top bushing. The outer circle of the top bushing is provided with a labyrinth seal groove, which works in cooperation with the labyrinth seal groove on the front cover for sealing. The inner circle end face supports the outer bearing inner ring. A sealing ring groove is provided on the outer end surface for the installation of the sealing ring, which cooperates with the belt pulley to seal, as shown in Figure 4-42.

项目 5

Project 5

转 向 架

Bogie

本项目以了解转向架的结构为工学任务，通过课堂任务的完成过程，着重介绍各型转向架的结构及性能参数、各部分的名称及作用，并以此为引导，掌握客、货车转向架的特点；通过课后任务，了解各型转向架的主要差别及用途。

The main task of this project is to understand the structure of bogies as the work-and-study task. In the classroom, the main focus is on introducing the structural performance parameters of various types of bogies, and names and functions of various parts. Through after-class tasks, students will grasp the characteristics of passenger car and freight car bogies and understand the main differences and uses of various types of bogies.

学生工作页
Student Worksheet

工学任务描述 Task description	预期目标 Expected goals
任务名称：认识转向架 Task name: Understanding of the bogie 任务编号：CJ-05 Task number: CJ-05 知识类型：认知型+结构原理型 Knowledge type: Cognitive + structural principle 适用范围：车辆系统各岗位群 Applicable scope: All post groups of the car system 完成时间：　　　　学时 Completion time:　　　　class hours	初级：了解各型转向架的基本构成、作用及适用车型 Elementary level: Understand the basic composition, function, and applicable vehicle types of various types of bogies. 中级：了解垂直载荷的传递顺序 Intermediate level: Understand the vertical load transfer sequence. 高级：了解转向架的分解及组装顺序 Advanced level: Understand the disassembly and assembly sequence of bogies.

知识回顾+小组讨论
Knowledge review + group discussion

1. 根据车辆的运行特点，总结转向架的基本任务。

Summarize the basic tasks of bogies based on the operation characteristics of the railway vehicles.

2. 总结转向架的基本组成与作用。

Summarize the basic composition and function of bogies.

基本组成 Basic composition	作　用 Function	相关知识点 Relevant knowledge points

3. 分析转向架的主要技术要求。

Analyze the main technical requirements of bogies.

4. 认识 209T 型转向架。

Understand bogie type 209T.

（1）认识 209T 型转向架的构架组成。

Understand the framework composition of bogie type 209T.

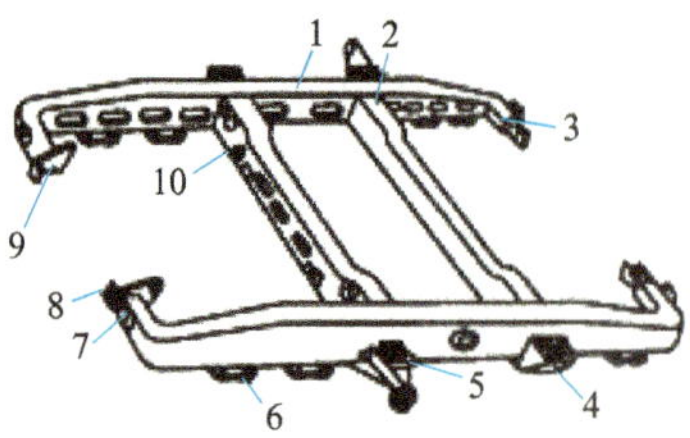

序号 S/N	名　称 Name	序号 S/N	名　称 Name	序号 S/N	名　称 Name
1		5		9	
2		6		10	
3		7			
4		8			

（2）认识 209T 型转向架摇枕弹簧装置的组成。

Understand the composition of the bolster spring device of bogie type 209T.

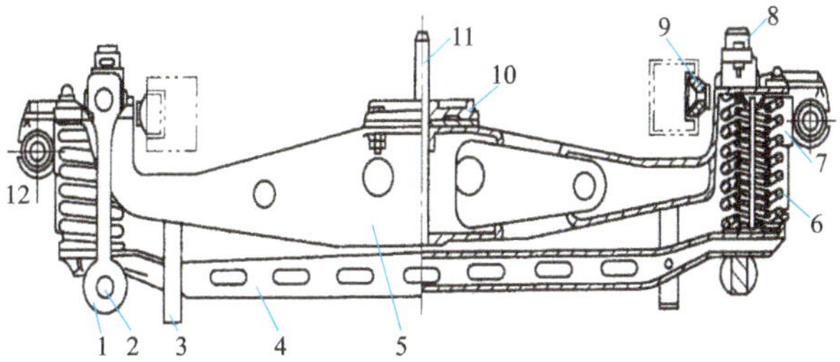

序号 S/N	名　　称 Name	序号 S/N	名　　称 Name	序号 S/N	名　　称 Name
1		5		9	
2		6		10	
3		7		11	
4		8		12	

（3）209T 型转向架采用哪种轴箱定位方式？主要解决了什么问题？这种定位方式的特点是什么？

Which axle box positioning method is used for bogie type 209T? What problems are mainly solved? What are the characteristics of this positioning method?

（4）识记 209T 型转向架基础制动装置的组成，分析制动时力的传递顺序。

Remember the composition of the foundation braking device of bogie type 209T and analyze the force transmission sequence during braking.

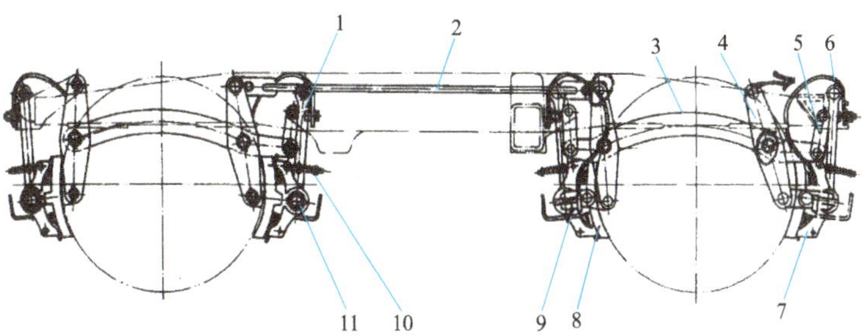

序号 S/N	名　称 Name	序号 S/N	名　称 Name	序号 S/N	名　称 Name
1		5		9	
2		6		10	
3		7		11	
4		8			

5. 认识 SW-160 型转向架。

Understand bogie type SW-160.

（1）识记 SW-160 型转向架的构架组成。

Remember the framework composition of bogie type SW-160.

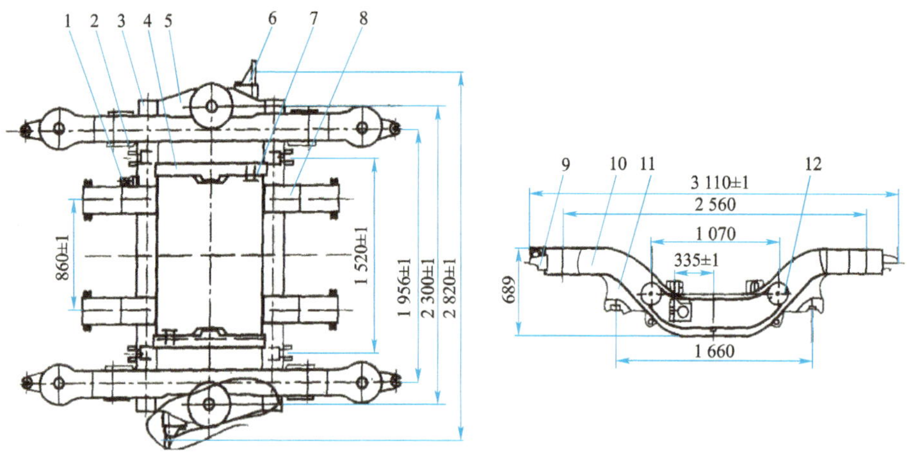

序号 S/N	名　称 Name	序号 S/N	名　称 Name	序号 S/N	名　称 Name
1		5		9	
2		6		10	
3		7		11	
4		8		12	

（2）识记 SW-160 型转向架中央悬挂装置的组成。

Remember the composition of the central suspension device of bogie type SW-160.

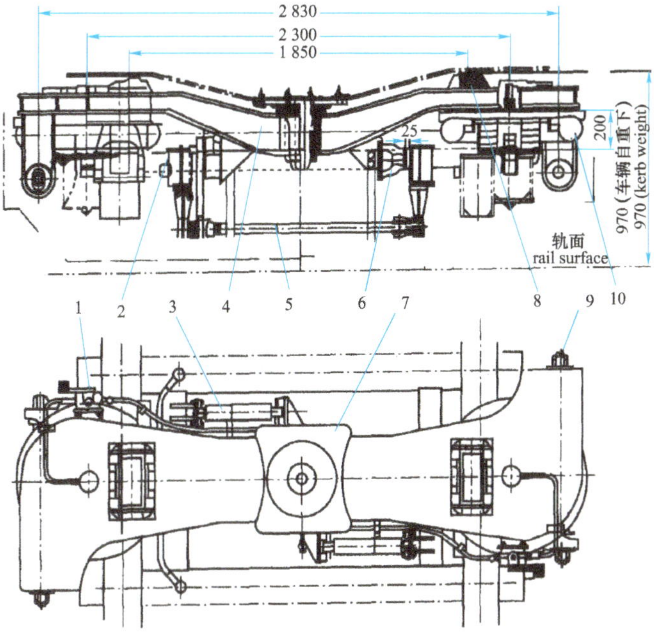

序号 S/N	名　称 Name	序号 S/N	名　称 Name	序号 S/N	名　称 Name
1		5		9	
2		6		10	
3		7			
4		8			

（3）识记 SW-160 型转向架轮对轴箱定位装置的组成。

Remember the composition of bogie type SW-160's wheelset axle box positioning device.

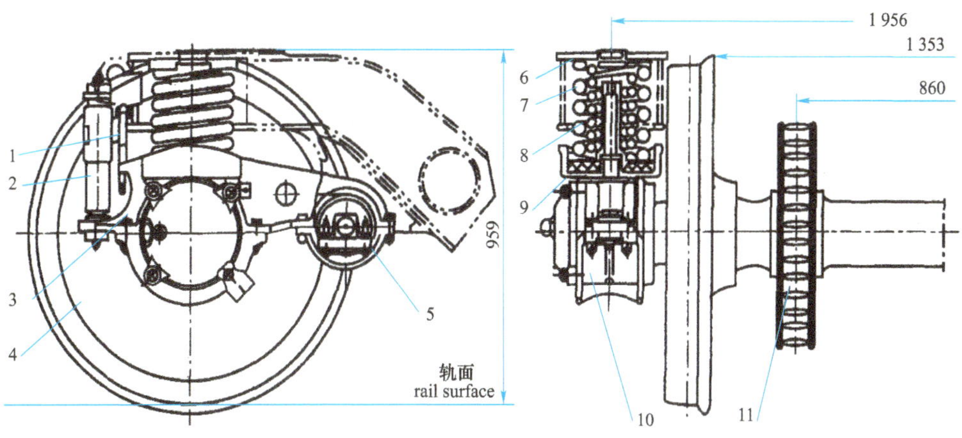

序号 S/N	名　称 Name	序号 S/N	名　称 Name	序号 S/N	名　称 Name
1		5		9	
2		6		10	
3		7		11	
4		8			

（4）总结 SW-160 型转向架基础制动装置的特点。

Summarize the characteristics of bogie type SW-160's foundation braking device.

6. 认识 SW-220K 型转向架。

Understand bogie type SW-220K.

（1）小组讨论：与 SW-220 型转向架相比，二者的差别在哪里？

Group discussion: What are the differences compared to bogie type SW-220?

（2）根据下图写出转向架的组成部分，并总结其特点。

Look at the picture and write down the components of the bogie, and summarize its characteristics.

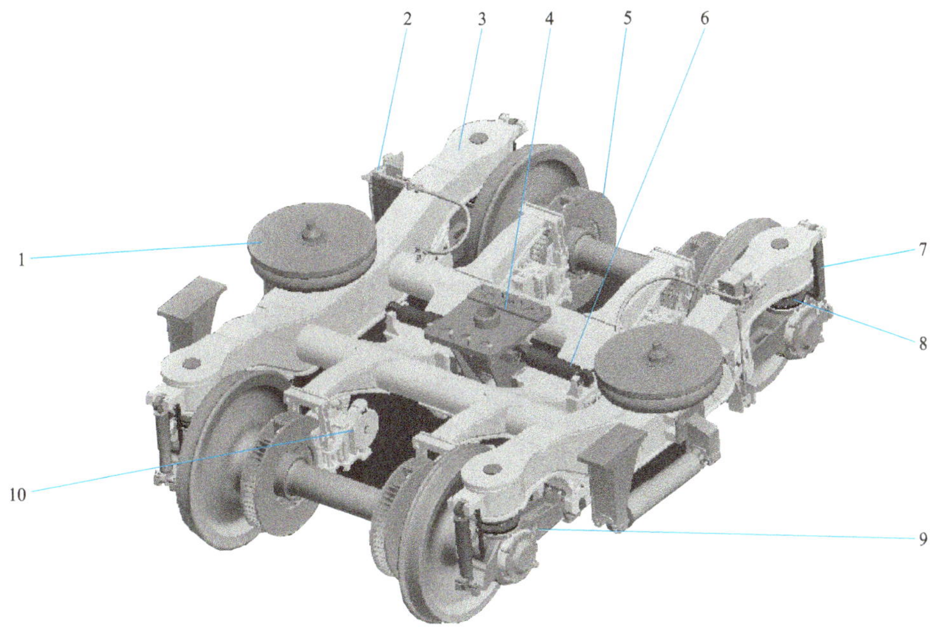

序号 S/N	名　称 Name	特　点 Characteristic
1		
2		
3		
4		
5		
6		
7		
8		
9		
10		

7. 认识转 K2 型转向架。

Understand bogie type ZK-2.

（1）识记转 K2 型转向架的组成。

Remember the composition of bogie type ZK-2.

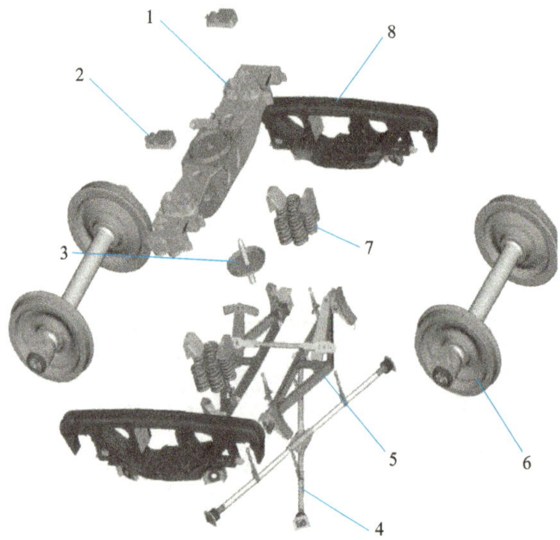

序号 S/N	名　　称 Name	序号 S/N	名　　称 Name	序号 S/N	名　　称 Name
1		4		7	
2		5		8	
3		6			

（2）识记转 K2 型转向架的侧架组成。

Remember the composition of bogie type ZK-2's side frame.

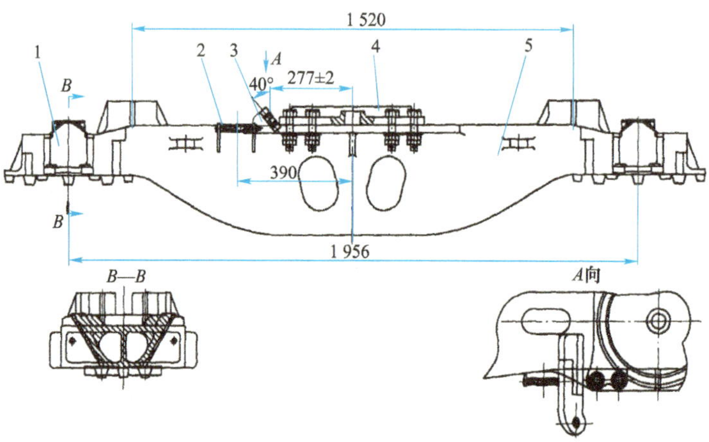

序号 S/N	名　　称 Name	序号 S/N	名　　称 Name
1		4	
2		5	
3			

8. 认识转 K5 型转向架。

Understand bogie type ZK-5.

（1）识记转 K5 型转向架的组成。

Remember the composition of bogie type ZK-5.

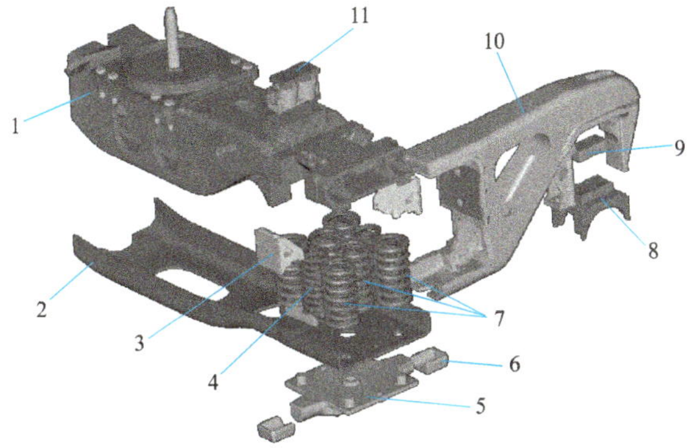

序号 S/N	名　称 Name	序号 S/N	名　称 Name	序号 S/N	名　称 Name
1		5		9	
2		6		10	
3		7		11	
4		8			

（2）对比转 K6 型和转 K2 型转向架，总结转 K5 型转向架的特点。

Compare bogie type ZK-6 and ZK-2, and summarize the characteristics of bogie type ZK-5.

（3）分析转 K5 型转向架垂向力的传递顺序。

Analyze the transmission sequence of the vertical force of bogie type ZK-5.

课后任务

After-class tasks

查阅资料，填写 SW-220K 型转向架的主要技术参数。

Refer to relevant documents and fill in the main technical parameters of bogie type SW-220K.

可持续运行速度/（km/h） Continuous operating speed/(km/h)		轴承型号 Bearing model	
最高试验速度/（km/h） Max. test speed/(km/h)		限界 Gauge	
轨距/mm Track gauge/mm		一系垂向阻尼系数/（kN·s/m） Primary vertical damping coefficient/(kN·s/m)	
轴距/mm Wheelbase/mm		二系横向阻尼系数/（kN·s/m） Secondary lateral damping coefficient/(kN·s/m)	
轴重/t Axle load/t		抗蛇行运动阻尼系数/（kN·s/m） Anti-hunting motion damping coefficient/(kN·s/m)	
轮径/mm Wheel diameter/mm		制动形式 Braking form	
车轮车轴型式 Wheel axle type			

学习效果评价
Learning effect evaluation

年 月 日
Year Month Day

专业班级： Major & class:	姓名： Name:	学号： Student number:	
工学小组及分工： Work-and-study team and responsibility division:			
专业（知识/技能）收获 Professional gains (knowledge/skills)	（非专业）能力素质收获 (Non-professional) ability and quality gains		
评价考核项目 Evaluation item	自我评价 Self-evaluation	小组评价 Group evaluation	教师评价 Teacher's evaluation
已掌握各型转向架的结构 Have mastered the structure of each type of bogie			
已掌握各型转向架的主要技术参数 Have mastered the main technical parameters of each type of bogie			
已理解各型转向架的用途 Have understood the purpose of each type of bogie			
已掌握相关知识点的数量 Number of knowledge points mastered			
主动提出问题的数量 Number of questions proposed			
课外学习时间（学时） After-school learning time (hours)			
其他类型转向架自主学习（收集相关知识点的数量） Autonomously learn other types of bogies (number of relevant knowledge points collected)			
工作态度（课堂、课后任务完成情况） Work attitude (completion condition of classroom tasks and after-class tasks)	☆☆☆☆ ☆☆☆☆	☆☆☆☆ ☆☆☆☆	☆☆☆☆ ☆☆☆☆
合作意识及协调能力 Cooperation consciousness and coordination ability	☆☆☆☆ ☆☆☆☆	☆☆☆☆ ☆☆☆☆	☆☆☆☆ ☆☆☆☆
正确表达和沟通能力 Correct expression and communication skills	☆☆☆☆ ☆☆☆☆	☆☆☆☆ ☆☆☆☆	☆☆☆☆ ☆☆☆☆
自律能力（缺勤/旷课/迟到/违纪次数） Self-discipline (absences/absenteeism/lateness/disciplinary violations)			

转向架是车辆的重要部件。车辆采用转向架是为了增加车辆的载重、长度、容积并提高列车运行速度。由于车辆用途的不同，以及运行条件、制造和检修能力的差异，转向架的种类、结构各异，但其基本组成部分是相同的。一般由轮对轴箱装置、基础制动装置、构架（侧架组成）、摇枕（摇枕悬挂装置）等四大部分组成。转向架的主要承载方式可分为心盘承载、心盘部分承载和非心盘承载 3 种。

Bogie is an important component of a railway vehicle. The purpose of using bogies for railway vehicles is to increase the load, length, volume, and speed of trains. Due to different uses of railway vehicles and differences in operating conditions, manufacturing, and maintenance capabilities, the types and structures of bogies vary. But the components are the same. It is generally composed of four parts, such as wheelset axle box device, foundation braking device, frame (side frame) and bolster (bolster suspension device). The bearing modes of main bogies can be divided into three types: center plate bearing, partial center plate bearing, and non-center plate bearing.

任务 5.1　货车转向架

Task 5.1　Freight car bogies

5.1.1　对货车转向架的要求

Requirements for passenger car bogies

货车转向架是铁路货车的关键部件，而且在车辆的组成中是一个相对独立的部件，因而对各型车辆具有较大的适应性。

Freight car bogies are key components of railway freight cars and are relatively independent components in the composition of s, so they have greater adaptability to various types of railway vehicles.

对货车转向架的一般要求是：结构简单合理，工作安全可靠，运行性能良好，制造成本低廉，维护检修方便等。

The general requirements for freight car bogies are simple and reasonable structure, safe and reliable operation, good operating performance, low manufacturing cost, convenient maintenance and repair, etc.

5.1.2　转 K2 型转向架

Bogie type ZK-2

转 K2 型转向架是一种新型货车转向架，采用交叉支撑装置、二级刚性弹簧悬挂等技术，对于增加转向架的抗菱刚度，改善空车的动力学性能起到了良好的作用，如图 5-1 所示。

Bogie type ZK-2 is a new type of freight car bogie provided with cross-support devices, two-stage rigid spring suspension, and other technologies, which play a good role in increasing the diamond-resistant rigidity of the bogies and improving the dynamic performance of empty vehicles, as shown in Figure 5-1.

图 5-1 转 K2 型转向架
Figure 5-1 Bogie type ZK-2

1. 转 K2 型转向架的结构特点
Structural characteristics of bogie type ZK-2

转 K2 型转向架为铸钢三大件式货车转向架。摇枕、侧架材质为 B 级铸钢，两侧架之间加装下交叉支撑装置；采用带变摩擦减振装置的中央枕簧悬挂系统，摇枕弹簧为两级刚度，采用锻造支撑座；下心盘内设有尼龙心盘磨耗盘；装用能满足提速要求的双列圆锥滚子轴承、50 钢车轴及采用磨耗型踏面的 HDSA 轻型辗钢或 HDZC 轻型铸钢车轮；采用双作用常接触弹性旁承；基础制动装置采用 L 型组合式制动梁、新型高摩合成闸瓦。

Bogie type ZK-2 is a kind of cast steel three-piece freight car bogie. The bolster and side frame are made of Grade B cast steel, and a lower cross-support device is installed between the two side frames; The central bolster spring suspension system with variable-friction vibration-damping devices is adopted. The bolster spring is two-stage rigidity spring and is subject to a forged support seat; a center plate wear plate is set in the lower center plate; it is equipped with double-row tapered roller bearings, 50 steel axles, and HDSA light rolled steel or HDZC light cast steel wheels with hollow tread that meet the speed increase requirements; double-acting constant-contact elastic side bearing is adopted; The foundation braking device is subject to an L-shaped combined brake beam and a new-type high-friction composite brake shoe.

2. 转 K2 型转向架的关键技术
Key technologies of bogie type ZK-2

1）侧架弹性下交叉支撑装置
Elastic lower cross-support device of the side frame

侧架弹性下交叉支撑装置如图 5–2 所示。侧架弹性下交叉支撑装置的功能如下。

The elastic lower cross-support device of the side frame is shown in Figure 5-2, and its functions are as follows.

（1）增加转向架抗菱刚度，从而提高转向架临界速度和货车直线运行稳定性。

Increase the diamond-resistant rigidity of the bogie, thereby improving the critical speed of the bogie and the stability of the freight car when running in a straight line.

（2）有效保持转向架正位状态，减少车辆在曲线运行时车轮与钢轨冲角，从而改善转向架的曲线通过性能，显著降低车轮轮缘磨耗。

Effectively maintain the upright position of the bogie and reduce the angle of attack between the wheel and the rail when the vehicle is running on a curve, thereby improving the curving performance of the bogie and significantly reducing wheel flange wear.

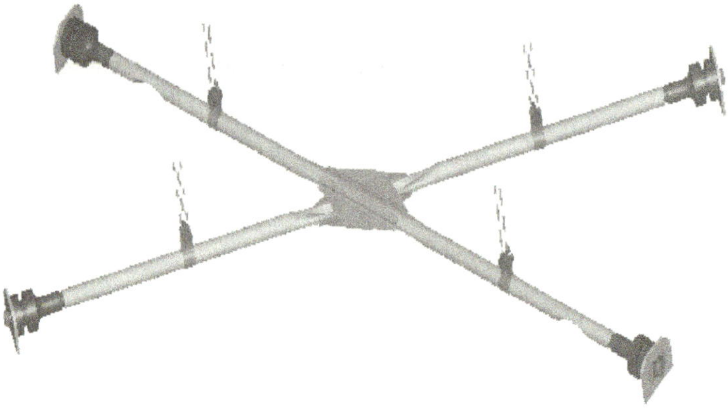

图 5-2 侧架弹性下交叉支撑装置

Figure 5-2 Elastic Lower Cross-support Device of Side Frame

2）双作用常接触弹性旁承

Double-acting constant-contact elastic side bearing

双作用常接触弹性旁承如图 5-3 所示。

The double-acting constant-contact elastic side bearing is shown in Figure 5-3, and its functions are as follows.

双作用常接触弹性旁承的功能如下。

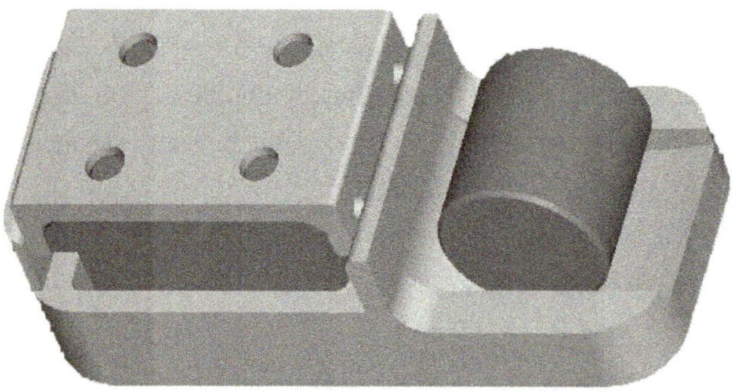

图 5-3 双作用常接触弹性旁承

Figure 5-3 Double-acting Constant-Contact Elastic Side Bearing

（1）增加车体与转向架间的回转阻尼，有效抑制转向架与车体的摇头运动和车体的侧滚振动，从而提高车辆高速运行时的平稳性和稳定性。

Increase the rotational damping between the car body and the bogie and effectively suppress the hunting motion and rolling vibration of the bogie and the car body, thereby improving the smoothness and stability of the railway vehicle during high-speed operation.

（2）车辆通过小半径曲线时，刚性滚子与上旁承接触，有效控制回转阻力矩于适当范围内，改善曲线通过性能。

When the railway vehicle passes through a small-radius curve, the rigid roller contacts the upper side bearing, effectively controls the rotational resistance moment within an appropriate range, and improves the curving performance.

（3）非金属磨耗板耐磨性好且性能稳定，可确保车辆动力学性能稳定。

The non-metallic wear plate has good wear resistance and stable performance, which can ensure the stable dynamic performance of the railway vehicle.

3）中央悬挂系统两级刚度弹簧

Two-stage rigidity spring of the central suspension system

中央悬挂系统两级刚度弹簧如图 5-4 所示。其功能为：提高空车弹簧静挠度，改善空车动力学性能。

The two-stage rigidity spring of the central suspension system is shown in Figure 5-4. Its function is: improve the static deflection of springs in the empty vehicle and improve the empty vehicle's dynamic performance.

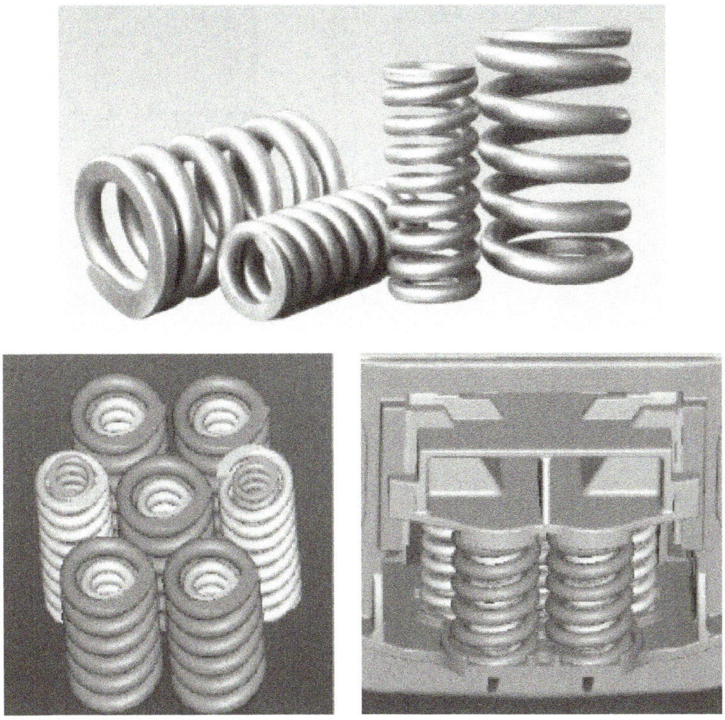

图 5-4　中央悬挂系统两级刚度弹簧

Figure 5-4　Two-stage Rigidity Spring of Central Suspension System

4）心盘磨耗盘

Center plate wear plate

心盘磨耗盘如图 5-5 所示。心盘磨耗盘为尼龙制造，能够有效减少上、下心盘的磨损，解决货车运用中的惯性问题，降低检修成本，保证车辆运行安全。

The center plate wear plate is shown in Figure 5-5. The center plate wear plate is made of nylon, which can effectively reduce the wear of the upper and lower center plates, solve the inertia problem in the use of freight cars, reduce maintenance costs, and ensure operational safety.

5）耐磨销套

Wear-resistant pin sleeve

耐磨销套如图 5-6 所示。其作用是减少零件的磨耗，延长零件的使用寿命，降低检修成本。

The wear-resistant pin sleeve is shown in Figure 5-6. Its function is to reduce the wear of parts, extend the service life of parts, and reduce the maintenance cost.

图 5-5　心盘磨耗盘
Figure 5-5　Center Plate Wear Plate

图 5-6　耐磨销套
Figure 5-6　Wear-resistant Pin Sleeve

采用以上关键技术后，既提高了转 K2 型转向架的动力学性能，又提高了易磨易损件的耐磨性，延长了转向架的检修期限和使用寿命。因此，转 K2 型转向架是一种运行平稳、安全可靠、方便检修的新型提速货车转向架。

The above key technology improves not only improves the dynamic performance of bogie type ZK-2 but also the wear resistance of easily worn parts, extending the maintenance period and service life of the bogie. Therefore, bogie type ZK-2 is a new type of speed-increasing freight car bogie that operate smoothly, safely, and reliably, and are convenient for maintenance.

3. 转 K2 型转向架的结构

Structure of bogie type ZK-2

由 RD_2 型轮对、352226X2-2R2 型圆锥滚子轴承、承载鞍、侧架、摇枕弹簧、减振弹簧、斜楔、摇枕、下心盘、侧架下交叉支撑装置、双作用常接触弹性旁承、中拉杆式基础制动装置等组成。

It is composed of RD_2 wheelsets, 352226X2-2R2 tapered roller bearings, bearing saddles, side frames, bolster springs, vibration-damping springs, wedges, bolster, lower center plates, side frame lower cross-support devices, double-acting constant-contact elastic side bearings, and center pull rod type foundation braking devices.

1）轮对组成及轴承

Wheelset composition and bearing

转 K2 型转向架的轮对组成及轴承如图 5-7 所示，车轮采用 HDS 或 HDSA 辗钢轮或 HDZC

铸钢轮，车轴为 RD_2 型 LZW50 钢，并采用 352226X2-2RZ 型滚动轴承（如图 5–8 所示）。

The wheelset composition and bearings of bogie type ZK-2 are shown in Figure 5-7. The wheels are made of HDS or HDSA rolled steel wheel or HDZC cast steel wheel. The axle is made of RD_2 LZW50 steel and 352226X2-2RZ roller bearings (shown in Figure 5-8).

图 5–7 轮对组成及轴承
Figure 5-7 Wheelset Composition and Bearing

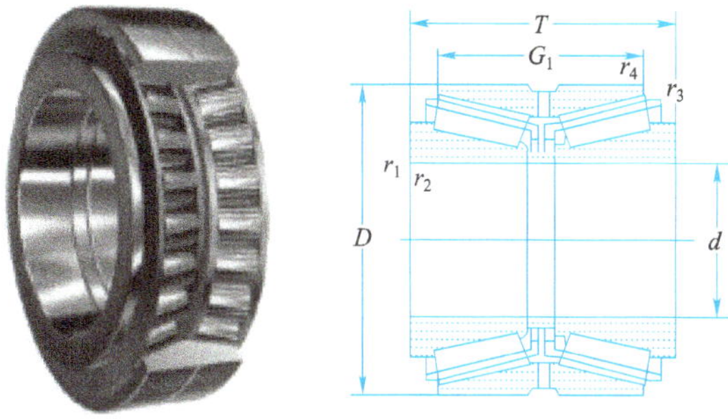

图 5–8 352226X2-2RZ 型滚动轴承
Figure 5-8 352226X2-2RZ Roller Bearing

2）侧架组成
Side frame composition

转 K2 型转向架的侧架组成如图 5–9 所示。

The side frame composition of bogie type ZK-2 is shown in Figure 5-9.

图 5–9 转 K2 型转向架的侧架组成
Figure 5-9 Side Frame Composition of Bogie Type ZK-2

侧架材质为 B 级铸钢；支撑座通过沿侧架大体中心线上下两条焊缝焊接在侧架上，如图 5–10 所示；组装位置必须采用专用组焊工装加以保证，配合面允许打磨修配；左、右滑槽磨耗板为卡入式，如图 5–11 所示；侧架立柱磨耗板（如图 5–12 所示）通过 2 个折头螺栓（如图 5-13 所示）与侧架立柱紧固。

The side frame is made of Grade B cast steel, and the support seat is welded to the side frame through two welds along the general centerline of the side frame, as shown in Figure 5-10; The assembly position must be guaranteed using a dedicated assembly welder kit, and the mating surface is allowed to be polished and repaired; The left and right chute wear plates are of the snap-in type, as shown in Figure 5-11; The side frame column wear plate, shown in Figure 5-12, is fastened to the side frame column by two folding-head bolts (shown in Figure 5-13).

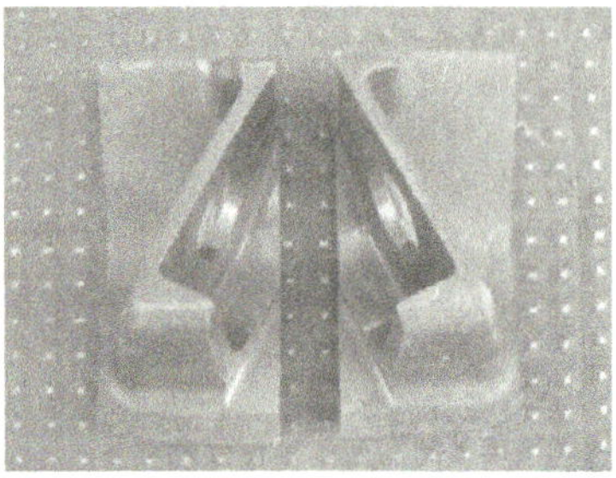

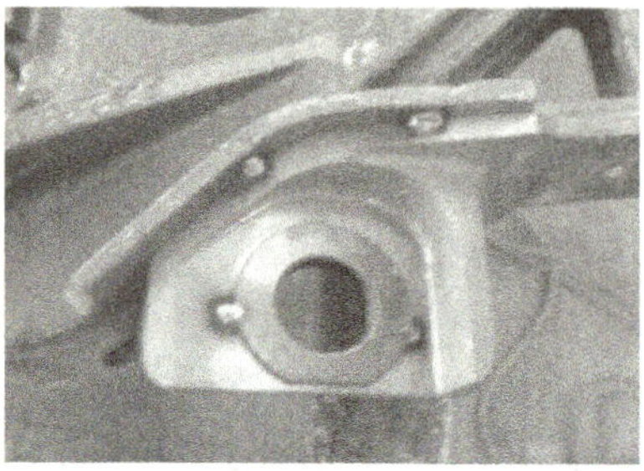

图 5–10　支撑座及支撑座焊装位置
Figure 5-10　Support Seat and Welding Position of Support Seat

图 5–11　卡入式滑槽磨耗板
Figure 5-11　Snap-in Chute Wear Plate

图 5–12　侧架立柱磨耗板
Figure 5-12　Side Frame Column Wear Plate

图 5–13　折头螺栓
Figure 5-13　Folding-head Bolt

3）摇枕组成

Bolster composition

转 K2 型转向架的摇枕组成如图 5–14 所示。

The bolster composition of bogie type ZK-2 is shown in Figure 5-14.

图 5–14　转 K2 型转向架的摇枕组成
Figure 5-14　Bolster Composition of Bogie Type ZK-2

转 K2 型转向架的摇枕组成由固定杠杆支点座、上拉杆托架组成、摇枕、下心盘、斜面磨耗板组成。摇枕材质为 B 级钢。下心盘螺栓为 GB/T 31.1—2013 中规定的 M22 螺栓（强度等级为 10.9 级），螺母为 BY-B 型、BY-A 型、FS 型防松螺母（强度等级为 10 级），因上拉杆越过摇枕上平面，为防止上拉杆磨损摇枕上平面而安装上拉杆托架组成。

The bolster of bogie type ZK-2 consists of a fixed lever fulcrum seat, upper pull rod bracket, bolster, lower center plate, and bevel wear plate. The material of bolster is Grade B steel. The lower center plate bolts are M22 bolts (strength grade 10.9) stipulated in GB/T 31.1—2013, and the nuts are BY-B, BY-A and FS lock nuts (strength grade 10). As the upper pull rod crosses the upper plane of the bolster, it is composed of an upper pull rod mounting bracket to prevent the upper pull rod from grinding the upper plane of the bolster.

4）中央悬挂系统

Central suspension system

中央悬挂系统由 10 个外圆弹簧、10 个内圆弹簧、4 组双卷减振弹簧组成，如图 5-15 所示。摇枕悬挂由摇枕内圆弹簧和摇枕外圆弹簧组成。在空车状态下，只压缩摇枕外圆弹簧。由于摇枕外圆簧刚度较小，使空车状态下的弹簧静挠度增大，可改善空车的动力学性能。重车时，摇枕外圆弹簧的压缩量增加。当其高度与内圆弹簧的高度一致时，内圆弹簧开始与外圆弹簧一起承载，弹簧总刚度增大，形成两级刚度悬挂特性。

The central suspension system consists of 10 outer helical springs, 10 inner helical springs, and 4 sets of double-coil vibration-damping springs, as shown in Figure 5-15. The bolster suspension is subject to an inner helical bolster spring and an outer helical bolster spring. In the empty vehicle state, only the outer helical bolster spring is compressed. Due to the small rigidity of the outer helical bolster spring, increasing the static deflection of the spring in the empty vehicle state can improve the dynamic performance of the empty vehicle. When the vehicle is loaded, the compression amount of the outer helical bolster spring increases. When its height coincides with the height of the inner helical spring, the inner helical spring begins to bear load together with the outer helical spring, and the total spring rigidity increases, forming a two-stage rigidity suspension characteristic.

图 5-15 转 K2 型转向架的中央悬挂系统
Figure 5-15 Central Suspension System of Bogie Type ZK-2

5）减振装置

Vibration-damping device

转 K2 型转向架的减振装置组成如图 5–16 所示。转 K2 型转向架的减振装置由侧架立柱磨耗板、组合式斜楔（如图 5–17、图 5–18 所示）、摇枕斜面磨耗板及双卷减振弹簧组成。侧架立柱磨耗板的材质为 T10，斜楔体的材质为针状铸铁，主摩擦板的材质为高分子材料，摇枕斜面磨耗板的材质为 0Cr18Ni9。2003 年下半年后，部分转 K2 型转向架装用了材质为 47Mn2Si2TiB 的侧架立柱磨耗板及 ADI 斜楔。

The composition of the vibration-damping device for bogie type ZK-2 is shown in Figure 5-16. The vibration-damping device for bogie type ZK-2 consists of a side frame column wear plate, combined wedge (as shown in Figure 5-17 and Figure 5-18), bolster bevel wear plate, and double-coil vibration-damping spring. The side frame column wear plate is made of T10 and the wedge is made of needle-shaped cast iron. The main friction plate is made of polymer material, and the bolster bevel wear plate is made of 0Cr18Ni9. After the second half of 2003, some bogies type ZK-2 were installed with 47Mn2Si2TiB side frame column wear plates and ADI wedges.

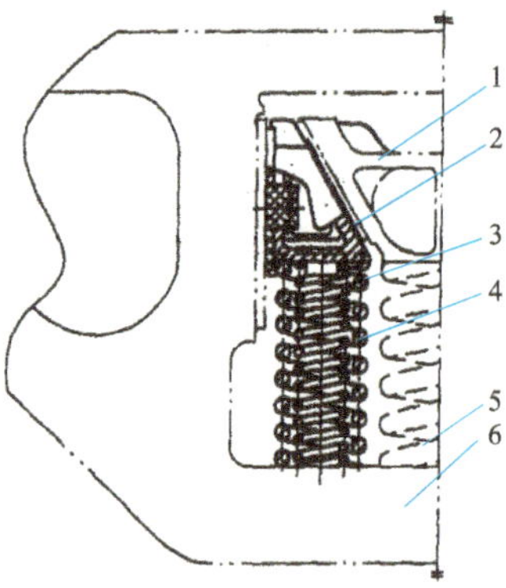

1—摇枕；2—组合式斜楔；3—减振内圆弹簧；
4—减振外圆弹簧；5—摇枕弹簧；6—侧架。
1—Bolster; 2—Combined wedge; 3—Inner vibration—damping helical spring; 4—Outer vibration-damping helical spring; 5—Bolster spring; 6—Side frame.

图 5–16 转 K2 型转向架的减振装置组成
Figure 5-16 Composition of Vibration-damping Device for Bogie Type ZK-2

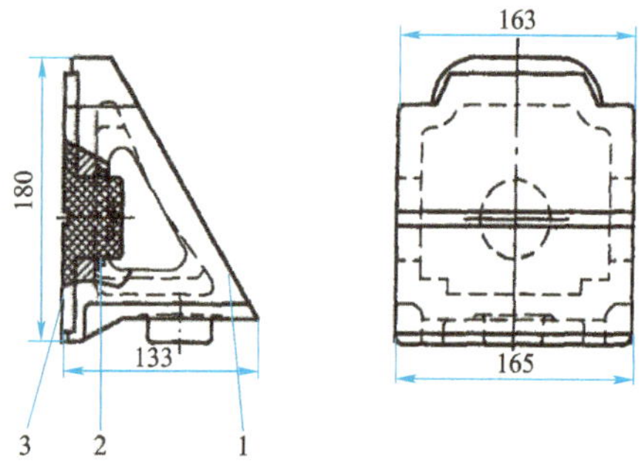

1—斜楔体；2—垫圈；3—主摩擦板。
1—Wedge; 2—Washer; 3—Main friction plate.

图 5–17 组合式斜楔
Figure 5-17 Combined Wedge

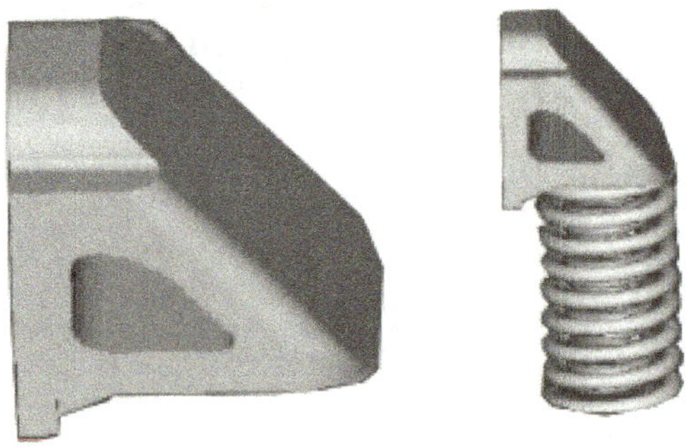

图 5–18 斜楔与减振弹簧
Figure 5-18 Wedge and Vibration-damping Spring

6）基础制动装置

Foundation braking device

转 K2 型转向架的基础制动装置如图 5-19 所示。

The foundation braking device of bogie type ZK-2 is shown in Figure 5-19.

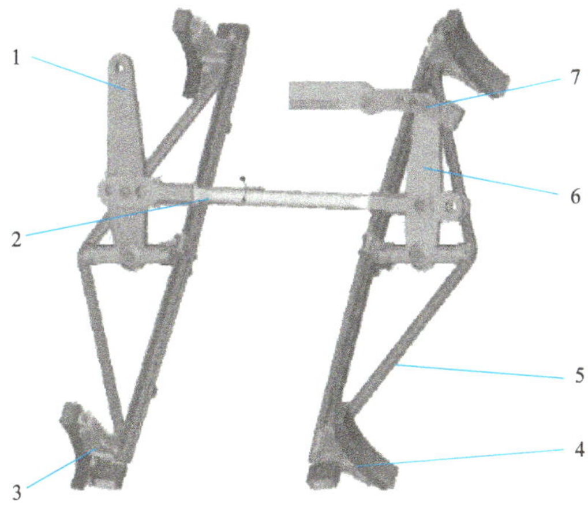

1—游动杠杆；2—中拉杆；3—闸瓦托；4—高摩合成闸瓦；
5—组合式制动梁；6—固定杠杆；7—固定杠杆支点。

1—Floating lever; 2—Center pull rod; 3—Brake shoe support; 4—High-friction composite brake shoe;
5—Combined brake beam; 6—Fixed lever; 7—Fixed lever fulcrum.

图 5-19　转 K2 型转向架的基础制动装置

Figure 5-19　Foundation Braking Device of Bogie Type ZK-2

转 K2 型转向架的基础制动装置由左、右组合式制动梁、中拉杆（分一位和二位）、固定杠杆、固定杠杆支点、游动杠杆、高摩合成闸瓦及各种规格的耐磨销套等组成。

The foundation braking device for bogie type ZK-2 consists of left and right combined brake beams, center pull rods (divided into “B” end and “A” end), fixed levers, fixed lever fulcrums, floating levers, high-friction composite brake shoes, various wear-resistant pin sleeves and others.

中拉杆采用整体锻造结构，夹板每端设三孔，配合固定杠杆支点调整闸调器 L 值。衬套为奥贝球铁耐磨衬套。圆销为 45 钢淬火圆销。

The center pull rod is subject to an integrally forged structure, with three holes at each end of the clamp plate, and is used to adjust the L value of the brake adjuster in conjunction with the fixed lever fulcrum. The bushing material is austempering ductile iron wear-resistant bushing. Round pins are 45 steel quenched round pins.

7）侧架弹性下交叉支撑装置

Elastic lower cross-support device of the side frame

侧架弹性下交叉支撑装置的三维及二维结构分别如图 5-20、图 5-21 所示。转 K2 型转向架下交叉支撑装置由 1 个下交叉杆、1 个上交叉杆、8 个橡胶垫、4 个双耳防松垫圈、4 个锁紧板、4 个标志板、4 个紧固螺栓组成。在上、下交叉杆中部焊有上、下夹板，利用 2 组 M12 螺栓、螺母、垫圈将夹板紧固，同时把螺母用电焊点固，上、下夹板间有 4 个外塞焊点和 2 个平焊缝，把上、下交叉杆点固定，形成一个整体。

The three-dimensional and two-dimensional structures of the cross-support device under the elastic side frame are shown in Figure 5-20 and Figure 5-21, respectively. The lower cross-support device for bogie type ZK-2 consists of one lower crossbar, one upper crossbar, eight rubber pads, four double flange lock washers, four locking plates, four sign plates, and four solid bolts. The upper and lower clamp plates are welded in the middle of the upper and lower cross bars. The clamp plates are fastened using two sets of M12 bolts, nuts, and washers. At the same time, the nuts are welded by electric welding. There are four external plug welds and two flat welds between the upper and lower clamp plates, securing the upper and lower cross bars as a whole.

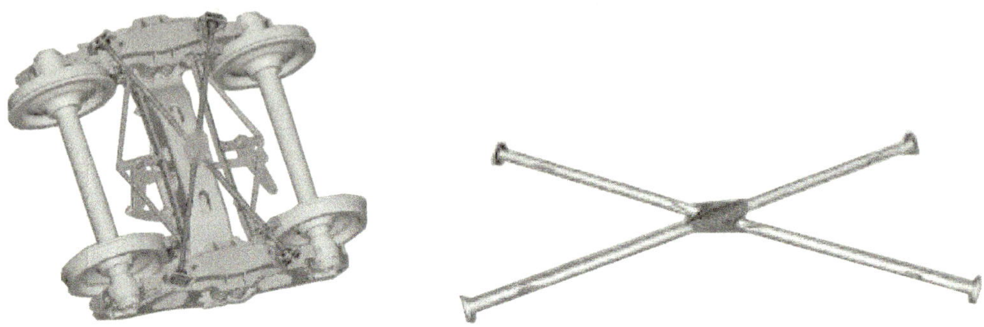

图 5-20　侧架弹性下交叉支撑装置的三维结构图

Figure 5-20　Three-dimensional Structure Diagram of Elastic Cross-support Device of Side Frame

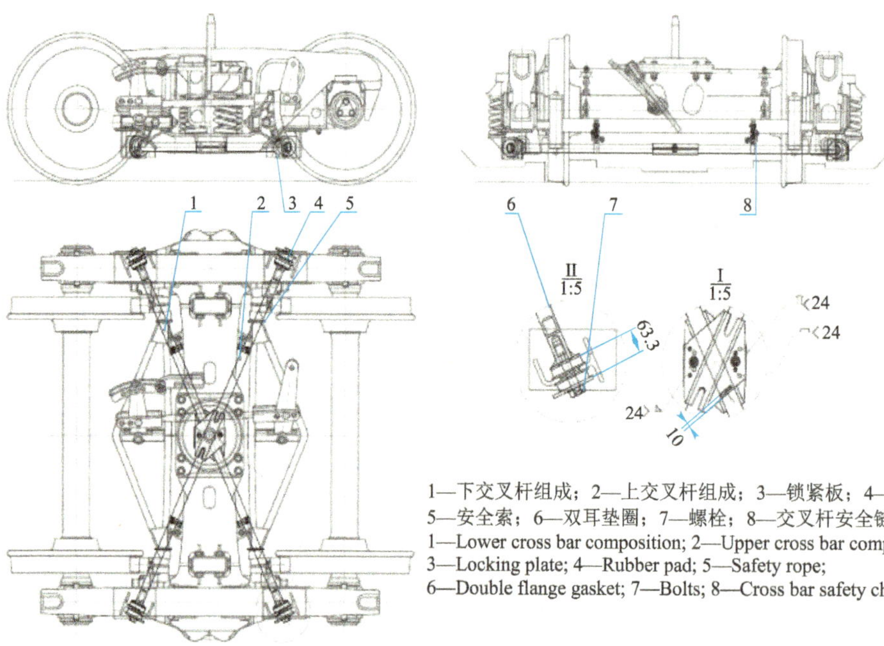

1—下交叉杆组成；2—上交叉杆组成；3—锁紧板；4—橡胶垫；5—安全索；6—双耳垫圈；7—螺栓；8—交叉杆安全链。
1—Lower cross bar composition; 2—Upper cross bar composition; 3—Locking plate; 4—Rubber pad; 5—Safety rope; 6—Double flange gasket; 7—Bolts; 8—Cross bar safety chain.

图 5-21　侧架弹性下交叉支撑装置的二维结构图

Figure 5-21　Two-dimensional Structure Diagram of Elastic Cross-support Device of Side Frame

8）双作用常接触弹性旁承

Double-acting constant-contact elastic side bearing

双作用常接触弹性旁承由旁承座、弹性旁承体、旁承磨耗板、滚子、滚子轴、调整垫板、垫板、垫片等零部件组成，如图 5-22 所示。

Double-acting constant-contact elastic side bearing consists of a side bearing seat, elastic side bearing body, side bearing wear plate, roller, roller bearing, adjusting pad, pad, gasket, and other components, as shown in Figure 5-22.

图 5-22　双作用常接触弹性旁承
Figure 5-22　Double-acting Constant-Contact Elastic Side Bearing

9）横跨梁

Cross beam

因空重车自动调整装置的需要，须在二位转向架上安装横跨梁。横跨梁由左横跨梁托、横跨梁组成、右横跨梁托、调整板、磨耗垫板、跨梁吊座及安全链组成，如图 5-23 所示。

Due to the need for an automatic adjustment device for empty and loaded vehicles, a cross beam is installed on a “A” end bogie. The cross beam consists of a left cross beam bracket, a cross beam, a right cross beam bracket, an adjustment plate, a wear pad, a cross beam hanger seat and safety chain, as shown in Figure 5-23.

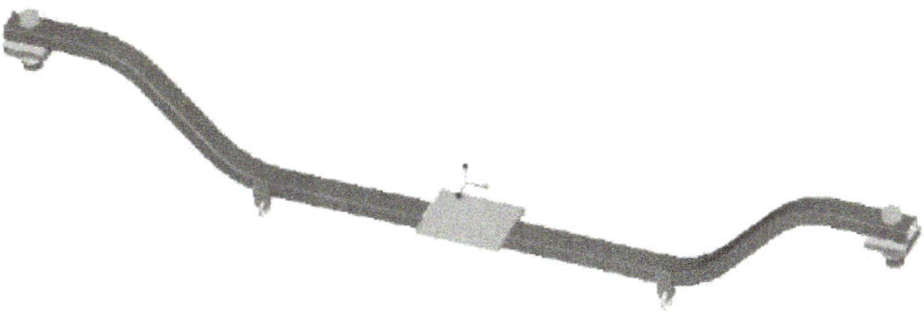

图 5-23　横跨梁
Figure 5-23　Cross Beam

4. 转 K2 型转向架的主要性能参数
Main performance parameters of bogie type ZK-2

转 K2 型转向架的主要性能参数如表 5–1 所示。

The main performance parameters of bogie type ZK-2 are shown in Table 5-1.

表 5–1　转 K2 型转向架的主要性能参数

Table 5–1　Main Performance Parameters of Bogie Type ZK–2

轨距 Track gauge	1 435 mm
轴重 Axle load	21 t
轴型 Axle type	RD_2
自重 Tare weight	≤4.2 t
商业运营速度 Commercial operation speed	120 km/h
通过最小曲线半径 Min. radius of curvature negotiated	100 m
限界 Gauge	符合《标准轨距铁路限界　第 1 部分：机车车辆限界》（GB 146.1—2020）的要求 Comply with the requirements of *Gauge for Standard Gauge Railways—Part 1: Rolling Stock Gauge* (GB 146.1—2020)
旁承中心距 Side bearing center distance	1 520 mm
下心盘面直径 Lower center plate diameter	355 mm
固定轴距 Fixed wheelbase	1 750 mm
下心盘面（含心盘磨耗盘）至弹性旁承顶面距离 Distance from the lower center plate surface (including center plate wear plate) to the top surface of the elastic side bearing	自由状态：71 mm Free state: 71 mm
	工作状态：62 mm Working state: 62 mm
侧架上平面至轨面高 Height from the upper plane of side frame to rail surface	743 mm
侧架下平面至轨面高 Height from the lower plane of side frame to rail surface	165 mm
车轮直径 Wheel diameter	840 mm
移动杠杆与车体纵向铅垂面的夹角 Angle between the moving lever and the longitudinal vertical surface of the car body	50°
基础制动装置制动倍率 Foundation braking device braking ratio	4

5.1.3 转 K4 型转向架 Bogie type ZK-4

它是由美国原 ABC-NACO 公司于 1970 年研制成功的摆动式转向架，装用在以较高速度运行的货车上。经运用实践和多次试验证明，该转向架性能优良、耐久性好。1990 年以后，广泛应用在对运行速度和运行品质要求高的多种货车上，并先后出口到加拿大、英国、泰国等国家，目前累计已生产 5 万余辆投入运用。

It is the swing-type bogie developed by the original ABC-NACO Company in the United States in 1970, which was installed on freight cars operating at higher speeds. Through application practice and multiple tests, the bogie has been proven to have excellent performance and good durability. After 1990, it has been widely used in a variety of freight cars with high requirements for operating speed and quality and has been exported to Canada, the United Kingdom, Thailand, and other countries. Currently, more than 50,000 vehicles have been produced and put into use.

为了更快、更好地将在美国和其他多个国家应用证明为先进成熟的摆动式转向架引入中国，株洲车辆厂以合资形式引进美国技术，并与美国原 ABC-NACO 公司联合进行改进设计。改进设计是在保持原摆动式转向架先进的设计原理、结构和成功的经验的基础上，按照中国的铁路标准及线路情况，即符合中国的限界、路况、轴重、制动距离及中国的制造、检修、运用的传统要求等，研制了中国铁路货车使用的摆动式转向架。

To introduce the advanced and mature swing-type bogies that have been applied in the United States and many other countries into China more quickly and better, Zhuzhou Locomotive has introduced the United States with joint venture technology and collaborated with the original ABC-NACO company in the United States to carry out the improved design. The improved design is based on maintaining the advanced design principles, structure, and successful experience of the original swing-type bogies, in accordance with Chinese railway standards and line conditions on meeting clearance, road conditions, axle load, braking distance, and traditional requirements for manufacturing, maintenance, and application. The swing-type bogies for railway freight cars in China have been developed.

研制的样机按照国标及铁标的有关要求，先后通过了侧架和摇枕的静强度、压吨、疲劳试验，摇动座的静载荷和疲劳试验，弹簧的疲劳试验，旁承的耐久性试验，侧架、摇枕及弹簧托板的动应力试验，以及装于 C_{64}、P_{65}、G_{70}、NX_{17} 等车型的线路动力学试验（试验最高速度达到 146 km/h）。

The developed prototype has successively passed the static strength, compression, and fatigue tests of the side frame and bolster, the static load and fatigue tests of the rolling seat, the fatigue test of the spring, the durability test of the side bearing, and the dynamic stress test of the side frame, bolster, and spring bracket in accordance with the relevant requirements of the national and iron standards. The line dynamics test has been carried out on C_{64}, P_{65}, G_{70}, NX_{17} and other models (the maximum speed of the test reaches 146 km/h).

2001 年 12 月，铁道部运输局会同科教司等，在株洲通过了摆动式转向架及 C_{64} 敞车安装摆动式转向架的技术审查。

In December 2001, the Transportation Bureau of the Ministry of Railways, together with the Department of Science and Education, passed the technical review of swing-type bogies and C_{64} gondola cars equipped with swing-type bogies in Zhuzhou.

转 K4 型转向架实物如图 5-24 所示。

The physical object of bogie type ZK-4 is shown in Figure 5-24.

图 5-24　转 K4 型转向架实物
Figure 5-24　Physical Object of Bogie Type ZK-4

1. 转 K4 型转向架的结构特点
Structural characteristics of bogie type ZK-4

（1）结构上属于铸钢三大件式转向架，具有结构简单、车轮均载性好、检修维护方便等优点。

Structurally, it belongs to a cast steel three-piece bogie, which has the advantages of simple structure, good wheel load sharing, and convenient maintenance.

（2）采用摇动台摆式机构，使转向架横向具有两级刚度特性，大大增加了车辆的横向柔性，提高了车辆的横向动力学性能，降低了轮轨间的磨耗。

The bogie is subject to a shaking table tilting mechanism, which enables the bogie to have two-stage lateral rigidity characteristics, greatly increasing the lateral flexibility of the railway vehicle, improving the lateral dynamic performance of the railway vehicle, and reducing the wear between wheels and rails.

在传统铸钢三大件式转向架的基础上增加一个弹簧托板，连接左、右侧架的弹性悬挂，并通过使摇动座坐落在侧架中央承台的支承座上，形成下摆点；同时，左、右侧架通过其顶部的导框摇动座分别支承在前后两承载鞍上，形成上摆点。两侧架通过上、下摆点连接成为横向可同步摆动的吊杆，并与弹簧托板铰接而形成一个矩形的摆动机构，可在车辆运行时实现横向摆动。摆动机构原理图如图 5-25 所示。

On the basis of traditional cast steel three-piece bogies, a spring bracket is added to connect the elastic suspension of the left and right side frames, and the rolling seat is located on the bearing seat of the central cushion cap of the side frame to form a lower swing point; In addition, the left and right side frames are respectively supported on the front and rear bearing saddles through their top guide frame rolling seats, forming an upper swing point. The two side frames are connected through the upper and lower swing points to form a horizontally synchronous swing suspender, which is hinged with the spring bracket to form a rectangular swing mechanism to achieve lateral swing during the operation of railway vehicles. The schematic diagram of the swing mechanism is shown in Figure 5-25.

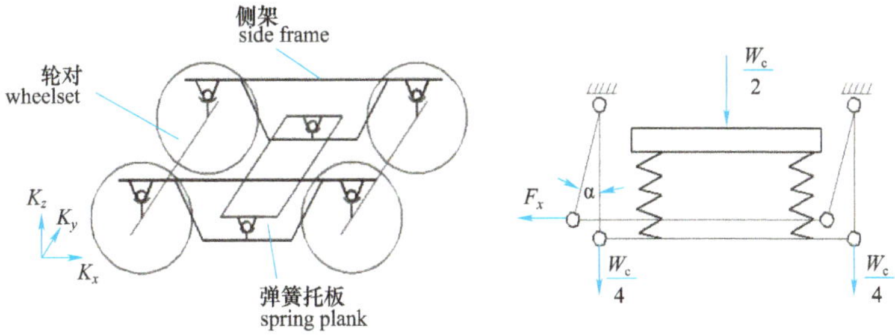

图 5-25　摆动机构原理图

Figure 5-25　Schematic Diagram of Swing Mechanism

（3）提高了车辆脱轨安全性。由于摆动式转向架的摇枕挡位置下移，使侧滚中心降低，对侧滚振动的控制加强，有效地减小了爬轨和脱轨的可能性，尤其是对于高重心的货车，大大提高了其脱轨安全性。

It improves the derailment safety of railway vehicles. Due to the downward movement of the bolster stop position of the swing-type bogie, the roll center is lowered, and the control of rolling vibration is strengthened, effectively reducing the possibility of track climbing and derailment, especially for freight cars with a high center of gravity, and greatly improving their derailment safety.

（4）具有较高的耐久性和可靠性，运用寿命长，维修工作量小，可运营 160 万 km 免检修。

With high durability and reliability, a long service life and a small maintenance workload, this bogie can operate 1.6 million km without inspection and repair.

2. 转 K4 型转向架的主要性能参数和尺寸参数

Main performance parameters and dimensional parameters of bogie type ZK-4

1）主要性能参数

Main performance parameters

转 K4 型转向架的主要性能参数如表 5-2 所示。

The main performance parameters of bogie type ZK-4 are shown in Table 5-2.

表 5-2　转 K4 型转向架的主要性能参数

Table 5-2　Main Performance Parameters of Bogie Type ZK–4

轴重 Axle load	21 t
自重 Tare weight	≤4.2 t
最高运行速度 Max. operating speed	120 km/h
轨距 Track gauge	1 435 mm

续表

Continued

轮型及轮径 Wheel type and diameter	HDSA 型，ϕ840 mm HDSA type, ϕ840 mm
车轮踏面形状 Wheel tread shape	磨耗型踏面 Hollow tread
轴型 Axle type	RD_2 型 RD_2 type
轴承 Bearing	SKF197726
基础制动杠杆倾角 Inclination angle of foundation brake lever	40°
基础制动装置制动倍率 Foundation braking device braking ratio	6.48
转向架中央弹簧垂向总刚度 Total vertical rigidity of bogie central spring	
空车垂向刚度 Vertical rigidity of empty vehicle	3 470 N/mm
重车垂向刚度 Vertical rigidity of loaded vehicle	8 960 N/mm
心盘允许载荷 Allowable load of center plate	371.42 kN
通过最小曲线半径 Min. radius of curvature negotiated	145 m
工作环境温度 Ambient operating temperature	±40 ℃
限界 Gauge	符合《标准轨距铁路限界　第 1 部分：机车车辆限界》（GB 146.1—2020）的要求 Comply with the requirements of *Gauge for Standard Gauge Railways—Part 1: Rolling Stock Gauge* (GB 146.1—2020)

2）主要尺寸参数

Main dimension parameters

转 K4 型转向架的主要尺寸参数如表 5-3 所示。

The main dimensional parameters of bogie type ZK-4 are shown in Table 5-3.

表 5-3　转 K4 型转向架的主要尺寸参数

Table 5-3　Main Dimensional Parameters of Bogie Type ZK-4

固定轴距 Fixed wheelbase	1 750 mm
轴颈中心距 Journal center distance	1 956 mm

续表

Continued

旁承中心距 Side bearing center distance	1 520 mm
下心盘直径 Lower center plate diameter	355 mm
下心盘面（含心盘衬垫）距轨面自由高 Free height from lower center plate surface (including center plate gasket) to rail surface	701 mm
侧架上平面距轨面高 Height from the upper plane of side frame to rail surface	743 mm
侧架下平面距轨面高 Height from the lower plane of side frame to rail surface	165 mm

3. 转 K4 型转向架的结构
Structure of bogie type ZK-4

转 K4 型转向架类似于传统铸钢三大件式转向架，主要由轮对和轴承装置、摇枕、侧架、弹性悬挂系统及减振装置、基础制动装置、常接触弹性旁承等组成，其三维结构图、主要结构示意图、分解图、主要结构分解图分别如图 5-26、图 5-27、图 5-28、图 5-29 所示。但该型转向架采用了独特的弹簧托板、摇动座等结构，使之具有更好的横向性能及其他优点。

Bogie type ZK-4 is similar to traditional cast three-piece bogie, mainly composed of wheelsets and bearing devices, bolster, side frame, elastic suspension system and vibration-damping device, foundation braking device, constant-contact elastic side bearings, etc., and its Three-dimensional Structure Diagram, Schematic Diagram of Main Structure, Exploded View, and Exploded View of Main Structure are shown in Figure 5-26, Figure 5-27, Figure 5-28, and Figure 5-29 respectively. However, this type of bogies adopts unique structures such as spring brackets and rolling seats, which provide better lateral performance and other advantages.

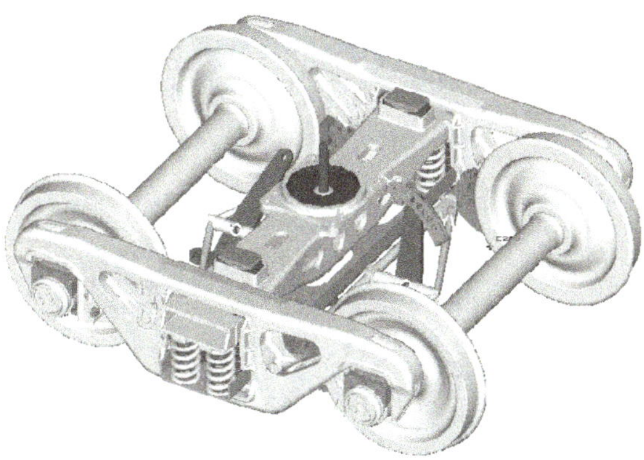

图 5-26　转 K4 型转向架三维结构图

Figure 5-26　Three-dimensional Structure Diagram of Bogie Type ZK-4

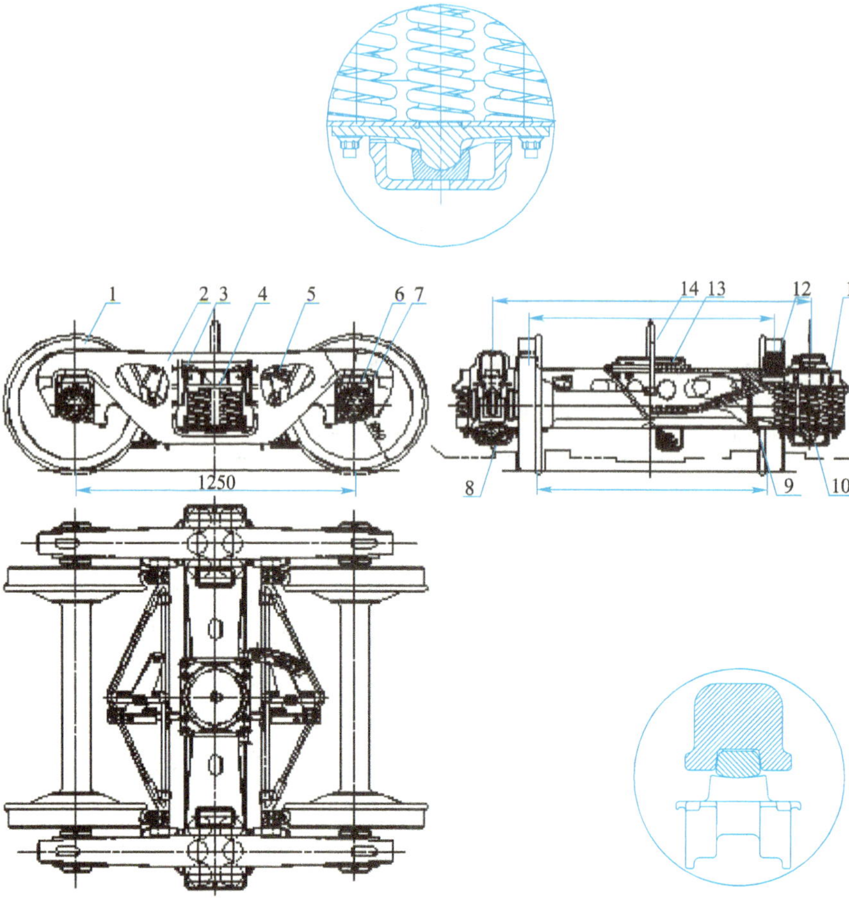

1—RD_3型轮对；2—侧架组成；3—斜楔减振装置；4—摇枕组成；5—基础制动装置；6—承载鞍；7—滚动轴承装置；8—摇动座支承；9—弹簧托板；10—摇动座；11—摇枕弹簧；12—常接触弹性旁承；13—心盘衬垫；14—中心销。

1—RD_3 wheelset; 2—Side frame composition: 3—Wedge vibration-damping device; 4—Bolster composition; 5—Foundation braking device; 6—Bearing saddle; 7—Roller bearing device; 8—Rolling seat support; 9—Spring bracket; 10—Rolling seat; 11—Bolster spring; 12—Constant-contact elastic side bearing; 13—Center plate gasket; 14—Center pin.

图 5–27　转 K4 型转向架主要结构示意图

Figure 5-27　Schematic Diagram of Main Structure of Bogie Type ZK-4

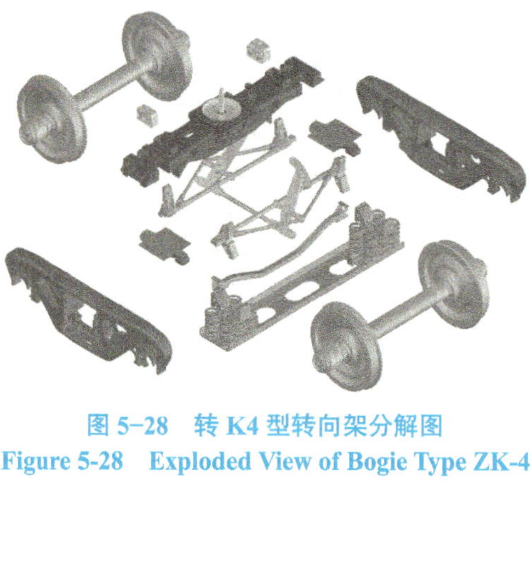

图 5–28　转 K4 型转向架分解图

Figure 5-28　Exploded View of Bogie Type ZK-4

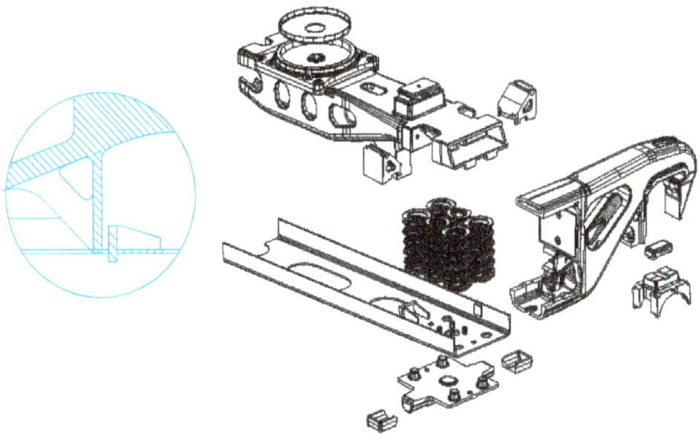

图 5-29 转 K4 型转向架主要结构分解图

Figure 5-29 Exploded View of Main Structure of Bogie Type ZK-4

1）摇枕及下心盘

Bolster and lower center plate

转 K4 型转向架采用直径分别为 355 mm 和 308 mm 的两种下心盘，但两种下心盘与摇枕上的螺栓孔位置相同。转 K4 型转向架采用了和转 K2 型、转 8G 型转向架相同尺寸的改型尼龙心盘衬垫。摇枕材质为 AAR M201 B 级钢。转 K4 型转向架的摇枕及下心盘如图 5-30 所示。

Two types of lower center plates with diameters of 355 mm and 308 mm are used for bogie type ZK-4, but the positions of the two lower center plates and the bolt holes on the bolster are the same. The modified nylon center plate gasket of the same size is used for bogie type ZK-4 as bogie type ZK-2 and bogie type Z8G. The bolster is made of AAR M201 Grade B steel. The bolster and lower center plate of bogie type ZK-4 are shown in Figure 5-30.

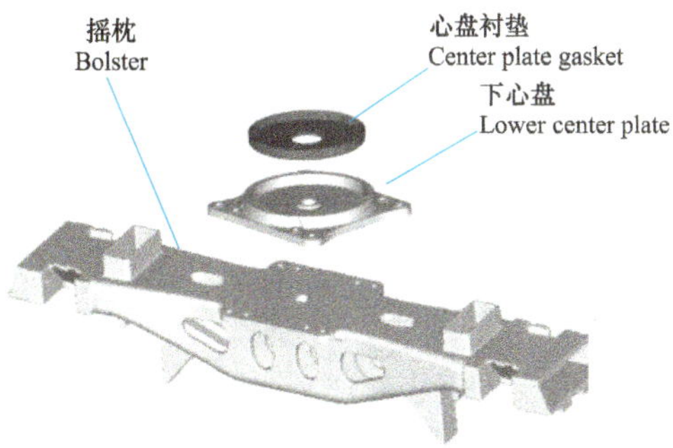

图 5-30 摇枕及下心盘

Figure 5-30 Bolster and Lower Center Plate

摇枕下部铸出两块三角形挡，其与弹簧托板上的挡块配合，限定了摇枕的最大横向位移（摆动加横移共为±32 mm），防止摇枕横向窜出，起到安全挡的作用。

Two triangular blocks are cast at the lower part of the bolster, which cooperate with the blocks on the spring bracket to limit the maximum lateral displacement of the bolster (Swing plus lateral displacement is ±32 mm in total), preventing the bolster from stringing out and acting as a safety block.

八字面磨耗板的材质为 Cr18Ni9，与摇枕组焊后，用 1 mm 塞尺塞入磨耗板与铸面之间，深度不得超过 12 mm。转 K4 型转向架的摇枕结构如图 5–31 所示。

The material of the octagonal wear plate is Cr18Ni9. After assembly and welding with the bolster, a 1 mm feeler gauge is used to plug between the wear plate and the casting surface, with a depth less than 12 mm. The bolster structure of bogie type ZK-4 is shown in Figure 5-31.

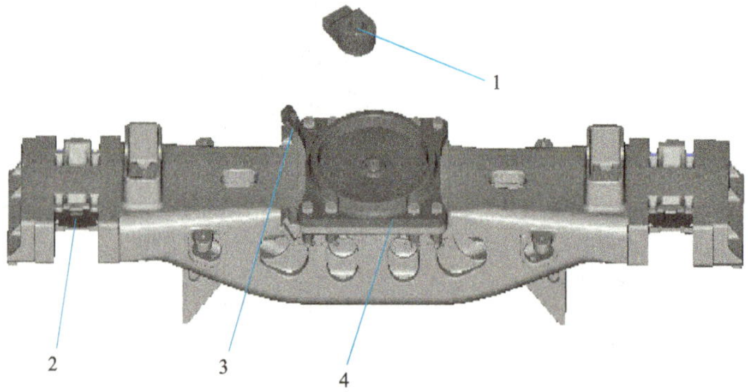

1—内外球套；2—八字面磨耗板；3—固定杠杆支点座；4—下心盘。

1—Inner and outer ball sleeve; 2—Octagonal wear plate; 3—Fixed lever fulcrum seat; 4—Lower center plate.

图 5–31　摇枕结构

Figure 5-31　Bolster Structure

2）侧架组成及承载鞍

Side frame composition and bearing saddle

转 K4 型转向架的侧架组成有侧架立柱磨耗板、侧架、导框摇动座等，如图 5–32 所示。

The side frame of bogie type ZK-4 consists of a side frame column wear plate, a side frame, a guide frame rolling seat, etc., as shown in Figure 5-32.

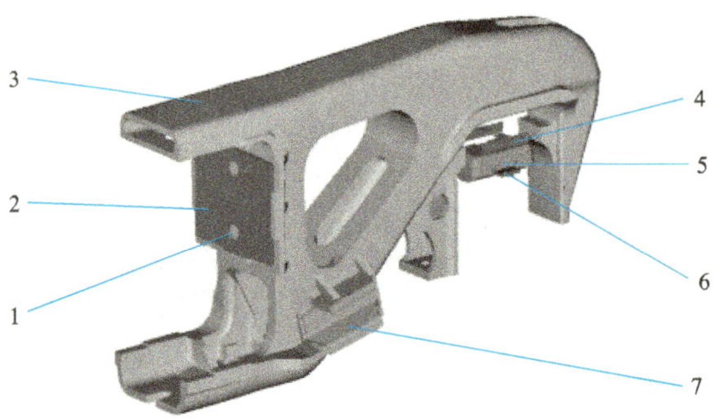

1—ZT 型折头螺栓；2—侧架立柱磨耗板；3—侧架；4—垫片；5—导框摇动座；6—固定块；7—侧架滑槽磨耗板。

1—ZT folding-head bolt; 2—Side frame column wear plate; 3—Side frame; 4—Gasket; 5—Guide frame rolling seat; 6—Fixing block; 7—Side frame chute wear plate.

图 5–32　侧架组成

Figure 5-32　Side Frame Composition

侧架立柱磨耗板的材质为 45 钢，用折头螺栓、防松螺母将其紧固在侧架上。同时，侧架上、下连接部位施以焊接。侧架中央方框下弦杆处是一腔形结构，用以安装摇动座支承及摇动座。其导框处是一腔形结构，用以安装导框摇动座。导框摇动座两侧可用不同厚度的垫片塞紧，再将固定块焊固，使导框摇动座定位于侧架导框顶部腔内。转 K4 型转向架的侧架、导框摇动座连接图如图 5-33 所示。

The side frame column wear plate is made of 45 steel, and it is fastened to the side frame with folding-head bolts and lock nuts. Moreover, the upper and lower connection parts of the side frame are welded. The lower chord of the central box of the side frame is a cavity-shaped structure used to install the rolling seat support and rolling seat. The guide frame has a cavity-shaped structure for installing the guide frame rolling seat. The two sides of the guide frame rolling seat can be plugged with gaskets of different thicknesses, and then the fixing block is welded firmly to fix the guide frame rolling seat in the top cavity of the side frame guide frame. The connection diagram of the side frame and guide frame rolling seat of bogie type ZK-4 is shown in Figure 5-33.

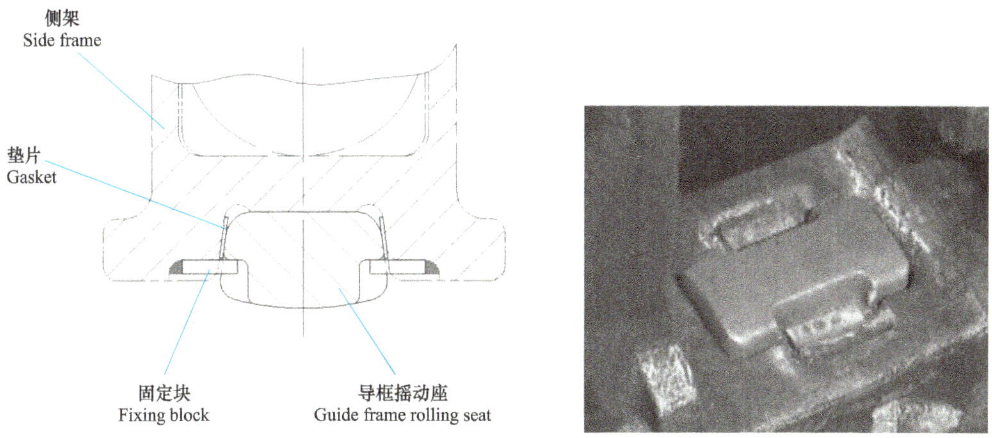

图 5-33　侧架、导框摇动座连接图

Figure 5-33　Connection Diagram of Side Frame and Guide Frame Rolling Seat

侧架导框摇动座底面为圆弧形，承载鞍顶面也是圆弧形，两圆弧形成滚动副，使侧架像吊杆一样，具有摆动的功能，以提高车辆的横向性能。转 K4 型转向架的承载鞍和导框摇动座如图 5-34 所示。

The bottom surface of the side frame guide frame rolling seat is arc-shaped, and the top surface of the bearing saddle is also arc-shaped. The two arcs form a rolling pair, making the side frame swing like a suspender and improving the lateral performance of the railway vehicle. The bearing saddle and guide frame rolling seat of bogie type ZK-4 are shown in Figure 5-34.

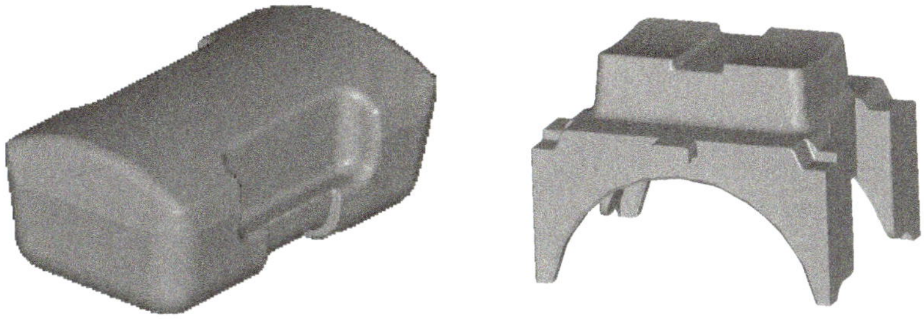

图 5-34　承载鞍和导框摇动座

Figure 5-34　Bearing Saddle and Guide Frame Rolling Seat

3）摇动座、摇动座支承及弹簧托板

Rolling seat, rolling seat support, and spring bracket

摇动座与弹簧托板用折头螺栓、防松螺母紧固，弹簧悬挂系统坐落在弹簧托板上；摇动座支承坐落在侧架中央方框下弦杆的腔形结构中，摇动座与摇动座支承的接触面为圆弧形结构，两圆弧形成滚动副，使侧架具有摆动的功能，如图 5–35 所示。

The rolling seat and the spring bracket are fastened with folding-head bolts and lock nuts, and the spring suspension system is located on the spring bracket; The rolling seat support is located in the cavity structure of the lower chord of the central box of thc side frame. The contact surface between the rolling seat and the rolling seat support is a circular arc structure, with two circular arcs forming a rolling pair, enabling the side frame to have a swinging function, as shown in Figure 5-35.

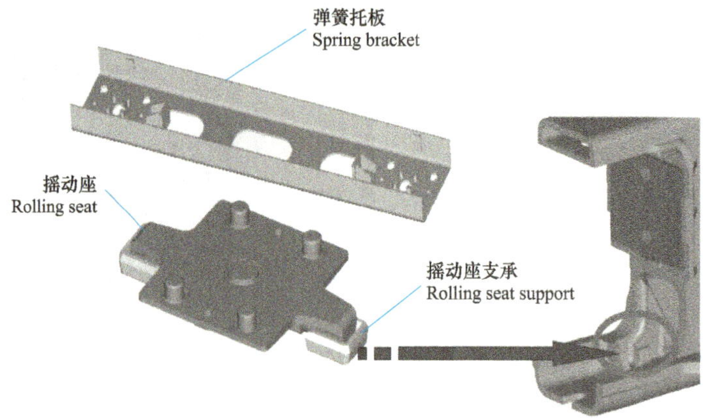

图 5–35　摇动座、摇动座支承及弹簧托板

Figure 5-35　Rolling Seat, Rolling Seat Support and Spring Bracket

4）弹性悬挂系统及减振装置

Elastic suspension system and vibration-damping device

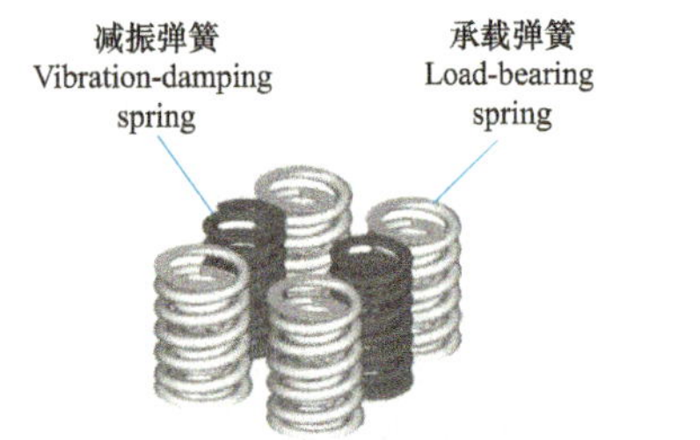

图 5–36　弹性悬挂系统

Figure 5-36　Elastic Suspension System

每侧的弹性悬挂系统及减振装置由 2 个斜楔组成、2 组减振内圆弹簧、2 组减振外圆弹簧、4 组承载内圆弹簧、4 组承载外圆弹簧组成，如图 5–36 所示。减振弹簧为两级刚度，减振内圆弹簧簧条直径为 17 mm，自由高度为 232 mm，减振外圆弹簧簧条直径为 21 mm，自由高度为 265 mm；承载弹簧也为两级刚度，承载内圆弹簧簧条直径为 20 mm，自由高度为 232 mm，承载外圆弹簧簧条直径为 24 mm，自由高度为 269 mm。这样就使空车、重车分别对应不同的空、重两级刚度，空车和重车都有优良的动力学性能。

The elastic suspension system and vibration-damping device on each side are composed of two wedges, two sets of inner vibration-damping helical springs, two sets of outer vibration-damping helical springs, four sets of load-bearing inner helical springs, and four sets of load-bearing outer helical springs, as shown in Figure 5-36. The vibration-damping spring has a two-stage rigidity, with a diameter of 17 mm and a free height of 232 mm for the inner vibration-damping helical spring, and a diameter of 21 mm and a free height of 265 mm for the outer vibration-damping helical spring; The load-bearing spring also has a two-stage rigidity, with a diameter of 20 mm and a free height of 232 mm for the inner load-bearing helical spring, and a diameter of 24 mm and a free height of 269 mm for the outer load-bearing helical spring; This allows the empty and loaded railway vehicles to correspond to different levels of rigidity, which both have excellent dynamic performance.

斜楔由材质为 ADI 的斜楔体及材质为高分子复合材料的摩擦板组成。部分由美国进口的斜楔，其复合材料摩擦板与斜楔体黏接。国产斜楔采用摩擦板嵌入斜楔体的组合结构，卸换方便。斜楔组成如图 5–37 所示。

The wedge is composed of a wedge made of ADI and a friction plate made of polymer composite material. Some of the wedges are imported from the United States, whose composite friction plates are bonded to the wedges. The domestic wedges adopt a combined structure with friction plates embedded in the wedges, which is convenient for removal and replacement. The composition of the wedge is shown in Figure 5-37.

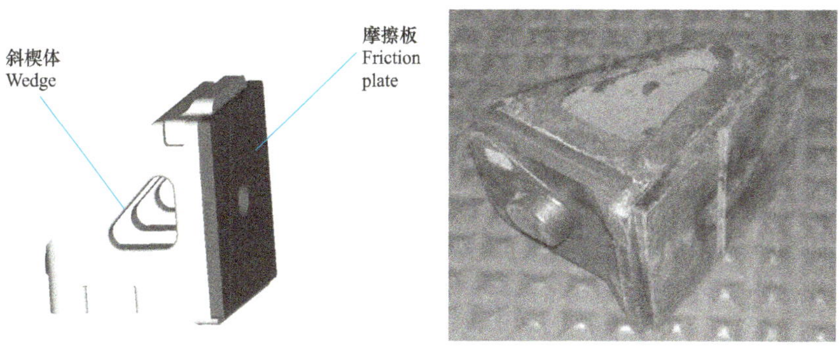

图 5–37　斜楔组成

Figure 5-37　Wedge Composition

5）常接触橡胶弹性旁承

Constant-contact rubber elastic side bearing

下旁承组成采用常接触橡胶弹性旁承，由旁承体组成、调整垫板、纵向锁紧斜铁组成，其中旁承体组成又由旁承体上部、旁承体下部、锥套形橡胶层、铆钉、旁承摩擦板等组成一个整体。图 5–38 所示为常接触橡胶弹性旁承。

The lower side bearing is subject to a constant-contact rubber elastic side bearing, which is composed of a side bearing body, an adjusting pad, and a longitudinal locking inclined iron. The side bearing body is composed of an upper part of the side bearing body, a lower part of the side bearing body, a conical sleeve-shaped rubber layer, rivets, a side bearing friction plate and others. Figure 5-38 shows a constant-contact rubber elastic side bearing.

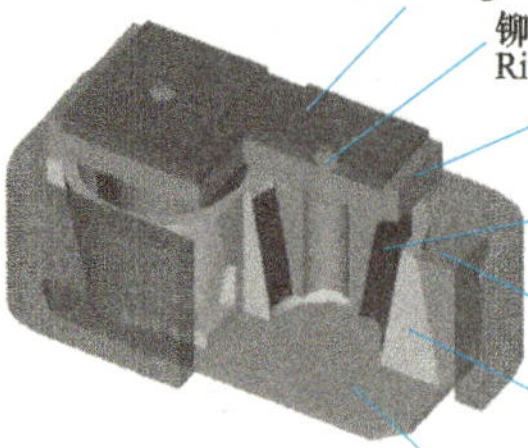

图 5-38　常接触橡胶弹性旁承

Figure 5-38　Constant-contact Rubber Elastic Side Bearing

常接触弹性旁承的主要特点如下。

The main characteristics of constant-contact elastic side bearings are as follows.

（1）结构简单紧凑，安装方便。由于旁承体组成通过橡胶将旁承体上部与旁承体下部硫化在一起，通过压入将旁承摩擦板与旁承上体连接成一个整体，所以结构简单紧凑。

Simple and compact structure, easy to install. Due to the composition of the side bearing body, the upper part of the side bearing body and the lower part of the side bearing body are vulcanized together through rubber, and the side bearing friction plate and the side bearing upper body are connected into a whole through pressing, with a simple and compact structure.

（2）检测、调整旁承压缩量方便。旁承体上部底面与旁承体下部顶面间距的变化量即为旁承压缩量。旁承压缩量不符要求时，可取出旁承体组成并加入适当厚度的调整垫板达到要求高度，然后插入纵向锁紧斜铁即可，操作方便。

Convenient to detect and adjust the compression amount of the side bearing. The variation in the distance between the upper bottom surface of the side bearing body and the lower top surface of the side bearing body is the compression amount of the side bearing. If the compression amount of the side bearing does not meet the requirements, the height required can be achieved by taking out the side bearing body, adding an adjusting pad with appropriate thickness, and inserting a longitudinal locking inclined iron, which is convenient for operation.

（3）纵向无间隙、无磨耗。采用纵向锁紧斜铁消除了旁承体下部与旁承盒之间的纵向间隙，采用锥套形橡胶层将旁承体上部与旁承体下部硫化在一起，消除了旁承体上、下部之间的间隙，实现了弹性旁承在纵向无间隙、无磨耗的条件下工作，可稳定地保持旁承抑制蛇行运动、提高临界速度的功能，并消除了旁承与旁承盒之间的磨耗，提高旁承的使用寿命，降低维护成本。

No longitudinal clearance and wear. The longitudinal locking inclined iron is used to eliminate the longitudinal gap between the entire lower part of the side bearing and the side bearing box. The tapered rubber sleeve is used to vulcanize the entire upper part of the side bearing and the lower part of the side bearing body together, eliminating the gap between the upper and lower parts of the side bearing body, realizing that the elastic side bearing works in a longitudinal gap-free and wear-free condition, stably maintaining the function of the side bearing to suppress hunting motion, improving the critical speed, eliminating the wear between the side bearing and the side bearing box, improving the service life of side bearings, and reducing maintenance costs.

（4）可靠性较好。橡胶弹性旁承在国内外有较多的使用，如美国的 Stcki 旁承。在橡胶质量有保证时，该旁承有较高的可靠性。在运行中，橡胶弹性旁承提供转向架相对于车体的回转力矩，以抑制车体的蛇行运动，约束车体侧滚振动，提高货车以较高速度运行时的平稳性和稳定性。

Good reliability. The rubber elastic side bearings are widely used at home and abroad, such as Stcki side bearings in the United States. When the quality of rubber is guaranteed, the side bearing has high reliability. During operation, the rotational torque of the bogie relative to the car body is provided by rubber elastic side bearings to suppress the hunting motion of the car body, restrain the rolling vibration of the car body, and improve the smoothness and stability of the freight car at higher speeds.

6）基础制动装置

Foundation braking device

转 K4 型转向架的基础制动装置如图 5-39 所示。

The foundation braking device of bogie type ZK-4 is shown in Figure 5-39.

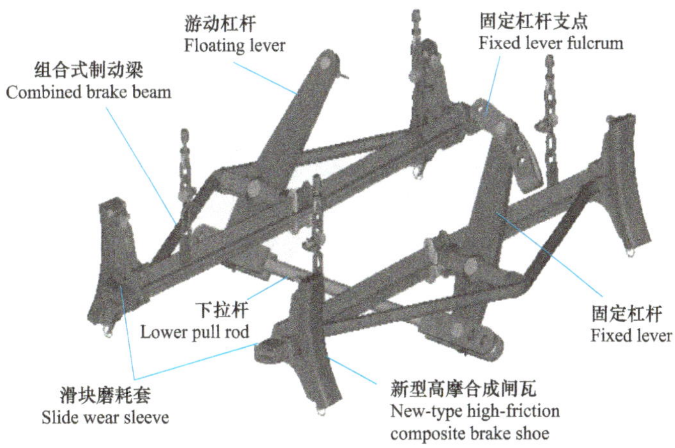

图 5-39　基础制动装置

Figure 5-39　Foundation Braking Device

制动杠杆中孔和固定杠杆支座孔装用球形销套，以利于侧架、摇枕的摆动。

The middle hole of the brake lever and the mounting hole of the fixed lever are equipped with ball-shaped pin sleeves to facilitate the swing of the side frame and bolster.

5.1.4　转 K5 型转向架

Bogie type ZK-5

转 K5 型转向架是在我国铁路大提速和重载战略下，由株洲车辆厂和美国原 ABC-NACO 公司在转 K4 型转向架的基础上联合开发的新产品。

Bogie type ZK-5 is a new product jointly developed by CRRC Zhuzhou Locomotive and the original ABC-NACO Company of the United States based on bogie type ZK-4 under the strategy of large railway speed increase and heavy load in China.

1. 转 K5 型转向架的结构特点

Structural characteristics of bogie type ZK-5

转 K5 型转向架适用于在标准轨距铁路上运用的载重为 70 t 级的各型铁路货车、载重为 76 t 和 80 t 的各型运煤专用敞车及其他总重为 100 t 的铁路专用货车。其主要特点与转 K4 型转向架相同。转 K5 型转向架及其悬挂装置分解图分别如图 5–40、图 5–41 所示。

Bogie type ZK-5 is applicable to various types of railway freight cars with a load of 70 t, various types of coal transport gondolas with a load of 76 t and 80 t, and other railway special freight cars with a total weight of 100 t used on standard track gauge railways. Its main characteristics are the same as those of bogie type ZK-4. The exploded views of bogie type ZK-5 and its suspension device are shown in Figure 5-40 and Figure 5-41, respectively.

图 5–40　转 K5 型转向架

Figure 5-40　Bogie Type ZK-5

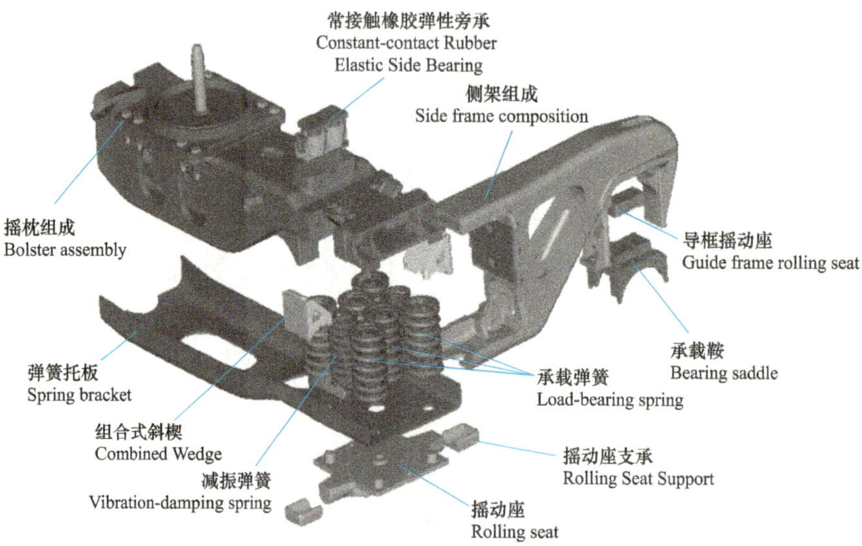

图 5–41　转 K5 型转向架悬挂装置分解图

Figure 5-41　Exploded View of Suspension Device for Bogie Type ZK-5

2. 转 K5 型转向架的主要性能参数及尺寸参数

Main performance parameters and dimensional parameters of bogie type ZK-5

转 K5 型转向架的主要性能参数及尺寸参数分别如表 5–4、表 5–5 所示。

The main performance parameters and dimensional parameters of bogie type ZK-5 are shown in Table 5-4 and Table 5-5.

表 5–4 转 K5 型转向架的主要性能参数

Table 5–4 Main Performance Parameters of Bogie Type ZK-5

轴重 Axle load	25 t
固定轴距 Fixed wheelbase	1 800 mm
自重 Tare weight	≤4.7 t
商业运行速度 Commercial operating speed	120 km/h
轨距 Track gauge	1 435 mm
轮径 Wheel diameter	840 mm
车轮踏面形状 Wheel tread shape	磨耗型踏面 Hollow tread
轴型 Axle type	RE_{2B} 型 RE_{2B}
轴承 Bearing	353130A 型、353130B 型或 353130C 型 Type 353130A, 353130B, or 353130C
基础制动装置制动倍率 Foundation braking device braking ratio	4

表 5–5 转 K5 型转向架的主要尺寸参数

Table 5–5 Main Dimensional Parameters of Bogie Type ZK-5

固定轴距 Fixed wheelbase	1 800 mm
轴颈中心距 Journal center distance	1 981 mm
旁承中心距 Side bearing center distance	1 520 mm
下心盘面直径 Lower center plate diameter	375 mm
下心盘面（含心盘衬垫）距轨面自由高 Free height from lower center plate surface (including center plate gasket) to rail surface	703 mm

续表

Continued

下心盘面至弹性旁承顶面距离 Distance from the lower center plate surface to the top surface of the elastic side bearing	83 mm
侧架上平面距轨面高 Height from the upper plane of side frame to rail surface	765 mm
侧架下平面距轨面高 Height from the lower plane of side frame to rail surface	160 mm

3. 转 K5 型转向架的结构

Structure of bogie type ZK-5

1）轮对与轴承

Wheelsets and bearings

采用 RE_{2B} 型轮对及 353130A、353130B 或 353130C 紧凑型滚动轴承，车轮为新结构轻型铸钢车轮（HEZB）或辗钢车轮（HESA），车轴为 RE_{2B} 车轴。转 K5 型转向架的轮对如图 5-42 所示。

RE_{2B} wheelsets and 353130A, 353130B, or 353130C compact roller bearings are used. The wheels are new structure lightweight cast steel wheels (HEZB) or rolled steel wheels (HESA), and the axles are RE_{2B} axles. The wheelset of bogie type ZK-5 is shown in Figure 5-42.

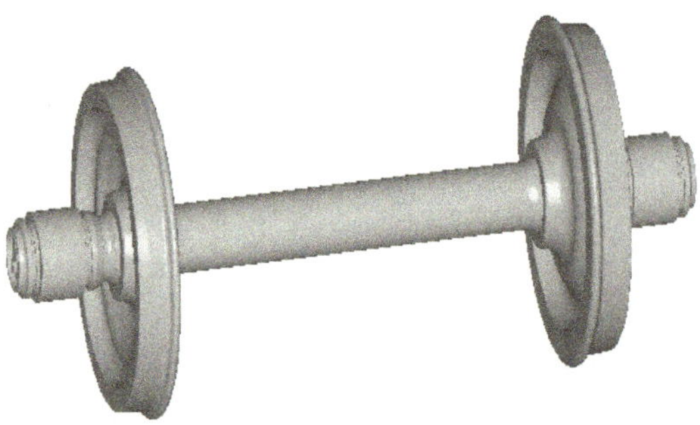

图 5-42　轮对

Figure 5-42　Wheelset

2）承载鞍

Bearing saddle

承载鞍的鞍顶面为经硬化处理的圆弧面，与导框摇动座组合成为摆动机构的上摆点，有摆动的功能，以提高车辆的横向性能。承载鞍的材质为 C 级钢。转 K5 型转向架的承载鞍如图 5-43 所示。

The saddle top surface of the bearing saddle is a hardened curved surface, which is combined with the guide frame rolling seat to form the upper swing point of the swing mechanism, providing a swing function and improving the lateral performance of the railway vehicle. The material of bearing saddle is Grade C steel. The bearing saddle of bogie type ZK-5 is shown in Figure 5-43.

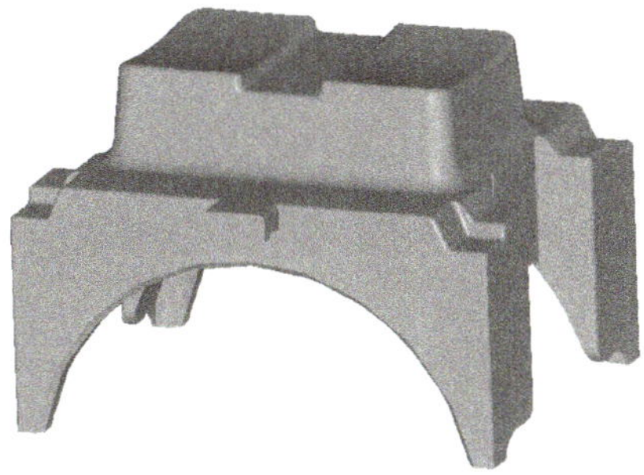

图 5-43　承载鞍
Figure 5-43　Bearing Saddle

3）侧架组成
Side frame composition

转 K5 型转向架的侧架组成由侧架、侧架立柱磨耗板、ZT 型平头折头螺栓、导框摇动座、导框摇动座固定块、侧架滑槽磨耗板组成，如图 5-44 所示。侧架的材质为 B 级钢，侧架立柱磨耗板的材质为 45 钢，侧架滑槽磨耗板的材质为 47Mn2Si2TiB 或 T10 钢。侧架立柱磨耗板用两个 ZT 型平头折头螺栓紧固在侧架立柱面上。导框摇动座为合金钢锻件，用固定块固定于侧架导框处。侧架立柱磨耗板、ZT 型平头折头螺栓及防松螺母均与转 K4 型转向架通用。

The side frame of bogie type ZK-5 consists of side frame, side frame column wear plate, ZT flat-head folding-head bolt, guide frame rolling seat, guide frame rolling seat fixing block, and side frame chute wear plate, as shown in Figure 5-44. The side frame is made of Grade B steel, the side frame column wear plate is made of 45 steel, and the side frame chute wear plate is made of 47Mn2Si2TiB or T10 steel. The side frame column wear plate is fastened to the side frame column surface with two ZT flat-head folding-head bolts. The guide frame rolling seat is made of alloy steel forgings, and is fixed to the side frame guide frame with a fixing block. The side frame column wear plate, ZT flat-head folding-head bolt, and lock nut are all common to bogie type ZK-4.

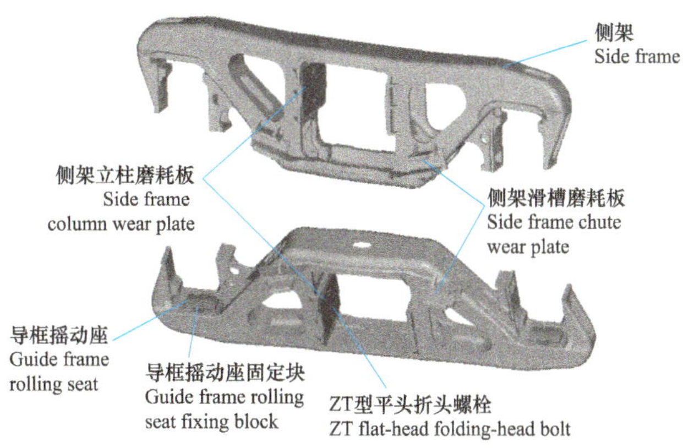

图 5-44　侧架组成
Figure 5-44　Side Frame Composition

4）摇枕组成

Bolster composition

转 K5 型转向架的摇枕组成由摇枕、固定杠杆支点座、下心盘、心盘磨耗盘、八字面磨耗板、上拉杆托架等组成，如图 5–45 所示。摇枕和下心盘的材质均为 B 级钢，下心盘直径为 375 mm。

The bolster of bogie type ZK-5 consists of a bolster, a fixed lever fulcrum seat, a lower center plate, a center plate wear plate, an octagonal wear plate, an upper pull rod bracket and others, as shown in Figure 5-45. The bolster and lower center plate are made of Grade B steel, and the diameter of the lower center plate is 375 mm.

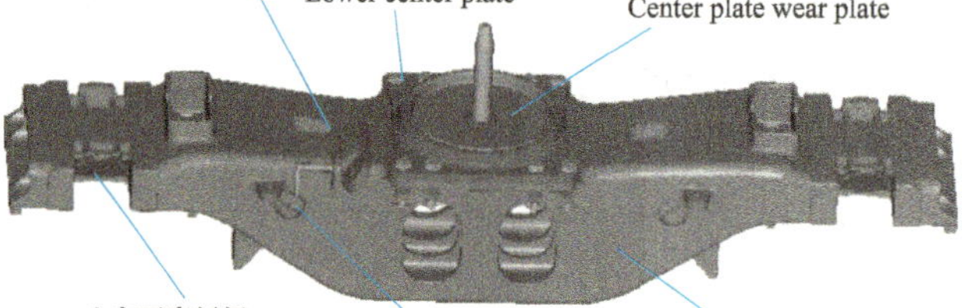

图 5–45 摇枕组成

Figure 5-45 Bolster Composition

摇枕组成内有材质为含油尼龙的心盘磨耗盘，心盘螺母采用 10 级 BY-A 24 或 BY-B 24 防松螺母，配套螺栓采用《六角头螺杆带孔螺栓》（GB/T 31.1—2013）中规定的螺栓，螺栓强度为 10.9 级。摇枕八字面采用不锈钢磨耗板，材质为 0Cr18Ni9，与转 K4 型转向架的磨耗板通用。

There is a center plate wear plate made of oil containing nylon inside the bolster. The center plate nut is a Grade 10 BY-A 24 or BY-B 24 lock nut, and the matching bolt is a bolt specified in *Hexagon Bolts with Split Pin Hole on Shank* (GB/T 31.1—2013), with a bolt strength of Grade 10.9. The splayed surface of the bolster is made of stainless steel wear plate made of 0Cr18Ni9, which is common to the wear plate of bogie type ZK-4.

摇枕下部铸出两块三角形挡，其与弹簧托板上的挡块配合，限定摇枕的最大横向位移（摆动加横移共为±32 mm），防止摇枕窜出，起到安全挡的作用。

Two triangular blocks are cast at the lower part of the bolster, which cooperate with the blocks on the spring bracket to limit the maximum lateral displacement of the bolster (Swing plus lateral displacement is ±32 mm in total), preventing the bolster from stringing out and acting as a safety block.

5）摇动座、摇动座支承及弹簧托板

Rolling seat, rolling seat support, and spring bracket

摇动座与弹簧托板用折头螺栓、防松螺母紧固，弹簧悬挂系统坐落在弹簧托板上。摇动座支承坐落在侧架中央方框下弦杆的腔形结构中，摇动座与摇动座支承的接触面为圆弧形结构，两圆弧形成滚动副，使侧架具有摆动的功能。摇动座与摇动座支承均沿用美国原ABC-NACO 公司的标准件，摇动座为 E 级钢铸件，摇动座支承为合金钢锻件，且摇动座支承、折头螺栓及防松螺母与转 K4 型转向架通用。

The rolling seat and the spring bracket are fastened with folding-head bolts and lock nuts, and the spring suspension system is located on the spring bracket. The rolling seat support is located in the cavity structure of the lower chord of the central box of the side frame. The contact surface between the rolling seat and the rolling seat support is a circular arc structure, with two circular arcs forming a rolling pair, enabling the side frame to have a swinging function. The standard parts of the original ABC-NACO Company of the United States are used for both the rolling seat and the rolling seat support. The rolling seat is made of Grade E steel castings, and the rolling seat support is made of alloy steel forgings. The rolling seat support, folding-head bolts, and lock nuts are common to bogie type ZK-4.

弹簧托板为高强度钢压型件，板厚为 10 mm。转 K5 型转向架的摇动座、摇动座支承及弹簧托板如图 5–46 所示。

The spring bracket is a high-strength steel compression member with a plate thickness of 10 mm. Figure 5-46 shows the rolling seat, rolling seat support and spring bracket of bogie type ZK-5.

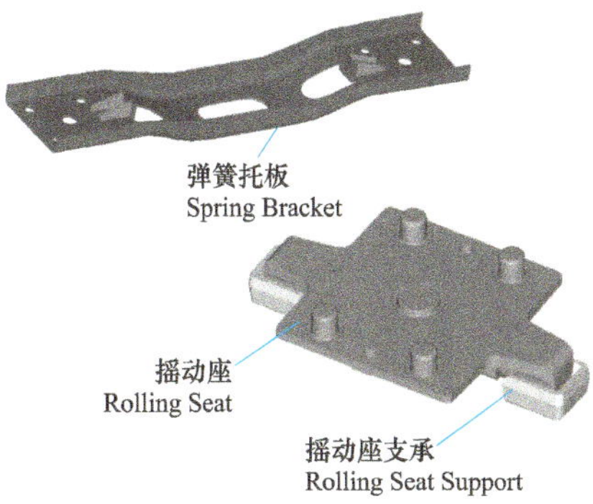

图 5–46 摇动座、摇动座支承及弹簧托板

Figure 5-46 Rolling Seat, Rolling Seat Support and Spring Bracket

6）弹簧悬挂系统及减振装置

Spring suspension system and vibration-damping device

每侧的弹性悬挂系统及减振装置由 2 个斜楔组成、2 组减振弹簧、6 组承载弹簧组成。减振弹簧与承载弹簧均为两级刚度，使空车、重车分别对应不同的空、重两级刚度，空车和重车均有优良的动力性能。

The elastic suspension system and vibration-damping device on each side are composed of two wedges, two sets of vibration-damping springs, and six sets of load-bearing springs. Both the vibration-damping spring and the load-bearing spring are of two-stage rigidity, allowing empty and loaded railway vehicles to correspond to different levels of rigidity, respectively, with excellent dynamic performance.

斜楔由材质为奥贝球铁的斜楔体及材质为高分子复合材料的主摩擦板组成，减振内、外圆弹簧和斜楔组成均与转 K4 型转向架通用。转 K5 型转向架的悬挂装置及斜楔如图 5–47 所示。

The wedge is composed of a wedge made of austempering ductile iron and a main friction plate made of polymer composite material. The inner and outer vibration-damping helical springs, and wedge components are common to bogie type ZK-4. The suspension device and wedge of bogie type ZK-5 are shown in Figure 5-47.

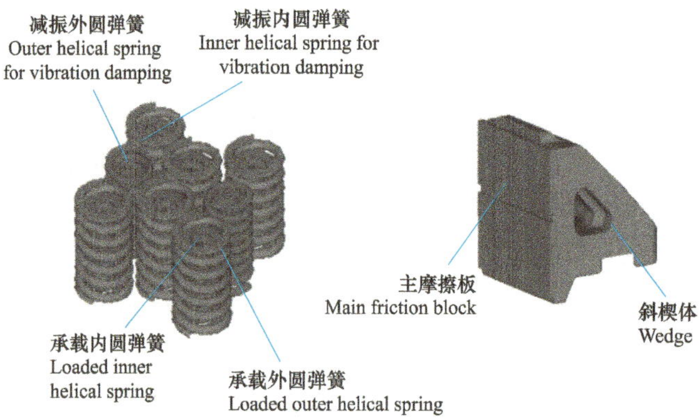

图 5–47 悬挂装置及斜楔

Figure 5-47 Suspension Device and Wedge

7）基础制动装置

Foundation braking device

基础制动装置为中穿拉杆形式，采用新型高摩合成闸瓦。采用奥贝球铁耐磨销套及相应圆销，固定杠杆支点与固定杠杆支点座之间用链蹄环连接，以利于侧架、摇枕的摆动。转 K5 型转向架的基础制动装置如图 5–48 所示。

The foundation braking device is in the form of a middle-through pull rod and a new-type high-friction composite brake shoe. Austempering ductile iron wear-resistant pin sleeves and corresponding round pins are used. The fixed lever fulcrum and the fixed lever fulcrum seat are connected with chain shoe rings to facilitate the swing of the side frame and bolster. The foundation braking device of bogie type ZK-5 is shown in Figure 5-48.

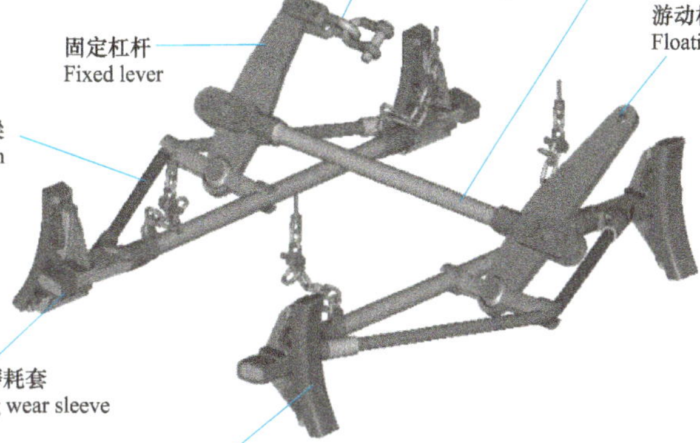

图 5-48 基础制动装置

Figure 5-48 Foundation Braking Device

8）下旁承组成

Lower side bearing composition

下旁承采用常接触橡胶弹性旁承，下旁承由旁承体组成、调整垫板、纵向锁紧斜铁组成，其中旁承体组成又由旁承体上部、旁承体下部、锥套形橡胶层、铆钉、旁承摩擦板等组成一个整体。转 K5 型转向架的常接触橡胶弹性旁承如图 5-49 所示。

The lower side bearing is subject to a constant-contact rubber elastic side bearing, which is composed of a side bearing body, an adjusting pad, and a longitudinal locking inclined iron. The side bearing body is composed of an upper part of the side bearing body, a lower part of the side bearing body, a conical sleeve-shaped rubber layer, rivets, and a side bearing friction plate. The constant-contact rubber elastic side bearings of bogie type ZK-5 are shown in Figure 5-49.

图 5-49 常接触橡胶弹性旁承

Figure 5-49 Constant-contact Rubber Elastic Side Bearing

9）横跨梁组成

Cross beam composition

横跨梁为 50 mm×50 mm×3 mm 方钢管压型件，中间焊有不锈钢磨耗板，两端分别落在横跨梁托上。横跨梁托焊在侧架上，用来与空重车调整阀接触以感知车重。转 K5 型转向架的横跨梁组成如图 5-50 所示。

The cross beam is a 50 mm × 50 mm × 3 mm square steel tube compression member, welded with a stainless steel wear plate in the middle, with both ends resting on the cross beam bracket, and the cross beam bracket welded to the side frame. It is used to sense the railway vehicle's weight by contacting the empty load regulating valve. The cross beam composition of bogie type ZK-5 is shown in Figure 5-50.

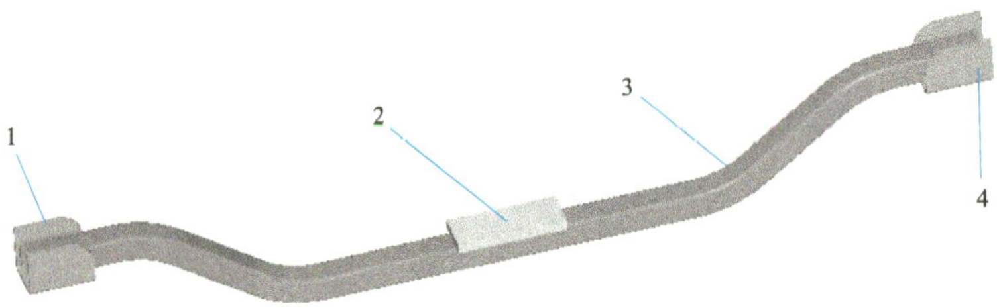

1—横跨梁托（一）；2—磨耗板；3—横跨梁；4—横跨梁托（二）。
1—Cross beam bracket (I); 2—Wear plate; 3—Cross beam; 4—Cross beam bracket (II).

图 5-50 横跨梁组成
Figure 5-50 Cross Beam Composition

5.1.5 转 K6 型转向架
Bogie type ZK-6

1. 转 K6 型转向架的用途
Purpose of bogie type ZK-6

转 K6 型转向架适用于标准轨距、轴重 25 t、最高商业运营速度 120 km/h 的各型铁路提速、重载货车。

Bogie type ZK-6 is suitable for various types of railway speed-up and heavy-haul freight cars with the standard track gauge, axle load of 25t, and maximum commercial operating speed of 120 km/h.

2. 转 K6 型转向架的结构特点
Structural characteristics of bogie type ZK-6

转 K6 型转向架为铸钢三大件式货车转向架。一系悬挂采用轴箱弹性剪切垫；二系悬挂采用带变摩擦减振装置的中央枕簧悬挂系统，摇枕弹簧为二级刚度；两侧架之间加装侧架弹性下交叉支撑装置；采用直径为 375 mm 的下心盘，下心盘内设有含油尼龙心盘磨耗盘；采用 JC 型双作用常接触弹性旁承；装用 25 t 轴重双列圆锥滚子轴承，采用轻型新结构 HEZB 型铸钢车轮或 HESA 型辗钢车轮；基础制动装置为中拉杆式单侧闸瓦制动装置，采用 L-A 型或 L-B 型组合式制动梁及新型高摩合成闸瓦。转 K6 型转向架的整体图和分解图分别如图 5-51、图 5-52 所示。

Bogie type ZK-6 is a kind of cast steel three-piece freight car bogie. The primary suspension is subject to axle box elastic shear pads; The secondary suspension is subject to a central bolster spring suspension system with variable-friction vibration-damping devices, and the bolster spring has a secondary rigidity; An elastic lower cross-support device of the side frame is installed between the two side frames; A lower center plate with a diameter of 375 mm is used, and an oil-containing nylon center plate wear plate is installed inside the lower center plate; JC double-acting constant-contact elastic side bearing is adopted; The 25 t axle load double-row tapered roller bearings are adopted, and lightweight new structure HEZB cast steel wheels or HESA rolled steel wheels are used; The foundation braking device is a center pull rod type single-side brake shoe braking device, using L-A or L-B combined brake beams, and a new-type high-friction composite brake shoe. The overall and exploded views of bogie type ZK-6 are shown in Figure 5-51 and Figure 5-52, respectively.

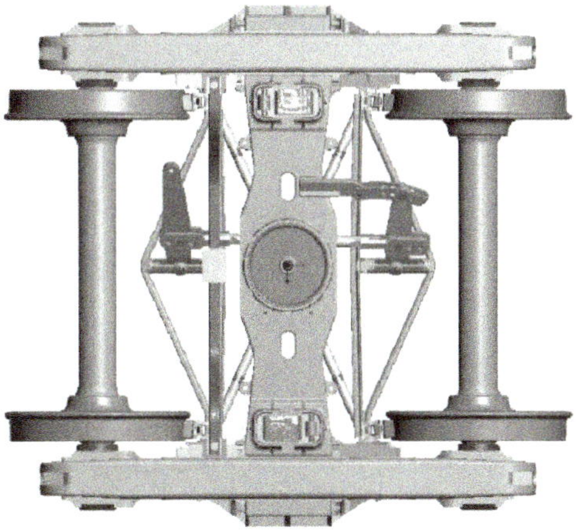

图 5–51　转 K6 型转向架的整体图
Figure 5-51　Overall View of Bogie Type ZK-6

图 5–52　转 K6 型转向架的分解图
Figure 5-52　Exploded View of Bogie Type ZK-6

3. 转 K6 型转向架的主要性能参数及尺寸参数
Main performance parameters and dimensional parameters of bogie type ZK-6

转 K6 型转向架的主要性能参数及尺寸参数如表 5–6、表 5–7 所示。

The main performance parameters and dimensional parameters of bogie type ZK-6 are shown in Table 5-6 and Table 5-7.

表 5–6　转 K6 型转向架的主要性能参数
Table 5-6　Main Performance Parameters of Bogie Type ZK–6

轨距 Track gauge	1 435 mm
轴重 Axle load	25 t
轴型 Axle type	RE_{2A} 或 RE_{2B} RE_{2A} or RE_{2B}
自重 Tare weight	4.8 t
最高商业运营速度 Max. commercial operation speed	120 km/h
通过最小半径（限速） Min. passing radius (speed limit)	145 m

表 5–7 转 K6 型转向架的主要尺寸参数

Table 5-7 Main Dimensional Parameters of Bogie Type ZK-6

<table>
<tr><td>固定轴距
Fixed wheelbase</td><td>1 830 mm</td></tr>
<tr><td>车轮直径
Wheel diameter</td><td>840 mm</td></tr>
<tr><td>移动杠杆自由端与铅垂面夹角
Angle between the free end of the moving lever and the vertical surface</td><td>53°</td></tr>
<tr><td>基础制动装置制动倍率
Foundation braking device braking ratio</td><td>4</td></tr>
<tr><td>轴颈中心距
Journal center distance</td><td>1 981 mm</td></tr>
<tr><td>旁承中心距
Side bearing center distance</td><td>1 520 mm</td></tr>
<tr><td>空车心盘至轨面高（心盘载荷 65.7 kN）
Height from empty center plate to rail surface (center plate load 65.7 kN)</td><td>680 mm</td></tr>
<tr><td>下心盘直径
Lower center plate diameter</td><td>375 mm</td></tr>
<tr><td rowspan="2">下心盘面至下旁承顶面距离
Distance from lower center plate surface to lower side bearing top surface</td><td>自由状态 93 mm
Free state 93 mm</td></tr>
<tr><td>工作状态 83 mm
Working state 83 mm</td></tr>
<tr><td>侧架上平面至轨面距离
Distance from the upper plane of side frame to rail surface</td><td>787 mm</td></tr>
<tr><td>侧架下平面至轨面距离
Distance from the lower plane of side frame to rail surface</td><td>162 mm</td></tr>
</table>

4. 转 K6 型转向架的结构

Structure of bogie type ZK-6

1）轴箱橡胶垫

Axle box rubber pad

转 K6 型转向架轴箱一系加装了内八字橡胶弹性剪切垫，实现轮对的弹性定位，减小转向架簧下质量及轮轨作用力，降低轮轨磨耗，隔离轮轨间高频振动、缓和轮轨冲击，有利于提高侧架等零部件的疲劳寿命。组装轴箱橡胶垫时，铜绞线在转向架内侧。转 K6 型转向架的轴箱橡胶垫如图 5–53 所示。

The axle box of bogie type ZK-6 is equipped with an inner octagonal rubber elastic shear pad to achieve elastic positioning of the wheelset and reduce the unsprung mass of the bogie, the wheel-rail force, and wheel-rail wear, isolate high-frequency vibration between wheels and rails, mitigate the wheel-rail impact, and it is beneficial to improving the fatigue life of components such as side frames. When the axle box rubber pad is assembled, the copper stranded wire is located inside the bogie. The axle box rubber pad of bogie type ZK-6 is shown in Figure 5-53.

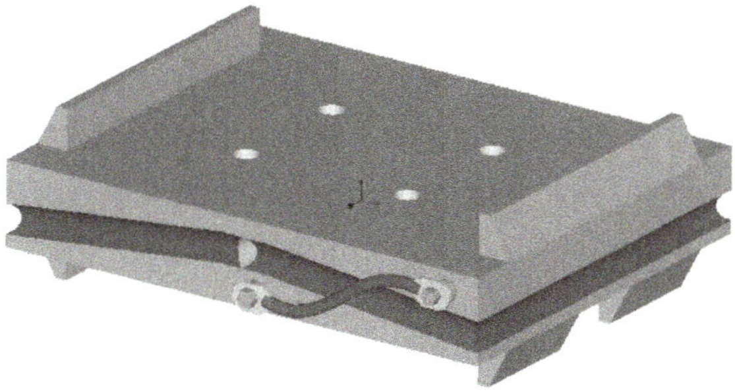

图 5–53 轴箱橡胶垫
Figure 5-53 Axle Box Rubber Pad

2）侧架弹性下交叉支撑装置

Elastic lower cross-support device of the side frame

转 K6 型转向架采用侧架弹性下交叉支撑装置，用以提高转向架的抗菱刚度，从而提高转向架的蛇行失稳临界速度及货车直线运行的稳定性。同时，支撑装置可有效保持转向架的正位状态，从而减小了车辆在直线和曲线运行时对钢轨的冲击，改善了转向架的曲线通过性能，显著减少了轮轨磨耗。

The elastic lower cross support device of the side frame is used for bogie type ZK-6 to improve the diamond-resistant rigidity of the bogie, thereby increasing the critical speed of hunting instability of the bogie and improving the stability of the freight car when running in a straight line. Besides, the support device can effectively maintain the upright position of the bogie, thereby reducing the impact against the rail when the railway vehicle is running in straight and curved lines, improving the curving performance of the bogie, and significantly reducing wheel-rail wear.

理论研究指出，三大件式转向架的抗菱刚度对转向架的蛇行运动稳定性有控制性作用。抗菱刚度小，两轮对容易产生同相摇头和反相横移运动，转向架直线运行的稳定性就差，容易发生蛇行失稳，并降低车辆平稳性。因此，提高三大件式转向架的抗菱刚度是非常重要的。

Theoretical research indicates that the diamond-resistant rigidity of a three-piece bogie has a controlling effect on the hunting stability of the bogie. If the diamond-resistant rigidity is small and two-wheel pairs are prone to in-phase shaking and reverse lateral movement, the stability of the straight running of the bogie will be poor and prone to hunting instability, thus reducing the railway vehicle’s stability. Therefore, it is very important to improve the diamond-resistant rigidity of three-piece bogies.

传统三大件式转向架的两侧架之间仅通过摇枕、弹簧、斜楔连接，抵抗菱形变形的能力有限。转 K6 型转向架的两侧架之间不但通过摇枕、弹簧、斜楔连接，而且增加了新的连接方式（交叉杆），转向架抗菱刚度显著增大。根据实测结果，交叉支撑转向架的空、重车抗菱刚度可比原三大件式转向架提高 3～6 倍。

The two side frames of the traditional three-piece bogies are only connected by bolsters, springs, and wedges, which have limited diamond-resistant deformation. The two side frames of bogie type ZK-6 are connected not only by bolsters, springs, and wedges but also by a new connection method (crossbar), significantly increasing the diamond-resistant rigidity of the bogie.

According to the measured results, the diamond-resistant rigidity of empty and heavy vehicles of cross-supported bogies can be 3–6 times higher than that of the original three-piece bogies.

下交叉支撑装置由 1 个下交叉杆、1 个上交叉杆、8 个橡胶垫、4 个双耳垫圈、4 个锁紧板、4 个紧固螺栓组成。转 K6 型转向架的侧架弹性下交叉支撑装置如图 5–54 所示。

The lower cross-support device consists of a lower crossbar, an upper crossbar, 8 rubber pads, 4 double flange washers, 4 locking plates, and 4 fastening bolts. The elastic lower cross-support device of the side frame of bogie type ZK-6 is shown in Figure 5-54.

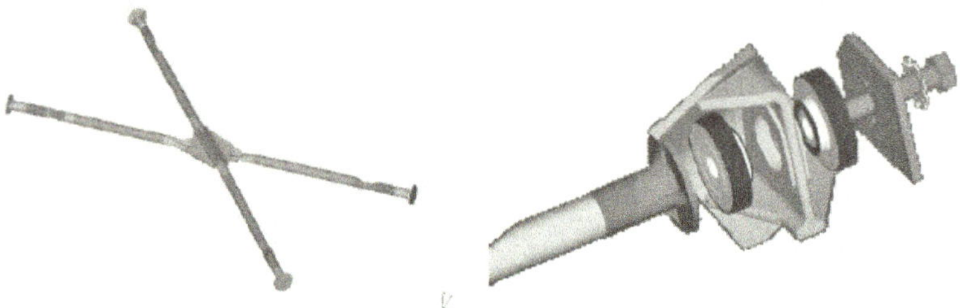

图 5–54　侧架弹性下交叉支撑装置
Figure 5-54　Elastic Lower Cross-support Device of Side Frame

在上、下交叉杆中部焊有上、下夹板，利用 2 组 M12 螺栓、螺母及垫圈将夹板紧固，同时把螺母用电焊点固，上、下夹板间有 4 处塞焊点和两条平焊缝，把上、下交叉杆点固成一个整体。

The upper and lower clamp plates are welded in the middle of the upper and lower cross bars. The clamp plates are fastened using two sets of M12 bolts, nuts, and washers. In addition, the nuts are welded by electric welding. There are four plug welds and two flat welds between the upper and lower clamp plates, securing the upper and lower cross bars as a whole.

3）双作用常接触弹性旁承

Double-acting constant-contact elastic side bearing

货车运行速度要求采用常接触旁承增大转向架与车体之间的回转阻尼，以有效抑制转向架与车体的摇头蛇行运动，同时约束车体侧滚振动，提高货车以较高速度运行时的平稳性和稳定性。对于常接触弹性旁承而言，由于上、下旁承之间无间隙而又有接触弹性，也增加了车体在转向架上的侧滚稳定性。同时，为了防止货车曲线运行时车体发生过大倾角，采用刚性滚子来限制弹性旁承的压缩量。一旦上旁承板压靠滚子，不仅车体侧倾角受到限制，而且因滚子的滚动而不致增大回转阻力矩，影响曲线通过性能。

The requirement for the running speed of freight cars is to use constant-contact side bearings to increase the rotational damping between the bogie and the car body to effectively suppress the shaking and hunting motion of the bogie and the car body, while restraining the rolling vibration of the car body and improving the smoothness and stability of the freight car when it operates at higher speeds. Constant-contact elastic side bearings also increase the rolling stability of the car body on the bogie due to the fact that there is no gap between the upper and lower side bearings with contact elasticity. Furthermore, to prevent excessive inclination of the car body during the curve operation of the freight car, rigid rollers are used to limit the compression amount of the elastic side bearings. Once the upper side bearing plate presses against the roller, the roll angle of the car body can be limited, and the rolling of the roller won't increase the rotational resistance moment and affect the curving performance.

JC 型双作用弹性旁承由弹性旁承体、旁承磨耗板、旁承座、滚子、滚子轴、调整垫板、垫片等零部件组成，如图 5-55 所示。

JC double-acting elastic side bearing consists of an elastic side bearing body, side bearing wear plate, side bearing seat, roller, roller bearing, adjusting pad, gasket, and other components, as shown in Figure 5-55.

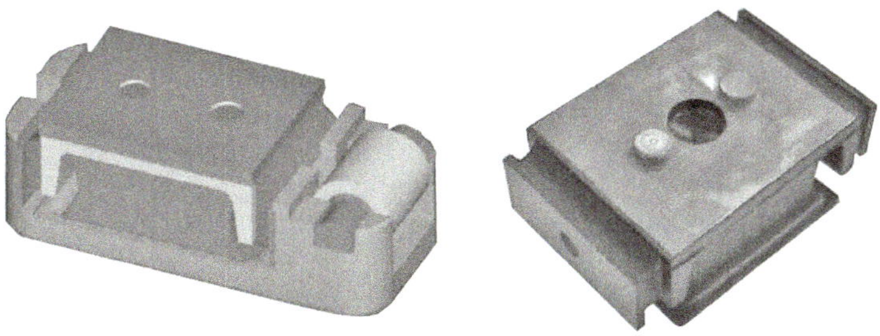

图 5-55 JC 型双作用弹性旁承
Figure 5-55 JC Double-acting Elastic Side Bearing

4）中央悬挂系统两级刚度弹簧
Two-stage rigidity spring of the central suspension system

众所周知，提高弹簧静挠度不仅可提高货车转向架的运行平稳性，而且还可以提高转向架对扭曲线路的适应性和脱轨安全性。现有货车空车运行性能和脱轨安全性不良，也与空车弹簧静挠度过小有关，因此有必要采取措施提高货车空车的弹簧静挠度。

It is well known that improving the static deflection of springs can improve not only the running stability of freight car bogies but also the adaptability of bogies to twisted lines and derailment safety. The poor running performance and derailment safety of existing freight cars are also related to the small static deflection of springs in the empty vehicle. Therefore, it is necessary to take measures to improve the static deflection of springs in the empty vehicle.

采用内、外枕簧不同高度的两级刚度弹簧是提高空车弹簧静挠度的有效措施，即在空车时弹簧具有较小的刚度，使空车弹簧静挠度提高，而在重车时弹簧具有较大的刚度，以承受重车的载荷，这样可使货车转向架的空、重车弹簧静挠度都在合理范围内。转 K6 型转向架所采用的两级刚度弹簧为内、外圈弹簧不等高结构，空车时仅外圈弹簧承重，重车时则由内、外圈弹簧共同承重。

Using two-stage rigidity springs with different heights of inner and outer bolster springs is an effective measure to improve the static deflection of empty-vehicle springs. That is, when the vehicle is empty, the spring has a smaller rigidity, which increases its static deflection. When the vehicle is loaded, the spring has a greater rigidity to withstand the load of the vehicle. In this way, the static deflection of empty and loaded vehicle springs of the freight car bogie can be kept in a reasonable range. The two-stage rigidity springs used for bogie type ZK-6 are of unequal height structures with inner and outer ring springs. When empty, only the outer ring springs bear the load, while when loaded, both the inner and outer ring springs bear the load.

转向架摇枕弹簧由 6 个外圆弹簧（一）、1 个外圆弹簧（二）和 7 个内圆弹簧组成。外圆弹簧（一）比内圆弹簧高 23 mm，外圆弹簧（二）与内圆弹簧同高。为便于识别，外圆弹簧（二）涂黄色厚浆醇酸漆。转 K6 型转向架的中央悬挂装置布置图如图 5–56 所示。

The bogie bolster spring consists of 6 outer helical springs (I), 1 outer helical spring (II), and 7 inner helical springs. The outer helical spring (I) is 23 mm higher than the inner helical spring, and the outer helical spring (II) is the same height as the inner helical spring. For easy identification, the outer helical spring (II) is coated with yellow thick alkyd paint. The layout of the central suspension device for bogie type ZK-6 is shown in Figure 5-56.

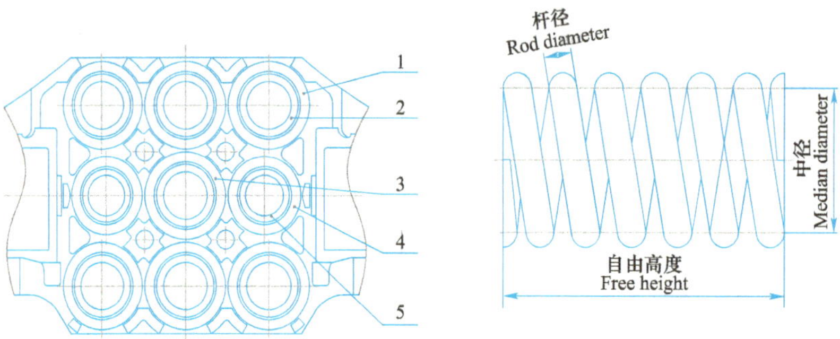

1—外圆弹簧（一）；2—内圆弹簧；3—外圆弹簧（二）；4—减振外圆弹簧；5—减振内圆弹簧。
1—Outer helical spring (I); 2—Inner helical spring; 3—Outer helical spring (II);
4—Outer helical spring for vibration damping; 5—Inner helical spring for vibration damping.

图 5–56　中央悬挂装置布置图

Figure 5-56　Layout of the Central Suspension Device

5）心盘磨耗盘

Center plate wear plate

货车上、下心盘的磨耗是由货车运用中的惯性引起的，其检修工作量较大，且检修质量的好与坏直接威胁行车的安全。为了减少货车上、下心盘的磨损，在转 K6 型转向架中采用了经过长期运用考验而证明耐磨性能优良的心盘磨耗盘，材质为铸模式特种含油尼龙。

The wear of the upper and lower center plates of freight cars is an inertial problem in the operation of freight cars, whose maintenance workload is large, and the maintenance quality directly threatens operation safety. To reduce the wear of the upper and lower center plates of freight cars, a center plate wear plate made of cast pattern special oil-containing nylon, which has been proven to have excellent wear resistance through long-term operation tests, is used in bogie type ZK-6.

该心盘磨耗盘介于上、下心盘之间，上、下心盘的平面和圆周边部分都被含油尼龙心盘磨耗盘隔离，这就完全避免了上、下钢质心盘间的直接磨损，也改善了上、下心盘面的承载均衡性。经运用考验，这种含油尼龙心盘磨耗盘运用 5～6 年后磨耗甚少，非常耐磨。因此，采用含油尼龙心盘磨耗盘可以有效提高上、下心盘的使用寿命。

The center plate wear plate is located between the upper and lower center plates. The plane and circular periphery of the upper and lower center plates are isolated by the oil-containing nylon center plate wear plate, which completely avoids direct wear between the upper and lower steel center plates and improves the bearing uniformity of the upper and lower center plates. After application testing, this oil-containing nylon center plate wear plate has little wear after 5–6 years of use while being wear-resistant. Therefore, using an oil-containing nylon center plate wear plate can effectively improve the service life of the upper and lower center plates.

6）耐磨销套

Wear-resistant pin sleeve

货车转向架在运用过程中，基础制动装置的销套磨损十分严重，特别是货车提速后，销套磨损将更为加剧。为了改善销套磨损，提高提速货车转向架销套的使用寿命，在转 K6 型转向架中全部采用耐磨销套，即采用奥贝球铁衬套和 45 钢淬火圆销，提高圆销表面硬度，同时减小销套间的间隙，提高销套装配精度，以改善销套的受力状态等。

During the operation of freight car bogies, the pin sleeve wear of the foundation braking device is very serious. After the freight car accelerates, the pin sleeve wear will become even more severe. To improve the wear of the pin sleeves and increase the service life of the pin sleeves of the speed-increasing freight car bogies, wear-resistant pin sleeves are used in bogie type ZK-6, that is, austempering ductile iron bushings and 45 steel quenched round pins are used to improve the surface hardness of the round pins, reduce the gap between the pin sleeves, improve the fitting accuracy of the pin sleeves, and improve the stress state of the large pins.

7）轮对组成及轴承

Wheelset composition and bearing

车轮为符合《铁道货车用辗钢整体车轮》（TB/T 2817—2018）的 HESA 型辗钢全加工车轮或符合《碳素钢铸钢车轮》（TB/T 1013—2011）的 HEZB840 碳素钢铸钢车轮。车轮进行静平衡测试，最大残余不平衡值不大于 125 g • m。同一辆车必须装用同一型号的车轮。车轴为符合标准车轴图样中几何尺寸的 RE_{2A} 型车轴或符合 SYST256-00-00-00 图样要求的 RE_{2B} 型车轴，材质为 LZW50 钢。滚动轴承采用 SKF TBU150 型、FAG TAROL150 型滚动轴承或 353130A 紧凑型滚动轴承，轴承轮廓尺寸为：内圈内径×外圈外径×轴承宽度（150 mm×250 mm×160 mm）。同一轮对必须装用同一型号的轴承。

The wheels shall be HESA rolled steel fully machined wheels conforming to *Solid Forged and Rolled Wheels for Railway Wagon Applications* (TB/T 2817—2018) or HEZB840 carbon steel cast steel wheels conforming to *Carbon Cast Steel Wheel* (TB/T 1013—2011). The wheels shall undergo static balance testing, with the maximum residual imbalance value no greater than 125 g·m. The same railway vehicle must be equipped with the same type of wheels. The geometric dimensions of the axle comply with the RE_{2A} axle in the standard axle drawing or the RE_{2B} axle in accordance with the requirements of the SYST256-00-00-00 drawing, and the material is LZW50 steel. The roller bearing is subject to SKF TBU150 type, FAG TAROL150 roller bearing or 353130A compact roller bearing, and the bearing outline dimension: inner diameter of inner ring × outer diameter of outer ring × bearing width (150 mm × 250 mm × 160 mm). The same wheelset must be equipped with bearings of the same model.

8）侧架

Side frame

转 K6 型转向架的侧架如图 5–57 所示。支撑座通过沿侧架大体中心线上、下两条焊缝焊接在侧架上，组装位置必须用专用组焊工装设备来保证，配合面允许打磨修配；立柱磨耗板通过 4 个折头螺栓与侧架立柱紧固。

The side frame of bogie type ZK-6 is shown in Figure 5-57. The support seat is welded to the side frame through two welds along the general centerline of the side frame. The assembly position must be ensured by using a dedicated assembly welder kit, and the mating surface is allowed to be polished and repaired; The column wear plate is fastened to the side frame column through four folding-head bolts.

9）减振装置

Vibration-damping device

转向架减振结构为斜楔式变摩擦减振装置，由侧架立柱磨耗板、组合式斜楔（如图 5–58 所示）、斜面磨耗板、双卷减振弹簧组成。减振弹簧比摇枕外圆弹簧（一）高 10 mm。

The damping structure of the bogie is a wedge variable-friction vibration-damping device, which is composed of a side frame column wear plate, a combined wedge (as shown in Figure 5-58), a bevel wear plate, and a double-coil vibration-damping spring. The vibration-damping spring is 10 mm higher than the outer helical bolster spring (I).

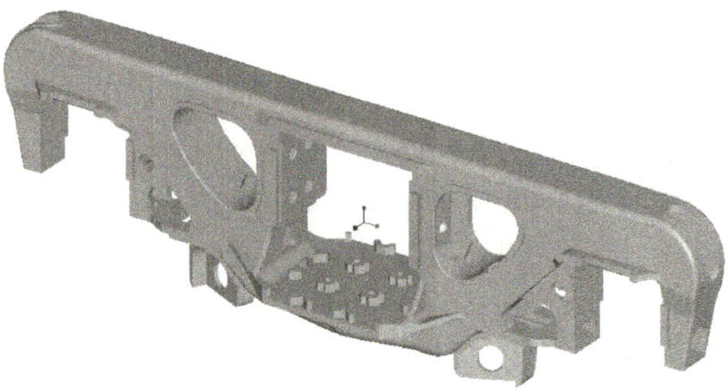

图 5–57　侧架

Figure 5-57　Side Frame

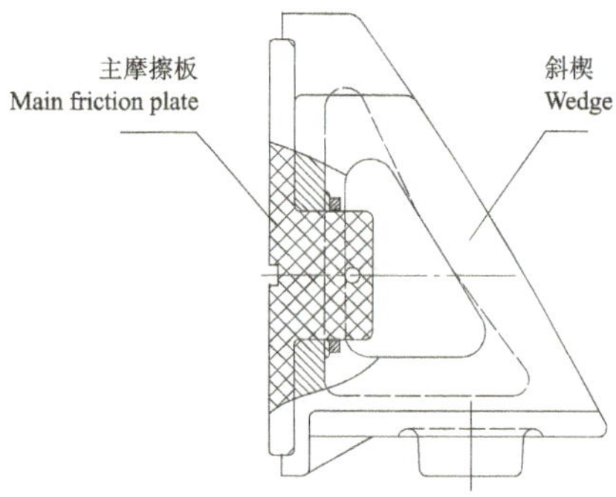

图 5–58　组合式斜楔

Figure 5-58　Combined Wedge

10）摇枕组成

Bolster composition

转 K6 型转向架的摇枕组成由固定杠杆支点座、摇枕、下心盘、斜面磨耗板组成，如图 5–59 所示。摇枕的材质为 B 级钢，下心盘螺栓为《六角头螺杆带孔螺栓》(GB/T 31.1—2013）中规定的 M24 螺栓（强度等级为 10.9 级），螺母为 BY-B 型、BY-A 型、FS 型防松螺母（强度等级为 10 级）。

The bolster of bogie type ZK-6 consists of a fixed lever fulcrum seat, a bolster, a lower center plate, and a bevel wear plate, as shown in Figure 5-59. The bolster is made of Grade B steel, the lower center plate bolt is M24 bolt (strength grade 10.9) specified in *Hexagon Bolts with Split Pin Hole on Shank* (GB/T 31.1—2013), and the nuts are BY-B, BY-A, and FS lock nuts (strength grade 10).

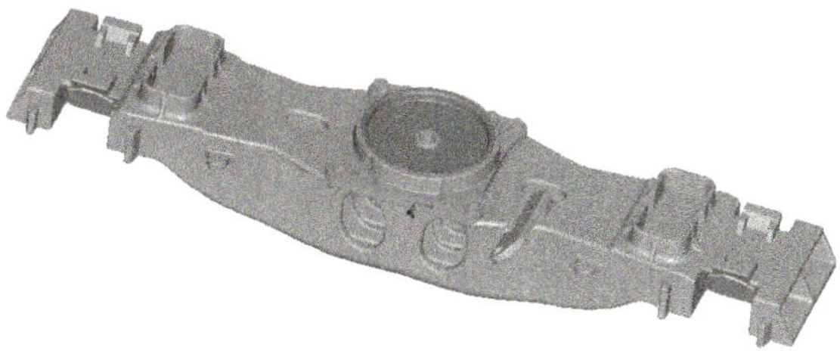

图 5-59 摇枕组成
Figure 5-59 Bolster Composition

11）基础制动装置

Foundation braking device

转 K6 型转向架的基础制动装置由左、右组合式制动梁，以及中拉杆、固定杠杆、固定杠杆支点、游动杠杆、新型高摩合成闸瓦和各种规格的耐磨销套组成，如图 5-60 所示。

The foundation braking device of bogie type ZK-6 consists of left and right combined brake beams, center pull rods, fixed levers, fixed lever fulcrums, floating levers, new high-friction composite brake shoes, and various specifications of wear-resistant pin sleeves, as shown in Figure 5-60.

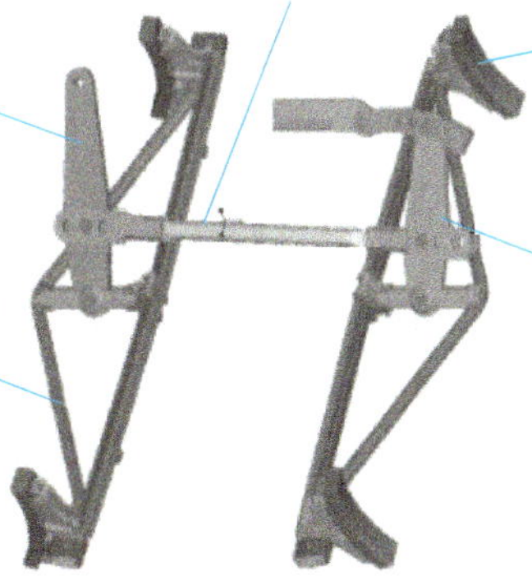

图 5-60 基础制动装置
Figure 5-60 Foundation Braking Device

任务 5.2 客车转向架

Task 5.2 Passenger car bogies

铁路客车是用来运送旅客和为旅客服务的，既要求安全正点，又要做到方便舒适，所以对客车转向架的要求比货车转向架的要求更严格。转向架担负着走行任务，同时承受各种垂向、纵向载荷，在具有足够强度的同时，还要有良好的运行平稳性和舒适性，将旅客安全地送到目的地。

Railway passenger cars are used to transport and serve passengers, requiring safety and punctuality as well as convenience and comfort. Therefore, the requirements for passenger car bogies are stricter than those for freight car bogies. The bogie is used for running tasks and also bears various vertical and longitudinal loads. While having sufficient strength, it should also have good running stability and comfort to safely deliver passengers to their destinations.

5.2.1 我国客车转向架的发展历史 Development history of passenger car bogies in China

转向架可以说是铁道车辆上最重要的部件之一，它直接承载车体重量，保证车辆顺利通过曲线。同时，转向架的各种参数也直接决定了车辆的稳定性和乘坐舒适性。自新中国成立以来，我国的客车转向架技术逐渐成熟，空气弹簧、盘型制动、电子防滑器等新技术的采用使转向架的性能得到了大幅度的提高。

Bogie can be said to be one of the most important components of railway vehicles, which directly carries the weight of the car body and ensures that the railway vehicles can smoothly pass through the curve. Furthermore, various parameters of the bogie also directly determine the stability and ride comfort of the railway vehicle. Since the founding of the PRC in 1949, the technology of passenger car bogies in China has gradually developed. The adoption of new technologies such as air springs, disc brakes, and electronic anti-skid devices has greatly improved the performance of bogies.

我国铁路客车从 20 世纪 50 年代的 21 型客车发展到如今的 25 型客车。客车最高运行速度从 20 世纪 50 年代的 100 km/h 逐步提高到 120 km/h、160 km/h，直至 200 km/h。客车运行速度之所以能够不断提高，关键在于技术先进、参数匹配、性能优良、运用安全可靠的客车转向架。

The railway passenger cars in China have developed from 21 type coaches in the 1950s to 25 type coaches today. The maximum operating speed of passenger cars has gradually increased from 100 km/h in the 1950s to 120 km/h, 160 km/h, and 200 km/h. The key to continuously improving the running speed of passenger cars lies in the use of safe and reliable passenger car bogies with advanced technology, parameter matching, and excellent performance.

5.2.2 对客车转向架的要求 Requirements for passenger car bogies

客车转向架应具有符合速度要求的运行安全性、平稳性、舒适性和曲线通过性能，并符合有关国家标准。

Passenger car bogies shall ensure operational safety, smoothness, comfort, and curving performance that meet the speed requirements and comply with relevant national standards.

（1）为了改善和提高客车在垂直方向的动力学性能，客车转向架上宜采用柔软的弹簧。一般要求客车转向架的弹簧静挠度大于 170 mm。为此，客车转向架通常采用两系弹簧：在轴箱与构架间设轴箱弹簧，又称第一系悬挂弹簧；在摇枕和构架间设摇枕弹簧，又称中央弹簧、第二系悬挂弹簧。

To improve and enhance the dynamic performance of passenger cars in the vertical direction, soft springs should be used on passenger car bogies. The general static deflection of springs of passenger car bogies is required to be greater than 170 mm. For this reason, typically, two types of springs are used for passenger car bogies: the axle box spring installed between the axle box and the frame, also known as the primary suspension spring; the bolster spring installed between the bolster and the frame, also known as the central spring or the secondary suspension spring.

（2）为了改善和提高客车的横向动力学性能，客车转向架上专门设置了横向弹性复原装置、横向减振装置；在高速客车转向架中，通过采用各种形式的轴箱定位装置，抑制转向架在线路上的蛇行运动。

To improve and enhance the lateral dynamic performance of passenger cars, the passenger car bogies are specially equipped with lateral elastic recovery devices and lateral vibration-damping devices; In high-speed passenger car bogies, various forms of axle box positioning devices are used to suppress the hunting motion of the bogies on the line.

① 转向架各零部件应有足够的强度和适宜的刚度。

Each component of the bogie shall have sufficient strength and appropriate rigidity.

② 尽可能实现轻量化，尤其要减少簧下质量。

The weight should be minimized, especially by reducing unsprung mass.

③ 尽量减少轮轨之间的作用力，减少轮轨磨耗及各部位的磨耗。

The force between wheels and rails should be minimized, and wheel-rail wear and the wear of various parts should be decreased.

④ 具有减少噪声、吸收高频振动的能力。

It should be able to reduce noise and absorb high-frequency vibration.

⑤ 具有良好的制动性能，保证在规定的制动距离内安全停车。

It should have good braking performance to ensure safe parking within the specified braking distance.

⑥ 积极开发、采用新技术、新材料、新工艺。

It is required to actively develop and adopt new technologies, materials, and processes.

⑦ 各零部件要尽可能实现通用化、标准化和产品系列化。

All parts and components should be generalized, standardized, and serialized as much as possible.

⑧ 转向架应具备结构简单、运用可靠、检修方便、制造容易、成本低廉的性能。

The bogie shall have the characteristics of simple structure, reliable operation, convenient maintenance, easy manufacturing, and low cost.

5.2.3 客车转向架的基本作用及要求
Basic functions and requirements for passenger car bogies

一般而言，客车转向架可分为轮对轴箱弹簧装置、中央弹簧弹性悬挂装置、构架、基础制动装置等部分。由于所装用的客车车型的不同和性能等方面的差别，各型转向架在结构上大都有一定的差别。

Generally speaking, passenger car bogies can be divided into wheelset axle box spring devices, central spring elastic suspension devices, frames, and foundation braking devices. Due to the differences in types of passenger cars and performance of the passenger cars installed, there are certain differences in the structure of various types of bogies.

1. 客车转向架的基本作用

Basic functions of passenger car bogies

（1）减少车辆运行阻力。

Reduce the running resistance of railway vehicles.

（2）车辆通过高低不平处时，能够减少车体的垂直位移。

Reduce the vertical displacement of the car body when passing through uneven places.

（3）安装多系弹簧及减振器，保证车辆有良好的运行品质，以适应不断提高的行车速度。

Install multi-stage springs and damper to ensure the good running quality of the railway vehicle to adapt to the constantly increasing driving speed.

（4）转向架容易从车体下推出，便于检修。

Can be easily pushed out from under the car body for easy maintenance.

（5）传递和放大制动缸产生的制动力，使车辆具有良好的制动效果。

Transmit and amplify the braking force generated by the brake cylinder for a good braking effect of the railway vehicle.

（6）支撑车体并将车体上的各种作用力和载荷传递给钢轨。

Support the car body and transfer various forces and loads on the car body to the rail.

2. 快速客车对转向架的要求

Requirements of bogies for high-speed passenger cars

（1）降低轴重，尤其是减少簧下质量，以减少轮轨之间垂向动力作用。

Reduce the axle load, especially the unsprung mass, to reduce the vertical dynamic interaction between the wheels and rails.

（2）尽力采取各种措施，保证高速客车有较高的失稳临界速度，同时兼顾车辆的曲线通过能力，减少轮轨之间的横向动力作用。

Try various measures to ensure that high-speed passenger cars have a high critical speed of instability. Take into account the curving performance of the railway vehicle to reduce the lateral dynamic action between the wheels and rails.

（3）为了使高速运行的车辆有良好的运行平稳性，应以超临界的观点进行设计和选择有关参数。

To ensure good running stability of the railway vehicles running at high speeds, the design and selection of relevant parameters should be carried out from a supercritical point of view.

（4）在高速转向架中采用空气弹簧和橡胶件，以降低噪声和隔离、吸收高频振动。同时，尽量形成相关零部件之间的无磨耗接触，以减少磨耗、延长寿命和便于维修，研究轮轨噪声的成因，并采取相应措施防止、减少噪声的污染。

Use air springs and rubber parts in high-speed bogies to reduce noise and isolate and absorb high-frequency vibrations. Furthermore, try to form a non-abrasive contact between relevant components to reduce wear, extend service life, and facilitate maintenance, study the causes of wheel/rail noise, and take corresponding measures to prevent and reduce noise pollution.

（5）为实现高速运行中的列车能够在规定的距离内安全停车，转向架的基础制动装置部分在传统的双侧闸瓦踏面制动的基础上，采用盘型制动、磁轨制动等方式，改善制动性能、提高制动功率。根据列车运行速度情况需要确定采取单一式制动方式还是复合式制动方式。

To achieve safe parking of trains in high-speed operation within a specified distance, the foundation braking device of the bogie is subject to disc braking, magnetic rail braking, and other methods on the basis of traditional dual-side brake shoe tread braking to improve braking performance and increase braking power. Determine whether to adopt a single braking mode or a composite braking mode according to the running speed as needed.

5.2.4　209 系列转向架
209 series bogie

209 系列转向架自 1972 年定型以来，经过不断的改进和发展，已形成 209T 型（T 表示踏面制动）、209P 型（P 表示盘型制动）、209PK 型（K 表示空气弹簧）、209HS 型、PW-200 型等系列转向架，主要由构架、摇枕弹簧装置、轮对轴箱定位装置和基础制动装置等组成。

Since its finalization in 1972, the 209 series bogies have been continuously improved and developed, and series have been formed such as bogie type 209T (T represents tread braking), 209P (P represents disc braking), 209PK (K represents air spring), 209HS, PW-200, mainly composed of frame, bolster spring device, wheelset axle box positioning device, and foundation braking device.

5.2.4.1　209T 型转向架
Bogie type 209T

209T 型转向架最大的特点就是采用了纵向牵引拉杆装置，用以代替传统的纵向摇枕挡，其结构如图 5-61 所示。该型转向架主要用于 25G 型客车上。

The most significant feature of bogie type 209T is the use of a longitudinal traction rod device to replace the traditional longitudinal bolster block. Its structure is shown in Figure 5-61. This type of bogie is mainly used on 25G type coaches.

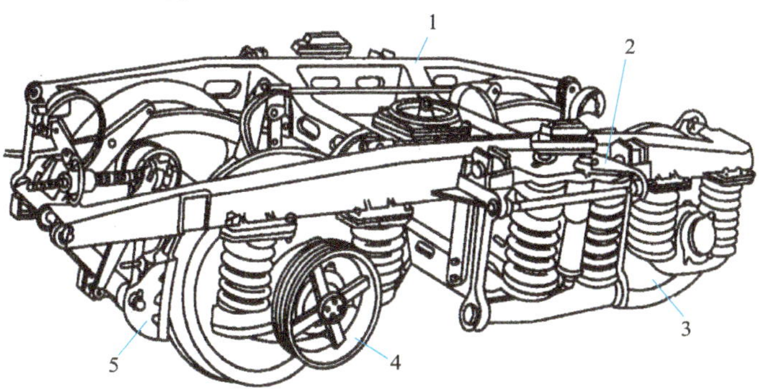

1—构架；2—摇枕弹簧装置；3—轮对轴箱弹簧装置；4—发电机皮带轮装置；5—基础制动装置。
1—Framework; 2—Bolster spring device; 3—Wheelset axle box spring device; 4—Generator pulley device; 5—Foundation braking device.

图 5-61　209T 型转向架的结构
Figure 5-61　Structure of Bogie Type 209T

1. 209T 型转向架的结构特点
Structural features of bogie type 209T

（1）H 型铸钢一体式构架。

H-shaped cast steel integrated frame.

（2）干摩擦导柱式轴箱弹性定位装置。

Dry friction guide pillar axle box elastic positioning device.

（3）摇动台式二系悬挂装置（长吊杆、圆弹簧、油压减振器）。

Shaking table type secondary suspension device (long suspender, helical spring and oil pressure damper).

（4）一系为圆簧悬挂。

The primary suspension is a helical spring suspension.

（5）吊挂式双侧闸瓦踏面基础制动装置。

Suspension two-side brake shoe tread foundation braking device.

2. 209T 型转向架的结构

Structure of bogie type 209T

1）构架组成

Framework device composition

209T 型转向架为铸钢一体式 H 形构架，由 2 根侧梁、2 根横梁及 4 根悬臂小端梁等组成，并铸有各种安装座，如图 5-62 所示。在构架侧梁外部装有横向缓冲器，由挡轴、缓冲橡胶组成，如图 5-63 所示。组装时，将缓冲橡胶压入构架侧梁外部的缓冲器座内即可。横向缓冲器和摇枕每侧间隙为(25±2)mm，两侧间隙之和不大于 50 mm。构架两侧梁中心距为 1 943 mm。

Bogie type 209T is a cast steel integrated H-shaped frame, consisting of 2 side beams, 2 cross beams, and 4 cantilever small end beams, and is cast with various mounting bases, as shown in Figure 5-62. A lateral buffer is installed outside the frame side beam, consisting of a retaining shaft stopper and buffer rubber, as shown in Figure 5-63. During assembly, the buffer rubber is pressed into the buffer seat outside the frame side beam. The gap between the lateral buffer and the bolster on each side is (25±2) mm, and the sum of the gaps on both sides is not greater than 50 mm. The center distance between beams on both sides of the frame is 1,943 mm.

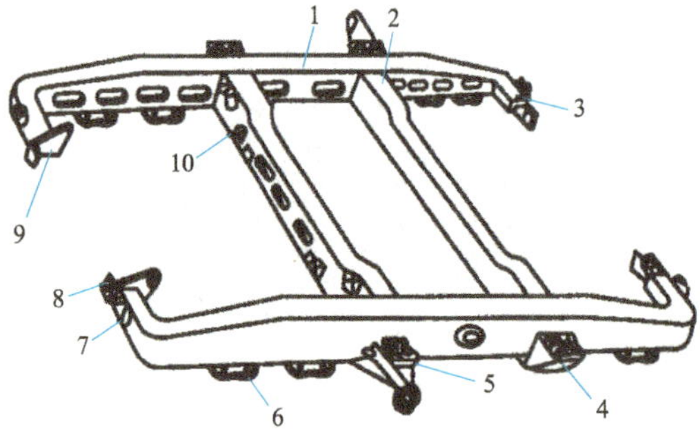

1—侧梁；2—横梁；3—小端梁；4—摇枕吊座托架；5—摇枕吊座；6—轴箱弹簧支柱座；7—闸瓦托吊座；8—缓解弹簧座；9—固定杠杆支点座；10—制动拉杆吊座。

1—Side beam; 2—Cross beam; 3—Small end beam; 4—Bolster hanger seat bracket; 5—Bolster hanger seat; 6—Axle box spring strut seat; 7—Brake shoe support crane seat; 8—Release spring seat; 9—Fixed lever fulcrum seat; 10—Brake rod hanger seat.

图 5-62　H 形构架

Figure 5-62　H-shaped Frame

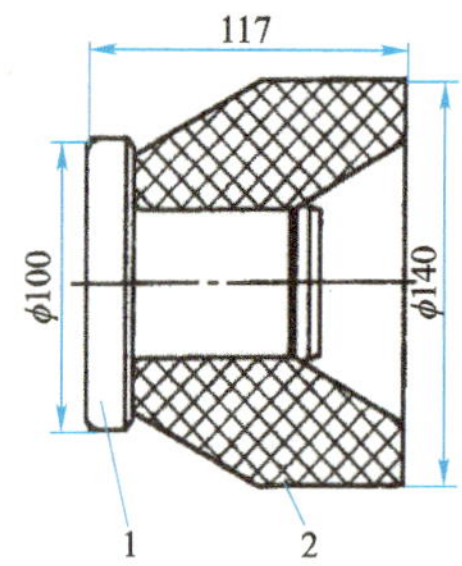

1—挡轴；2—缓冲橡胶。

1—Retaining shaft; 2—Buffer rubber.

图 5-63　横向缓冲器

Figure 5-63　Lateral Buffer

2）摇枕弹簧装置

Bolster spring device

209T 型转向架的摇枕弹簧装置为摇动台式，采用单节长吊杆、带油压减振器的摇枕圆弹簧组，其结构如图 5-64 所示。下旁承用螺栓组装在摇枕端部，位于构架侧梁外侧。两旁承中心距为 2 390 mm。

The bolster spring device of bogie type 209T is a shaking table type, using a single-section long suspender, and a helical bolster spring set with an oil pressure damper. Its structure is shown in Figure 5-64. The lower side bearings are assembled with bolts at the end of the bolster, located outside the frame side beam, with a center distance of 2,390 mm between the two side bearings.

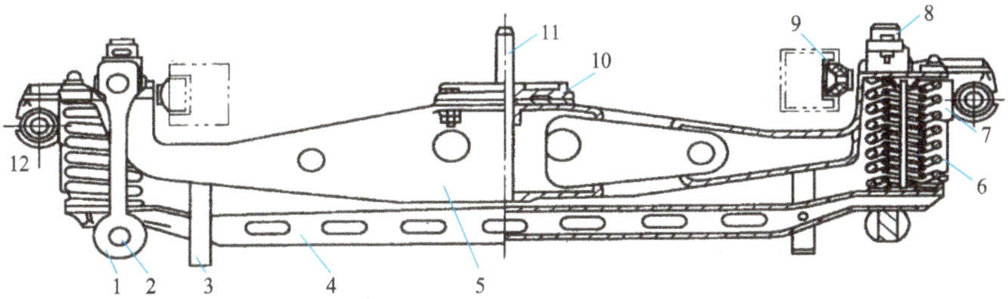

1—摇枕吊；2—摇枕吊轴；3—安全吊；4—弹簧托梁；5—摇枕；6—摇枕弹簧；7—油压减振器；8—下旁承；9—横向缓冲器；10—下心盘；11—中心销；12—纵向牵引拉杆。

1—Bolster hanger; 2—Bolster suspension shaft; 3—Safety crane; 4—Spring joist; 5—Bolster; 6—Bolster spring; 7—Oil pressure damper; 8—Lower side bearing; 9—Lateral buffer; 10—Lower center plate; 11—Center pin; 12—Longitudinal traction rod.

图 5-64　摇枕弹簧装置的结构

Figure 5-64　Structure of Bolster Spring Device

在构架侧梁外侧和摇枕两端斜对称焊有牵引拉杆座，用具有橡胶弹性节点的牵引拉杆（见图 5-65）将摇枕和构架相连。牵引拉杆的组装应在落车找平后进行。

A traction rod seat is diagonally and symmetrically welded on the outer side of the frame side beam and both ends of the bolster, and a traction rod with rubber elastic nodes (see Figure 5-65) is used to connect the bolster and the frame. The assembly of the traction rod should be carried out after landing and leveling.

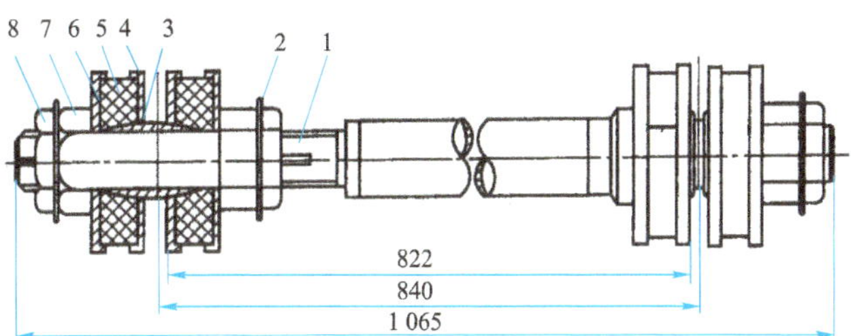

1—拉杆；2—止推垫圈；3—隔套；4—内夹板；5—橡胶垫；6—外夹板；7—螺母 M42；8—薄螺母 M。

1—Pull rod; 2—Thrust washer; 3—Spacer sleeve; 4—Inner clamp plate; 5—Rubber pad; 6—Outer clamp plate; 7—Nut M42; 8—Thin nut M.

图 5-65　牵引拉杆

Figure 5-65　Traction Rod

摇枕弹簧装置由圆弹簧组和油压减振器组成。摇枕弹簧横向中心距为 2 510 mm。

The bolster spring device consists of a helical spring set and an oil pressure damper. The lateral center distance of the bolster spring is 2,510 mm.

摇枕吊通过摇枕吊销及两块支承板垂直悬挂在摇枕吊座上。摇枕吊座及托架如图 5-66 所示。支承板上的圆孔做成上、下偏心 25 mm，支承板下部还可安放厚度 10 mm 以内的垫板，形成了钩高调整装置。车钩高度的调整范围最大可达 30 mm。

The bolster hanger is vertically suspended on the bolster hanger seat through the bolster suspension and two support plates. The bolster hanger seat and bracket are shown in Figure 5-66. The circular holes on the support plate are made to have an upper and lower eccentricity of 25 mm, and a cushion plate with a thickness of less than 10 mm can be placed at the lower part of the support plate, forming a hook height adjustment device. The adjustment range of the coupler height can be up to 30 mm.

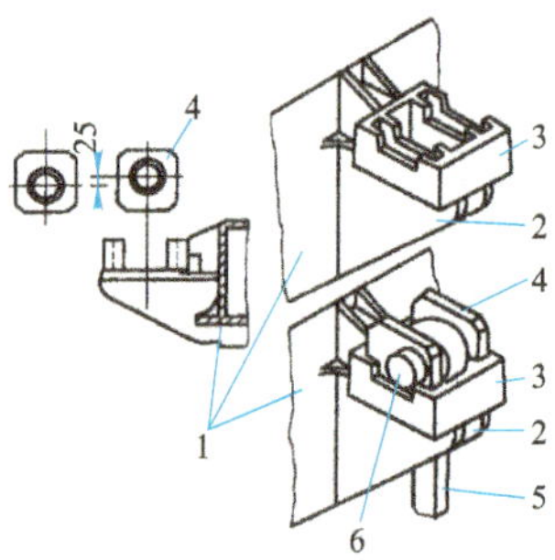

1—构架侧梁；2—摇枕吊座托架；3—摇枕吊座；4—吊销支承板；5—摇枕吊；6—摇枕吊销。

1—Frame side beam; 2—Bolster hanger seat bracket; 3—Bolster hanger seat; 4—Suspension support plate; 5—Bolster hanger; 6—Suspension of bolster.

图 5-66　摇枕吊座及托架

Figure 5-66　Bolster Hanger Seat and Bracket

3）轮对轴箱定位装置

Wheelset axle box positioning device

209T 型转向架的轮对轴箱弹簧装置为无导框式结构，采用 RD_3 型滚动轴承轮对，装用的轴承型号为 42726QT、152726QT 单列向心短圆柱滚子轴承，轴箱弹簧采用单卷圆柱螺旋弹簧，轴箱定位装置采用了干摩擦导柱式弹性定位结构，如图 5-67 所示。

The wheelset and axle box spring device of bogie type 209T is of a frameless structure, using RD_3 roller bearing wheelsets. The installed bearing models are 42726QT and 152726QT single-row radial short cylindrical roller bearings. The axle box spring uses a single-coil cylindrical spiral spring, and the axle box positioning device is subject to a dry friction guide pillar elastic positioning structure, as shown in Figure 5-67.

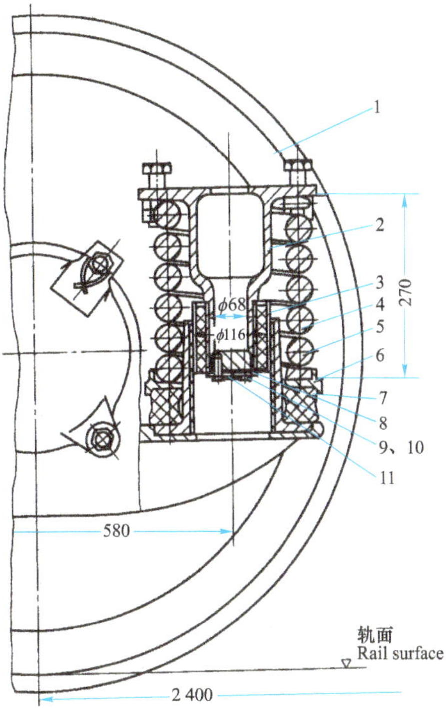

1—轮对；2—弹簧支柱；3—弹性定位套组成；4—定位座组成；5—轴箱弹簧；6—支持环；7—橡胶缓冲垫；8—挡盖；9—螺栓（M10×25）；10—弹簧垫圈；11—低碳素结构钢丝（ϕ1.6×170）。

1—Wheelset; 2—Spring strut; 3—Elastic positioning sleeve composition; 4—Positioning seat composition; 5—Axle box spring; 6—Support ring; 7—Rubber cushion; 8—Cover; 9—Bolt (M10x25); 10—Low carbon structural steel wire (ϕ1.6x170).

（a）干摩擦导柱式弹性轴箱定位装置

Dry friction guide pillar elastic axle box positioning device

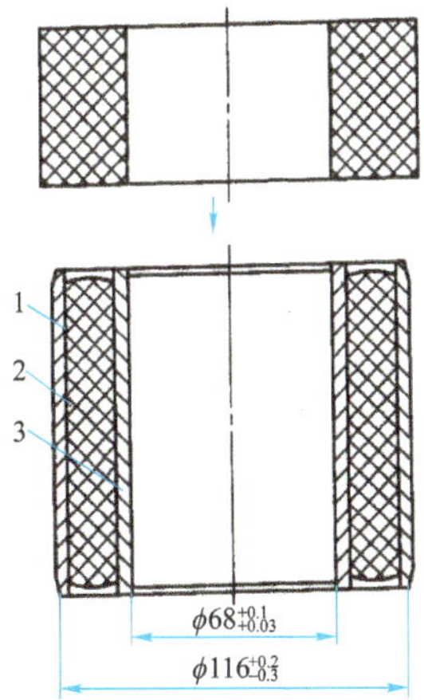

1—外套；2—橡胶套；3—内套。

1—Outer sleeve; 2—Rubber sleeve; 3—Inner sleeve.

（b）弹性定位套

Elastic positioning sleeve

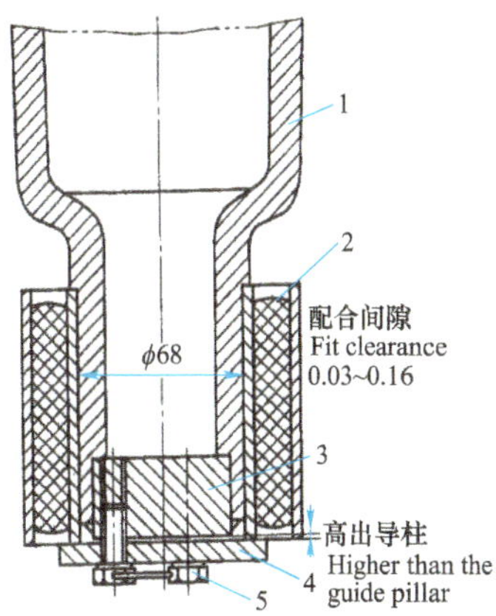

1—弹簧支柱；2—弹性定位套组成；3—端盖；4—挡盖；5—螺栓、垫圈、钢丝。

1—Spring strut; 2—Elastic positioning sleeve composition; 3—End cap; 4—Cover; 5—Bolts, washers, steel wires.

（c）弹性定位套与支柱组装

Elastic positioning sleeve and strut composition

图 5-67 轮对轴箱定位装置

Figure 5-67 Wheelset Axle Box Positioning Device

4）基础制动装置

Foundation braking device

209T 型转向架的基础制动装置采用杠杆传动，双侧闸瓦制动，为双片吊挂直接作用式。209T 型转向架的基础制动装置由移动杠杆、制动拉杆、移动杠杆上拉杆、制动梁、闸瓦托、闸瓦间隙调整装置等组成，其结构如图 5-68 所示。

The foundation braking device of bogie type 209T is subject to lever transmission and dual-side brake shoe tread braking. It is a double-piece suspension direct-acting type. The foundation braking device of bogie type 209T consists of a moving lever, a brake rod, an upper pull rod of moving lever, a brake beam, a brake shoe support, and a brake shoe clearance adjustment device, as shown in Figure 5-68.

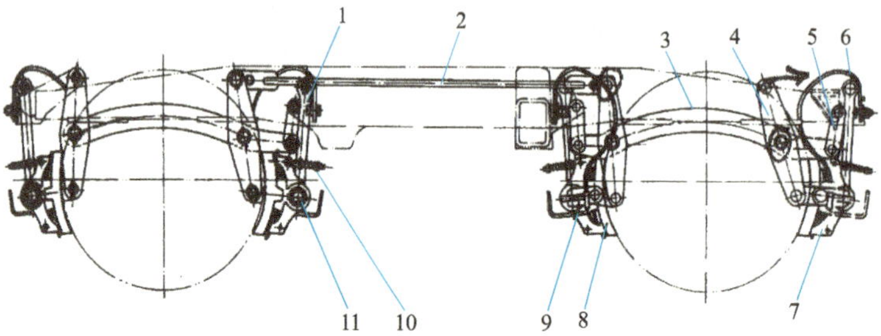

1—闸瓦托吊；2—移动杠杆上拉杆；3—移动杠杆下拉杆；4—移动杠杆；5—拉杆吊；6—缓解弹簧；7—闸瓦托；8—闸瓦；9—拉环；10—闸瓦托弹簧；11—制动梁。

1—Brake shoe support crane; 2—Upper pull rod of moving lever; 3—Lower pull rod of moving lever; 4—Moving lever; 5—Trolley crane; 6—Release spring; 7—Brake shoe support; 8—Brake shoe; 9—Pull ring; 10—Brake shoe support spring; 11—Brake beam.

图 5-68 基础制动装置的结构

Figure 5-68 Structure of Foundation Braking Device

3. 209T 型转向架的主要技术参数

Main technical parameters of bogie type 209T

209T 型转向架的主要技术参数如表 5-8 所示。

The main technical parameters of bogie type 209T are shown in Table 5-8.

表 5-8 209T 型转向架的主要技术参数

Table 5-8 Main Technical Parameters of Bogie Type 209T

最高运行速度 Max. operating speed	140 km/h
固定轴距 Fixed wheelbase	2 400 mm
车轮型式及直径 Wheel type and diameter	整体辗钢车，945 mm Monobloc rolled steel car, 945mm
车轴型号 Axle model	RD_3，RD_4
轴承型号 Bearing model	42726QT，152726QT

续表

Continued

<table>
<tr><td colspan="2">轴箱定位方式
Axle box positioning method</td><td>干摩擦导柱式定位
Dry friction guide pillar positioning</td></tr>
<tr><td colspan="2">心盘允许最大载荷
Max. allowable load of center plate</td><td>290 kN</td></tr>
<tr><td colspan="2">车体自重下，下心盘面距轨面高
Height from the lower center plate surface to the rail surface under the tare weight of the car body</td><td>780 mm</td></tr>
<tr><td colspan="2">车体自重下，下旁承面距轨面高
Height from the lower side bearing surface to the rail surface under the tare weight of the car body</td><td>970 mm</td></tr>
<tr><td colspan="2">两旁承中心间距
Center distance between two side bearings</td><td>2 390 mm</td></tr>
<tr><td colspan="2">弹簧型式
Spring type</td><td>一、二系均为圆柱螺旋弹簧
Both the primary and secondary springs are cylindrical spiral springs</td></tr>
<tr><td colspan="2">减振型式及阻尼系数
Vibration-damping type and damping coefficient</td><td>枕弹簧处加装油压减震器，阻尼系数为 2×100 kN • s/m
Install an oil pressure damper at the pillow spring, with a damping coefficient of 2 × 100 kN·s/m</td></tr>
<tr><td colspan="2">摇枕吊有效长度
Effective length of bolster hanger</td><td>590 mm</td></tr>
<tr><td colspan="2">摇枕吊倾角
Bolster suspension angle</td><td>0°</td></tr>
<tr><td colspan="2">牵引方式
Traction mode</td><td>纵向牵引拉杆
Longitudinal traction rod</td></tr>
<tr><td colspan="2">摇枕横向缓冲装置
Bolster lateral buffer</td><td>橡胶缓冲器
Rubber buffer</td></tr>
<tr><td colspan="2">摇枕弹簧横向间距
Lateral spacing of bolster spring</td><td>2 510 mm</td></tr>
<tr><td colspan="2">基础制动装置
Foundation braking device</td><td>双侧踏面制动
Dual-side tread braking</td></tr>
<tr><td colspan="2">每台转向架制动倍率
Braking ratio of each bogie</td><td>4</td></tr>
<tr><td colspan="2">每台转向架质量
Mass of each bogie</td><td>6.8 t</td></tr>
<tr><td colspan="2">轨距
Track gauge</td><td>1 435 mm</td></tr>
<tr><td rowspan="2">通过最小曲线半径
Min. radius of curvature negotiated</td><td>正线运行
Mainline operation</td><td>145 mm</td></tr>
<tr><td>缓行调车
Slow switching</td><td>100 mm</td></tr>
</table>

5.2.4.2　209P 型转向架

Bogie type 209P

209P 型转向架（如图 5–69 所示）是为适应铁路客车提速的使用要求，在 209T 型转向架的基础上改进设计的。209P 型转向架的制动装置采用盘型制动单元和踏面清扫单元。209P 型转向架主要装用于构造速度为 140 km/h 的各种 25 型客车。

Bogie type 209P (as shown in Figure 5-69) is an improved design based on bogie type 209T to meet the operational requirements of increasing the speed of railway passenger cars, and the disc braking device is adopted. The disc braking unit and tread cleaning unit are used for the braking device of bogie type 209P. Bogie type 209P is mainly installed on various 25 type coaches with a construction speed of 140 km/h.

图 5–69　209P 型转向架
Figure 5-69　Bogie Type 209P

1. 209P 型转向架的结构
Structure of bogie type 209P

209P 型转向架的结构如图 5–70 所示。

The structure of bogie type 209P is shown in Figure 5-70.

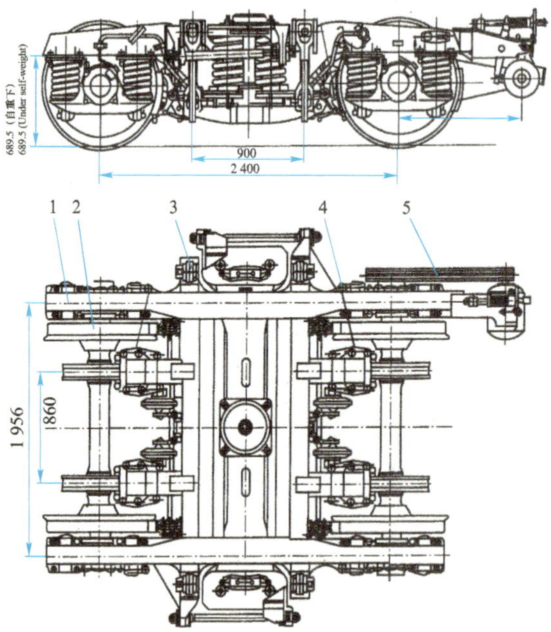

1—构架装置；2—轮对轴箱定位装置；3—摇枕弹簧装置；4—基础制动装置；5—轴端发电装置。
1—Framework device; 2—Wheelset axle box positioning device; 3—Bolster spring device;
4—Foundation braking device; 5—Axle-end power generation device.

图 5–70　209P 型转向架的结构
Figure 5-70　Structure of Bogie Type 209P

1）构架装置

Framework device

构架装置主要由构架、定位挡圈、制动吊座、摇枕吊销支承板座、安全吊安装座、牵引拉杆座、制动缸吊座、闸瓦托吊座等零件焊接而成。

The framework device is mainly composed of welded parts such as the framework, positioning retainer, brake hanger seat, bolster suspension support plate seat, safety crane mounting plate, traction rod seat, brake cylinder hanger seat, brake shoe support crane seat, etc.

构架有铸钢构架和焊接构架两种形式。铸钢构架采用 ZG230-450 制造；焊接构架由侧梁、横梁、摇枕吊座及发电机吊架等零部件组焊而成，侧梁、横梁均采用压型结构，各零部件所用板材采用 Q235A 低碳钢钢板。

There are two forms of framework: cast steel framework and welded framework. The cast steel frame is manufactured using ZG230-450; The welded frame consists of side beams, cross beams, bolster hanger seats, generator hangers, and other components. The side beams and cross beams are of profiled structure, and the plates used for each component are Q235A low-carbon steel plates.

2）轮对轴箱定位装置

Wheelset axle box positioning device

209P 型转向架的轮对轴箱定位装置由轮对轴箱装置、轴箱弹簧装置及轴箱定位装置三部分组成。

The wheelset axle box positioning device of bogie type 209P consists of three parts: wheelset axle box device, axle box spring device, and axle box positioning device.

209P 型转向架的轮对采用 RD_{3A}、RD_{4A} 车轴，在车轴中部 860 mm 中心距上设有 2 个宽度为 180 mm、直径为 198 mm 的制动盘座；采用《铁路用辗钢整体车轮》(GB/T 8601—2021）中规定的 PD 型 A 级全加工辗钢整体车轮。轮对需做动平衡试验，以减少轮轨之间的动作用力。轮位差不大于 2 mm，同一轮对两车轮的滚动圆直径之差不大于 1 mm。

The wheelset of bogie type 209P is subject to RD_{3A} and RD_{4A} axles, with two 180 mm wide and thick axles arranged at a center distance of 860 mm in the middle of the axle ϕ198 mm brake disc holder; The PD Class A fully machined rolled steel monobloc wheels specified in *Forged and Rolled Solid Wheels for Railway* (GB/T 8601—2021) shall be used. The dynamic balance test should be performed for the wheelset to reduce the movement force between the wheels and rails. The wheel position difference shall not be greater than 2 mm, and the difference between the rolling circle diameters of two wheels of the same wheelset shall not be greater than 1 mm.

轴箱装置采用整体金属迷宫式密封轴箱，内装 NJ3226X1 型或 NJP3226Xl 型轴承，以及新的橡胶密封元件。

The axle box device is subject to an integral metal labyrinth-sealed axle box, with NJ3226X1 or NJP3226Xl bearings and new rubber sealing elements installed inside.

轴箱定位采用干摩擦导柱式弹性定位结构。采用整体硫化一次成型的弹性定位套，通过 3 个 M12 螺栓将弹性定位套固定在导柱上，以提高运用可靠性；定位座组成中装有内表面覆聚四氟乙烯的钢背摩擦套或奥贝球铁摩擦套，这两种摩擦套均具有自润滑性能，适于在干摩擦的环境中使用，无需加油润滑。组装后，定位座与弹性定位套之间的间隙为

0.5～0.8 mm。

The axle box is positioned using a dry friction guide pillar elastic positioning structure. The elastic positioning sleeve is integrally vulcanized and formed in one step. The elastic positioning sleeve is fixed to the guide pillar through three M12 bolts to improve application reliability; The positioning seat assembly is equipped with a steel-backed friction sleeve with an inner surface coated with polytetrafluoroethylene or an austempering ductile iron friction sleeve. Both of these friction sleeves have self-lubricating properties and are suitable for use in dry friction environments without the need for oil lubrication. After assembly, the gap between the positioning seat and the elastic positioning sleeve is 0.5–0.8 mm.

在轴箱两侧弹簧托盘上依次安放有定位座、缓冲胶垫、支持环、轴箱弹簧，以提高缓冲、吸振能力。轴箱弹簧采用综合性能良好的 60Si2Mn 弹簧钢制造。

A positioning seat, buffer rubber pad, support ring, and axle box spring are placed on the spring trays on both sides of the axle box to improve the buffering and vibration absorption capabilities. The axle box spring is made of 60Si2Mn spring steel with good comprehensive performance.

3）摇枕弹簧悬挂装置

Bolster spring suspension device

209P 型转向架的摇枕弹簧悬挂装置与 209T 型转向架的基本相同。

The bolster spring suspension device of bogie type 209P is basically the same as that of bogie type 209T.

摇枕弹簧采用双卷螺旋钢弹簧，内、外弹簧的旋向相反。内、外弹簧均采用综合性能良好的 60Si2Mn 弹簧钢制造。为降低车体的自振频率，增加平稳性，在载重条件下，转向架两系弹簧的静挠度不小于 160 mm（邮政车、行李车、特种车除外）。

The bolster spring is subject to a double-coil spiral steel spring, with the inner and outer coils rotating in opposite directions. The inner and outer springs are made of 60Si2Mn spring steel with good comprehensive performance. To reduce the natural vibration frequency of the car body and increase its stability, under load conditions, the static deflection of the two springs of the bogie shall not be less than 160 mm (except for mail cars, luggage vehicles, and special vehicles).

209P 型转向架采用国产或进口的新型油压减振器。这类减振器具有密封、防尘、防锈性能好，阻力稳定，调整、拆卸容易，重量轻等特点。减振器阻尼系数为 100 kN·s/m。

Domestic or imported new oil pressure dampers are adopted for bogie type 209P. This type of damper has the characteristics of good sealing, dust prevention, rust prevention, stable resistance, easy adjustment and disassembly, and lightweight. The damper damping coefficient is 100 kN·s/m.

209P 型转向架采用座式中心销，以利于防腐，如图 5–71 所示。

Seat-type center pins are used for bogie type 209P to facilitate corrosion protection, as shown in Figure 5-71.

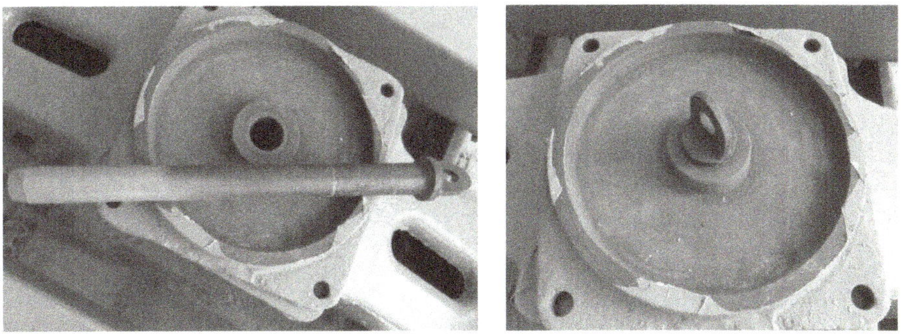

图 5-71 209P 型转向架的座式中心销
Figure 5-71 Seat-type Center Pin of Bogie Type 209P

摇枕、托梁均为铸钢件。摇枕为等强度箱形鱼腹梁，托梁为多孔箱形梁，既保证了强度，又减轻了质量。针对 209T 型转向架摇枕与牵引拉杆座连接的筋板处强度相对薄弱的缺点，209P 型转向架的摇枕将该处筋板加强，提高了运用可靠性。

The bolster and joist are all cast steel. The bolster is a constant strength box-shaped fish-belly sill, and the joist is a perforated box-shaped beam, which not only ensures strength but also reduces mass. For the weakness of relatively weak strength at the rib plate connecting the bolster of bogie type 209T and the traction rod seat, the bolster of bogie type 209P strengthens the rib plate at this point, improving application reliability.

4）基础制动装置

Foundation braking device

209P 型转向架的基础制动装置采用盘型制动单元和踏面清扫单元，其结构如图 5-72 所示。

The disc braking unit and tread cleaning unit are used for the foundation braking device of bogie type 209P, as shown in Figure 5-72.

每个制动盘有一个盘型制动单元，由单元制动缸、手制动杠杆、内外侧杠杆、杠杆吊、闸片托、闸片、闸片托吊、闸片吊销等零部件组成，以三点悬挂式悬挂在构架制动吊座上。根据车重不同，将杠杆比分为 4 个档次，如表 5-9 所示。每个车轮有一个踏面清扫单元，由踏面清扫器、闸瓦托吊及其横向连接杆等零部件组成。

Each brake disc has a disc braking unit, which is composed of a unit brake cylinder, hand brake lever, inner and outer levers, lever crane, brake pad holder, brake pad, brake pad support crane, brake pad suspension, and other components, and is suspended on the frame brake hanger seat in a three-point suspension type. According to different vehicle weights, the leverage ratio is divided into four gears, as shown in Table 5-9. Each wheel has a tread cleaning unit, which is composed of parts such as a tread cleaner, a brake shoe support crane, its lateral connecting rod and others.

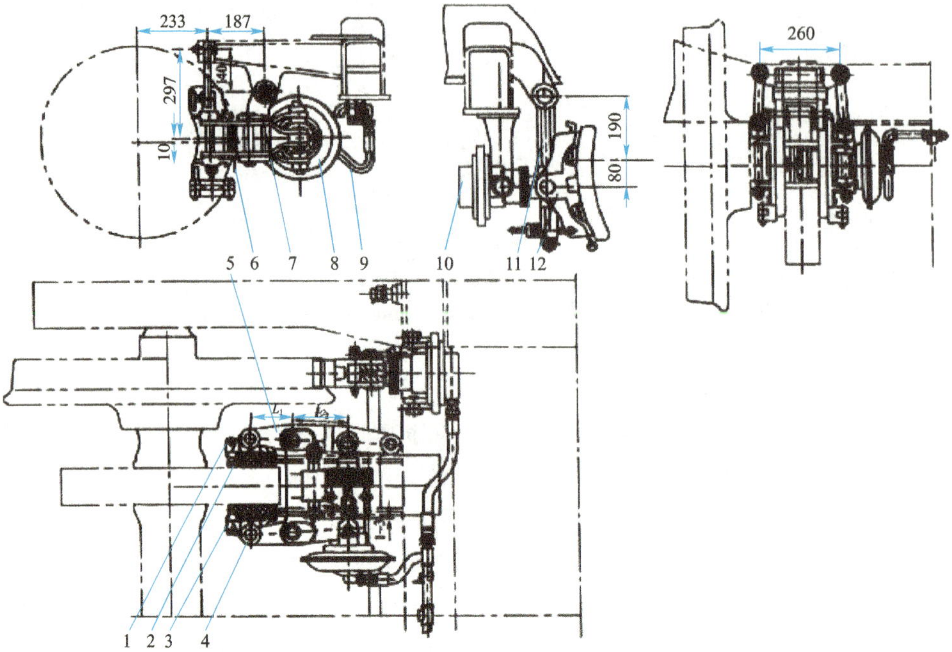

1—左闸片托装置；2—闸片组成；3—右闸片组成；4—内侧杠杆；5—手制动杠杆；6—外侧杠杆；7—杠杆吊座；8—英寸单元制动缸；9—软管组成；10—6 英寸单元制动缸；11—闸瓦托吊及横向连接装置；12—闸瓦托组成。
1—Left brake pad support device; 2—Brake pad composition; 3—Right brake pad composition; 4—Inner lever; 5—Hand brake lever; 6—Outer lever; 7—Lever hanger seat; 8—inch unit brake cylinder; 9—Hose composition; 10—6-inch unit brake cylinder; 11—Brake shoe support crane and lateral connecting device; 12—Brake shoe support composition.

图 5-72　209P 型转向架基础制动装置的结构

Figure 5-72　Structure of Foundation Braking Device for Bogie Type 209P

表 5-9　杠杆比档次对照表

Table 5-9　Comparison Table of Leverage Ratio Grades

自重范围/t Tare weight range/t	杠杆比（L_2/L_1） Leverage Ratio (L_2/L_1)		杠杆吊座 *A* 值 Lever hanger seat *A* value		使用车型 Vehicle type
	104 阀 104 valve	F8 阀 F8 valve	104 阀 104 valve	F8 阀 F8 valve	
42～46 42-46	146/154	134/166	33	21	XL_{25G}、UZ_{25G}、YZ_{25G}、XL_{25B}、UZ_{25B}、YZ_{25B}
46～50 46-50	155/145	143/157	42	30	YW_{25G}、RW_{25G}、CA_{25G}、YW_{25B}、RW_{25B}、CA_{25B}
50～55 50-55	163/137	150/150	50	37	宿营 YW_{25B}、RW_{25B} Camping YW_{25B}、RW_{25B}
55 以上 Above 55	171/129	160/140	58	47	KD_{25G}

2. 209P 型转向架的主要技术参数

Main technical parameters of bogie type 209P

209P 型转向架的主要技术参数如表 5-10 所示。

The main technical parameters of bogie type 209P are shown in Table 5-10.

表 5-10 209P 型转向架的主要技术参数
Table 5-10 Main Technical Parameters of Bogie Type 209P

最高运行速度 Max. operating speed		140 km/h
适用轨距 Applicable track gauge		1 435 mm
固定轴距 Fixed wheelbase		2 400 mm
车轮型式及滚动圆直径 Wheel type and rolling circle diameter		PD 型 A 级整体辗钢车轮，ϕ915 mm PD Class A monobloc rolled steel wheel, ϕ915 mm
车轴型式 Axle type		RD_{3A}、RD_{4A} 型车轴 RD_{3A} and RD_{4A} axles
自重下心盘面距轨面高 Height from lower center plate surface to rail surface under the tare weight		780 mm
自重下旁承面距轨面高 Height from side bearing surface to rail surface under the tare weight		970 mm
通过最小曲线半径 Min. radius of curvature negotiated	车辆连挂 Vehicle coupling	145 mm
	单车调车 Single car switching	100 mm
弹簧形式 Spring type		一系、二系均为圆柱螺旋钢弹簧 Both the primary and secondary springs are cylindrical spiral steel springs
减振方式及其阻尼系数 Damping method and damping coefficient		二系垂向油压减振器，2×100 kN • s/m Secondary vertical oil pressure damper, 2 × 100 kN·s/m
轴承 Bearing		NJ(P)3226X1（42726QT，152726QT）
轮对轴箱定位方式 Positioning method of wheelset and axle box		干摩擦导柱式弹性定位 Dry friction guide pillar elastic positioning
转向架制动型式 Bogie braking type		单元式盘型制动+单侧踏面清扫 Unit disc braking + single-side tread cleaning
限界 Gauge		符合《标准轨距铁路限界 第 1 部分：机车车辆限界》（GB 146.1—2020）的要求 Comply with the requirements of *Gauge for Standard Gauge Railways—Part 1: Rolling Stock Gauge* (GB 146.1—2020)
转向架质量 Bogie mass		约 7 032 kg（装 5 kW 轴端发电装置时，约 7 265 kg） About 7,032 kg (about 7,265 kg when a 5 kW axle-end power generation device is installed)

5.2.5 206 型系列转向架
206 series bogies

206 型系列转向架是为国际联运客车设计制造的新 U 形转向架，它的主要结构特点是构架侧梁中部下凹成 U 形，使摇枕得以从构架侧梁上部通过。这样的结构形式，便于增加摇枕弹簧的静挠度和加大摇枕弹簧的横向距离。经过不断地改进和发展，已形成 206G 型、206P 型、206KP 型、SW-160 型、SW-200 型等系列转向架。

206 series bogies are new U-shaped bogies designed and manufactured for international intermodal passenger cars. Their main structural feature is that the middle of the frame side beam is recessed into a U-shaped shape, allowing the bolster to pass through the upper part of the frame side beam. This structural form facilitates increasing the static deflection and the lateral distance of the bolster spring. Through continuous improvement and development, series bogies such as 206G, 206P, 206KP, SW-160, and SW-200 have been formed.

206 型系列转向架主要由构架、中央悬挂装置、轮对轴箱装置和基础制动装置等组成。

The 206 series bogies are mainly composed of a frame, a central suspension device, a wheelset axle box device, and a foundation braking device.

5.2.5.1. 206G 型转向架

Bogie type 206G

206G 型转向架的构架分铸钢结构和钢板焊接结构两种形式，除构架组成、摇枕组成及弹簧托梁不同外，其他零部件可以互换，其结构如图 5-73 所示。

The framework of bogie type 206G is divided into two forms: cast steel structure and steel

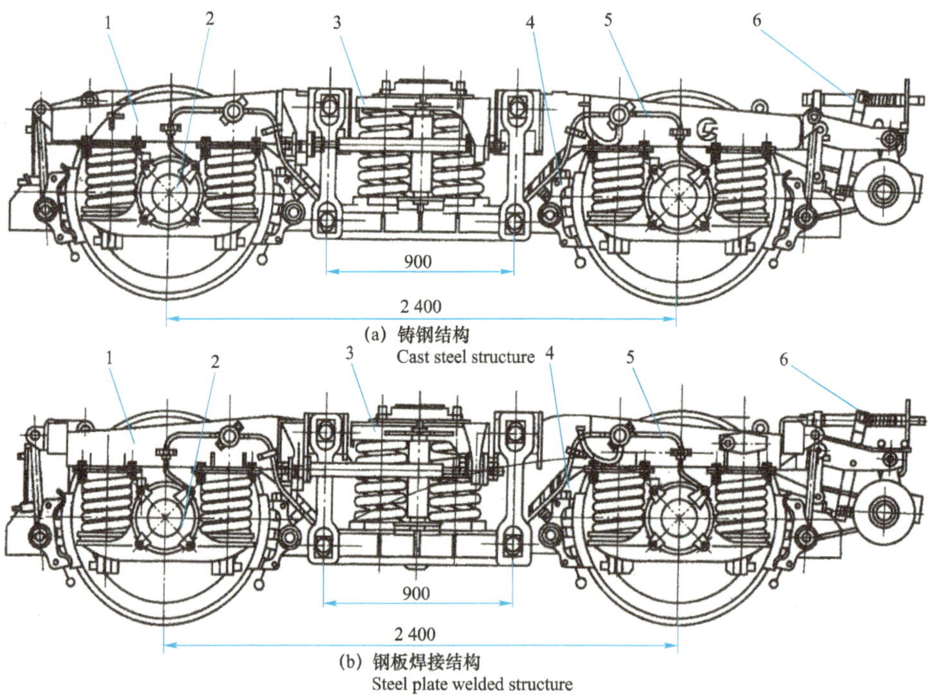

1—构架组成；2—轮对轴箱装置；3—中央悬挂装置；4—制动装置；5—轴温报警装置；6—轴端传动装置。

1—Framework composition; 2—Wheelset axle box device; 3—Central suspension device; 4—Braking device; 5—Axle temperature alarm device; 6—Axle-end transmission device.

图 5-73　206G 型转向架的结构

Figure 5-73　Structure of Bogie Type 206G

plate welded structure. Except for the differences in frame composition, bolster composition and spring joist, other components can be interchanged, as shown in Figure 5-73.

1）构架组成

Framework composition

206G 转向架侧梁中央下凹成 U 形，也称 U 形构架，如图 5-74 所示。与 206 型不同的是取消了纵向摇枕挡座和磨耗板，在每侧左边的一个摇枕吊座附近焊有牵引拉杆座，在侧梁中部内侧增设了油压减振器座等。

The center of side beam for bogie type 206G is recessed into a U-shaped shape, also known as a U-shaped frame, as shown in Figure 5-74. Unlike bogie type 206, the longitudinal bolster seat and wear plate are eliminated, and a traction rod seat is welded near a bolster hanger seat on the left side of each side; An oil pressure damper seat is added inside the middle of the side beam.

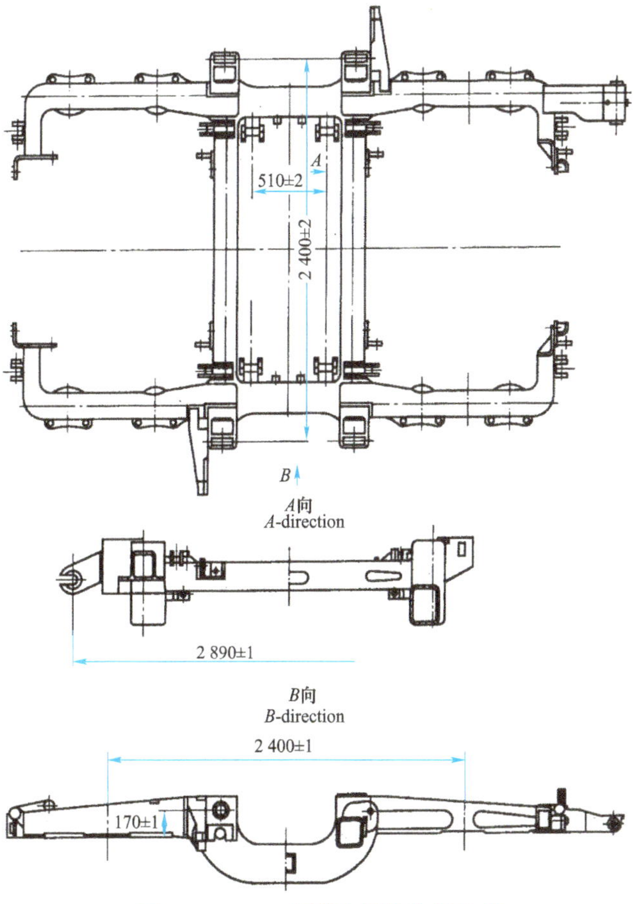

图 5-74　206G 型转向架的构架组成

Figure 5-74　Framework Composition of Bogie Type 206G

2）中央悬挂装置

Central suspension device

206 型转向架的中央悬挂装置属于小摇动台结构，使用无磨耗的牵引拉杆，加设横向油压减振器（阻尼系数为 2×25 kN · s/m）等，其结构如图 5-75 所示。垂向油压减振器的阻尼系数为 80 kN • s/m。

The central suspension device of bogie type 206 belongs to a small shaking table structure, using a non-abrasive traction rod, and is equipped with a lateral oil pressure damper (damping coefficient of 2 × 25 kN·s/m), etc., as shown in Figure 5-75. The damping coefficient of the vertical oil pressure damper is 80 kN·s/m.

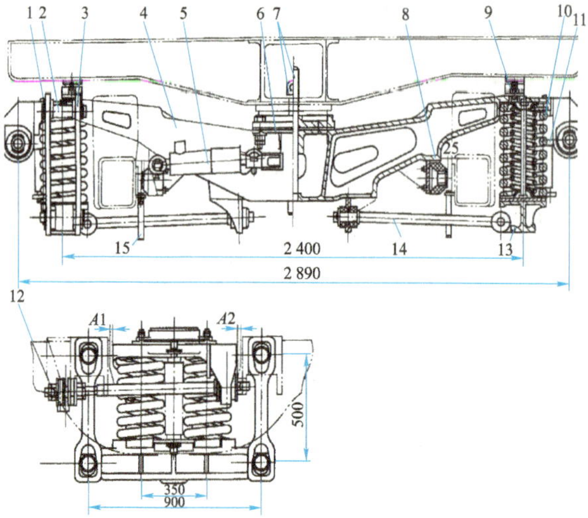

1—摇枕吊环座；2—摇枕吊销；3—摇枕吊；4—摇枕；5—横向油压减振器；6—下心盘垫；7—中心销；8—横向缓冲器；9—下旁承；10—摇枕弹簧；11—油压减振器；12—纵向牵引拉杆；13—弹簧托梁；14—横向拉杆；15—横向拉杆安全吊。
1—Bolster hanger ring seat; 2—Suspension of bolster; 3—Bolster hanger; 4—Bolster; 5—Lateral oil pressure damper; 6—Lower center plate pad; 7—Center pin; 8—Lateral buffer; 9—Lower side bearing; 10—Bolster spring; 11—Oil pressure damper; 12—Longitudinal traction rod; 13—Spring joist; 14—Lateral pull rod; 15—Lateral pull rod safety crane.

图 5-75 206G 型转向架中央悬挂装置的结构

Figure 5-75 Central Suspension Device for Bogie Type 206G

3）轮对轴箱定位装置

Wheelset axle box positioning device

206G 型转向架采用导柱式弹性定位装置。定位套的材质为粉末冶金（铸钢型式）、氟塑料金属。

Bogie type 206G is subject to a guide pillar elastic positioning device. The positioning sleeve is made of powder metallurgy (cast steel type) and fluoroplastic metal.

4）基础制动装置

Foundation braking device

206G 型转向架采用双侧闸瓦踏面制动。

Bogie type 206G is subject to dual-side brake shoe tread braking.

5.2.5.2 206P 型转向架

Bogie type 206P

206P 型转向架是在 206G 型转向架的基础上加装盘型制动装置设计而成的，它可用于 25B 型、25G 型的各式客车。206P 型转向架的结构如图 5-76 所示。

Bogie type 206P is designed based on bogie type 206G and equipped with a disc braking device. It can be used for various types of passenger cars, such as 25B and 25G. The structure of bogie type 206P is shown in Figure 5-76.

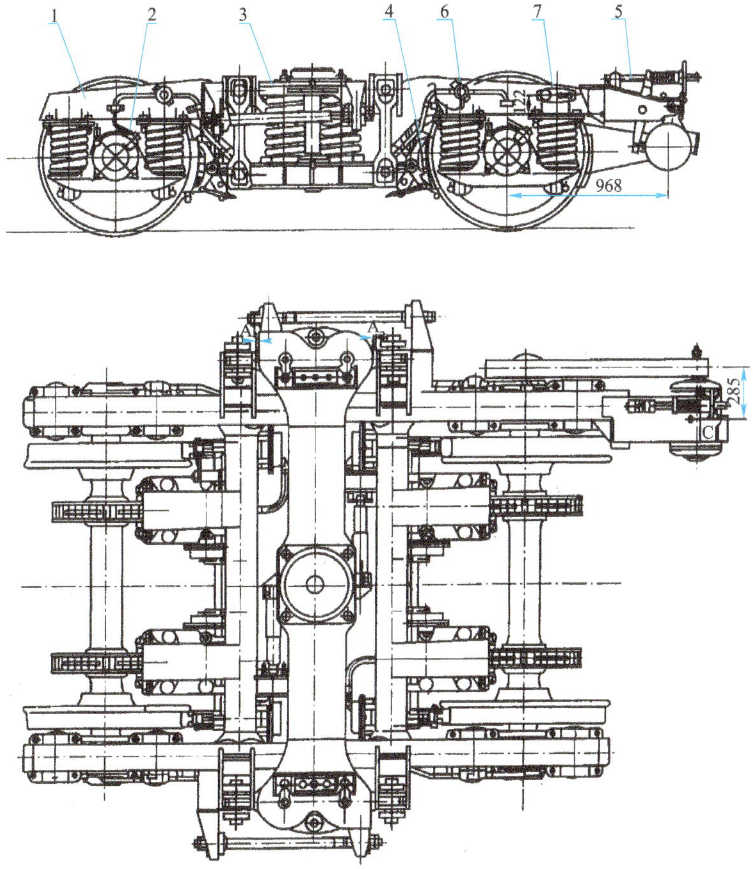

1—构架组成；2—轮对轴箱定位装置；3—中央悬挂装置；4—制动装置；5—轴端传动装置；6—轴温报警装置；7—铭牌。
1—Framework composition; 2—Wheelset axle box positioning device; 3—Central suspension device; 4—Braking device; 5—Axle-end transmission device; 6—Axle temperature alarm device; 7—Nameplate.

图 5-76　206P 型转向架的结构
Figure 5-76　Structure of Bogie Type 206P

1）构架组成
Framework composition

构架为钢板压型后组焊而成的 U 形结构，保留了其安全可靠及组装分解方便的特点。

The framework is a U-shaped structure formed by assembling and welding steel plates after pressing, which retains its characteristics of safety and reliability with convenient assembly and disassembly.

2）中央悬挂装置
Central suspension device

中央悬挂装置与 206G 型转向架基本相同。垂向、横向油压减振器采用进口件。

The central suspension device is basically the same as bogie type 206G. The vertical and lateral oil pressure dampers are made of imported parts.

3）轮对轴箱装置
Wheelset axle box device

轮对轴箱装置与 206G 型转向架基本相同。其弹性定位套和定位座可与 209G 型转向架互换；采用 RD_{3A}、RD_{4A} 型车轴。

The wheelset axle box device is basically the same as bogie type 206G. Its elastic positioning sleeve and positioning seat can be interchanged with bogie type 209G; RD_{3A} and RD_{4A} axles are used.

5.2.6 SW 型系列转向架
SW series bogies

5.2.6.1 SW–160 型转向架
Bogie type SW-160

1997 年，四方机车车辆厂在 206KP 型、206WP 型转向架设计、制造和运用经验的基础上，为 25K 型快速客车及高档快速客车研制、开发了 SW-160 型转向架，如图 5–77 所示。

In 1997, on the basis of experience in the design, manufacturing, and application of bogie type 206KP and bogie type 206WP, Sifang Factory developed and developed bogie type SW-160 for 25K and high-end high-speed passenger cars, as shown in Figure 5-77.

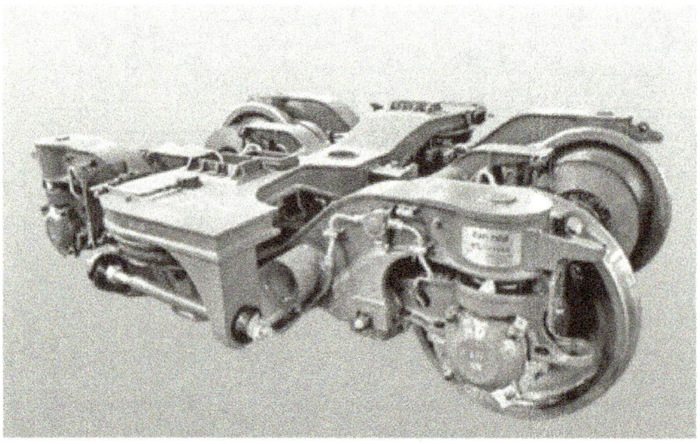

图 5–77 SW-160 型转向架
Figure 5-77 Bogie Type SW-160

1. SW–160 型转向架的结构特点
Structural characteristics of bogie type SW-160

（1）构架由 4 块钢板拼焊而成。

The frame is welded from 4 steel plates.

（2）空气弹簧横向间距增大，以实现外侧悬挂，不仅有利于提高运行稳定性和抗侧滚性能，也有利于取消抗侧滚扭杆装置，简化转向架结构。

Increasing the lateral spacing of air springs to achieve outer suspension is conducive not only to improving operational stability and anti-roll performance but also to eliminating anti-roll torsion bar devices and simplifying the bogie structure.

（3）采用转臂式弹性轴箱定位装置，但进一步优化了结构和定位参数。

The rotary arm elastic axle box positioning device is adopted, but the structure and positioning parameters are further optimized.

2. SW-160 型转向架的结构

Structure of bogie type SW-160

SW-160 型转向架由构架组成、中央悬挂装置、轮对轴箱定位装置和基础制动装置组成。具体结构如下。

Bogie type SW-160 is composed of a framework, a central suspension device, a wheelset axle box positioning device, and a foundation braking device. The specific structure is as follows.

1）构架组成

Framework composition

SW-160 型转向架的构架组成采用焊接结构，如图 5-78 所示。其侧梁由 4 块钢板拼焊而成；空气弹簧座在侧梁外侧，以增大空气弹簧支点横向距离；在侧梁之外的两横梁间设一箱形空管支承梁，并和横梁相连通作为附加空气室；横梁采用圆管型材，贯通并延伸出两个侧梁之外；加设二纵向辅助梁；将构架上的定位臂根部与侧梁焊接处改为圆弧过渡结构，定位臂的定位面改为梯形槽结构。

The framework composition of bogie type SW-160 is of a welded structure, as shown in Figure 5-78. Its side beam is welded by 4 steel plates; Sitting outside the side beam, the air spring seat is provided to increase the lateral distance of the air spring fulcrum; A box-shaped empty pipe support beam is arranged between two transverse beams outside the side beam and communicates with the beam as an additional air chamber; The cross beams are still made of circular tubular profiles that penetrate and extend beyond the two side beams; Two longitudinal auxiliary beams are added; The welding position between the root of the positioning rotary arm and the side beam on the frame is changed to a circular arc transition structure, and the positioning surface of the positioning rotary arm is changed to a trapezoidal groove-shaped structure.

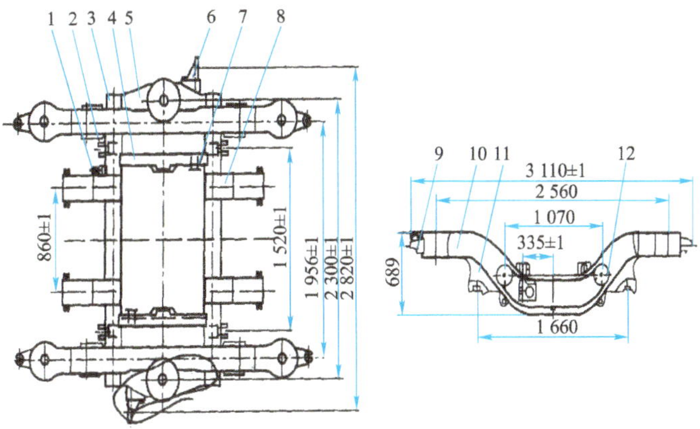

1—手制动转轴座；2—闸瓦托吊座；3—横梁；4—纵向辅助梁；5—空气弹簧支撑座；6—牵引拉杆座；7—横向减振器座；8—制动吊座；9—轴箱减振器座；10—侧梁；11—定位臂；12—制动梁吊座。

1—Hand brake rotary shaft seat; 2—Brake shoe support cane seat; 3—Cross beam; 4—Longitudinal auxiliary beam; 5—Air spring support seat; 6—Traction rod seat; 7—Lateral damper seat; 8—Brake hanger seat; 9—Axle box damper seat; 10—Side beam; 11—Positioning arm; 12—Brake beam hanger seat.

图 5-78　SW-160 型转向架的构架组成

Figure 5-78　Framework Composition of Bogie Type SW-160

2）中央悬挂装置

Central suspension device

SW-160 型转向架的中央悬挂装置（如图 5-79 所示）采用无摇动台结构和新研制的 SYS640 型自密封空气弹簧（如图 5-80 所示），并将空气弹簧横向间距增大至 2 300 mm，构成外侧悬挂，增大了转向架的抗侧滚刚度，使取消抗侧滚扭杆装置成为可能（通过试验决定是否安装）。

The central suspension device of bogie type SW-160 is subject to a structure without shaking tables (as shown in Figure 5-79) and a newly developed SYS640 self-sealing air spring (as shown in Figure 5-80), and the lateral spacing of the air spring is increased to 2,300 mm to form an outer suspension, which increases the anti-roll rigidity of the bogie and makes it possible to cancel the anti-roll torsion bar device (whether to install it is determined through testing).

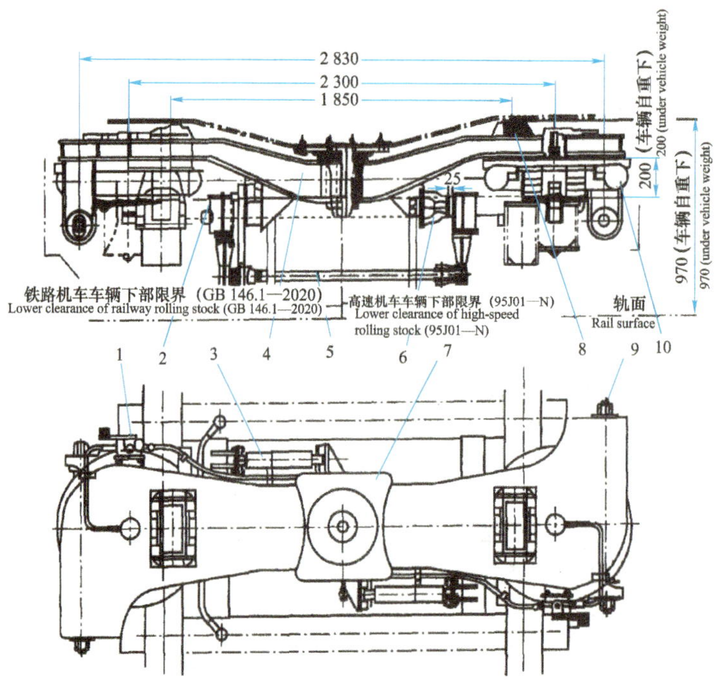

1—高度控制阀；2—差压阀；3—油压减振器；4—摇枕组成；5—扭杆组成；6—横向缓冲器；7—牵引销组成；8—旁承组成；9—牵引拉杆组成；10—SYS550D（SYS640）型自密封空气弹簧。

1—Height control valve; 2—Differential pressure valve; 3—Oil pressure damper; 4—Bolster composition; 5—Torsion bar composition; 6—Lateral buffer; 7—Traction pin composition; 8—Side bearing composition; 9—Traction rod composition; 10—SYS550D (SYS640) self-sealing air spring.

图 5-79　SW-160 型转向架中央悬挂装置的结构

Figure 5-79　Structure of Central Suspension Device for Bogie Type SW-160

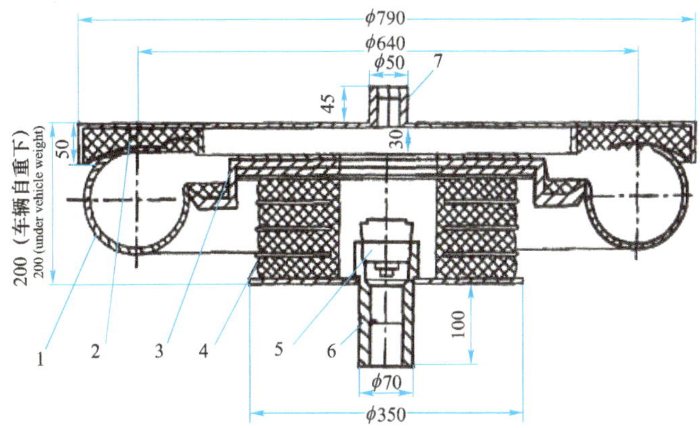

1—橡胶囊；2—上盖组成；3—下座组成；4—橡胶堆；5—节流阀；6、7—O 形密封圈。

1—Rubber capsule; 2—Upper cover composition; 3—Lower seat composition; 4—Rubber pile; 5—Throttle valve; 6/7—O-ring.

图 5-80　SYS640 型自密封空气弹簧

Figure 5-80　SYS640 Self-sealing Air Spring

摇枕采用封闭式箱形结构，增强了承载部位的强度和刚度，并将空气弹簧的供风改为上进式。

The bolster is subject to a closed box structure, which enhances the strength and rigidity of the bearing part and changes the air supply of the air spring to an upward type.

采用全旁承支重，选用 65Mn 上旁承与具有自润滑特性的氟塑料金属摩擦块；采用圆柱截面牵引销、套（内、外钢套中间为硫化橡胶）配合的新型结构，使其只传递水平载荷。

It is needed to adopt full side bearing support and select 65Mn upper side bearing and fluoroplastic metal friction block with self-lubricating characteristics; A new structure with a cylindrical section traction pin, and a sleeve (with vulcanized rubber in the middle of the inner and outer steel sleeves) is used to transmit only horizontal loads.

3）轮对轴箱定位装置

Wheelset axle box positioning device

SW-160 型转向架的轮对轴箱定位装置采用和 206KP 型转向架相同的单转臂无磨耗弹性轴箱定位和轴箱顶部单组双圈螺旋弹簧加橡胶垫及垂向油压减振器的形式，其结构如图 5-81 所示。

The wheelset and axle box positioning device of bogie type SW-160 is subject to the same form as bogie type 206KP, which is a single arm abrasion-free elastic axle box positioning device, and a single group of double-coil spiral springs on the top of the axle box with rubber pads and a vertical oil pressure damper, as shown in Figure 5-81.

SW-160 型转向架将原 206KP 型转向架的圆形销轴改为梯形槽结构；在轴箱底部、两侧均设轴温传感器安装位；大大增加了轴箱弹簧筒和轴箱弹簧间的间隙，尤其是纵向，将原圆形断面改为长圆孔断面；轴箱弹簧两端设有弹簧夹板，在组装、分解定位转臂时，可避免弹性定位套产生过大的扭转角。

The circular pin shaft on bogie type 206KP is changed into a trapezoidal groove structure by bogie type SW-160; Shaft temperature sensors are installed at the bottom and both sides of the axle box; The gap between the axle box spring cylinder and the axle box spring has been greatly increased, especially in the longitudinal direction. The original circular section has been changed to a long circular hole section; Spring clamp plates are provided at both ends of the axle box spring to prevent excessive torsion angles caused by the elastic positioning sleeve during assembly and disassembly of the positioning rotary arm.

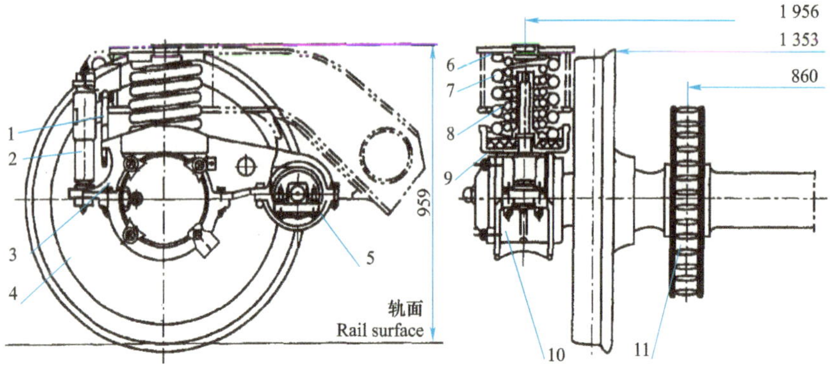

1—轮对提吊；2—垂向油压减振器；3—定位转臂组成；4—轮对；5—定位挡板；6—上弹簧夹板组成；7—轴箱弹簧组；8—下夹板组成；9—缓冲胶垫；10—轴箱；11—制动盘。

1—Wheelset lifting; 2—Vertical oil pressure damper; 3—Positioning rotary arm composition; 4—Wheelset; 5—Positioning baffle; 6—Upper spring clamp plate composition; 7—Axle box spring set; 8—Lower clamp plate composition; 9—Buffer rubber pad; 10—Axle box; 11—Brake disc.

图 5-81　SW-160 型转向架轮对轴箱定位装置的结构

Figure 5-81　Structure of Wheelset Axle Box Positioning Device for Bogie Type SW-160

4）基础制动装置

Foundation braking device

SW-160 型转向架的基础制动装置采用盘型制动。盘型制动缸为浮动式吊挂，两种单元制动缸均设有单向自动闸瓦间隙调整器，一位转向架的一位盘型制动单元具有手制动作用。

The disc braking is used for the foundation braking device of bogie type SW-160. The disc brake cylinder is a floating suspension type. Both types of unit brake cylinders are equipped with a one-way automatic brake shoe clearance adjuster. The “B” end bogie and “B” end disc braking units have a hand brake function.

5.2.6.2　SW-220K 型转向架

Bogie type SW-220K

SW-220K 型转向架是在 SW-220 型转向架的基础上，根据 160 km/h 速度等级客车的要求，经局部改造而成的，如图 5-82 所示。SW-220K 型转向架采用无摇动台、无摇枕、单转臂无磨耗弹性轴箱定位、空气弹簧、盘型制动的技术。SW-220K 型转向架适合各种 160 km/h 速度等级的客车（除制动装置外，该转向架可满足 220 km/h 速度等级的运用要求）使用。

Bogie type SW-220K is partially modified based on bogie type SW-220 according to the requirements of 160 km/h speed class passenger cars, as shown in Figure 5-82. Bogie type SW-220K is subject to the technology of non-shaking tables, non-bolster, single arm abrasion-free elastic axle box positioning, air spring, and disc brake. Bogie type SW-220K can be used for various passenger cars with a speed level of 160 km/h (Except for braking devices, the bogie can meet the application requirements of 220 km/h).

图 5-82 SW-220K 型转向架
Figure 5-82 Bogie Type SW-220K

1. SW-220K 型转向架的结构特点
Structural characteristics of bogie type SW-220K

SW-220K 型转向架的结构特点如下。

The structural characteristics of bogie type SW-220K are as follows.

（1）构架由 4 块钢板拼焊而成，为 U 形构架。

The frame is welded from 4 steel plates, as a U-shaped frame.

（2）采取了无摇枕的空气弹簧二系悬挂结构，车体直接坐落于空气弹簧上。

The secondary suspension structure of air spring without bolster is adopted, and the car body is directly located on the air spring.

（3）外侧悬挂，提高了抗侧滚性能；未设抗侧滚扭杆装置。

The outer suspension improves the anti-roll performance; No anti-roll torsion bar device is provided.

（4）采用了抗蛇行减振器，提高了转向架蛇行运动的稳定性。

The anti-hunting damper is adopted to improve the stability of the hunting motion of the bogies.

（5）采用转臂式弹性轴箱定位装置。

The rotary arm elastic axle box positioning device is adopted.

2. SW-220K 型转向架的结构
Structure of bogie type SW-220K

SW-220K 型转向架由构架组成、轮对轴箱定位装置、中央空气弹簧悬挂系统、基础制动装置等组成，其结构如图 5-83 所示。

Bogie type SW-220K is composed of a framework, a wheelset axle box positioning device, a central air spring suspension device, a foundation braking device and others, as shown in

Figure 5-83.

图 5-83 SW-220K 型转向架的结构
Figure 5-83 Structure of Bogie Type SW-220K

1）构架组成

Framework composition

（1）SW-220K 型转向架的构架组成为钢板焊接结构，平面呈“H”形，主要由侧梁组成、横梁组成、纵向辅助梁、空气弹簧支撑梁和定位臂等组成，如图 5-84 和图 5-85 所示。侧梁的中部为凹形，横梁的内腔与空气弹簧支撑梁的内腔组成空气弹簧的附加空气室。

The framework of bogie type SW-220K is a welded steel plate structure with an H-shaped plane, mainly composed of side beams, cross beams, longitudinal auxiliary beams, air spring support beams, and positioning rotary arms, as shown in Figure 5-84 and Figure 5-85. The middle of the side beam is concave, and the inner cavity of the beam and the inner cavity of the air spring support beam form an additional air chamber for the air spring.

图 5-84 SW-220K 型转向架的构架组成
Figure 5-84 Framework Composition of Bogie Type SW-220K

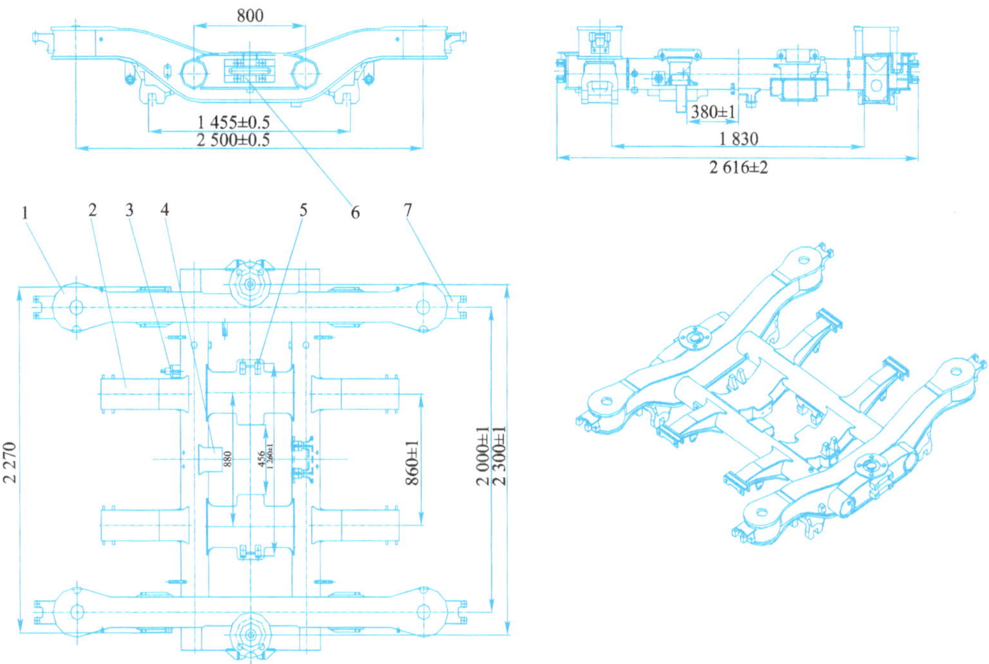

1—构架；2—制动吊梁组成；3—手制动转轴；4—防过冲座；5—横向减振器座；
6—抗蛇行油压减振器安装座；7—垂向减振器座。

1—Framework; 2—Anti-overshoot seat; 3—Anti-hunting damper mounting base; 4—Brake lifting beam composition;
5—Hand brake rotary shaft; 6—Vertical damper seat; 7—Lateral damper seat.

图 5-85　SW-220K 型转向架构架组成的结构

Figure 5-85　Structure of Framework Composition of Bogie Type SW-220K

（2）侧梁组成。侧梁采用由 4 块 Q345E 焊接结构用轧制钢板组成箱形断面的焊接结构，上、下盖板厚分别为 12 mm、16 mm，腹板厚 12 mm，侧梁中部为 U 形。与弹性节点连接的定位臂为铸钢件（材质为 ZG25MnNi），其与侧梁连接部为圆滑过渡，力求应力缓和。

Side frame composition. The side beam is of a welded structure with a box section composed of four Q345E rolled steel plate for welding structure. The upper and lower cover plates are respectively 12 mm and 16 mm thick, and the web plate is 12 mm thick. The middle of the side beam is U-shaped. The positioning rotary arm connected to the elastic node is a steel casting (material: ZG25MnNi), and its connection to the side beam has a smooth transition, for stress relaxation.

（3）横梁组成。横梁采用ϕ203×12 mm 无缝钢管（材质为 Q345E），表面经酸洗磷化处理。其内腔作为空气弹簧的附加空气室。在横梁上焊有制动吊座、牵引座及空气弹簧的防过冲座等。

Cross beam composition. Beam is made of ϕ 203 × 12 mm seamless steel pipe (material: Q345E), with its surface subjected to acid pickling and phosphating treatment. The inner chamber serves as an additional air chamber for the air spring. The beam is welded with a brake hanger seat, a traction seat, and an air spring anti-overshoot seat.

（4）纵向辅助梁。为提高构架刚度，在两横梁之间由纵向辅助梁连接，其上安装有横向减振器座和横向缓冲器座等。辅助梁采用箱形断面的焊接结构。

Longitudinal auxiliary beam. To improve the rigidity of the frame, the two cross beams are connected by a longitudinal auxiliary beam, on which a lateral damper seat and a lateral buffer seat are installed. The auxiliary beam is of a welded structure with a box section.

（5）空气弹簧支撑梁。位于侧梁外侧的两横梁之间，由 3 块钢板组焊而成的槽形结构，它与侧梁外侧腹板组成的密闭腔与横梁内腔相通，共同组成空气弹簧的附加空气室。

Air spring support beam. Located between the two cross beams on the outer side of the side beam, it is a groove-shaped structure composed of three steel plates assembled and welded. It is connected to the closed cavity formed by the outer web of the side beam and the inner cavity of the cross beam, forming an additional air chamber for the air spring.

2）轮对轴箱定位装置

Wheelset axle box positioning device

（1）轮对轴箱。轮对轴箱采用 KKD 车轮、RD_{3A1} 车轴、轴装制动盘、804468/804469（进口于 FAG 公司），或 BC1B322880/BC1B322881（进口于 SKF 公司）轴承。另外，轮对轴箱的轴端有两种：防滑速度传感器轴端和接地装置轴端。转向架的 2、4、6、8 轴端接有接地电阻。各车轴端布置如表 5-11 所示。

Wheelset axle box. The wheelset and axle box are subject to KKD wheels, RD_{3A1} axles, axle-mounted brake discs, 804468/804469 (imported from FAG), or BC1B322880/BC1B322881 (imported from SKF) bearings. In addition, there are two types of axle ends for the wheelset axle box: axle ends with anti-skid speed sensors and grounding device axle ends. The 2, 4, 6, and 8 axle ends of the bogie are connected to ground resistors. The arrangement of each axle end is shown in Table 5-11.

表 5-11　各车轴端布置

Table 5-11　Arrangement of Each Axle End

	防滑速度传感器轴端 Anti-skid speed sensor axle end	接地装置轴端 Grounding device axle end
位　数 Number of positions	2，4，6，8	1，3，5，7

轮对轴箱与定位转臂采用跨接的形式，定位转臂通过 4 个 M20 螺栓与压盖连接，定位转臂跨落入轴箱外部的槽内。若需要更换轮对，只需松开 4 个 M20 螺栓和接地线等，便可以使轮对轴箱与转向架分离。

The wheelset axle box and the positioning rotary arm are connected in a bridging manner. The positioning rotary arm is connected to the gland through four M20 bolts, and the positioning rotary arm straddles into the groove outside the axle box. If a wheelset needs to be replaced, it is needed to just loosen four M20 bolts and ground wires to separate the wheelset axle box from the bogie.

SW-220K 型转向架轮对轴箱定位装置的结构及其外形分别如图 5-86、图 5-87 所示。

The wheelset and axle box positioning device of bogie type SW-220K and its outline are shown in Figure 5-86 and Figure 5-87.

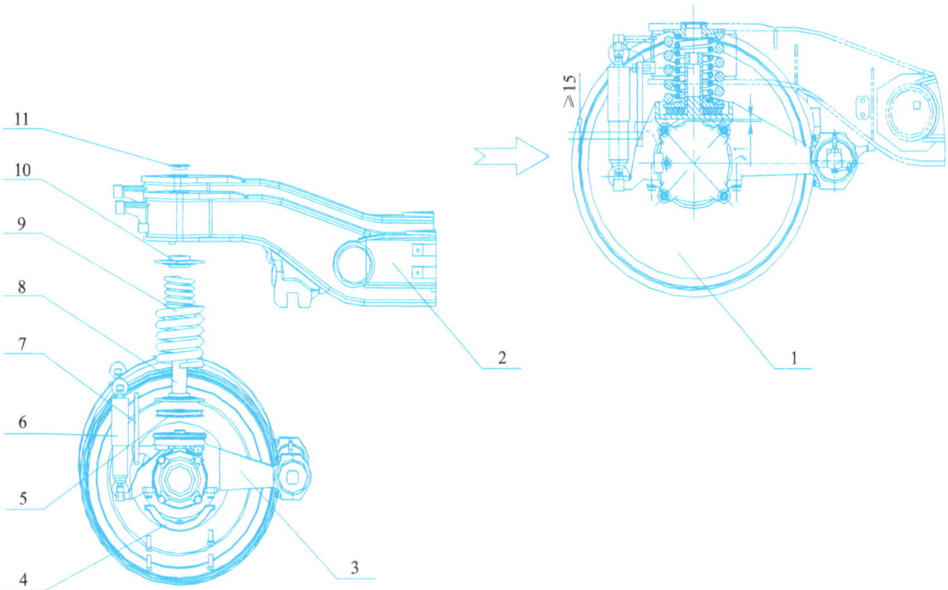

1—轮对轴箱组成；2—构架组成；3—定位转臂组成；4—压盖；5—缓冲胶垫；6—垂向油压减振器；
7—轮对提吊；8—下弹簧夹板；9—轴箱弹簧组；10—上弹簧夹板；11—防锈帽。

1—Composition of wheelset and axle box; 2—Framework composition; 3—Positioning rotary arm composition;
4—Gland; 5—Buffer rubber pad; 6—Vertical oil pressure damper; 7—Wheelset lifting; 8—Lower spring clamp plate;
9—Axle box spring set; 10—Upper spring clamp plate; 11—Anti-rust cap.

图 5-86　SW-220K 型转向架轮对轴箱定位装置的结构

Figure 5-86　Structure of Wheelset Axle Box Positioning Device for Bogie Type SW-220K

图 5-87　SW-220K 型转向架轮对轴箱定位装置的外形

Figure 5-87　Outline of Wheelset Axle Box Positioning Device for Bogie Type SW-220K

（2）轴箱定位装置。轴箱定位装置为单转臂无磨耗弹性定位，定位转臂是该装置中的骨架，是轮对轴箱与构架的联系纽带，为减小定位节点刚度对一系垂向刚度的附加影响，定位转臂选择尽可能长，为 550 mm 长的铸钢件（材质为 ZG25MnNi）。SW-220K 型转向架轴箱定位装置的结构如图 5-88 所示。

Axle box positioning device. The axle box positioning device is a s single-arm abrasion-free elastic axle box positioning device. The positioning rotary arm is the skeleton of the device and serves as the connecting link between the wheelset axle box and the frame. To reduce the additional impact of the positioning node rigidity on the primary vertical rigidity, the positioning rotary arm is selected as long as possible, the steel castings (material: ZG25MnNi) with a length of 550 mm are used. The structure of axle box positioning device of bogie type SW-220K is shown in Figure 5-88.

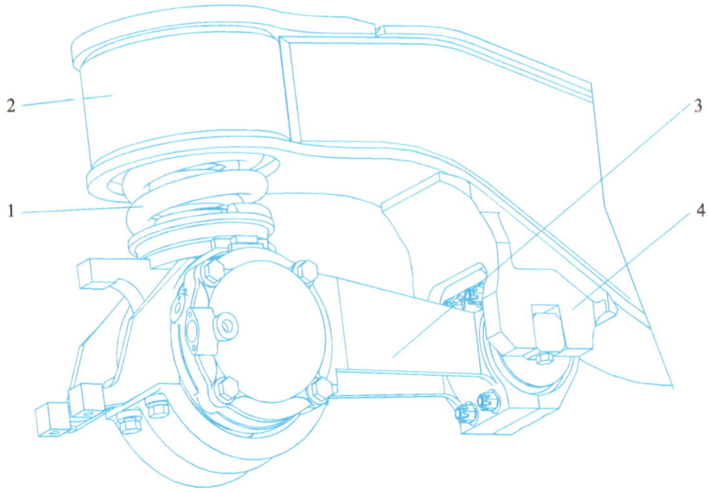

1—轴箱弹簧；2—构架；3—轴箱转臂；4—定位座。
1—Axle box spring ;2—Framework; 3—Axle box rotary arm; 4—Positional seat.

图 5-88 SW-220K 型转向架轴箱定位装置的结构

Figure 5-88 Structure of Axle Box Positioning Device of Bogie Type SW-220K

轴箱定位装置具有以下特点。

The axle box positioning device has the following characteristics.

① 可利用弹性节点自由地选择纵向和横向的刚度。

Elastic nodes can be used to freely select the longitudinal and lateral rigidity.

② 垂向采用轴箱顶置钢弹簧，弹簧刚度选择范围大，并且与纵向、横向刚度几乎无关，可以单独设计。

Vertically, a steel spring mounted on the top of the axle box is used, with a wide selection of spring rigidity, which is almost independent of longitudinal and lateral rigidity and can be designed independently.

③ 没有滑动和摩擦部分，橡胶件几乎不外露，从而延缓老化，可以长期运用而免维修。

With no sliding and friction parts, the rubber parts are hardly exposed, which delays aging and makes it possible to use it for a long time without maintenance.

④ 与其他定位方式相比，零部件少，不必进行轴距控制，因此组装、分解中均不需特殊工装设备。

Compared to other positioning methods, there are fewer components with no need for wheelbase control, so special tooling is not required during assembly and disassembly.

（3）弹性节点。弹性节点是由橡胶与金属硫化成一体的梯形结构，只有将其安装于定位转臂中才能体现弹性节点的特性。

Elastic nodes. The elastic node is a trapezoidal structure made of rubber and metal vulcanization, which can only reflect the characteristics of the elastic node after being installed in the positioning rotary arm.

（4）钢弹簧组成。钢弹簧组成包括内、外圈钢簧，缓冲胶垫和上、下夹板。钢弹簧的材质为 60Si2CrVA。

Steel spring composition. The steel spring consists of inner and outer steel springs, buffer rubber pads, and upper and lower clamp plates. The steel spring is made of 60Si2CrVA.

缓冲胶垫主要作用为消除和衰减部分来自轮轨的高频振动，其外形尺寸为：220 mm×64 mm×16 mm（外径×内径×厚度）。

The main function of the buffer rubber pad is to eliminate and attenuate some high-frequency vibrations from the wheel/rail. Its overall dimension: 220 mm × 64 mm × 16 mm (outer diameter × internal diameter × thickness).

上弹簧夹板为锻钢件（材质为 Q235-A），上部加工有安装防尘罩用的凹槽。

The upper spring clamp plate is a forged steel piece (material: Q235-A), and the upper part is machined with a groove for installing the dust cover.

下弹簧夹板由锻钢件和圆钢焊接制成，上部有 Tr32 螺纹孔。利用该螺纹，通过工艺螺栓和上、下弹簧夹板将钢簧预压在一起，便于轴箱定位装置的组装、拆卸。

The lower spring clamp plate is made of forged steel and round steel by welding, and the upper part has Tr32 threaded holes. Using this thread, the steel springs are pre-pressed together through process bolts and upper and lower spring clamp plates, facilitating the assembly and disassembly of the axle box positioning device.

（5）一系垂向减振器。在定位转臂和构架弹簧座之间设置了油压减振器，以防止高频振动的传递并减小转向架的点头振动。轴箱减振器参数如表 5-12 所示。

Primary vertical damper. An oil pressure damper is installed between the positioning rotary arm and the frame spring seat to prevent the transmission of high-frequency vibration and reduce the nodding vibration of the bogie. The parameters of the axle box damper are shown in Table 5-12.

表 5-12　轴箱减振器参数

Table 5-12　Parameters of Axle Box Damper

阻尼系数 Damping coefficient	20 kN·s/m
位移 Displacement	190 mm
最大/最小长度 Max./Min. length	570/380 mm
安装长度 Installation length	453 mm
节点结构及刚度 Node structure and rigidity	两端球铰，刚度为 10 MN/m Ball joint at both ends, stiffness of 10 MN/m
防尘罩直径 Dust cover diameter	84 mm

（7）轴端形式。转向架的 1、3、5、7 位轴端装有炭刷式接地装置，2、4、6、8 位轴端装有速度传感器的测速齿轮。

Axle end form. The axle ends at positions 1, 3, 5, and 7 of the bogie are equipped with carbon brush-type grounding devices, and the axle ends at positions 2, 4, 6, and 8 are equipped with speed-measuring gears for speed sensors.

（8）轴端接地装置。轴端接地装置为铁路客车轴承提供简单、有效、经济的保护和防护，防止工作电流或系统故障电流及雷电电流通过轴承造成的轴承损伤。

Axle-end grounding device. The axle-end grounding device provides simple, effective, and economical protection for railway passenger car bearings, preventing bearing damage caused by working current or system fault current as well as lightning current flowing through the bearings.

SW-220K 型转向架轴端接地装置的结构如图 5–89 所示。

The structure of bogie type SW-220K is shown in Figure 5-89.

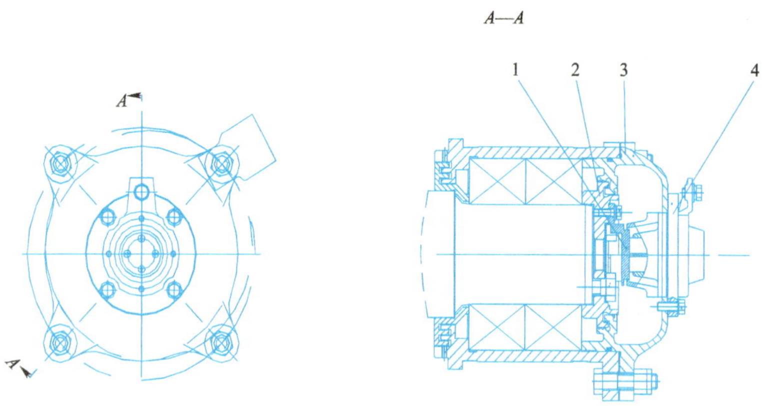

1—摩擦片；2—轴承压板；3—轴箱盖；4—接地装置。

1—Friction plate; 2—Bearing press plate; 3—Axle box cover; 4—Grounding device.

图 5–89　SW-220K 型转向架轴端接地装置的结构

Figure 5-89　Structure of Axle-end Grounding Device of Bogie Type SW-220K

轴端接地装置的主要性能如下。

The main performance of axle-end grounding device is as follows.

① 额定电流为 300 A。

Rated current of 300 A.

② 瞬态电流不小于 10 kA RMS，持续时间为 100 ms。

Transient current of no less than 10 kA RMS for a duration of 100 ms.

③ 峰值电流不小于 25 kA。

Peak current of no less than 25 kA.

④ 正常工作条件下电刷的更换寿命不小于 80 万 km。

Replacement life of the electric brush under normal working conditions of no less than 800,000 km.

⑤ 装置对轴承的温升增加不超过 3℃。

Temperature rise of the device to the bearing of no higher than 3℃.

3）中央空气弹簧悬挂系统

Central air spring suspension system

SW-220K 型转向架中央空气弹簧悬挂系统的结构如图 5-90 所示。

The structure of central air spring suspension system of bogie type SW-220K is shown in Figure 5-90.

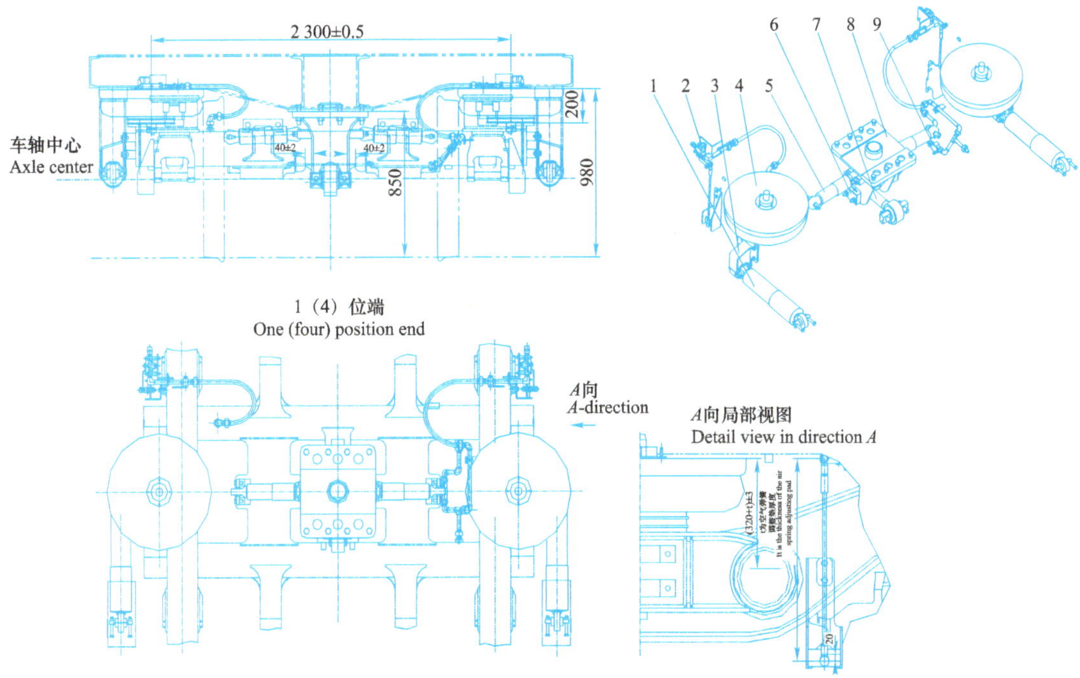

1—抗蛇行油压减振器；2—高度控制阀；3—减振器座；4—空气弹簧组成；5—横向油压减振器；6—横向止挡；7—牵引拉杆组成；8—中心销组成；9—差压阀。

1—Anti-hunting oil pressure damper; 2—Height control valve; 3—Damper seat; 4—Air spring composition; 5—Lateral oil pressure damper; 6—Lateral stop; 7—Traction rod composition; 8—Center pin composition; 9—Differential pressure valve.

图 5-90　SW-220K 型转向架中央空气弹簧悬挂系统的结构

Figure 5-90　Structure of Central Air Spring Suspension System of Bogie Type SW-220K

（1）空气弹簧。空气弹簧是由气囊和附加的橡胶弹簧组合而成的自由膜型式，适用于水平位移大的无摇枕转向架，其结构如图 5-91 所示。空气弹簧的特性参数如表 5-13 所示。

Air spring. The air spring is a free film type composed of an airbag and an additional rubber spring, suitable for bolsterless bogies with large horizontal displacement, as shown in Figure 5-91. The characteristic parameters of the air spring are shown in Table 5-13.

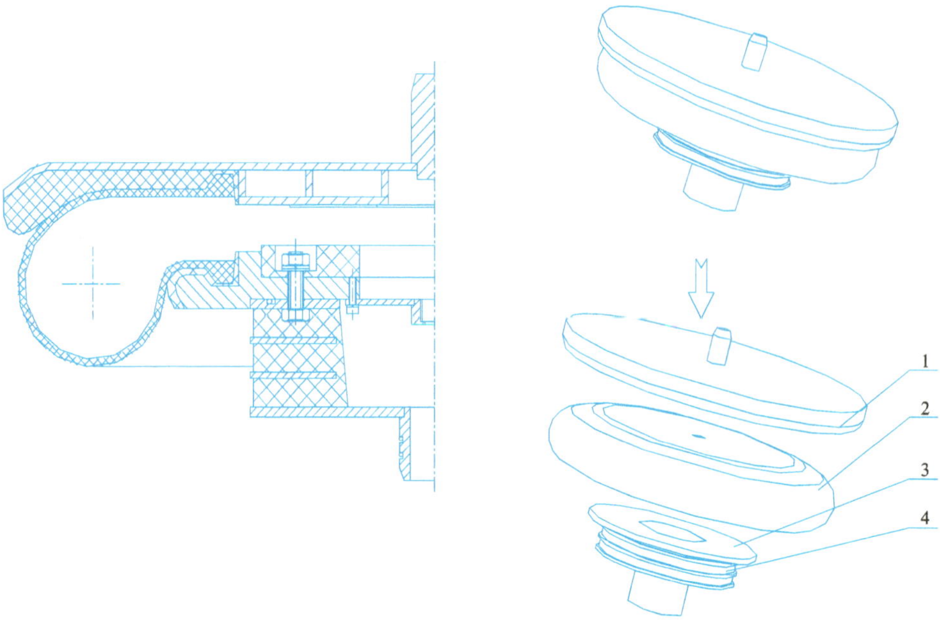

1—上盖组成；2—橡胶囊；3—下座组成；4—橡胶堆。

1—Upper cover composition; 2—Rubber capsule; 3—Lower seat composition; 4—Rubber pile.

图 5-91　SW-220K 型转向架空气弹簧的结构

Figure 5-91　Structure of Air Spring on Bogie Type SW-220K

表 5-13　空气弹簧的特性参数

Table 5-13　Characteristic Parameters of Air Spring

有效直径（F_z=100 kN） Effective diameter (F_z=100 kN)		580 mm
空载（内压 400 kPa）F_z No load (internal pressure 400 kPa) F_z 满载（内压 500 kPa）F_z Full load (internal pressure 500 kPa) F_z		106 kN 130 kN
最大垂向位移 Max. vertical displacement 最大水平偏移 Max. horizontal offset		±40 mm ±120 mm
附加空气室 V_a Additional air chamber V_a		80 L
节流孔当量阻尼 Equivalent damping of orifice		60 kN·s/m
垂向刚度 Vertical rigidity	空载时 c_z c_z at no load	320 N/mm
横向刚度 Lateral rigidity	空载时 c_y c_y at no load	180 N/mm
	满载时 c_y c_y at full load	260 N/mm

气囊的上、下支口为自密封结构。上盖板上设有定位柱，与车体相连；下部通气口与构架相连，为圆柱面并用 O 形橡胶圈密封。为使空气弹簧无气状态时转向架能够运行，在下支座上面设有特殊的滑板，以提高转向架的曲线通过性能。当空气弹簧破损无气时，附加的橡胶弹簧提供二系垂向刚度，确保车辆运行安全。空气弹簧在附加弹簧内设置了固定阻尼孔，以提供二系垂向阻尼。二系横向油压减振器参数如表 5-14 所示。

The upper and lower branches of the airbag are self-sealing structures. The upper cover plate is provided with a positioning column connected to the car body, and the lower vent port is connected to the frame, which is a cylindrical surface and sealed with an O-ring. To enable the bogie to operate when the air spring is in an airless state, a special sliding plate is installed on the lower support to improve the curving performance of the bogie. When the air spring is damaged without air, additional rubber springs provide secondary vertical rigidity to ensure safe vehicle operation. The air spring is provided with a fixed damping hole in the additional spring to provide secondary vertical damping. The parameters of the secondary lateral oil pressure damper are shown in Table 5-14.

表 5-14 二系横向减振器参数

Table 5-14 Parameters of Secondary Lateral Damper

阻尼系数 Damping coefficient	40 kN·s/m
行程 Stroke	160 mm
最大/最小长度 Max./Min. length	510 mm/350 mm
安装长度 Installation length	420 mm
节点结构及刚度 Node structure and rigidity	球铰，刚度为 10 MN/m Ball joint, stiffness of 10 MN/m
防尘罩直径 Dust cover diameter	84 mm

（2）牵引装置。牵引装置采用单拉杆结构，安装在车体的中心销组成与带缓冲的拉杆连接，传递牵引力和制动力。为降低转向架传递给车体的振动，每台转向架的前后牵引刚度设置为 5 MN/m。SW-220K 型转向架牵引装置的结构如图 5-92 所示。

Traction device. The traction device is of a single pull rod structure, and the center pin installed on the car body is connected with a buffered pull rod to transmit traction and braking force. To reduce the vibration transmitted from the bogie to the car body, the front and rear traction rigidity of each bogie is set to 5 MN/m. The structure of bogie type SW-220K is shown in Figure 5-92.

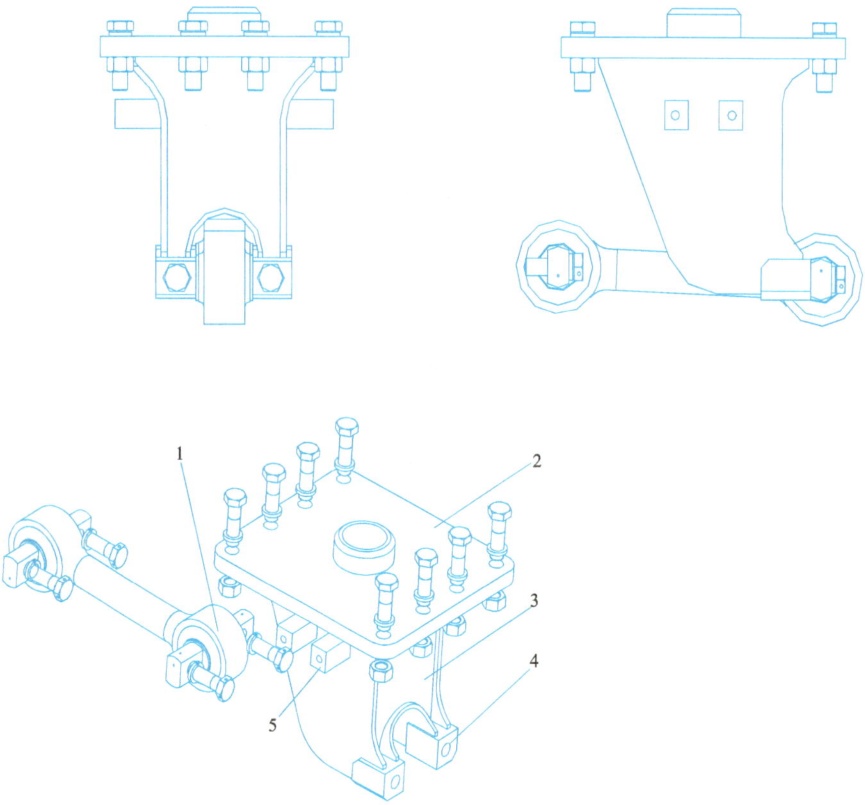

1—牵引拉杆；2—安装座；3—中心销连接体；4—拉杆安装块；5—减振器安装块。

1—Traction rod; 2—Damper mounting block; 3—Mounting seat; 4—Center pin connector; 5—Tie rod mounting block.

图 5-92　SW-220K 型转向架牵引装置的结构

Figure 5-92　Structure of Traction Device for Bogie Type SW-220K

SW-220K 型转向架的牵引装置具有以下特点。

The traction device of bogie type SW-220K has the following characteristics.

① 转向架相对于车体的回转依靠牵引拉杆端部节点中橡胶的弹性变形。

The rotation of the bogie relative to the car body depends on the elastic deformation of the rubber in the end nodes of the traction rod.

② 转向架横向（垂向）移动时的回复力，除依靠空气弹簧横向（垂向）刚度外，还依靠两拉杆两端橡胶节点的刚度，但这部分的作用很小。

The restoring force of the bogie during lateral (vertical) movement depends not only on the lateral (vertical) rigidity of the air spring, but also on the rigidity of the rubber joints at both ends of the two pull rods, but it only plays a small role.

③ 牵引装置内无相对滑动部分，为无磨耗结构。

There is no relative sliding part in the traction device, which is an abrasion-free structure.

④ 转向架和车体的分离应先拆卸牵引杆两端螺栓。

To separate the bogie from the car body, it is required to first remove the bolts at both ends of the traction rod.

（3）横向缓冲器。横向缓冲器是为限制车体运行中（特别是曲线上）过大的横向位移而设置的。为了避免运行中车体频繁碰撞缓冲器或者接触后出现硬性冲击，将缓冲器与止挡的间隙设置为（40±2）mm，同时将缓冲器设计成非线性的特性，它与空气弹簧的横向刚度共同限制车体的横向位移，且位移较大时，可提供非线性增长的复原力。

Lateral buffer. The lateral buffer is set to limit excessive lateral displacement during the operation of railway vehicles (especially on curves). To avoid frequent collision of the car body with the buffer or hard impact after contact during operation, the gap between the buffer and the stop is set to 40±2 mm. At the same time, the buffer is designed to have nonlinear characteristics. Together with the lateral rigidity of the air spring, it limits the lateral displacement of the car body and can provide nonlinear growth of resilience when the displacement is large.

（4）防过冲座。由于采用无摇枕转向架，应设置防过冲座来防止因意外造成车体过度地上升。该转向架在横梁上设有防过冲座，与牵引拉杆头部之间设置了 70 mm 的间隙，具有限制车体过高上升的功能。

Anti-overshoot seat. Due to the use of bolsterless bogies, anti-overshoot seats should be provided to prevent the accidental excessive rise of the car body. This bogie is equipped with an anti-overshoot seat on the crossbeam, and a clearance of 70 mm is set between it and the head of the traction rod, which has the function of limiting the excessive rise of the car body.

（5）抗蛇行油压减振器。为了获得稳定的回转阻力力矩，以抑制转向架的蛇行运动，采用了抗蛇行油压减振器，代替了以往转向架使用旁承摩擦副提供回转阻力力矩的方式。从运行稳定性方面考虑，该减振器的活塞速度较小，减小了车体的蛇行运动。抗蛇行油压减振器的主要参数如表 5–15 所示。

Anti-hunting oil pressure damper. To obtain a stable rotational resistance torque and suppress the hunting motion of the bogie, an anti-hunting oil pressure damper is used instead of the traditional method of using side bearing friction pairs to provide rotational resistance torque for the bogie. From the perspective of operational stability, the piston speed of this damper is smaller, which reduces the hunting motion of the car body. The main parameters of the anti-hunting oil pressure damper are shown in Table 5-15.

表 5–15　抗蛇行油压减振器的主要参数

Table 5-15　Main Parameters of Anti–hunting Oil pressure Damper

阻尼系数 Damping coefficient	600 kN·s/m
行程 Stroke	320 mm
最大/最小长度 Max./Min. length	880 mm/560 mm
安装长度 Installation length	720 mm
节点结构及刚度 Node structure and rigidity	球铰，刚度为 25 MN/m Ball joint, stiffness of 25 MN/m
防尘罩直径 Dust cover diameter	125 mm

（6）高度控制阀和差压阀。高度控制阀是根据载荷的变化自动调整空气弹簧内压而使车体保持一定高度的装置。高度控制阀有机械式的纯空气阀（SAB）或日本的液压式 LV-3 型高度控制阀。这两种高度控制阀均分左、右。

Height control valve and differential pressure valve. The height control valve is a device that automatically adjusts the internal pressure of the air spring according to changes in load to maintain a certain height of the car body. The height control valves used in this system include mechanical pure air valves (SAB) or hydraulic Japanese LV-3 type, both of which are equally divided.

差压阀是在左、右空气弹簧出现超过规定的压力差时，使压力高的一端的空气流向较低的一端，以防止车体异常倾斜的装置。差压阀设定的压力差为 150 kPa。

The differential pressure valve is a device that allows the air at the high-pressure end to flow to the lower end when the left and right air springs exceed the specified pressure difference to prevent abnormal tilting of the car body. The pressure difference set for this valve is 150 kPa.

4）基础制动装置

Foundation braking device

基础制动装置与 25K 型客车相同，可与 SW-160 型转向架的所有配件互换。SW-220K 型转向架基础制动装置的结构如图 5-93 所示。

The foundation braking device is the same as 25K type coach and can be interchanged with all accessories of bogie type SW-160. The structure of foundation braking device of bogie type SW-220K is shown in Figure 5-93.

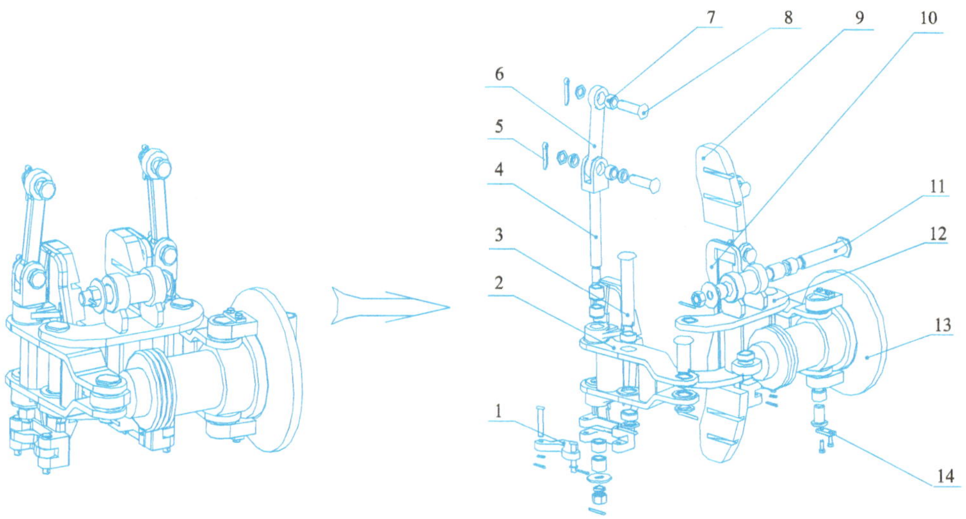

1—锁铁；2—夹钳杠杆；3—圆销；4—闸片托销；5—扁开口销；6—闸片托吊；7—钢衬套（氟塑料金属里衬）；8—扁孔圆销；9—闸片；10—闸片托；11—螺头圆销；12—连杆组成；13—单元制动缸；14—锁紧压板。

1—Lock iron; 2—Clamp lever; 3—Round pin; 4—Brake pad support pin; 5—Flat cotter pin; 6—Brake pad support crane; 7—Steel bushing (fluoroplastic metal lining); 8—Flat hole round pin; 9—Brake pad; 10—Brake pad holder; 11—Stud round pin; 12—Connecting rod composition; 13—Unit brake cylinder; 14—Locking pressing plate.

图 5-93 SW-220K 型转向架基础制动装置的结构

Figure 5-93 Structure of Foundation Braking Device of Bogie Type SW-220K

（1）单元制动缸。制动缸为 8 英寸活塞式单元制动缸，其内部带有间隙调整器，可自动调整闸片间隙。制动缸的主要特性如表 5–16 所示。

Unit brake cylinder. The brake cylinder is an 8-inch piston-type unit brake cylinder with a clearance adjuster inside, which can automatically adjust the brake pad clearance. The main characteristics of the brake cylinder are shown in Table 5-16.

表 5–16　制动缸的主要特性

Table 5-16　Main Characteristics of Brake Cylinder

制动缸直径 Brake cylinder diameter	203 mm
制动缸最大压力 Max. pressure of brake cylinder	480 kPa（F8 阀）或 420 kPa（104 阀） 480 kPa (F8 valve) or 420 kPa (104 valve)
初始制动压力 Initial brake pressure	20 kPa 或 30 kPa
安装尺寸 Installation dimensions	（240±2）mm
活塞杆最大行程 Max. stroke of piston rod	（28±2）mm
丝杆有效伸出量 Effective extension of lead screw	4 mm 或 6 mm
丝杆每次伸出量 Each extension of lead screw	（14±2）mm
丝杆最大伸出量 Max. extension of lead screw	120 mm

每辆车的一位转向架设有一个带手制动装置的杠杆。

The “B” end bogie of each railway vehicle has a lever with a hand brake mounted on one steering wheel.

（2）制动盘和闸片。

Brake disc and brake pad.

① 制动盘。SW-220K 型转向架采用轴装制动盘，制动盘的结构和材质同提速客车，由整体式铸铁结构的制动盘环和盘毂组成。制动盘环与盘毂通过螺栓、垫块和弹性套等连接。制动盘毂与车轴为过盈配合，过盈量为 0.14～0.22 mm，压装力为 200～400 kN。制动盘同提速客车的制动盘，其主要结构参数如表 5–17 所示。

Brake disc. Bogie type SW-220K is of axle-mounted brake discs, which are of the same structure and material as those of speed-increasing passenger cars. They are composed of integrally cast iron structure brake disc rings and disc hubs. The brake disc and disc hub are connected by bolts, pads, elastic sleeves, etc. The brake disc hub and axle have an interference fit, with an interference amount of 0.14–0.22 mm, and a press mounting force of 200–400 kN. The main structural parameters of the brake disc are shown in Table 5-17, which is the same as the brake disc of the speed-increasing passenger car.

表 5-17 制动盘的主要结构参数

Table 5-17 Main Structural Parameters of Brake Discs

制动盘直径 Brake disc diameter	640 mm
制动盘摩擦半径 Brake disc friction radius	247 mm
制动盘允许磨耗量（单面） Allowable wear of brake disc (single side)	7 mm

② 闸片。转向架采用与现有提速客车相同的闸片，可完全互换。

Brake pad. The bogie is subject to the same brake pads as the existing speed-increasing passenger cars, which are completely interchangeable.

3. SW-220K 型转向架的主要技术参数

Main technical parameters of bogie type SW-220K

SW-220K 型转向架的主要技术参数如表 5-18 所示。

The main technical parameters of bogie type SW-220K are shown in Table 5-18.

表 5-18 SW-220K 型转向架的主要技术参数

Table 5-18 Main Technical Parameters of Bogie Type SW-220K

连续运行速度 Continuous running speed	160 km/h
最高试验速度 Max. test speed	250 km/h
轴距 Wheelbase	2 500 mm
适用轨距 Applicable track gauge	1 435 mm
车轮直径 Wheel diameter	915 mm（新轮），845 mm（旧轮） 915 mm (new wheel), 845 mm (old wheel)
最大轴重 Max. axle load	15.5 t（行包车 16.5 t） 15.5 t (charter car 16.5 t)
通过最小曲线半径 Min. radius of curvature negotiated	连挂 145 m，单车调车 100 m Coupling 145 m, single car switching 100 m
弹簧型式 Spring type	一系钢弹簧，二系为空气弹簧 Primary steel spring, secondary air spring
车轮车轴型式 Wheel axle type	KKD 车轮，RD_{3A1} 轴 KKD wheel, RD_{3A1} axle
轴箱轴承 Axle box bearing	进口 SKF BC1B322880（AB）/BC1B322881（AB）或 FAG 804468A/804469A Imported SKF BC1B322880 (AB)/BC1B322881 (AB) or FAG 804468A/804469A

续表

Continued

制动型式 Braking type	轴装盘型制动 Axle-mounted disc braking
制动盘型式及直径 Brake disc type and diameter	轴装铸铁盘，640 mm Axle-mounted cast iron disk, 640 mm
制动缸型式 Brake cylinder type	8 英寸单元制动缸（每车一位制动缸带手制动） 8" unit brake cylinder ("B" end brake cylinder of each vehicle with hand brake)
轮对定位方式 Wheelset positioning method	单转臂无磨耗弹性轴箱定位 Single arm abrasion-free elastic axle box positioning
转向架质量 Bogie mass	约 5 800 kg About 5,800 kg

5.2.7 CW 型系列转向架 CW series bogies

CW 型系列转向架有 CW–1 型、CW–2 型、CW–200 型、CW–200K 型等。字母 C 代表长春，字母 W 代表客车工厂。CW–1 型转向架的摇枕弹簧采用钢弹簧，CW–2 型转向架则采用空气弹簧。快速客车上使用 CW–2C 型转向架和 CW–1B 型转向架；CW–2 型转向架经过对构架的改进和加强，在国内客车上已装用有 CW–2B 型、CW–2C 型和 CW–2E 型 3 种转向架。CW-200 型和 CW-200K 型转向架为高速客车转向架。

CW series bogies include CW-1, CW-2, CW-200, CW-200K, etc. The letter C represents Changchun, and the letter W represents the passenger car factory. The bolster springs of bogie type CW-1 are steel springs, while those of bogie type CW-2 are air springs. Bogie type CW–2C and bogie type CW-1B are used on high-speed passenger cars; After improving and strengthening the structure of bogie type CW-2, three types of bogies have been installed on domestic passenger cars, namely, CW-2B, CW–2C, and CW–2E. Bogie type CW-200 and bogie type CW-200K are high-speed passenger car bogies.

5.2.7.1 CW–2C 型转向架 Bogie type CW-2C

1. CW–2C 型转向架的结构特点 Structural characteristics of bogie type CW-2C

CW–2C 型转向架的结构特点如下。

The structural characteristics of bogie type CW-2C are as follows.

（1）采用双列向心短圆柱滚子轴承：这种轴承设计提供了良好的支撑和稳定性。

Using the double-row radial short cylindrical roller bearings: This bearing design provides good support and stability.

（2）采用转臂式轴箱定位：通过转臂设计，实现了轴箱的精确定位，有助于提高车辆的稳定性和安全性。

Using the rotary arm axle box positioning: through the design of rotary arm, the precise positioning of the axle box is realized, which helps to improve the stability and safety of the railway vehicle.

（3）圆柱螺旋弹簧安装在轴箱外侧端：弹簧的设计有助于吸收和分散车辆运行过程中的震动和冲击。

The cylindrical spiral spring is installed on the outside end of the axle box: the spring is designed to help absorb and disperse the vibration and shock during the operation of the railway vehicle.

（4）增设垂直油压减振器：通过减振器的使用，进一步减少了车辆运行过程中的震动，提高了乘坐舒适度。

Add vertical oil pressure damper: through the use of damper, further reduce the vibration during the operation of railway vehicles, improve the ride comfort.

（5）同一轮对两轴箱用横向控制杆相连：这种设计有助于提高车辆的横向稳定性，减少侧向力对车辆运行的影响。

The same wheel to the two axle boxes are connected with transverse control levers: this design helps to improve the lateral stability of the railway vehicle and reduce the impact of lateral forces on the operation of the railway vehicle.

2. CW-2C 型转向架的结构

Structure of bogie type CW-2C

CW-2C 型转向架的结构如图 5-94 所示。

The structure of bogie type CW-2C is shown in Figure 5-94.

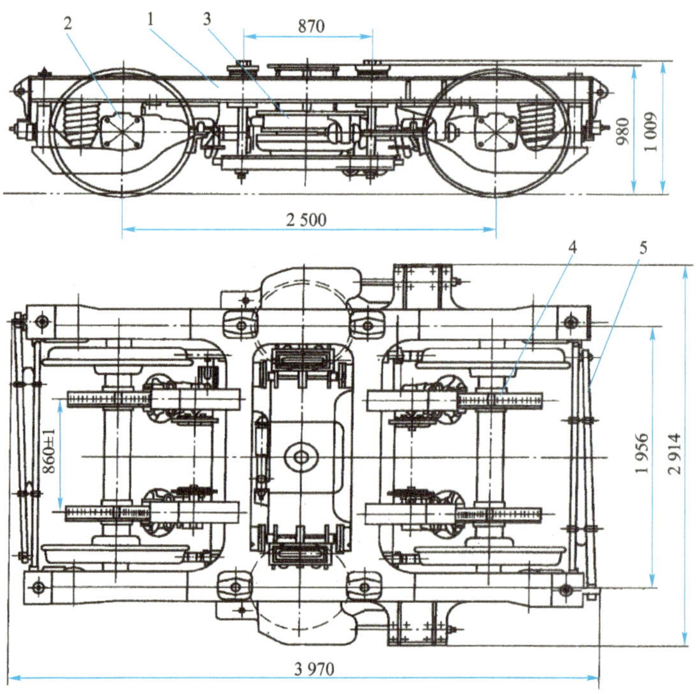

1—构架；2—轮对轴箱弹簧装置；3—摇枕弹簧装置；4—基础制动装置；5—横向控制杆。

1—Framework; 2—Wheelset axle box spring device; 3—Bolster spring device; 4—Foundation braking device; 5—Lateral control lever.

图 5-94　CW-2C 型转向架的结构

Figure 5-94　Structure of Bogie Type CW-2C

1）构架组成

Framework composition

CW-2C 型转向架采用 16MnR 或 16Mn 低合金结构钢焊接 H 形构架，如图 5–95 所示。构架由 2 个直侧梁和 2 个直横梁组成，两侧梁端部斜对称焊接 2 个横向控制杆安装座，两侧梁中部的 4 个 116 mm×116 mm 方孔是为安装摇枕吊杆而设。4 个轴箱节点定位座和 2 个牵引拉杆座用螺栓固定在侧梁上。横梁外侧焊有盘型制动吊座，侧梁下部焊有踏面清扫器座。

16MnR or 16Mn low alloy structural steel welded H-shaped frames are used for bogie type CW-2C, as shown in Figure 5-95. The framework is composed of two straight side beams and two straight cross beams. The ends of the beams on both sides are diagonally and symmetrically welded with two transverse control lever mounting seats. The four 116 mm × 116 mm square holes in the middle of the beams on both sides are designed for installing the bolster suspender. Four axle box node positioning seats and two traction rod seats are fixed to the side beam with bolts. The outer side of the beam is welded with a disc-shaped brake hanger seat, and the lower part of the side beam is welded with a tread cleaner seat.

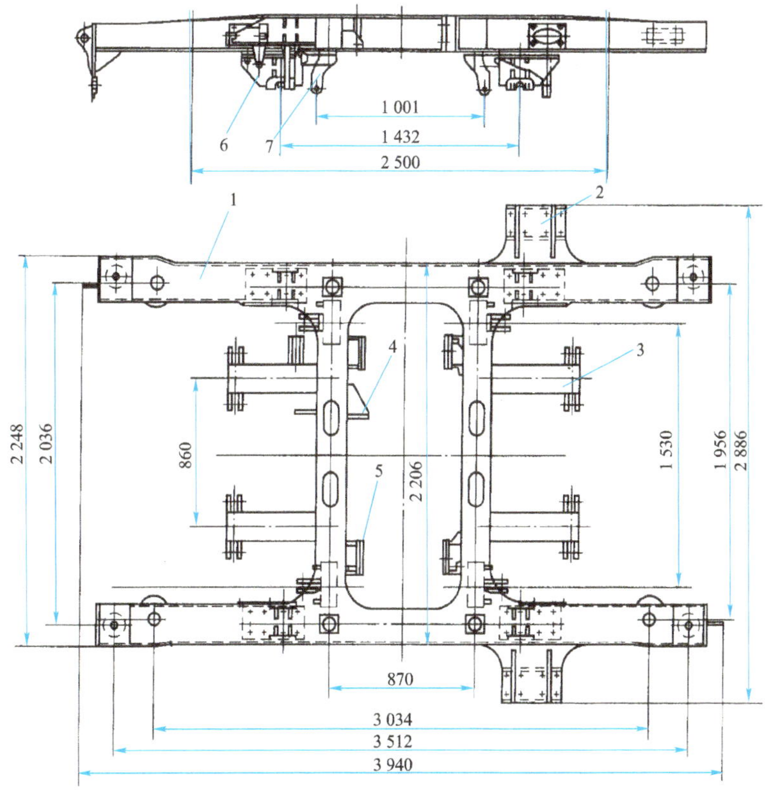

1—构架；2—牵引拉杆座；3—盘型制动吊座；4—横向减振器座；5—纵向挡；6—定位座；7—踏面清扫器座。

1—Framework; 2—Traction rod seat; 3—Disc brake hanger seat; 4—Lateral damper seat; 5—Longitudinal stop; 6—Positioning seat; 7—Tread cleaner seat.

图 5–95　CW-2C 型转向架的构架组成

Figure 5-95　Framework Composition of Bogie Type CW-2C

2）中央悬挂装置

Central suspension device

CW-2C 型转向架的中央悬挂装置采用带有空气弹簧的摇动台结构，由摇枕、空气弹簧、弹簧托梁、摇枕吊杆、下旁承、横向油压减振器、抗侧滚扭杆装置、牵引拉杆、横向拉杆和横向止挡等零部件组成，其结构如图 5–96 所示。摇枕为箱形焊接结构，其内分为左、右两个部分，分别作为左、右两个空气弹簧的附加空气室，每个附加空气室的容积为 60 L。

The central suspension device of bogie type CW-2C is subject to a shaking table structure with air springs, which is composed of components such as a bolster, air spring, spring joist, bolster suspender, lower side bearing, lateral oil pressure damper, anti-roll torsion bar device, traction rod, lateral pull rod, and lateral stop, as shown in Figure 5-96. The bolster is a box-shaped welded structure, which is divided into left and right parts, serving as additional air chambers for the left and right air springs. Each additional air chamber has a volume of 60 L.

CW-2C 型转向架采用全旁承支重，旁承磨耗板为钢板上涂覆聚四氟乙烯复合层（复合层厚度为 1.5 mm）；为防止灰沙侵入磨耗板摩擦表面，在旁承座板上开有沟槽，内装密封毡条。

Full side bearing is used to support the weight of bogie type CW-2C, and the side bearing wear plate is coated with a polytetrafluoroethylene composite layer (The thickness of the composite layer is 1.5 mm) on the steel plate; To prevent dust and sand from invading the friction surface of the wear plate, grooves are opened on the side bearing seat plate and sealing felt strips are installed inside.

摇枕两端与构架间装有弹性横向止挡，以限制摇枕的横向位移。摇枕与构架间装有牵引拉杆起牵引作用，牵引拉杆端部均为橡胶套连接。摇枕与构架间还装设 1 个横向油压减振器，以控制横向振动。

Elastic lateral stops are installed between both ends of the bolster and the frame to limit the lateral displacement of the bolster. A traction rod is installed between the bolster and the frame for traction, and the ends of the traction rod are connected by rubber sleeves. A lateral oil pressure damper is also installed between the bolster and the frame to control lateral vibration.

空气弹簧有效直径为 600 mm；在充气状态下，空气弹簧标准高为 150 mm。空气弹簧利用节流阀可调阻尼有效地控制垂直振动而代替了垂向液压减振器。

The effective diameter of the air spring is 600 mm. Under the inflated state, the standard height of the air spring is 150 mm. The use of throttle valve adjustable damping of the air spring effectively controls vertical vibration instead of vertical hydraulic dampers.

弹簧托梁由 16MnR 钢板焊接而成。弹簧托梁通过 4 根摇枕吊杆悬挂于侧梁上，组成摇动台结构。摇枕吊杆上、下两端通过一对球面接触的凹凸垫、橡胶垫及开口螺母与构架侧梁和弹簧托梁相连接，该弹性悬挂结构既可保证摇动台摇动自由，又不产生磨耗。

The spring joist is welded from 16MnR steel plates. The spring joist is suspended on the side beam through four bolster suspenders, forming a shaking table structure. The upper and lower ends of the bolster suspender are connected to the frame side beam and spring joist through a pair of spherical contact concave and convex pads, rubber pads, and open nuts. This elastic suspension structure can ensure that the shaking table moves freely without wear.

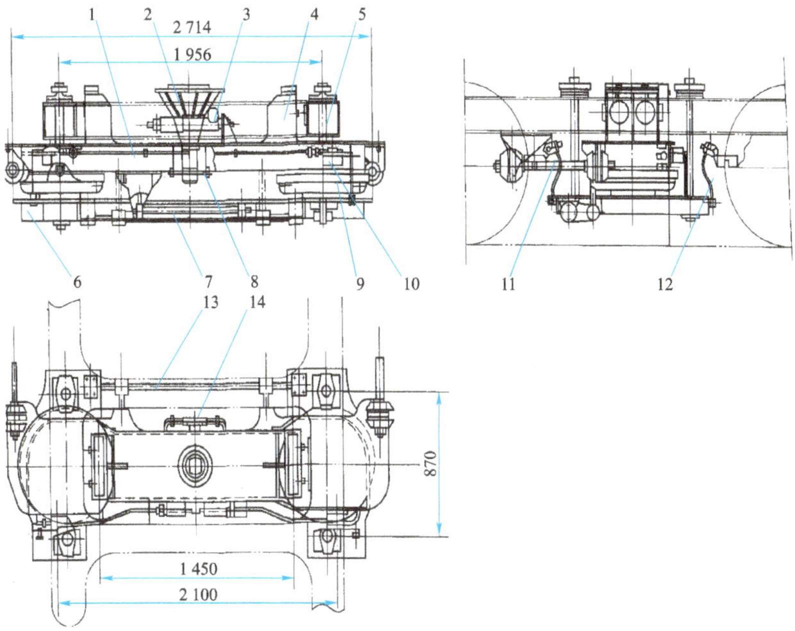

1—摇枕；2—回转支座；3—横向减振器；4—旁承；5—摇枕吊杆；6—弹簧托梁；7—横向拉杆；8—中心销套；9—空气弹簧；10—高度调整阀；11—牵引拉杆；12—安全钢丝绳；13—扭杆；14—差压阀。

1—Bolster; 2—Rotary bearing; 3—Lateral damper; 4—Side bearing; 5—Bolster suspender; 6—Spring joist; 7—Lateral pull rod; 8—Center pin sleeve; 9—Air spring; 10—Height adjustment valve; 11—Traction rod; 12—Safety wire rope; 13—Torsion bar; 14—Differential pressure valve.

图 5-96 CW-2C 型转向架中央悬挂装置的结构

Figure 5-96 Structure of Central Suspension Device for Bogie Type CW-2C

弹簧托梁与摇枕间设有横向拉杆，以防止摇枕相对于弹簧托梁发生相对位移。弹簧托梁与构架之间装有 4 根不锈钢的钢丝绳作为摇动台的安全吊。

A lateral pull rod is provided between the spring joist and the bolster to prevent relative displacement of the bolster relative to the spring joist. Four stainless wire ropes are installed between the spring joist and the frame as a safety crane for the swing table.

抗侧滚扭杆装置安装在摇枕与弹簧托梁之间。扭杆与扭臂之间的连接为圆锥花键，扭杆两端支承在装有关节轴承的支承座内。吊杆两端装有橡胶密封圈和防尘盖，支承座与扭杆连接处也装有橡胶油封。

The anti-roll torsion bar device is installed between the bolster and the spring joist. The connection between the torsion bar and the torsion arm is a conical spline, and both ends of the torsion bar are supported in a bearing seat equipped with joint bearings. Rubber sealing rings and dust covers are installed at both ends of the suspender, and rubber sealing rings are also installed at the connection between the bearing seat and the torsion bar.

安装在车体枕梁上的铸钢中心销穿过装于摇枕中央的橡胶套作为回转轴。

The cast steel center pin installed on the sleeper beam of the car body passes through a rubber sleeve installed in the center of the bolster as a rotary shaft.

3）轴箱定位装置

Axle box positioning device

CW-2C 型转向架采用转臂式轴箱定位装置及与其匹配的横向控制杆，其结构如图 5-97 所示。其轴承采用进口 SKF 或 NSK 滚动轴承。转向架的 1、3、5、7 位轴头装有防滑器的传感器和测速齿轮。

Bogie type CW-2C adopts a rotary arm axle box positioning device and its matching lateral control lever, as shown in Figure 5-97. The bearings are imported SKF or NSK roller bearings. The axle heads at positions 1, 3, 5, and 7 of the bogie are equipped with anti-skid sensors and speed-measuring gears.

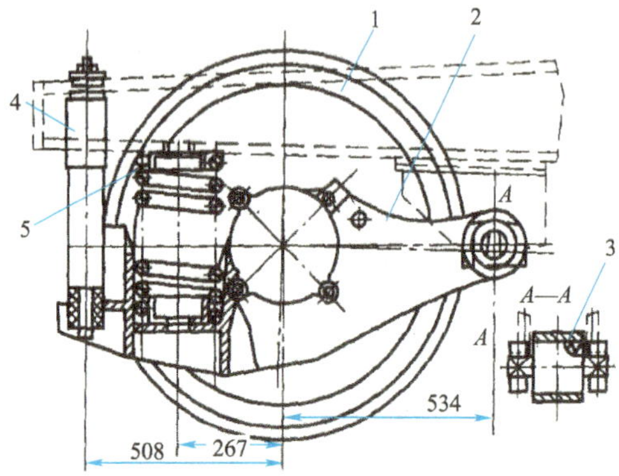

1—轮对；2—轴箱体；3—弹性定位套；4—油压减振器；5—轴箱弹簧。

1—Wheelset; 2—Axle box body; 3—Elastic positioning sleeve; 4—Oil pressure damper; 5—Axle box spring.

图 5-97 CW-2C 型转向架轴箱定位装置的结构

Figure 5-97 Structure of Axle Box Positioning Device for Bogie Type CW-2C

4）基础制动装置

Foundation braking device

CW-2C 型转向架基础制动装置采用单元式盘型制动系统和轴端式电子防滑器。

The foundation braking device of bogie type CW-2C is subject to a unit disc braking system and an axle-end electronic anti-skid device.

5.2.7.2 CW-200K 型转向架

Bogie type CW-200K

CW-200K 型转向架是在 CW-200 型转向架的基础上加以改进，同时借鉴和吸收了国外高速转向架的结构而自主研制开发的。CW-200K 型转向架专门用于 160 km/h 速度等级的客车。

Bogie type CW-200K is improved on the basis of bogie type CW-200 and is independently developed by drawing on and absorbing the structure of foreign high-speed bogies. Bogie type CW-200 is specially used for passenger cars with a speed class of 160 km/h.

1. CW-200K 型转向架的结构特点

Structural characteristics of bogie type CW-200K

CW-200K 型转向架的总体结构采用无摇枕、无摇动台、无旁承的三无结构。车体和转向架间通过牵引拉杆传递拉、压力，并装有抗蛇行油压减振器。中央悬挂装置采用大变位空气弹簧，轴箱悬挂采用转臂式定位，并安装有垂向减振器。基础制动采用每轴两个制动盘和防滑器。

The overall structure of bogie type CW-200K can be summarized as a structure without a bolster, shaking table, or side bearing. Traction and pressure are transmitted between the car body and the bogie through traction rods, and anti-hunting oil pressure dampers are installed. The central suspension device is subject to a large deflection air spring, and the axle box suspension is of a rotary arm positioning, which is installed with a vertical damper. The foundation braking is subject to two brake discs and anti-skid devices per axle.

2. CW–200K 型转向架的结构

Structure of bogie type CW-200K

CW-200K 型转向架主要由构架组成、轴箱定位装置、中央悬挂装置、基础制动装置和轴温报警装置等组成，如图 5–98 所示。

Bogie type CW-200K mainly consists of a framework, an axle box positioning device, a central suspension device, a foundation braking device, and an axle temperature alarm device, as shown in Figure 5-98.

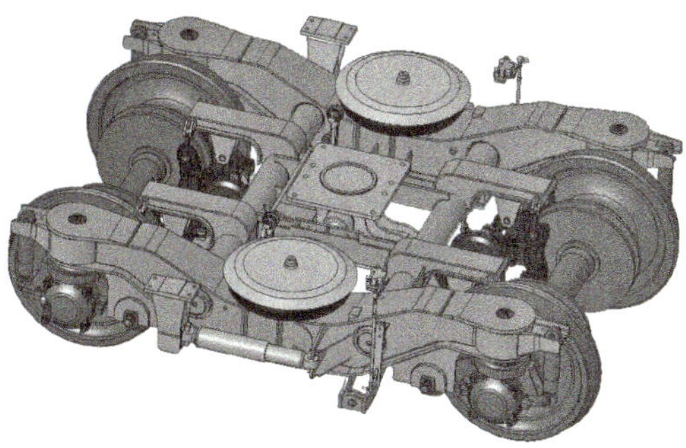

图 5–98　CW-200K 型转向架
Figure 5-98　Bogie Type CW-200K

1）构架组成

Framework composition

构架的所有板材均采用 16MnR 材质，为 H 形钢板焊接结构，由 2 根侧梁和 2 根横梁组成，2 根横梁间设有纵向梁，如图 5–99 所示。侧梁为中间下凹的鱼腹形，由 4 块钢板组焊成箱形封闭结构。侧梁内有密封隔板，使侧梁内腔成为空气弹簧的附加空气室。横梁采用日本进口无缝钢管，外径为 165.2 mm，壁厚为 14.3 mm。在侧梁上焊有定位座、横向减振器座、高度阀座和防过充座等；在横梁上焊有盘型单元制动吊座、抗侧滚扭杆座和牵引拉杆座等。通过优化设计，在保证足够强度和刚度的基础上，CW-200K 型转向架尽量减轻质量，构架组成质量约为 1 435 kg。

All plates of the frame are made of 16MnR material and are of an H-shaped steel plate welded structure, consisting of two side beams and two cross beams. A longitudinal beam is provided between the two cross beams, as shown in Figure 5-99. The side beam is a fish-belly shape with a concave center and is welded into a box-shaped closed structure by four steel plates. A sealing partition is provided in the side beam, making the inner chamber of the side beam an additional air chamber for the air spring. The cross beam is made of seamless steel pipes imported from Japan, with an outer diameter of 165.2 mm with a wall thickness of 14.3 mm. The side beam is welded with positioning seats, lateral damper seats, height valve seats, and anti-overshoot seats. The cross beam is welded with disc-shaped unit brake hanger seats, anti-roll torsion bar seats, and traction rod seats. Through optimized design and by ensuring sufficient strength and rigidity, the mass of bogie type CW-200K is reduced as much as possible, and the composition mass of the framework is about 1,435 kg.

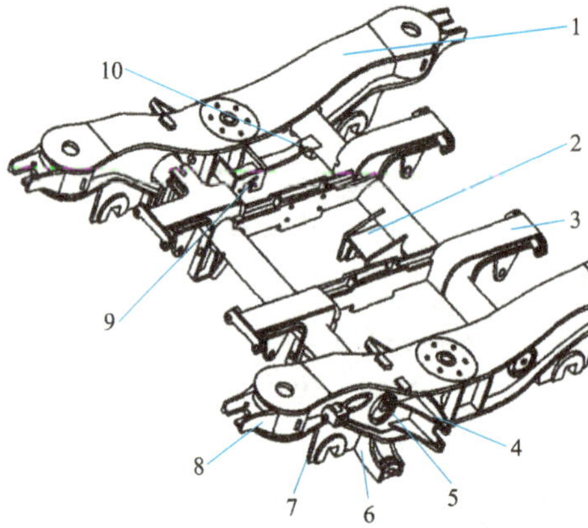

1—构架；2—牵引座；3—制动吊座；4—抗蛇行油压减振器座；5—高度调整阀座；6—防过充座；7—定位座；8—垂向减振器座；9—横向减振器座；10—差压阀座。

1—Framework; 2—Traction seat; 3—Brake hanger seat; 4—Anti-hunting oil pressure damper seat; 5—Height adjustment valve seat; 6—Anti-overshoot seat; 7—Positioning seat; 8—Vertical damper seat; 9—Lateral damper seat; 10—Differential pressure valve seat.

图 5-99　CW-200K 型转向架的构架组成

Figure 5-99　Framework Composition of Bogie Type CW-200K

2）轴箱定位装置

Axle box positioning device

轴箱定位装置包括轮对组成、弹簧装置、轴端装置、轴箱减振器、节点装置、转臂和箍，其结构如图 5-100 所示。轴箱定位采用分体式轴箱结构的无磨耗转臂式定位方式，轴箱转臂

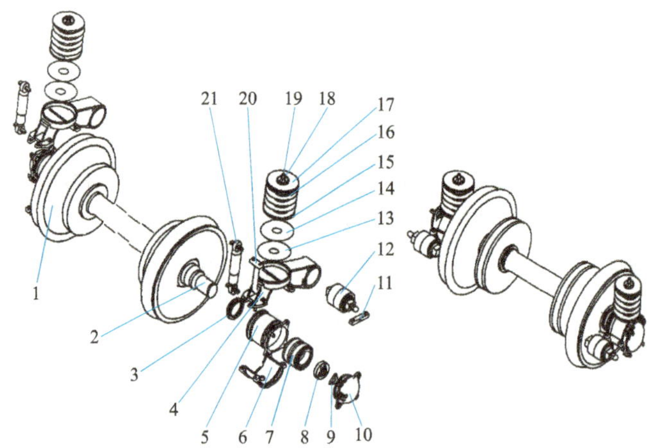

1—车轮；2—车轴；3—防尘挡圈；4—转臂；5—轴箱；6—箍；7—轴承；8—压板；9—防松片；10—轴箱盖；11—锁紧板；12—节点；13—橡胶垫；15—下夹板；16—弹簧；17—上夹板；18—螺母；19—螺栓；20—吊；21—轴箱减振器。

1—Wheel; 2—Axle; 3—Dust retaining ring; 4—Rotary arm; 5—Axle box; 6—Hoop; 7—Bearing; 8—Pressing plate; 9—Lock washer; 10—Axle box cover; 11—Locking plate; 12—Node; 13—Rubber pad; 15—Lower clamp plate; 16—Spring; 17—Upper clamp plate; 18—Nut; 19—Bolts; 20—Crane; 21—Axle box damper.

图 5-100　CW-200K 型转向架轴箱定位装置的结构

Figure 5-100　Structure of Axle Box Positioning Device for Bogie Type CW-200K

一端与轴箱体连接，另一端压装于定位节点并通过定位座与构架相连。轴箱定位的纵、横向刚度靠橡胶节点保证，其中转臂和箍为整体加工，分解时只需将转臂和箍间的连接螺栓拧开即可将轮对推出。

The axle box positioning device includes wheelset composition, spring device, axle-end device, axle box damper, node device, rotary arm, and hoop, as shown in Figure 5-100. The axle box is positioned using a split axle box structure with a wear-free rotary arm. One end of the axle box rotary arm is connected to the axle box body, and the other end is pressed onto a positioning node and connected to the frame through a positioning seat. The longitudinal and lateral rigidity of the axle box positioning is ensured by rubber joints, wherein the rotary arm and hoop are integrally processed. During disassembly, only the connecting bolts between the rotary arm and the hoop need to be unscrewed to push out the wheelset.

（1）轮对组成。车轮采用整体辗钢车轮，为磨耗型踏面的 KKD 型车轮。车轴轴重为 15.5 t，轴颈中心距为 2 000 mm，轴型为 RD_{3A1} 型。每轴两个制动盘，车轴轴承采用 SFK 公司生产的短圆柱滚子轴承。

Wheelset composition. The wheels are integrally rolled steel wheels, which are KKD wheels with hollow treads. The axle load is 15.5 t. The journal center distance is 2,000 mm, and the axle type is RD_{3A1}. There are two brake discs per axle, and the axle bearings are short cylindrical roller bearings produced by SFK.

（2）弹簧装置。弹簧装置由内、外圈弹簧，上、下夹板及预压紧螺栓、螺母组成为一体。螺母上开有销孔，弹簧组装后须穿开口销。整套轴箱弹簧装在轴箱顶部。

Spring device. The spring device is composed of inner and outer ring springs, upper and lower clamp plates, pre-pressing bolts, and nuts. The nut is provided with a pinhole, and the cotter pin must be threaded after the spring is assembled. The complete set of axle box springs is installed on the top of the axle box.

（3）轴端装置。轴承为进口短圆柱滚子轴承，轮廓尺寸为 130 mm×250 mm×（2×80 mm）。其中的一端安装有轴端接地装置，用于防止轴承发生电蚀。轴端装置、带接地装置的轴端装置、带速度传感器的轴端装置的结构分别如图 5–101、图 5–102、图 5–103 所示。

Axle-end device. The bearing is an imported short cylindrical roller bearing with a contour dimension of 130 mm × 250 mm × (2 × 80 mm). A shaft-end grounding device is installed at one end to prevent electrical corrosion of the bearing. Axle-end device, axle-end device with grounding device, and axle-end device with speed sensor are shown in Figure 5-101, Figure 5-102, and Figure 5-103, respectively.

（4）节点装置。节点装置包括 2 个橡胶节点、转轴、转轴套和盖形螺母，其结构如图 5–104 所示。一系定位的纵、横向刚度均由橡胶节点决定，组装时要求同一转向架各位置节点的刚度值应做原始记录，相差值应为 0.2 MN/m。定位节点的纵、横向刚度可根据整车的动力学优化及试验进行调整。定位套从转臂定位孔两端分别压入后用定位轴和盖形螺母锁紧。

Node device. The joint assembly consists of two rubber joints, a rotary shaft, a rotary shaft sleeve, and a cap nut, as shown in Figure 5-104. The longitudinal and lateral rigidities of the primary positioning are determined by the rubber nodes. During assembly, it is required that the rigidity values of the nodes at each position of the same bogie should be recorded in an original manner, with a difference of 0.2 MN/m. The longitudinal and lateral rigidity of the positioning nodes can be adjusted based on the dynamic optimization and testing of the entire vehicle. The positioning sleeve is pressed from both ends of the positioning hole of the rotary arm and locked with a positioning shaft and a cap nut.

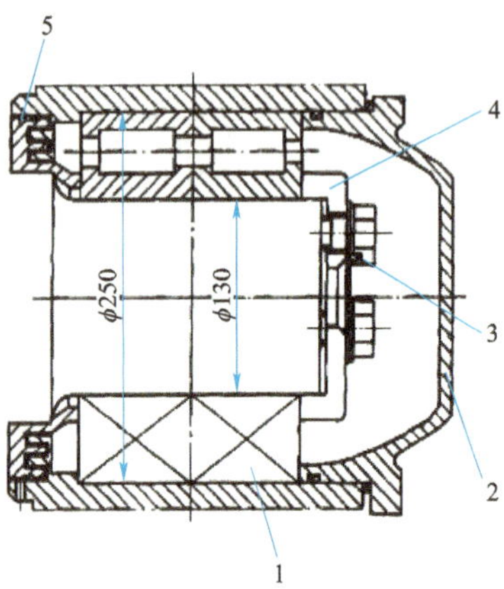

1—轴承；2—轴箱盖；3—防松片；
4—压板；5—防尘挡圈。
1—Bearing; 2—Axle box cover; 3—Lock washer;
4—Pressing plate; 5—Dust retaining ring.

图 5-101 轴端装置的结构
Figure 5-101 Structure of Axle-end Device

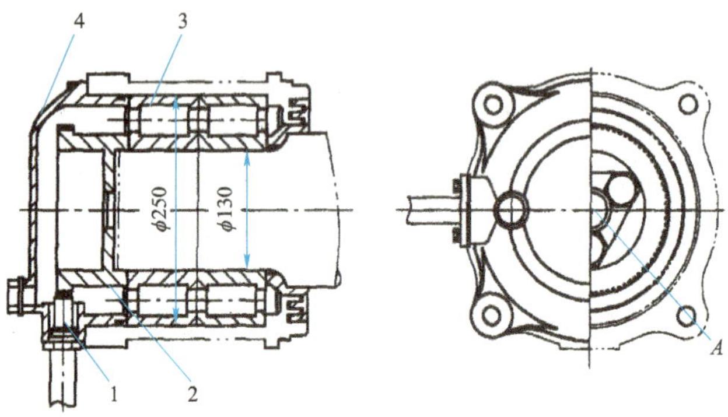

1—轴承压板；2—摩擦盘；3—接地装置；4—轴箱盖。
1—Bearing press plate; 2—Friction disc;
3—Grounding device; 4—Axle box cover.

图 5-102 带接地装置轴端装置的结构
Figure 5-102 Structure of Axle-end Device with Grounding Device

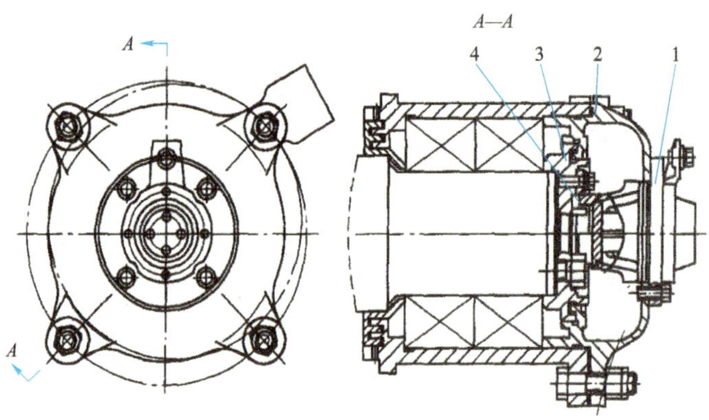

1—轴承；2—轴箱盖；3—传感器组成；4—测速齿轮。
1—Bearing; 2—Axle box cover; 3—Sensor composition; 4—Speed-measuring gear.

图 5-103 带速度传感器轴端装置的结构
Figure 5-103 Structure of Axle-end Device with Speed Sensor

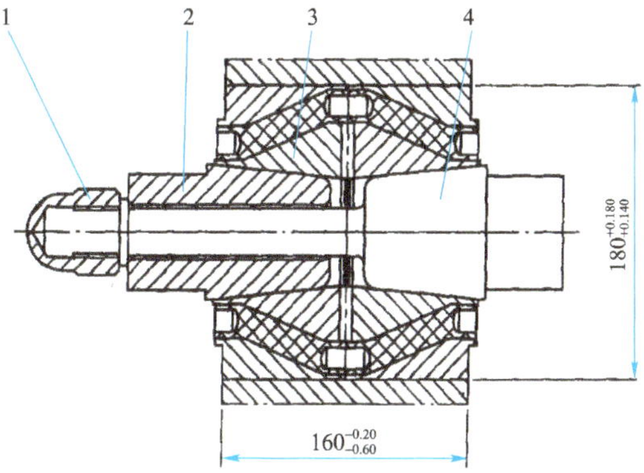

1—盖形螺母；2—转轴套；3—橡胶节点；4—转轴。

1—Cap nut; 2—Rotary shaft sleeve; 3—Rubber node; 4—Rotary shaft.

图 5-104 节点装置的结构

Figure 5-104 Structure of Node Device

3）中央悬挂装置

Central suspension device

中央悬挂装置包括空气弹簧、高度阀、差压阀、牵引装置、抗侧滚扭杆和安全钢丝绳等，其结构如图 5-105 所示。

The central suspension device includes air springs, height valves, differential pressure valves, traction devices, anti-roll torsion bars, and safety wire ropes, as shown in Figure 5-105.

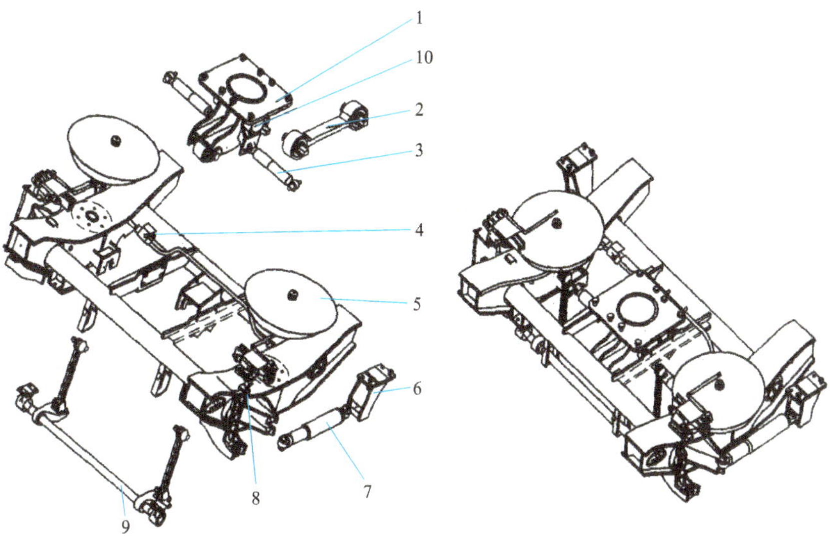

1—牵引支座；2—牵引拉杆；3—横向减振器；4—差压阀；5—空气弹簧；
6—抗蛇行油压减振器座；7—抗蛇行油压减振器；8—高度阀；9—抗侧滚扭杆；10—横向止挡。

1—Traction support; 2—Traction rod; 3—Lateral damper; 4—Differential pressure valve; 5—Air spring; 6—Anti-hunting oil pressure damper seat; 7—Anti-hunting oil pressure damper; 8—Height valve; 9—Anti-roll torsion bar; 10—Lateral stop.

图 5-105 CW-200K 型转向架中央悬挂装置的结构

Figure 5-105 Structure of Central Suspension Device for Bogie Type CW-200K

中央悬挂装置为无摇枕结构，采用高柔性空气弹簧。两侧设 2 个横向减振器、2 个横向止挡，横向止挡与小纵向梁的间隙为（40±2）mm。车体与转向架装有 2 个对称的抗蛇行油压减振器，使车辆在高速运行时减小轮缘磨耗和悬挂系统的作用力，提高车辆运行的稳定性和平稳性。

The central suspension device is a bolsterless structure with highly flexible air springs. Two lateral dampers and two lateral stops are provided on both sides, and the clearance between the lateral stop and the small longitudinal beam is (40 ± 2) mm. Two symmetrical anti-hunting dampers are installed between the car body and the bogie, which can reduce the wheel flange wear and the force of the suspension system when the railway vehicle is running at high speed, improving the running stability and smoothness.

（1）空气弹簧。空气弹簧横向变位可达 110 mm 以上，车辆通过曲线时依靠空气弹簧的水平变位实现转向功能，同时又不会形成过大的回转阻力，使车辆产生较大的侧向力，从而增大轮轨磨耗。

Air spring. The lateral displacement of the air spring can reach more than 110 mm. When the railway vehicle passes through a curve, it relies on the horizontal displacement of the air spring to achieve the steering function, while at the same time, it does not form excessive rotational resistance that causes the railway vehicle to generate large lateral forces, thereby increasing wheel/rail wear.

转向架构架侧梁内部作空气弹簧的附加空气室，空气弹簧的下部通风口与附加空气室连接，上部进风口与车体的管路连接。空气弹簧的胶囊气室与附加空气室间的节流孔，对车体的垂向振动起到一定的衰减作用，因此不需要加装垂向油压减振器。

The interior of the bogie frame side beam is provided with an additional air chamber for the air spring. The lower vent of the air spring is connected to the additional air chamber, and the upper air inlet is connected to the pipeline of the car body. The orifice between the capsule air chamber and the additional air chamber of the air spring can attenuate the vertical vibration of the car body to a certain extent, so it is not necessary to install a vertical oil pressure damper.

安装空气弹簧时，上部进风口和下部通风口的外部表面须涂润滑脂防锈，O 形密封圈须涂润滑脂进行保护。

When an air spring is installed, the outer surfaces of the upper air inlet and lower air outlet must be coated with grease for rust prevention, and the O-ring must be coated with grease for protection.

（2）差压阀和高度阀。在两个附加空气室管路之间设有差压阀。一旦其中一个空气弹簧失压，压差值达到 120 kPa 时差压阀即打开，以使两空气弹簧之间的压力保持均衡，确保行车安全。每个空气弹簧有一个高度控制阀，用于维持车体在不同静载荷下均与轨面保持一定的高度。

Differential pressure valve and height valve. A differential pressure valve is provided between the pipelines of the two additional air chambers. Once one of the air springs loses pressure, the differential pressure valve opens when the pressure difference reaches 120 kPa to maintain a balanced pressure between the two air springs and ensure driving safety. Each air spring has a height control valve to maintain the car body at a certain height from the rail surface under different static loads.

（3）牵引装置。牵引装置主要由牵引支座、牵引拉杆、横向止挡和横向减振器等组成。各零部件的功能如下。

Traction device. The traction device mainly consists of traction support, traction rod, lateral stop, and lateral damper. The functions of each component are as follows.

① 牵引支座。牵引支座起着车体与转向架之间的衔接作用，它的一端与车体连接，另一端与转向架上的牵引拉杆、横向减振器连接。

Traction support. The traction support serves as a connection between the car body and the bogie, with one end connected to the car body and the other end connected to the traction rod and lateral damper on the bogie.

② 牵引拉杆。牵引装置采用单拉杆结构，杆身为整体锻件，两端装有相同的球形橡胶节点，一端与构架相连，另一端与车辆牵引座连接。牵引装置对悬挂系统的附加横向刚度很小，具有良好的随动性。

Traction rod. The traction device is of a single pull rod structure, and the rod body is an integral forging. Both ends are equipped with the same spherical rubber nodes. One end is connected to the frame, and the other end is connected to the traction seat of the railway vehicle. The additional lateral stiffness of the traction device to the suspension system is very small with good follow-up performance.

③ 横向止挡。为适应于低横向刚度的空气弹簧，采用柔性横向缓冲器，能有效地缓解车辆的横向振动。

Lateral stop. To adapt to air springs with low lateral stiffness, flexible lateral buffers are used to effectively alleviate the lateral vibration of the railway vehicle.

④ 横向减振器。在车辆发生横向振动时，横向减振器会施加适当的阻尼力，以改善车辆的横向运动的平稳性。

Lateral damper. When a railway vehicle is subject to lateral vibration, the lateral damper applies an appropriate resistance to improve the smoothness during lateral movement of the railway vehicle.

（4）抗侧滚扭杆。构架与车体间装有抗侧滚扭杆。抗侧滚扭杆由扭杆、扭臂连杆、支承座、纤维轴承及球关节轴承组成。车辆通过曲线时依靠扭杆的扭转变形限制车体的侧滚角度，而当车体上下振动时扭杆不发生扭转，对车体不产生作用。

Anti-roll torsion bar. An anti-roll torsion bar is installed between the frame and the car body. The anti-roll torsion bar consists of a torsion bar, a torsion arm connecting rod, a bearing seat, fiber bearings, and ball joint bearings. When the railway vehicle passes through a curve, the torsional deformation of the torsion bar limits the rolling angle of the car body. However, when the car body vibrates up and down, the torsion bar does not twist with no effect on the car body.

（5）安全钢丝绳。在构架的两外侧各有一根安全钢丝绳。安全钢丝绳的功能是：当车辆出现异常状态时，即空气弹簧处于过充状态及高度调整阀、差压阀同时处于故障状态时，由安全钢丝绳将车体和构架拉住，限制空气弹簧的高度，保证车辆与限界之间的有效安全距离，从而保证车辆的行车安全。

Safety wire rope. There is a safety steel wire rope on both outer sides of the frame. The function of the safety wire rope is: When the railway vehicle is in an abnormal state, that is, when the air spring is in an overcharged state and the height adjustment valve and differential pressure valve are both in a fault state, the safety wire rope pulls the car body and the frame, limiting the height of the air spring and ensuring an effective safety distance between the railway vehicle and the gauge, thereby ensuring the driving safety of the railway vehicle.

安全钢丝绳由调整端头和钢丝绳组成。调整端头可以使钢丝绳的长度在 0～35 mm 的范围内进行调整，以满足车轮旋修后对车钩高度的调整。

The safety wire rope consists of an adjusting end and a wire rope. The adjusting end can adjust the length of the steel wire rope within the range of 0–35 mm to meet the adjustment of the coupler height after wheel rotation repair.

4）基础制动装置

Foundation braking device

基础制动装置每轴安装 2 个轴装式制动盘和 2 个带有间隙调整器的单元制动缸，闸片的材质为粉末冶金，可满足最高运行速度 200 km/h 的要求。该制动盘与闸片组成一对摩擦副，具有摩擦系数稳定、导热率高等特点。

The foundation braking device is equipped with two axle-mounted brake discs and two unit brake cylinders with clearance adjusters per axle. The brake pads are made of powder metallurgy, which can meet the requirements of a maximum operating speed of 200 km/h. The brake disc and brake pad form a pair of friction pairs, which have the characteristics of stable friction coefficient and high thermal conductivity.

5）轴温报警装置

Axle temperature alarm device

在构架侧梁外侧安装有轴温报警装置的接线盒和连接线，温度传感头安装在轴箱体上，用来检测车辆运行过程中轴箱内部温度的变化，一旦轴箱内部的温度高于外界温度 40℃，车上的轴温报警器立即发出警报，此时必须立即停车进行检查，排除故障并进行彻底修复后方可继续运行。

A junction box and connecting line for an axle temperature alarm device are installed on the outer side of the frame side beam, and a temperature sensing head is installed on the axle box body to detect changes in the internal temperature of the axle box during the operation of railway vehicle. Once the temperature inside the axle box is 40℃ higher than the outside temperature, the axle temperature alarm on the railway vehicle will immediately give an alarm. At this time, the railway vehicle must be stopped immediately for inspection, troubleshooting, and thorough repair before continuing operation.

项目 6

Project 6

车钩缓冲装置

Coupler and Draft Gear

本项目以认识车钩缓冲装置为工学任务，通过课堂任务的完成过程，着重介绍车钩缓冲装置的基本组成，并以此为引导，介绍各种类型车辆（动车组）车钩缓冲装置的结构组成；通过课后任务，了解各种类型车钩缓冲装置的技术、工艺要求。

The main task of this project is to understand the coupler and draft gear. In the classroom, the main focus is on introducing the basic composition of the coupler and draft gear, and the structural composition of various types of railway vehicles (EMU) coupler and draft gears. Through after-class tasks, students will gain an understanding of the technical and technological requirements of various types of coupler and draft gears.

学生工作页 Student Worksheet

工学任务描述 Task description	预期目标 Expected goals
任务名称：认识车钩缓冲装置 Task name: Understanding of the coupler and draft gear 任务编号：CJ-6 Task number: CJ-6 任务类型：认知型+结构原理型+工作过程型 Task type: Cognitive + structural principle + work process 适用范围：车辆系统各岗位群 Applicable scope: All post groups of the car system 完成时间：　　学时 Completion time:　　class hours	初级：了解车钩缓冲装置的基本组成、作用及技术要求 Elementary level: Understand the basic composition, function, and technical requirements of the coupler and draft gears 中级：认识各型的车钩缓冲装置；了解机车与车辆、车辆与车辆连挂的要求；掌握车钩三态作用及检查方法；掌握车钩缓冲装置的结构及检查要点 Intermediate level: Understand various types of the coupler and draft gears; understand the requirements for locomotive and railway vehicle, railway vehicle and railway vehicle coupling; master the three-state action and inspection methods of the coupler; master the structure and inspection points of the coupler and draft gear 高级：从设计者的角度考虑车钩缓冲装置如何适应牵引设备更高速、安全、平稳地运行 Advanced level: Consider how can coupler and draft gears adapt to higher speed, safe, and stable operation of traction equipment from the perspective of the designer.

知识回顾+小组讨论

Knowledge review + group discussion

1. 尝试列出车钩缓冲装置的基本组成。

Try to list the basic components of the coupler and draft gear.

	基本组成 Basic composition	相关知识点 Relevant knowledge points
1		
2		
3		
4		
5		

2. 小组讨论：车钩缓冲装置的基本功能有哪些？如何实现这些功能（连挂、缓冲、力的传递）？

Group discussion: What are the basic functions of the coupler and draft gear? How to achieve these functions (coupling, buffering, force transfer)?

3. 思考一下，对于高速牵引设备的车钩缓冲装置，在设计上有哪些特殊要求？

What are the special requirements for the design of the coupler and draft gears of high-speed traction equipment?

4. 认识车钩缓冲装置。

Understand the coupler and draft gear.

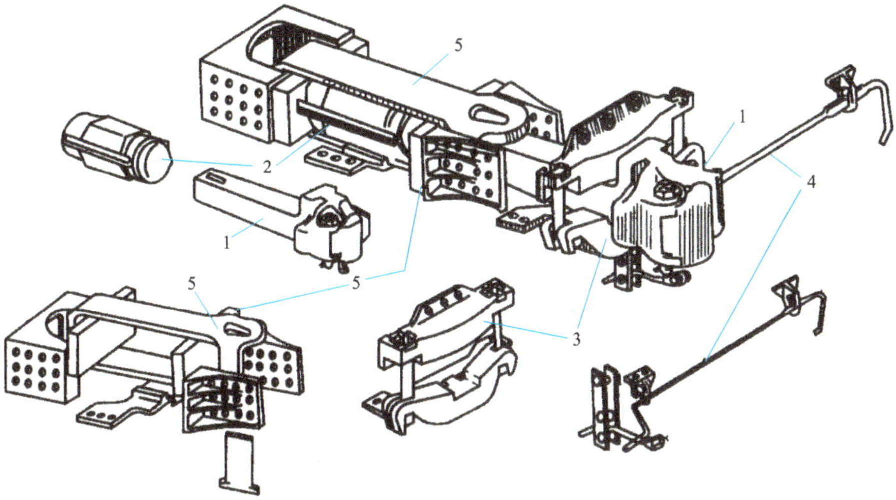

序号 S/N	名　称 Name	序号 S/N	名　称 Name	序号 S/N	名　称 Name
1		3		5	
2		4			

5. 认识上作用式车钩缓冲装置。

Understand the upper-acting coupler and draft gear.

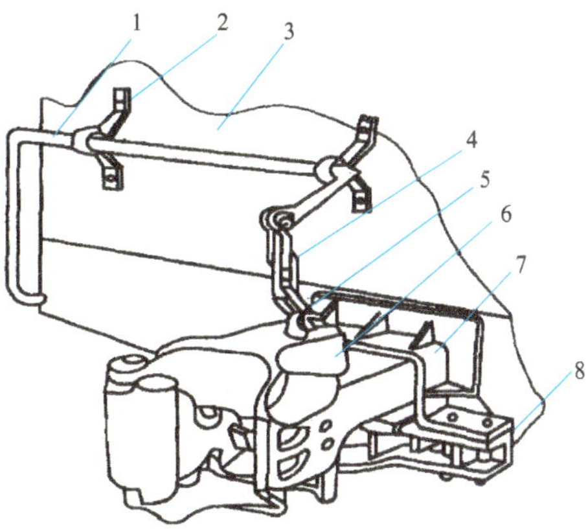

序号 S/N	名　称 Name	序号 S/N	名　称 Name	序号 S/N	名　称 Name
1		4		7	
2		5		8	
3		6			

6. 认识 15 型车钩钩体和配件。

Understand the coupler body and accessories of the No.15 coupler.

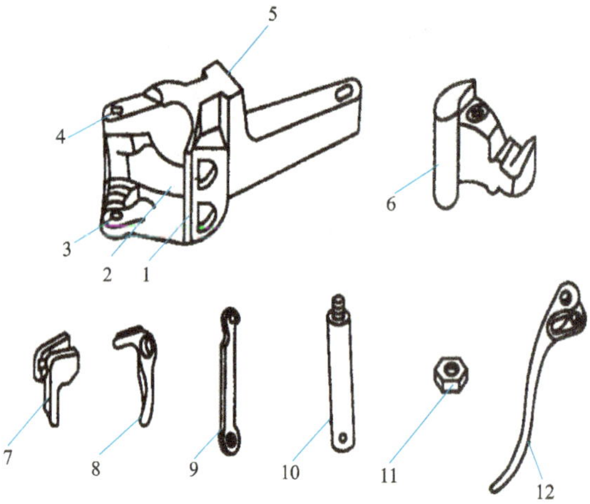

序号 S/N	名　称 Name	序号 S/N	名　称 Name	序号 S/N	名　称 Name
1		5		9	
2		6		10	
3		7		11	
4		8		12	

7. 认识密接式车钩缓冲装置。

Understand the tight-lock coupler and draft gear.

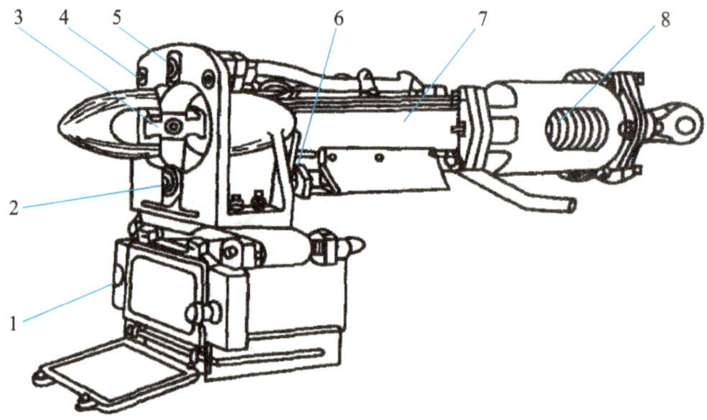

序号 S/N	名　称 Name	序号 S/N	名　称 Name	序号 S/N	名　称 Name
1		4		7	
2		5		8	
3		6			

8. 认识 16 型、17 型联锁式固定和转动车钩。

Understand the No.16 and No.17 interlocking fixed and rotating couplers.

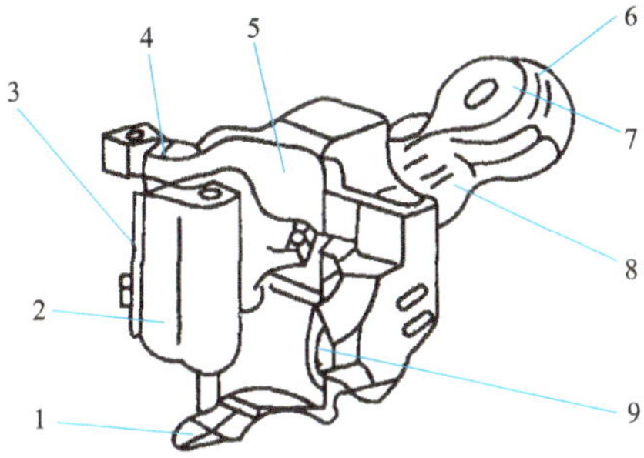

序号 S/N	名　称 Name	序号 S/N	名　称 Name	序号 S/N	名　称 Name
1		4		7	
2		5		8	
3		6		9	

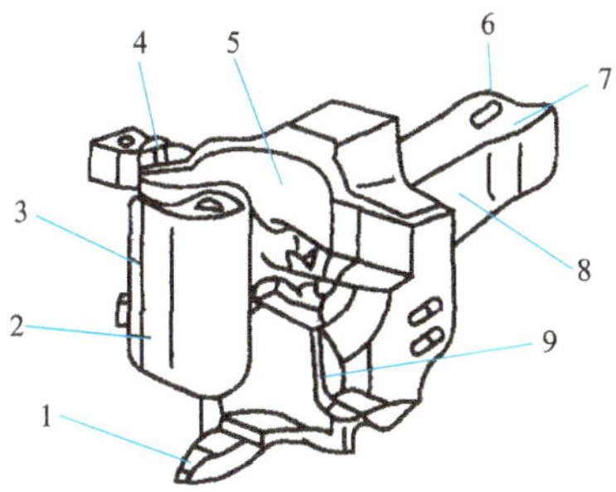

序号 S/N	名　称 Name	序号 S/N	名　称 Name	序号 S/N	名　称 Name
1		4		7	
2		5		8	
3		6		9	

9. 认识 ST 型缓冲器。

Understand the ST draft gear.

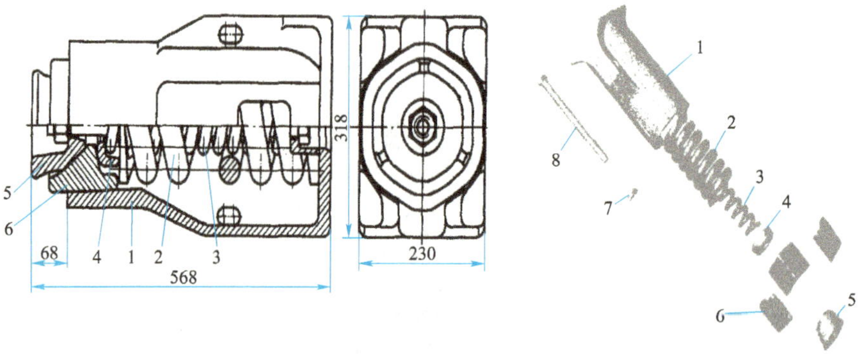

序号 S/N	名　称 Name	序号 S/N	名　称 Name	序号 S/N	名　称 Name
1		4		7	
2		5		8	
3		6			

10. 认识 MT-2 型、MT-3 型缓冲器。
    MT-2 and MT-3 buffers.

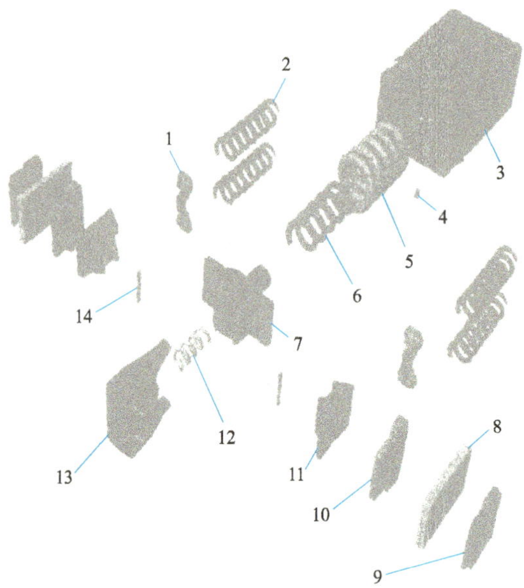

序号 S/N	名　称 Name	序号 S/N	名　称 Name	序号 S/N	名　称 Name
1		6		11	
2		7		12	
3		8		13	
4		9		14	
5		10			

11. 认识弹性胶泥缓冲器。

Understand the elastic clay draft gear.

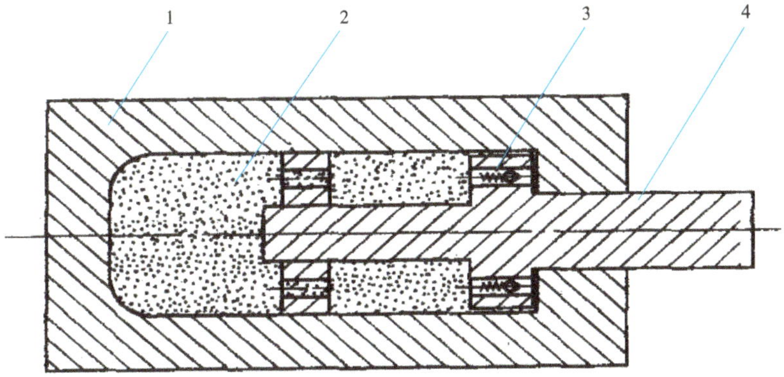

序号 S/N	名　称 Name	序号 S/N	名　称 Name
1		3	
2		4	

12. 实训任务。

Practical training tasks.

实训任务一：拆装车钩

Practical training task 1: Disassembly and assembly of couplers

车钩实物或模型拆装实训记录

Practical Training Record of Disassembly and Assembly of Coupler Physical or Model

准备工作 Preparation	
注意事项 Notes	

续表

Continued

<table>
<tr><td>整体结构观察
Overall structure observation</td><td>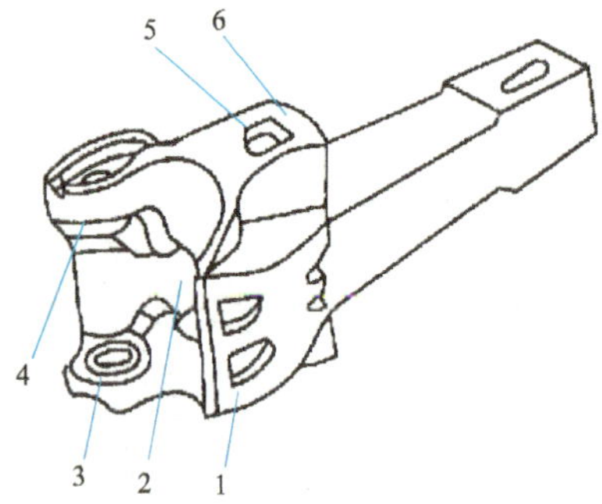
</td></tr>
<tr><td>拆解过程
Disassembly process</td><td></td></tr>
<tr><td>认识零部件
Understanding components</td><td>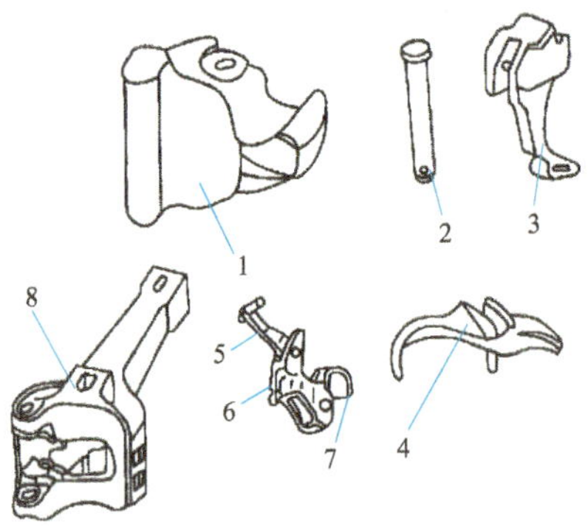

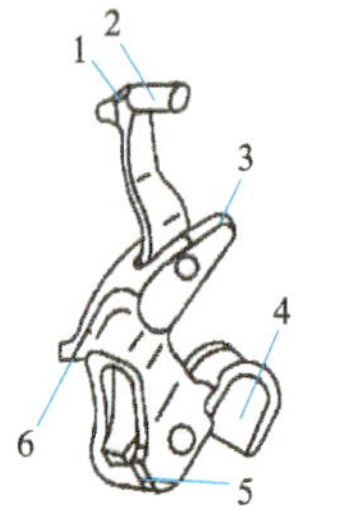

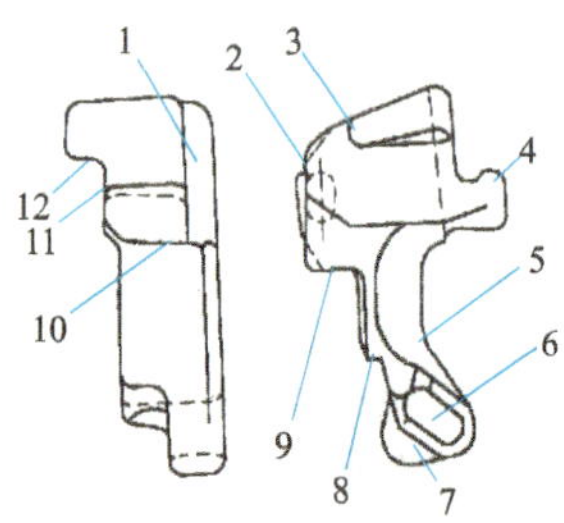

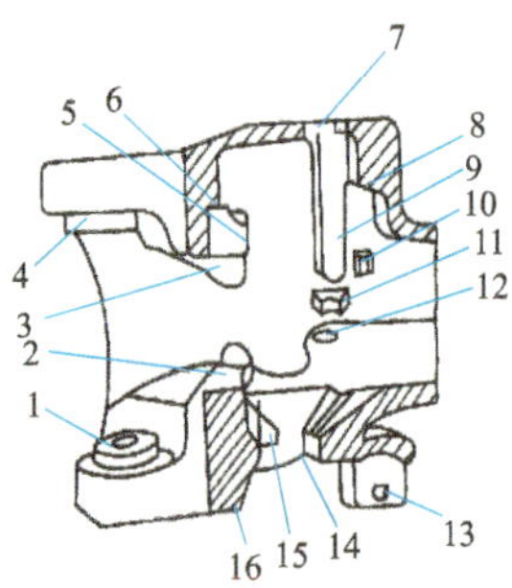

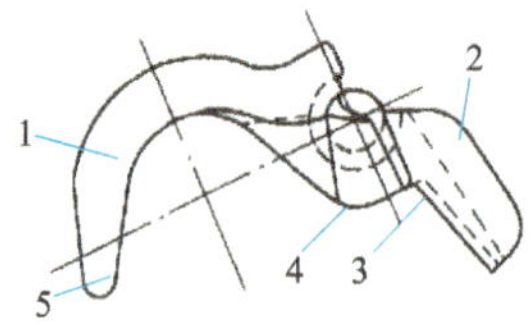
</td></tr>
<tr><td>安装过程
Assembly process</td><td></td></tr>
</table>

总结并记录：车钩的基本组成、作用及相关技术

Summarize and record: Basic composition, function, and related technology of coupler

基本组成 Basic composition	作　用 Function

分析并记录：13 型下作用式自动车钩满足连挂装置要求的办法

Summarize and record: Method for satisfying the requirements of the coupling device for No.13 lower-acting automatic coupler

应满足的要求 Requirements to be met	相应措施 Corresponding measures

实训任务二：检查车钩的三态作用[①]
Training task 2: Check the “three-state action” of coupler

检查车钩的三态作用实训记录
and check the “three-state action” training record of couplers

序　　号 No.	检查部位 Inspection site	检查内容及标准 Inspection content and standards
1		
2		
3		
4		
5		
6		
7		

总结并记录：13 型下作用式自动车钩三态作用位置、特征及作用

Summarize and record: Characteristics and functions of the three-state action position of the No.13 lower-acting automatic coupler

位　　置 Location	特　　征 Features	进入方式 Entry method	作用方式 Mode of action	作用结果 Action results

学习并记录：动车组牵引缓冲装置的基本组成、作用及相关技术

Learn and record: Basic composition, function, and related technology of traction draft gear for EMUs

基本组成 Basic composition	作　　用 Function	关键技术 key technology

① 技术标准：《机车车辆自动车钩缓冲装置》（TB/T 456—2019）

Technical standard: *Automatic Coupler and Draft Gears for Rolling Stock* (TB/T 456—2019)

课后任务

After-class tasks

1. 查阅资料，尝试总结比较以下车辆车钩缓冲装置的基本结构。

Refer to relevant documents and try to summarize and compare the basic structures of the following coupler and draft gears.

车辆类型 Type	70 型货车 70 freight car	25T 客车 25T passenger car	动车组 （介绍一种型号） EMU (introduce a model)	地铁 （介绍一种型号） Metro (introduce a model)	轻轨 （介绍一种型号） Light rail (introduce a model)
基本组成 Basic composition					

2. 提出你的问题。

Ask your question.

问题（1）：

Question (1): ____________________

答案：

Answer: ____________________

____

问题（2）：

Question (2): ____________________

答案：

Answer: ____________________

____

学习效果评价
Learning effect evaluation

年 Year　　月 Month　　日 Day

专业班级： Major & class:	姓名： Name:	学号： Student number:
工学小组及分工： Work-and-study team and responsibility division:	兴趣车型： Interested vehicle types:	
专业（知识/技能）收获 Professional gains (knowledge/skills)	（非专业）能力素质收获 (Non-professional) ability and quality gains	

评价考核项目 Evaluation item	自我评价 Self-evaluation	小组评价 Group evaluation	教师评价 Teacher's evaluation
已掌握车钩的结构原理 Have mastered the structural principle of the coupler			
已掌握车钩三态作用的检查方法 Have mastered the inspection method for the three-state action of the coupler			
已掌握缓冲装置的结构原理和检查方法 Have mastered the structural principle and inspection method of the draft gear			
已掌握动车组连接装置的结构原理 Have mastered the structural principle of the EMU connection device			
主动提出问题的数量 Number of questions proposed			
课外学习时间（学时） After-school learning time (hours)			
工作态度（课堂、课后任务完成情况） Work attitude (completion condition of classroom tasks and after-class tasks)	☆☆☆☆ ☆☆☆☆	☆☆☆☆ ☆☆☆☆	☆☆☆☆ ☆☆☆☆
合作意识及协调能力 Cooperation consciousness and coordination ability	☆☆☆☆ ☆☆☆☆	☆☆☆☆ ☆☆☆☆	☆☆☆☆ ☆☆☆☆
正确表达和沟通能力 Correct expression and communication skills	☆☆☆☆ ☆☆☆☆	☆☆☆☆ ☆☆☆☆	☆☆☆☆ ☆☆☆☆
自律能力（缺勤/旷课/迟到/违纪次数） Self-discipline (absences/absenteeism/lateness/disciplinary violations)			

任务 6.1　车钩缓冲装置概述

Task 6.1　Overview of coupler and draft gear

6.1.1　车钩缓冲装置的作用及类型

Function and type of coupler and draft gear

车钩缓冲装置是车辆最基本的、最重要的部件之一，其中车钩的作用是实现机车与车辆之间或车辆与车辆之间的连挂，以及传递牵引力和冲击力，并使车辆之间保持一定距离。缓冲装置的作用是缓和列车在运行中由于机车牵引力变化或在起动、制动及调车作业时车辆相互碰撞而引起的纵向冲击和振动。

Coupler and draft gear is one of the most basic and important components of a railway vehicle. The function of the coupler is to achieve coupling between the locomotive and the railway vehicle or between the railway vehicles, transmit traction and impact forces, and maintain a certain distance between the railway vehicles. The function of the draft gear is to mitigate the longitudinal impact and vibration caused by changes in locomotive traction during train operation or railway vehicle collisions during starting, braking, and switching operations.

在车钩缓冲装置中，如果牵引、连挂和缓和冲击的作用是由同一装置来承担的，那么该装置称为牵引缓冲装置；如果它们的作用分别由不同的装置来承担，则分别称为牵引连挂装置和缓冲装置。牵引连挂装置用来实现车辆之间的彼此连挂、传递及缓和牵引（拉伸）力的作用；缓冲装置（缓冲盘）用来传递和缓和冲击（压缩）力的作用，并且使车辆彼此之保持一定的距离。

In a coupler and draft gear, if the functions of traction, coupling, and impact mitigation are assumed by the same device, the device is called a traction draft gear; If their functions are assumed by different devices, they are called traction coupling devices and draft gears respectively. The traction coupling device is used to achieve the mutual coupling between railway vehicles, transfer, and mitigate the traction (tensile) force; The draft gear (buffer disk) is used to transmit and mitigate the impact (compression) force and maintain a certain distance between railway vehicles.

按照牵引连挂装置的连挂方式，车钩可分为自动车钩和非自动车钩。自动车钩不需要人工参与就能实现车辆之间的连挂，非自动车钩则要由人工来完成车辆之间的连挂。我国铁路车辆均采用自动车钩。

According to the coupling mode of the traction coupling device, the coupler can be divided into automatic coupler and non-automatic coupler. Automatic couplers can achieve the coupling between railway vehicles without manual participation, while non-automatic couplers require manual participation for coupling between railway vehicles. All railway vehicles in China are automatic couplers.

自动车钩又可分为两种基本类型：非刚性车钩和刚性车钩。非刚性车钩允许两个相连挂的车钩在垂直方向上有相对位移，其结构如图 6-1（a）所示、实物如图 6-2（a）所示。当两个车钩的纵轴线存在高度差时，连挂着的两个车钩呈阶梯形状，并且各自保持水平位置。刚性车钩不允许两相连挂车钩在垂直方向彼此存在位移，但是在水平方向可产生少许转角，其结构如图 6–1（b）所示、实物如图 6–2（b）所示。如果在车辆连挂之前两车钩的纵向轴线高度存在偏差，那么在连挂后，两车钩的轴线处在同一直线上并呈倾斜状态。两车钩的尾端采用销接的方式，从而保证了两连挂车辆之间的位移和偏角。

Automatic couplers can be divided into two basic types: non-rigid couplers and rigid couplers. Non-rigid couplers allow two coupled couplers to have relative displacement in the vertical direction (see Figure 6-1 (a)), and the actual object is shown in Figure 6-2 (a). When there is a height difference between the longitudinal axis lines of two couplers, the two couplers connected take on a stepped shape and each maintains a horizontal position. Rigid couplers do not allow two coupled couplers to displace each other in the vertical direction but can generate a small amount of rotation angle in the horizontal direction (see Figure 6-1 (b)). The actual object is shown in Figure 6-2 (b). If there is a deviation in the height of the longitudinal axes of the two couplers before the railway vehicle is coupled, after coupling, the axes of the two couplers are in the same straight line and inclined. The tail ends of the two couplers are connected by pins to ensure the displacement and deflection angle between the two coupled railway vehicles.

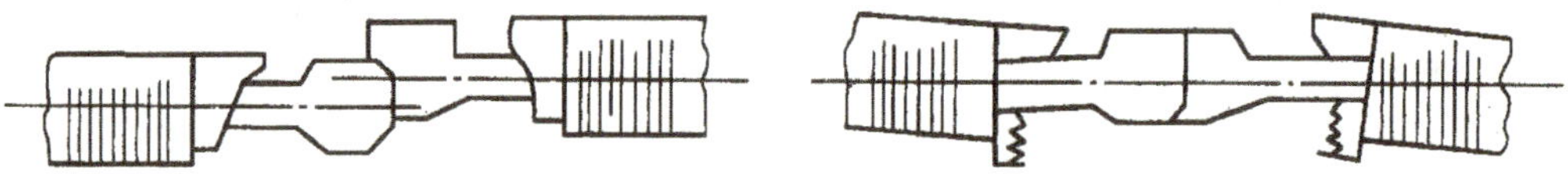

(a) 非钢性车钩的结构
Non-rigid coupler

(b) 刚性车钩的结构
Rigid coupler

图 6–1 非刚性车钩与刚性车钩的结构

Figure 6-1 Structure of Non-rigid Coupler and Rigid Coupler

(a) 非刚性车钩
Non-rigid coupler

(b) 刚性车钩
Non-rigid coupler

图 6–2 非刚性车钩与刚性车钩

Figure 6-2 Non-rigid Coupler and Rigid Coupler

刚性车钩减小了两个连挂车钩之间的间隙，从而大大降低了列车运行中的纵向冲击，提高了列车运行的平稳性，同时也降低了车钩零件的磨耗和噪声。另外，刚性车钩有可能同时实现车辆间的气路和电路的自动连挂。非刚性车钩结构较简单、强度高、重量轻，与车体的连挂较为简单。

The rigid coupler reduces the gap between the two coupled couplers, greatly reducing the longitudinal impact during train operation, improving the smoothness of train operation, and reducing the wear and noise of coupler parts. In addition, it is possible for rigid couplers to achieve automatic coupling of air and electrical circuits between railway vehicles simultaneously. The non-rigid coupler has a simple structure, high strength, lightweight, and simple coupling to the car body.

我国铁路客车采用的是非刚性的自动车钩，对于高速列车和城市的地铁、轻轨车辆则应采用刚性的自动车钩，即密接式车钩。

In China, non-rigid automatic couplers are used for railway passenger cars. For high-speed trains and urban metro and light rail vehicles, rigid automatic couplers, that is, tight-lock couplers, should be used.

6.1.2 车钩缓冲装置的组成及功能 Composition and function of coupler and draft gear

1. 车钩缓冲装置的组成 Composition and function of coupler and draft gear

车钩缓冲装置由车钩、缓冲器、钩尾框、从板等零部件组成。图 6-3 为车钩缓冲装置的一般结构形式。在钩尾框内依次装有前从板、缓冲器和后从板（有时不需后从板），并借助钩尾销把车钩和钩尾框连成一个整体，从而使车辆具有连挂、牵引和缓冲 3 种功能。

The coupler and draft gear consists of a coupler, draft gear, coupler yoke, slave plate, and other components. Figure 6-3 shows the general structure of coupler and draft gear. A front slave plate, a draft gear, and a rear slave plate (sometimes without a rear slave plate) are sequentially installed in the coupler yoke. The coupler and the coupler yoke are connected as a whole with the

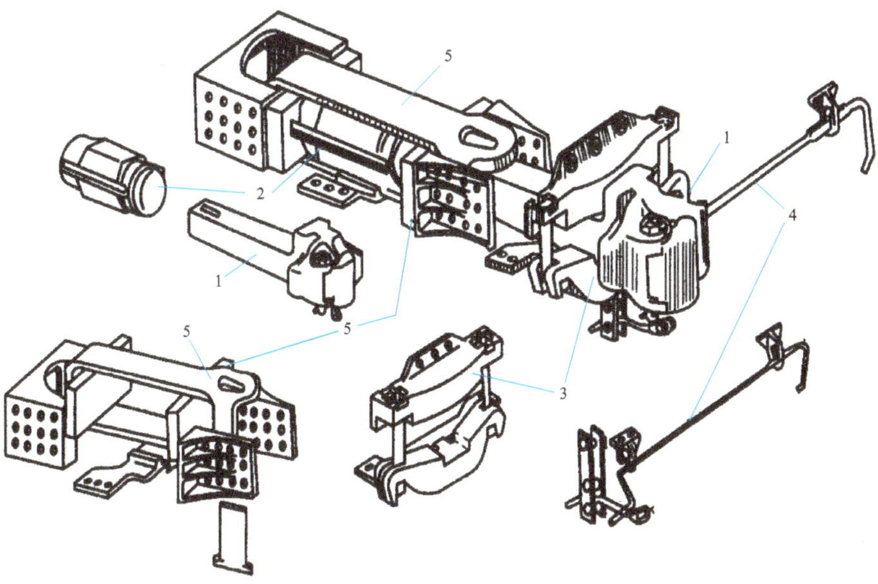

1—车钩；2—缓冲器；3—车钩复原装置；4—解钩装置；5—钩尾框及从板。

1—Coupler; 2—Draft gear; 3—Coupler recovery device; 4—Uncoupling device; 5—Coupler yoke and slave plate.

图 6-3 车钩缓冲装置的一般结构形式

Figure 6-3 General Structure of Coupler and Draft Gear

aid of coupler tail pins, thereby enabling the railway vehicle to have three functions: coupling, traction, and draft gearing.

2. 车钩缓冲装置的功能

Function of coupler and draft gear

车钩缓冲装置是车辆最重要的部件之一，通过它使机车和车辆或车辆和车辆之间实现连挂，并且传递和缓和列车在运行或在调车作业时所产生的牵引力和冲击力。

The coupler and draft gear is one of the most important components of a railway vehicle, which enables thc coupling between the locomotive and the railway vehicle or between the railway vehicles, and transmits and mitigates the traction and impact forces generated by the train during operation or switching operations.

6.1.3 车钩缓冲装置在车辆上的安装及作用力的传递

Installation of the coupler and draft gear on the railway vehicle and transmission of force

车钩缓冲装置一般组成一个整体，安装于车底架两端的牵引梁内，其前、后从板及缓冲器卡装在牵引梁的前、后从板座之间，下部靠钩尾框托板及钩体托梁（货车）或复原装置（客车）托住，各部相互位置如图 6-4（a）所示。

The coupler and draft gear is generally installed as a whole in the traction beam at both ends of the railway vehicle underframe. Its front and rear slave plates and draft gears are clamped between the front and rear slave plate seats of the traction beam, and the lower part is supported by the coupler yoke support plate and coupler body support beam (freight car) or recovery device (passenger car). The mutual positions of each part are shown in Figure 6-4 (a).

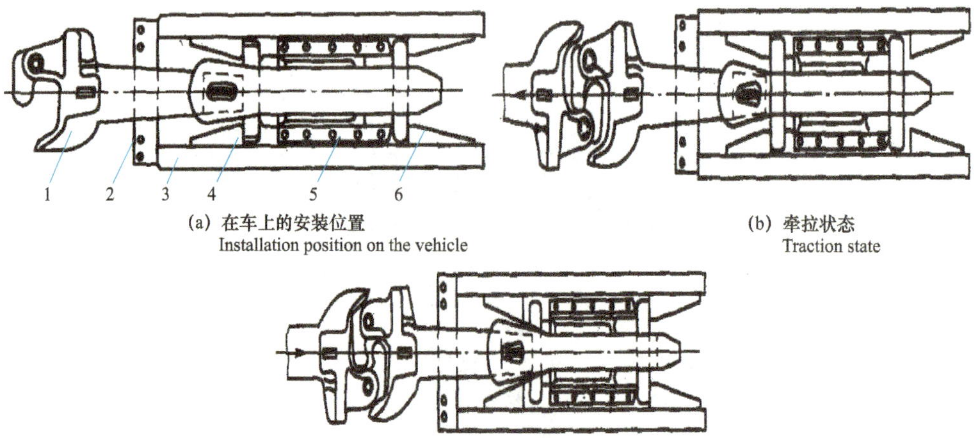

(a) 在车上的安装位置
Installation position on the vehicle

(b) 牵拉状态
Traction state

(c) 压缩状态
Compression state

1—车钩缓冲装置；2—冲击座或复原装置；3—中梁（牵引梁）；4—前从板座；5—钩尾框托板；6—后从板座。

1—Coupler and draft gear; 2—Impact seat or recovery device; 3—Center beam (traction beam);
4—Front slave plate seat; 5—Coupler yoke bracket; 6—Rear slave plate seat.

图 6-4 车钩缓冲装置在车辆上的安装位置及受力状态

Figure 6-4 Installation Position and Stress State of Coupler and Draft Gear on the Railway Vehicle

当车辆受牵拉时，作用力的传递过程为：车钩→钩尾框→后从板→缓冲器→前从板→前从板座→牵引梁，如图 6-4（b）所示。当车辆受冲击时，作用力的传递过程为：车钩→前从板→缓冲器→后从板→后从板座→牵引梁，如图 6-4（c）所示。

When the railway vehicle is pulled, the transmission process of the force is as follows: coupler → coupler yoke → rear slave plate → draft gear → front slave plate → front slave plate seat → traction beam, as shown in Figure 6-4 (b). When the railway vehicle is impacted, the transmission process of the force is as follows: coupler → front slave plate → draft gear → rear slave plate → rear slave plate seat → traction beam, as shown in Figure 6-4 (c).

由此可见，车钩缓冲装置无论是承受牵引力，还是冲击力，都要经过缓冲器将力传递给牵引梁，这样就有可能使车辆间的纵向冲击振动得到缓和和消减，从而改善了运行条件，保护车辆及货物不受损坏。

It can be seen that whether the coupler and draft gear is subjected to traction force or impact force, it must pass through the draft gear to transmit the force to the traction beam, which may alleviate and reduce the longitudinal impact vibration between the railway vehicles, thereby improving operating conditions and protecting the railway vehicles and goods from damage.

为了保证车辆连挂安全可靠和车钩缓冲装置安装的互换性，我国机车车辆有关规程规定：客车车钩中心线至钢轨顶面高度最小为 830 mm，最大为 890 mm；两连挂车钩中心高度之差不得大于 75 mm；牵引梁前、后从板座之间的距离为 625 mm。

To ensure the safety and reliability of railway vehicle coupling and the interchangeability of coupler and draft gear installation, the relevant regulations for railway vehicle in China stipulate that the minimum height from the center line of the passenger car coupler to the top surface of the rail should be 830 mm, and the maximum height should be 890 mm; The difference between the central heights of the two coupled couplers shall not be greater than 75 mm; The distance between the front and rear slave plate seats of the traction beam is 625 mm.

6.1.4　车钩的开启方式及复原装置 Opening method and recovery device of coupler

车钩的开启方式分为上作用式及下作用式两种。对于上作用式车钩装置，车钩提升机构位于钩头上方；对于下作用式车钩装置，车钩提升机构位于钩头下方。对于客车，因车体端部有折棚和平渡板装置，故无法采用上作用式车钩装置，而采用下作用式车钩装置。这时，借助于设在钩头下部的推顶杆的动作来实现开启，它不如上作用式车钩装置轻便。图 6-5 和图 6-6 分别为上作用式车钩装置和下作用式车钩装置的结构。图 6-7 和图 6-8 分别为上作用式车钩装置和下作用式车钩装置的实物。

The opening methods of the coupler are divided into two types: upper-acting and lower-acting. The coupler lifting mechanism of the upper-acting coupler device is located above the coupler head; The coupler lifting mechanism of the lower-acting coupler device is located below the coupler head. For passenger cars, due to the fact that there are folding sheds and flat crossover devices at the end of the car body, the upper-acting coupler device cannot be used, but the lower-acting coupler device is used. At this time, the opening is realized by the action of the push rod located at the lower part of the hook head, which is not as light as the upper-acting coupler device. Figure 6-5 shows the structure of upper-acting coupler device, and Figure 6-6 shows the structure of lower-acting coupler device. Figure 6-7 shows the actual object of upper-acting coupler device, and Figure 6-8 shows the actual object of lower-acting coupler device.

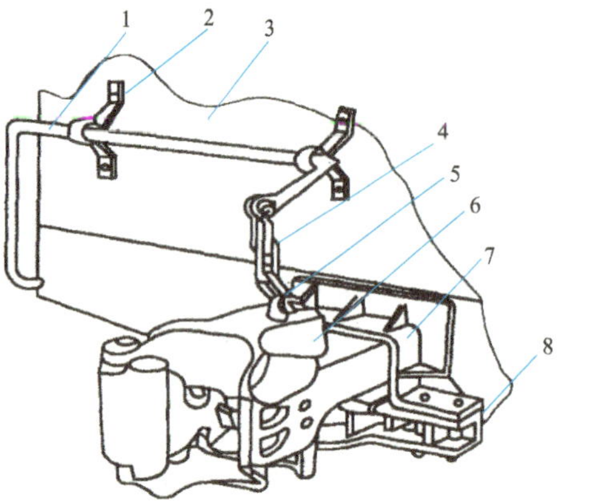

1—车钩提杆；2—车钩提杆座；3—车体端墙；4—提钩链；5—锁提销；6—钩头；7—冲击座；8—钩身托梁。

1—Coupler lifting rod; 2—Coupler lifting rod seat; 3—End wall of car body; 4—Lifting hook chain; 5—Lock lifting pin; 6—Coupler head; 7—Impact seat; 8—Coupler body joist.

图 6–5　上作用式车钩装置的结构

Figure 6-5　Structure of Upper-acting Coupler Device

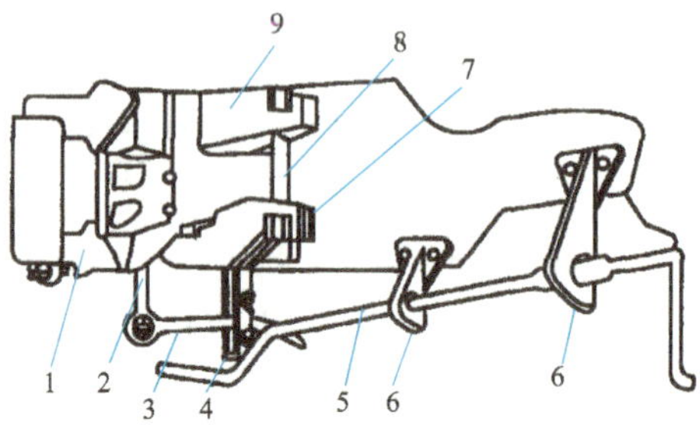

1—钩头；2—锁推销；3—下锁销杆；4—下锁销托吊；5—车钩提杆；6—车钩提杆座；7—摆块；8—摆块吊；9—冲击座。

1—Coupler head; 2—Lock push pin; 3—Lower lock pin rod; 4—Lower lock pin support crane; 5—Coupler lifting rod; 6—Coupler lifting rod seat; 7—Swing block; 8—Swing block hanger; 9—Impact seat.

图 6–6　下作用式车钩装置的结构

Figure 6-6　Structure of Lower-acting Coupler Device

图 6–7　上作用式车钩装置

Figure 6-7　Upper-acting Coupler Device

图 6–8　下作用式车钩装置

Figure 6-8　Lower-acting Coupler Device

客车车钩的解钩提杆安装在二、三位车端。当车辆在曲线上运行时，车钩中心线与车体纵向中心线之间将产生一偏角。由于客车车体较长，在曲线上车钩的偏移量较大，如果车钩偏移后不能迅速地恢复到正常位置，势必会增加车辆运行时的摆动量，而且还会造成车辆摘挂困难。因此，在客车上均装有车钩复原装置。我国铁路客车上采用摆块式车钩复原装置，它由摆块吊和摆块组成，结构如图 6–9 所示。

The uncoupling lever of the passenger car coupler is installed at the "A" end and "C" end of car. When the railway vehicle runs on a curve, there will be a deflection angle between the coupler centerline and the longitudinal centerline of the car body. Due to the long body of the passenger car, the deviation of the coupler on the curve is large. If the coupler cannot quickly recover to the normal position after the deviation, it will inevitably increase the amount of swing during the operation of railway vehicles and cause difficulties in railway vehicle uncoupling. Therefore, all passenger cars are equipped with coupler recovery devices, and Chinese passenger cars are equipped with swing block coupler recovery devices, which are composed of swing block hangers and swing blocks. The structure is shown in Figure 6-9.

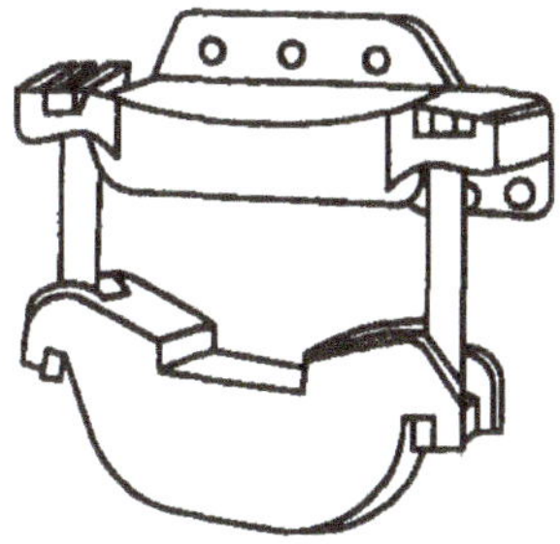

图 6-9　摆块式车钩复原装置
Figure 6-9　Swing Block Coupler Recovery Device

6.1.5　车钩的种类及组成 Type and composition of couplers

我国铁路客车上所使用的车钩属于非刚性自动车钩，所谓自动车钩即在拉动钩提杆或两车互相碰撞时就能自动完成解开或连挂，所以也称为关节式车钩。

The couplers used on railway passenger cars in China are non-rigid automatic couplers. Automatic couplers are also known as articulated couplers, which can be automatically released or coupled when the coupler lifting rod is pulled or two railway vehicles collide with each other.

我国铁路客车上采用 1 型、15 型车钩。随着列车运行速度的提高，对车钩的强度提出了更高的要求，1 型车钩不再能适应运输的要求，已经被淘汰。现在新造的客车上全部采用 15 型车钩。15 型车钩的结构特点及主要几何尺寸如表 6–1 所示。

No.1 and No.15 couplers are used on railway passenger cars in China. With the improvement of train operation speed, higher requirements have been put forward for the strength of the coupler. The No.1 coupler can no longer meet the requirements of transportation and has been eliminated. Now, all new passenger cars are provided with No.15 couplers. The structural characteristics and main geometric dimensions of the No.15 coupler are shown in Table 6-1.

表 6–1　15 型车钩的结构特点及主要几何尺寸
Table 6-1　Structural Characteristics and Main Geometric Dimensions of No.15 Coupler

钩舌高 Coupler knuckle height	钩颈（宽×高）Coupler neck (width × height)	钩尾至钩舌连接线距离 Connecting line distance from coupler tail to coupler knuckle	钩尾至钩头台肩距离 Distance from coupler tail to coupler head shoulder	钩身壁厚 Coupler body wall thickness	钩耳孔形状 Coupler ear hole shape	钩舌销直径 Coupler knuckle pin diameter	钩尾（宽×高）Coupler tail (width × height)	尾销孔 Tail pin hole	钩尾销 Coupler tail pin	质量 Mass
280 mm	176 mm × 130 mm	1 000 mm	663 mm	25 mm	ϕ(42+0.620) mm	(42–0.72–0.50) mm	圆弧面 Circular arc surface 130 mm×130 mm	长圆孔 Oblong hole 130 mm×50 mm	长圆 Oblong circle 92 mm×32 mm	166.4 kg

15 型车钩由铸钢制成，材料为 ZG230-450/ZG25 MNCrNiMo，抗拉强度为 1 600～1 700 kN/2 300～2 400 kN。车钩一般可分为钩体、钩舌、钩舌销及钩体头部内的钩锁、钩舌推铁、钩锁销等。当钩体头部内的零件处于不同的位置时，起着不同的作用，从而使车钩具有闭锁、开锁、全开三种作用，俗称车钩的三态作用。

The No.15 coupler is made of cast steel, made of ZG230-450/ZG25 MNCrNiMo, and has a tensile strength of 1,600 – 1,700 kN/2,300 – 2,400 kN. Couplers can generally be divided into coupler body, coupler knuckle, coupler knuckle pin, coupler lock, coupler knuckle push iron, coupler lock pin, etc. in the coupler head. When the parts in the head of the coupler body are in different positions, they play different roles, resulting in three functions of the coupler: locking, unlocking, and full-open, commonly known as the three-state function of the coupler.

任务 6.2 货 车 车 钩
Task 6.2 Freight car coupler

6.2.1 13 型、13A 型车钩
No.13 and 13A couplers

1. 主要结构及技术参数
Main structure and technical parameters

13 型车钩曾是我国铁路货车的主型车钩，一度约占全路货车车钩的 80%，随着铁路货车重载、提速工作的不断推进，13 型车钩暴露出了很多问题，已经不适应重载、提速的要求。13A 型车钩是为适应我国铁路货车重载、提速工作的需要而研制的，该车钩缩小了车辆的连挂间隙，可改善列车的纵向动力学性能，减小列车的纵向冲击。图 6-10 为 13A 型车钩连挂间隙示意图。13A 型车钩于 2003 年开始在全路推广。

No.13 coupler used to be the main type of coupler for railway freight cars in China, once accounting for about 80% of the total number of freight car couplers on the railway. With the continuous advancement of heavy load and speed increase work for railway freight cars, the No.13

图 6-10 13A 型车钩连挂间隙示意图
Figure 6-10 Schematic Diagram of Coupling Clearance of 13A Coupler

coupler has proven to have many problems and is no longer suitable for the requirements of heavy load and speed increase. The 13A coupler is developed to meet the needs of heavy load and speed increase work of railway freight cars in China. This coupler reduces the coupling clearance of railway vehicles, improves the longitudinal dynamic performance of trains, and reduces the longitudinal impact of trains. Figure 6-10 shows the schematic diagram of the coupling clearance of 13A coupler. The 13A coupler has been promoted throughout the railway since 2003.

图 6-11 所示为我国铁路货车上使用的 13 型车钩及钩头零件。13 型车钩的设计较合理地安排了钩头与钩舌及钩舌与钩舌销之间的间隙。在锁闭位置时，可使钩舌销不受或较少地分担作用力，从而更充分地发挥了车钩各部材料的承载能力，故车钩的强度较大。由普通铸钢制造的 13 型车钩的抗拉破坏强度约为 2.5 MN，当采用 AAR 标准 C 级低合金高强度铸钢时，其抗拉破坏强度可达 3 MN 以上。

Figure 6-11 shows the No.13 coupler and coupler head parts used on freight cars in China. The design of the No.13 coupler reasonably arranges the clearance between the coupler head and the coupler knuckle, as well as between the coupler knuckle and the coupler knuckle pin. When in the locked position, the coupler knuckle pin cannot bear or share less force, thereby giving full play to the bearing capacity of various materials of the coupler, so the strength of the coupler is relatively large. The tensile failure strength of the No.13 coupler made of ordinary cast steel is about 2.5 MN. When AAR standard Grade C low alloy high-strength cast steel is used, the tensile failure strength can reach more than 3 MN.

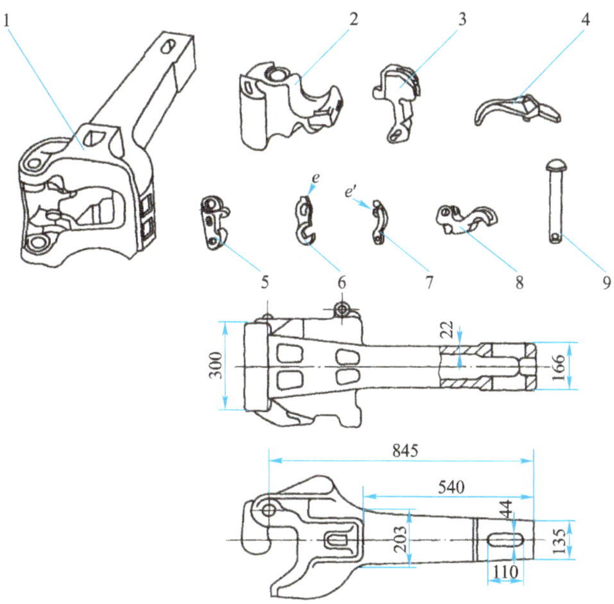

1—钩头；2—钩舌；3—钩锁铁；4—钩舌推铁；5—上锁销杆（上作用）；6—上锁销（上作用）；7—下锁销（下作用）；8—下锁销杆（下作用）；9—钩舌销。

1—Coupler head; 2—Coupler knuckle; 3—Coupler lock iron; 4—Coupler knuckle push iron; 5—Upper lock pin rod (upper-acting); 6—Upper lock pin (upper-acting); 7—Lower lock pin (lower-acting); 8—Lower lock pin (lower-acting); 9—Coupler knuckle pin.

图 6-11 13 型车钩及钩头零件

Figure 6-11 No.13 Coupler and Coupler Head Parts

13 型车钩钩头与钩舌上、下两个牵引突缘之间的间隙 δ_1 最小，两个护销突缘之间的间隙 δ_2 稍大，钩耳孔与钩舌销之间的间隙 δ_3 最大，即 $\delta_1<\delta_2<\delta_3$。车钩受牵拉时，两个牵引突缘最先受力，当牵引突缘受磨耗间隙增大后，它与护销突缘一起传递牵引力。当各突缘间经磨耗后间隙均增大时，则牵引突缘、护销突缘与钩舌销三者共同承受牵引力。此外，将钩耳孔做成长圆形，既可保证纵向的合理间隙，又避免了横向的间隙过大。13 型车钩钩头的结构如图 6–12 所示。

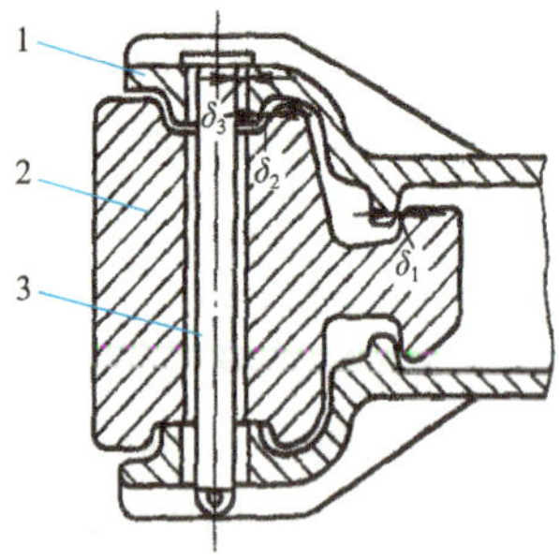

图 6-12　13 型车钩钩头的结构
Figure 6-12　Structure of No.13 Coupler Head

The gap δ_1 between the upper and lower traction lugs of the No.13 coupler head and the coupler knuckle is the smallest. The gap δ_2 between the two guard pin lugs is slightly larger, and the gap δ_3 between the coupler ear hole and the coupler knuckle pin is the largest, that is, $\delta_1 < \delta_2 < \delta_3$. When the coupler is pulled, the two traction lugs bear the force first. When the wear clearance of the traction lugs increases, it transmits the traction force together with the guard pin lug. When the clearance between each flange increases after wear, the traction lug, the guard pin lug, and the hook knuckle pin jointly bear the traction force. In addition, making the coupler ear hole into a long circular shape not only ensures a reasonable longitudinal clearance but also avoids excessive lateral clearance. The structure of the No.13 coupler head is shown in Figure 6-12.

图 6–13 所示为 13A 型车钩。13A 型车钩是在 13 型车钩的基础上改进后研制开发的，其钩头零件与 13 型车钩基本相同，主要是对钩舌外形尺寸进行了重要改进。其中，S 形连接面尺寸的改变使车钩连挂间隙明显缩小，13A 型车钩的连挂间隙为 11.5 mm，比 13 型车钩的连挂间隙（19.5 mm）减少了约 41%，可有效地降低列车的纵向冲击，改善列车的动力学性能。该型车钩从 2002 年开始在新造的铁路货车上推广使用。13A 型车钩的结构如图 6–14 所示。

Figure 6-13 shows the 13A coupler. The 13A coupler is developed based on the improvement of the No.13 coupler. Its coupler head parts are basically the same as the No.13 coupler, mainly due to significant improvements in the overall dimensions of the coupler knuckle. The change in the

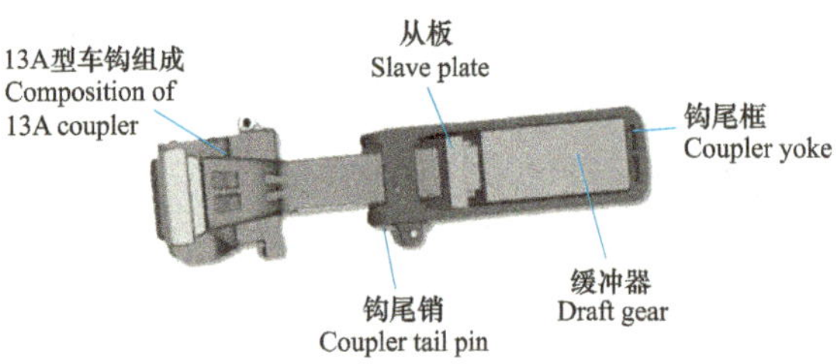

图 6–13　13A 型车钩
Figure 6-13　13A Coupler

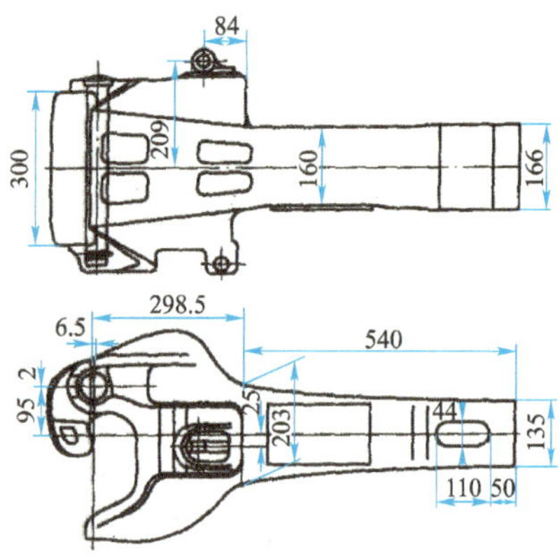

图 6–14　13A 型车钩的结构
Figure 6-14　Structure of 13A Coupler

size of the S-shaped connection surface has significantly reduced the coupling clearance of the coupler. The coupling clearance of the 13A coupler is 11.5 mm, 41% less than the (19.5 mm) coupling clearance of the No.13 coupler. This can effectively reduce the longitudinal impact of the train and improve the dynamic performance of the train. This type of coupler has been widely used on newly built freight cars since 2002. The structure of the 13A coupler is shown in Figure 6-14.

13A 型车钩可以与 13 型车钩互换，并能与 13 型、16 型、17 型车钩实现自由连挂。13A 型车钩增加安装了钩体磨耗板，以适应厂修、段修工作的需要，可方便运用和检修，提高了车钩的使用寿命和可靠性。13A 型车钩钩体、钩舌上的型号铸造标记为“13A”。

The 13A coupler can be interchanged with the No.13 coupler and can be freely coupled with the No.13, No.16, and No.17 couplers. The coupler body wear plate has been added and installed for 13A coupler to meet the needs of factory and depot repairs, which can facilitate use and maintenance, and improve the service life and reliability of the coupler. The model casting mark on the coupler body and knuckle of 13A coupler is “13A”.

13A 型车钩的主要技术参数如表 6–2 所示。

The main technical parameters of 13A coupler are shown in Table 6-2.

表 6–2 13A 型车钩的主要技术参数

Table 6-2 Main Technical Parameters of 13A Coupler

车钩连接线至钩肩长度 Length from coupler connecting line to coupler shoulder		298.5 mm
钩肩截面外形尺寸 Overall dimension of coupler shoulder section		160 mm×203 mm
最大相对转角 Max. relative rotation angle	在水平面内 In horizontal plane	6°
	在垂直面内 In the vertical plane	2°11′
最大纵向移动间隙 Max. longitudinal movement clearance		11.5 mm
横向最大连挂范围 Transverse max. coupling range		88 mm
最大允许两车钩中心线高度差 Max. allowable height difference between center lines of two couplers		75 mm
钩体最小静拉破坏载荷 Min. static tensile failure load of coupler body		≥3 225 kN
钩舌最小静拉破坏载荷 Min. static tensile failure load of coupler knuckle		≥2 950 kN

13A 型车钩由钩体、钩舌、钩头配件等组成，其中钩体由钩头、钩身、钩尾等 3 部件构成，钩头配件包括钩舌销、钩舌推铁、钩锁铁、上锁销组件等。13A 型车钩钩锁腔的结构如图 6–15 所示。

13A coupler consists of a coupler body, a coupler knuckle, a coupler head accessory, etc. The coupler body is composed of a coupler head, a coupler body, a coupler tail, and other components.

The coupler head accessories include a coupler knuckle pin, a coupler push iron, a coupler lock iron, an upper lock pin assembly and others. The structure of the 13A coupler lock cavity is shown in Figure 6-15.

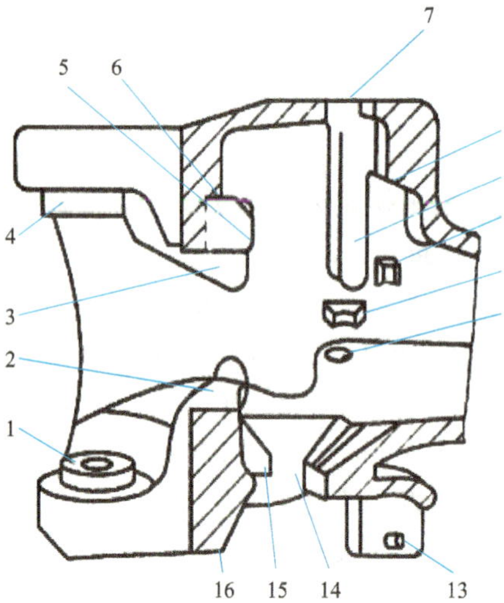

1—下护销突缘；2—下牵引突缘；3—上牵引突缘；4—上护销突缘；5—导向挡；6—全开作用台；7—上锁销孔；8—上防脱（跳）台；9—钩锁导向壁；10—钩锁后部定位挡；11—钩舌推铁挡铁；12—钩舌推铁轴孔；13—下锁销钩转轴；14—下锁销孔；15—下防脱（跳）台；16—二次防脱（跳）台。

1—Lower guard pin lug; 2—Lower traction lug; 3—Upper traction lug; 4—Upper guard pin lug; 5—Guide stop: 6—Full-open action platform; 7—Upper lock pin hole; 8—Upper anti-falling (creeping) platform; 9—Coupler lock guide wall; 10—Coupler lock rear positioning stop; 11—Coupler knuckle push iron stopper; 12—Coupler knuckle push iron shaft hole; 13—Lower lock pin coupler rotary shaft; 14—Lower lock pin hole; 15—Lower anti-falling (creeping) platform; 16—Secondary anti-falling (creeping) platform.

图 6-15 13A 型车钩钩锁腔的结构

Figure 6-15 Structure of 13A Coupler Lock Cavity

13A 型车钩钩舌的结构如图 6-16 所示。

The structure of the 13A coupler knuckle is shown in Figure 6-16.

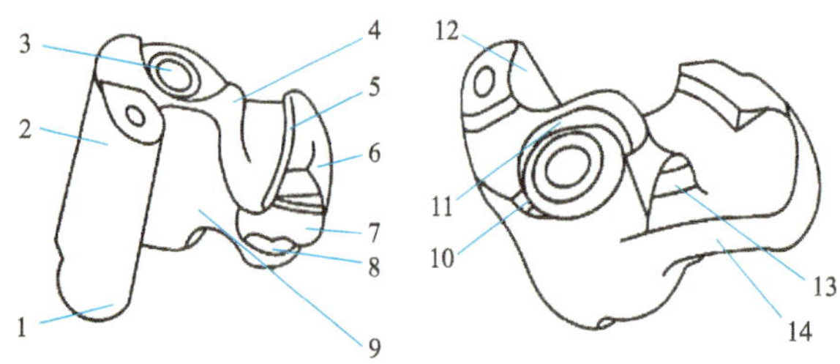

1—钩舌鼻；2—钩舌正面；3—钩舌销孔；4—冲击突肩（冲击台）；5—牵引突缘（牵引台）；6—钩舌尾端面；7—钩舌锁面；8—钩锁承台；9—钩舌内腕；10—全开止挡；11—护销突缘；12—钩腕牵引面（钩舌内侧面）；13—钩舌推铁面；14—钩舌尾止端。

1—Coupler knuckle nose; 2—Front face of coupler knuckle; 3—Pin hole of coupler knuckle; 4—Impact shoulder (impact table); 5—Traction lug (traction platform): 6—Coupler knuckle tail end face; 7—Coupler knuckle lock surface; 8—Coupler lock cushion cap; 9—Coupler knuckle inner wrist: 10—Full-open stop; 11—Guard pin lug; 12—Coupler wrist traction surface (inner side of coupler knuckle); 13—Coupler knuckle push iron surface; 14—Coupler knuckle stop end.

图 6-16 13A 型车钩钩舌的结构

Figure 6-16 Structure of 13A Coupler Knuckle

13A 型车钩钩锁铁的结构如图 6–17 所示。

The structure of the 13A coupler lock iron is shown in Figure 6-17.

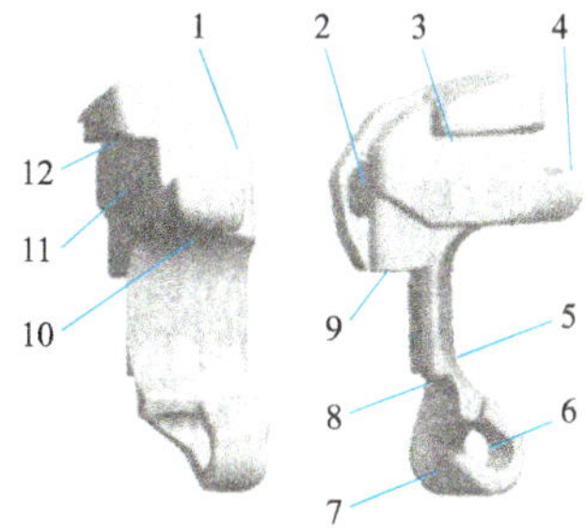

1—前导向面；2—上锁销杆转轴；3—后导向面；4—全开回转支点；5—锁腿；6—下锁销轴孔；7—后踢足面；8—开锁座面，9—后座锁面；10—前座锁面；11—锁面；12—侧座锁面。

1—Front guide surface; 2—Upper lock pin rod rotary shaft; 3—Rear guide surface; 4—Full-open rotary fulcrum; 5—Lock leg; 6—Lower lock pin shaft hole; 7—Rear skirting surface; 8—Unlocking seating surface, 9—Rear seating surface; 10—Front seating surface; 11—Lock surface;

图 6–17　13A 型车钩钩锁铁的结构

Figure 6-17　Structure of 13A Coupler Lock Iron

13A 型车钩钩舌推铁、上锁销体的结构分别如图 6–18 和图 6–19 所示。

The structure of the 13A coupler knuckle push iron and upper lock pin body is shown in Figure 6-18 and Figure 6-19.

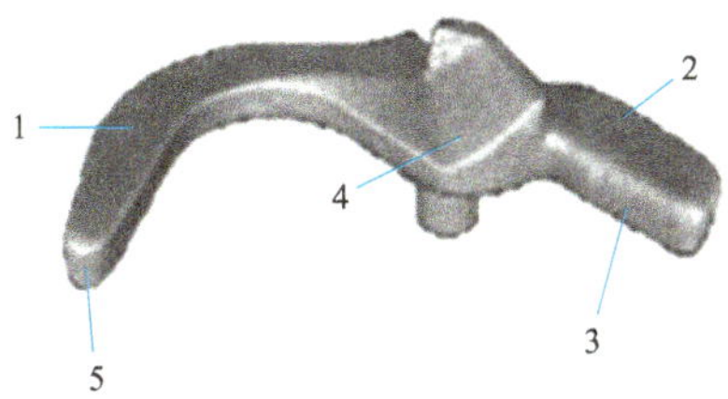

1—钩舌推铁腿；2—锁座；3—踢足推动面；4—锁腿导向面；5—推铁踢足。

1—Coupler knuckle push iron leg; 2—Lock seat; 3—Kick pushing surface; 4—Lock leg guide surface; 5—Push iron and kick.

图 6–18　13A 型车钩钩舌推铁的结构

Figure 6-18　Structure of 13A Coupler Knuckle Push Iron

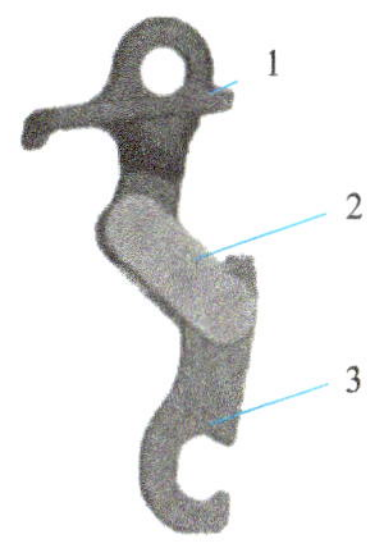

1—上锁提；2—上锁销；3—上锁销杆。

1—Upper lock body; 2—Upper lock pin; 3—Upper lock pin rod.

图 6–19　13A 型车钩上锁销体的结构

Figure 6-19　Structure of Upper Lock Pin Body of 13A Coupler

2. 车钩的三态作用

Three-state action of coupler

1）闭锁位置

Locking position

钩舌尾部转入钩腔内，钩锁铁以自重下落，后坐锁面坐在钩舌推铁的锁座上，前坐锁面坐在钩舌尾部侧面，侧坐锁面坐在钩舌尾部顶面，钩锁铁卡在钩舌锁面和钩腔立壁之间，挡住钩舌，使其不能转动。由于上锁销定位凸檐的支点作用，上锁销及上锁销杆呈弓形，上锁销及上锁销杆的防跳台卡住钩锁腔后壁的上防跳台下方，钩锁铁虽然受到振动却不能跳起，此种作用称为车钩的防跳作用。

The tail side of the coupler knuckle is transferred into the coupler cavity, the coupler lock iron falls with its own weight, the locking rear seating surface sits on the lock seat of the knuckle push iron, the locking front seating surface sits on the side of the tail side of the coupler knuckle, the side locking surface sits on the top surface of the tail side of the coupler knuckle, the coupler lock iron is stuck between the coupler knuckle locking surface and the wall of the coupler cavity, blocking the coupler knuckle so that it can not turn. Due to the fulcrum function of the upper locking pin positioning convex eaves, the upper locking pin and the upper locking pin rod are arched, and the upper locking pin and the upper locking pin rod's anti-creep platform are stuck below the upper anti-creep platform on the back wall of the coupler lock cavity. Although the coupler lock iron is subject to vibration, it can not creep. This effect is called the anti-creep effect of the coupler.

钩锁铁的右侧被钩头的内壁所阻挡，而其左侧又挡住了钩舌尾部，使钩舌在钩头内不能绕钩舌销转动，此为闭锁位置。

The right side of the coupler lock iron is blocked by the inner wall of the coupler head, while the left side of the coupler blocks the tail of the coupler knuckle, making it impossible for the coupler knuckle to turn around the coupler knuckle pin in the coupler head, and this is the locking position.

上作用式车钩的闭锁位置如图 6–20 所示。

The locking position of the upper-acting coupler is shown in Figure 6-20.

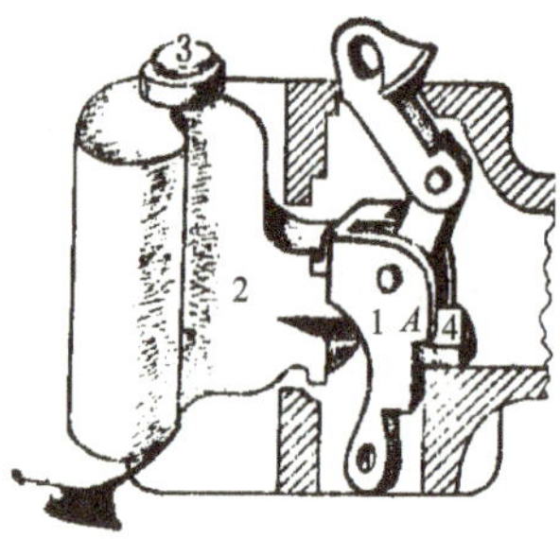

图 6–20　上作用式车钩的闭锁位置

Figure 6-20　Locking Position of Upper-acting Coupler

2）开锁位置

Unlocking position

两连挂着的车辆需要分开时，必须有一个车钩处于开锁位置。

To separate two coupled cars, one coupler is required to be in the unlocking position.

由闭锁位置提起车钩提杆，通过提钩链带动上锁销，上锁销以定位下凸檐为支点旋转，同时上移，带动上锁销杆外转，脱离防跳位置。当继续提起车钩提杆时，上锁销杆则带动钩锁铁上移，越过钩舌尾部；放下车钩提杆时，由于钩锁铁偏重，腿部后移，脚部的开锁坐锁面坐在钩舌推铁的锁座上，使钩锁铁不能落下，形成开锁位置。

Lift the coupler lifting rod from the locking position, and drive the upper locking pin through the lifting hook chain. The upper locking pin rotates with the lower convex eave as the fulcrum, and moves upward at the same time to drive the upper locking pin rod to turn outward and leave the anti-creep position. When continuing to lift the coupler lifting rod, the upper locking pin lever drives the coupler lock iron to move upward and pass over the tail of the coupler knuckle; When putting down the coupler lifting rod, because the coupler lock iron is too heavy, the leg is moved back, and the unlocking seating surface is seated on the locking seat of the knuckle push iron, so that the coupler lock iron cannot fall and the unlocking position is formed.

上作用式车钩的开锁位置如图 6–21 所示。

The unlocking position of the upper-acting couplers is shown in Figure 6-21.

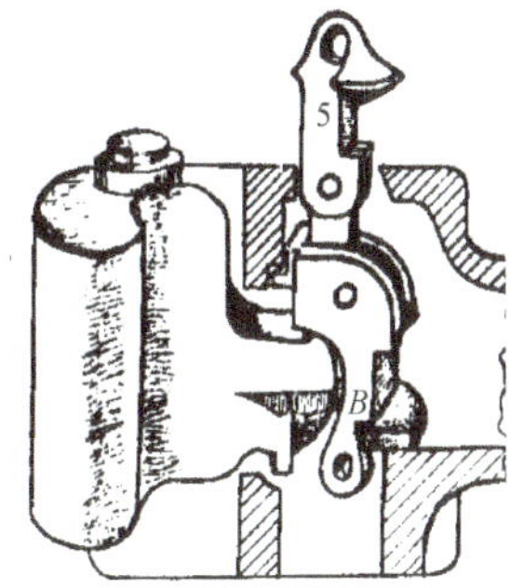

图 6–21 上作用式车钩的开锁位置

Figure 6-21 Unlocking Position of Upper-acting Coupler

3）全开位置

Full-open position

在车辆彼此连挂之前，必须有一个车钩处于全开位置，才能达到自动连挂的目的。

Before railway vehicles are coupled to each other, a coupler must be in the full-open position to achieve the purpose of automatic coupling.

用力提起车钩提杆，通过提钩链带动上锁销及上锁销杆上移，从而带动钩锁铁也充分上移，钩锁铁的全开回转支点以钩锁腔前壁全开作用台为点，脚部向后转动，踢动钩舌推铁，使钩舌推铁绕钩舌推铁轴转动，推铁踢足推动钩舌尾部外侧面，使钩舌以钩舌销为轴向内转动张开，形成全开位置。

Lift the coupler lifting rod forcefully, and drive the upper locking pin and upper locking pin rod to move up through the lifting hook chain, thus driving the coupler lock iron to move up fully. The full-open rotary fulcrum of the coupler lock iron takes the full-open action platform on the front wall of the coupler lock cavity as the point, the foot turns backward, kicks the knuckle push iron, so that the knuckle push iron rotates around the knuckle push iron shaft, and the push iron and kick pushes the outer side of the tail of the coupler knuckle. Make the coupler knuckle turn inward and open with the coupler knuckle pin as the axis to form a full-open position.

当两车连挂时，由于钩舌尾部与坐落在其上的钩锁铁接触部分是一弧面，当钩舌向闭锁位旋转时，使钩锁铁前部往上抬起，钩锁铁下脚 h 处的缺口即可摆脱钩头内挡棱 b，而垂直落下，恢复成闭锁位置。因此，此时只需两车相互碰撞就能实现自动连挂。

In the event that two cars are coupled, as the contact part between the tail of the coupler knuckle and the coupler lock iron located on it is an arc surface, when the coupler knuckle rotates towards the locking position, the front of the coupler lock iron is lifted upward, and the gap at the lower leg h of the coupler lock iron can be freed from the inner retaining rib b of the coupler head and fall down vertically to restore to the locking position. So, it only requires two cars to collide with each other to achieve automatic coupling.

上作用式车钩的全开位置如图 6–22 所示。

The full-open position of the upper-acting couplers is shown in Figure 6-22.

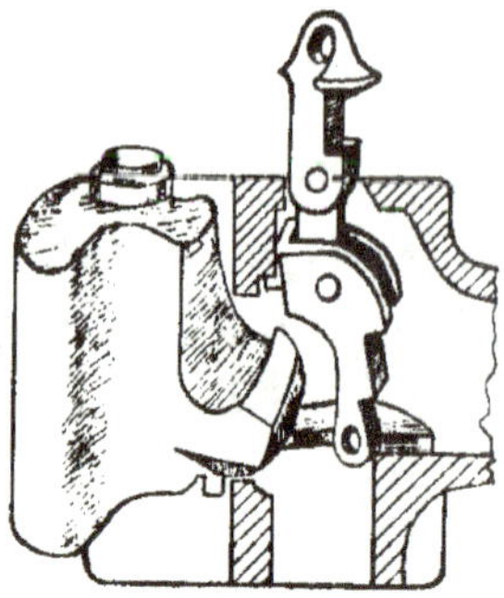

图 6–22　上作用式车钩的全开位置

Figure 6-22　Full-open Position of Upper-acting Coupler

6.2.2　16 型、17 型车钩
No.16 and No.17 couplers

1. 主要结构及技术参数
Main structure and technical parameters

16 型、17 型联锁式固定和转动车钩是为我国大秦线运煤万吨单元列车配置的重要车辆部件，也用于 70 t 级的货车。整个列车固定编组，在卸煤场设有自动列车定位机和翻车机，当装有转动车钩的车辆进入翻车机位翻转卸煤时，可不摘钩连续作业，从而大大缩短了卸货作业的辅助时间，提高了运输效率。

No.16 and No.17 interlocking fixed and rotating couplers are important car components configured for 10,000-ton coal unit trains of China's Datong-Qinhuangdao Railway, which are also used for 70 t grade freight cars. The whole train is in fixed cars, with an automatic train positioning machine and a car dumper provided in the coal unloading yard. When a car equipped with a rotating coupler enters the car dumper position to overturn and unload coal, it can work continuously without uncoupling, thus greatly shortening the auxiliary time for unloading operations and improving transportation efficiency.

运煤敞车（C_{63} 型）一端装 16 型转动车钩，另一端装 17 型固定车钩，整列车上每组相连接的两个车钩，一为转动车钩，一为固定车钩，彼此相互搭配。当车辆进入翻车机位时，翻车机带动待翻车辆以车钩纵向中心线为转轴翻转 180°，被翻转车辆和装有转动车钩的钩尾框相对于转动车钩钩身旋转，转动车钩由于受相邻车辆上与其连挂的固定车钩的约束而静止不动，被翻转车辆另一端的固定车钩带动相邻车辆上与其连挂的转动车钩一起旋转，完成自动卸货作业。翻车作业如图 6–23 所示。

Coal transporting gondola car (C_{63}) is provided with a No.16 rotating coupler at one end and a

No.17 fixed coupler at the other end. Two couplers connected in each group of cars on the entire train include a rotating coupler and a fixed coupler, which are matched with each other. When a car enters the car dumper position, the car dumper drives the car to be overturned to rotate 180° with the longitudinal centerline of the coupler as the rotary shaft. Then the overturned car and the coupler yoke equipped with a rotating coupler rotate relative to the rotating coupler body. Next, the rotating coupler is stationary due to the constraint of the fixed coupler on the adjacent car, while the fixed coupler on the other end of the overturned car drives the rotating coupler on the adjacent car to rotate together with it, thus completing the automatic unloading operation. The tipping operation is shown in Figure 6-23.

(a) 翻车作业准备
Preparation for tipping operation

(b) 翻车作业过程中
Tipping operation in process

图 6–23 翻车作业
Figure 6-23 Tipping Operation

16 型、17 型联锁式固定和转动车钩采用 AAR 标准 F 型连接轮廓，其纵向间隙比一般货车车钩小，为 9.5 mm。车钩连挂后有联锁功能及能够适应车辆翻转作业要求的特点，并且有三态作用和能够与 13 型或 13A 型车钩连挂的性能。16 型、17 型联锁式固定和转动车钩的结构如图 6–24 所示。

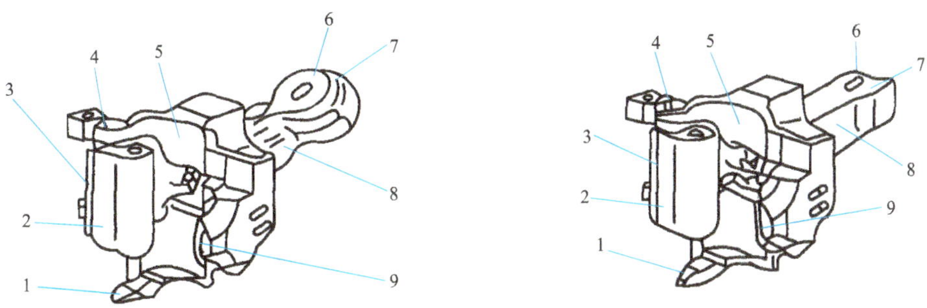

(a) 16号联锁式转动车钩
No. 16 interlocking rotating couple

(b) 17号联锁式固定车钩
No. 17 interlocking fixed coupler

1—联锁辅助支架；2—钩舌；3—联锁套口；4—钩舌销；5—钩头；6—钩尾端面；
7—球台状钩尾（16 型）、钩尾凸肩（17 型）；8—钩身；9—联锁套头。

1—Interlocking auxiliary support; 2—Coupler knuckle; 3—Interlocking socket; 4—Coupler knuckle pin; 5—Coupler head; 6—Coupler tail end surface; 7—Ball table shaped coupler tail (No.16), coupler tail shoulder (No.17); 8—Coupler body; 9—Interlocking sleeve.

图 6–24 16 型、17 型联锁式固定和转动车钩的结构
Figure 6-24 Structure of No.16 and No.17 Interlocking Fixed and Rotating Couplers

No.16 and No.17 interlocking fixed and rotating couplers are connected using AAR standard F-type connection profile, whose longitudinal clearance is 9.5 mm and smaller than general freight car couplers. The couplers are coupled with interlocking functions and can meet the requirements of car tipping operation. Moreover, the couplers are characterized by three-state action and can be linked with No.13 or 13A couplers. The structure of the No.16 and No.17 interlocking fixed and rotating couplers is shown in Figure 6-24.

图 6–25 所示为 16 型转动车钩及其与车体连接部分的旋转系统图。为使车钩相对于车辆底架转动灵活，减少钩身与车钩支承座间的转动阻力，钩身制成圆柱形，并将车钩尾端与从板接触部制成球面。图 6–25 中的转动套可在钩尾框头部直径为 270 mm 的内圆柱体空腔内做 360°回转，转动套的前端由钩尾框的前端凸缘挡住，通过钩尾销将车钩与转动套连成一体，并由钩尾销托托住，钩尾销托装设于钩尾框销托安装槽中并由插销锁定。由于钩尾框内缓冲器的弹力，使车钩尾端的球面紧顶在带有球面凹坑的从板上。当钩头受到扭转力矩的作用时，钩身连同钩尾销及与其连接的转动套相对于钩尾框绕钩身纵向轴线转动。

Figure 6-25 shows the rotating system diagram of No.16 rotating coupler and its connecting part with the car body. For the purpose of making the coupler rotate flexibly relative to the underframe and reducing the rotation resistance between the coupler body and the coupler bearing seat, the coupler body is made into a cylindrical shape, and the contact part between the tail end of the coupler and the slave plate is made into a spherical surface. As shown in the figure 6-25, the rotating sleeve can rotate 360° in the inner cylindrical cavity of the coupler yoke with a head diameter of 270 mm. The front end of the rotating sleeve is blocked by the front flange of the coupler yoke, and the coupler is integrated with the rotating sleeve by the coupler tail pin and held by the coupler tail pin bracket that is installed in the mounting groove of coupler yoke pin bracket and locked by the pin. The spherical surface of the tail end of the coupler is pressed against the slave plate with a spherical pit due to the elasticity of the buffer in the coupler yoke. When the coupler head is subjected to torsional moment, the coupler body together with the coupler tail pin and the rotating sleeve attached to it rotates around the longitudinal axis of the coupler body with respect to the coupler yoke.

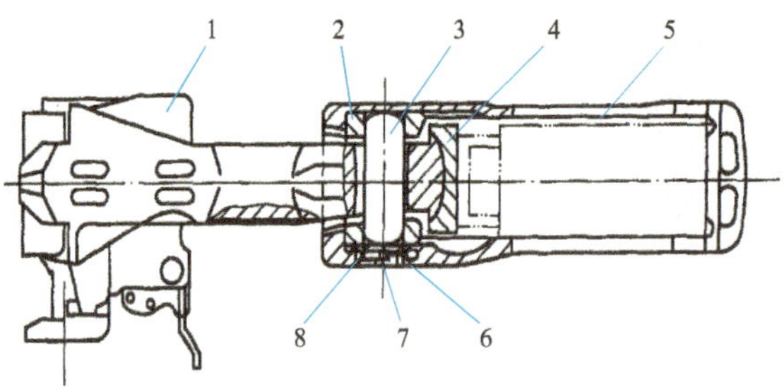

1—钩头；2—转动套；3—钩尾销；4—从板；5—钩尾框；6—钩尾销托；7—开口销；8—插销。

1—Coupler head; 2—Rotating sleeve; 3—Coupler tail pin; 4—Slave plate; 5—Coupler yoke; 6—Coupler tail pin bracket; 7—Cotter pin; 8—Pin.

图 6–25　16 型转动车钩及其与车体连接部分的旋转系统图

Figure 6-25　Rotating System Diagram of No.16 Rotating Coupler and Its Connecting Part with Car Body

16 型车钩的结构如图 6–26 所示。16 型车钩由钩体、钩舌、钩舌推铁、钩舌销、锁铁组成、下锁销转轴和下锁销组成等零部件组成。

The structure of the No.16 coupler is shown in Figure 6-26. The No.16 coupler comprises parts and components such as a coupler body, a coupler knuckle, a coupler knuckle push iron, a coupler knuckle pin, a lock iron, a lower lock pin rotary shaft, and a lower lock pin.

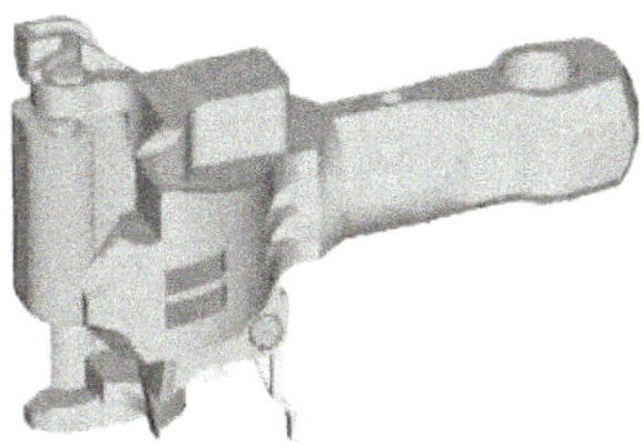

(a) 车钩整体结构图
Overall Structure Diagram of Coupler

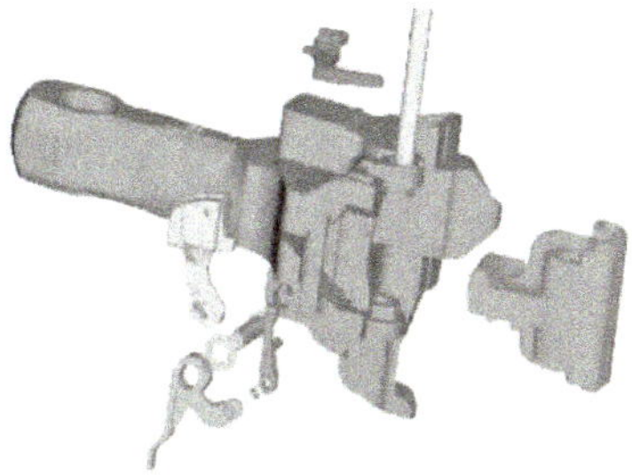

(b) 车钩分散结构图
Coupler Dispersed Structure Diagram

图 6-26 16 型车钩的结构
Figure 6-26 Structure of No.16 Coupler

16 型车钩的部分组成结构如图 6-27 所示。

The partial compositional structure of the No.16 coupler is shown in Figure 6-27.

17 型车钩钩体的钩头部分有联锁套头、联锁套口及防脱装置，钩身的形状与其他车钩相似，为箱形截面，钩尾端面（与从板接触的部位）为半径 133.5 mm 的球面，并在球形端面两侧有自动对中的凸肩。

With regard to the No.17 coupler, the coupler head part of its body is provided with an interlocking sleeve, an interlocking socket, and an anti-falling device. It has a similar coupler body to that of other couplers, with a box-shaped section provided. The coupler tail end surface (the part in contact with the slave plate) is a spherical surface with a radius of 133.5 mm, with automatic centering shoulders on both sides of the spherical end surface.

17 型车钩缓冲装置的结构如图 6-28 所示。

The structure of the No.17 coupler and draft gear device is shown in Figure 6-28.

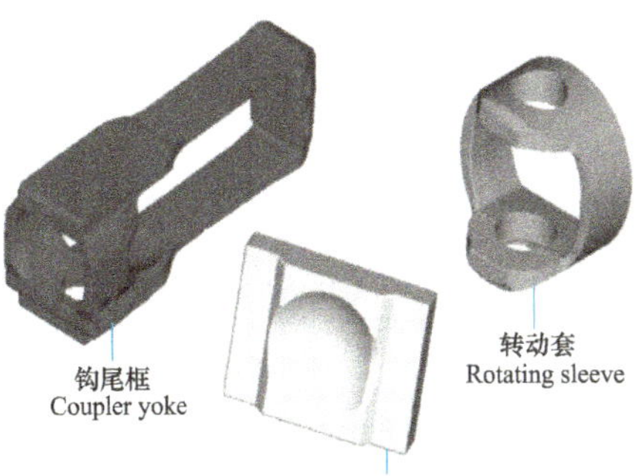

图 6-27 16 型车钩的部分组成结构
Figure 6-27 Partial Compositional Structure of No.16 Coupler

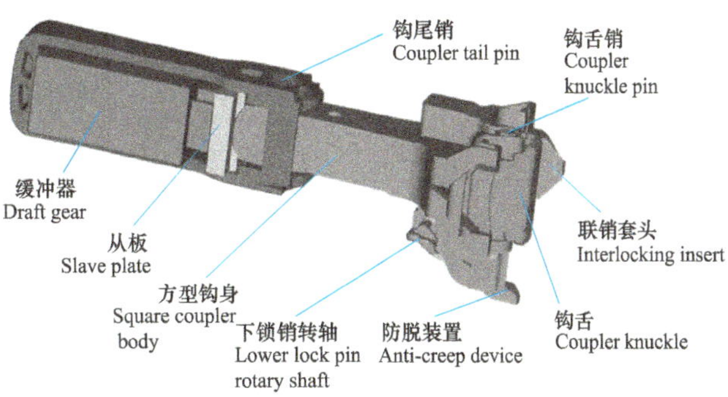

图 6-28 17 型车钩缓冲装置的结构
Figure 6-28 Structure of No.17 Coupler and Draft Gear

17 型车钩的结构如图 6–29 所示。

The structure of the No.17 coupler is shown in Figure 6-29.

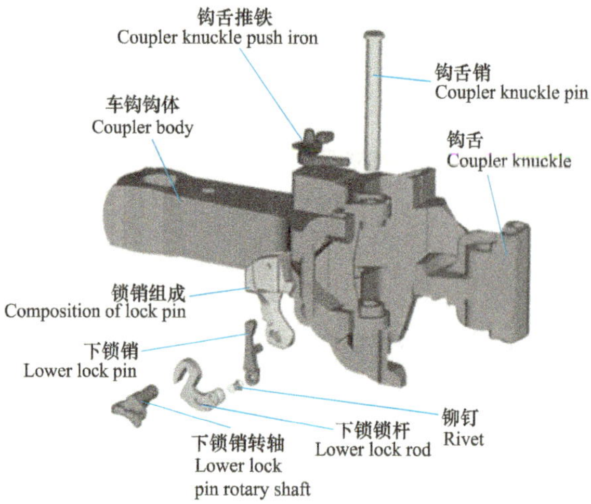

图 6–29　17 型车钩的结构

Figure 6-29　Structure of No.17 Coupler

17 型车钩钩体的结构如图 6–30 所示。

The structure of the No.17 coupler body is shown in Figure 6-30.

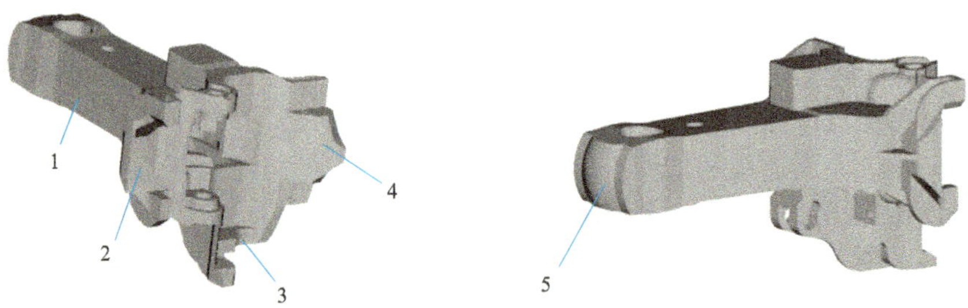

1—箱形钩身；2—联锁套口；3—防脱装置；4—联锁套头；5—球形端面及对正凸肩。

1—Box-shaped coupler body; 2—Interlocking socket; 3—Anti-falling device; 4—Interlocking sleeve; 5—Spherical end surface and alignment shoulder.

图 6–30　17 型车钩钩体的结构

Figure 6-30　Structure of No.17 Coupler Body

17 型车钩配件的结构如图 6–31 所示。

The structure of No.17 coupler accessories is shown in Figure 6-31.

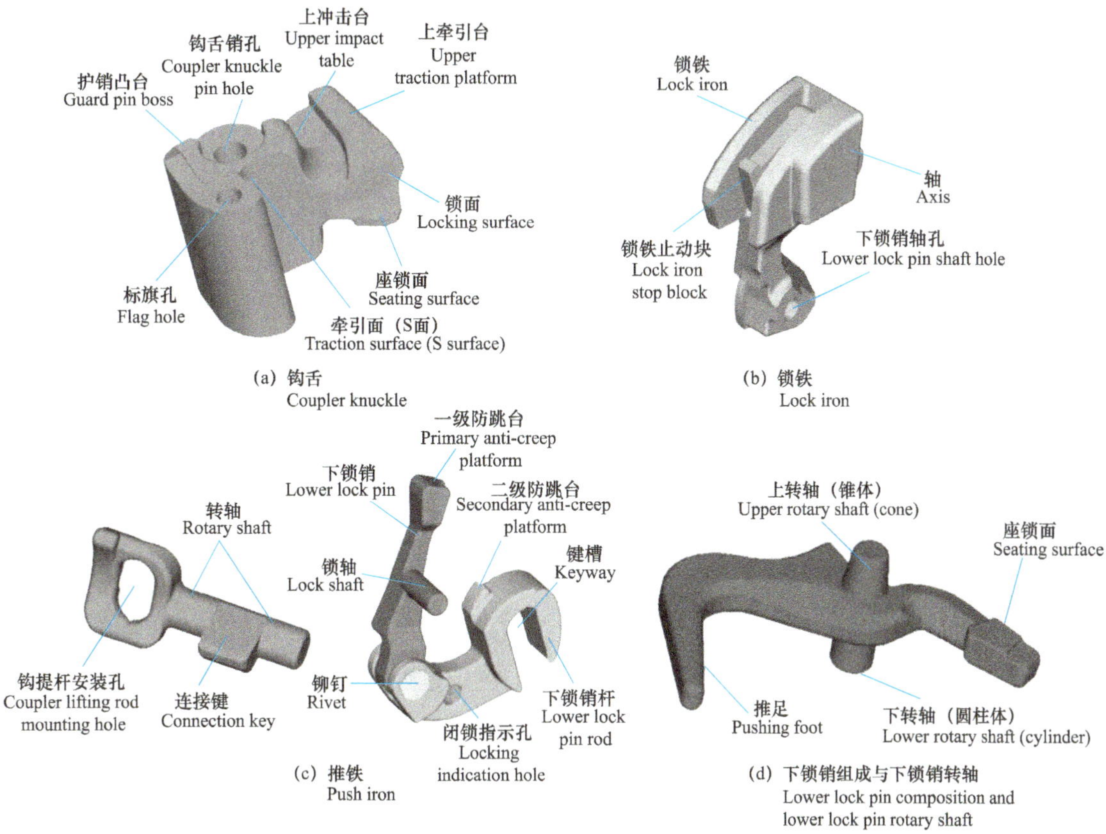

图 6–31　17 型车钩配件的结构

Figure 6-31　Structure of No.17 Coupler Accessories

17 型车钩为联锁式固定车钩，钩头结构与 16 型车钩相同，零件可以互换。17 型车钩与钩尾框的连接与一般车钩相同。

The No.17 coupler is a chain-type fixed coupler with the same coupler head structure as the No.16 coupler, the parts of which can be interchanged. Its connection of No.17 coupler to the coupler yoke is the same as that of a general coupler.

16 型、17 型车钩及钩尾框、转动套、从板等均采用 QG-E1 高强度低合金铸钢制造。钩舌静拉破坏强度达 3 432 kN，钩体与钩尾框达 4 MN 以上。

The No.16 and No.17 couplers, coupler yoke, rotating sleeve, slave plate, etc. are all made of QG-E1 high-strength low-alloy cast steels. The static tensile failure strength of the coupler knuckle can reach 3,432 kN, while the coupler body and coupler yoke can reach over 4 MN.

16 型、17 型车钩的主要技术参数如表 6–3 所示。

The main technical parameters of the No.16 and No.17 couplers are shown in Table 6-3.

表 6-3　16 型、17 型车钩的主要技术参数
Table 6-3　Main Technical Parameters of No.16 and No.17 Couplers

<table>
<tr><th colspan="2" rowspan="2">主要技术参数
Main technical parameters</th><th colspan="2">参数值
Parameter value</th></tr>
<tr><th>16 型车钩
No.16 coupler</th><th>17 型车钩
No.17 coupler</th></tr>
<tr><td colspan="2">车钩有效长度
Effective length of coupler</td><td>732.5 mm</td><td>735 mm</td></tr>
<tr><td colspan="2">钩身长度
Coupler body length</td><td>427.5 mm</td><td>430 mm</td></tr>
<tr><td rowspan="2">最大相对转角
Max. relative rotation angle</td><td>在水平面内
In horizontal plane</td><td colspan="2">13°</td></tr>
<tr><td>在垂直面内
In the vertical plane</td><td colspan="2">向上 5°30′
Upward 5°30′</td></tr>
<tr><td colspan="2">最大纵向移动间隙
Max. longitudinal movement clearance</td><td colspan="2">9.5 mm</td></tr>
<tr><td colspan="2">横向最大连挂范围
Transverse max. coupling range</td><td colspan="2">167 mm</td></tr>
<tr><td rowspan="2">最大垂向移动间隙
Max. vertical movement clearance</td><td>向上
Upward</td><td colspan="2">71 mm</td></tr>
<tr><td>向下
Downward</td><td colspan="2">90.5 mm</td></tr>
</table>

2. 车钩的三态作用

Three-state action of coupler

16 型、17 型车钩的钩头内部结构基本一致，也具有闭锁、开锁、全开 3 种作用位置，即三态作用。在结构上与 13 型和 13A 型车钩的区别是：钩头零件中的钩舌推铁不是竖立地放置在钩头腔内，钩舌带有突出的转轴成水平位置插在钩头腔内相应的孔中。在装配位置方面，钩锁铁不像 2 型车钩那样坐在钩头腔内的台阶上，而是坐在钩舌推铁的一端。16 型、17 型车钩钩头内腔和钩锁铁形状都较复杂，不易检查控制，但具有防分离可靠性高、车钩强度高、耐磨性能好、连挂间隙小、曲线通过性能好、连挂性能好等技术特点。

The No.16 and No.17 couplers have basically the same internal structure on their coupler heads, which are provided with three action positions such as locking, unlocking, and full-open, namely, the three-state action. The difference in structure from No.13 and 13A couplers is that the coupler knuckle push iron in the coupler head parts is not placed vertically in the coupler head cavity, the coupler knuckle is inserted in the corresponding hole in the coupler head cavity with a protruding rotary shaft in a horizontal position. With regard to the assembly position, the coupler lock iron is not placed on the step inside the coupler head cavity like the No.2 coupler, but on the end of the coupler knuckle push iron. Both the coupler head cavity and coupler lock iron of No.16 and No.17 couplers are complicated in shape, which is not easy to check and control, but this coupler is characterized by high reliability of anti-separation, high coupler strength, good wear resistance, small coupling clearance, good curving performance, good coupling performance, and other technical features.

1）闭锁位置

Locking position

车辆连挂后，车钩必须处于闭锁位才能传递牵引力。

The coupler is required to be in the unlocking position to transmit traction after the car is coupled.

当钩舌转动到闭锁位时，锁铁坐于钩舌尾部的座锁面上，钩舌不能绕钩舌销转动打开，车钩处于闭锁位，如图 6–32 所示。

When the coupler knuckle turns to the locking position, the lock iron is placed on the seating surface at the tail of the coupler knuckle, and the coupler knuckle cannot be opened by turning around the coupler knuckle pin, leaving the coupler in the locking position, as shown in Figure 6-32.

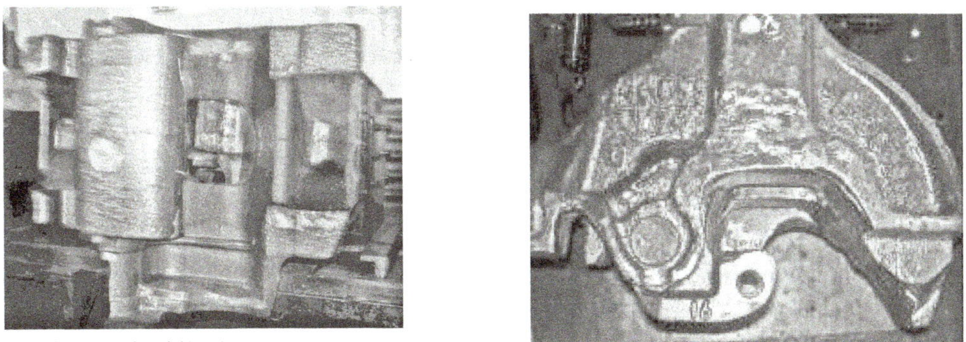

(a) 锁铁坐于钩舌座锁面上

Lock iron placed on the seating surface of the coupler knuckle

(b) 钩舌未打开

Coupler knuckle unopened

图 6–32　车钩处于闭锁位

Figure 6-32　Coupler in Locking Position

2）开锁位置

Unlocking position

两连挂着的车辆需分开时，必须有一个车钩处于开锁位。

To separate the two coupled cars, one coupler is required to be in the unlocking position.

提起车钩提杆手柄，带动锁铁上升到一定的高度，然后放下车钩提杆，锁铁停留在钩舌推铁座锁面上，此时钩舌不能自动打开；如果钩舌受到牵引力就能绕钩舌销转动，此时为开锁位，如图 6–33 所示。

Lift the handle of the coupler lifting rod to raise the lock iron up to a certain height, put down the coupler lifting rod, the lock iron stay in the coupler knuckle push iron seating surface. At this time, the coupler can not automatically open. If the coupler knuckle is subject to traction, the coupler can be turned around the coupler knuckle pin, and the coupler knuckle is in the unlocking position, as shown in Figure 6-33.

(a) 操作车钩提杆
Operate the coupler lifting rod

(b) 钩舌打开
Coupler knuckle open

图 6-33 车钩处于开锁位
Figure 6-33 Coupler in Unlocking Position

3）全开位置
Full-open position

在车钩彼此连挂之前，必须有一个车钩处于全开位，才能进行自动连挂操作。

Before the couplers are coupled to each other, one coupler must be in the full-open position to perform the automatic coupling operation.

继续扳动车钩提杆至极限位置，钩舌绕钩舌销转动打开，此时为全开位，如图 6-34 所示。

The coupler lifting rod is pulled to the limit position, and the coupler knuckle rotates around the coupler knuckle pin to open. Then it is in the fully-open position, which is shown in Figure 6-34.

(a) 操作车钩提杆
Operate the coupler lifting rod

(b) 钩舌转动打开
Coupler knuckle opens by rotating

图 6-34 车钩处于全开位
Figure 6-34 Coupler in Full-open Position

3. 主要技术特点
Main technical features

（1）良好的防跳性能，防分离可靠性高。16 型、17 型车钩具有下锁销防跳和下锁销杆防跳两级防跳功能，与上作用式车钩相比，具有更好的防跳性能。锁铁上部设有防跳止动块，可防止翻车作业时锁铁窜动，从而避免车钩自动开锁。

Good anti-creep performance and high anti-separation reliability. No.16 and No.17 couplers are provided with the two-stage anti-creep function of a lower lock pin and lower lock pin rod, which are better in terms of anti-creep performance compared with the upper-acting couplers. The upper part of the lock iron is provided with anti-creep stop blocks, which can prevent the lock iron from moving during the tipping operation to avoid the automatic unlocking of the coupler.

（2）具有联锁功能和防脱功能。16 型、17 型车钩的钩头部位均设有联锁装置，车钩连挂后可自动实现联锁；在车钩钩头下面设有防脱装置，列车发生事故时仍能保持车钩的连挂性能，防止列车颠覆。

With interlocking function and anti-falling function. The coupler heads of the No.16 and No.17 couplers are provided with an interlocking device, which can automatically achieve interlocking after coupling. Moreover, there is an anti-falling device installed under the coupler head, which can still maintain the coupling performance of the coupler in case of a train accident and prevent the train from overturning.

（3）耐磨性能好。16 型、17 型车钩采用高强度的材质，钩体、钩舌和钩尾框的硬度为 241～311 HBS，车钩的钩尾端面及钩尾销孔后圆弧面经特殊热处理，硬度可达到 375～476 HBS。钩身下平面与车钩支撑座接触部位焊装磨耗板，提高了钩身的耐磨性能。

Good wear resistance. The No.16 and No.17 couplers are made of high-strength materials, with the hardness of the coupler body, coupler knuckle, and coupler yoke being 241–311 HBS. The coupler tail end surface and the back circular arc surface of the coupler tail pin hole are specially heat-treated, with a hardness reaching 375–476 HBS. The contact part between the lower plane of the coupler body and the coupler support seat is welded with a wearing plate, which improves the wear resistance of the coupler body.

（4）车钩强度高。16 型、17 型车钩的结构合理，主要零部件均采用了 TB/T 2942–E 级（与 AAR M201–E 级相当）铸钢制造，钩舌的最小破坏载荷可达到 3 430 kN，钩体的最小破坏载荷可达到 4 005 kN，钩尾框的最小极限载荷为 4 005 kN。

High coupler strength. With reasonable structure, the main parts of the No.16 and No.17 couplers are made of cast steel of TB/T 2942-Grade E (equivalent to AAR M201-Grade E), with a minimum breaking load of 3,430 kN for coupler knuckle, 4,005 kN for coupler body, and 4,005 kN for coupler yoke.

（5）具有自动对中功能，曲线通过性能好。17 型车钩尾部设有自动对中凸肩，可以使车钩在运行中一直保持正位；采用了竖圆钩尾销与钩尾框连接，提高了车辆的曲线通过能力。

Automatic centering function for a good curving performance. No.17 coupler is provided with an automatic centering shoulder at the end of the coupler, which can keep the coupler in a constant positive position during operation. The vertical round coupler tail pin is connected with the coupler yoke, which improves the curve passing ability of the car.

（6）连挂间隙小。16 型、17 型车钩的连挂间隙为 9.8 mm，比 13 型车钩减少了 52%，从而可降低列车的纵向冲击，改善列车的动力学性能，提高铁路货运的安全可靠性，延长车辆的使用寿命。

Small coupling clearance. The coupling clearance of the No.16 and No.17 couplers is 9.8 mm, 52% less than that of the No.13 coupler, thus reducing the longitudinal impact of the train, improving the dynamics of the train, enhancing the safety and reliability of railroad freight, and extending the service life of the car.

（7）连挂性能好。16 型、17 型车钩可与我国现在使用的 13 型、13A 型及 15 型车钩实现正常连挂。

Good coupling performance. The No.16 and No.17 couplers can be coupled with the No.13 coupler, 13A coupler, and No.15 coupler currently used in China.

任务 6.3 客 车 车 钩

Task 6.3 Passenger Car Coupler

6.3.1 15 型车钩

No. 15 coupler

15 型车钩在 20 世纪 90 年代之前用 ZG230-450 铸钢制造；为了提高车钩强度，20 世纪 90 年代后改用 C 级钢（ZG25MnCrNiMo）制造了 15 型高强度车钩，这种车钩的纵向连挂间隙较大（约 27.5 mm），运行时车辆之间的纵向力也较大，严重影响旅客列车的舒适性，也是制约客车提速的重要因素之一。为了改善这种情况，21 世纪初四方车辆研究所研制开发了 15 型小间隙车钩，其纵向连接间隙减小到 3.5～7 mm。目前，15 型高强度车钩主要用于 25B 型、25G 型铁路客车，15 型小间隙车钩主要用于 25G 型、25K 型铁路客车。

No.15 coupler was made of cast steel ZG230-450 before the 1990s, and the No.15 high-strength coupler was made of grade C steel (ZG25MnCrNiMo) after the 1990s to enhance the strength of the coupler, which has a large longitudinal coupling clearance (about 27.5 mm) and a large longitudinal force between cars during movement. It seriously affects the comfort of passenger cars and is one of the factors limiting the speed of the passenger car. To improve this situation, from the beginning of this century, the Sifang Rolling Stock Research Institute developed the No.15 small gap coupler, with its longitudinal connection gap reduced to 3.5–7 mm. At present, No.15 high-strength couplers are mainly applied to 25B and 25G passenger cars, while No.15 small gap couplers are mainly applied to 25G and 25K passenger cars.

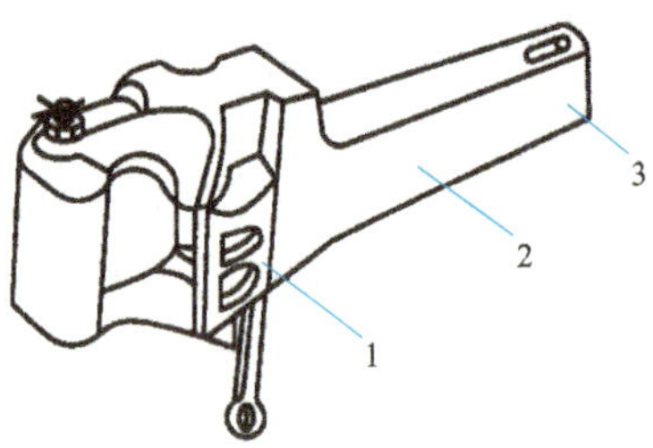

1—钩头；2—钩身；3—钩尾。
1—Coupler head; 2—Coupler body; 3—Coupler tail.

图 6-35 15 型车钩的结构
Figure 6-35 Structure of No.15 Coupler

1. 基本组成

Basic composition

15 型车钩由钩体、钩舌及钩头配件等组成，其中钩体分为钩头、钩身、钩尾三部分，如图 6-35 所示。钩头与钩舌通过钩舌销相连接，钩舌可绕钩舌销转动，钩头内部装有钩锁铁、钩舌推铁、锁销等零件。

The No.15 coupler is composed of a coupler body, coupler knuckle, coupler head fittings, etc., among which the coupler body consists of three parts, namely, a coupler head, coupler body, and coupler tail, as shown in Figure 6-35. The coupler head and the coupler knuckle are connected through the coupler knuckle pins. The coupler knuckle can rotate around the coupler knuckle pin. The coupler head is internally equipped with a coupler lock iron, coupler knuckle push iron, coupler pin, and other parts.

2. 构造及作用

Structure and functions

1）钩体

Coupler body

钩体是车钩的基础部分，其他零件与其配合共同完成车钩的作用，可分为钩头、钩身和钩尾三部分。图 6–36 为 15 型车钩的钩体及配件。

The coupler body is the basic part of the coupler, with which other parts cooperate to complete the function of the coupler. It can be divided into three parts of the coupler head, the coupler body, and the coupler tail. Figure 6-36 represents the coupler body and accessories of the No.15 coupler.

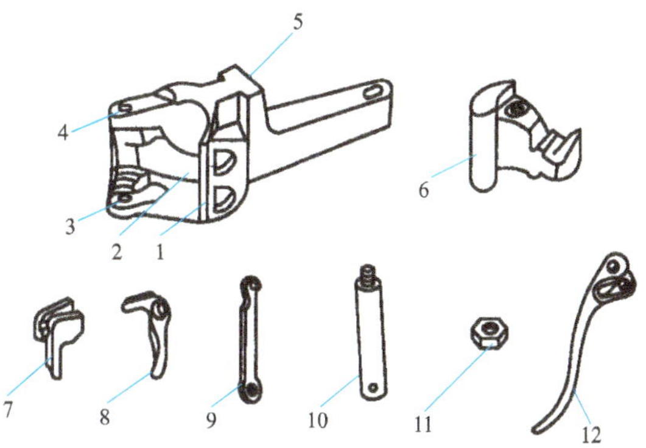

1—钩腕；2—钩锁腔；3—下钩耳孔；5—钩肩；6—钩舌；7—钩锁；8—钩舌推铁；9—下锁销；10—钩舌销；11—销螺母；12—圆棒形下锁销杆。

1—Coupler wrist; 2—Coupler lock cavity; 3—Lower coupler ear hole; 5—Coupler shoulder; 6—Coupler knuckle; 7—Coupler lock; 8—Coupler knuckle push iron; 9—Lower lock pin; 10—Coupler knuckle pin; 11—Pin nut; 12—Round rod-shaped lower lock pin rod.

图 6–36　15 型车钩的钩体及配件

Figure 6-36　Coupler Body and Accessories of No.15 Coupler

2）钩头

Coupler head

钩头是车辆摘挂的重要部分。

The coupler head is an important part of car uncoupling.

（1）钩腕：在两车钩连挂时，可容纳对方钩舌并控制其横向移动。

Coupler wrist: It can accommodate the opposite coupler knuckle and control its lateral movement when two couplers are coupled.

（2）钩锁腔：钩头中空部，安装钩头配件，图 6–37 为 15 型车钩钩锁腔的内部结构。

Coupler lock cavity: The hollow part of the coupler head is used for the installation of the coupler head fittings. The internal structure of the coupler lock cavity of No.15 couplers is shown in Figure 6-37.

（3）钩耳：供安装钩舌用，分上、下钩耳。

Coupler ear: It is used for the installation of coupler knuckles, which can be divided into upper and lower coupler ears.

（4）钩耳孔：供安装钩舌销用。

Coupler ear hole: It is used for the installation of the coupler knuckle pin.

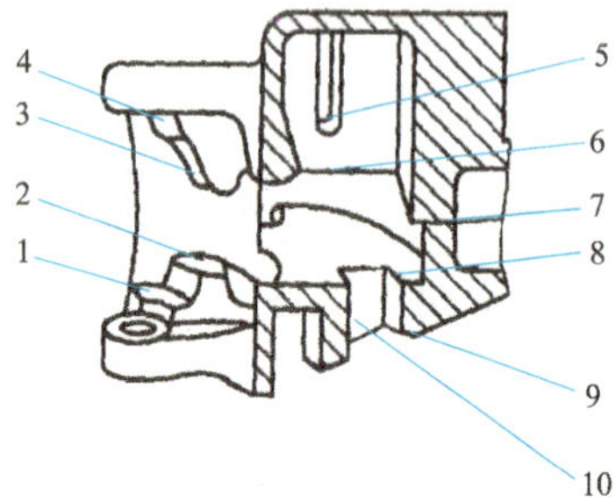

1—下冲击凸肩；2—下牵引凸缘；3—上牵引凸缘；4—上冲击凸肩；5—钩舌推铁槽；6—导向挡；7—上防脱（跳）台；8—开锁坐面；9—下防脱（跳）台；10—下锁销孔。

1—Lower impact shoulder; 2—Lower traction flange; 3—Upper traction flange; 4—Upper impact shoulder; 5—Coupler knuckle push iron groove; 6—Guide block; 7—Upper anti-falling (anti-creep) platform; 8—Unlocking seating surface; 9—Lower anti-falling (anti-creep) platform; 10—Lower lock pin hole.

图 6-37　15 型车钩钩锁腔的内部结构

Figure 6-37　Internal Structure of Coupler Lock Cavity of No.15 Coupler

（5）钩肩：车辆发生较大冲击时，钩肩与冲击座接触，使部分冲击力直接传递给底架，避免缓冲器破损。

Coupler shoulder: In the case of a large impact on the car, the coupler shoulder contacts the impact seat to let part of the impact force be directly transmitted to the underframe, to avoid damage to the buffer.

（6）下锁销孔：供安装下锁销用，也是锁脚起落的孔。

Lower lock pin hole: It is used for the installation of the lower lock pin and is also the hole for lifting and lowering the lock foot.

（7）钩身：传递牵引力和冲击力的部位，做成中空方形结构，具有较大的强度和刚度。

The coupler body: It is the part that transmits traction and impact force. It is a hollow square structure with greater strength and stiffness.

（8）钩尾：供安装钩尾框用，其上开有钩尾销孔，钩尾端面为圆弧面。

The coupler tail: It is used for installing the coupler yoke. The coupler tail is provided with a coupler tail pin hole, with a circular arc surface end surface.

15 型车钩钩体上铸有型号等标志，如图 6-38 所示。

The model and other marks cast on the coupler body of the No.15 coupler are shown in Figure 6-38.

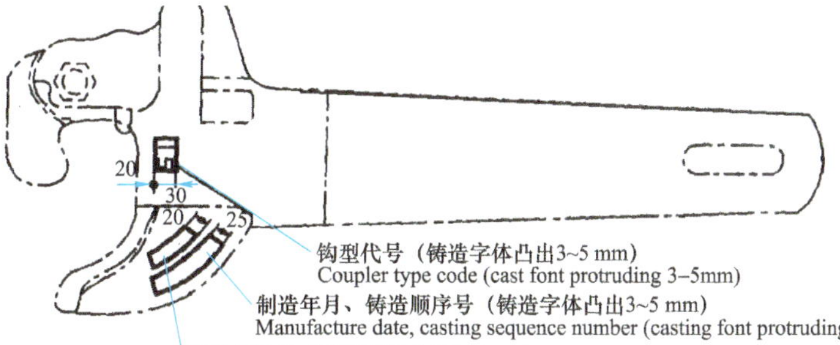

图 6–38 15 型车钩钩体铸造标志
Figure 6-38 Casting Mark of No.15 Coupler Body

3）钩舌及钩舌销

Coupler knuckle and coupler knuckle pin

钩舌装在上、下钩耳之间，插入钩舌销后以钩舌销为轴而转动；利用钩舌的开闭可进行车辆互相连挂和摘解。15 型车钩钩舌的结构如图 6–39 所示，其上有牵引突缘，传递牵引力。

The coupler knuckle is installed between the upper and lower coupler ears, which rotates with the coupler knuckle pin as the axis after inserting the coupler knuckle pin. The opening and closing of the coupler knuckle can be used for car coupling and uncoupling. The structure of the coupler knuckle of the No.15 coupler is shown in Figure 6-39, with traction lugs on it to transmit traction.

钩舌销穿过钩耳孔及钩舌销孔，将钩舌与钩体联系在一起，钩舌可绕其转动。正常情况下，钩舌销不受牵引力、冲击力，仅起到转轴作用。

The coupler knuckle pin passes through the coupler ear hole and the coupler knuckle pin hole to connect the coupler knuckle and the coupler body, and the coupler knuckle can rotate around the coupler knuckle pin. Normally, the coupler knuckle pin is not subject to traction or impact forces and only acts as a pivot.

4）钩头内部零件

Internal parts of coupler head

钩头内部零件包括钩锁铁、钩舌推铁和下锁销。

It includes a coupler lock iron, a coupler knuckle push iron, and a lower lock pin.

（1）钩锁铁。装在钩锁腔内钩舌尾部侧面，在闭锁位置时挡住钩舌尾部，起锁钩作用，在全开位置时推动钩舌推铁而使钩舌张开。其背部及两侧均为垂直平面，并有导向面，与钩锁腔内的导向壁吻合，借以保持钩锁铁上、下移动时的正位。钩锁铁下部为锁脚，锁脚下部有开锁坐锁面。在开锁位置时，钩锁铁由于偏心向前倾斜，锁脚向后翘，开锁坐锁面恰好落在钩头内开锁坐锁面上。钩锁铁背部有锁销作用槽，其中内有十字销凹槽，使下锁销的十字销在其上、下滑动。钩锁铁的结构如图 6–40 所示。

Coupler lock iron. It is installed on the tail side of the coupler knuckle in the coupler lock cavity, which blocks the coupler knuckle tail at the locked position to lock the coupler and pushes the coupler knuckle push iron to open the coupler knuckle at the full-open position. The back and both sides of the coupler lock are vertical planes with guide surfaces that coincide with the guide walls in the coupler lock cavity to maintain the correct position of the coupler lock when the coupler lock iron moves up and down. The lower part of the coupler lock iron is a lock foot, the lower part of which is provided with an unlocking seating surface. At the unlocking position, the coupler lock iron tilts forward and the lock foot tilts backward due to deviation from the center of gravity, causing the unlocking seating surface to fall right on the unlocking seating surface inside the coupler head. The back of the coupler lock iron is provided with a lock pin action groove, in which a cross pin groove is provided to slide the cross pin of the lower lock pin up and down. The structure of the coupler lock iron is shown in Figure 6-40.

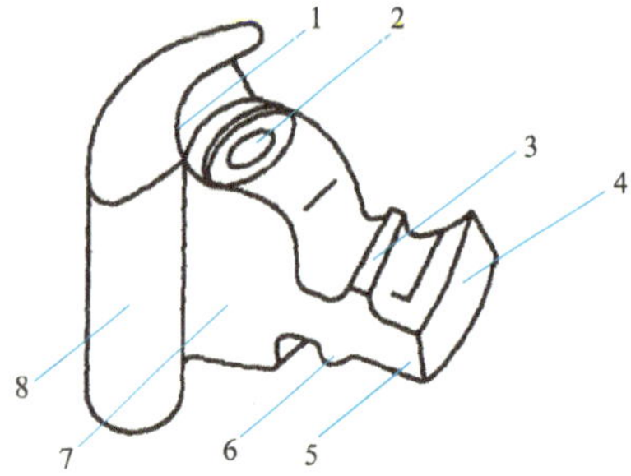

1—钩腕牵引面；2—钩舌销孔；3—上牵引凸缘；4—钩舌尾端面；5—钩舌锁面；6—下牵引凸缘；7—内腕；8—钩舌鼻。

1—Coupler wrist traction surface; 2—Coupler knuckle pin hole; 3—Upper traction flange; 4—Coupler knuckle tail end surface; 5—Coupler knuckle lock surface; 6—Lower traction flange; 7—Inner wrist; 8—Coupler knuckle nose.

图 6-39　15 型车钩钩舌的结构

Figure 6-39　Structure of No.15 Coupler Knuckle

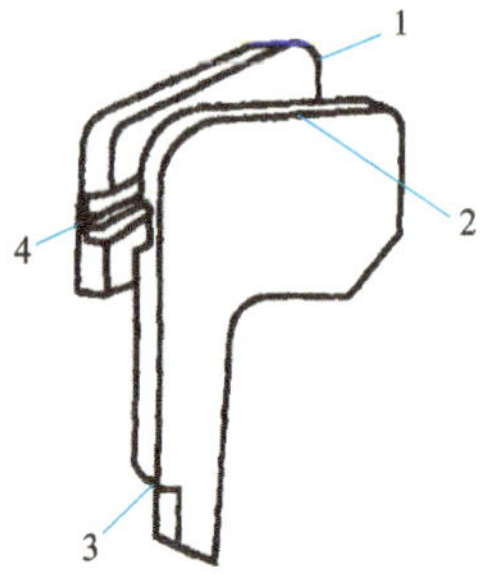

1—导向角；2—全开作用面；3—开锁座锁面；4—锁销作用槽（十字销凹槽）。

1—Guide angle; 2—Full-open action surface; 3—Unlocking seating surface; 4—Lock pin action groove (cross pin groove).

图 6-40　15 型车钩钩锁铁的结构

Figure 6-40　Structure of No.15 Coupler Lock Iron

（2）钩舌推铁。悬挂在钩腔内，上部嵌入钩舌推铁槽内，下端靠在钩舌尾部侧面，全开位置时能够踢动钩舌转动。钩舌推铁的结构如图 6-41 所示。

Coupler knuckle push iron. It is suspended in the coupler cavity, with its upper part embedded in the knuckle push iron groove, and its lower end leans against the coupler knuckle tail side. The coupler knuckle can be kicked to rotate when it is in the full-open position. The structure of the coupler knuckle push iron is shown in Figure 6-41.

（3）下锁销及下锁销杆。下锁销在其一端两侧有圆柱形十字销，置于钩锁背部十字销凹槽内，以便推起钩锁铁。端部除十字销外，还有防脱（跳）止端，以便在闭锁位置起防脱（跳）作用（见图 6-42）。下锁销杆是下作用式车钩用以保持下锁销正确作用位置的配件，一端安装在钩舌销下部，另一端与下锁销及下作用式车钩提杆套装在一起。

Lower lock pin and lower lock pin rod. The lower lock pin is provided with a cylindrical cross pin on both sides of its end, which is placed in the cross pin groove on the back of the coupler lock to push up the coupler lock iron. In addition to the cross pin, there is also an end provided with an anti-falling (anti-creep) stop end for the anti-falling (anti-creep) function at the locked position (see Figure 6-42). The lower lock pin rod is an accessory for a lower-acting coupler to maintain the correct position of the lower lock pin. One end of the lower lock rod is installed at the lower part of the coupler knuckle pin, while the other end is packaged with the lower lock pin and the lower-acting coupler lifting rod.

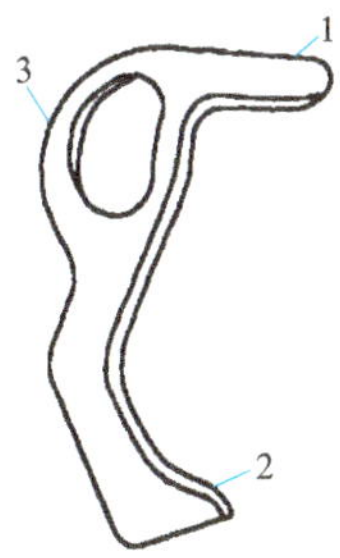

1—全开作用端；2—推铁踢足；3—全开支点。
1—Full-open action end; 2—Push iron and kick; 3—Full-open fulcrum.

图 6-41　15 型车钩钩舌推铁的结构
Figure 6-41　Structure of No.15 Coupler Knuckle Push Iron

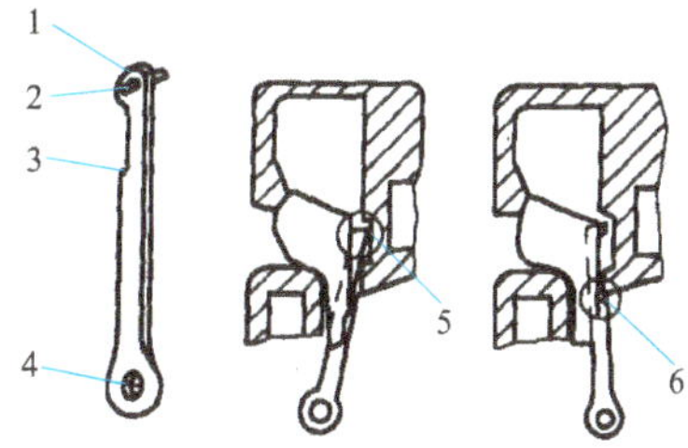

1—上防脱（跳）止端；2—十字销；3—下防脱（跳）止端；4—下锁销杆销孔；5—上防脱（跳）位置；6—下防脱（跳）位置。
1—Upper anti-falling (creeping) stop end; 2—Cross pin; 3—Lower anti-falling (creeping) stop end; 4—Lower lock pin rod pin hole; 5—Upper anti-falling (creeping) position; 6—Lower anti-falling (creeping) position.

图 6-42　下锁销及其在钩腔内的状态
Figure 6-42　Lower Lock Pin and Its Status in Coupler Cavity

3. 车钩的三态作用
Three-state action of coupler

车钩的自动连挂和自动摘解是通过它的三态作用完成的。当钩体内钩舌、钩锁铁、钩舌推铁、锁销等零件处于不同位置时，可使车钩具有开锁、闭锁、全开 3 种作用，俗称三态作用。

The automatic coupling and uncoupling of the coupler are carried out by its “three-state” action. It means that the coupler is provided with three functions when the coupler knuckle, coupler lock iron, coupler knuckle push iron, lock pin, and other parts within the coupler body are in different positions, namely, unlocking, locking, and full-open, which is collectively known as the “three-state” action.

1）闭锁位置
Locking position

车辆连挂后，两个车钩均须处于闭锁位置时才能传递牵引力。

After the car is coupled, both couplers have to be in the locked position to transfer traction.

钩舌转入钩锁腔内，钩锁铁靠自重落下，坐在钩锁腔底部，卡在钩舌尾部侧面和钩锁腔侧壁之间，挡住钩舌的转动。这时，下锁销沿着钩锁背部的锁销槽下滑，下锁销的上防跳台卡在钩锁腔后壁防跳台下；下防跳台卡在下锁销孔的后缘下防跳台处，起防跳作用，形成闭锁位置，如图 6-43 所示。

The coupler knuckle is rotated into the coupler lock cavity, and the coupler lock iron falls by its own weight and is placed at the bottom of the coupler lock cavity, where it is stuck between the tail side of the coupler knuckle and the side wall of the coupler lock cavity, blocking the rotation of the coupler knuckle. Then, the lower lock pin slides along the lock pin slot on the back of the coupler lock, and the upper anti-creep platform of the lower lock pin is stuck under the anti-creep platform on the rear wall of the coupler lock cavity, while the lower anti-creep platform is stuck at the lower anti-creep platform at the trailing edge of the lower lock pin hole to act as anti-creep and form a locking position, which is shown in Figure 6-43.

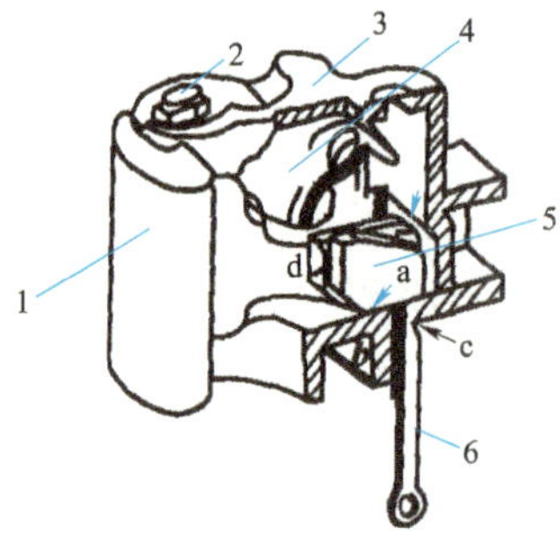

1—钩舌；2—钩舌销；3—钩头；4—钩舌推铁；5—钩锁铁；6—下锁销。

1—Coupler knuckle; 2—Coupler knuckle pin; 3—Coupler head; 4—Coupler knuckle push iron; 5—Coupler lock iron; 6—Lower lock pin.

图 6-43　15 型车钩的闭锁位置

Figure 6-43　Locking Position of No.15 Coupler

2）开锁位置

Unlocking position

两连挂着的车辆需要分开时，必须有一个车钩处于开锁位置。

To separate two coupled cars, one coupler is required to be in the unlocking position.

由闭锁位置提起车钩提杆，推动下锁销，锁销轴沿着钩锁背部的锁销槽上移，使下锁销上、下防跳台脱离防跳位置；当下锁销继续上移时，则顶动钩锁铁上移；由于钩锁铁的偏重上部向前倾转，而腿部向后转动，当放下车钩提杆时，钩锁的开锁坐锁面就坐在下锁销孔后部的锁座上，钩锁不能落下，形成开锁位置，如图 6-44 所示。这时，只要两辆车向相反的方向运动，就可以将相互连挂的车辆分开。

By lifting the coupler lift rod from the locking position and pushing the lower lock pin, the lock pin shaft moves up along the lock pin groove on the back of the coupler lock, removing the upper and lower anti-creep platforms of the lower lock pin from the anti-creep position; As the lower lock pin remains upward, the jacking coupler lock also moves up; As the weighted upper part of the coupler lock iron tilts forward while the legs turn backward, the unlocking seating surface of the coupler lock is placed at the lock seat at the rear of the lower lock pin hole, with the coupler lock cannot falling, resulting in an unlocking position, as shown in Figure 6-44. At this time, as long as the two cars are moving in opposite directions, the coupled cars can be separated.

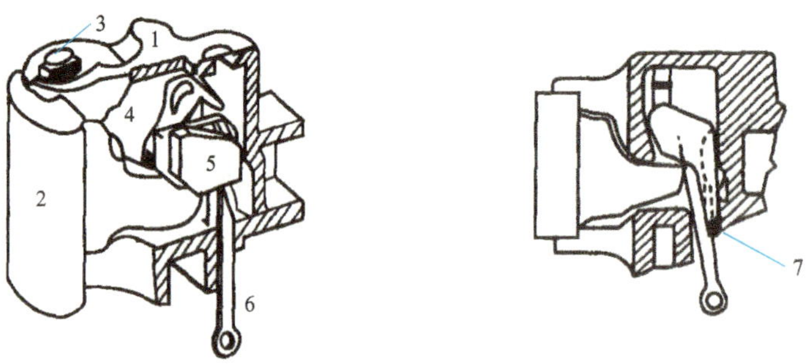

1—钩头；2—钩舌；3—钩舌销；4—钩舌推铁；5—钩锁铁；6—下锁销；7—开锁坐锁面位置。

1—Coupler head; 2—Coupler knuckle; 3—Coupler knuckle pin; 4—Coupler knuckle push iron; 5—Coupler lock iron; 6—Lower lock pin; 7—Position of unlocking seating surface.

图 6-44　15 型车钩的开锁位置

Figure 6-44　Unlocking Position of No.15 Coupler

3）全开位置

Full-open position

在车辆彼此连挂之前，必须有一个车钩处于全开位置，才能达到自动连挂的目的。

Before railway vehicles are coupled to each other, a coupler must be in the full-open position to achieve the purpose of automatic coupling.

由闭锁位或开锁位用力提起车钩提杆，使钩锁被充分顶起，钩锁的全开作用面顶动钩舌推铁的全开作用端，钩舌推铁以背部全开支点和钩锁腔内壁接触面为支点回转，其下部推铁踢足踢动钩舌尾部侧面，使钩舌以钩舌销为轴转动张开，放下车钩提杆后，钩锁铁靠自重落下，坐在钩舌尾部上，形成全开位置，如图 6–45 所示。

By lifting the coupler lift rod with force from the locking position or the unlocking position, the coupler lock is fully jacked up, with the full-open action surface of the coupler lock topping the full-open action end of the coupler knuckle push iron. Then the coupler knuckle push iron rotates with the full-open fulcrum on the back and the contact surface of the inner wall of the coupler lock cavity as the fulcrum, and the lower push iron and kick kicks the side of the coupler knuckle tail, so that the coupler knuckle rotates and opens with the coupler knuckle pin as the axis. After lowering the coupler lift rod, the coupler lock iron falls by its own weight on the coupler knuckle tail, forming a full-open position as shown in Figure 6-45.

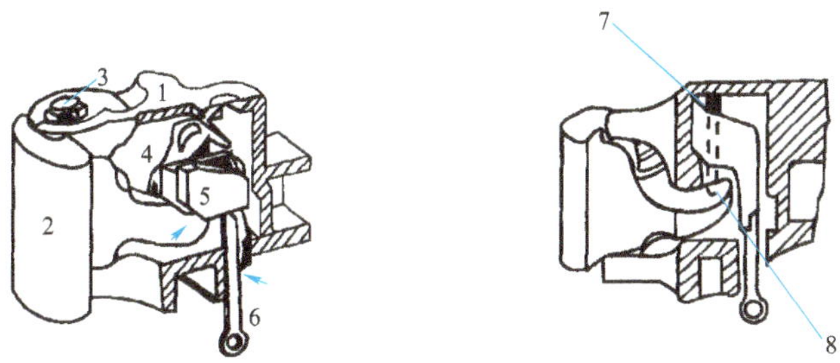

1—钩头；2—钩舌；3—钩舌销；4—钩舌推铁；5—钩锁铁；6—下锁销；
7—钩锁顶动钩舌推铁；8—钩舌推铁踢动钩舌尾。

1—Coupler head; 2—Coupler knuckle; 3—Coupler knuckle pin; 4—Coupler knuckle push iron; 5—Coupler lock iron; 6—Lower lock pin; 7—Coupler lock jacks coupler knuckle push iron; 8—Coupler knuckle push iron kicks the coupler knuckle tail.

图 6–45　15 型车钩的全开位置

Figure 6-45　Full-open Position of No.15 Coupler

6.3.2　密接式车钩

Tight-lock couplers

对于高速列车、城市地铁和轻轨车辆的车钩缓冲装置，常采用机械气路、电路均能同时实现自动连挂的密接式车钩。这种车钩属刚性自动车钩，要求在两钩连挂后，其间没有上下和左右的移动，而且纵向间隙也限制在很小的范围之内（约 1～2 mm）。这对提高列车运行平稳性、降低车钩零件的磨耗和噪声均有重要意义。

The coupler and draft gear of high-speed trains, urban subways, and light rail cars often use a tight-lock coupler that can automatically couple both mechanical and electrical circuits at the same time. This type of coupler is a rigid automatic coupler, which requires no movement up and down or left and right after the two couplers are coupled, as well as restriction of the longitudinal clearance to a small range (about 1–2 mm). This is significant for improving the smoothness of train operation and reducing the wear and noise of coupler parts.

密接式车钩的构造和工作原理与上述的一般车钩完全不同，目前国内外常见的有以下 4 种结构形式。

The structure and working principle of the tight-lock coupler are quite different from the above-mentioned general couplers, and there are four common structural forms at home and abroad.

（1）MJGH-25T 型密接式车钩。

MJGH-25T tight-lock coupler.

（2）日本新干线高速列车上所采用的柴田式密接式车钩。我国北京地铁车辆的车钩即属此种车钩。

The Shibata-type tight-lock couplers used on high-speed trains on Shinkansen in Japan, are also used on Beijing metro cars in China.

（3）德国的沙库（Schafenberg）型密接式车钩，常见于欧洲国家所制造的地铁、轻轨及高速车辆上。德国制造的上海地铁车辆亦装用这种车钩。

Schafenberg tight-lock couplers from Germany, which are commonly used on metro, light rail, and high-speed cars made in European countries, are also used in Shanghai metro cars made in Germany.

（4）德国的 BSI-COMPACT 型密接式车钩。

BSI-COMPACT tight-lock coupler from Germany.

任务 6.4　缓冲器
Task 6.4　Buffer

6.4.1　缓冲器的类型、结构及性能
Type, structure and performance of buffer

缓冲器的作用是用来缓和列车在运行中由于机车牵引力的变化或在起动、制动及调车作业时车辆相互碰撞而引起的纵向冲击和振动，有消散车辆之间冲击和振动能量的功能，从而减轻对车体结构和装载货物的破坏作用，提高列车运行的平稳性。

The buffer is used to alleviate the longitudinal impact and vibration arising from the changes in locomotive traction during train operation or car collisions during starting, braking, and switching operations. The buffer serves to dissipate the impact and vibration energy between cars, to reduce the damage to the car structure and loaded goods, and improve the smoothness of train operation.

缓冲器的工作原理是借助于压缩弹性元件来缓和冲击作用力，同时在弹性元件变形过程中利用金属摩擦、液压阻尼和胶质阻尼等吸收冲击能量。

The working principle of the buffer is to alleviate the impact force by means of compression of the elastic element and absorption of the impact energy by using metal friction, hydraulic damping, and gum damping during the deformation process of the elastic element.

根据缓冲器的结构特征和工作原理，一般可将缓冲器分为弹簧式缓冲器、摩擦式缓冲器、橡胶缓冲器、摩擦橡胶式缓冲器、弹性胶泥缓冲器、液压缓冲器及空气缓冲器等。目前应用最广泛的是摩擦式缓冲器和摩擦橡胶式缓冲器。这两种缓冲器具有结构简单、制造方便、成本低的优点。随着我国铁路的几次大提速，对缓冲器的容量和阻抗力要求越来越高，根据车辆使用要求的多样化，缓冲器的多样化、系列化要求已经成为共识，近年来弹性橡胶泥缓冲器也因此得到了发展和运用。

The buffers can be generally classified into the following types based on their structural features and working principles: spring buffers, friction buffers, rubber buffers, friction rubber buffers, elastic clay draft gears, hydraulic buffers, air buffers, etc. At present, friction buffers and friction rubber buffers are the types most widely used. These two buffers have the advantages of simple structure, convenient manufacturing, and low cost. As China's railroads have increased speed several times, the capacity and impedance of buffers have become increasingly demanding. Due to the diverse requirements for car use, the diversification and serialization requirements of buffers have become a consensus, which has led to the development and application of elastic rubber clay buffers in recent years.

以前我国铁路车辆上所采用的缓冲器，客车上为 1 号缓冲器，货车上为 2 号缓冲器、MX-1 缓冲器和 3 号缓冲器等。3 号缓冲器容量太小，性能不稳，基本上已被淘汰。为了改进现有的几种缓冲器的性能，以满足铁路运输发展的要求，因而提出了多种改进方案，如 G1 型、G2 型等，在保持原 1 号缓冲器、2 号缓冲器等结构形式基本不变的前提下，增大了容量，改善了性能。

In the past, the buffers used on China's railway cars were No.1 buffers on passenger cars, No.2 buffers, MX-1 buffers and No.3 buffers on freight cars. Since the No.3 buffer is small in capacity and unstable in performance, it is basically eliminated. To improve the performance of several existing buffers to meet the requirements of railway transportation development, various improvement schemes have been proposed, such as G1 type, G2 type, etc., to increase the capacity and improve the performance while leaving the original structural forms such as No.1 buffers, No.2 buffers and other structural forms basically unchanged.

随着我国列车运行速度和牵引总重的提高，5 000～6 000 t 的重载货物列车和万吨单元列车得以开行，对缓冲器容量、性能提出了更高的要求，诸多缓冲器已经不能适应运输发展的需要。20 世纪 90 年代我国借鉴美国 Mark-50 型缓冲器的技术研制的 MT-2 型、MT-3 型缓冲器已投入批量生产，满足了我国重载列车和单元列车对缓冲器的要求。2006 年以来，我国在运煤专线上开行了 20 000 t 级的重载货物列车，对缓冲器提出了更进一步的高要求。

The increase in train speed and traction weight in China and the operation of heavy-haul freight cars of 5,000–6,000 t and 10,000-ton unit trains demand higher buffer capacity and performance, and many buffers can no longer meet the needs of transportation development. For example, in the 1990s, MT-2 and MT-3 buffers developed by China with the technology of

American Mark-50 buffers have been put into mass production to meet the requirements of buffers for heavy-haul freight cars and unit trains in China. Heavy-haul freight cars of 20,000 t grade have been running on special coal transportation lines in China since 2006, which demands high requirements for buffers.

我国铁道车辆强度设计规范规定货车结构允许的最大纵向力为 2.25 MN，要求货车缓冲器的最大阻抗力不大于 2 000～2 500 kN，容量不小于 45～100 kJ，客车缓冲器的最大阻抗力为 800 kN，容量不小于 20 kJ。因此，我国货车缓冲器应该是低阻抗、大容量的，为此应在钩肩间隙允许范围内尽可能地增大缓冲器的行程（例如可将行程增大至 80～100 mm），以限制最大作用力。

The specification for strength design and test appraisement for railway vehicle specifies that the maximum longitudinal force allowed for freight car structures should be 2.25 MN. It is required that the maximum impedance force for freight car buffers should be not greater than 2,000–2,500 kN, the capacity should be not less than 45–100 kJ, while the maximum impedance force for passenger car buffers should be 800 kN, and the capacity should be not less than 20 kJ. Therefore, freight car buffers in China should have low impedance and large capacity, that is, the stroke of the buffer should be increased as much as possible within the allowable range of coupler shoulder clearance (for example, the stroke can be increased to 80–100 mm) to limit the maximum force.

6.4.2 缓冲器的主要性能参数及容量确定 Determination of Main Performance Parameters and Capacity of Buffers

缓冲器的性能直接影响着列车的牵引总重、运行速度、车辆的总重、编组作业效率、货物的完好率等涉及铁路运输效能的主要技术经济指标。决定缓冲器特性的主要参数是缓冲器的行程、最大作用力、容量、初压力及能量吸收率等。

The performance of the buffer directly affects main technical and economic indicators related to the effectiveness of railroad transportation, such as the total tractive weight of the train, the operating speed, the gross weight of the train, the efficiency of the grouping operation, and the intactness of the cargo. The main parameters determining the characteristics of the buffer are the stroke, maximum force, capacity, initial pressure and energy absorption rate of the buffer.

（1）行程：缓冲器受力后产生的最大变形量称为行程。此时，弹性元件处于全压缩状态，如再加大外力，变形量也不再增加。

Stroke: The maximum deformation of the buffer after being subjected to the force is called the stroke. The elastic element is in full compression at this moment, and its deformation will no longer increase if the external force is increased.

（2）最大作用力：缓冲器产生最大变形量时所对应的作用外力。

Maximum force: The external force corresponding to the maximum deformation of the buffer.

（3）容量：缓冲器在全压缩过程中，作用力在其行程上所做的功的总和称为容量。容量是衡量缓冲器能量大小的主要指标。如果容量太小，当冲击力较大时就会使缓冲器全压缩而导致车辆受到刚性冲击。

Capacity: The sum of the work done by the force on its stroke during the full compression is called the capacity. The capacity is the main indicator for measuring the energy level of the buffer. If it is too small, the buffer will be fully compressed and lead to a rigid impact on the car when the impact force is large.

（4）初压力：缓冲器的静预压力。初压力的大小影响列车的纵向舒适度。

Initial pressure: the static preload of the buffer. The initial pressure will affect the comfort of the train in the longitudinal direction.

（5）能量吸收率：缓冲器在全压缩过程中，有一部分能量被阻尼所消耗，其所消耗部分的能量与缓冲器容量之比称为能量吸收率。能量吸收率越大，缓冲器吸收冲击能量的能力就越大，反冲作用就越小，否则，缓冲器必须往复工作几次方能将冲击能量消耗尽，这将导致车钩、车底架过早疲劳损伤，并且加剧列车的纵向冲击。根据使用要求，缓冲器的吸收率也不能设计为 100%，一般要求能量吸收率不低于 70%。

Energy absorption rate: During the full compression process of a buffer, some of the energy is consumed by damping, and the ratio of the consumed energy to the buffer capacity is called the energy absorption rate. The greater the energy absorption rate, the stronger the ability of the buffer to absorb the impact energy, and the smaller the recoil effect, or else the buffer must work several times to consume the impact energy, resulting in premature fatigue damage to the coupler and underframe, and increasing the longitudinal impact of the train. The buffer's absorption rate cannot be designed to be 100% according to the usage requirements, which generally require the energy absorption rate to be no less than 70%.

表 6–4 为我国采用的几种主型缓冲器和改进型缓冲器的性能参数。

Table 6-4 shows the performance parameters of several main and improved buffers used in China.

表 6–4　我国采用的几种主型缓冲器和改进型缓冲器的性能参数

Table 6–4　Performance Parameters of Several Main and Improved Buffers Used in China

缓冲器型号 Buffer model	1 号 No. 1	2 号 No. 2	3 号 No. 3	MX–1 型 MX-1 type	G1 型 G1 type	G2 型 G2 type	MX–2 型 MX-2 type	MT–2 型 MT-2 type	MT–3 型 MT-3 type
类型 Type	摩擦式 Friction type	摩擦式 Friction type	摩擦式 Friction type	摩擦橡胶式 Friction rubber type	摩擦式 Friction type	摩擦式 Friction type	摩擦橡胶式 Friction rubber type	摩擦式 Friction type	摩擦式 Friction type
外形尺寸/mm Overall dimension/mm	514×317×228	514×317×228	568×317×225	568×318×226	514×317×228	514×317×228	563×318×228	555×7′n×227	555×19（1×227
最大作用力/kN Max. force/kN	580	1 200	900	1 700	800	1 630	1 800	2 000～2 300	2 000
行程/mm Stroke/mm	61～68	64～68	58～60	65	73	73	76	83	83
容量/kJ Capacity/kJ	14	23～24	18～20	40～43	18	42	45	54～65	45

续表

Continued

缓冲器型号 Buffer model	1 号 No.1	2 号 No.2	3 号 No.3	MX–1 型 MX-1 type	G1 型 G1 type	G2 型 G2 type	MX–2 型 MX-2 type	MT–2 型 MT-2 type	MT–3 型 MT-3 type
吸收能量/kJ Absorbed energy/kJ	10	13～14	14～17	35～40	13.5	37～41	38	46～55	37
能量吸收率/% Energy absorption rate/%	72	57	78～85	90	75	75	85	80	380
质量/kg Mass/kg	106	116	194	133	106	116	160	175	175

缓冲器的行程受到钩肩间隙（从车钩钩肩到冲击座的距离）的限制。缓冲器装车的一个重要原则是：车辆的钩肩间隙必须大于缓冲器的行程。这样，才能保证车辆的纵向冲击力从车钩经由缓冲器传到底架牵引梁，从而避免冲击力直接从车钩到冲击座传到底架端梁。我国新造车辆的车钩钩肩间隙原定为 76 mm。如果装用 MT-2 型或 MT-3 型缓冲器，则钩肩间隙应扩大至 91 mm。

The stroke of the buffer is limited by the coupler shoulder clearance (the distance from the coupler shoulder to the impact seat). An important principle for buffer installation is that the coupler shoulder clearance of the car must be greater than the buffer stroke. As a result, the longitudinal impact force of the car is transmitted from the hook to the underframe traction beam through the buffer, avoiding the transmission of the impact force directly from the hook to the impact seat to the underframe end beam. The coupler shoulder clearance of newly built car couplers in China was originally set at 76 mm. The coupler shoulder clearance should be expanded to 91 mm for the installation of MT-2 or MT-3 buffers.

缓冲器的最大作用力，也称最大阻抗力，其值应与货车结构所能承受的最大允许纵向力相适应。我国车辆强度设计规范规定货车结构允许的最大纵向力为 2.25 MN，缓冲器的最大作用力应不大于该值，这样缓冲器才能起到保护车辆和所载货物的作用。

The maximum force of the buffer, also known as the maximum impedance force, should be consistent with the maximum allowed longitudinal force that the freight car structure can withstand. The specification for strength design and test appraisement for railway vehicles specifies that the maximum allowed longitudinal force for freight car structures should be 2.25 MN, a value that the maximum force of the buffer should not exceed so that the buffer can protect the car and the loaded goods.

缓冲器所需的容量取决于列车的运行工况和调车工况。列车运行工况对缓冲器容量的要求与列车总重、列车编组方式、制动机的性能、车钩的纵向间隙及列车的操纵方法等诸多因素有关，可以根据列车动力学试验或仿真模拟计算予以确定。对于货车缓冲器容量，很大程度上取决于调车冲击工况，根据货车允许连挂速度和车辆总重，可按动量守恒和能量守恒定律计算出各种载重货车在不同组合和不同冲击速度下所需的缓冲器容量值。

The required capacity of the buffer relies on the operating conditions and switching conditions of the train. The buffer capacity required by the train operating conditions is related to many factors such as the total weight of the train, the train grouping method, the performance of the braking machine, the longitudinal clearance of the hook, and the train operation method, which can be determined according to the train dynamics test or simulation calculation. The buffer capacity for freight cars mostly depends on the switching impact circumstances. The needed buffer capacity values for various types of freight cars under various combinations and impact speeds can be determined based on the permitted coupling speed of freight cars and the overall car weight in accordance with the rules of momentum and energy conservation.

我国货车总数中，载重 50 t、总重 70 t 的货车仍占有一定的比例。20 世纪 70 年代后期生产的货车大都为载重 60～65 t、总重为 84 t 的 4D 轴货车。从 2006 年开始，我国大批量生产轴重为 23 t 的 70 t 级货车，在运煤专用线上主要是总重为 100 t 的 4E 轴货车。

Freight cars with a load of 50 t and a total weight of 70 t still make up a certain proportion of the entire number of freight cars in China. Most 4D axle freight cars with a load of 60 – 65 t and a total weight of 84 t were manufactured in the late 1970s. Since 2006, China has been mass-producing 70 t grade freight cars with a 23 t axle load. On the designated coal transportation lines, the majority of these freight cars are 4E axle freight cars with a total load of 100 t.

在计算缓冲器容量时，车辆的总重可取为 70 t、84 t 及 100 t 三种，分别考虑其 6 种不同组合的工况（见表 6–5）。我国编组站货车允许的安全连挂速度现规定为 5 km/h。为了提高编组站的作业效率，将来有必要将货车允许的安全连挂速度提高到 7 km/h，甚至提高到 10 km/h。

In the calculation of the buffer capacity, the gross weight of the car can be taken as 70 t, 84 t, and 100 t respectively in consideration of its six different combinations of operating conditions (see Table 6 -5). The safe coupling speed of the freight cars allowed in China's marshaling stations is now stipulated as 5 km/h. It is necessary to increase the permitted safe coupling speed of freight cars to 7 km/h or even to 10 km/h in the future to improve the operational efficiency of the marshaling station.

表 6–5　不同冲击工况下的缓冲器容量值

Table 6-5　Buffer Capacity Values under Different Impact Conditions

工况 Working condition	W_1/kN	W_2/kN	$\frac{W_1W_2}{W_1+W_2}$/kN	*E*/kJ					
				5 km/h	6 km/h	7 km/h	8 km/h	9 km/h	10 km/h
1	840	840	420	20.66	29.76	40.44	52.83	66.90	82.59
2	840	700	382	18.79	27.06	36.77	48.03	60.84	75.12
3	1 000	840	457	22.50	32.38	44.07	57.57	72.79	89.86
4	700	1 000	412	20.77	29.19	39.74	51.90	65.62	81.01
5	700	700	360	17.25	24.81	33.76	44.09	57.34	70.79
6	1 000	1 000	500	24.64	35.43	48.14	62.89	79.64	98.32

表 6–5 为两辆不同重量车辆在 6 种不同组合工况下相互冲击时，计算出的冲击速度为 5、6、7、8、9、10 km/h 时所需的缓冲器容量值。从表 6–5 中所列的计算值可见，冲击速度为 5 km/h 时，要求缓冲器容量为 18～24 kJ。我国 3 号缓冲器的容量为 18～20 kJ，2 号缓冲器的容量为 24 kJ，故目前我国装用这两种缓冲器的货车允许的安全连挂速度只能限制在 5 km/h 左右。

Table 6-5 shows the required buffer capacity values that can be calculated for two cars of different weights impacting each other in impact speeds of 5, 6, 7, 8, 9, and 10 km/h under six different combinations of operating conditions. It can be seen from the calculated values listed in Table 6-5 that the buffer capacity of 18–24 kJ is required when the impact speed is 5 km/h. Since the capacity of No.3 buffers in China is 18–20 kJ and the capacity of No.2 buffers is 24 kJ, the safety coupling speed allowed for the freight cars with these two buffers can only be limited to about 5 km/h.

如果将允许的安全连挂速度提高到 7 km/h，缓冲器的容量至少应达到 35～48 kJ。

A minimum buffer capacity of 35–48 kJ should be achieved if the allowed safe coupling speed is increased to 7 km/h.

6.4.3 我国常用缓冲器的类型、结构及性能 Type, structure, and performance of commonly used buffers in China

1. MT–2 型、MT–3 型缓冲器 MT-2 and MT-3 buffers

MT–2 型、MT–3 型缓冲器是为了适应我国大秦线开行 6 000～10 000 t 重载列车、主要干线开行 5 000 t 级重载列车，以及发展 25 t 轴重大型货车的需要而研发和开发的新一代大容量通用货车缓冲器，是参照美国 AAR901E 标准批准的 Mark–50 结构所研制的一种弹簧摩擦式缓冲器。MT–2 型与 MT–3 型缓冲器的结构和外形尺寸完全相同。

The MT-2 and MT-3 buffers are developed to meet the needs of China's Datong-Qinhuangdao Railway for heavy-haul trains of 6,000–10,000 t, the main trunk lines for heavy-haul trains of 5,000 t, and the development of large freight cars with 25 t axle load, which belong to spring friction buffers developed in accordance with the Mark-50 structure approved by the American AAR901E standard, with exactly the same structure and external dimensions.

MT–2 型缓冲器的容量为 54～65 kJ，用于大秦线专用敞车及 70 t 级通用货车；MT–3 型缓冲器的容量为 45 kJ，可用于 60 t 级通用货车。

The MT-2 with a capacity of 54–65 kJ is used for special open freight cars and 70 t grade general-purpose freight cars on the Datong–Qinhuangdao Railway, while the MT-3 with a capacity of 45 kJ is used for 60 t grade general-purpose freight cars.

MT 型缓冲器的作用原理如下所述。

The working principle of MT buffers is described below.

如图 6–46 所示，当缓冲器受冲击时，中心楔块与楔块沿着固定斜板滑动，同时夹紧动板。当楔块移动到一定距离后与动板一起移动，这时动板、固定斜板和外固定板构成另一组摩擦部分，消耗、吸收一部分动能，并共同推动弹簧座压缩外圆弹簧、内圆弹簧和角弹簧，将一部分冲击动能转变为弹簧的位能。当缓冲器卸载时，复原弹簧借助弹力使中心楔块复位，防止卡滞。

As shown in Figures 6-46, the central wedge and wedge slide along the fixed inclined plate while clamping the moving plate when the buffer is impacted. When wedges move with moving plate after moving to a certain distance, the moving plate, fixed inclined plate, and outer fixing plate constitute another set of friction parts, which consume and absorb part of the kinetic energy, and together push the spring seat to compress the outer helical spring, inner helical spring and angle spring to make part of the impact kinetic energy converted into the potential energy of the spring. When the buffer is unloaded, the restoring spring resets the center wedge with the help of the elastic force to prevent stuck.

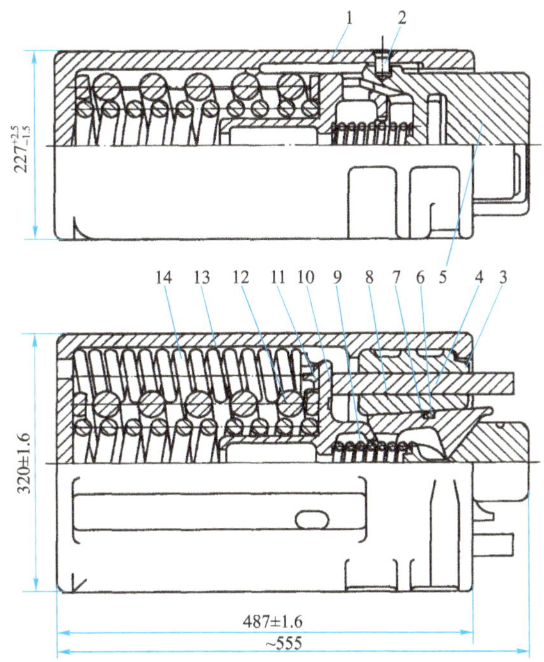

1—箱体；2—销子；3—外固定板；4—动板；5—中心楔块；6—铜条；7—楔块；8—固定斜板；9—复原弹簧；10—弹簧座；11—角弹簧座；12—外圆弹簧；13—内圆弹簧；14—角弹簧。

1—Box body; 2—Pin; 3—Outer fixing plate; 4—Moving plate; 5—Central wedge; 6—Copper bar; 7—Wedge; 8—Fixed inclined plate; 9—Restoring spring; 10—Spring seat; 11—Angle spring seat; 12—Outer helical spring; 13—Inner helical spring; 14—Angle spring.

图 6–46　MT–2 型、MT–3 型缓冲器

Figure 6-46　MT-2 and MT-3 Buffers

为满足纵向动力学性能要求，新造货车一般都采用 MT–2 型、MT–3 型缓冲器。MT–2 型、MT–3 型缓冲器由摩擦金属弹性元件和缓冲弹簧两部分组成。MT–2 型、MT–3 型缓冲器的结构如图 6–47 所示。

To satisfy the longitudinal dynamics performance requirements, MT-2 and MT-3 buffers are generally used in newly built freight cars. The MT-2 and MT-3 buffers are composed of two parts: a friction metal elastic element and a spring buffer. The structures of MT-2 and MT-3 buffers are shown in Figure 6-47.

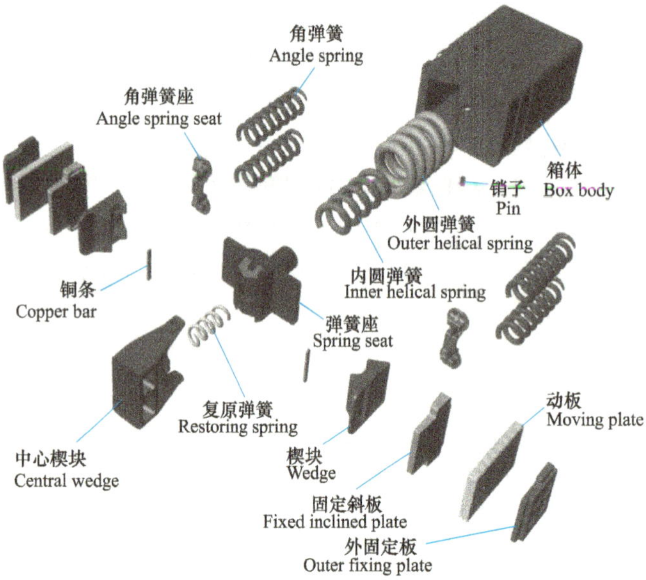

图 6-47　MT-2 型、MT-3 型缓冲器的结构
Figure 6-47　Structure of MT-2 and MT-3 Buffers

MT-2 型、MT-3 型缓冲器的挠力特征为：在车辆空载或在较低冲击速度时，缓冲器的刚度小且变化平缓；当车辆满载或为大型车，且冲击速度在 7 km/h 以上时，刚度增长较快。MT-2 型、MT-3 型缓冲器结构合理，容大，稳定性好，其检修周期可达 16 年，较适合我国大秦线开行重载单元列车和主要干线发展重载货物列车运输对缓冲器的要求。装设 MT-2 型、MT-3 型缓冲器的总重为 84～100 t 的大型货车，调车允许连挂速度可提高到 7 km/h 以上，是一种具有广阔发展前景的新型货车缓冲器。

As for the deflection characteristics of MT-2 and MT-3 buffers, the stiffness of the buffer is small and changes stably and slowly when the car is empty or is subject to a lower impact speed, and its stiffness grows faster when the car is fully loaded or is a large car subject to the impact speed of above 7 km/h. The MT-2 and MT-3 buffers are reasonable in structure, large in capacity, and good in stability, with a maintenance cycle of up to 16 years, which are suitable for the requirements of the buffer for the operation of heavy-haul unit trains on the Datong-Qinhuangdao Railway and the development of heavy-haul cargo train transportation on the main trunk lines in China. The MT-2 and MT-3 buffers installed on large freight cars with a total weight of 84–100 t allow a coupling speed to be increased to more than 7 km/h, which are the new type of freight car buffers with broad development prospects.

2. MX-1 型、MX-2 型橡胶缓冲器
MX-1 and MX-2 rubber buffers

为了解决我国货车上所使用的 2 号、3 号缓冲器容量太小，不能满足运输发展需要的矛

盾，设计制造了橡胶缓冲器。MX–1 型橡胶缓冲器为当前大批量生产和装车的摩擦橡胶缓冲器，容量达 40 kJ，其结构如图 6–48 所示。

The rubber buffers were designed and manufactured to solve the contradiction that the capacity of No.2 and No.3 buffers used on freight cars in China were too small to meet the needs of transportation development. MX-1 rubber buffer is the current mass-produced and loaded friction rubber buffer with a capacity of 40 kJ, whose structure is shown in Figure 6-48.

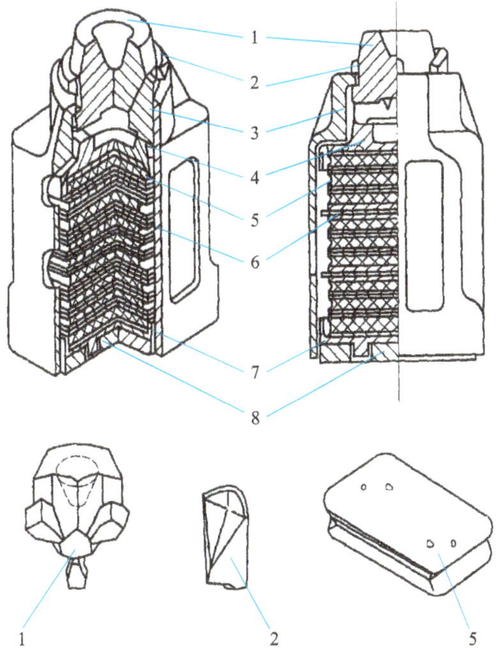

1—压头；2—楔块；3—顶隔板；5—橡胶片；6—中隔板；7—底隔板；8—底板。

1—Pressure head; 2—Wedge; 3—Top bulkhead; 5—Rubber sheet; 6—Middle bulkhead; 7—Bottom bulkhead; 8—Base plate.

图 6–48　MX–1 型橡胶缓冲器的结构

Figure 6-48　Structure of MX-1 Rubber Buffer

MX–1 型橡胶缓冲器的头部为楔块摩擦部分，由 3 个形状完全相同且带倾角的楔块、压头和小口箱体部分组成。楔块介于压头与箱体之间，其倾角为 52°和 1°3′。MX–1 型橡胶缓冲器的后部为弹性元件部分，有 9 片形状相同的橡胶片，用顶隔板、2 块中间隔板及底隔板将其分隔成 3 层，每层 3 片。橡胶片的两面与 2 mm 厚的钢板连接，并经硫化处理。钢板上带有两个定位用的球形凹凸脐。底板与箱体大敞口边缘的凹槽卡合，使整个缓冲器封闭在箱体内。

The head of the MX-1 rubber buffer is the wedge friction part, which consists of three wedges with identical shapes and inclined angles, a pressure head, and a small opening part of the box. The wedge is inserted between the pressure head and the box, with inclination angles of 52° and 1°3′. The rear part of the MX-1 rubber buffer is the elastic element part containing 9 pieces of rubber sheets in the same shape, which are separated into three layers with three pieces each by the top partition, two middle partitions, and the bottom partition. The rubber sheet is joined to a 2 mm thick steel plate on both sides and has been vulcanized. The steel plate is provided with two spherical concave and convex navels for positioning. The base plate snaps into the groove at the edge of the large openings of the box, leaving the entire buffer enclosed within the box.

MX–1 型橡胶缓冲器组装时，由箱体底部依次将各零件放入，并在压机上把橡胶片压缩，使底板倾斜进入箱体，并卡合在箱体对应位置的凹槽内。MX–1 型缓冲器的外部尺寸与 3 号缓冲器相同，装车时可与 2 号、3 号缓冲器互换使用。

To assemble the MX-1 rubber buffer, each part is put into the box in turn from the bottom of the box, and the rubber sheet is compressed on the press so that the base plate is tilted into the box and stuck in the groove in the corresponding position of the box. The external dimension of the MX-1 rubber buffer is the same as that of the No.3 buffer, which can be interchanged with No.2 and No.3 buffers during assembly.

橡胶缓冲器的工作原理是：借助于橡胶分子内摩擦和弹性变形起到缓和冲击和消耗能量的作用。为了增大缓冲器容量，在头部装有金属摩擦部分，借助 3 个带有倾角的楔块，在受压时与箱体及压头间各接触斜面产生相对位移，通过摩擦而消耗冲击能量。

The working principle of rubber buffers is to alleviate the impact and consume energy by means of internal friction and elastic deformation of rubber molecules. To increase the capacity of the buffer, the head is provided with a metal friction part, which consumes the impact energy through friction by means of three wedges with an inclined angle displaced relative to each contact slope between the box and the pressure head when under pressure.

MX–1 型橡胶缓冲器的优点是：容量大，可达 35 kJ 以上；性能良好，其能量吸收率高达 90%，能适应于各种不同的冲击能量，缓冲器的变形随着冲击力的增大而渐趋缓慢，阻抗显著增大。另外，缓冲器的结构较简单，零件少、重量轻、成本低、制造方便、检修容易。

MX-1 rubber buffer has the following advantages: a large capacity of more than 35 kJ, and a good performance with an energy absorption rate of up to 90% that is adaptable to a variety of different impact energy. Its deformation tends to slow down with the increase of the impact force, with a significant increase in impedance. Moreover, the buffer is simple in structure, with few parts, lightweight, and low cost, which is convenient to manufacture and easy to repair and maintain.

MX–1 型橡胶缓冲器在运用中存在的主要问题是：橡胶的性能不稳定，容易受气温的影响和老化；箱体结构不合理，容易产生裂纹；箱体采用底部大敞口结构，当橡胶片损坏需调换时，检修操作不便。此外，橡胶的弹性反作用的速度较快，调车作业时易引起车辆分离，而且当冲击力超过橡胶强度时，容易将使橡胶破损。所以，这种缓冲器对于更大的冲击力和更高的调车冲击速度已不能适应。

The problems of MX-1 rubber buffers in the application are mainly the unstable performance of rubber, the influence of temperature, and aging problems, as well as the unreasonable structure of the box body that is easy to crack; The box body has a large open structure at the bottom, making the maintenance operation inconvenient when the rubber piece is damaged and needs to be exchanged. Besides, due to the high speed of the elastic reaction of rubber, it is easy to cause car separation during switching operation, and the rubber will be easily broken when the impact force exceeds the rubber strength. So, this type of buffer is no longer adaptable to greater impact force and higher switching impact speed.

MX-2 型橡胶缓冲器是在原 MX-1 型橡胶缓冲器的基础上研制的一种改进型橡胶缓冲器：将原来整体式底部大敞口的箱体改成上下组合式底部封闭箱体，以便于组装和检修；橡胶片由原来的 9 片改为 8 片，每片的厚度由原来的 35 mm 增大至 40 mm。MX-2 型橡胶缓冲器的最大作用力为 1 800 kN，行程为 76 mm，容量可达 45 kJ。

The MX-2 rubber buffer is an improved type of rubber buffer developed based on the original MX-1 buffer, which changes the original integral box with a large open bottom into a closed box with an upper and lower combination bottom, to facilitate assembly and maintenance. The rubber piece is changed from the original 9 pieces to 8 pieces, with the thickness of each piece increased from the original 35 mm to 40 mm. The MX-2 rubber buffer can withstand a maximum force of 1,800 kN, with a stroke of 76 mm and a capacity of up to 45 kJ.

3. 1 号、2 号、3 号缓冲器
No.1, No.2, and No.3 buffers

1 号缓冲器为一种摩擦式缓冲器，它由前、后两部分组成。前部为螺旋弹簧，后部为内、外环弹簧，彼此以锥面相配合，两部分之间有弹簧座板分隔。金属弹簧用来缓和冲击作用力，环弹簧两滑动斜面间的摩擦力用来消耗冲击动能，起到吸收能量的作用。

No.1 buffer is a friction buffer, which consists of the front and rear parts. The front part is a spiral spring, while the rear part is an inner and outer ring spring. They are compatible with each other by conical surface and separated by a spring seat plate between the two parts. The metal spring is used to alleviate the impact force, while the friction between the two sliding ramps of the ring spring is used to consume the kinetic energy of impact, both of which play the role of energy absorption together.

1 号缓冲器的结构如图 6-49 所示。弹簧盒借助螺栓将两个半环状盒体连成一体，前端有一盒盖，其中部有六角形凸缘，与盒盖的折缘部分卡住，从而保证盒盖受压后沿盒体方向移动。弹簧盒的后端有底板，构成一封闭的缓冲器盒。盒内前端为双卷螺旋弹簧，后端装环弹簧，共有 6 个外环弹簧、5 个内环弹簧及 2 个半环弹簧。内环的外面和外环的内面都做成 V 形锥面，锥度为 15°。组装时，要求有 15 kN 的初压力，以保证环弹簧锥面间的密贴配合。

The structure of the No.1 buffer is shown in Figure 6-49. The spring box connects two semicircular boxes into one body by using bolts. There is a box cover at the front end, of which a hexagonal flange is at the middle part and can be stuck with the folding edge of the box cover, to ensure the box cover under pressure can move along the direction of the box body. The rear end of the spring box is provided with a base plate, together with which a closed buffer box is formed. The box is equipped with a double-coil spiral spring at the front end and a ring spring at the back with a total of six outer ring springs, five inner ring springs, and two half-ring springs, where the outside of the inner ring and the inner surface of the outer ring are made into a V-shaped conical surface, with a taper of 15°. During assembly, an initial pressure of 15 kN is required to ensure a close fit between the conical surfaces of the ring springs.

当 1 号缓冲器受冲击力时，盒盖向内移动，压缩螺旋弹簧，并将力通过弹簧座板传递给

环弹簧。由于内、外环为锥面配合，受力后外环扩张，内环缩小，产生轴向弹性变形，起到缓冲作用。与此同时，内、外环锥面间有相对滑动，因摩擦而做功，从而使部分冲击能变为摩擦功而耗散。当外力去除后，各内、外环由于弹力而复原，此时同样也要消耗部分冲击能量。

When the No.1 buffer is subjected to impact force, the box cover moves inward, compressing the spiral spring and transferring the force to the ring spring through the spring seat plate. Since the inner and outer rings are tapered fits, the outer ring expands and the inner ring shrinks after being subject to forces, producing the axial elastic deformation to act as a buffer. In the meantime, there is relative sliding between the inner and outer ring conical surfaces, which causes the dissipation of part of the impact energy due to friction work. After the external force is removed, the inner and outer rings are recovered due to the elastic force, which consumes part of the impact energy.

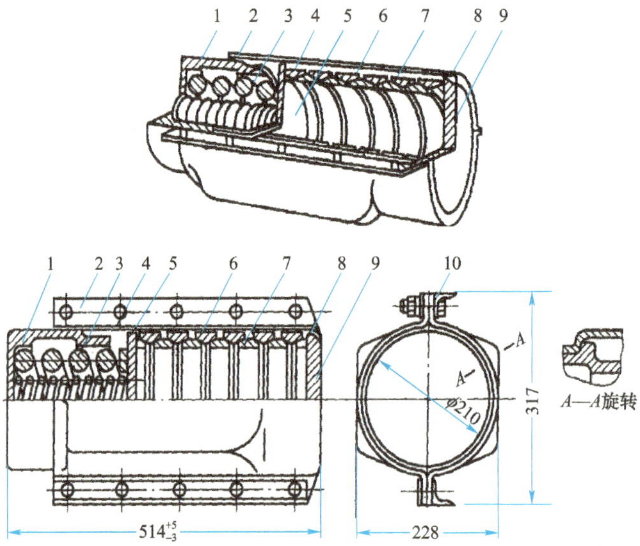

1—盒盖；2—簧盒；3—外圈圆弹簧；4—内圈圆弹簧；5—弹簧座板；6—外环弹簧；7—内环弹簧；8—半环弹簧；9—底板；10—角铁、螺栓。

1—Box cover; 2—Spring box; 3—Outer ring helical spring; 4—Inner ring helical spring; 5—Spring seat plate; 6—Outer ring spring; 7—Inner ring spring; 8—Half-ring spring; 9—Base plate; 10—Angle iron and bolt.

图 6-49　1 号缓冲器的结构

Figure 6-49　Structure of No.1 Buffer

1 号缓冲器由于具有刚度较小的螺旋弹簧，灵敏性好，初始刚度小，在受到较小的冲击力时也能起到缓冲作用，故较适合于客车的要求。但是 1 号缓冲器容量仅为 14 kJ，不能满足扩编旅客列车和双层客车对缓冲器容量的要求。另外，1 号缓冲器维修工作量大，使用寿命短，在新生产的客车上已停止使用。

The No.1 buffer is suitable for the requirements of passenger cars for it has spiral springs with less rigidity, good sensitivity, and small initial stiffness, and can play a buffering role when it is subjected to smaller impact force. But the No.1 buffer capacity is only 14 kJ, which cannot meet the requirements of buffer capacity for expanded passenger cars and double-deck passenger cars.

Besides, due to the large maintenance workload and short service life of the No.1 buffer, it has been discontinued in the newly produced passenger cars.

2 号缓冲器的外形与 1 号缓冲器完全相同，二者在结构上的主要区别在于：2 号缓冲器盒内前部的螺旋弹簧也用环弹簧代替，前部环弹簧的外径和断面的厚度较后部的环弹簧要小，且其中有两个内环开有切口，其目的是减小初始刚度，增加缓冲器的灵敏性。2 号缓冲器的结构如图 6-50 所示。

The shape of the No.2 buffer is the same as that of No.1. The main difference in its structure is that the spiral spring in the front part of the No.2 buffer box is replaced by a ring spring, the outer diameter and thickness of the front ring spring section are smaller than those of the rear ring spring, and there are two inner rings with cutouts, which are designed to reduce the initial stiffness and increase the sensitivity of the buffer.

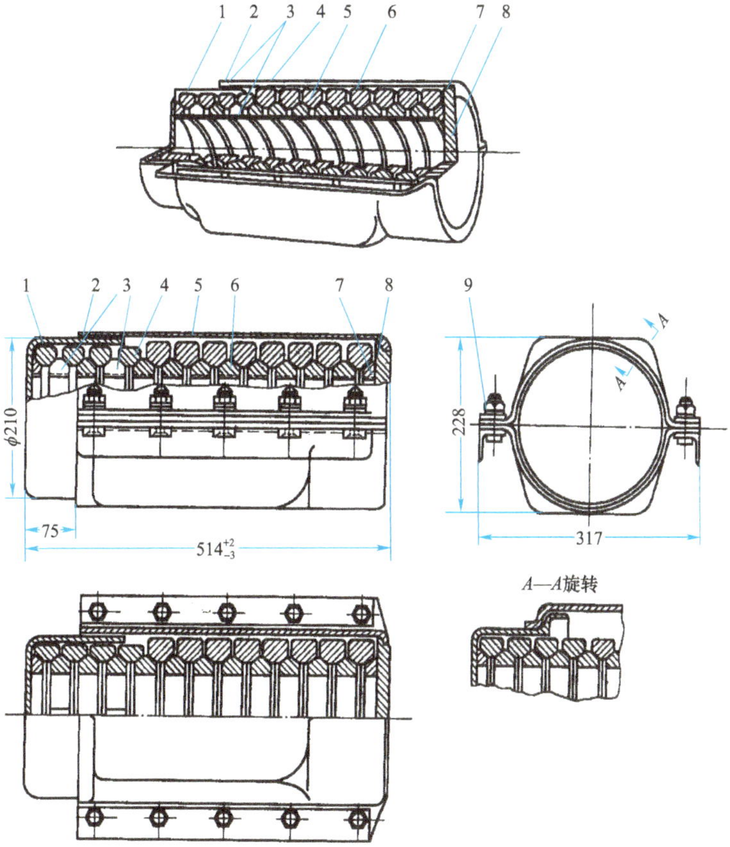

1—盒盖；2—簧盒；3—开有切口的内环弹簧；4—小外环弹簧；5—大外环弹簧；6—内环弹簧；7—半环弹簧；8—底板；9—角铁、螺栓。

1—Box cover; 2—Spring box; 3—Inner ring spring with cutout; 4—Small outer ring spring; 5—Large outer ring spring; 6—Inner ring spring; 7—Half-ring spring; 8—Base plate; 9—Angle iron and bolt.

图 6-50　2 号缓冲器的结构

Figure 6-50　Structure of No.2 Buffer

2 号缓冲器主要在货车上使用。为了增加缓冲器的容量，环弹簧断面尺寸较 1 号缓冲器的环弹簧要大些。2 号缓冲器共有 25 个环弹簧，其中大外环弹簧 8 个、小外环弹簧 4 个、内环弹簧 9 个、开有切口的内环弹簧及半环弹簧各 2 个。

The No.2 buffer is mainly installed on freight cars. To increase the capacity of the buffer, the ring spring section size is larger than that of the ring spring of the No.1 buffer. A total of 25 ring springs are installed in the No.2 buffer, of which eight are large outer ring springs, four are small outer ring springs, nine are inner ring springs, two are inner ring springs with cutouts, and two are half-ring springs.

2 号缓冲器的特点如下。

The characteristics of No.2 buffers are as follows.

（1）环弹簧受力较合理，能充分发挥材料的作用。

It is subjected to forces in a reasonable manner and can give full play to the material.

（2）性能较稳定，即使少数环弹簧折损，仍能起缓冲作用。

It has a stable performance and can act as a buffer even if a few bad springs are broken.

（3）使用中磨损较少，检修容易。

It is worn less in use and easy to overhaul.

（4）制造时对材质、加工要求较高，加工量大。

It is manufactured with high requirements for material and processing, with a large processing volume.

（5）内、外环弹簧容易产生永久变形，外环弹簧尺寸扩大，内环弹簧缩小，致使环弹簧在箱体内处于松弛状态，运用中加剧列车的纵向冲击。

The inner and outer ring springs are prone to permanent deformation, with an expansion of the outer ring spring size and a reduction of the inner ring spring, which causes the ring spring to be in a relaxed state inside the box and intensifies the longitudinal impact of the train in operation.

3 号缓冲器亦称华氏缓冲器，也是一种摩擦式缓冲器，其容量仅为 18～20 kJ。3 号缓冲器由 6 种零件组成，即箱体、2 个导板（摩擦楔块）、2 组瓦片弹簧（每组 8 片）、1 块矩形弹簧压板及内、外圆弹簧，其结构如图 6-51 所示。

No.3 buffer, also called Fahrenheit buffer, is also a friction buffer, with a capacity of only 18–20 kJ. The No.3 buffer is composed of six parts, such as the box body, two guide plates (i.e., friction wedges), two groups of tile springs (eight pieces each), a rectangular spring pressing plate, and inner and outer helical springs, the structure of which is shown in Figure 6-51.

导板的斜面与箱体开口端的相应部分接触，并借助于瓦片弹簧的弹力使之紧密贴合，导板的一端顶在弹簧压板上，弹簧压板的另一端顶住安放在箱体内的双卷圆弹簧。箱体的中部开有弹簧检查孔及导板预压加垫孔。

The slant of the guide plate is in contact with the corresponding part of the open end of the box, and closely fitted with the elasticity of the tile spring, with one end of the guide plate jacked on the spring pressing plate while the other end of the spring pressing plate jacked on the double-coil helical springs placed in the box. There are spring inspection holes and guide plate pre-pressure padding holes in the middle of the box.

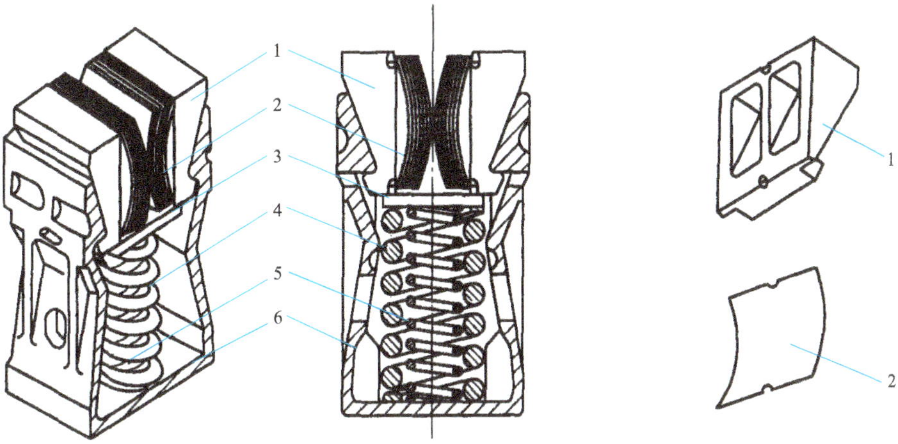

1—导板；2—瓦片弹簧；3—弹簧压板；4—外圆弹簧；5—内圆弹簧；6—箱体。

1—Guide plate; 2—Tile spring; 3—Spring pressing plate; 4—Outer helical spring; 5—Inner helical spring; 6—Box body.

图 6–51　3 号缓冲器的结构

Figure 6-51　Structure of No.3 Buffer

当缓冲器受压缩时，导板沿箱体的斜面向内滑动，一方面推动弹簧压板压缩螺旋弹簧，另一方面也压紧瓦片弹簧。这时，作用在缓冲器上的冲击能，一部分由导板与箱体斜面间的摩擦转变为热能而消失，另一部分动能变为弹簧的弹性势能。当压力去除后，弹簧的弹力使导板复位，在此过程中又消耗了部分动能。

When the buffer is compressed, the guide plate slides inward along the slanting surface of the box, which pushes the spring pressing plate to compress the spiral spring on the one hand and compresses the tile spring on the other hand. At this time, part of the impact energy acting on the buffer changes from the friction between the guide plate and the slope of the box to the heat energy and disappears, and the other part of the kinetic energy becomes the elastic potential energy of the spring. After the pressure is removed, the guide plate is reset through the elastic force of the spring with some kinetic energy consumed in the process.

4. G1 型、G2 型缓冲器

G1 and G2 buffers

为提高原 1 号、2 号缓冲器的容量，有关科研单位和制造工厂提出了两种改进型缓冲器——G1 型、G2 型缓冲器。G1 型缓冲器可用于双层旅客列车和扩编旅客列车，G2 型缓冲器可供 5 000 t 重载列车和大秦线重载列车使用。G1 型缓冲器的结构如图 6–52 所示。

Two types of improved buffers G1 and G2 have been proposed by relevant scientific research units and manufacturing plants to improve the capacity of the original No.1 and No.2 buffers. The G1 buffer can be used for double-deck passenger cars and expanded passenger cars, while the G2 buffer can be used for 5,000 t heavy-haul trains and heavy-haul trains on the Datong-Qinhuangdao Railway. The structure of the G1 buffer is shown in Figure 6-52.

G1 型、G2 型缓冲器在保持原 1 号、2 号缓冲器外形尺寸和簧盒内的内、外环弹簧总数不变的前提下将环弹簧的材料由原来的 60Si2Mn 弹簧钢（屈服极限为 1 200 MPa）改为高强度的 60Si2CrVA 弹簧钢（屈服极限为 1 000 MPa），并适当改变环弹簧断面及缓冲器的结构尺寸，行程从原来的 68 mm 增加至 73 mm，最大作用力分别达到 0.8 MN 和 1.33～1.63 MN，从而使 G1 型缓冲器的容量达 18 kJ，G2 型缓冲器的容量达 42 kJ，较之原 1 号、2 号缓冲器的容量有较大幅度的提高。

The material of the ring spring of G1 and G2 buffers is changed from 60Si2Mn spring steel (yield limit of 1,200 MPa) to high-strength 60Si2CrVA spring steel (yield limit of 1,000 MPa) while maintaining the same dimensions of the original No.1 and No.2 buffers and the total number of inner and outer ring springs in the spring box. The appropriate change of the ring spring section and the structure size of the buffer increases the stroke from the original 68 mm to 73 mm, with the maximum force reaching 0.8 MN and 1.33–1.63 MN respectively, so that the capacity of G1 and G2 buffers reaching 18 kJ and 42 kJ respectively, which is a substantial increase compared with the capacity of the original No.1 and No.2 buffers.

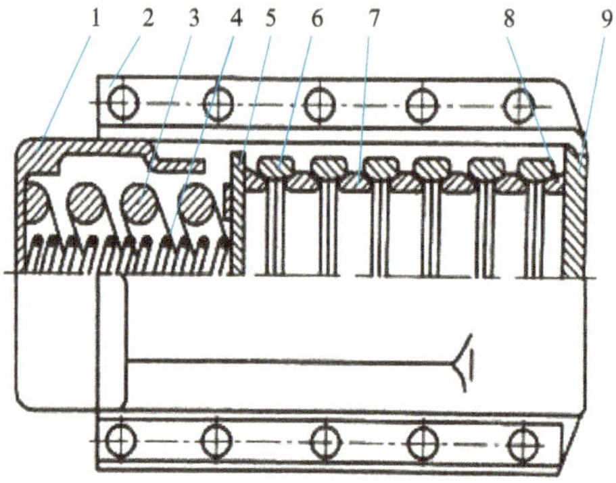

1—弹簧盒盖；2—弹簧盒；3—外圆弹簧；4—内圆弹簧；5—弹簧座；
6—外环弹簧；7—内环弹簧；8—半环弹簧；9—底板。

1—Spring box cover; 2—Spring box; 3—Outer helical spring; 4—Inner helical spring; 5—Spring seat;
6—Outer ring spring; 7—Inner ring spring; 8—Half-ring spring; 9—Base plate.

图 6-52 G1 型缓冲器的结构

Figure 6-52 Structure of G1 Buffer

G1 型、G2 型缓冲器环弹簧的受力较为合理，其最大的工作应力在内环弹簧断面。例如，缓冲器内环弹簧的最大工作应力为 1 437 MPa，低于环弹簧材料 60Si2CrVA 弹簧钢的屈服极限，而原 2 号缓冲器内环弹簧的最大工作应力高达 1 622 MPa，超过环弹簧材料 60Si2Mn 弹簧钢的屈服极限，从而避免了原 1 号、2 号缓冲器运用中出现环弹簧产生永久变形、断裂、卡环及容量不稳等缺陷，提高了缓冲器的使用寿命。

The ring springs of G1 and G2 buffers are subjected to forces in a reasonable manner, with the maximum working stress at the inner ring spring section. For instance, the maximum working stress of the inner ring spring of the buffer is 1,437 MPa, lower than the yield limit of the ring spring material 60Si2CrVA spring steel, while the maximum working stress of the inner ring spring of the original buffer No.2 is 1,622 MPa, higher than the yield limit of the ring spring material 60Si2Mn spring steel. This prevents permanent deformation of the ring spring, ring spring breakage, ring jamming, unstable capacity and other faults in the application of the original No.1 and No.2 buffers, thus improving the service life of the buffers.

项目 7

Project 7

客 车 车 体

Passenger Car Body

本项目以认识客车车体为工学任务，通过课堂任务的完成过程，着重介绍客车车体的基本组成，并以此为引导介绍铁路客车车体的结构及特点；通过课后任务，了解各种类型客车（动车组）车体的结构组成。

The main task of this project is to understand the passenger car body. In the classroom, the main focus is on introducing the basic components of the passenger car body, and the structure and characteristics of railway passenger car body. Through after-class tasks, students will gain an understanding of structural components of the passenger car body for various types of cars (EMU).

学生工作页 Student Worksheet

工学任务描述 Task description	预期目标 Expected goals
任务名称：认识客车车体 Task name: Understanding of the passenger car body 任务编号：CJ-7 Task number: CJ-7 任务类型：认知型+结构原理型 Task type: Cognitive + structural principle 适用范围：车辆系统各岗位群 Applicable scope: All post groups of the car system 完成时间：　　学时 Completion time:　　class hours	初级：了解客车车体的基本组成、作用及技术要求 Elementary level: Know the basic composition, function, and technical requirements of the passenger car body 中级：认识各型客车的车体、车内设备 Intermediate level: Understand various types of passenger car body and interior equipment 高级：从车体结构、材质、工艺角度考虑客车车体如何适应牵引设备更高速、安全、平稳地运行 Advanced level: How to adapt the passenger car body to the traction equipment from the perspective of body structure, material, and technology?

知识回顾+小组讨论

Knowledge review + group discussion

1. 尝试列出客车车体的基本组成。

   Try to list the basic components of a passenger car body.

序号 S/N	基本组成 Basic composition	相关知识点 Related knowledge points
1		
2		
3		
4		
5		
6		
7		
8		
9		

2. 小组讨论：客车的基本功能有哪些？为实现这些功能需要哪些设备？

Group discussion: What are the basic functions of a passenger car? What equipment is required to achieve these functions?

3. 思考：你都知道哪些型号的客车，尝试说明一下异同。

Thinking: Which models of passenger cars do you know? Try to explain their similarities and differences.

4. 认识底架，写出图中各部分的名称。

Understand the underframe and write the name of each part in the figure.

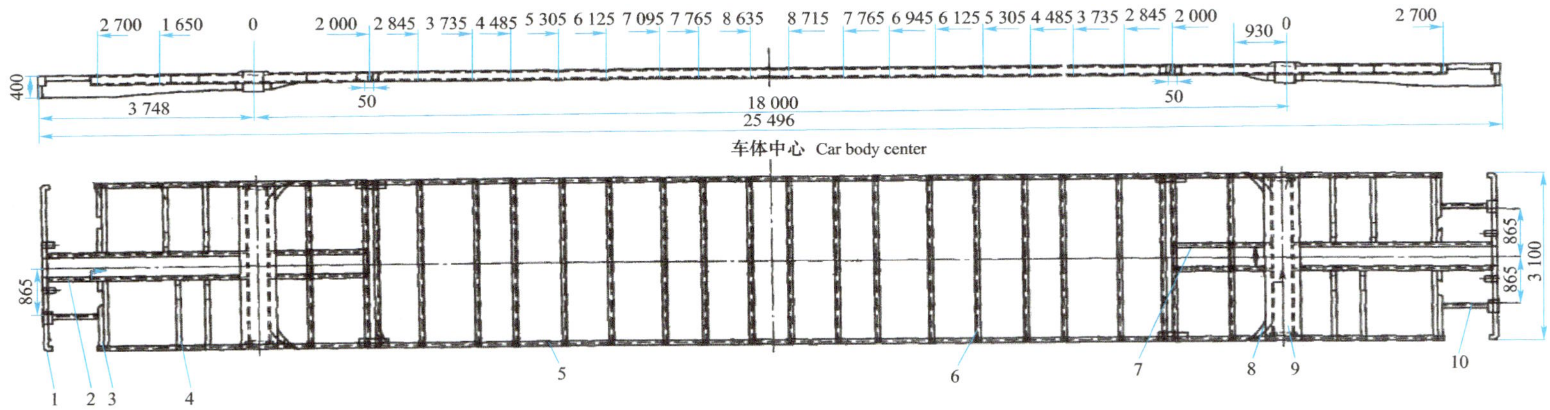

	名　称 Name	序号 Serial number	名　称 Name	序号 Serial number	名　称 Name
1		5		9	
2		6		10	
3		7			
4		8			

5. 认识底架牵枕组成，只写图中各部分的名称。

Understand the composition of undexframe traction sleepers, and write the name of each part in the figure only.

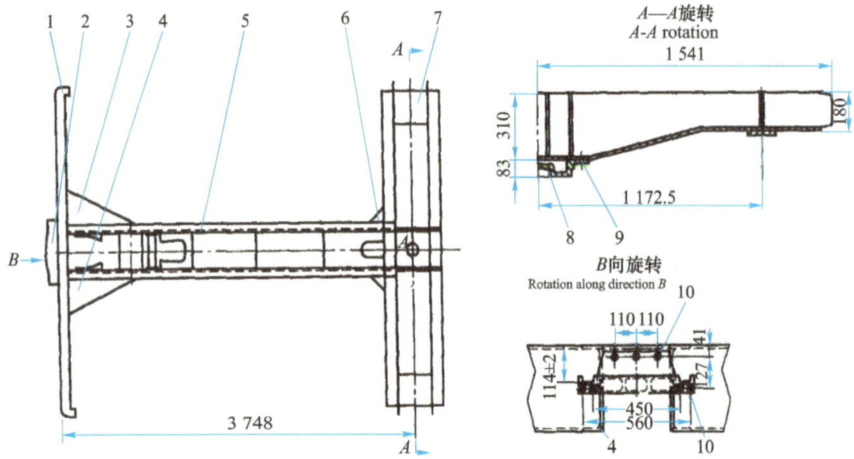

序号 S/N	名　称 Name	序号 S/N	名　称 Name	序号 S/N	名　称 Name
1		5		9	
2		6		10	
3		7			
4		8			

6. 认识侧墙，写出图中各部分的名称。

Understand the side wall and write the name of each part in the figure.

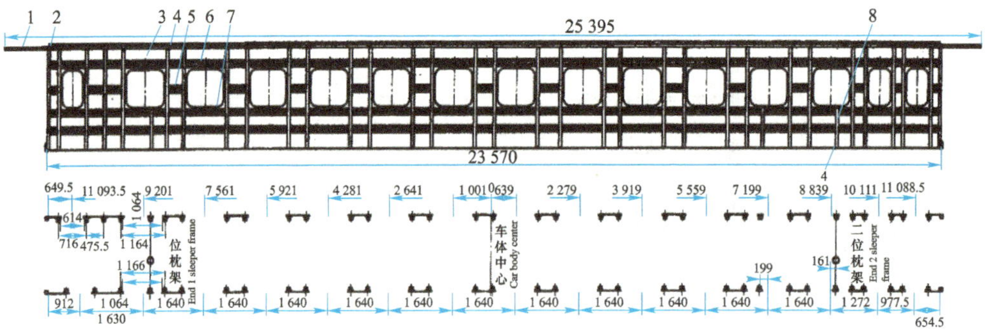

序号 S/N	名　称 Name	序号 S/N	名　称 Name	序号 S/N	名　称 Name
1		4		7	
2		5		8	
3		6			

7. 认识脚蹬翻板组成，写出图中各部分的名称。

Understand the composition of the pedal flip-board and write the name of each part in the figure.

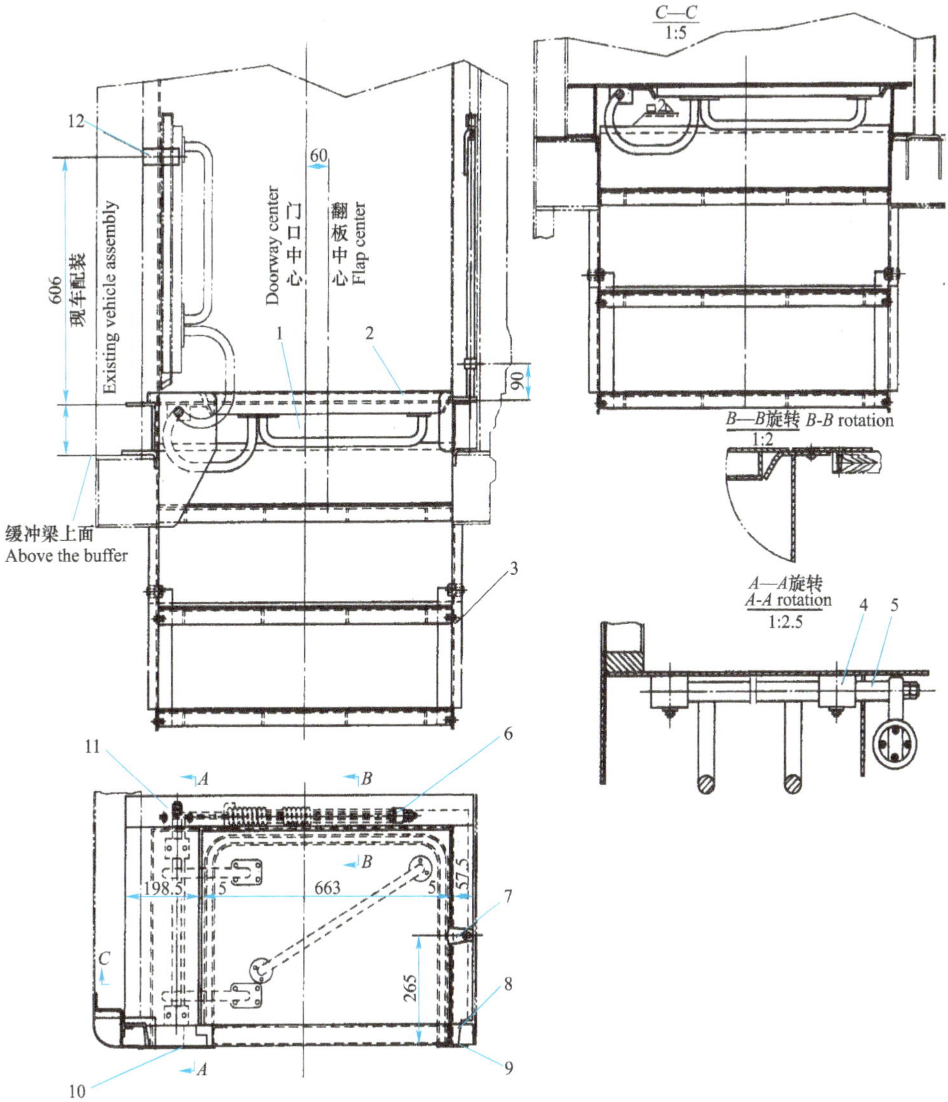

序号 S/N	名　称 Name	序号 S/N	名　称 Name	序号 S/N	名　称 Name
1		5		9	
2		6		10	
3		7		11	
4		8		12	

8. 认识端墙，写出图中各部分的名称。

Understand the end wall and write the name of each part in the figure.

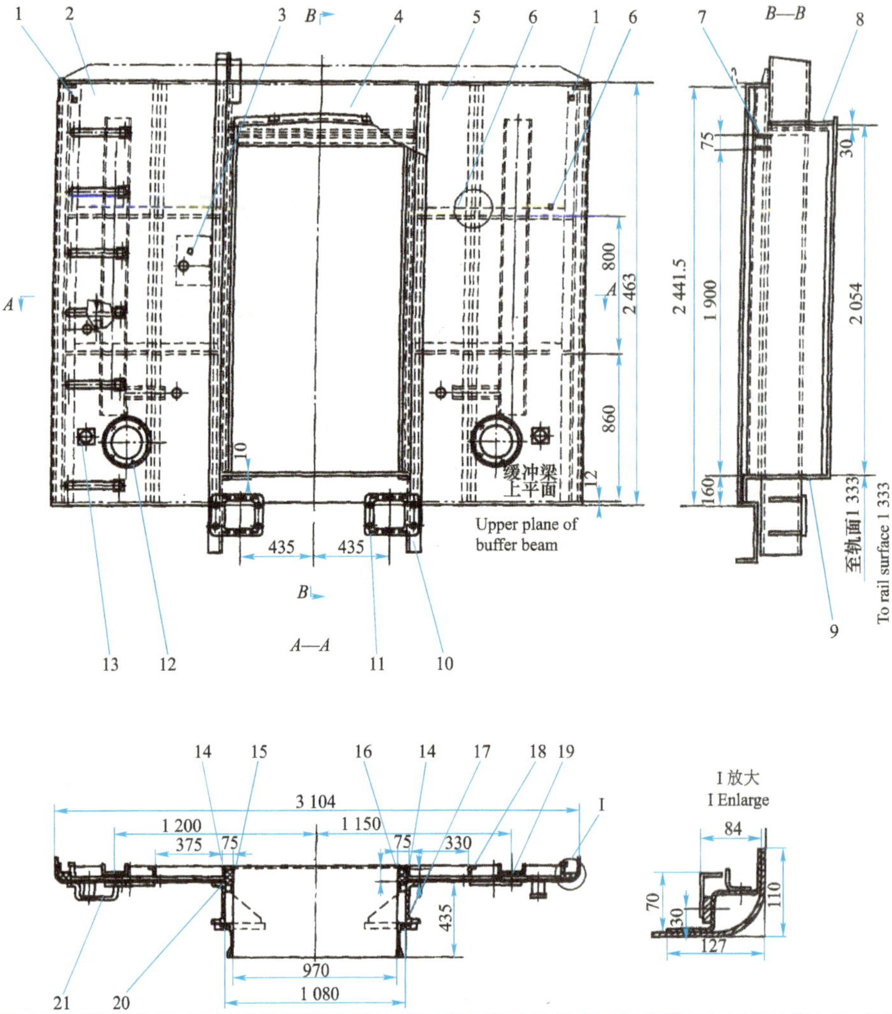

序号 S/N	名　称 Name	序号 S/N	名　称 Name	序号 S/N	名　称 Name
1		8		15	
2		9		16	
3		10		17	
4		11		18	
5		12		19	
6		13		20	
7		14		21	

9. 认识车顶，写出图中各部分的名称。

Understand the roof and write the name of each part in the figure.

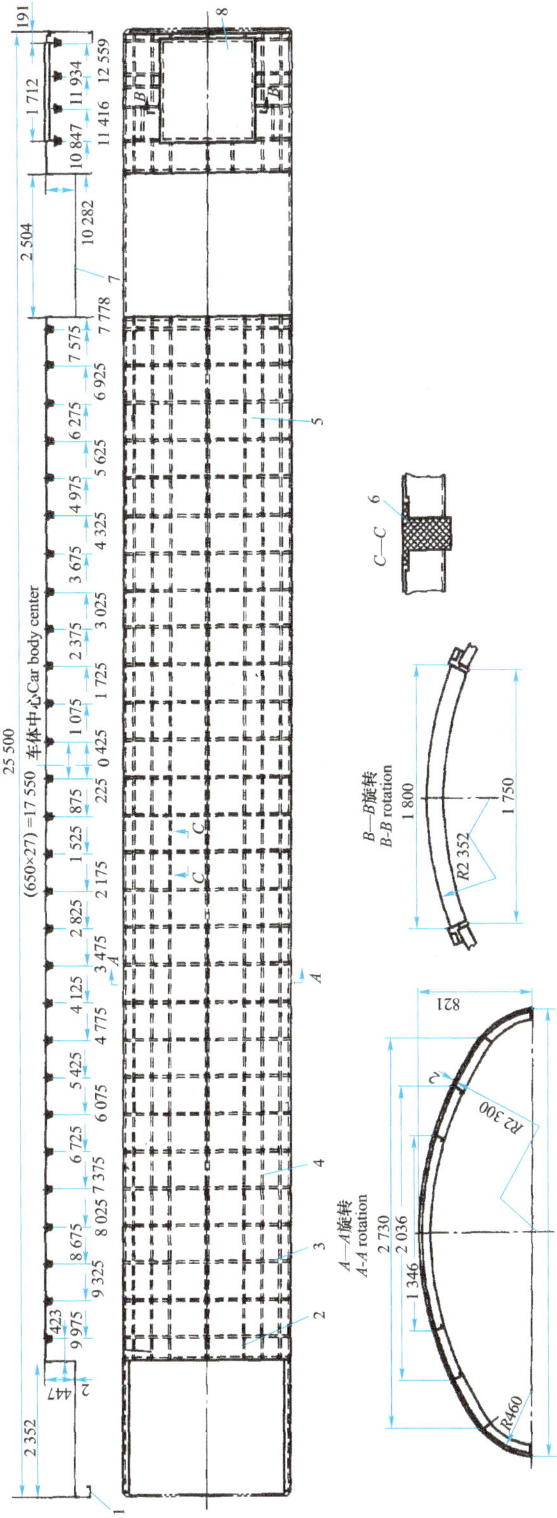

序号 Serial number	名称 Name	序号 Serial number	名称 Name	序号 Serial number	名称 Name
1		4		7	
2		5			
3		6			

10. 认识车体钢结构组成，写出图中各部分的名称。

Understand the composition of the car body's steel structure and write the name of each part in the figure.

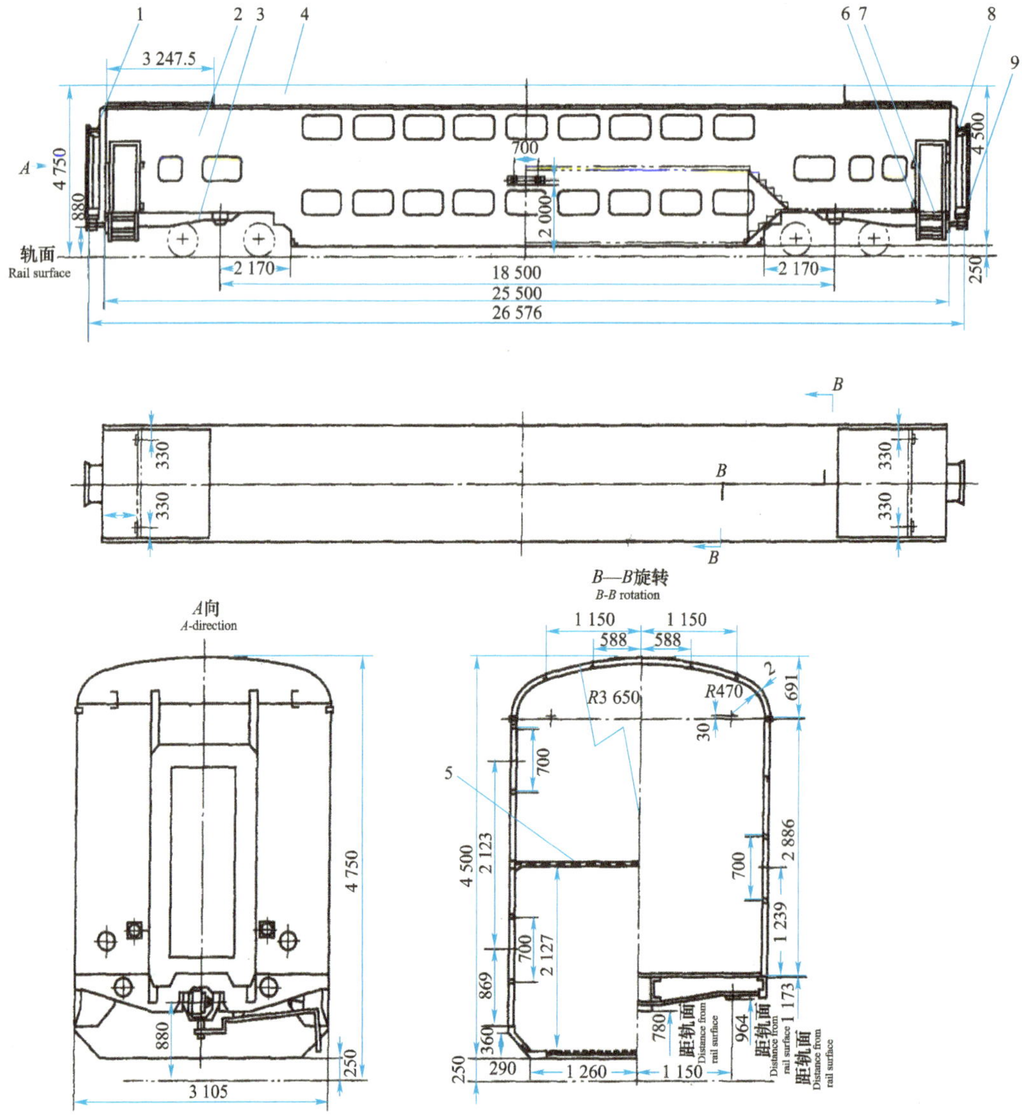

序号 S/N	名　称 Name	序号 S/N	名　称 Name	序号 S/N	名　称 Name
1		4		7	
2		5		8	
3		6		9	

课后任务

After-class tasks

1. 查阅资料，尝试总结比较以下客车车体的基本结构。

Refer to relevant documents and try to summarize and compare the basic structures of the following passenger car body.

客车类型 Type of passenger car	双层客车 Double-deck passenger car	发电车 Generator car	餐车 Dining car	CRH2 型动车组 CRH2 EMU	邮政车 Mail car
基本组成 Basic composition					

2. 提出你的问题。

Ask your question.

问题（1）：

Question (1) : ______

答案：

Answer: ______

问题（2）：

Question (2): ______

答案：

Answer: ______

学习效果评价
Learning effect evaluation

年 Year　月 Month　日 Day

专业班级： Major & class:	姓名： Name:	学号： Student number:
工学小组及分工： Work-and-study team and responsibility division:		

专业（知识/技能）收获 Professional gains (knowledge/skills)	（非专业）能力素质收获 (Non-professional) ability and quality gains

评价考核项目 Evaluation item	自我评价 Self-evaluation	小组评价 Group evaluation	教师评价 Teacher's evaluation
已掌握客车车体的基本组成 Have mastered the basic composition of passenger car body			
已掌握客车车体的作用 Have mastered the functions of passenger car body			
已掌握车内设备及布置情况 Have mastered the equipment and layout in cars			
对本书中未介绍车型车体结构的掌握情况 Mastery of models and car body structure not introduced in the book			
主动提出问题的数量 Number of questions proposed			
课外学习时间（学时） After-school learning time (hours)			
兴趣客车车体自主学习（收集相关知识点数量） Autonomous learning of interested passenger car body (the number of knowledge points collected)			
工作态度（课堂、课后任务完成情况） Work attitude (completion condition of classroom tasks and after-class tasks)	☆☆☆☆ ☆☆☆☆	☆☆☆☆ ☆☆☆☆	☆☆☆☆ ☆☆☆☆
合作意识及协调能力 Cooperation consciousness and coordination ability	☆☆☆☆ ☆☆☆☆	☆☆☆☆ ☆☆☆☆	☆☆☆☆ ☆☆☆☆
正确表达和沟通能力 Correct expression and communication skills	☆☆☆☆ ☆☆☆☆	☆☆☆☆ ☆☆☆☆	☆☆☆☆ ☆☆☆☆
自律能力（缺勤/旷课/迟到/违纪次数） Self-discipline (absences/absenteeism/lateness/disciplinary violations)			

任务 7.1　客车车体概述

Task 7.1　Overview of passenger car body

铁路以其快速、安全、节能和环保等特点，一直是人类最为重要的交通运输工具之一。为了增强铁路与公路、水运和航空运输竞争的能力，必须提高旅客列车的运行速度，缩短旅行时间，改善乘车条件，保证行车安全，制造出轻、快、稳的铁路客车。

Due to its fast, safe, energy-saving, and environment-friendly features, the railroad has been one of the most important means of transportation for human beings. For the purpose of strengthening the competitiveness of railroads with road, water, and air transportation, it is necessary to improve the running speed of passenger cars, shorten the travel time, improve the riding conditions, and ensure the safety of traffic to create light, fast, and stable railroad coaches.

回顾我国铁路客车发展的历史，随着国民经济的发展、科学技术的进步和人民生活水平的提高，铁路客车的设计制造水平也不断提高。铁路客车制造业从 1953 年开始自行设计生产我国的第一代产品，即 21 型系列客车产品。其中包括硬座车、硬卧车、餐车、行李车和邮政车等，先后共生产了 3 110 辆，1961 年停止生产。该型客车构造速度为 100 km/h，由于其构造速度、制造工艺、技术经济指标和舒适性等方面都满足不了要求，所以被 22 型客车所取代。22 型客车是我国的第二代铁路客车，其构造速度为 120 km/h，各种性能均较 21 型客车先进。22 型客车系列产品包括硬座车、硬卧车、软座车、软卧车、餐车、行李车、邮政车和发电车等，至 1992 年年底共生产了 26 000 余辆。22 型客车车体钢结构由普通碳钢制造，钢结构腐蚀严重，其结构及车辆性能满足不了时代的要求，需要更新换代，由产品性能和技术经济指标更先进的新型客车来替代，即第三代客车——25 型客车。该型客车从 1966 年开始研制，20 世纪 80 年代中期进入批量生产，1993 年定型为主型客车。车体长为 25.5 m，车辆定距为 18 m，采用耐候钢制车体结构，车辆寿命可达 25～30 年。

Looking back at the history of the development of China's railroad passenger cars, the level of design and manufacturing has improved with the development of the national economy, the progress of science and technology, and the improvement of people's living standards. Since 1953, the railroad passenger cars manufacturing industry started to design and produce our first generation of products on its own, namely the series of 21 type coaches. It includes semi-cushioned seat coaches, semi-cushioned berth sleeper, dining cars, baggage cars, mail cars, and other cars, with a total of 3,110 units produced. This type of car stopped production in 1961. It was replaced by 22 type coaches for its low construction speed of 100 km/h, poor manufacturing process, unsatisfying technical and economic indicators, and declining comfort, etc. As the second generation of passenger cars in China, 22 type coaches are constructed at a speed of 120 km/h and are more advanced than 21 type coaches in various aspects. The series products of 22 type coaches include semi-cushioned seat coaches, semi-cushioned berth sleepers, cushioned seat coaches, upholstered berth sleepers, dining cars, baggage cars, mail cars, generator cars, etc., which were produced for more than 26,000 units by the end of 1992. The steel structure of the car body for 22 type coach is made of ordinary carbon steel, with serious corrosion of the steel structure, whose structure and performance cannot meet the requirements of the times, and needs to be updated and replaced by a new passenger car with more advanced product performance and technical and economic indicators, namely the third generation of passenger cars, 25 type coaches. This type of passenger car began to develop in 1966, entered into mass production in the mid-1980s, and was determined to be the main passenger car in 1993. The car body is 25.5 m long and the fixed distance for the car is 18 m, with a weather-resistant steel body structure and a service life of 25–30 years.

25 型客车也发展了系列产品，从车型上分为 25 型（试验型）、25A 型（空调）、25B 型（燃煤、空调）、25D 型（动车组）、25G 型（25A 改型）、25K 型（快速）、25S 型（双层）、25Z 型（准高速）、25T 型（提速）等。25 型客车的主要技术参数如表 7–1 所示。

A series of products have also been developed for 25 type coaches, which are divided into 25 (test type), 25A (air-conditioning), 25B (coal-fired, air-conditioning), 25D (EMU), 25G (25A modified), 25K (fast), 25S (double-deck), 25Z (quasi-high-speed) and 25T (speed-up), etc. from the models. The main technical parameters of Type 25 passenger cars are shown in Table 7-1.

表 7–1　25 型客车的主要技术参数

Table 7-1　Main Technical Parameters of 25 Type Coaches

<table>
<tr><th rowspan="3">项目
Item</th><th colspan="11">型别
Model</th></tr>
<tr><th rowspan="2">25</th><th rowspan="2">25A</th><th colspan="2">25B</th><th rowspan="2">25D</th><th rowspan="2">25G</th><th rowspan="2">25S</th><th rowspan="2">25K</th><th rowspan="2">25Z</th><th rowspan="2">25T</th></tr>
<tr><th>燃煤
Coal burning</th><th>空调
Air conditioning</th></tr>
<tr><td>构造速度
Construction speed</td><td>140 km/h</td><td>140 km/h</td><td colspan="2">140 km/h</td><td>160 km/h</td><td>140 km/h</td><td>140 km/h</td><td>160 km/h</td><td>160 km/h</td><td>160 km/h</td></tr>
<tr><td>转向架型式
Bogie type</td><td>209
206</td><td>209
206</td><td colspan="2">209
206</td><td>SW-160
CW-2</td><td>2096
2066</td><td>209PK</td><td>209HS
206KP</td><td>GW-2
206KP</td><td>CW-200K
SW-220K</td></tr>
<tr><td>采暖型式
Heating type</td><td>电
Electric</td><td>电
Electric</td><td colspan="2">水
Water</td><td>水
Water</td><td>电
Electric</td><td>电
Electric</td><td>电
Electric</td><td>电
Electric</td><td>电
Electric</td></tr>
<tr><td>空调装置
Air conditioning unit</td><td>有
Yes</td><td>有
Yes</td><td colspan="2">无
None</td><td>有
Yes</td><td>有
Yes</td><td>有
Yes</td><td>有
Yes</td><td>有
Yes</td><td>有
Yes</td></tr>
<tr><td>制动机型式
Brake type</td><td>104</td><td>104</td><td colspan="2">104</td><td>JZ-7</td><td>104</td><td>104</td><td>104+电控
104 + electric control</td><td>18+电控
18 + electric control</td><td>104+电控
104 + electric control</td></tr>
<tr><td>基础制动
Foundation braking</td><td>闸瓦
Brake shoe</td><td>闸瓦
Brake shoe</td><td colspan="2">闸瓦
Brake shoe</td><td>盘型
Disc brake</td><td>闸瓦
Brake shoe</td><td>盘型
Disc brake</td><td>盘型
Disc brake</td><td>盘型
Disc brake</td><td>盘型
Disc brake</td></tr>
</table>

续表

Continued

项目 Item	型别 Model									
	25	25A	25B 燃煤 Coal burning	25B 空调 Air conditioning	25D	25G	25S	25K	25Z	25T
防滑器 Anti-skid device	无 None	无 None	无 None		有 Yes	无 None	有 Yes	有 Yes	有 Yes	有 Yes
列车信息系统 Train information system	无 None	无 None	无 None		有 Yes	无 None	无 None	有 Yes	有 Yes	有 Yes
轴报器型式 Axle annunciator type	单 Single	单 Single	单 Single		集中 Centralized	集中 Centralized	单 Single	集中 Centralized	单 Single	集中 Centralized

25 型客车发展的过程是一个技术上逐渐成熟的过程，不断改善了工艺设备，引进国外先进技术和样车，这些均为 25 型客车的设计、制造提供了成熟的技术及可借鉴的经验。

The development process of 25 type coaches is a process of gradual technical maturity, with continuous improvement of process equipment and the introduction of advanced foreign technology and prototypes, all of which provide mature technology and experience to draw on for the design and manufacture of 25 type coaches.

25 型客车的主要技术经济指标明显优于 22 型客车，现以非空调硬座客车为例将两种客车的主要技术经济指标进行对比，如表 7–2 所示。

It is obvious that the main technical and economic indicators of 25 type coaches are better than those of 22 type coaches, and the main technical and economic indicators of the two passenger cars are compared with those of non-air-conditioned semi-cushioned seat coaches, as shown in Table 7-2.

表 7–2　25 型、22 型非空调硬座客车的主要技术经济指标对比

Table 7-2　Comparison of Main Technical and Economic Indexes of 25 Type and 22 Type Non-air-conditioned Semi–cushioned Seat Coaches

项　目 Item	车　型 Model	
	YZ_{22B}	YZ_{25B}
构造速度 Construction speed	120 km/h	140 km/h
车体长度 Vehicle body length	23.6 m	25.5 m

续表
Continued

项　目 Item	车　型 Model	
	YZ_{22B}	YZ_{25B}
车顶距轨面高 Height from roof to rail surface	4.283 m	4.433 m
平稳性指标 Stability index	2.75 W	2.5 W
客室内噪声 Noise in saloon	68 dB（80 km/h 运行时） 68 dB (at 80 km/h operation)	68 dB（120 km/h 运行时） 68 dB (at 120 km/h operation)
自重 Tare weight	42.1 t	45.3 t
每延米重 Weight per linear meter	1.784 t/m	1.776 t/m
定员 Passenger capacity	118 人	128 人
每定员占自重 Tare weight per passenger capacity	0.356 t/人	0.353 t/人
钢结构自重 Tare weight of steel structure	14.2 t	14 t
钢结构型式 Steel structure type	有中梁、有压筋、整体承载结构 With center beam, compression reinforcement, and overall bearing structure	无中梁、无压筋、薄板筒形整体承载结构 Without center beam, compression reinforcement, and thin-plate cylindrical integral bearing structure
钢结构除锈 Derusting of steel structures	整体打砂 Overall sanding	钢材料预处理 Steel material pretreatment
风挡 Windshield	22 型通用铁风挡 Type 22 universal iron windshield	耐磨耗低噪声风挡 Wear-resistant and low-noise windshield
车窗 Car window	玻璃钢框、上开式 Glass fiber reinforced plastic frame, upper opening type	铝合金双层中空玻璃、上窗下开单元式 Aluminum alloy double-layer insulating glass, upper window lower-opening unit type
轮对 Wheelset	无动平衡要求 No dynamic balance requirements	有动平衡要求 There are dynamic balance requirements
阻燃材料 Flame retardant materials	无要求 No requirements	采用阻燃材料 Use of flame retardant materials
车内设备 In-car equipment		座椅及车内设备有所改善 Improved seating and interior equipment
车钩 Coupler	15 型 15	15 型低合金钢高强度车钩 No.15 low-alloy steel high-strength coupler
缓冲器 Draft gear	1 号 No. 1	G1 型 G1
制动 Brake		提高了销套的配合精度，部分采用了 ST_1–500 型自动闸瓦间隙调整器 The fitting accuracy of the pin sleeve is improved, and ST_1-500 automatic brake shoe clearance adjuster is partially adopted

通过表 7–2 中的对比，可以得出以下结论。

The following conclusions can be drawn from the comparison in Table 7-2.

（1）25 型客车比 22 型客车增加了定员，其中硬座车可增加 10 个，硬卧车可增加 6 个，软卧车可增加 4 个。每个定员所占车辆自重降低，经济效益提高。

There has been an increase in the passenger capacity of passengers in 25 type coaches compared with that of 22 type coaches, in which the number of passengers has been increased by 10 in semi-cushioned seat coaches, 6 in semi-cushioned berth sleepers and 4 in upholstered berth sleepers. The tare weight of the car that per passenger occupies has been reduced with higher economic efficiency.

（2）构造速度提高到 140 km/h 以上，比 22 型客车的 120 km/h 高出约 17%，标志着技术含量增大，是更新换代产品。

The construction speed has been increased to more than 140 km/h, which is 17% higher than the 120 km/h of 22 type coaches, indicating an increase in technical content and a newer product.

（3）改进了车体钢结构，采用无中梁底架整体承载结构，在车体加长 1.9 m 及车体高出 150 mm 的情况下，钢结构自重仍较 22 型客车有所降低。试验表明，25 型客车的钢结构具有足够的强度和刚度，标志着设计、制造水平的提高。车体钢结构取消了压筋，简化了工艺，同时也对墙板的平度提出了较高的要求，使其金属包板不平度值低于 22 型客车。

The steel structure of the car body has been improved using the overall load-bearing structure without the center beam underframe, and in the case of the car body being 1.9 m longer and 150 mm higher, the tare weight of the steel structure is still lower than that of 22 type coaches. The test showed sufficient strength and stiffness of the steel structure for 25 type coaches, which represents the improvement of the design and manufacturing level. After the cancellation of the compression reinforcement in the steel structure of the car body, and simplification of the process, as well as the higher requirements for the flatness of the wall plate, so that the unevenness value of its metal cladding is lower than that of the 22 type coaches.

（4）采用低噪声、耐磨耗风挡，克服了 22 型客车铁风挡缓冲杆磨耗严重，车辆连挂通过小曲线半径、反向曲线及岔道时，面板错动量大、难以复原，运行中冲击噪声大，甚至危及行车安全等问题。

The use of low-noise and wear-resistant windshields has overcome the serious wear and tear of the iron windshield buffer rod for 22 type coaches, and problems such as large panel misalignment, difficulty in recovery, loud impact noise, and even traffic safety hazards when the cars pass through small radius curves, reverse curves and turnouts during operation.

（5）提高了乘坐舒适性、安全性。舒适性是一个综合性指标，它包括平稳性好、噪声低、内部设备改善等，这些都可以提高旅客乘坐的舒适度。另外，防火、阻燃材料的应用，提高了旅客乘坐的安全性。

The ride comfort and safety has been improved. Comfort is a comprehensive indicator, including good smoothness, low noise, improved interior equipment and others. These have improved the comfort of passengers riding. Moreover, fireproof and flame-retardant materials have been applied to improve the safety of passengers' journey.

（6）新型铝合金单元车窗的采用，提高了车窗的密封性，改善了通风条件，减轻了窗口钢结构的腐蚀，同时也起到美观的作用。对轮对进行动平衡试验，这对减少轮轨间的冲击力、改善振动性能、提高轴承寿命、减少燃轴事故都是有益的。

The application of new aluminum alloy unit windows has strengthened the sealing of the windows, improved the ventilation, reduced the corrosion of the steel structure of the windows, and contributed to the aesthetic effect. The dynamic balance test for wheelsets helps to reduce the impact force between wheels and rails, improve the vibration performance, increase the bearing life, and reduce the accident of axle burning.

22 型客车向 25 型客车的过渡，将会增加一次性投资。一辆 25B 型硬座车的造价将比 22B 型硬座车提高 50%左右，但是由于定员的增加及舒适度的提高，由此增加的客票收入，在两年左右的时间内即可补偿所提高的造价。所以说，25 型客车的经济效益和社会效益是极为显著的。

The transition from 22 type coaches to 25 type coaches will require additional one-time investment. A 25B type semi-cushioned seat coach will cost about 50% more than a 22B type semi-cushioned seat coach, but the resulting increase in passenger ticket revenue will compensate for the increase in cost in about two years due to the increased passenger capacity and improved comfort. In this regard, the economic and social benefits of 25 type coaches are extremely significant.

目前，我国各客车制造厂家为适应提速的要求，以生产 25K 型的各型客车为主。统计资料显示，全国客车的拥有量为 75 000 辆。

At present, China's passenger car manufacturers are mainly producing 25K type coaches to meet the requirements of speed increase. Statistical information showed that the number of passenger cars nationwide is 75,000.

25 型系列客车，其构造速度有 140 km/h 和 160 km/h 两种。前者为普通 25 型客车，后者为提速 25 型客车。25 型系列客车包括硬座车、硬卧车、软卧车、软座车、餐车、行李车、邮政车和发电车等。

There are two types of 25 type coaches, which are constructed at 140 km/h and 160 km/h. The former are ordinary 25 type coaches, while the latter are accelerated 25 type coaches. 25 type coaches include semi-cushioned seat coaches, semi-cushioned berth sleepers, cushioned seat coaches, upholstered berth sleepers, dining cars, baggage cars, mail cars, and generator cars.

25 型双层旅客列车由硬座车、硬卧车、软座车、软卧车和发电车等组成。该列车的最高运行速度为 140 km/h，中短途、中长途双层旅客列车在客流繁忙的区域对于缓解乘车难的问题起着重要的作用。

The 25 type double-deck coach consists of the semi-cushioned seat coach, semi-cushioned berth sleeper, cushioned seat coach, upholstered berth sleeper, generator car, etc. The maximum operating speed of this train is 140 km/h. The short- and medium-distance and long-distance double-deck passenger cars contribute significantly to alleviating the problem of difficult travel in areas with busy passenger flow.

随着社会主义市场经济的发展，我国铁路的旅客运输从 20 世纪 90 年代中期开始连续进行了多次大提速，因此在发展常规客车的同时，也研制生产了不少动车组。这其中包括各速度级的、内燃的和电力牵引的、动力集中的和动力分散的等类型。在车体的主要结构和常规客车相差不是很大。限于篇幅，本书中不再专门讲述。

Railroad passenger transportation in China has continuously sped up several times since the mid-1990s with the development of a socialist market economy in China. While developing conventional passenger cars, a number of EMUs have also been developed and produced. These include various speed classes, internal combustion and electric traction, power-centralized and power-decentralized, and other types of trains. However, the main structure of the car body is not very different from that of conventional passenger cars. This book is not dedicated to this topic due to the limitation of space.

除了上述干线旅客列车中的各型客车外，我国在城市轨道交通方面，稳步地发展了地铁交通系统。从 20 世纪 70 年代起，首先在北京、天津两大城市开通了地下铁道交通运营线路。进入 20 世纪 90 年代之后，为了缓解大城市的市内交通拥堵，北京、上海、广州、天津、深圳及重庆等大城市均大力发展了城市轨道交通系统，因此城市轨道交通客车的需求量也在逐年增加，其车辆型式也越来越多。城市轨道交通车辆中有较大部分是我国自行设计制造的，也有一部分是通过进口或者技术合资引进的国外车辆。

In addition to the above-mentioned passenger cars of various types in the mainline passenger cars, the subway transportation system has been steadily developed in China in terms of urban rail transportation, with underground rail transportation operating lines first opened in two major cities, Beijing and Tianjin, since the 1970s. Later in the 1990s, the urban rail transit system was developed in Beijing, Shanghai, Guangzhou, Tianjin, Shenzhen, and Chongqing to alleviate the traffic congestion in big cities, resulting in an increase in the demand for urban rail transit passenger cars year by year with an increasing number of car types. There is a larger part of its urban rail transit vehicles designed and manufactured independently in China, and there is also a part of foreign cars introduced through imports or technical joint ventures.

随着我国国民经济的发展、人员交往的增多，以及旅游业的兴旺，将需要生产出现代化的、满足不同层次旅客需要的各种新型客车、高级旅游车和高速客车等。

It is necessary to produce modern passenger cars, senior tour passenger cars, and high-speed passenger cars to meet the needs of different levels of passengers with the development of China's national economy, the increase of personnel interaction, and the prosperity of tourism.

部分国产主型客车（25 型）的性能及尺寸如表 7-3 所示。

The performance and dimensions of some domestic main passenger cars (25 type coaches) are shown in Table 7-3.

表 7-3　部分国产主型客车（25 型）的性能及尺寸

Table 7-3　Performance and Dimensions of Domestic Main Type Passenger Cars (25 Type Coaches)

<table>
<tr><th rowspan="2">车辆型号
Vehicle model</th><th rowspan="2">定员
Seating capacity</th><th rowspan="2">自重/t
Curb weight/t</th><th rowspan="2">车体材质
Body material</th><th colspan="5">车体主要尺寸/mm
Main dimensions of the vehicle/mm</th><th colspan="2">钩缓装置
Hook buffer device</th><th colspan="2">电气装置
Electrical device</th><th rowspan="2">取暖装置
Heating device</th><th rowspan="2">给水装置形式及容量/L
Form and capacity of water supply device/L</th><th rowspan="2">通风装置
Ventilation system</th><th rowspan="2">平稳性指标/W
Stability index/W</th><th rowspan="2">车体平均传热系数/[W/(m²·K)]
Average heat transfer coefficient of the car body/[W/(m²·K)]</th><th rowspan="2">风挡形式
Windshield form</th></tr>
<tr><th>车体长
Car body length</th><th>车辆定距
Vehicle spacing</th><th>车体外宽
Vehicle width</th><th>车顶距轨面高
Height of vehicle roof from track</th><th>渡板距轨面高
Height of boarding bridge from track</th><th>车钩型号
Type of vehicle hook</th><th>缓冲器型号
Buffer model</th><th>电压/V
Voltage/V</th><th>供电方式
Power supply mode</th></tr>
<tr><td>YZ_{25A}</td><td>128
122 车长席
122 car length seat</td><td></td><td rowspan="4">Corten 钢
Corten steel</td><td rowspan="4">25 500</td><td rowspan="4">18 000</td><td rowspan="4">3 104</td><td rowspan="4">4.433</td><td rowspan="4">1 333</td><td rowspan="4">15 型高强度车钩
High-strength vehicle hook No. 15</td><td rowspan="4">G1</td><td rowspan="4">AC380</td><td rowspan="4">发电车集中供电
Centralized power supply for power generation vehicles</td><td rowspan="4">电热取暖
Electric heating</td><td>车下水箱，≥1 000
Under-car water tank, ≥1000</td><td rowspan="4">车顶单元式空调机组
Roof-mounted unitary air conditioning unit</td><td rowspan="4">≤2.5</td><td rowspan="4">≤1.1</td><td rowspan="4">低噪声耐磨风挡
Low noise and wear-resistant windscreen</td></tr>
<tr><td>YW_{25A}</td><td>66</td><td>45.5</td><td>车上水箱，1 300
On-board water tank, 1300</td></tr>
<tr><td>RW_{25A}</td><td>36</td><td></td><td>车上水箱，1 000
On-board water tank, 1000</td></tr>
<tr><td>CA_{25A}</td><td>48</td><td>46.6</td><td>车下水箱，1 200
Under-car water tank, 1200</td></tr>
<tr><td>YZ_{25B}</td><td>128
122 车长席
Seat for 122 car length</td><td>44.5</td><td rowspan="4">耐候钢
Weathering steel</td><td rowspan="4">25 500</td><td rowspan="4">18 000</td><td rowspan="4">3 104</td><td rowspan="4">4 433</td><td rowspan="4">1 333</td><td rowspan="4">15 型高强度车钩
High-strength car hook No. 15</td><td rowspan="4">G1</td><td rowspan="4">DC48，AC380</td><td rowspan="4">5 kW 感应发电机发电车集中供电
5 kW induction sub-generator for centralized power supply of the vehicle</td><td rowspan="4">燃煤锅炉取暖
Coal-fired boiler heating</td><td>车上水箱，1 200
On-board water tank, 1200</td><td rowspan="4">车顶单元式空调机组
Rooftop unit air conditioner</td><td rowspan="4">≤2.5</td><td rowspan="4">1.16</td><td rowspan="4">低噪声耐磨风挡
Low noise and wear-resistant windscreen</td></tr>
<tr><td>YW_{25B}</td><td>66
60 播音车
60 broadcasting vehicle</td><td>47</td><td rowspan="3">车上水箱，1 000
On-board water tank, 1000</td></tr>
<tr><td>RW_{25B}</td><td>36</td><td>51.5</td></tr>
<tr><td>CA_{25B}</td><td>48</td><td>54.2</td></tr>
</table>

续表

Continued

车辆型号 Vehicle model	定员 Seating capacity	自重/t Curb weight/t	车体材质 Body material	车体主要尺寸/mm Main dimensions of the vehicle/mm					钩缓装置 Hook buffer device		电气装置 Electrical device		取暖装置 Heating device	给水装置形式及容量/L Form and capacity of water supply device/L	通风装置 Ventilation system	平稳性指标/W Stability index/W	车体平均传热系数/[W/(m²·K)] Average heat transfer coefficient of the car body/[W/(m²·K)]	风挡形式 Windshield form
				车体长 Car body length	车辆定距 Vehicle spacing	车体外宽 Vehicle width	车顶距轨面高 Height of vehicle roof from track	渡板距轨面高 Height of boarding bridge from track	车钩型号 Type of vehicle hook	缓冲器型号 Buffer model	电压/V Voltage/V	供电方式 Power supply mode						
YZ_{25G}	128 122 车长席 122 car length seat	46	耐候钢 Weathering steel	25 500	18 000	3 104	4 433	1 333	15 型高强度车钩 High-strength car hook No. 15	G1	AC380	发电车集中供电 Centralized power supply for power generation vehicles	电热取暖 Electric heating	车上水箱，1 200 On-board water tank, 1200	车顶单元式空调机组 Roof-mounted split air conditioning unit	≤2.5	1.1	低噪声耐磨风挡 Low noise and wear-resistant windscreen
YW_{25G}	66													车上水箱，1 150 On-board water tank, 1150			<1.1	
RW_{25C}	36													车上水箱，1 000 On-board water tank, 1000			1.16	
CA_{25G}	48													车下水箱，1 200 Under-car water tank, 1200		≤2.75	1.16	
XL_{25G}	17.7 t	46												车上水箱，≥440 On-board water tank, ≥440		≤2.5	1.2	
$RZ1_{25Z}$	76	48.5	耐候钢 Weather-resistant steel	25 500	18 000	3 104	4 050	1 333	15 型高强度车钩 High-strength car hook No. 15	G1	AC380	发电车集中供电 Centralized power supply for power cars	电热取暖 Electric heating	车上水箱，1 150 On-board water tank, 1150	车顶单元式空调机组 Unit-type air conditioning system on the roof of the car	≤2.5	1.16	橡胶风挡 Rubber windshield
$RZ2_{25Z}$	96	48.5																
$RZX2_{25Z}$	56/5.6 t																	
CA_{25Z}	32																	
YZ_{25K}	118	46.7	耐候钢 Weather-resistant steel	25 500	18 000	3 105	4 433	1 333	15 型高强度车钩 High-strength car hook No. 15	G1	AC380	发电车集中供电 Centralized power supply for power generation vehicles	电热取暖 Electric heating	车上水箱，1 000 On-board water tank, 1000	车顶单元式空调机组 Roof-mounted unitary air conditioning unit	≤2.5	<1.16	低噪声耐磨风挡 Low noise and wear-resistant windscreen
YW_{25K}	66/60	46.5																

续表
Continued

车辆型号 Vehicle model	定员 Seating capacity	自重/t Curb weight/t	车体材质 Body material	车体主要尺寸/mm Main dimensions of the vehicle/mm					钩缓装置 Hook buffer device		电气装置 Electrical device		取暖装置 Heating device	给水装置形式及容量/L Form and capacity of water supply device/L	通风装置 Ventilation system	平稳性指标/W Stability index/W	车体平均传热系数/[W/(m²·K)] Average heat transfer coefficient of the car body/[W/(m²·K)]	风挡形式 Windshield form
				车体长 Car body length	车辆定距 Vehicle spacing	车体外宽 Vehicle width	车顶距轨面高 Height of vehicle roof from track	渡板距轨面高 Height of boarding bridge from track	车钩型号 Type of vehicle hook	缓冲器型号 Buffer model	电压/V Voltage/V	供电方式 Power supply mode						
RW_{25K}	36	48.1	耐候钢 Weather-resistant steel	25 500	18 000	3 105	4 433	1 333	15 型高强度车钩 High-strength car hook No. 15	G1	AC380	发电车集中供电 Centralized power supply for power generation vehicles	燃煤锅炉取暖 Coal-fired boiler heating	车上水箱，1 040 On-board water tank, 1040	车顶单元式空调机组 Roof-mounted unitary air conditioning unit	≤2.5	<1.16	低噪声耐磨风挡 Low noise and wear-resistant windscreen
CA_{25K}	48												电热取暖 Electric heating	车下水箱，1 200 Under-car water tank, 1200				
UZ_{25K}	18 t	46												车上水箱，600 On-board water tank, 600		≤2.75	≤1.16	
YZ_{25T}	118	46.7	耐候钢 Weathering steel	25 500	18 000	3 105	4 433	1 333	小间隙密接式车钩 Close-coupled hook with small gap	Gl	AC380	发电车集中供电 Centralized power supply for generator car	电热取暖 Electric heating	车上水箱，1 500 On-board water tank, 1500	车顶单元式空调机组 Roof-mounted unitary air conditioning unit	≤2.5	<1.16	折叠风挡 Foldable windshield
YW_{25T}	66	46.5												车上水箱，1 000 On-board water tank, 1000				
RW_{25T}	36	48.1											锅炉取暖 Boiler heating	车上水箱，1 040 On-board water tank, 1040				
CA_{25T}	48													车下水箱，1 200 Under-car water tank, 1200				

任务 7.2　25 型客车的车体结构

Task 7.2　Structure of car body for 25 type coach

25 型客车车体钢结构为全钢焊接结构，由底架、侧墙、车顶和端墙等 4 部分焊接而成。在侧墙、端墙、车顶钢骨架外面，分别焊有侧墙板、端墙板、车顶板和纵向波纹地板及平地板，形成一个上部带圆弧、下部为矩形的封闭壳体，俗称薄壁筒形车体结构。壳体内面或外面用纵向梁和横向梁、柱加强，形成整体承载的合理结构。

The steel structure of car body for 25 type coach car is an all-steel welded structure, which is welded from four parts, including the underframe, side walls, the roof, and end walls. There are sidewall plate, end wall plate, roof plate, and longitudinal corrugated floor and flat floor welded outside the side wall, end wall, roof steel skeleton, which forms a closed shell with a circular arc at the top and rectangular shape at the bottom, commonly known as thin-walled cylindrical body structure. The inside or outside of the shell is strengthened with longitudinal beams and transverse beams and columns to form a reasonable structure for overall bearing.

虽然 25 型各种客车的结构不完全相同，但其外形尺寸和结构形式则基本一致。图 7–1 为 1996 年以后生产的 25 型硬座客车车体钢结构，按其大部件的生产方式，可划分为底架、侧墙、车顶、外端墙、内端墙及其他零部件。

Despite that the structure of various 25 type coaches is not all the same, their external dimensions and structural forms are basically the same. Figure 7-1 shows that the steel structure of car body for 25 type semi-cushioned seat coach produced after 1996 can be divided into underframe, side wall, roof, outer end wall, inner end wall and other parts according to the production mode of large parts.

7.2.1　底架

Underframe

底架由牵引梁、枕梁、缓冲梁、下围梁（或称下侧梁）、枕梁间的纵向金属波纹地板及枕外金属平地板等组成，其结构如图 7–2 所示。

The underframe is composed of a traction beam, a sleeper beam buffer beam, a lower perimeter beam (or lower side beam), a longitudinal corrugated metal floor between the sleeper beams, and a flat metal floor outside the pillow, as shown in Figure 7-2.

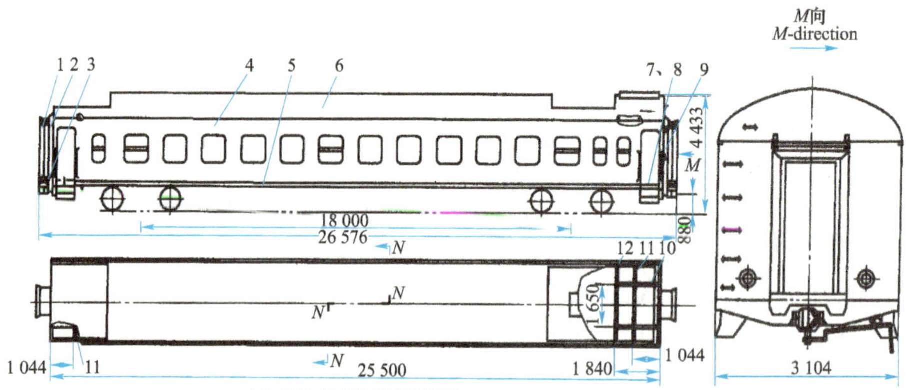

(a) 硬座车整体外部结构图
Overall external structure diagram of semi-cushioned seat coach

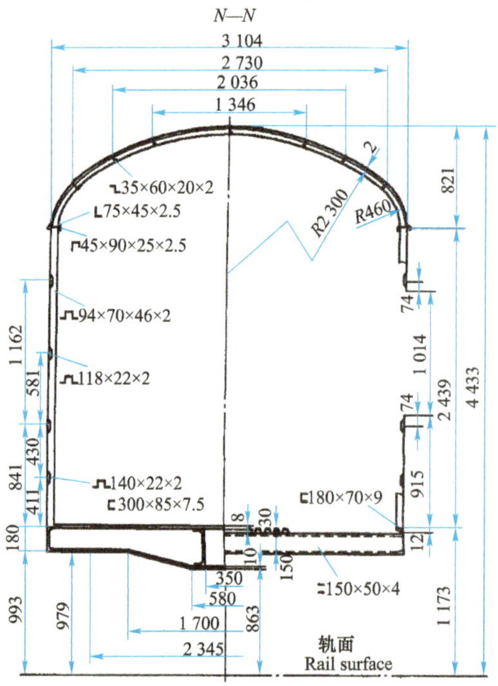

(b) 硬座车车体横断面剖视图
Cross-sectional view of the semi-cushioned seat coach body

1—风挡；2—端墙钢结构；3—钩缓装置；4—侧墙钢结构；5—底架钢结构；6—车顶钢结构；7—一、四位翻板安装；8—二、三位翻板安装；9—脚蹬组成；10—水箱吊梁；11—横梁；12—水箱横梁。

1—Windshield; 2—End wall steel structure; 3—Hook buffer device; 4—Side wall steel structure; 5—Underframe steel structure; 6—Roof steel structure; 7—Installation of "B" end and "D" end flaps; 8—Installation of "A" end and "C" end flaps; 9—Pedal composition; 10—Water tank lifting beam; 11—Cross beam; 12—Water tank beam.

图 7-1 硬座客车车体钢结构

Figure 7-1 Steel Structure of Semi-cushioned Seat Passenger Car Body

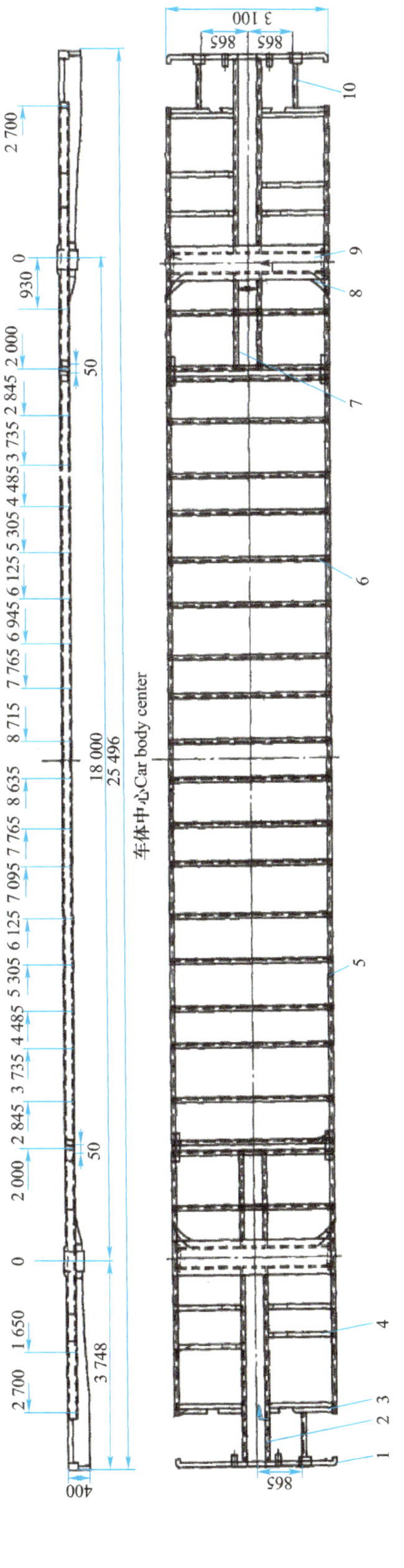

1—缓冲梁；2—牵引梁；3—端梁；4—枕外横梁；5—侧梁；6—横梁；7—纵向加强梁；8—加强板；9—枕梁；10—纵向梁。

1—Buffer beam; 2—Traction beam; 3—End beam; 4—Outer sleeper beam; 5—Side beam; 6—Cross beam; 7—Longitudinal reinforcement beam; 8—Reinforcement plate; 9—Sleeper beam; 10—Longitudinal beam.

图 7-2　底架的结构

Figure 7-2　Structure of Underframe

底架自上心盘中心到缓冲梁间的中梁称为牵引梁，由两根 30a 型槽钢及牵引梁上、下盖板组焊而成。其上盖板厚 8 mm、宽 490 mm，下盖板厚 10 mm、宽 490 mm。为了符合在牵引梁腹板间安装缓冲器的尺寸要求，两槽钢腹板的间距为 350 mm，并将牵引梁端部的一段加高至 400 mm 或 420 mm，为适应安装车钩缓冲装置而设计。两槽钢腹板内侧铆接有前、后从板座，焊有磨耗板和防跳板。

The central beam between the center of the upper center plate of the underframe and the buffer beam is called the traction beam, which is welded by two 30a channel steels and the upper and lower cover plates of the traction beam. Its upper cover is 8 mm thick and 490 mm wide, while its lower cover is 10 mm thick and 490 mm wide. It is designed to meet the dimensional requirements for the installation of buffers between the webs of the traction beam, with the two-channel webs spaced at 350 mm and a section at the end of the traction beam raised to 400 mm or 420 mm to accommodate the installation of the coupler and draft gears. The inner side of the two-channel steel webs is riveted with front and rear slave plates, and welded with wear plates and anti-creep plates.

缓冲梁是由 6 mm 厚钢板压制而成的槽形断面梁，两腹板高 180 mm，中部腹板高 400 mm。在缓冲梁中部开有安装车钩用的缺口，缓冲梁的中央部分与牵引梁端部相互组焊在一起，缓冲梁与端梁间有两根角断面的纵向梁，以增加其连接强度和刚度。

The buffer beam is a slotted section beam pressed from a 6 mm thick steel plate, with two webs 180 mm high and a central web 400 mm high. In the middle of the buffer beam is a gap for installing the coupler, and the central part of the buffer beam and the end of the traction beam are welded to each other on the longitudinal beam with two angular sections between the buffer beam and the end beam to increase its connection strength and stiffness.

枕梁是由厚 8 mm、间距 350 mm 的两块腹板，厚 10 mm、宽 600 mm 的下盖板，厚 8 mm、宽 600 mm 的上盖板组焊而成的闭口箱形断面。枕梁近侧梁端为小端，近牵引梁端为大端，它是一个近似的等强度鱼腹梁。在与牵引梁交叉处安装有心盘座，以增强该处的承载作用，提高枕梁和牵引梁的连接强度和刚度。在枕梁两端的上旁承安装处焊有旁承加强筋板，枕梁端部还焊有供顶车用的防滑垫板。

The sleeper beam is a closed box-shaped section composed of two webs with a thickness of 8 mm and a spacing of 350 mm, a lower cover plate with a thickness of 10 mm and a width of 600 mm, and an upper cover plate with a thickness of 8 mm and a width of 600 mm, which is an approximately equal strength fish-belly sill with a small end near the side beam and a large end near the traction beam. A center plate seat is installed at the intersection with the traction beam to improve the bearing effect there and to increase the connection strength and stiffness of the sleeper beam and the traction beam. At both ends of the sleeper beam, there is a side bearing reinforcement plate welded to the upper side bearing, and the end of the sleeper beam is also welded with an anti-skid pad for the top car.

枕梁、缓冲梁与牵引梁组成的结构称为牵枕缓结构，如图 7-3 所示。

The structure composed of the sleeper beam, buffer beam, and traction beam is called the traction sleeper buffer structure, which is shown in Figure 7-3.

底架两侧有沿底架两端梁间全长纵向布置的两侧梁，其断面为 18a 型槽钢。在横向，底架的枕梁及全部横梁的端部都与侧梁焊接，金属地板也与侧梁的上翼缘表面搭接；侧墙的立柱、侧墙板分别焊在侧梁的上翼缘表面和腹板外表面上，所以侧梁是连接侧墙和底架的重要构件。其连接关系如图 7–1 所示。

Both sides of the underframe are provided with two side beams arranged longitudinally along the full length between the two end beams of the underframe, whose sections are Type 18a channel steel. Transversely, the sleeper beams of the underframe and all the ends of the cross beams are welded to the side beams, and the metal floor is also lapped with the upper flange surface of the side beams; Besides, the columns and sidewall plates of the side walls are welded to the upper flange surface and the outer surface of the web of the side beams respectively, making the side beams an important member connecting the side walls and the underframe. The connection relationship is shown in Figure 7-1.

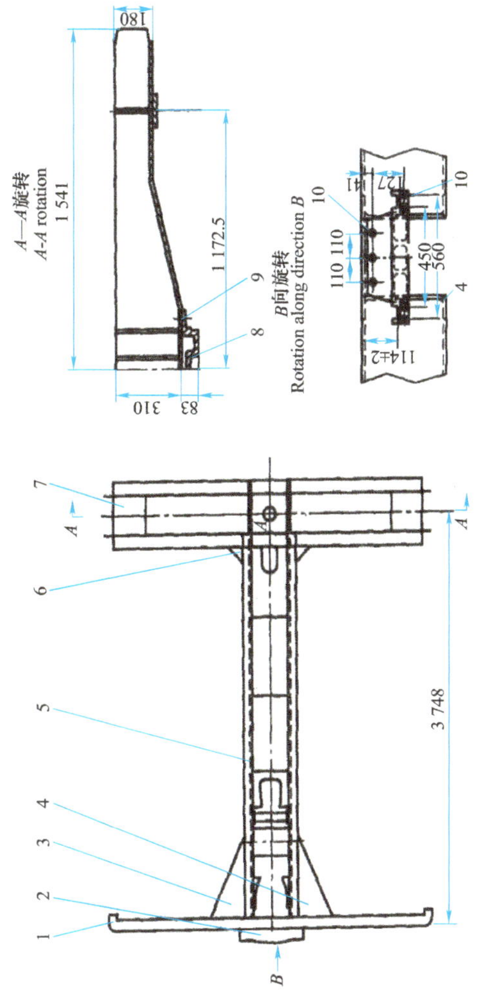

1—缓冲梁组成；2—冲击座；3、4、6—补强板；5—牵引梁组成；7—枕梁组成；8—上心盘；9、10—铆钉。

1—Buffer beam composition; 2—Impact seat; 3, 4, 6—Reinforcement plate; 5—Traction beam composition; 7—Sleeper beam composition; 8—Upper center plate; 9, 10—Rivet.

图 7–3　底架的牵枕缓结构

Figure 7-3　Traction Sleeper Buffer Structure of Underframe

在底架缓冲梁和枕梁之间、两枕梁之间均设置有较均布的横梁。这些横梁的两端分别与下侧梁和牵引梁或是与下侧梁焊接。这样，底架的牵枕缓、侧梁和横梁共同形成底架钢结构骨架。在骨架的上面焊上金属地板。缓冲梁和枕梁上盖板间为平地板，板厚为 2 mm；两枕梁间为纵向波纹金属地板，板厚为 1.5 mm。由底架钢结构骨架和金属地板共同组成底架钢结构。每端缓冲梁和枕梁间设有 2 对 50 mm×180 mm×50 mm×4 mm 的槽形断面横梁；在两枕梁间设置有 22 根 50 mm×150 mm×50 mm×4 mm 的槽形断面横梁。这些横梁的作用：一是把牵枕缓结构与侧梁连接起来形成底架钢结构骨架，从而保证底架有足够的强度和刚度，以承受作用于底架上的各种载荷；二是成为平地板和纵向波纹地板的支撑，在纵向力作用下防止纵向波纹地板的失稳，所以横梁间距均布在 1 m 以内。地板、横梁及下侧梁的连接如图 7-1（b）所示。由于两枕梁间无贯通的中梁，因而作用于底架上的纵向拉压力均由波纹地板和底架侧梁来承担。这种结构的底架称为无中梁底架。车体钢结构静强度试验表明，纵向波纹地板能承受三分之一以上的总纵向拉伸或压缩力。

There are evenly distributed cross beams arranged between the underframe buffer beam and the sleeper beam, as well as between the two sleeper beams. The two ends of these cross beams are welded to the lower side beam and traction beam respectively, or both ends are welded to the lower side beam. In this manner, the traction sleeper buffer structure, the side beam, and the cross beam of the underframe together form the underframe steel structure skeleton. A metal floor is welded to the top of the skeleton. A flat floor with a thickness of 2 mm is provided between the buffer beam and the upper cover plate of the sleeper beam, and a longitudinal corrugated metal floor with a thickness of 1.5 mm is provided between the two sleeper beams. The underframe steel structure is composed of an underframe steel structure skeleton and a metal floor. 2 pairs of slotted section cross beams with dimensions of 50 mm × 180 mm × 50 mm × 4 mm are arranged between the buffer beam and sleeper beam at each end, and 22 slotted section cross beams with dimensions of 50 mm × 150 mm × 50 mm × 4 mm are arranged between the two sleeper beams. One of the roles of these cross beams is to link the traction sleeper buffer structure with the side beams to form the underframe steel skeleton, to ensure that the underframe has sufficient strength and stiffness to withstand the various loads acting on the underframe; and the other is to become the support of the flat floor and the longitudinal corrugated floor, to prevent the destabilization of the longitudinal corrugated floor under the action of the longitudinal force, so the spacing of the cross beams is evenly distributed within 1 m. The connection of the floor, cross beam, and lower side beam is shown in Figure 7-1 (b). As there is no through center beam between the two sleeper beams, the longitudinal tensile forces acting on the underframe are borne by the corrugated floor and the side beams of the underframe. The underframe of this structure is called the underframe without a center beam. The static strength test of the steel structure of the car shows that the longitudinal corrugated floor can bear more than one-third of the total longitudinal tensile or compressive force.

7.2.2 侧墙

Side wall

25 型客车车体钢结构的侧墙外表面为平板无压筋，在平整的外墙板内侧焊有垂直立柱和水平纵向梁，形成板梁式平面承载侧墙结构，如图 7–4 所示。

The outer surface of the side walls of the 25 type coach's carbody steel structure is a flat plate without compression reinforcements, with vertical columns and horizontal longitudinal beams welded to the inner side of the flat outer wall plate, forming a plate and beam type flat bearing sidewall structure, as shown in Figure 7-4.

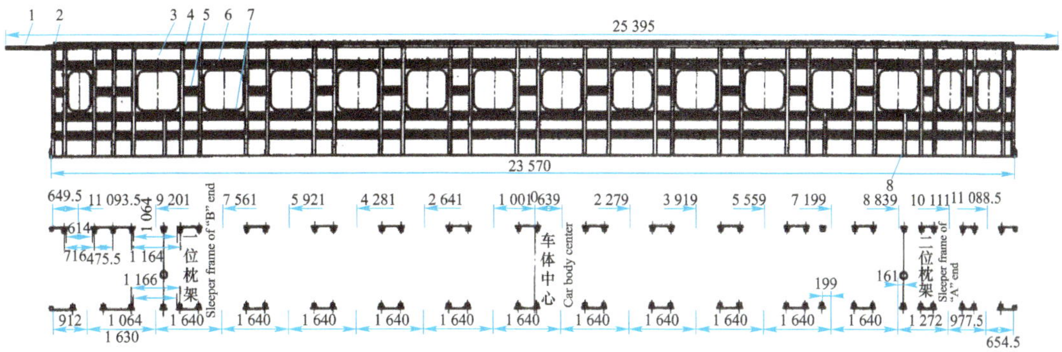

1—上侧梁；2—门立柱；3—侧墙板；4—立柱；5—窗间纵梁；6—窗上纵向梁；7—窗下纵向梁；8—窗下立柱。

1—Upper side beam; 2—Door column; 3—Sidewall plate; 4—Column; 5—Longitudinal beam between windows; 6—Longitudinal beam on the window; 7—Longitudinal beam under the window; 8—Column under the window.

图 7–4　侧墙的结构

Figure 7-4　Structure of Side Wall

侧墙上侧梁（上围梁）为 45 mm×90 mm×25 mm×2.5 mm 的槽形断面梁，长度为侧墙全长。侧墙水平纵向梁共 3 根，窗上 1 根，窗下 2 根，为 24 mm×22 mm×46 mm×22 mm×24 mm×2 mm 的帽形梁。这 3 根纵向梁起到加强侧墙的垂直弯曲强度和刚度的作用，同时也减少了侧墙板自由表面的面积。在侧墙窗口间有一条短的窗间小纵向梁，设置的目的是增强窗间板的强度与刚度。在各窗口两侧共有 31 根垂向的窗边侧立柱，它们与所有纵梁、上侧梁、下侧梁连接起来，组成侧墙钢骨架，并与侧墙板焊接形成侧墙钢结构。侧墙板为厚 2.5 mm 的耐候钢（09CuPCrNiB）。侧墙板上开有 11 个大窗孔，尺寸为 1 064 mm×1 014 mm；4 个小窗孔，尺寸为 614 mm×1 014 mm。每侧侧墙端部有两个侧门孔。门窗开孔处是侧墙的薄弱区域，通过周边的梁柱予以加强，并选择合适的窗角板的圆角半径来降低其应力集中。侧墙与底架的结合方式如图 7–1 所示。

The side beams (upper perimeter beams) on the side walls are slotted section beams with a dimension of 45 mm × 90 mm × 25 mm × 2.5 mm and a length of the full length of the side walls. There are three horizontal longitudinal beams on the side wall, including one on the window and two under the window, which are cap-shaped beams with a dimension of 24 mm × 22 mm × 46 mm × 22 mm × 24 mm × 2 mm. These three longitudinal beams act to strengthen the vertical bending strength and stiffness of the sidewall and reduce the area of the free surface of the sidewall plate. A short longitudinal beam is provided between the windows of the sidewalls to enhance the strength and stiffness of the inter-window plates. A total of 31 vertical window side columns on both sides of each window are connected with all longitudinal beams, upper side beams, and lower side beams to form the sidewall steel skeleton and weld to the sidewall plate for the sidewall steel structure. Sidewall plates are made of 2.5 mm thick weather-resistant steel (09CuPCrNiB). Sidewall plates are provided with 11 large window holes with the dimensions of 1,064 mm × 1,014 mm and 4 small window holes with the dimensions of 614 mm × 1,014 mm. Each side of the side walls is provided with two side door openings at the end. As the door and window openings are the weak areas of the side walls, they are strengthened by the surrounding beams, and the proper fillet radius of the window corner plates is selected to reduce their stress concentration. The side walls and the underframe are combined in the way shown in Figure 7-1.

7.2.3 车顶 Roof

车顶是由上边梁、车顶弯梁、车顶纵向梁、空调机组安装座平台、水箱盖等组成的钢骨架，在钢骨架的外面焊有车顶板，共同组成车顶钢结构，如图 7–5 所示。

The roof is a steel skeleton composed of upper boundary beams, roof bending beams, roof longitudinal beams, air conditioning unit mounting seat platform, water tank cover, etc. There are roof plates welded on the outside of the skeleton, which together form the roof steel structure, as shown in Figure 7-5.

车顶上边梁沿车顶两侧全长，为 45 mm×72 mm×2.5 mm 的钢板压制成角形断面。上边梁与顶端横梁组成车顶下部框架。车顶一、二位端各有一个空调机组安装座平台钢结构，作为安装空调机组的基础。二位端还有一个水箱盖组成。车顶的中间部分结构，其上焊有 30 根 26 mm×70 mm×46 mm×70 mm×26 mm×2 mm 的帽形断面车顶弯梁。车顶端部的弯梁为 30 mm×55 mm×62.5 mm×45 mm×2 mm 的折角形钢板压型件。在车顶的横断面上，除两根车顶上边梁外，还有 5 根 30 mm×60 mm×20 mm×2 mm 的“乙”字形车顶纵向梁。

The upper boundary beam of the roof is provided with an angular section pressed by steel plates with a dimension of 45 mm × 72 mm × 2.5 mm along the full length of both sides of the roof. The upper boundary beams and the top cross beams form the lower frame of the roof. “B” end and “A” end of the roof are respectively provided with an air conditioning unit mounting seat platform steel structure that serves as the basis for the installation of air conditioning units. “A” end also contains a water tank cover. The middle part of the structure of the roof is welded with 30 roof bending beams with a cap-shaped section of a dimension of 26 mm × 70 mm × 46 mm × 70 mm × 26 mm × 2 mm. The bending beam at the roof end is a folded corner-shaped steel plate compression member with a dimension of 30 mm × 55 mm × 62.5 mm × 45 mm × 2 mm. On the cross-section of the roof, there are 5 sigmoidal roof longitudinal beams with a dimension of 30 mm × 60 mm × 20 mm × 2 mm apart from two roof upper boundary beams.

车顶板由侧顶板和中顶板两部分组成。侧顶板是冷轧型钢，将雨檐与小圆弧板（R458）及纵向梁合为一体制造成型，从而提高了侧顶板的平整度，并提高了小圆弧部分的抗弯刚度和强度，还简化了制造工艺。中顶板为大圆弧板（*R*2 300 mm），车顶板厚度均为 2 mm。

The roof plate consists of the side roof plate and the middle roof plate. The side roof plate is made of cold-rolled steel, which is manufactured by integrating the rain eaves with the small circular arc plate (R458) and the longitudinal beams, thus improving the flatness of the side roof plate, enhancing the bending stiffness and strength of the small circular arc part, and simplifying the

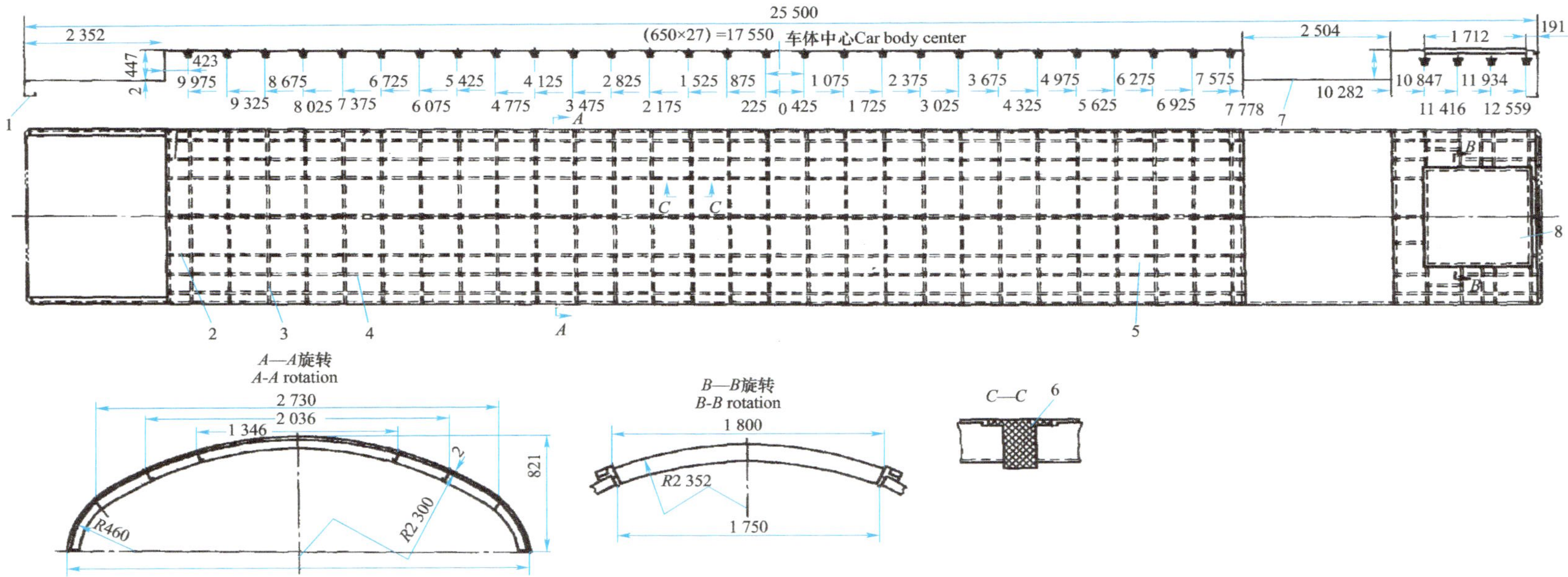

1—顶端弯梁；2—纵梁；3—车顶弯梁；4—侧板；5—中顶板；6—防寒材料；7—平顶结构；8—水箱活盖。

1—Top bending beam; 2—Longitudinal beam; 3—Roof bending beam; 4—Side plate; 5—Middle roof plate; 6—Cold-proof material; 7—Flat roof structure; 8—Water tank flap.

图 7-5 车顶钢结构

Figure 7-5 Roof

manufacturing process. The middle roof plate is a large circular arc plate (R2 300 mm), with a thickness of 2 mm for each roof plate.

车顶一、二位端平顶部分钢结构是安装单元式空调机组的支撑结构。两端各有一根 18a 型槽钢制成的顶端横梁。

The steel structure of the flat roof part of “B” end and “A” end of the roof serves as a support structure for the installation of cellular air conditioning units. There is a top cross beam made of 18a channel steel at each end.

车顶钢结构是由纵横梁件组成的空间梁系，其上焊有曲面金属包板（端部为平板）组成的梁板结构，共同承受作用于其上的各种载荷。车顶结构具有足够的强度和刚度，并通过防漏雨试验。

The roof steel structure is a spatial cross beam system composed of longitudinal and transverse beam members, on which a curved metal cladding plate (flat plate at the end) is welded to form a beam-plate structure to jointly withstand various loads acting on it. The roof structure is strong and rigid enough and has passed the rainproof test.

7.2.4 端墙
End wall

客车车体钢结构的两外端，通常称为外端墙。外端墙钢结构如图 7–6 所示。

The two outer ends of the steel structure of a passenger car body are commonly referred to as the outer end walls. The steel structure of the outer end wall is shown in Figure 7-6.

外端墙有 2 根强大的 24b 型槽钢制成的折棚立柱；2 根 59.5 mm×65.5 mm×50.5 mm×61.5 mm×2 mm 钢板压制成折角形的角柱；2 根位于端门两侧的 40 mm×70 mm×35 mm×2.5 mm 的“乙”字形门边立柱，还有位于端门立柱和角柱之间的同上述断面一样的“乙”字形立柱。上述所有立柱的上端与车顶的顶端横梁相焊接，下端焊在底架缓冲梁的上翼缘上。在角柱与门边立柱之间焊有两根角形断面的水平横梁，门上横梁是“乙”字形断面，上述梁柱构成端墙钢骨架。在骨架的外表面焊有 2 mm 厚的墙板，与钢骨架组成梁板组焊结构。此外，还有与端墙垂直的门板、门上板、踏板等与风挡连接，形成由一节车通向相邻车的安全通道。

The outer end wall is equipped with two folding shed columns made of strong channel steel 24b; two corner columns which are made of 59.5 mm × 65.5 mm × 50.5 mm × 61.5 mm × 2 mm steel plates being pressed into a folded angle shape; two 40 mm × 70 mm × 35 mm × 2.5 mm Z-shaped door side columns located on both sides of the end door, as well as the Z-shaped columns with the same cross-section located between the end door columns and corner columns. The upper ends of all the above columns are welded to the top cross beam of the roof, and the lower ends are welded to the upper flange of the underframe bumper beam. There are two horizontal cross beams with angular sections welded between the corner column and the door side column. The upper door cross beam is a Z-shaped cross-section, and the above beams and columns constitute the steel skeleton of the end wall. A 2 mm thick wall plate is welded on the outer surface of the skeleton, which forms the assembly welding structure of the beam-plate with the steel skeleton. In addition, there are door plates, upper door plates, and pedals that are perpendicular to the end wall and connected to the windshield, which form a safe passage from one car to the adjacent car.

在外端墙板内外面还焊装一些如电线槽、角铁、电力连接器座、连接器座、风挡缓冲杆座、扶手等附件。

Some accessories such as wire slots, angle irons, power connector base, connector base, windshield bumper bar base, and handholds are also welded on the inner and outer surfaces of the outer end wall plate.

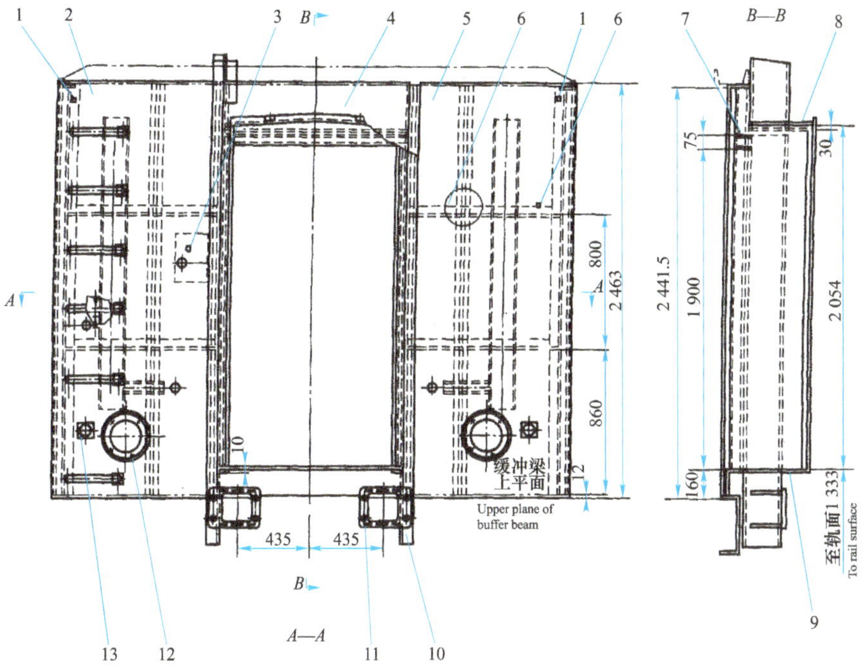

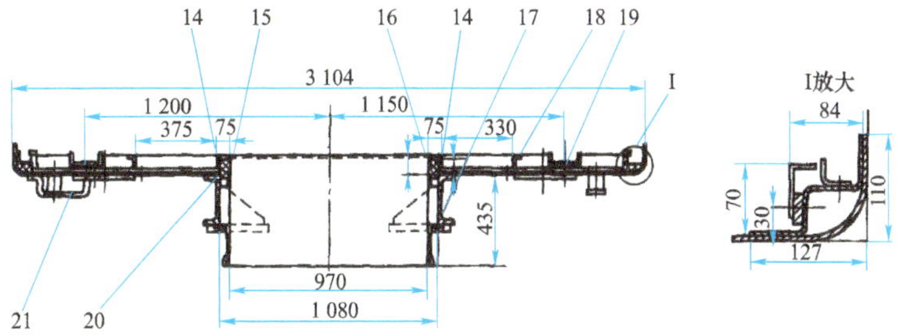

1—角柱；2—左墙板；3—垫板；4—上墙板；5—右墙板；6—横梁；7—门上横梁；8—门上板；9—踏板；10—折棚柱；11—风挡缓冲器座；12—电力连接器座；13—连接器座；14—门立柱；15—左门板组成；16—右门板组成；17—角铁；18—立柱；19—线槽；20—防寒材料；21—扶手。

1—Corner column; 2—Left wall plate; 3—Base plate; 4—Upper wall plate; 5—Right wall plate; 6—Cross beam; 7—Upper door cross beam; 8—Upper door plate; 9—Pedal; 10—Folding shed column; 11—Windshield buffer seat; 12—Power connector base; 13—Connector base; 14—Door column; 15—Left door plate composition; 16—Right door plate composition; 17—Angle iron; 18—Column; 19—Trunking; 20—Cold-proof material; 21—Handhold.

图 7-6 端墙的结构

Figure 7-6 Structure of End Wall

端墙结构应具有足够的强度和刚度，特别是抗纵向冲击的强度。

The end wall structure should have sufficient strength and stiffness, especially the strength against longitudinal impact.

为了防止风沙、雨水侵入车内及运行时便于旅客安全地在列车内通行，在车辆两端连接处装有风挡装置，也称折棚装置。

To prevent the invasion of sand and rain into the vehicle and to facilitate the safe passage of passengers in the train during operation, the windshield device, also known as the folding shed device, is installed at the connection between both ends of the railway vehicle.

脚蹬翻板装置如图 7-7 所示，由翻板组成、框组成、轴组成、轴座组成、拉簧安装、翻板固定器安装、脚蹬组成及面板等组成。

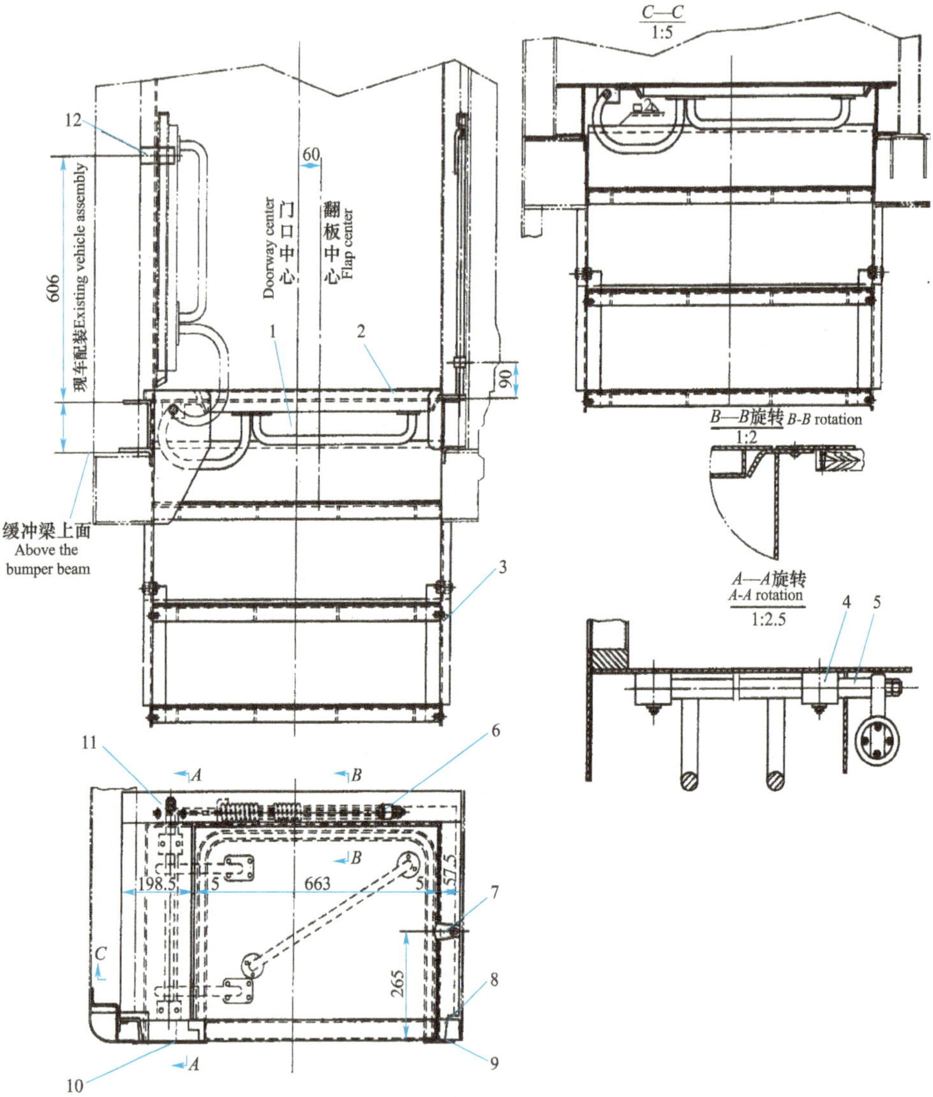

1—框组成；2—翻板组成；3—脚蹬组成；4—轴座组成；5—轴组成；6—拉簧组成；7—翻板固定器安装；8—门槛；9、10—面板；11—踏板；12—锁卡板。

1—Frame composition; 2—Flip-board composition; 3—Pedal composition; 4—Axle seat composition; 5—Axle composition; 6—Tension spring composition; 7—Installation of flip-board fixator; 8—Doorsill; 9, 10—Panel; 11—Pedal; 12—Lock card plate.

图 7-7 脚蹬翻板装置

Figure 7-7 Pedal Flip-board Device

The pedal flip-board device is shown in Figure 7-7, which consists of a flip-board composition, a frame composition, an axle composition, an axle seat composition, installation of tension spring, installation of flip-board fixator, pedal composition, panel composition, etc.

脚蹬翻板装置的作用是：当列车运行时，通过翻板固定器和车侧门使翻板处于水平位置，使通过台形成封闭空间；当旅客在停站上、下车时，翻板在拉簧的作用下，可以自动绕着转轴向内端墙侧翻转至垂直位置，旅客可以通过脚蹬踏板上、下车。该脚蹬翻板装置既适用于低站台，也适用于高站台。

The function of the pedal flip-board device is to keep the flip-board in a horizontal position through the flip-board fixator and the side door of the railway vehicle when the train is running, to form a closed space on the vestibule; When passengers get on and off the train at the stop, the flip-board can automatically turn around the rotary shaft towards the inner end wall side to a vertical position under the action of the tension spring, and passengers can get on and off through the pedal. The pedal flip-board device is suitable for both low and high platforms.

项目 8

Project 8

货 车 车 体

Freight Car Body

本项目以认识货车车体为工学任务，通过课堂任务的完成过程，着重介绍货车车体的基本结构、作用和要求，并以此为引导，简单介绍货车车体在结构、加工工艺、材料方面的特点。

The main task of this project is to understand the freight car body. In the classroom, the main focus is on introducing the basic structure, functions, and requirements of the freight car body and briefly introducing the characteristics of the freight car body in terms of structure, processing technology, and materials.

学生工作页
Student Worksheet

工学任务描述 Task description	预期目标 Expected goals
任务名称：认识货车车体 Task name: Understanding of the freight car body 任务编号：CJ-08 Task number: CJ-08 知识类型：认知型+结构原理型 Knowledge type: Cognitive + structural principle 适用范围：车辆系统各岗位群 Applicable scope: All post groups of the car system 完成时间：　　学时 Completion time:　　class hours	初级：了解货车车体的基本结构、作用和要求 Elementary level: Know the basic structure, functions, and requirements of freight car body 中级：掌握货车车体的作用和要求 Intermediate level: Understand the functions and requirements of freight car body 高级：了解不同货车车型的车体在结构、加工工艺、材料方面的特点。 Advanced level: Understand the characteristics of different vehicle types and car bodies in terms of structure, processing technology, and materials.

知识回顾+小组讨论

Knowledge review + group discussion

1. 按照你对铁路货车车厢的印象，尝试描述或绘制车体的大致结构和组成。

Based on your impression of the car of a railway freight car, try to describe or draw the general structure and composition of the car body.

2. 指出下图中所示的货车车体各部分的名称。

Indicate the names of various parts of the freight car body shown in the following figure.

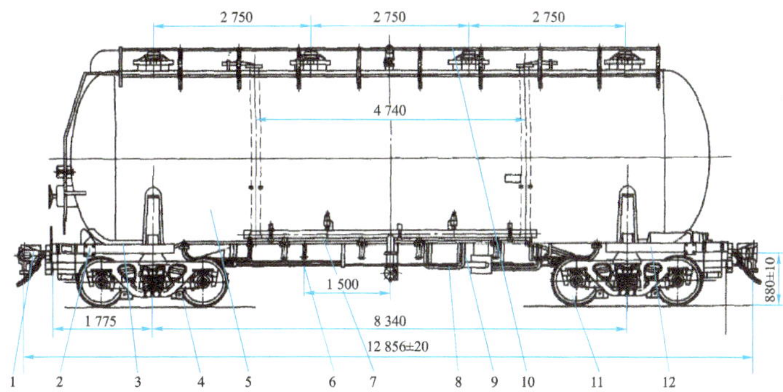

序号 S/N	名　　称 Name	序号 S/N	名　　称 Name	序号 S/N	名　　称 Name
1		5		9	
2		6		10	
3		7		11	
4		8		12	

3. 你认为货车车体应具备哪些功能？

What functions do you think the freight car body should have?

4. 你认为货车车体应满足哪些要求？货车车体的刚度与强度有何区别？

What requirements do you think the freight car body should meet? What is the difference between the stiffness and strength of the freight car body?

归纳总结+学习记录

Summary + learning record

1. 货车车体的基本组成与作用。

Basic composition and function of the freight car body.

1	基本组成部分 Basic components	作　　用 Function
2		
3		
4		
5		
6		
7		
8		

2. 基于 $C_{70(H)}$敞车的特点，你认为对敞车的车体都应有哪些特殊要求？

Based on the characteristics of the $C_{70(H)}$ gondola car, what special requirements do you think should be placed on the body of the gondola car?

	敞车的特点 Characteristics of gondola cars	特殊要求 Special requirements
1		
2		
3		
4		
5		
6		
7		

课后任务

After-class tasks

1. 查阅 C_{76A}、C_{80}、C_{70} 型货车车体的资料，对照后找出不同点。

Refer to relevant documents on the freight car body of C_{76A}, C_{80}, and C_{70} freight cars to find out the differences.

	C_{76A} 型货车 C_{76A} freight car	C_{80} 型货车 C_{80} freight car	C_{70} 型货车 C_{70} freight car
1			
2			
3			

续表

Continued

	C_{76A} 型货车 C_{76A} freight car	C_{80} 型货车 C_{80} freight car	C_{70} 型货车 C_{70} freight car
4			
5			
6			
7			
8			
9			
10			
11			
12			
13			
14			
15			
16			

2. 查找资料，了解你所喜欢车型的车体结构特点。

Search for information to understand the structural characteristics of the car body of your favorite vehicle type.

____________________的车体结构特点如下：

The structural characteristics of the car body for ____________________ are as follows:

3. 提出你的问题。

Put forward your questions.

问题（1）：

Question (1):

答案：

Answer:

问题（2）：

Question (2):

答案：

Answer:

学习效果评价
Learning effect evaluation

年 Year　　月 Month　　日 Day

专业班级： Major & class:	姓名： Name:	学号： Student number:
工学小组及分工： Work-and-study team and responsibility division:		

专业（知识/技能）收获 Professional gains (knowledge/skills)	（非专业）能力素质收获 (Non-professional) ability and quality gains

评价考核项目 Evaluation item	自我评价 Self-evaluation	小组评价 Group evaluation	教师评价 Teacher's evaluation
已了解货车车体的基本结构、作用和要求 The basic structure, functions, and requirements of freight car body have been understood			
已掌握相关知识点的数量 Number of knowledge points mastered			
主动提出问题的数量 Number of questions proposed			
课外学习时间（学时） After-school learning time (hours)			
工作态度（课堂、课后任务完成情况） Work attitude (completion condition of classroom tasks and after-class tasks)	☆☆☆☆ ☆☆☆☆	☆☆☆☆ ☆☆☆☆	☆☆☆☆ ☆☆☆☆
合作意识及协调能力 Cooperation consciousness and coordination ability	☆☆☆☆ ☆☆☆☆	☆☆☆☆ ☆☆☆☆	☆☆☆☆ ☆☆☆☆
正确表达和沟通能力 Correct expression and communication skills	☆☆☆☆ ☆☆☆☆	☆☆☆☆ ☆☆☆☆	☆☆☆☆ ☆☆☆☆
自律能力（缺勤/旷课/迟到/违纪次数） Self-discipline (absences/absenteeism/lateness/disciplinary violations)			

任务 8.1　货车车体概述
Task 8.1　Overview of freight car body

货车按用途可分为通用货车和专用货车两类。通用货车有敞车、棚车、平车等。专用货车有罐车、保温车、长大货物车、漏斗车、自翻车和集装箱专用平车等。每种车都包括几种不同构造和特点的车型。

Freight cars can be divided into two categories according to their use: general-purpose freight cars and special-purpose freight cars. General-purpose freight cars include gondola cars, box cars, flat cars, etc. Special freight cars include tank cars, refrigerator cars, high-capacity freight cars, hopper cars, self-dumping cars, and special flat cars for containers. Each car includes several models with different construction and characteristics.

货车的数量和车种的配备应根据货物运量和所运货物的性质来确定。截止到 2022 年底，全国铁路货车拥有量为 99.7 万辆。

The number of freight cars and the equipment of their types should be determined based on the volume of goods and the nature of the goods being transported. By the end of 2022, the number of railway freight cars in China was 997,000.

任务 8.2　敞　　车
Task 8.2　Gondola cars

8.2.1　敞车的发展简述
Overview of development of gondola cars

敞车是铁路运输中的主型车辆。在我国目前的货车总数中，敞车数量最多，约占 60%。新中国成立初期，我国铁路上使用的敞车多数是 1949 年前遗留下来的旧车，车型很复杂，约有 30 多种；它们的吨位都很小，多数为 30 t 级的，有一部分为 20 t、40 t 级的，少数为 50 t 级的。这些旧车的共同缺点是：运行性能差、载重量小、强度低、零部件复杂、检修不便等。后来，这些车中的一部分经检修后改了型，另一部分则被逐步淘汰。国产的新型敞车则大量地投入了运用。

The gondola car is the main type of railway vehicle in railway transportation. In the current total number of freight cars in China, the number of gondola cars is the largest, accounting for about 60%. In the early days of the founding of the PRC in 1949, most of the gondola cars used on the railways were old cars left over before 1949, with complex models, about 30 types; their tonnage is very small, with most of them in the 30 t grade, some of them in the 20 t or 40 t grade, and a few in the 50 t grade. The common disadvantages of these old cars are poor operating performance, low load-carrying capacity, low strength, complex components, inconvenience in maintenance, etc. Later, some of these railway vehicles were overhauled and modified, while others were phased out. A large number of new domestic gondola cars have been put into use.

20 世纪 50—60 年代，我国先后设计了载重 30 t 的 C_1 型敞车和载重为 40 t 的 C_6 型敞车，投入运用后均发现强度不足。这两种车型的生产数量不多。

In the 1950s and 1960s, China successively designed the C_1 gondola car with a load capacity of 30 t and the C_6 gondola car with a load capacity of 40 t. After they were put into use, it was found that the strength was insufficient, and the production quantity of these two types of railway vehicles was not large.

为了提高敞车的载重吨位，1952 年设计了载重为 50 t 的 C_{50} 型敞车，自 1953 年试制并投产到 1976 年，共计生产约 35 000 辆，是当时敞车中的主型车。在长达 24 年的生产期间内，C_{50} 型敞车做过多次设计修改，各工厂生产的车也因各自工艺的不同而有差别。

To improve the deadweight tonnage of gondola cars, the C_{50} gondola car with a load capacity of 50 t was designed in 1952. From trial production and put into production in 1953 until 1976, a total of about 35,000 gondola cars were produced, which was the main type of gondola cars at that time. During the production period of up to 24 years, the C_{50} gondola car has been modified and designed many times, and the cars produced by various factories also differ due to their respective processes.

1958 年，在铁道部组织的修改设计会议上，由 15 个工厂的设计人员联合提出了底架为单中梁结构、桁架式侧壁承载的载重为 60 t 的 C_{60} 型敞车设计方案，经过一系列的试验后投入了批量生产。与其他旧车型相比，该车型具有自重轻、载重大的优点，采用了独特的单中梁结构。但由于刚度不足等先天性缺陷，C_{60} 型敞车仅生产了一小批。

In 1958, designers from 15 factories jointly proposed the design proposal of C_{60} gondola cars with a single center beam structure underframe and a 60 t load-bearing truss side wall at a modification design meeting organized by the Ministry of Railways. After a series of tests, it was put into mass production. This type of railway vehicle offered benefits over other older railway vehicles in terms of lightweight and heavy load, and the unique single center beam structure was adopted. Only a small batch of C_{60} gondola cars have been produced due to congenital defects such as insufficient stiffness.

1959 年，在总结 C_{50} 型敞车运用经验的基础上设计了 C_{13} 型敞车。它的主要特点是：缩小了心盘距，加长了牵引梁，载重提高到了 60 t。为克服当时 C_{50} 型敞车端部卸货困难的问题，C_{13} 型敞车在端部增设了下侧门，同时取消了侧柱连铁，方便了大件货物在中、小站的装卸。但是 C_{13} 型敞车投入运用后，发现中梁横向弯曲变形大，牵引梁下垂甩头严重，导致修程大，原型修复出厂后仍不能解决根本问题。

In 1959, the C_{13} gondola car was designed based on the summary of the application experience of the C_{50} gondola car. Its main characteristics are to reduce the distance between centers and discs, lengthen the traction beam, and increase the load capacity to 60 t. To overcome the difficulty of unloading at the end of the C_{50} gondola car at that time, a lower side door was added to the end of the C_{13} gondola car, and the side pillar connecting iron was canceled, which facilitated the loading and unloading of large cargo at small and medium-sized stations. After the C_{13} gondola car was put into operation, it was found that the transverse bending and deformation of the center beam were large, and the sagging and shaking of the traction beam were serious, which caused a large repair process. After the prototype was repaired, the fundamental problem remained unresolved.

1965 年铁道科学研究院、四方车辆研究所、齐齐哈尔车辆工厂组成联合调查组对站段、货场做了广泛调查，并做了结构模拟试验，在此基础上设计完成了全钢结构侧壁承载的新型敞车。该车型采用了 09Mn2、09Mn2Cu 低合金钢，投入批量生产后，定型为 C_{65} 型敞车。它是我国在大量生产的货车上采用低合金钢的第一个车型，具有自重轻、载重大的特点。C_{65} 型敞车运用后也暴露出一些质量问题，如燃轴、切轴事故多，以及端墙外胀、枕梁裂纹等。据此，1971 年将 C_{65} 型敞车的载重由 65 t 降为 60 t，容积也相应减小。同年，在 C_{65} 型敞车的基础上缩短底架、降低车体，定型为 C_{62} 型敞车，于 1972 年起投入大批生产。

In 1965, extensive investigations were conducted in stations, depots, and freight yards by a joint investigation team composed of China Academy of Railway Sciences, Sifang Rolling Stock Research Institute and Qiqihar Rolling Stock Factory, and structural simulation tests were conducted. On this basis, a new type of gondola car with a full steel structure and side wall bearing was designed and completed. The 09Mn2 and 09Mn2Cu low alloy steel were adopted for this type of railway vehicle. It was finalized as the C_{65} gondola car after being put into mass production. It was the first vehicle type of using low alloy steel on a mass-produced freight car in China, with the characteristics of lightweight and heavy load. The C_{65} gondola car also had some quality problems after being used, such as frequent axle burning, axle cutting accidents, end wall external expansion, and cracks in sleeper beams. Based on this, the load capacity of the C_{65} gondola was reduced from 65 t to 60 t in 1971, and the volume was also reduced accordingly. In the same year, based on the C_{65} gondola car, the underframe was shortened and the car body was lowered, and the C_{62} was finalized for mass production in 1972.

为了提高敞车装载性能，以适应铁路运输事业的发展，1972 年在低边型敞车的基础上设计了车内高为 2 m，侧、端墙及车门为钢木结构的 C_{62M} 型敞车，并于 1974 年至 1975 年间进行了小批量试制、运用和考验。1976 年，C_{50} 型敞车停产，大批生产 C_{62} 型敞车。当时 C_{65}、C_{62}、C_{62M} 型敞车为我国的主型敞车（至 1980 年，这 3 种车型分别生产了约 8 500、20 000、14 000 辆）。1980 年还在 C_{62M} 的基础上，设计了车体的端、侧墙及门由钢架木衬改为全钢结构的 C_{62A} 型敞车。改进后的 C_{62A} 型敞车，结构坚固耐用，当时很受用户欢迎，至 1994 年共生产近 90 000 辆。为提高敞车的使用年限，延长检修周期，于 1986 年将 C_{62A} 型敞车的主要零部件改用耐候钢，相应车型也改为 $C_{62A(N)}$，后定型为 C_{62B} 型敞车。

In 1972, the C_{62M} gondola car with an interior height of 2 m and a steel wood structure of its side, end walls, and doors were designed on the basis of a low-sided gondola car, to improve the loading performance of gondola cars and adapt to the development of railway transportation. From 1974 to 1975, it was tested for trial production in small batches. In 1976, the production of C_{50} gondola cars was discontinued and the C_{62} gondola cars were mass-produced. At that time, the C_{65}, C_{62}, and C_{62M} gondola cars were the main types of gondola cars in China (by 1980, approximately 8,500, 20,000, and 14,000 vehicles were produced for these three types respectively). In 1980, the C_{62A} gondola car was designed on the basis of the C_{62M}, with the end, side walls, and doors of the car body changed from a steel frame and wood lining to an all-steel structure. The improved C_{62A} gondola car, with a sturdy and durable structure, was very popular with users at that time, and nearly 90,000 vehicles were produced by 1994. The main components of the C_{62A} gondola car were changed to weather-resistant steel in 1986, to improve the service life of gondola cars and extend the maintenance cycle. The corresponding type was also changed to $C_{62A(N)}$, which was later finalized as C_{62B} gondola car.

为了使通用敞车也能适应重载组合列车和翻车机卸货的要求，1988 年在 $C_{62A(N)}$型敞车的基础上，对端墙、侧墙、车门做了较大的改进和加强，制动装置采用引进消化的国外及国内研制的新制动技术，转向架采用改进的转 8A 型转向架，改进后定型为 C_{64} 型敞车。此后，C_{64} 型敞车开始投入批量生产，并成为我国铁路主型通用敞车。2001 年，为适应我国铁路货车提速的发展要求，在 C_{64} 型敞车的基础上研制了采用转 8AG 和转 8G 型转向架的 C_{64T}、采用转 K2 型转向架的 C_{64K}、采用转 K4 型转向架的 C_{64H} 型系列通用敞车。

In 1988, significant improvements and enhancements were made to the end walls, side walls, and doors on the basis of the $C_{62A(N)}$ gondola car, to make the general gondola car adapt to the requirements of heavy load combination trains and car dumper unloading. The new braking technology developed abroad and domestically was adopted for the braking device, and the bogie was changed to the improved Z8A bogie, which was finalized as the C_{64} gondola car after improvement. Since then, the C_{64} gondola car has been put into mass production and become the main type of general gondola car for China's railways. In 2001, based on the C_{64} gondola car, the C_{64T} series of general gondola cars with Z8AG and Z8G bogies, the C_{64K} series of general gondola cars with bogie type ZK-2, and the C_{64H} series of general gondola car with bogie type ZK-4 bogies were developed for meeting the development requirements of speed increase of railway freight cars in China.

为适应我国既有铁路线路、桥梁的实际承载能力，加快铁路装备现代化进程，满足铁路货车由 60 t 向 70 t 升级换代的要求，齐齐哈尔铁路车辆（集团）有限责任公司于 2003 年开始 70 t 新型通用敞车的研制，2005 年初完成了载重 70 t 新型通用敞车工作图设计、小批量试制和各项性能试验工作，并于同年 6 月通过了样车的部级审查，定型为 C_{70} 型敞车。该车型载重 70 t、自重 23.8 t，2005 年开始投入生产。齐齐哈尔轨道交通装备有限责任公司于 2005 年投产了 C_{70H} 型敞车（采用转 K5 型转向架）。

CRRC Qiqihar Railway Rolling Stock (Group) Co., Ltd. began the development of a new type of general gondola car with a load capacity of 70 t in 2003, to adapt to the actual carrying capacity of existing railway lines and bridges in China, accelerate the modernization process of railway equipment, and meet the upgrading requirements of railway freight cars from 60 t to 70 t. In early 2005, it completed the working drawing design, small batch trial production, and various performance tests of the new type of general gondola car with a load capacity of 70 t. In June of the same year, it passed the ministerial-level review of the prototype railway vehicle, and the new type of general gondola car was finalized as C_{70}. The railway vehicle has a load capacity of 70 t and a tare weight of 23.8 t. It was put into production in 2005. Qiqihar Railway Equipment Co., Ltd. put into production the C_{70H} gondola car (using bogie type ZK-5) in 2005.

8.2.2 敞车的用途
Purpose of gondola cars

通用敞车是供中国标准轨距铁路使用的通用铁路车辆，主要用于装运煤炭、矿石、建材、机械设备、钢材及木材等货物。

General gondola car is a general railway vehicle used for China's standard gauge railways, mainly for transporting coal, ore, building materials, mechanical equipment, steel, wood, and other cargo.

8.2.3 C_{64} 型敞车
C_{64} gondola car

C_{64} 型敞车是 C_{62B} 型敞车的升级换代产品，采用全钢焊接结构，充分吸收了 C_{65} 和 C_{62} 等各型敞车结构性能的优点，并进行了不断的改进。其车辆载重为 61 t，比容系数为 1.2 m^3/t；每延米轨道载重为 6.2 t/m，能适应翻车机卸货的要求。为承受翻车机压车力的作用，C_{64} 型敞车的上侧梁及上端梁均采用冷弯专用型钢；为改善因长期使用翻车机卸货而导致的侧开门上门锁锁闭机构变形较大的问题，改进了中侧门结构，加粗了侧开门上门锁轴并增加了侧开门中部支点等。C_{64} 型敞车的结构如图 8-1 所示。

The C_{64} gondola car is an upgraded product of the C_{62B} gondola car. It adopts an all-steel welded structure, which fully absorbs the structural performance advantages of various types of gondola cars such as the C_{65} and C_{62} series with continuous improvement. Its vehicle load is 61 t,

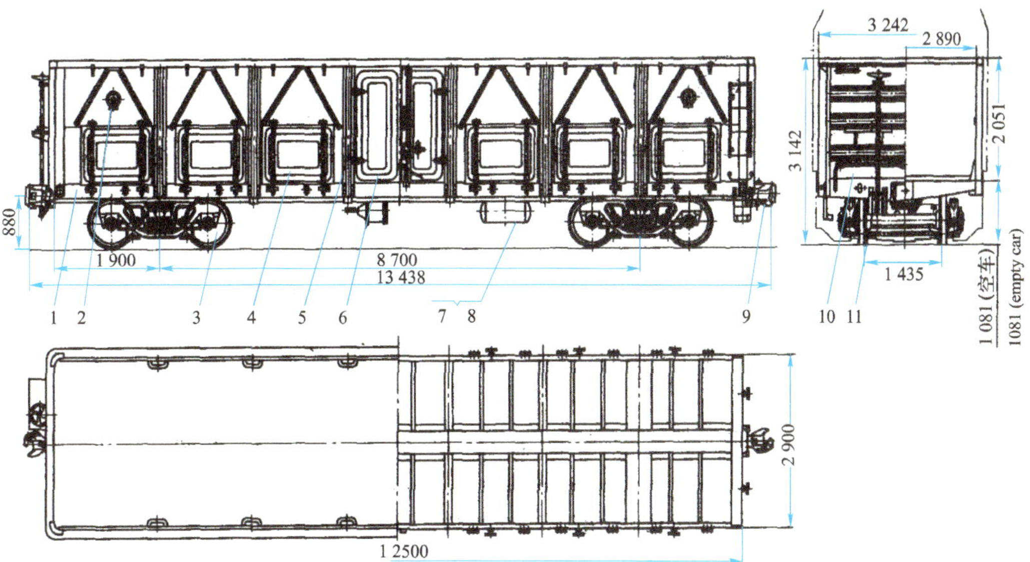

1—底架组成；2—标记；3—转向架；4—下侧门组成；5—侧墙组成；6—侧开门组成；7—底架附属件；8—风制动装置；9—车钩缓冲装置；10—端墙组成；11—手制动装置。

1—Underframe composition; 2—Marking; 3—Bogie; 4—Lower side door composition; 5—Side wall composition; 6—Side door composition; 7—Underframe accessories; 8—Pneumatic braking device; 9—Coupler and draft gear; 10—End wall composition; 11—Hand brake device.

图 8-1 C_{64} 型敞车的结构

Figure 8-1 Structure of C_{64} Gondola Car

and its specific volume coefficient is 1.2 m^3/t; the rail load per meter of track is 6.2 t/m, which meets the requirements of unloading by car dumpers. The upper side beam and upper end beam of the C_{64} gondola car are made of cold-formed special section steel for withstanding the pressure of the car dumper; to improve the large deformation of the locking mechanism of the upper door lock of the side door due to the long-term use of the car dumper for unloading, measures such as improving the structure of the middle side door, thickening the axle of the upper door lock of the side door, and adding the middle fulcrum of the side door have been taken. The structure of the C_{64} gondola car is shown in Figure 8-1.

1. 底架

Underframe

底架为全钢焊接结构，由中梁、侧梁、枕梁、端梁、小横梁及钢地板等组成，如图 8–2 所示。中梁用两根材质为 09v 的 310“乙”字形钢组焊而成，侧梁采用 24 型槽钢制成等截面直梁，侧梁上组装有绳栓、下侧门搭扣、脚蹬及中侧门的锁销插等。枕梁为箱型变截面结构，其上盖板厚 8 mm、下盖板厚 12 mm、腹板厚 8 mm。端梁用 7 mm 厚的钢板压成角形断面。全车共有 4 根大横梁，它用厚 8 mm 的上、下盖板及厚 6 mm 的腹板组焊成“工”字形变截面梁。全车 28 根小横梁均用 12 型槽钢制成。底架上铺厚 8 mm 的钢地板，底架四角设置牵引钩。

The underframe is an all-steel welded structure, consisting of the center beam, side beam, sleeper beam, end beam, small cross beam, steel floor, etc., as shown in Figure 8-2. The center beam is installed and welded by two sheets of 310 Z-shaped steel made of 09v material, and the side beam is the straight beam with a uniform cross-section made of Type 24 channel steel. The side beam is assembled with rope bolts, lower-side door buckles, foot pedals, and lock pin inserts for the middle-side door. The sleeper beam is a box-shaped variable cross-section structure with an upper

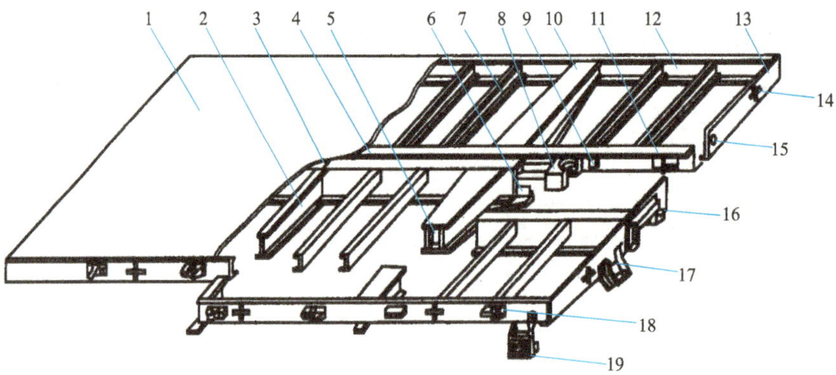

1—钢地板；2—大横梁；3—中梁隔板；4—中梁；5—枕梁隔板；6—心盘座角钢；7—小横梁；8—后从板座；9—磨耗板；10—枕梁；11—前从板座；12—侧梁；13—端梁；14—绳栓；15—制动主管孔；16—冲击座；17—手制动轴托；18—下侧门搭扣；19—脚蹬。

1—Steel floor; 2—Large cross beam; 3—Center beam partition; 4—Center beam; 5—Sleeper beam partition; 6—Center plate seat angle steel; 7—Small cross beam; 8—Rear slave plate seat; 9—Wearing plate; 10—Sleeper beam; 11—Front slave plate seat; 12—Side beam; 13—End beam; 14—Rope bolt; 15—Braking main pipe hole; 16—Impact seat; 17—Hand brake axle support; 18—Lower side door buckle; 19—Pedal.

图 8–2 C_{64} 型敞车的底架

Figure 8-2 Underframe of C_{64} Gondola Car

cover plate thickness of 8 mm, a lower cover plate thickness of 12 mm, and a web thickness of 8 mm. The end beam is pressed into an angular section with a 7 mm steel plate. The complete car has four large cross beams, which are installed and welded into I-shaped variable cross-section beams using 8 mm thick upper and lower cover plates and 6 mm thick webs. The 28 small cross beams of the complete car are made of Type 12 channel steel. The steel floor with a thickness of 8 mm is paved on the underframe, and traction hooks are set at the four corners of the underframe.

2. 侧墙

Side wall

侧墙为板柱式侧壁承载结构，由上侧梁、侧柱、侧板、斜撑、侧柱连铁、侧门、内补强座和侧柱补强板组焊而成，如图 8-3 所示。侧墙上半部为板梁结构，两侧柱间设“人”字形斜撑。侧墙下半部由侧柱、连铁和侧梁组成刚性框架，中间开设门孔。侧墙刚度较大，也是主要承载部件之一。其内高从 C_{62B} 型敞车的 2 000 mm 提高到 2 050 mm。为适应翻车机作业要求，上侧梁采用断面尺寸为 116 mm×140 mm 的耐候冷弯型钢制造。上侧梁在中央侧门孔的部分焊有 8 mm 厚钢板压制成的槽形门檐、12 mm 厚的门孔补强板和 8 mm 厚的三角形门孔补强筋板。在上侧梁的外侧焊有吊起下侧门的钩链。为解决侧柱连铁腐蚀严重问题，侧柱连铁采用的材质为耐候钢，且上翼缘为斜面的槽形断面梁制造，侧柱连铁开口向外，与侧墙板组焊成封闭形断面，连铁两端部用钢板封堵，以防货物、尘土及水分等浸入。全车 12 根侧柱用 22 号帽型钢制成，侧柱下半部焊有 10 mm 厚的加强板，其内焊有铸钢内补强座。角柱下部焊有 8 mm 厚的加强板，侧柱与侧梁采用铆接。上部侧板为 5 mm 厚的钢板，上面焊有 75 mm×50 mm×6 mm 的“人”字形斜撑加强并支撑上侧梁。在一、四位端的侧墙上设有扶梯。

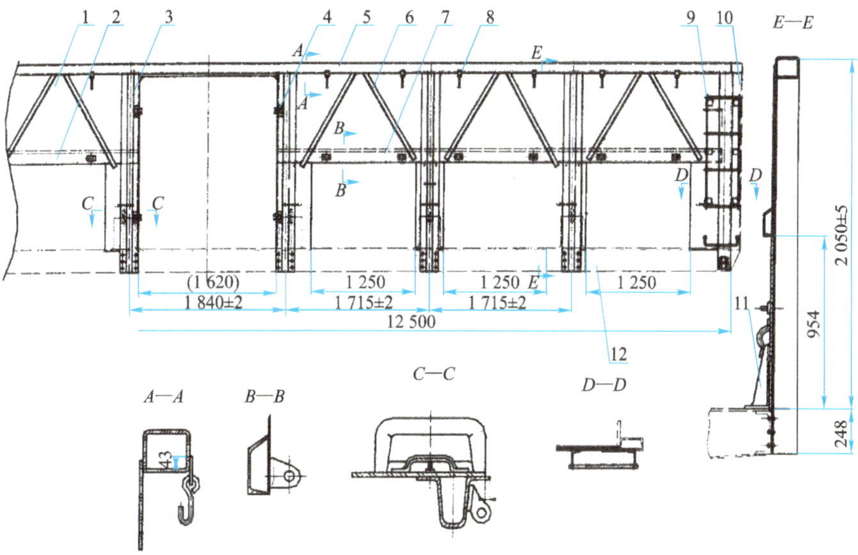

1—侧壁板；2—下侧门折页座；3—侧柱；4—侧开门折页座；5—上侧梁；6—斜撑；
7—侧柱连铁；8—钩链；9—扶梯；10—角柱；11—侧柱内补强座；12—侧梁。

1—Sidewall plate; 2—Lower side door folding seat; 3—Side column; 4—Side door folding seat; 5—Upper side beam; 6—Bracing; 7—Side column connecting iron; 8—Hook chain; 9—Escalator; 10—Corner column; 11—Internal reinforcement seat of side column; 12—Side beam.

图 8-3　C_{64} 型敞车的侧墙

Figure 8-3　Side wall of C_{64} Gondola Car

The side wall is a plate column type side wall bearing structure, which is installed and welded by the upper side beam, side column, side plate, bracing, side column connecting iron, side door, internal reinforcement seat, and side column reinforcement plate, as shown in Figure 8-3. The upper half of the side wall is a plate beam structure, and herringbone bracing is set between the two side columns. The lower half of the side wall is a rigid frame consisting of side columns, connecting iron, and side beams, with a door opening in the middle. The side wall has a large stiffness and is also one of the main load-bearing components. The interior height of the car has been increased from 2,000 mm of the C_{62B} gondola car to 2,050 mm. The upper side beam is made of weather-resistant cold-formed steel with a cross-sectional dimension of 116 mm × 140 mm to meet the operational requirements of the car dumper. The upper side beam is welded to the central side door hole with a groove-shaped eave pressed by 8 mm thick steel plates, a 12 mm thick door opening reinforcement plate, and an 8 mm thick triangular door opening reinforcement plate. A hook chain for lifting the lower side door is welded on the outer side of the upper side beam. The side column connecting iron is made of weathering-resistant steel and a slotted section beam with an inclined upper flange, to solve the serious corrosion of the side column connecting iron. The opening of the side column connecting iron is outward, and it is installed and welded with the sidewall plate into a closed section. Both ends of the connecting iron are sealed with steel plates to prevent the immersion of goods, dust, and moisture. The 12 side columns of the complete car are made of No.22 cap-shaped steel, and the lower half of the side columns are welded with a 10 mm thick reinforcement plate, which is welded with a cast steel internal reinforcement seat. The lower part of the corner column is welded with an 8 mm thick reinforcement plate, and the side column and side beam are riveted. The upper side plate is a 5 mm thick steel plate welded with 75 mm × 50 mm × 6 mm herringbone bracing to strengthen and support the upper side beam. Escalators are provided on the side walls of "B" end and "D" end.

敞车侧门的位置、数量及开启方式对于装卸作业、侧墙强度和刚度影响颇大。侧门的开度既要便于装卸，又要保证侧壁的承载能力不受太大影响。全车有 12 扇下侧门及 2 对对开式中侧门。下侧门与 C_{62B} 型敞车的下侧门通用，其门孔的开度为 1 250 mm×954 mm，中侧门结构与 C_{62B} 型敞车类似。为改变通用敞车上门锁机构易失灵及两门板对接处门板易外涨变形等问题，C_{64} 型敞车的上门锁采用带有偏心压紧机构的新型门锁装置，在上门锁处，门板变形小于 40 mm 时仍可锁闭。同时，在右侧门左边框处焊一通长的门锁垫板，以加强此处的强度，改善上、下门锁机构的承载能力。为改善采用翻车机卸货时中侧门不利的受力状况，在通长的门锁垫板上增设顶面与侧柱外平面平齐的支点，改善了门板的受力工况。下门锁仍沿用 C_{62A} 型敞车的下门锁机构。

The position, number, and opening method of the side doors of gondola cars have a significant impact on loading and unloading operations, and the strength and stiffness of the side walls. The opening of the side door should not only facilitate loading and unloading but also ensure that the bearing capacity of the side wall is not greatly affected. The complete car has 12 lower side doors and 2 pairs of split middle side doors. The lower side door is in common use with the lower side door of the C_{62B} gondola car, with an opening of 1,250 mm × 954 mm of the door hole. The structure of the middle side door is similar to that of the C_{62B} gondola car. To solve problems such as the failure of the door lock mechanism on the general gondola car and the deformation of the door plate at the junction of the two-door plates, a new door lock device with an eccentric pressing mechanism is adopted for the upper door lock of the C_{64} gondola car, which can still be locked when the deformation of the door plate at the upper door lock is less than 40 mm. In addition, a full-length door lock base plate is welded at the left frame of the right door to strengthen the strength here and improve the bearing capacity of the upper and lower door lock mechanisms. To improve the unfavorable stress condition of the middle side door when the car dumper is used for unloading, a fulcrum with the top surface flush with the outer plane of the side column is added to the full-length door lock base plate to improve the stress condition of the door panel. The lower door lock mechanism of the C_{62A} gondola car is used.

侧开门为双合式车门，分左、右侧，如图 8-4 所示。右侧门由门板、折页及上、下门锁等组成；左侧门除没有门锁及扶手外，其他与右侧门相同。门板由 5 mm 厚的钢板压制成型，中部向内凹入，四周压成凹筋以代替门框。侧开门的两侧均焊有折页。

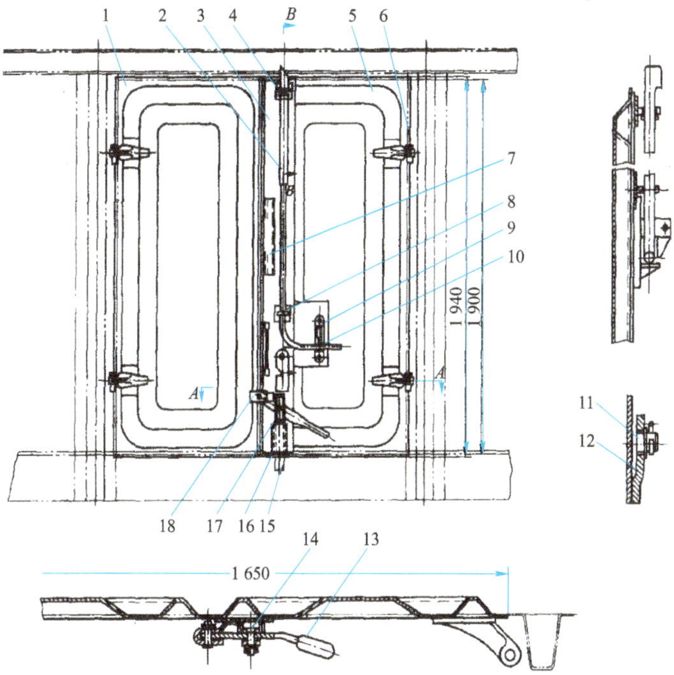

1—左侧门板；2—上门锁杆；3—门锁垫板；4—上导架；5—右侧门板；6—折页；7—支承；8—下导架；9—侧门锁杆固定座；10—垫板；11—圆销；12—锁铁；13—下门锁手柄；14—沉头锁轴；15—下门锁销；16—下门锁销座；17—上、下门锁销支点；18—下门锁手柄支点。

1—Left door plate; 2—Upper door lock rod; 3—Door lock base plate; 4—Upper guide frame; 5—Right side door plate; 6—Folding parts; 7—Support; 8—Lower guide frame; 9—Side door lock rod fixing seat; 10—Base plate; 11—Round pin; 12—Lock iron; 13—Lower door lock handle; 14—Countersunk head lock shaft; 15—Lower door lock pin; 16—Lower door lock pin seat; 17—Upper and lower door lock pin fulcrum; 18—Lower door lock handle fulcrum.

图 8-4　C_{64} 型敞车的侧开门

Figure 8-4　Side Door of C_{64} Gondola Car

The side door is a double-open type door, divided into left and right sides, as shown in Figure 8-4. The right door consists of door plate, folding parts, and upper and lower door locks and others; the left door is the same as the right door, except that there is no door lock and handhold. The door plate is pressed and formed from a 5 mm thick steel plate, with the center recessed inward and the four sides pressed into concave bars to replace the door frame. Folding parts are welded on both sides of the side door.

上门锁由上门锁杆、导架、侧门锁杆固定座及垫板等组成。各零件间用圆销连接，可相对转动。当关闭侧门时，先关左侧门，再关右侧门。此时将门锁杆往下拉，侧杠杆绕支点的圆销沿顺时针方向转动，推动上锁销沿上导架向上滑动，插入门孔加强铁之内。为了防止车体振动时上锁销下滑而侧开门自动开启，开闭杆下端带有弯钩，可轻便地卡入固定座中，锁铁靠自重转到铅垂位置挡住开闭杆弯钩部分，使其不能上升和滑出，起到锁闭作用。

The upper door lock consists of the upper door lock rod, guide frames, the side door lock rod fixing seat, the base plate, etc. The parts are connected with round pins and can rotate relative to each other. At the time of closing the side door, the left door should be closed first, and then the right door should be closed. At this time, the door lock rod should be pulled down, the side rod should be rotated around the round pin of the fulcrum in a clockwise direction. The upper lock pin should be pushed to slide upward along upper guide frame to insert into the door hole reinforcement iron. To prevent the upper lock pin from sliding down and the side door from automatically opening when the car body vibrates, the lower end of the opening and closing rod is equipped with a hook, which can be easily stuck in the fixed seat. The lock iron is rotated by its own weight to the vertical position to block the hook part of the opening and closing rod, preventing it from rising and sliding out, thereby playing a locking role.

下门锁由手柄和下锁销等组成，同样用圆销连接。侧门关好后放下手柄，下锁销沿着锁销座下滑，插入底架侧梁上的锁销插中，从而关闭侧门。此时下门锁铁也靠自重落至最低位置，挡住下锁销自动升起，达到锁闭作用。

The lower door lock consists of a handle, a lower lock pin, etc., which are connected with a round pin. After the side door is closed, the handle should be put down, and the lower lock pin should slide along the lock pin seat to insert into the lock pin on the side beam of the underframe, thereby closing the side door. At this time, the lower door lock iron also falls to the lowest position by its own weight, to block the lower lock pin from automatically rising and play a locking role.

侧门关闭时，必须把上、下门锁一起锁住，才能保证侧门严密。开启侧门时，只要先转动锁铁，采用与上述相反方向的推或拉即可开启。

At the time of closing the side door, the upper and lower door locks should be locked together to ensure that the side door is tight. At the time of opening the side door, the lock iron should be turned first and the side door should be pushed or pulled in the opposite direction to be opened.

下侧门由门板和折页等组成，如图 8-5 所示。门板由 5 mm 厚的钢板压成中间凹入及四周带凹筋的压型板。折页由扁钢制成，其端部卷有圆环，焊接于门板上，借助圆销与侧柱连铁上的折页连接。折页下部伸出板外，关门时插入底架侧梁上的下侧门搭扣座内。折页中部焊有挂环，下侧门开启后，借助上侧梁上的钩链吊挂起来。

The lower door consists of the door plate, folding part, etc., as shown in Figure 8-5. The door plate is pressed from a 5 mm thick steel plate into a contour plate with a concave center and concave bars on four sides. The folding part is made of flat steel, with a circular ring wound at its end, which is welded to the door plate and connected to the folding part on the side column with the help of a round pin. The lower part of the folding part extends out of the plate and is inserted into the lower side door buckle seat on the side beam of the underframe when the door is closed. A hanging ring is welded in the middle of the folding part, and after the lower side door is opened, it is hung up with the help of a hook chain on the upper side beam.

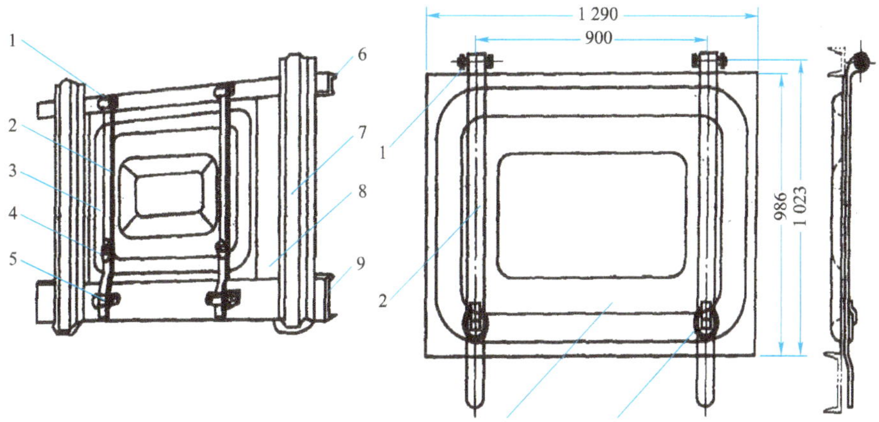

1—圆销；2—折页；3—门板；4—挂环；5—下侧门搭扣；6—侧柱连铁；7—侧柱；8—侧柱加强板；9—侧梁。

1—Round pin; 2—Folding part; 3—Door plate; 4—Hanging ring; 5—Lower side door buckle; 6—Side column connecting iron; 7—Side column; 8—Side column reinforcement plate; 9—Side beam.

图 8-5 C_{64} 型敞车的下侧门

Figure 8-5 Lower Side Door of C_{64} Gondola Car

3. 端墙

End wall

端墙由上端缘、角柱、横带及端板等组焊而成。上端梁采用断面尺寸为 116 mm×140 mm 的冷弯型钢制造，在与上侧梁连接处焊有篷布护铁压型件。角柱用 14a 型槽钢与 7 mm 厚的角柱板组焊而成。角柱板与侧墙板及角柱加强板搭接。3 根横带用 140 mm 厚的耐候冷弯型钢制成，横带两端部与角柱焊成一体，提高了端墙的整体刚度和强度。端墙板采用 5 mm 厚的钢板制造。

The end wall is installed and welded by the upper end edge, corner column, transverse strip, end plate, etc. The cold-formed steel with a section size of 116 mm × 140 mm is used for the upper end beam, and the tarpaulin back iron compression member is welded at the connection with the upper side beam. The corner column is installed and welded with 14a channel steel and a 7mm thick corner column plate. The corner column plate is overlapped with the sidewall plate and corner column reinforcement plate. The three transverse strips are made of 140 mm weather-resistant cold-formed steel, and both ends of the transverse strips are welded with corner columns, which improves the overall stiffness and strength of the end wall. The end wall plate is made of a 5 mm thick steel plate.

8.2.4 C_{70}型、C_{70H}型敞车
C_{70} and C_{70H} gondola car

1. 主要特点
Main characteristics

（1）采用屈服极限为 450 MPa 的高强度钢和新型中梁，载重大、自重轻；优化了底架结构，提高了纵向承载能力，适应万吨重载列车的运输要求。

High-strength steel with a yield limit of 450 MPa and the new type of center beam are used, with heavy load and lightweight; the underframe structure has been optimized, and the longitudinal bearing capacity has been improved to meet the transportation requirements of 10,000-ton heavy haul trains.

（2）车体内长 13 m，满足较长货物的运输要求；对底架结构进行了优化，车辆中部集载能力达到 39 t，较 C_{64} 型敞车提高了 70%，可运输的集载货物范围更广。

The length inside the car body is 13 m, which meets the transportation requirements for longer goods; the underframe structure has been optimized to achieve a concentrated loading capacity of 39 t in the middle of the car, which is 70% higher than that of the C_{64} gondola car. The range of concentrated loading goods that can be transported is wider.

（3）采用新型中立门结构，提高了车门的可靠性，可解决现有 C_{64} 型敞车最大的惯性质量问题。

The new neutral door structure is used to improve the reliability of the door, which can solve the maximum inertia mass problem of the existing C_{64} gondola car.

（4）采用 E 级钢 17 型高强度车钩和 MT-2 型缓冲器，提高了车钩缓冲装置的使用可靠性。

The No.17 high-strength coupler made of E-grade steel and MT-2 buffer is used to improve the serviceability of the coupler and draft gear.

（5）采用转 K6 型或转 K5 型转向架，确保车辆运营速度达 120 km/h，满足提速要求；改善了车辆运行品质，降低了轮轨间的作用力，减轻了轮轨磨耗。

Bogie type ZK6 or ZK5 is used to ensure that the operating speed can reach 120 km/h, meeting the speed increase requirements; the running quality of railway vehicles is improved, the force between wheels and rails is reduced, and the wheel-rail wear is reduced.

（6）侧柱采用新型双曲面冷弯型钢，提高了强度和刚度，更适应翻车机作业。

The new hyperboloid cold-formed steel is adopted for the side column, which improves the strength and stiffness and is more suitable for the operation of car dumpers.

（7）满足现有敞车的互换性要求，主要零部件与现有敞车通用互换，方便维护和检修。

The interchangeability requirements of existing gondola cars are met, and the main components are interchangeable with existing gondola cars, which facilitates maintenance and overhaul.

2. 主要性能参数

Main performance parameters

C_{70} 型、C_{70H} 型敞车的主要性能参数如表 8–1 所示。

The main performance parameters of the C_{70} and C_{70H} gondola cars are shown in Table 8-1.

表 8–1　C_{70} 型、C_{70H} 型敞车的主要性能参数

Table 8-1　Main Performance Parameters of C_{70} and C_{70H} Gondola Cars

<table>
<tr><td>载重
Load capacity</td><td colspan="2">70 t</td></tr>
<tr><td>自重
Tare weight</td><td colspan="2">≤23.8 t</td></tr>
<tr><td>轴重
Axle load</td><td colspan="2">23 t（允许−1%～+2%）
23 t (allowable −1% to +2%)</td></tr>
<tr><td>容积
Volume</td><td colspan="2">77 m³</td></tr>
<tr><td>比容
Specific volume</td><td colspan="2">1.1 m³/t</td></tr>
<tr><td>自重系数
Ratio of tare weight to loading capacity</td><td colspan="2">0.33</td></tr>
<tr><td>每延米重
Weight per linear meter</td><td colspan="2">≤6.71 t/m</td></tr>
<tr><td>商业运营速度
Commercial operation speed</td><td colspan="2">120 km/h</td></tr>
<tr><td>通过最小曲线半径
Min. radius of curvature negotiated</td><td colspan="2">145 m</td></tr>
<tr><td>全车制动倍率
Braking leverage of the complete car</td><td colspan="2">11.2</td></tr>
<tr><td rowspan="2">全车制动率（常用制动位）
Braking ratio of the complete car (service braking position)</td><td>空车
Empty car</td><td>19.4%</td></tr>
<tr><td>重车
Full car</td><td>17.4%</td></tr>
<tr><td>制动距离（重车、紧急）
Braking distance (full car, emergency)</td><td colspan="2">1 400 m</td></tr>
<tr><td>限界
Gauge</td><td colspan="2">符合《标准轨距铁路限界　第 1 部分：机车车辆限界》（GB 146.1—2020）的要求
Comply with the requirements of Gauge for Standard Gauge Railways—Part 1: Rolling Stock Gauge (GB 146.1—2020)</td></tr>
</table>

3. 主要尺寸参数

Main dimension parameters

C_{70} 型、C_{70H} 型敞车的主要尺寸参数如表 8–2 所示。

The main dimension parameters of the C_{70} and C_{70H} gondola cars are shown in Table 8-2.

表 8-2　C_{70} 型、C_{70H} 型敞车的主要尺寸参数
Table 8-2　Main Dimension Parameters of C_{70} and C_{70H} Gondola Cars

<table>
<tr><td>车辆长度
Vehicle length</td><td colspan="2">13 976 mm</td></tr>
<tr><td>车辆定距
Fixed distance</td><td colspan="2">9 210 mm</td></tr>
<tr><td>最大宽度
Max. width</td><td colspan="2">3 242 mm</td></tr>
<tr><td>车辆最大高度
Max. height of car</td><td colspan="2">3 143 mm</td></tr>
<tr><td>车体内长
Interior length of car body</td><td colspan="2">13 000 mm</td></tr>
<tr><td rowspan="2">车体内宽
Interior width of car body</td><td>上侧板处
Upper side plate</td><td>2 892 mm</td></tr>
<tr><td>连铁处
Connecting rail</td><td>2 792 mm</td></tr>
<tr><td>车体内高
Interior height of car body</td><td colspan="2">2 050 mm</td></tr>
<tr><td>地板面距轨面高（空车）
Height from floor surface to rail surface (empty car)</td><td colspan="2">1 083 mm</td></tr>
<tr><td>车钩中心线高（空车）
Height of coupler centerline (empty car)</td><td colspan="2">880 mm</td></tr>
<tr><td rowspan="2">门孔尺寸（宽×高）
Door opening size (width × height)</td><td>侧开门孔
Side door opening</td><td>1 620 mm×1 900 mm</td></tr>
<tr><td>下侧门孔
Lower side door opening</td><td>1 250 mm×951 mm</td></tr>
<tr><td rowspan="2">固定轴距
Fixed wheelbase</td><td>转 K6 型
Bogie type ZK-6</td><td>1 830 mm</td></tr>
<tr><td>转 K5 型
Bogie type ZK-5</td><td>1 800 mm</td></tr>
<tr><td>车轮直径
Wheel diameter</td><td colspan="2">840 mm</td></tr>
</table>

4. 主要结构
Main structure

C_{70} 型、C_{70H} 型敞车主要由车体、转向架、车钩缓冲装置及制动装置等组成，如图 8-6 所示。

The C_{70} and C_{70H} gondola cars are mainly composed of a car body, bogie, coupler and draft gear, braking device, etc., as shown in Figure 8-6.

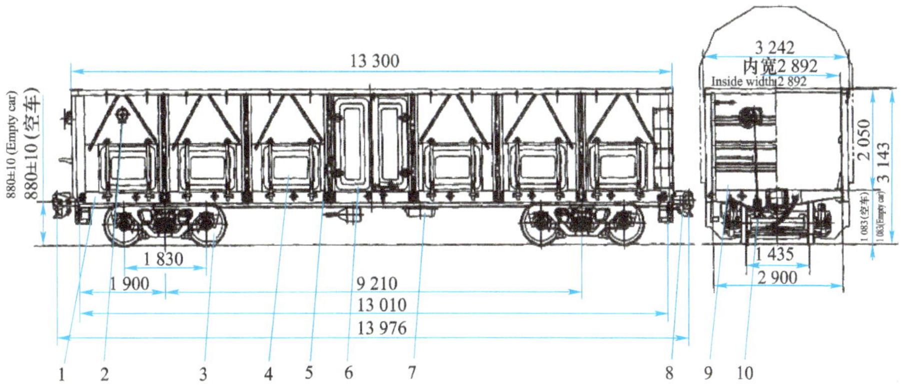

1—底架；2—标记；3—转向架；4—下侧门；5—侧墙；6—侧开门；7—空气制动装置；
8—车钩缓冲装置；9—端墙；10—手制动装置。

1—Underframe; 2—Marking; 3—Bogie; 4—Lower side door; 5—Side wall; 6—Side door; 7—Pneumatic braking device;
8—Coupler and draft gear; 9—End wall; 10—Hand brake device.

图 8-6 C_{70} 型、C_{70H} 型敞车的结构

Figure 8-6 Structure of C_{70} and C_{70H} Gondola Cars

1）车体

Car body

C_{70} 型、C_{70H} 型敞车的车体为全钢焊接结构，由底架、侧墙、端墙、车门等部件组成。车体主要材料采用屈服强度为 450 MPa 的耐大气腐蚀钢。

The car body of C_{70} and C_{70H} gondola cars is an all-steel welded structure, composed of underframe, side walls, end walls, doors, and other components. The main material of the car body is weather-resisting steel with a yield strength of 450 MPa.

（1）底架。底架由中梁、侧梁、枕梁、大横梁、端梁、纵向梁、小横梁及钢地板组焊而成。中梁采用 310 乙字型钢，允许采用冷弯中梁，侧梁为 240 mm×80 mm×8 mm 的槽形冷弯型钢；枕梁、大横梁为钢板组焊结构，底架上铺 6 mm 厚的耐候钢地板；采用锻造上心盘（直径为 358 mm）及材质为 C 级铸钢的前、后从板座，前、后从板座与中梁间，以及脚蹬、牵引钩、绳栓、下侧门搭扣与侧梁间均采用专用拉铆钉连接。

Underframe. The underframe is installed and welded by the center beam, side beam, sleeper beam, large cross beam, end beam, longitudinal beam, small cross beam, and steel floor. The center beam is made of 310 Z-shaped steel, and the cold-formed center beams are allowed, with a side beam of 240 mm × 80 mm × 8 mm groove-shaped cold-formed steel; the sleeper beam and large cross beam are of steel plate assembly welding structure, and the 6 mm thick weather-resistant steel floor is paved on the underframe; the forging upper center plate (with a diameter of 358 mm) and the front and rear slave plate seats made of grade C cast steel are used. The front and rear slave plate seats are connected to the center beam, and the pedals, traction hooks, rope bolts, lower side door buckles, and side beams are connected using special pulling rivets.

（2）侧墙。侧墙为板柱式结构，由上侧梁、侧柱、侧板、连铁、斜撑、侧柱补强板及侧柱内补强座等组焊而成，如图 8-7 所示。上侧梁采用 140 mm×100 mm×5 mm 的冷弯矩形钢管制造，侧柱采用 8 mm 厚的冷弯双曲面帽型钢制造。侧柱与侧梁采用专用拉铆钉连接。

Side wall. The side wall is a plate column structure, which is installed and welded by the upper side beam, side column, side plate, connecting iron, bracing, side column reinforcement plate, and side column internal reinforcement seat, as shown in Figure 8-7. 140 mm × 100 mm × 5 mm cold-formed rectangular steel pipe is used for upper side beam, and 8 mm thick cold-formed hyperbolic cap-shaped steel is used for the side columns. The side columns and side beams are connected with special pulling rivets.

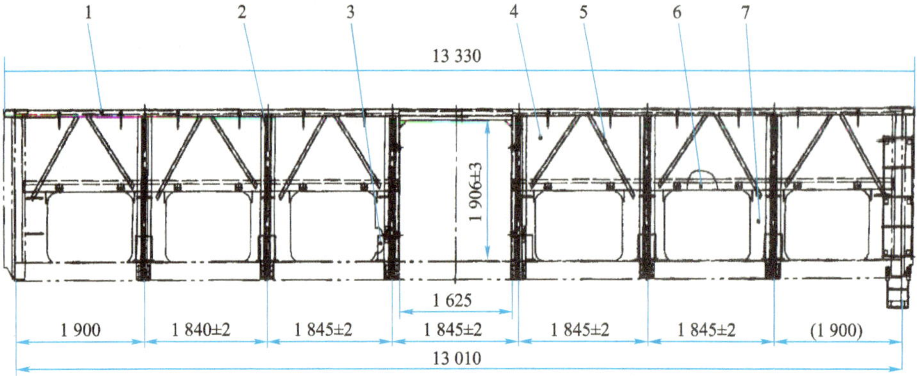

1—上侧梁；2—侧柱；3—侧柱内补强座；4—侧板；5—斜撑；6—侧柱连铁；7—侧柱补强板。

1—Upper side beam; 2—Side column; 3—Internal reinforcement seat of side column; 4—Side plate; 5—Bracing; 6—Side column connecting iron; 7—Side column reinforcement plate.

图 8-7　C_{70} 型、C_{70H} 型敞车的侧墙

Figure 8-7　Side Wall of C_{70} and C_{70H} Gondola Cars

（3）端墙。端墙由上端梁、角柱、横带及端板等组焊而成，如图 8-8 所示。上端梁、角柱采用 160 mm×100 mm×5 mm 的冷弯矩形钢管制造，横带采用断面高度为 150 mm 的帽形冷弯型钢制造。

End wall. The end wall is installed and welded by upper end beams, corner columns, transverse strips, end plates, etc., as shown in Figure 8-8. 160 mm × 100 mm × 5 mm cold-formed rectangular steel pipe is used for the upper end beam and corner column, the cap-shaped cold-formed steel with a cross-sectional height of 150 mm is used for the transverse strip.

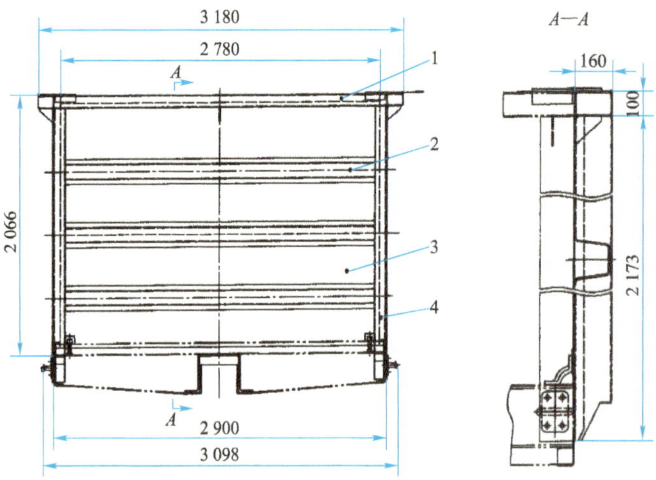

1—上端梁；2—横带；3—端板；4—角柱。

1—Upper end beam; 2—Transverse strip; 3—End plate; 4—Corner column.

图 8-8　C_{70}、C_{70H} 型敞车的端墙

Figure 8-8　End Wall of C_{70} and C_{70H} Gondola Cars

（4）侧开门及下侧门。在车体两侧的侧墙上各安装一对侧开式侧开门及 6 扇上翻式下侧门，以方便手动卸货。侧开门采用了新型的锁闭装置，门边处组焊了槽形冷弯型钢，增强了刚度并将通长式上锁杆封闭。下门锁采用偏心压紧机构，当车门关闭后，通长式上锁杆可防止下门锁窜出，操作简单，安全可靠，如图 8–9 所示。下侧门的结构与 C_{64} 型敞车相同，如图 8–5 所示。

Side door and lower side door. A pair of side-opening side doors and six upturning lower side doors should be installed on the side walls on both sides of the car body to facilitate manual unloading. The new type of locking device is adopted for the side door, and the groove-shaped cold-formed steel is installed and welded at the door edge to enhance the stiffness and close the full-length locking rod. The eccentric pressing mechanism is adopted for the lower door lock. When the door is closed, the full-length locking rod can prevent the lower door lock from popping out, which is simple to operate, safe, and reliable, as shown in Figure 8-9. The structure of the lower side door is the same as that of the C_{64} gondola car, as shown in Figure 8-5.

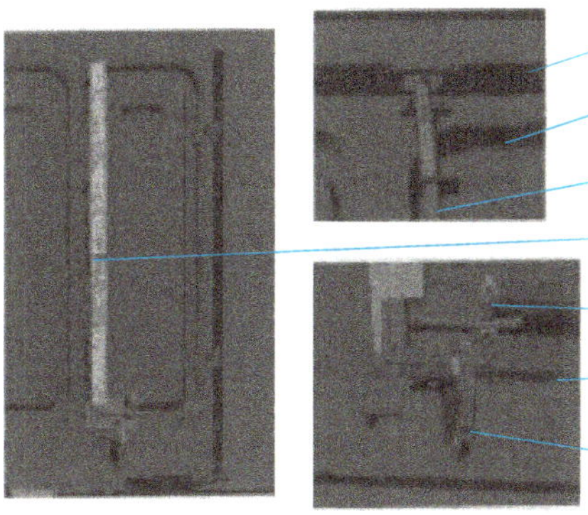

图 8–9　C70 型、C_{70H} 型敞车的侧开门开闭机构

Figure 8-9　Opening and Closing Mechanisms of Side Door for C_{70} and C_{70H} Gondola Cars

2）车钩缓冲装置

Coupler and draft gear

C_{70} 型、C_{70H} 型敞车采用 E 级钢 17 型车钩、配套采用 17 型锻造钩尾框、合金钢钩尾销、MT–2 型或新型缓冲器、含油尼龙钩尾框托板磨耗板。钩尾销托梁、钩尾框托板、安全托板采用 BY-B 型或 FS 型防松螺母。

The No.17 coupler made of E-grade steel, and the No.17 forged coupler yoke, alloy steel coupler tail pin, MT-2 or new type buffer, oil-containing nylon coupler yoke supporting plate, and wearing plate are used as supporting material for C_{70} and C_{70H} gondola cars. The BY-B or FS lock nuts are adopted for the coupler tail pin joist, coupler yoke supporting plate, and safety joist.

3）制动装置

Braking device

C_{70} 型、C_{70H} 型敞车采用制动主管压力满足 500 kPa 和 600 kPa 的空气制动装置，主要由 120 型控制阀、直径为 254 mm 的整体旋压密封式制动缸、ST2-250 型双向闸瓦间隙自动调整器、KZW-A 型空重车自动调整装置、货车脱轨自动制动装置等组成。制动装置也采用编织制动软管总成、奥贝球铁衬套、高摩合成闸瓦、不锈钢制动配件和管系。手制动装置采用 NSW 型手制动机。

The pneumatic braking device with a main brake pipe pressure of 500 kPa and 600 kPa is adopted for C_{70} and C_{70H} gondola cars, mainly composed of a Type 120 control valve, an integral spinning sealed brake cylinder with a diameter of 254 mm, an ST2-250 automatic adjuster for two-way brake shoe gap, a KZW-A automatic adjustment device for empty and full cars, and an automatic braking device for the derailment of the freight car. Braided brake hose assembly, austempering ductile iron bushing, high-friction composite brake shoe, stainless steel brake accessories, and pipe system are adopted for braking device. The NSW hand brake is adopted as a hand braking device.

4）转向架

Bogie

C_{70} 型、C_{70H} 型敞车采用转 K6 或转 K5 型转向架，装用转 K6 型转向架时车型为 C_{70}，装用转 K5 型转向架时车型为 C_{70H}。

Bogie type ZK6 or ZK5 is used for C_{70} and C_{70H} gondola cars. The vehicle type is C_{70} when bogie type ZK6 is installed, and the vehicle type is C_{70H} when bogie type ZK5 is installed.

任务 8.3　棚　　车

Task 8.3　Box cars

8.3.1　棚车的发展简述

Overview of development of box cars

解放初期，我国铁路上运用的棚车从国外进口，车型多达 80 多种。这些车辆结构较复杂、载重小、容积小，已全部被淘汰。新中国成立以来，我国铁路棚车不论在品种、质量、数量上都有很大的发展。1951 年至 1953 年间，我国自行设计制造了载重 30 t 的 P_1、P_3 型棚车，但由于其载重小，结构落后，已全部被淘汰。1953 年开始制造载重 50 t 的 P_{50} 型棚车，起初设计的 P_{50} 型棚车为全铆结构，随着电焊工艺的不断发展而改成底架电焊、上部铆接的结构；后来薄板焊接水平提高，上部各梁柱与包板也采用电焊结构，现该车型已全部被淘汰。1958 年开始设计试制载重 60 t、容积 120 m^3 的 P_{13} 型棚车，并于 1963 年投入了批量生产；该车型的车体为电焊结构，侧、端、顶板均采用薄钢板压型，并取消了端柱、斜撑及车顶弯梁等件；为了适应散装货物的装卸，车顶设有装货口，侧墙下角设有卸货口。其运用表明：装卸货口在散装粮谷时发挥了良好的作用，但在装载一般货物时，易造成失盗。为了方便制造、检修和运用管理，以后生产了与 P_{13} 型棚车结构基本相同但取消了装卸货口的棚车，改型为 P_{60}。P_{13}、P_{60} 型棚车曾是我国铁路货车中的主型棚车，P_{60} 型棚车的数量最多，至 1994 年共生产了 11 300 余辆。

In the early 1949, the box cars used on China’s railways were imported from abroad, with more than 80 vehicle types. These railway vehicles have been eliminated due to their complex structure, small load capacity, and small volume. Since the founding of the PRC in 1949, there has been overwhelming development in the variety, number, and quantity of railway box cars in China. From 1951 to 1953, China independently designed and manufactured P_1 and P_3 box cars with a load capacity of 30 t. Due to their small load capacity and backward structure, they have all been eliminated. In 1953, the P_{50} box car with a load capacity of 50 t was started to be manufactured. Initially, the P_{50} box car was designed as a fully riveted structure. With the continuous development of the welding process, it was changed to the structure with an underframe welded and upper riveted; later, the welding level of thin plates was improved, and the upper beams, columns, and cladding plates were welded. Now, this type of railway vehicle has been eliminated. The design and trial production of the P_{13} box car started in 1958, which with a load capacity of 60 t and a volume of 120 m^3. The P_{13} box car was put into mass production in 1963; the car body is an electric welding structure. The side, end, and top plates are profiled with thin steel plates, and the end columns, bracing, roof bending beams, and other parts are canceled; a loading port is provided on the roof, and an unloading port is provided at the lower corner of the side wall, to adapt to the loading and unloading of bulk goods. The application indicates that the loading and unloading port plays a good role in bulk grain loading, but it is easy to attract theft when general goods are loaded. To facilitate manufacturing, maintenance, and operation management, the box car with the same structure as the P_{13} box car was produced later, but the loading and unloading port was canceled, and the type was changed to P_{60}. P_{13} and P_{60} box cars used to be the main type of box cars in China's railway freight cars, with the largest quantity of P_{60} cars. By 1994, more than 11,300 cars had been produced.

随着机械化装卸作业的不断发展，2 m 宽的车门在叉车作业时不太方便，为此研制了 3 m 宽车门的棚车，将 P_{60} 型棚车修改定型为 P_{61} 型棚车，并于 1974 年投入批量生产。投入运用后，由于木地板改为了铁地板，空车地板面高度由 1 144 mm 改为 1 077 mm，不利于在标准货物站台上进行机械化装卸作业，同时也不适宜运输人员及马匹。因此，在 1979 年提出了 P_{62} 型棚车方案，采用了刀把形牵引梁，车窗改为百叶式通风口，于 1982 年投入批量生产，至 1994 年共计生产了 45 700 余辆。为提高车辆的耐腐蚀性能、延长检修周期，于 1987 年将 P_{62} 型棚车主要板材件改用为耐候钢，并定型为 $P_{62A(N)}$型棚车。

As the mechanized loading and unloading operation is continuously developing, the 2 m wide door is not very convenient for forklift operation. Therefore, the box car with a 3 m wide door was developed, and the P_{60} car was modified to P_{61}, which was put into mass production in 1974. After it was put into use, the height of the empty car floor was changed from 1,144 mm to 1,077 mm due to the conversion of wooden flooring to iron flooring, which was not conducive to mechanized loading and unloading operations on standard goods platforms, and the iron flooring was not suitable for transporting personnel and horses. Therefore, the P_{62} box car scheme was proposed in 1979, which adopted the knife holder-shaped traction beam, and the window was changed to a louvered ventilation opening. It was put into mass production in 1982, and a total of 45,700 vehicles had been produced by 1994. To improve the corrosion resistance of vehicles and extend the maintenance cycle, the main plate parts of P_{62} box cars were changed to weather-resistant steel in 1987, and they were finalized as $P_{62A(N)}$ box cars.

1993 年，在 P_{62N} 型棚车的基础上设计制造了具有内衬结构的 P_{64} 型棚车，1994 年通过部级技术审查并批量生产至 1998 年。1997 年又研制成功了具有圆弧顶、大容积、新型车门和下翻式车窗的 P_{64A} 型通用棚车，在自重没有增加的前提下，容积增大了 10 m^3；1998 年装用转 K2 型转向架的 P_{65} 型行包快运棚车研制成功并投入运用，该车型的商业运营速度可以达到 120 km/h。2001 年通过采用新材料、新工艺、新技术，完成了 P_{64GK} 型棚车的研制，该车型采用了 09CuPCrNi-A 高耐候结构钢、新型竹编内衬板及新型棚车门锁，开发应用了 10 余种新型冷弯型钢，并采用转 K2 型转向架、13A 型小间隙车钩，在优化车体结构前提下，有效减轻了车辆自重，载重较 P_{6Q} 型棚车增加了 2 t，商业运营速度达到 120 km/h。P_{64} 系列棚车是目前运营的主型棚车。

In 1993, P_{64} box cars with a lining structure were designed and manufactured on the basis of P_{62N} box cars. In 1994, they passed ministerial-level technical reviews and were mass-produced until 1998. In 1997, the P_{64A} general box car with a circular arc roof, large volume, new doors, and downwardly turning windows was successfully developed. The volume was increased by 10 m^3 without increasing its tare weight; In 1998, the P_{65} luggage and parcel express box car with bogie type ZK-2 was successfully developed and put into operation. The commercial operation speed of this type can reach 120 km/h. In 2001, the development of P_{64GK} box cars was completed by adopting new materials, new processes, and new technologies. The car uses 09CuPCrNi-A high weathering resistant structural steel, a new bamboo woven lining plate, and a new type of box car door lock. More than ten new types of cold-formed steel have been developed and applied, including bogie type ZK2 and 13A small gap couplers. Under the premise of optimizing the car body structure, the vehicle's tare weight has been effectively reduced, and the load has increased by 2 t compared to that of P_{6Q} box cars, The commercial operation speed reaches 120 km/h. P_{64} series box cars are the main type of box cars currently in operation.

为适应我国既有铁路线路、桥梁的实际承载能力要求，加快铁路装备现代化进程，齐车公司于 2003 年开始 70 t 级新型通用棚车的研制，于 2005 年初完成了 70 t 级新型通用棚车工作图设计、小批量试制及各项性能试验工作，并于同年 8 月通过了样车的部级审查。该车型载重 70 t、自重 24.6 t。装用转 K6 型转向架时定型为 P_{70} 型棚车，装用转 K5 型转向架时定型为 P_{70H} 型棚车。

CRRC Qiqihar began the development of the new type of 70 t grade general purpose box car in 2003, to meet the actual bearing capacity requirements of existing railway lines and bridges in China and accelerate the modernization process of railway equipment. At the beginning of 2005, it completed the working drawing design, small batch trial production, and various performance tests of the 70 t new type general purpose box car. In August of the same year, it passed the ministerial-level review of the prototype car, with a load capacity of 70 t and a tare weight of 24.6 t. The vehicle type is P_{70} when bogie type ZK6 is installed, and the vehicle type is P_{70H} when bogie type ZK5 is installed.

表 8-3 为我国主型棚车的主要技术参数一览表。

Table 8-3 List of Main Technical Parameters of Main Box Cars in China

表 8-3　我国主型棚车的主要技术参数一览表

Table 8-3　Overview of the main technical parameters of China's main type of box cars

型号 Model	重量参数 Weight parameters			容积参数 Capacity parameter		车辆尺寸/mm Vehicle size/mm			车辆定距/mm Vehicle fixed distance/mm	车体尺寸/mm Body size/mm				底架尺寸/mm Chassis size/mm		轴重/t Axle load / t	每延米载重/（t/m） Load per meter / (t/m)	门、窗孔（宽×高）/mm Door and window opening (width x height) / mm
	载重/t Load capacity/t	自重/t Self-weight/t	自重系数 Self-weight coefficient	容积/m³ Volume/m³	比容 Specific volume	最大宽度 Maximum width	最大高度 Maximum height	车辆长度 Vehicle length		内长 Inner length	内宽 Inner width	地板面距轨面高 Floor height from rail surface	内高 Inner height	长度 Length	宽度 Width			
P_{13}	60	22.6	0.38	120	2.0	3 338	4 547	16 442	11 500	15 470	2 830	1 144	2 740	15 500	3 030	20.7	5.0	门孔: 1 954×2 578 Door hole: 1 954×2 578 窗孔: 494×394 Window hole: 494×394
P_{60}	60	22.2	0.37	120	2.0	3 338	4 547	16 442	11 500	15 470	2 830	1 144	2 740	15 500	3 030	20.6	5.0	门孔: 1 950×2 578 Door opening: 1 950×2 578 窗孔: 494×394 Window opening: 494×394
P_{61}	60	23.9	0.40	120	2.0	3 338	4 540	16 442	11 500	15 480	2 850	1 072	2 765	15 500	3 030	21.0	5.1	门孔: 2 960×2 685 Door hole: 2 960×2 685 窗孔: 492×391 Window opening: 492×391
P_{62}	60	24.0	0.40	120	2.0	3 312	4 220	16 438	11 700	15 490	2 820	1 141	2 760	15 500	2 820	21.0	5.1	门孔: 2 964×2 597 Door opening: 2 964×2 597
P_{64}	58	25.4	0.43	116	2.0	3 312	4 160	16 438	11 700	15 466	2 796	1 143	2 705	15 500	2 820	21.0	5.1	门孔: 2 964×2 542 Door opening: 2 964×2 542 窗孔: 690×415 Window opening: 690×415
P_{65}	40	25.9	0.65	135	3.38	3 320	4 675	16 438	11 700	15 462	2 790	1 130		15 500	2 820	18	4.3	门孔: 2 964×2 531 Door hole: 2 964×2 531
P_{66}	60	24	0.4	135	2.25	3 170	4 585	16 430	11 700	15 476	2 800	1 124	2 852	15 500	2 800	21	5.1	门孔: 7 670×2 535 Door opening: 7 670×2 535
P_{70}	70	24.6	0.35	145	2.07	3 300	4 770	17 066	12 100	16 087	2 793	1 136	2 855	16 100		23	5.5	门孔: 3 012×2 539 Door hole: 3 012×2 539
P_{31}	31	16.1	0.52	65.8	2.12	2 994	3.556	12 868	8 400	11 920	2 310	1 062				12	3.66	

8.3.2 P_{70}型、P_{70H}型棚车
P_{70} and P_{70H} box cars

1. 主要特点
Main characteristics

（1）P_{70}型、P_{70H}型棚车的容积为 145 m^3，载重为 70 t，容积比 P_{64}型棚车增加 10 m^3，载重比 P_{64GK}型棚车增加 10 t，单车载重量提高了 16.7%。

The P_{70} and P_{70H} box cars have a volume of 145 m^3 and a load capacity of 70 t. The volume is 10 m^3 more than that of the P_{64} box car, the load capacity is 10 t more than that of P_{64GK} box cars, and the load capacity of a single vehicle increases by 16.7%.

（2）P_{70}型、P_{70H}型棚车每延米重 5.5 t/m，比 P_{64GK}型棚车增加 0.4 t/m，在既有 850 m 站场及线桥条件下，列车运能可提高 300 t。

The weight of P_{70} and P_{70H} box cars per linear meter is 5.5 t/m, 0.4 t/m more than that of P_{64GK} box cars. Under the condition of the existing 850 m station yard and railway bridge, the train transportation capacity is increased by 300 t.

（3）P_{70}型、P_{70H}型棚车采用转 K6 型或转 K5 型转向架，改善了车辆运行品质，在既有线桥条件下车辆商业运营速度可达 120 km/h；采用 17 型车钩、MT−2 型缓冲器、高强度钢中梁，提高了纵向承载能力，可适应编组万吨重载列车的要求。

The running quality of vehicles is improved by using bogie type ZK6 or ZK5 for P_{70} and P_{70H} box cars, which meet the commercial operating speed of 120 km/h under the conditions of existing railway bridges; the longitudinal bearing capacity is improved by using No.17 couplers, MT-2 buffers, and high-strength steel center beams, which can meet the requirements of marshaling 10,000-ton heavy haul trains.

（4）在既有棚车运用经验的基础上优化了结构，提高了车体的疲劳强度及耐腐蚀性能；转向架、车钩缓冲装置及制动系统的主要零部件通过可靠性设计和完善的工艺、质量保证，实现了寿命管理；延长检修周期，取消辅修修程，段修周期由 1.5 年提高到 2 年，降低了检修维护成本。

Based on the existing experience of box cars, the structure has been optimized to improve the fatigue strength and corrosion resistance of the car body; the life management of the main components of the bogie, coupler and draft gear, and braking system have been achieved through reliability design, complete technology, and quality assurance. The maintenance cycle has been extended and the auxiliary repair process has been canceled. The depot repair cycle has been increased from 1.5 years to 2 years, and the maintenance costs have been reduced.

（5）采用高强度耐候钢及冷弯型钢，并应用可靠性设计理念优化断面结构，对大应力部位进行细部设计，对整车进行疲劳寿命预测，以提高结构可靠性，有效减轻车辆自重，满足铁路货车提速、重载的要求。

High-strength weather-resistant steel and cold-formed steel are used, and the application of reliability design concepts is made to optimize the section structure. Detailed design is conducted for large stress parts, and fatigue life prediction is carried out for the complete car, to improve structural reliability, effectively reduce the tare weight of the vehicle, and meet the requirements for speed increase and heavy-loading of railway freight cars.

（6）为改善车内装货环境、避免聚集在车顶上部的潮浊空气对车顶板的腐蚀，在车顶部采用了 4 个通风器来加强车内空气流通。

Four ventilators are installed on the top of the vehicle to enhance the air circulation inside the vehicle, to improve the loading environment inside the vehicle and avoid the corrosion of the roof plate caused by the accumulation of damp and turbid air on the top of the roof.

（7）为确保重载编组、高速运行工况下从板座与中梁的连接强度及抗振、防松性能，提高车辆的运用可靠性，前后从板座与中梁之间采用专用拉铆钉铆接。

To ensure the connection strength, vibration resistance, and looseness prevention performance of the slave plate seat and the center beam under heavy load marshaling and high-speed operation conditions, and to improve the operational reliability of the vehicle, the special pulling rivet is used for riveting the front and rear slave plate seats and the center beam.

（8）为解决从棚车底门缝进行盗窃散粒货物的问题，对推拉式车门下部结构进行了改进，提高了车门的防盗性能。

The lower structure of the push-pull door has been improved to solve the problem of stealing bulk goods from the bottom door seam of the box car, which improves the anti-theft performance of the door.

（9）车窗、车门及部分冷弯型钢等与现有棚车通用互换，方便维护和检修。

Windows, doors, and some cold-formed steel are interchangeable with existing box cars to facilitate maintenance and overhaul.

2. 主要性能参数

Main performance parameters

P_{70} 型、P_{70H} 型棚车的主要性能参数如表 8–4 所示。

The main performance parameters of P_{70} and P_{70H} box cars are shown in Table 8-4.

表 8–4 P_{70} 型、P_{70H} 型棚车的主要性能参数

Table 8-4 Main Performance Parameters of P_{70} and P_{70H} Box Cars

<table>
<tr><td>载重
Load capacity</td><td colspan="2">70 t</td></tr>
<tr><td rowspan="2">自重
Tare weight</td><td>无内衬板
Without inner lining plate</td><td>≤23.8 t</td></tr>
<tr><td>有内衬板
With inner lining plate</td><td>≤24.6 t</td></tr>
<tr><td>轴重
Axle load</td><td colspan="2">23 t（允差–1%～+2%），有内衬板
23 t (tolerance –1% to +2%) with inner lining plate
23 t（允差–1.0%～+2.8），无内衬板
23 t (tolerance –1.0% to +2.8%) without inner lining plate</td></tr>
<tr><td>容积
Volume</td><td colspan="2">145 m³</td></tr>
</table>

续表

Continued

比容 Specific volume	2.07 m³/t	
换长 Change length	1.6	
自重系数 Ratio of tare weight to loading capacity	无内衬板 Without inner lining plate	≤0.34
	有内衬板 With inner lining plate	≤0.35
每延米重 Weight per linear meter	5.5 t/m	
通过最小曲线半径 Min. radius of curvature negotiated	145 m	
商业运营速度 Commercial operation speed	120 km/h	
制动距离（重车、紧急） Braking distance (full car, emergency)	1 400 m	
制动率 Braking ratio	空车 Empty car	22%
	重车 Full car	17.3%

3. 主要尺寸参数

Main dimension parameters

P_{70} 型、P_{70H} 型棚车的主要尺寸参数如表 8-5 所示。

The main dimension parameters of P_{70} and P_{70H} box cars are shown in Table 8-5.

表 8-5　P_{70} 型、P_{70H} 型棚车的主要尺寸参数

Table 8-5　Main Dimension Parameters of P_{70} and P_{70H} Box Cars

车辆长度 Vehicle length	17 066 mm
车辆定距 Fixed distance	12 100 mm
车辆最大高度（空车） Max. height of car (empty car)	4 770 mm
车辆最大宽度 Max. width of car	3 300 mm

续表
Continued

车体内长 Interior length of car body	无内衬板 Without inner lining plate	16 094 mm
	有内衬板 With inner lining plate	16 087 mm
车体内宽 Interior width of car body	无内衬板 Without inner lining plate	2 800 mm
	有内衬板 With inner lining plate	2 793 mm
车钩中心线距轨面高（空车） Height from coupler center line to rail surface (empty car)	880 mm	
地板面距轨面高（空车） Height from floor surface to rail surface (empty car)	1 136 mm	
车门门孔尺寸（高×宽） Door opening size (height × width)	2 539 mm×3 012 mm	
固定轴距 Fixed wheelbase	转 K6 型 Bogie type ZK-6	1 830 mm
	转 K5 型 Bogie type ZK-5	1 800 mm
车轮直径 Wheel diameter	840 mm	

4. 主要结构 Main structure

P_{70} 型、P_{70H} 型棚车主要由车体、转向架、车钩缓冲装置及制动装置等组成。

The P_{70} and P_{70H} box cars are mainly composed of a car body, bogie, coupler and draft gear, braking device, etc.

1）车体 Car body

P_{70} 型、P_{70H} 型棚车的车体为全钢焊接整体承载结构，主要由底架、侧墙、端墙、车顶、车门、车窗等组成，如图 8-10 所示。底架主要型钢板材为 Q450NQR1 高强度耐候钢，端、侧墙及车顶的主要型钢板材为 09CuPCrNi-A 耐大气腐蚀钢。

The car body of P_{70} and P_{70H} box cars is an all-steel welded integral bearing structure, mainly composed of an underframe, side walls, end walls, roof, doors, windows, etc., as shown in Figure 8-10. The main section steel plates of the underframe are made of Q450NQR1 high-strength weather-resistant steel, and the main section steel plates of the end, side walls, and roof are made of 09CuPCrNi-A weather-resisting steel.

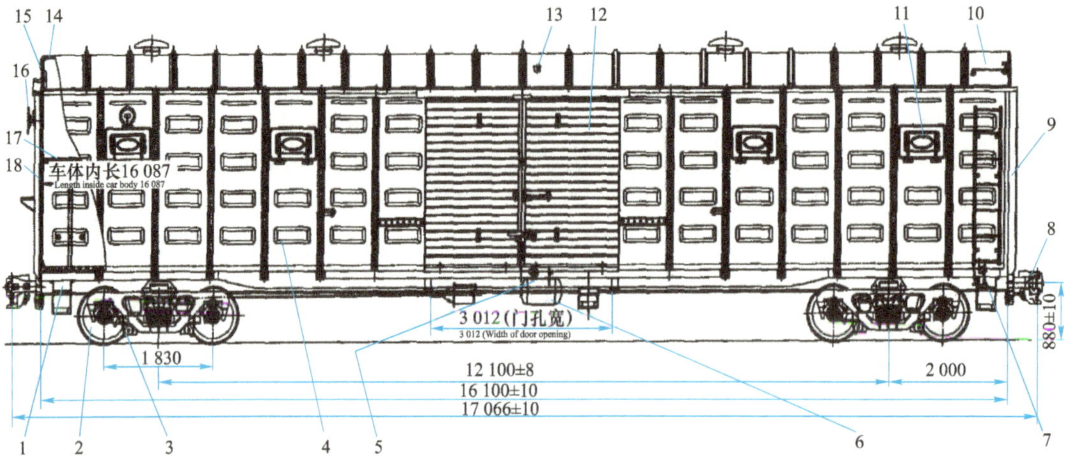

1—底架组成；2—转 K6 型转向架；3—底架木结构；4—侧墙组成；5—底架附属件；6—空气制动装置；7—便器组成；8—车钩缓冲装置；9—端墙组成；10—车顶组成；11—车窗组成；12—车门组成；13—烟囱座组成；14—车顶木结构；15—电气安装；16—手制动装置；17—侧墙木结构；18—端墙木结构。

1—Underframe composition; 2—Bogie type ZK6; 3—Underframe wooden structure; 4—Side wall composition; 5—Underframe accessories; 6—Pneumatic braking device; 7—Toilet composition; 8—Coupler and draft gear; 9—End wall composition; 10—Roof composition; 11—Window composition; 12—Door composition; 13—Composition of chimney base; 14—Roof wooden structure; 15—Electrical installation; 16—Hand brake device; 17—Side wall wooden structure; 18—End wall wooden structure.

图 8-10　P_{70} 型、$P70_H$ 型棚车的车体结构

Figure 8-10　Structure of the Car Body for P_{70} and P_{70H} Box Cars

（1）底架。底架由中梁、枕梁、下侧梁、大横梁、端梁、小横梁、纵向梁、地板等组成，如图 8-11 所示。中梁采用屈服强度为 450 MPa 的热轧 310 乙字型钢或冷弯中梁；上心盘和前、后从板座分别采用直径为 358 mm 的锻钢和 C 级铸钢；下侧梁为冷弯型钢组焊成的鱼腹形结构；枕梁为双腹板、单层上下盖板组焊而成的变截面箱形结构；大横梁为“工”字形组焊结构；底架铺设铁路货车用竹木复合层积材地板，门口处装 3 mm 厚的扁豆形花纹钢地板；装用车号自动识别标签，预留便器安装座及火炉安装孔。前、后从板座与中梁间，以及脚蹬与侧梁间均采用专用拉铆钉连接。

Underframe. The underframe is composed of a center beam, sleeper beam, lower side beam, large cross beam, end beam, small cross beam, longitudinal beam, floor, etc., as shown in Figure 8-11. The center beam is made of hot-rolled 310 Z-shaped steel or cold-formed center beam with a yield strength of 450 MPa; the forged steel upper center plate with a diameter of 358 mm and the front and rear slave plate seat of C-grade cast steel is adopted; the lower side beam is a fish-belly structure installed and welded by welding cold-formed steel; the sleeper beam is a variable cross-section box structure composed of double web plates and single layer upper and lower cover plates installed and welded; the large cross beam is of I-shaped assembly welding structure; the underframe is paved with composite laminated timber flooring made of bamboo wood for railway freight cars, and a 3 mm thick lenticular patterned steel floor is installed at the entrance. Automatic identification labels for vehicle numbers are installed, and toilet mounting seats and furnace mounting holes are reserved. Special pulling rivets are used to connect the front and rear slave plate seats with the center beam, as well as the pedals and the side beam.

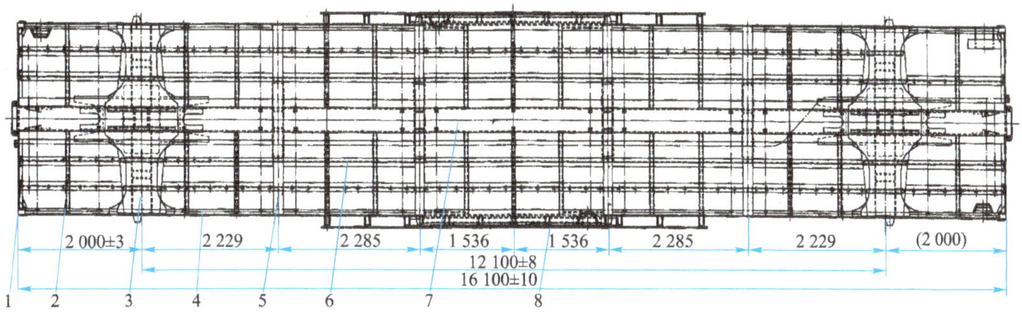

1—端梁；2—小横梁；3—枕梁；4—下侧梁；5—大横梁；6—纵向梁；7—中梁；8—导轨。

1—End beam; 2—Small cross beam; 3—Sleeper beam; 4—Lower side beam; 5—Large cross beam; 6—Longitudinal beam; 7—Center beam; 8—Guide rail.

图 8-11 P_{70} 型、$P70_H$ 型棚车的底架组成

Figure 8-11 Underframe Composition of P_{70} and P_{70H} Box Cars

（2）侧墙。侧墙为板柱式结构，由侧板、侧柱、门柱、上侧梁等组焊而成，如图 8-12 所示。侧板为 2.3 mm 厚的钢板压型结构，侧柱采用 4 mm 厚的 U 形冷弯型钢，上侧梁为冷弯矩形管与冷弯角形钢组焊而成。

Side wall. The side wall is a plate column structure, installed and welded by side plates, side columns, door columns, and upper side beams, as shown in Figure 8-12. The side plate is a profiled structure of a 2.3 mm thick steel plate, the side columns are made of 4 mm thick U-shaped cold-formed steel, and the upper side beams are installed and welded by cold-formed rectangular tubes with cold-formed angle steel.

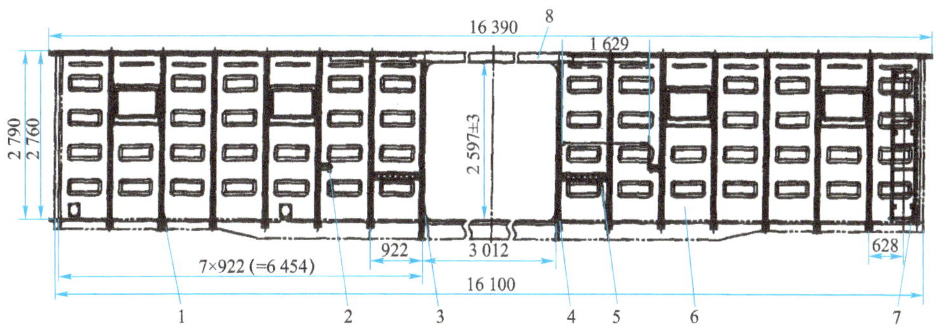

1—侧柱；2—车门止挡；3—左门柱；4—右门柱；5—开门座；6—侧板；7—扶梯；8—上侧梁。

1—Side column; 2—Door stop; 3—Left door column; 4—Right door column; 5—Door opening seat; 6—Side plate; 7—Escalator; 8—Upper side beam.

图 8-12 P_{70} 型、$P70_H$ 型棚车的侧墙组成

Figure 8-12 Side Wall Composition of P_{70} and P_{70H} Box Cars

（3）端墙。端墙为板柱式结构，由端板、端柱、角柱、上端梁等组焊而成。端板采用 3 mm 厚的钢板，端柱采用热轧槽钢，角柱采用 125 mm×125 mm×7 mm 压型角钢，上端梁采用 140 mm× 60 mm×6 mm 压型角钢，端板上预留电源线通过孔及照明设施安装座。

End wall. The end wall is a plate column structure, installed and welded by end plates, end columns, corner columns, upper end beams, etc. The end plate is made of a 3 mm thick steel plate, the end column is made of hot-rolled channel steel, and the corner column is made of 125 mm × 125 mm × 7 mm profiled angle steel. The upper end beam is made of 140 mm × 60 mm × 6 mm profiled angle steel, and power cable clearing holes and lighting installation seats are reserved on the end plate.

（4）车顶。车顶由车顶板、车顶弯梁、车顶侧梁、端弯梁等组焊而成。车顶弯梁为圆弧形结构，车顶侧梁采用冷弯型钢。车顶外部安装 4 个通风器和 1 个烟囱座，车顶弯梁处设有照明设施安装板。车顶内衬采用厚度为 5 mm 的 PVC 板，侧端墙内衬采用厚度为 3.5 mm 的竹材板。

Roof. The roof is installed and welded by the roof plate, roof bending beam, roof side beam, end bending beam, etc. The roof bending beam is of a circular arc structure, and the roof side beam is made of cold-formed steel. Four ventilators and one chimney seat are installed outside the roof, and the lighting installation plate is provided at the roof bending beam. The inner lining of the roof is made of PVC plate with a thickness of 5 mm, and the side end wall inner lining is made of bamboo plate with a thickness of 3.5 mm.

（5）车门、车窗。车体每侧安装一组推拉式对开车门，车门板采用 1.5 mm 厚的冷弯波纹板，车体每侧设 4 扇下翻式车窗。P_{70} 型、P_{70H} 型棚车的车门组成如图 8-13 所示。

Doors and windows. A set of push-pull split doors are installed on each side of the car body. The door plates are made of 1.5 mm thick cold-formed corrugated plates, and each side of the car body is equipped with four downwardly turning windows. The door composition of P_{70} and P_{70H} box cars is shown in Figure 8-13.

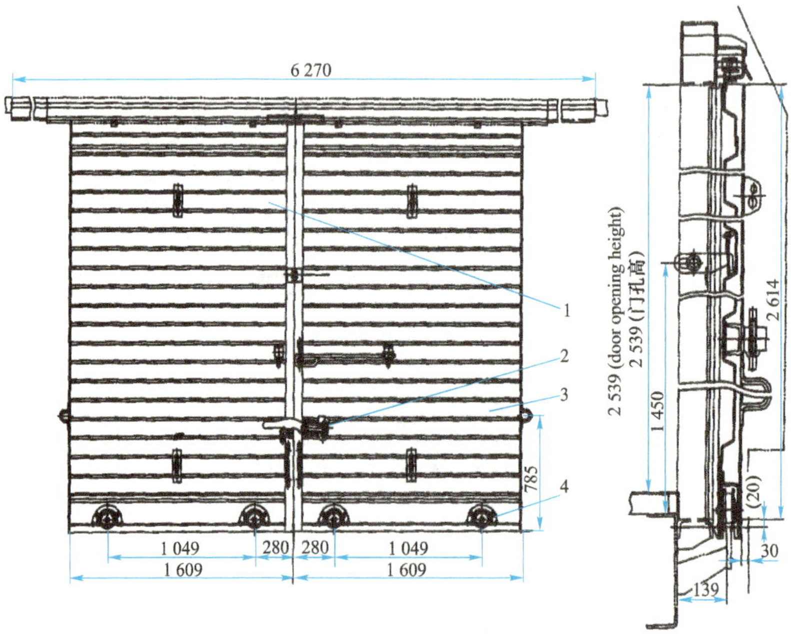

1—左门组成；2—门锁安装；3—右门组成；4—滑轮组装。

1—Left door composition; 2—Door lock installation; 3—Right door composition; 4—Pulley assembly.

图 8-13　P_{70} 型、P_{70H} 型棚车的车门组成

Figure 8-13　Door Composition of P_{70} and P_{70H} Box Cars

2）车钩缓冲装置

Coupler and draft gear

P_{70}型、P_{70H}型棚车采用 E 级钢 17 型车钩、17 型锻造或铸造钩尾框、合金钢钩尾销、MT−2 型缓冲器、含油尼龙钩尾框托板磨耗板。

No.17 coupler made of E-grade steel, No.17 forged or cast coupler yoke, alloy steel coupler yoke pin, MT-2 buffer, and oil-containing nylon coupler yoke bracket wearing plate are adopted for P_{70} and P_{70H} Box Cars.

3）制动装置

Braking device

P_{70}型、P_{70H}型棚车采用主管压力满足 500 kPa 和 600 kPa 的空气制动装置。

The pneumatic braking device with a main pipe pressure of 500 kPa and 600 kPa is used for P_{70} and P_{70H} Box Cars.

P_{70}型、P_{70H}型棚车的制动装置主要由 120 型控制阀、直径为 254 mm 的整体旋压密封式制动缸、ST2-250 型双向闸瓦间隙自动调整器、KZW-A 型空重车自动调整装置、货车脱轨自动制动装置等组成。制动装置也采用编织制动软管总成、奥贝球铁衬套、高摩合成闸瓦、不锈钢制动配件和管系。手制动装置采用 NSW 型手制动机。

The braking device of P_{70} and P_{70H} box cars is mainly composed of a Type 120 control valve, an integral spinning sealed brake cylinder with a diameter of 254 mm, an ST2-250 automatic adjuster for two-way brake shoe gap, a KZW-A automatic adjusting device for empty and full cars, and an automatic braking device for the derailment of the freight car. Braided brake hose assembly, austempering ductile iron bushing, high-friction composite brake shoe, stainless steel brake accessories, and pipe system are adopted for braking device. The NSW hand brake is adopted as a hand braking device.

4）转向架

Bogie

P_{70}型、P_{70H}型棚车采用转 K6 型或转 K5 型转向架。

The P_{70} and P_{70H} box cars use bogie type ZK6 or ZK5.

5）油漆

Paint

（1）隔热胶方案。车体底漆采用环氧云铁防锈底漆，漆膜厚度不小于 60 μm；车顶板内表面（车顶侧梁以上）采用专用防腐隔热胶，胶层厚度为 1～2 mm，颜色为中灰；端、侧墙及车门内表面采用厚浆醇酸面漆，颜色为中灰，干膜总厚度不小于 120 μm；车体外表面涂专用隔热漆，即漆膜总厚度不小于 120 μm 的车体外表面蓝灰色油漆。

Thermal insulation adhesive scheme. The primer of the car body should be epoxy micaceous iron antirust primer with a film thickness of not less than 60 μm; the inner surface of the roof plate (above the roof side beam) should adopt special anti-corrosion and thermal insulation adhesive, with an adhesive thickness of 1−2 mm and a color of medium gray; the end, side walls, and interior surfaces of the doors should be coated with a thick slurry alkyd finish paint with a color of medium gray and a total dry film thickness of not less than 120 μm; the exterior surface of the car body should be coated with special thermal insulation paint, with a total paint film thickness of not less than 120 μm, and the paint color of the exterior surface of the car body should be blue-gray.

（2）竹材板内衬方案。车体内表面采用溶剂型（或水溶性）厚浆醇酸漆底、面漆；车体、底架及其附属件外表面底漆采用环氧云铁防锈漆，面漆采用溶剂型（或水溶性）厚浆醇酸漆，底漆干膜厚度不小于 60 μm，油漆干膜总厚度不小于 120 μm。车体、底架及其附属件外表面的油漆颜色（含制动部分）为蓝灰色，内表面的颜色为中灰。

Bamboo wood plate lining scheme. The interior surface of the car body should adopt solvent-based (or water-soluble) alkyd resin build primer and finish paint; the primer for the exterior surface of the car body, underframe, and their accessories should be epoxy micaceous iron antirust paint. The finish paint should be solvent-based (or water-soluble) alkyd resin build paint. The dry film thickness of the primer should not be less than 60 μm, and the total dry film thickness of the paint should not be less than 120 μm. The exterior surface paint color of the car body, underframe, and accessories (including braking parts) should be blue-gray, and the interior surface color should be medium gray.

转向架各铸钢件、车钩、钩尾框、轮对、心盘等的表面应涂醇酸树脂漆，转向架摇枕弹簧涂沥青清漆，其中侧架导框顶面、车轮轮辋内外表面、心盘与心盘磨耗盘接触的工作表面不涂漆。

The surface of each steel casting, coupler, coupler yoke, wheelset, center plate, etc. of the bogie should be coated with alkyd resin paint, and the swing bolster spring of the bogie should be coated with asphalt varnish. The top surface of the side frame guide frame, the inner and outer surfaces of the wheel bearing, and the working surface where the center plate contacts the center plate wear plate should not be painted.

6）车辆标记

Markings of railway vehicle

车辆标记按《铁道车辆标记　一般规则》（TB/T 1.1—1995）、《铁道车辆标记　文字与字体》（TB/T 1.2—1995）的要求涂打。

The markings on railway vehicles should be painted in accordance with the requirements of *Lettering and Marking of Railway Cars—General Regulations* (TB/T 1.1—1995) and *Lettering and Marking of Railway Cars—Letter and Style of Calligraphy* (TB/T 1.2—1995).

7）车辆寿命及检修周期

Life and maintenance cycle of railway vehicle

车辆寿命：25 年。

Life of railway vehicle: 25 years.

检修周期：厂修 8 年，段修 2 年。

Maintenance cycle: 8 years for shop repair and 2 years for depot repair.

5. 与 P_{64GK} 型通用棚车对比

Comparison with P_{64GK} general box car

P_{70} 型、P_{70H} 型棚车与 P_{64GK} 型棚车主要技术参数的对比如表 8-6 所示。

The comparison of main technical parameters and accessories between P_{70} and P_{70H} box cars and P_{64GK} box cars is shown in Table 8-6.

表 8-6　P_{70} 型、P_{70H} 型棚车与 P_{64GK} 型棚车主要参数的对比
Table 8-6　Comparison of Main Parameters of P_{70}, P_{70H} Box Cars and P_{64GK} Box Cars

主要技术参数 Main technical parameters	P_{70} 型、P_{70H} 型棚车 P_{70} and P_{70H} box cars	P_{64GK} 型棚车 P_{64GK} box cars
载重 Load capacity	70 t	60 t
自重 Tare weight	23.8 t，2 406 t	24 t
轴重 Axle load	23 t	21 t
容积 Volume	145 m^3	135 m^3
每延米重 Weight per linear meter	5.5 t/m	5.1 t/m
商业运营速度 Commercial operation speed	120 km/h	120 km/h
车辆定距 Fixed distance	12 100 mm	11 700 mm
车辆长度 Vehicle length	17 066 mm	16 430 mm
车辆最大宽度 Max. width of car	3 300 mm	3 340 mm
车辆最大高度 Max. height of car	4 770 mm	4 448 mm
车辆内长 Vehicle interior length	16 094 mm	15 478 mm
车厢宽 Vehicle width	2 800 mm	2 804 mm
车辆内高 Vehicle interior height	2 855 mm	2 855 mm
地板面距轨面高 Height from floor surface to rail surface	1 136 mm（空车） 1,136 (empty car)	1 136 mm（空车） 1,136 (empty car)
车门门孔 Door opening	2 539 mm×3 012 mm	2 539 mm×2 963 mm
车钩 Coupler	17 型 17	13A 型 13A type
缓冲器 Draft gear	MT–2 型 MT-2 type	MT–3 型 MT-3 type
转向架 Bogie	转 K6 型或转 K5 型 Bogie type ZK-6 or ZK-5	转 K2 型 Bogie type ZK-2
主要钢材牌号 Main designations of steel	Q450NQR1	09CuPCRNI-A

P_{70}型、P_{70H}型棚车与P_{64GK}型棚车主要部件的对比如表 8-7 所示。

The comparison of main accessories between P_{70} and P_{70H} box cars and P_{64GK} box cars is shown in Table 8-7.

表 8-7 P_{70}型、P_{70H}型棚车与P_{64GK}型棚车主要部件的对比

Table 8-7 Comparison of Main Accessories of P_{70}, P_{70H} Box Cars and P_{64GK} Box Cars

主要部件 Main Accessories	P_{70}型、P_{70H}型棚车 P_{70} and P_{70H} box cars	P_{64GK}型棚车 P_{64GK} box cars
车钩 Coupler	17 型 17	13A 型 13A type
缓冲器 Draft gear	MT−2 型 MT-2 type	MT−3 型 MT-3 type
转向架 Bogie	转 K6 或转 K5 型 Bogie type ZK-6 or ZK-5	转 K2 型 Bogie type ZK-2

项目 9

Project 9

动力集中电动车组

Power-centralized EMUs

本项目以了解动力集中电动车组的结构为工学任务，通过课堂任务的完成过程，着重介绍动力集中电动车组的结构性能参数、各部分的名称及作用，并以此为引导，掌握动力集中电动车组的特点；通过课后任务，了解动力车、拖车、控制车的主要差别。

The main task of this project is to understand the structure of power-centralized EMUs. In the classroom, the main focus is on introducing the structural performance parameters, names, and functions of various parts of power-centralized EMUs and knowing the characteristics of power-centralized EMUs. Through after-class tasks, students will gain an understanding of the main differences between power cars, trailer cars, and control cars.

学生工作页 Student Worksheet

工学任务描述 Task description	预期目标 Expected goals
任务名称：认识动力集中电动车组 Task name: Understanding of the power-centralized EMUs 任务编号：CJ-9 Task number: CJ-9 任务类型：认知型+结构原理型 Task type: cognitive + structural principle 适用范围：车辆系统各岗位群 Applicable scope: All post groups of the car system 完成时间：　　学时 Completion time: Class hours	初级：了解动力集中电动车组的基本组成、作用及技术参数 Elementary level: understanding the basic composition, function, and technical parameters of power-centralized EMUs 中级：认识动力车、拖车、控制车的结构及车内设备 Intermediate level: understanding the structure and internal equipment of power cars, trailer cars, and control cars 高级：从车体结构、材质、工艺角度考虑动力集中电动车组如何适应牵引设备更高速、安全、平稳地运行 Advanced level: considering how power-centralized EMUs can adapt to the faster, safer, and stable operation of traction equipment from the perspective of vehicle structure, material, and technology

知识回顾+小组讨论

Knowledge review + group discussion

1. 尝试列出动力集中电动车组的基本结构。

Try to list the basic structure of the power-centralized EMUs.

序号 S/N	基本组成 Basic composition	相关知识点 Relevant knowledge points
1		
2		
3		
4		
5		
6		
7		
8		
9		

2. 小组讨论：动力车的基本功能和动力车内、外部的设备。

Group discussion: Basic functions of power cars and internal and external equipment of power cars.

3. 思考：说明动力集中电动车组与25T型客车的异同。

Thinking: Try to explain the similarities and differences between power-centralized EMUs and 25T type coaches.

4. 根据动力车的平面布局，写出图中各部分的名称。

Write the name of each part in the figure according to the plane layout of the power cars.

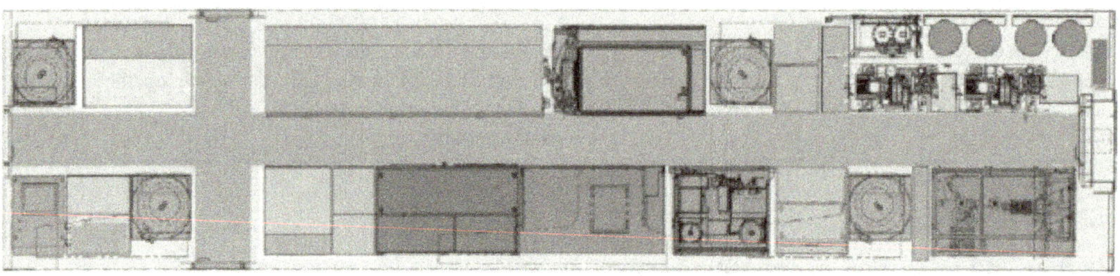

5. 简述拖车和控制车车体系统的组成，并加以区别。

Briefly describe the composition of the carbody system of the trailer car and control car, and distinguish them.

6. 简述拖车和控制车制动系统的组成，并加以区别。

Briefly describe the composition of the braking system of the trailer car and control car, and distinguish them.

课后任务

After-class tasks

1. 查阅资料，尝试总结比较动车组的基本结构。

Refer to relevant documents and try to summarize and compare the basic structures of the power EMUs.

客车类型 Type of passenger car	CRH1	CRH2	CRH5	CRH380BL	CRH380
基本组成 Basic composition					

2. 提出你的问题。

Ask your question.

问题（1）：____

Question (1): ____

答案：

Answer:____

____

问题（2）：____

Question (2): ____

答案：

Answer:____

____

学习效果评价
Learning effect evaluation

年 Year　　月 Month　　日 Day

专业班级： Major & class:	姓名： Name:	学号： Student number:
工学小组及分工： Work-and-study team and responsibility division:		

专业（知识/技能）收获 Professional gains (knowledge/skills)	（非专业）能力素质收获 (Non-professional) ability and quality gains

评价考核项目 Evaluation item	自我评价 Self-evaluation	小组评价 Group evaluation	教师评价 Teacher's evaluation
已掌握动力集中电动车组的基本组成 Have mastered the basic composition of power-centralized EMUs			
已掌握相关知识点的数量 Number of knowledge points mastered			
主动提出问题的数量 Number of questions proposed			
课外学习时间（学时） After-school learning time (hours)			
工作态度（课堂、课后任务完成情况） Work attitude (completion condition of classroom tasks and after-class tasks)	☆☆☆☆ ☆☆☆☆	☆☆☆☆ ☆☆☆☆	☆☆☆☆ ☆☆☆☆
合作意识及协调能力 Cooperation consciousness and coordination ability	☆☆☆☆ ☆☆☆☆	☆☆☆☆ ☆☆☆☆	☆☆☆☆ ☆☆☆☆
正确表达和沟通能力 Correct expression and communication skills	☆☆☆☆ ☆☆☆☆	☆☆☆☆ ☆☆☆☆	☆☆☆☆ ☆☆☆☆
自律能力（缺勤/旷课/迟到/违纪次数） Self-discipline (absences/absenteeism/lateness/disciplinary violations)			

任务 9.1 背 景

Task 9.1 Background

为加快推进铁路装备现代化，充分利用既有线路和机车、客车的检修资源，提高既有线铁路运输服务品质，满足我国铁路运输经营发展的要求，在中国铁路总公司和中国中车股份有限公司（以下简称“中国中车”）的统一指挥下，各机车厂、客车厂及科研院所组建联合团队，共同开展时速 160 km 动力集中电动车组关键技术研究及样车研制工作。

Under the unified command of China State Railway Group Co., Ltd. and CRRC Corporation Limited (hereinafter referred to as “CRRC”), various locomotive factories, passenger car factories, and research institutes have established joint teams to jointly carry out the research on key technologies and prototype vehicle development of 160 km/h power-centralized EMUs, to accelerate the modernization of railway equipment, make full use of the maintenance resources of existing lines, locomotives, and passenger cars, improve the quality of existing railway transportation services, and meet the transportation and business development requirements of railway in China.

2016 年 8 月，中国中车所属唐山公司、浦镇公司、株机公司和大连公司分别与中国铁路总公司科技管理部签订了《时速 160 km 动力集中电动车组关键技术研究——控制车和拖车关键技术研究》课题合同和《时速 160 km 动力集中电动车组关键技术研究——动力车关键技术研究》课题合同。

In August 2016, the Tangshan, Puzhen, Zhuzhou Locomotive, and Dalian companies affiliated with China State Railway Group Co., Ltd. signed project contracts with the Science and Technology Management Department of China State Railway Group Co., Ltd. for *Research on Key Technologies of 160 km/h Power-centralized EMUs — Research on Key Technologies of Control Cars and Trailer Cars* and *Research on Key Technologies of 160 km/h Power-centralized EMUs — Research on Key Technologies of Power Cars*.

2015 年 11 月，中国铁路总公司和中国中车在北京组织召开了“动力集中电动车组技术方案及研制工作方案研讨会”，会议明确了动车组的各项顶层指标。

In November 2015, China State Railway Group Co., Ltd. and CRRC organized and held the “Seminar on Technical Scheme and Development Scheme of Power-centralized EMUs” in Beijing. The various top-level indicators for the EMU have been clarified in the meeting.

2016 年 4 月，中国中车下发《中国中车 2016 年科技研究开发计划》，动力集中电动车组被列入开发计划。

In April 2016, CRRC issued the *CRRC Scientific and Technological Research and Development Plan in 2016*, and the power-centralized EMUs were included in the development plan.

2016 年 8 月，中国铁路总公司运输局车辆部在北京组织召开了“时速 160 km 动力集中电动车组拖车技术条件研讨会”，成立联合设计团队，短编拖车、控制车项目启动。

In August 2016, the Vehicle Department of the Transportation Bureau of China State Railway Group Co., Ltd. organized and held a “Seminar on the Technical Conditions of Trailer Cars of 160 km/h Power-centralized EMUs” in Beijing, with joint design teams established and the project of short-marshaling trailer cars and control cars launched.

2016 年 9 月，首台动力车落车。

In September 2016, the first power car was completed.

2016 年 10 月，动力车深度简统化完成。

In October 2016, the deep simplification of the power car was completed.

2016 年 12 月，控制车与动力车接口确定完毕。联合设计团队完成短编组二等座车、控制车和餐吧车的工程设计及资料编写。

In December 2016, the interface between the control car and the power car was determined. The joint design teams completed the engineering design and data compilation of the short-marshaling second-class seat car, control car, and dining bar car.

2017 年 4 月，首列短编组拖车下线。

In April 2017, the first short-marshaling trailer car was offline.

2017 年 5 月，首列短编组列车完成联调联试。

In May 2017, the joint commissioning and test of the first short-marshaling train were completed.

2017 年 8 月，短编组动力车、拖车、控制车技术条件、设计方案、试验评审通过。

In August 2017, the technical conditions, design schemes, and tests of short marshaling power cars, trailer cars, and control cars were reviewed and approved.

2017 年 9 月，中国铁路总公司机辆部在唐山召开时速 160 km 动力集中电动车组（长编）启动会，长编联合设计启动。

In September 2017, the Locomotive and Vehicle Department of China State Railway Group Co., Ltd. held a kickoff meeting for the 160 km/h power-centralized EMUs (long-marshaling) in Tangshan, with the joint design of the long marshaling launched.

2017 年 12 月，短编组列车完成环线试验和正线型式试验。

In December 2017, the loop line tests and main-line type tests of short-marshaling trains were completed.

2017 年 12 月，长编组二等卧车、一等卧车、二等座车/餐车（厨房式）工程设计及资料编写完成；短编组二等座车、控制车和餐吧车优化设计完成。

In December 2017, the engineering design and data compilation of the second-class sleeping car, first-class sleeping car, and second-class seat car/dining car (kitchen type) for the long marshaling were completed. The optimization design of the second-class seat car, control car, and dining bar car for short marshaling has been completed.

2018 年 2 月，短编组试用评审及长编组设计方案、试验评审通过。

In February 2018, the trial review of the short marshaling, the design scheme, and the test review of the long marshaling were passed.

2018 年 3 月，首列长编组拖车下线。

In March 2018, the first long marshaling trailer car was offline.

2018 年 4 月，短编组列车开始运用考核。

In April 2018, the application assessment of short marshaling trains began.

任务 9.2　设 计 原 则

Task 9.2　Design principles

动力车在八轴客运电力机车技术平台的基础上，参照中国既有动车组经验及要求，进行优化设计。拖车以既有 25T 型客车为基础，在平面布置、内部装饰、人机界面等方面参照既有 CRH 动车组进行优化设计。

Based on the 8-axle electric locomotive technology platform for passenger transport, the power car is optimized and designed with reference to the experience and requirements of existing EMUs in China. Based on the existing 25T type coaches, the trailer car is optimized with reference to the existing CRH EMUs in terms of plane layout, interior decoration, human-machine interface, etc.

动力集中电动车组坚持技术一体化设计原则，同时在外观、内装方面与既有的 CRH 动车组相似，从而提高密封性能、减小纵向冲动、降低噪声、提高乘坐舒适性，适应既有客车线路及运用适度考虑研制周期。

Power-centralized EMUs adhere to the technical integration design principles; the appearance and interior decoration are similar to the existing CRH EMUs; the sealing performance is improved, and the longitudinal impulse and noise are reduced to improve the riding comfort; it is needed to adapt to the existing passenger car routes and appropriately consider the development cycle for application.

任务 9.3　接 口 要 求

Task 9.3　Requirements for interface

1. 动力车与拖车之间的接口

Interface between power car and trailer car

动力车与拖车之间的接口如表 9-1 所示。

The interface between the power car and the trailer car is shown in Table 9-1.

表 9–1 动力车与拖车之间的接口

Table 9–1 Interface between Power Car and Trailer Car

类 型 Type	部 件 Component	接 口 Interface
机械 Mechanics	风挡 Windshield	双层气密折棚风挡 Double-layer airtight folding shed windshield
	车钩 Coupler	25T 型密接式车钩 25T tight-lock coupler
	车端阻尼 Vehicle end damping	25T 型车端阻尼器 25T vehicle end damper
电气 Electrical	列供 Train supply	短编组：DC600V 2 路各 200 kW Short marshaling: DC600V, 200 kW each for two circuits
		200 kW 长编组：每个动力车 DC600V 1 路 400 kW 200 kW long marshaling: each power car DC600V, 400kW for one circuit
	网络 Network	动力车与控制车之间或动力车与动力车之间：WTB 总线 Between power car and control car or between power car and power car: WTB bus 拖车与动力车：网关传输信息（车门状态、轴温报警、火警、制动报警） Trailer car and power car: gateway transmits information (door status, axle temperature alarm, fire alarm, braking alarm)
	硬线 Hardwire	传输控制指令：门控、列车电空制动等 Transmission of control instructions: door control, train electro-pneumatic braking, etc.
制动 Brake	气路 Gas circuit	总风管和列车管 Main air duct and train pipe

2. 短编重联接口

Short marshaling reconnection interface

短编重联接口如表 9–2 所示。

The short marshaling reconnection interface is shown in Table 9-2.

表 9–2 短编重联接口

Table 9-2 Short Marshalling Reconnection Interface

类 型 Type	部 件 Component	接 口 Interface
机械 Machinery	开闭机构 Opening and closing mechanism	自动开闭机构 Automatic opening and closing mechanism
	车钩 Coupler	带电气钩的密接式车钩 Tight-lock coupler with electrical coupler
电气 Electrical	网络 Network	动力车与控制车之间或动力车与动力车之间：WTB 总线 Between power car and control car or between power car and power car: WTB bus 拖车与动力车：网关传输信息（车门状态、轴温报警、火警、制动报警） Trailer car and power car: gateway transmits information (door status, axle temperature alarm, fire alarm, braking alarm)
	硬线 Hardwire	传输控制指令：门控、列车电空制动等 Transmission of control instructions: door control, train electro-pneumatic braking, etc.
制动 Brake	气路 Gas circuit	总风管和列车管 Main air duct and train pipe

任务 9.4　总 体 方 案

Task 9.4　Overall programme

1. 编组参数

Marshaling parameters

1）短编组

Short marshaling

短编组动力集中电动车组的编组参数如表 9–3 所示。

The marshaling parameters of short-marshaling power-centralized EMUs are shown in Table 9-3.

表 9–3　短编组动力集中电动车组的编组参数

Table 9-3　Marshaling Parameters of Short-marshaling Power-centralized EMUs

序号 S/N	1	2	3	4	5	6	7	8	9
等级 Class	—	二等 Second class	二等 Second class	二等 Second class	二等 Second class	二等 Second class	二等 Second class	二等 Second class	一等 First class
定员 Passenger capacity	—	98	98	98	76	98	98	98	56

9 辆编组，1 动 7 拖 1 控，全部为座车，总定员 720 人（一等座定员 56 人，二等座定员 664 人）。2、3、4、6、7、8 号车设二等座椅；9 号车设一等座椅；5 号车设无障碍卫生间及轮椅存放区，以及餐吧区和机械师室，6 号车设播音室。短编组动力集中电动车组如图 9–1 所示。

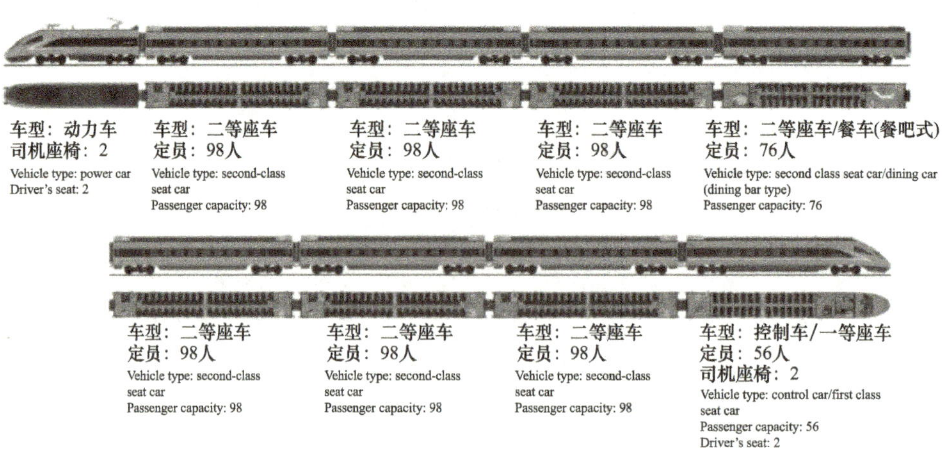

图 9–1　短编组动力集中电动车组

Figure 9-1　Short-marshaling Power-centralized EMUs

9-car, with one power car, seven trailer cars, and one control car, all of which are passenger cars, with a total passenger capacity of 720 people (first class passenger capacity of 56 people, second class passenger capacity of 664 people). No.2, 3, 4, 6, 7, and 8 are equipped with second-class seats; No.9 car is equipped with first-class seats; No.5 car is equipped with an accessible toilet and wheelchair storage area, a dining bar area, and a mechanic room, and No.6 car is equipped with a broadcasting room. The short marshaling power-centralized EMUs are shown in Figure 9-1.

2）典型长编组

Typical long marshaling

20 辆编组，2 动 18 拖；总定员 1 102 人，二等座席 242 人，硬卧 660 人，软卧 200 人。典型长编组动力集中电动车组的编组参数如表 9–4 所示。

20-car, with 2 power cars and 18 trailer cars; the total passenger capacity is 1102 people, with 242 second-class seats, 660 semi-cushioned berths, and 200 cushioned berths. The marshaling parameters of a typical long marshaling power-centralized EMUs are shown in Table 9-4.

典型的动车组长编由二等卧车、一等卧车、二等座车/餐车（厨房式）和二等座车组成，编组形式为：1 辆动力车+4 辆二等卧车+5 辆一等卧车+1 辆二等座车/餐车+2 辆二等座车+6 辆二等卧车+1 辆动力车。典型长编组动力集中电动车组如图 9–2 所示。

A typical long marshaling EMU consists of second-class sleeping cars, first-class sleeping cars, second-class seat cars/dining cars (kitchen type), and second-class seat cars. The marshaling form is: 1 power car + 4 second-class sleeping cars + 5 first-class sleeping cars + 1 second-class seat car/dining car + 2 second-class seat cars + 6 second-class sleeping cars + 1 power car. The typical long marshaling power-centralized EMUs are shown in Figure 9-2.

图 9–2　典型长编组动力集中电动车组

Figure 9-2　Typical Long Marshaling Power-centralized EMUs

表 9-4 典型长编组动力集中电动车组的编组参数

Table 9-4 Marshalling Parameters of Typical Long Marshalling Power-centralized Electric Vehicle Group

序号 Serial number	1	2	3	4	5	6	7	8	9	10	11	12	13	14	15	16	17	18	19	20
车型 Vehicle model	动力车 Power car	二等卧车 Second-class sleeping car	二等卧车 Second-class sleeping car	二等卧车 Second-class sleeping car	二等卧车 Second-class sleeping car	一等卧车 First-class sleeping car	一等卧车 First-class sleeping car	一等卧车 First-class sleeping car	一等卧车 First-class sleeping car	一等卧车 First-class sleeping car	二等座车/餐车（厨房式） Second class car/dining car (kitchen type)	二等座车 Second-class car	二等座车 Second-class car	二等卧车 Second-class sleeping car	二等卧车 Second-class sleeping car	二等卧车 Second-class sleeping car	二等卧车 Second-class sleeping car	二等卧车 Second-class sleeping car	二等卧车 Second-class sleeping car	动力车 Power car
席别 Farewell	—	硬卧 Hard sleeper	硬卧 Hard sleeper	硬卧 Hard sleeper	硬卧 Hard sleeper	软卧 Hard sleeper	软卧 Soft sleeper	软卧 Soft sleeper	软卧 Soft sleeper	软卧 Soft sleeper	二等座席 Second-class seat	二等座席 Second-class seat	二等座席 Second-class seat	硬卧 Hard sleeper	硬卧 Hard sleeper	硬卧 Hard sleeper	硬卧 Hard sleeper	硬卧 Hard sleeper	硬卧 Hard sleeper	—
定员 Staffing	—	66	66	66	66	40	40	40	40	40	46[①]	98	98	66	66	66	66	66	66	—

注：① 包含 2 个无障碍座席。

2 accessible seats included.

2. 主要技术参数
Main technical parameters

动力集中电动车组的主要技术参数如表 9–5 所示。

The main technical parameters of the power-centralized EMUs are shown in Table 9-5.

表 9–5　动力集中电动车组的主要技术参数
Table 9-5　Main Technical Parameters of Power-centralized EMUs

<table>
<tr><td colspan="2">设计寿命
Design life</td><td>不少于 30 年或 900 万 km
Not less than 30 years or 9 million km</td></tr>
<tr><td colspan="2">轴重
Axle load</td><td>动力车：≤21 t
Power car: ≤ 21 t
拖车和控制车：≤16.5 t
Trailer car and control car: ≤ 16.5 t</td></tr>
<tr><td colspan="2">速度
Speed</td><td>最高运营速度：160 km/h
Max. operating speed: 160 km/h</td></tr>
<tr><td colspan="2">加速度
Acceleration</td><td>0～40 km/h 平均加速度：≈0.35 m/s²
0–40 km/h Average acceleration: ≈ 0.35 m/s²
160 km/h 时剩余加速度：≈0.13 m/s²
At the speed of 160 km/h, the residual acceleration: ≈ 0.13 m/s²</td></tr>
<tr><td colspan="2">二等座车
Second-class seat car</td><td>98 人
98 people</td></tr>
<tr><td colspan="2">二等座车/餐车（餐吧式）
Second-class seat car/dining car (dining bar style)</td><td>76 人
76 people</td></tr>
<tr><td colspan="2">二等座车/餐车（厨房式）
Second-class seat car/dining car (kitchen type)</td><td>46 人
46 people</td></tr>
<tr><td colspan="2">控制车
Control car</td><td>56 人
56 people</td></tr>
<tr><td colspan="2">二等卧车
Second-class sleeping car</td><td>66 人
66 people</td></tr>
<tr><td colspan="2">一等卧车
First-class sleeping car</td><td>40 人
40 people</td></tr>
<tr><td colspan="2">供电制式
Power supply system</td><td>DC600V 集中供电，分散变流
DC600V centralized power supply, decentralized converter</td></tr>
<tr><td colspan="2">动力车车体长度
Length of power car body</td><td><20 000 mm</td></tr>
<tr><td colspan="2">控制车车体长度
Length of control car body</td><td>27 955 mm</td></tr>
<tr><td colspan="2">中间车体长度
Length of intermediate car body</td><td>25 500 mm</td></tr>
<tr><td colspan="2">车辆间距
Vehicle spacing</td><td>1 076 mm</td></tr>
<tr><td colspan="2">车体宽度
Width of car body</td><td>3 105 mm</td></tr>
<tr><td rowspan="2">车辆高度（新轮，不包括空调）
Vehicle height (new wheels, excluding air conditioning)</td><td>动力车
Power car</td><td>4 030 mm</td></tr>
<tr><td>控制车/拖车
Control car/trailer car</td><td>4 433 mm</td></tr>
</table>

续表

Continued

客室地板面距轨面高度 Height from passenger compartment floor to rail surface	1 283 mm
转向架中心距 Center distance of bogie	拖车和控制车：18 000 mm Trailer car and control car: 18,000 mm 动力车：9 000/10 055 mm Power car: 9,000/10,055 mm
转向架轴距 Wheelbase of bogie	拖车和控制车：2 500 mm/2 600 mm Trailer car and control car: 2,500 mm/2,600 mm 动力车：2 900 mm/2 800 mm Power car: 2,900 mm/2,800 mm
车钩中心线距轨面高度 Height from coupler centerline to rail surface	880 mm
通过最小曲线半径 Min. radius of curvature negotiated	整列：R145 m Whole train: R145 m 单节调车：动力车：R125 m Single car switching: power car: R125 m 拖车和控制车：R100 m Trailer car and control car: R100 m
动力车轮周牵引功率 Peripheral traction power of power wheel	持续制：5 600 kW Continuous system: 5,600 kW 半小时：6 400 kW Half hour: 6,400 kW
紧急制动距离（平直道） Emergency braking distance (straight road)	初速度为 160 km/h 时：≤1 400 m At an initial speed of 160 km/h: ≤ 1,400 m 初速度为 120 km/h 时：≤800 m At an initial speed of 120 km/h: ≤ 800 m
网络系统 Network system	动力车：WTB/MVB Power car: WTB/MVB 拖车和控制车：Lonworks Trailer car and control car: Lonworks

3. 平面布局

Plane layout

1）动力车的平面布局

Plane layout of power car

动力车由单司机室、机械间、贯穿中间走廊结构（宽度≥600 mm）组成。机械间设备根据设备重量按照斜对称布置的原则进行布置，并在机械间两侧各设有一扇铰链式的动力车入口门。全车设备布置可分为车顶设备布置、司机室设备布置、机械间设备布置、车下设备布置、辅助设备布置及动力车布线等几个部分。动力车的平面布局如图 9–3 所示。

The power car adopts a single cab, and the mechanical room is a structure that runs through the middle corridor (width≥600 mm). The equipment in the mechanical room is arranged according to the principle of oblique and symmetrical arrangement based on the weight of the equipment, and a hinged power car entrance door is provided on both sides of the mechanical room.

The layout of complete car equipment can be divided into several parts, including roof equipment layout, cab equipment layout, mechanical room equipment layout, equipment layout under the vehicle, auxiliary equipment layout, and power car wiring. The plane layout of the power car is shown in Figure 9-3.

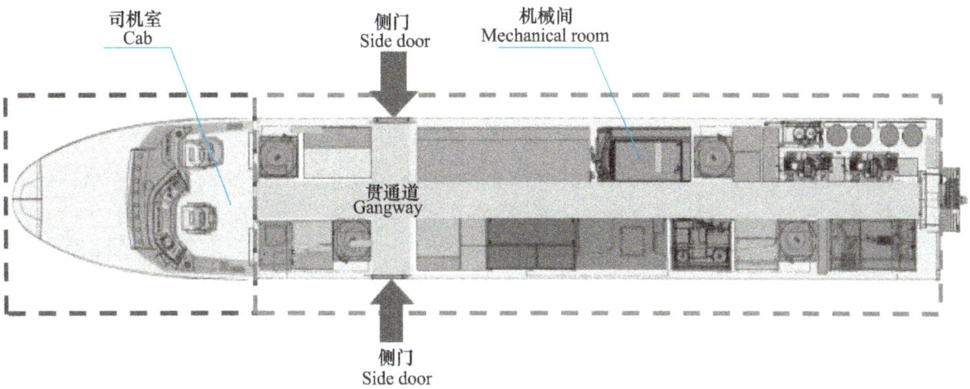

图 9–3　动力车的平面布局

Figure 9-3　Plane Layout of Power Car

2）控制车的平面布局

Plane layout of control car

控制车定员 56 人。两端设通过台；一位端设蹲式便器卫生间、乘务员室、电气控制柜、电热开水器；车体中部为客室，设置“2+2”一等座椅；二位端设坐式便器卫生间、单人洗面间、司机室。控制车的平面布局如图 9–4 所示。

Passenger capacity of control car: 56 people. With vestibule at both ends; “B” end of car is equipped with a eastern type toilet, a crew room, an electrical control cabinet, and an electric water heater; the middle part is the passenger compartment with “2+2” first-class seats; “A” end of car is provided with a western type toilet, a single person washroom, and a cab. The plane layout of the control car is shown in Figure 9-4.

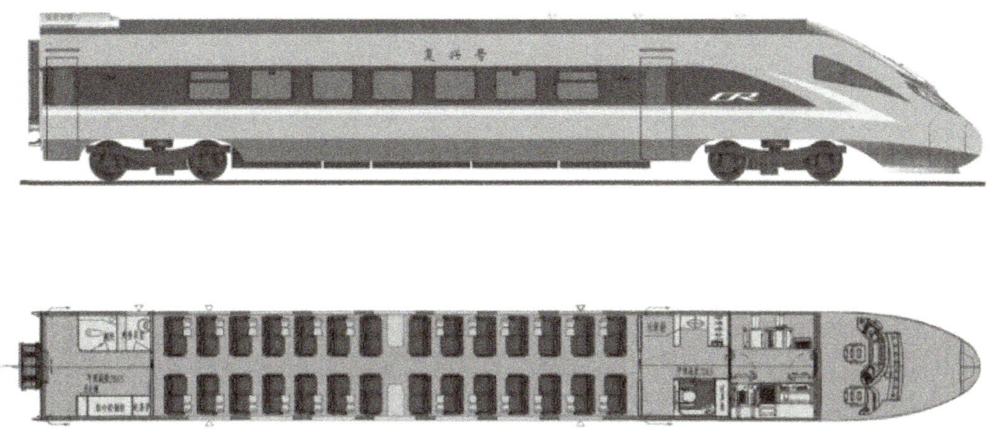

图 9–4　控制车的平面布局

Figure 9-4　Plane Layout of Control Car

3）二等座车的平面布局

Plane layout of second-class seat cars

二等座车定员 98 人。两端设通过台；一位端设坐式便器卫生间、乘务员室、电气控制柜、电热开水器；车体中部为客室，设置“2+3”普通座椅；二位端设蹲式便器卫生间、单人洗面间、大件行李区。二等座车的平面布局如图 9–5 所示。

Passenger capacity of second-class seat car: 98 people. With vestibule at both ends; “B” end of car is equipped with a western type toilet, a crew room, an electrical control cabinet, and an electric water heater; the middle is the passenger compartment with “2+3” common seats; “A” end of car is equipped with a eastern type toilet, a single washroom, and a large luggage area. The plane layout of the second-class seat car is shown in Figure 9-5.

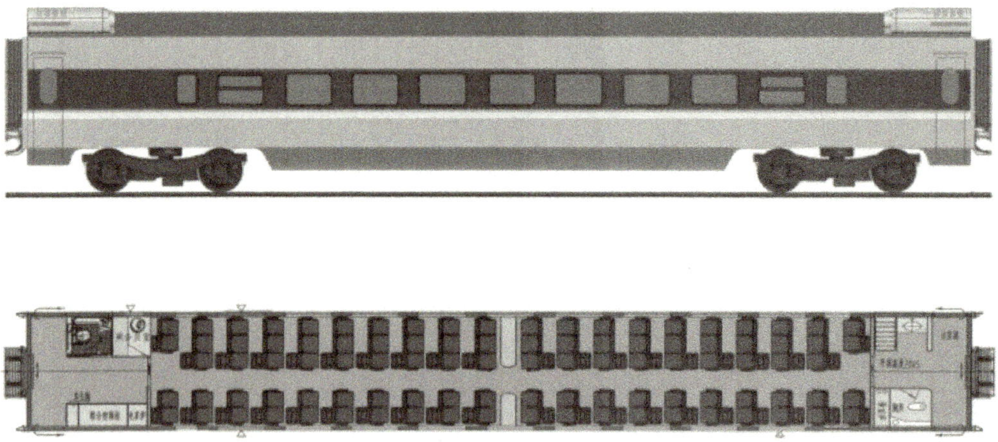

图 9–5　二等座车的平面布局

Figure 9-5　Plane Layout of Second-class Seat Car

4）二等座车/餐车（餐吧式）的平面布局

Plane layout of second-class seat car/dining car (dining bar style)

二等座车/餐车（餐吧式）定员 76 人。一位端设通过台、垃圾箱和无障碍卫生间；车体中部为客室、播音室及机械师室，设置“2+3”普通座椅，客室设有无障碍座位和残障人士轮椅存放区；二位端设配电柜、餐吧区，餐吧区设方便于售卖的展示柜及储藏设备。二等座车/餐车（餐吧式）的平面布局如图 9–6 所示。

Passenger capacity of second-class seat car/dining car (dining bar style): 76 people. With “B” end of car is equipped with a vestibule, a garbage bin, and an accessible toilet; in the middle of the car body, there are passenger compartments, broadcasting rooms, and mechanic rooms, with “2+3” common seats. The passenger compartment is equipped with accessible seats and wheelchair storage areas for the disabled; “A” end of car is equipped with a distribution cabinet and a dining bar area. The dining bar area is equipped with display cabinets and storage equipment that are convenient for sale. The plane layout of the second-class seat car/dining car (dining bar type) is shown in Figure 9-6.

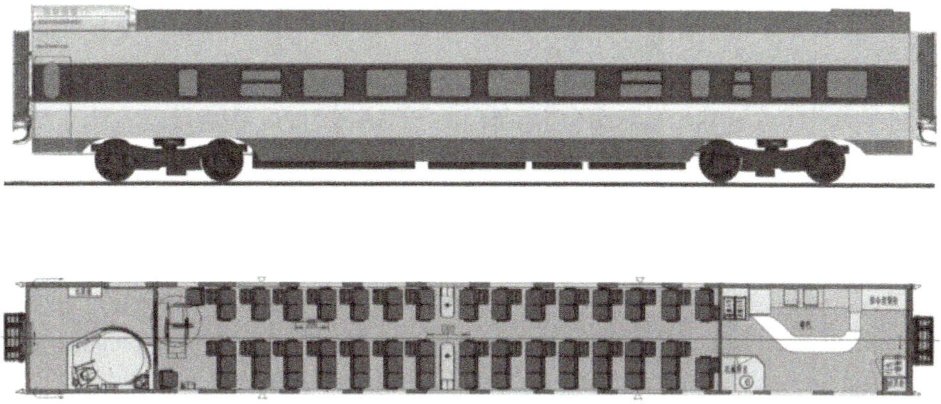

图 9-6 二等座车/餐车（餐吧式）的平面布局
Figure 9-6 Plane Layout of Second-class Seat Car/Dining Car (Dining Bar Style)

5）二等座车/餐车（厨房式）的平面布局

Plane layout of second-class seat car/dining car (kitchen type)

二等座车/餐车（厨房式）定员 46 人。一位端设通过台；一位端小走廊设隐藏式垃圾箱和一个无障碍卫生间；车体中部为客室及机械师室，设置“2+3”普通座椅及 4 个安全锤，客室设有无障碍座位和残障人士轮椅存放区；二位端设综合控制柜、配餐式厨房、行包专用柜及侧走廊。二等座车/餐车（厨房式）的平面布局如图 9-7 所示。

Passenger capacity of second-class seat car/dining car (kitchen type): 46 people. With vestibule at “B” end of car; the small corridor at “B” end of car is equipped with a concealed garbage bin and an accessible toilet; in the middle of the car body, there are the passenger compartment and the mechanic room, which are equipped with “2+3” common seats and 4 safety hammers. The passenger compartment is equipped with accessible seats and wheelchair storage areas for the disabled; “A” end of car is equipped with a comprehensive control cabinet, a catering kitchen, a special cabinet for luggage, and side corridors. The plane layout of the second-class seat car/dining car (kitchen type) is shown in Figure 9-7.

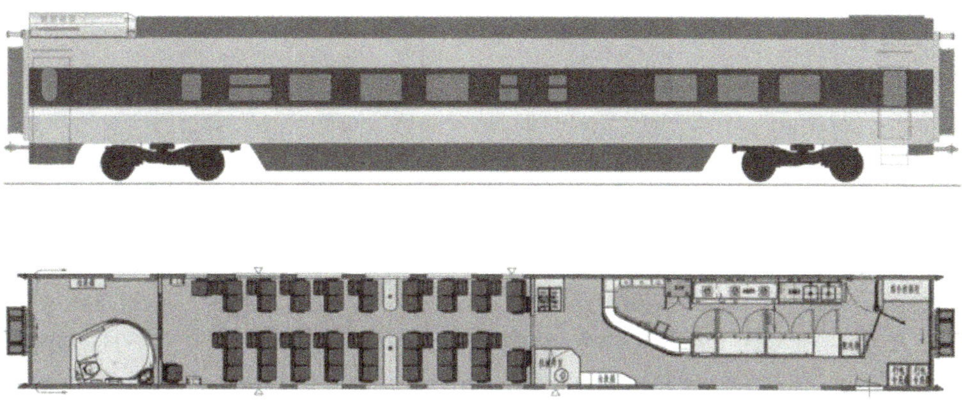

图 9-7 二等座车/餐车（厨房式）的平面布局
Figure 9-7 Plane Layout of Second-class Seat Car/Dining Car (Kitchen Type)

6）二等卧车的平面布局

Plane layout of second-class sleeping cars

二等卧车定员 66 人。一位端设通过台、坐式便器卫生间、乘务员室及小走廊，乘务室内设电热开水器，小走廊内设电气控制柜、卧具柜；车体中部设 11 个半封闭式卧铺包间及侧走廊，上铺与中铺、中铺与下铺间设脚蹬；二位端设三人洗面间及隐藏式洁具柜、垃圾箱、蹲式便器卫生间及小走廊。二等卧车的平面布局如图 9–8 所示。

Passenger capacity of second-class sleeping car: 66 people. “B” end of car is equipped with a vestibule, a western type toilet, a crew room, and a small corridor. The crew compartment is equipped with an electric water heater, and the small corridor is equipped with an electrical control cabinet and bedding cabinet; there are 11 semi-enclosed sleeper compartments and side corridors in the middle of the car body, and pedals are provided between the upper and middle berths, and between the middle and lower berths; “A” end of car is equipped with a three-person washroom, a concealed sanitary cabinet, a garbage bin, a eastern type toilet, and a small corridor. The plane layout of the second-class sleeping car is shown in Figure 9-8.

图 9–8　二等卧车的平面布局

Figure 9-8　Plane Layout of Second-class Sleeping Car

7）一等卧车的平面布局

Plane layout of first-class sleeping car

一等卧车定员 40 人。一位端设通过台、坐式便器卫生间、乘务员室及小走廊，乘务室内设电热开水器，小走廊内设电气控制柜、卧具柜；车体中部设 10 个封闭式卧铺包间及侧走廊；二位端设三人洗面间及隐藏式洁具柜、垃圾箱、蹲式便器卫生间及小走廊。一等卧车的平面布局如图 9–9 所示。

Passenger capacity of first-class sleeping car: 40 people. “B” end of car is provided with a vestibule, a western type toilet, a crew room, and a small corridor. The crew compartment is equipped with an electric water heater, and the small corridor is equipped with an electrical control cabinet and bedding cabinet; there are 10 enclosed sleeper compartments and side corridors in the middle of the car body; “A” end of car is equipped with a three-person washroom, a concealed sanitary cabinet, a garbage bin, a eastern type toilet, and a small corridor. The plane layout of the first-class sleeping car is shown in Figure 9-9.

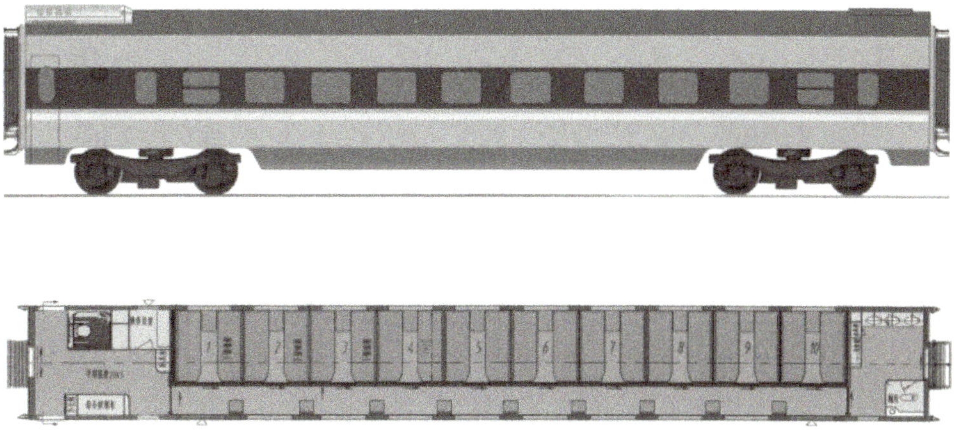

图 9–9　一等卧车的平面布局
Figure 9-9　Plane Layout of First-class Sleeping Car